1937

1937
Stalin's Year of Terror

Vadim Z. Rogovin

Translated by Frederick S. Choate

Mehring Books, Inc.
Oak Park, Michigan

Published by Mehring Books, Inc.
United States: 25900 Greenfield Road, Oak Park, MI 48237
Australia: PO Box 367, Bankstown, NSW 2200 Australia
Britain: PO Box 1306, Sheffield S9 3UW England

Printed in the United States of America

Library of Congress Cataloging-in-Publications Data

Rogovin, Vadim Zakharovich
   [1937, English]
   1937: Stalin's year of terror/Vadim Z. Rogovin : translated by Frederick S. Choate.
   p.   cm.
   Includes bibliographical references and index.
   ISBN 0-929087-77-1 (paperback)
   1. Soviet Union—Politics and government—1936–1953.   2. Stalin, Joseph, 1879-1953.
3. Kommunisticheskaia partiia Sovetskogo Soiuza—Purges.   4. Political purges—Soviet
Union—History.   I. Title.
   DK267.R47613   1998
   947.084'2—dc21
                                                97-50514
                                                  CIP

Cover photographs: Top left: Stalin. Top right, Vyshinsky.
Bottom left to right: Rykov, Bukharin, Pyatakov, Tukhachevsky, Radek.

Contents

FOREWORD

IN GATHERING MATERIAL for this book, great help was provided at home and abroad by readers of the previous volumes of the series, "Was There an Alternative?" The author expresses his gratitude to M. V. Goloviznin, T. I. Isaeva-Voronskaya, Iu. V. Primakov, R. A. Medvedev (Moscow), S. Samulenkov (Riga), Michel Le Hevel (Paris), Frederick Choate (San Francisco), Felix Kreisel (Boston) and Frank Goodwin (Los Angeles).

Chapters 10 and 52 were written with N. F. Naumova, and Chapters 14 and 55 with the help of M. V. Goloviznin.

Introduction

> *Once upon a time, unintentionally,*
> *And probably hazarding a guess,*
> *Hegel called the historian a prophet*
> *Predicting in reverse.*
>
> > B. Pasternak

AFTER KHRUSHCHEV'S REPORT at the Twentieth Congress of the CPSU, which rocked the whole world, the most consistent defenders of socialism felt that this official exposé of the great terror of 1936–38 would be the beginning of extensive work devoted to reexamining the essence of Stalinism and overcoming it completely in all the socialist countries and within the Communist Parties. Pointing out the enormous complexity of this task, Bertolt Brecht wrote: "The liquidation of Stalinism can take place only if the party mobilizes the wisdom of the masses on a gigantic scale. Such a mobilization lies along the road to communism."[1]

Analogous thoughts were expressed by the German Communist poet, Johannes Becher, who noted that the tragic content of the Stalinist epoch was incomparable with the tragedy of any preceding epoch. "This tragedy," he wrote, "can be overcome only when it is acknowledged as such, and when the forces chosen to overcome it are equal to its tragic nature." Herein lies the guarantee that "the system of socialism on a world scale will not cease to develop." Becher correctly noted that "the sense of tragedy can only be fully passed on by those people who participated in it, tried to fight it, and who suffered through the entire tragedy from within, i.e., by those who were socialists and who remained socialists forever."[2]

Alas, by the time of the Twentieth Congress, the people who were capable of effectively fighting against Stalinism and who retained genuine communist convictions had almost ceased to exist in the Soviet Union and in the foreign

Communist Parties: the overwhelming majority of them had been exterminated in the ruthless purges. Almost all of the leaders of the CPSU and other
Communist Parties were in one way or another tainted by participating in the
Stalinist crimes, or at least in their ideological justification and preparation;
their thinking was deeply scarred by the metastases of Stalinism. This couldn't
help but affect the content of Khrushchev's report, which in essence was directed not against Stalinism, but only against the most monstrous crimes committed by Stalin. The main conception of the report was contained in assertions according to which Stalin until 1934 "actively fought for Leninism, against
the opponents and distorters of Lenin's teachings." He led the "fight against
those who tried to divert the country from the only correct, Leninist path,—
against Trotskyists, Zinovievists, rightists and bourgeois nationalists." It was
only after Kirov's murder, Khrushchev declared, that Stalin "increasingly abused
power and began to victimize prominent members of the party and state, applying terrorist methods against honest Soviet people."[3]

Moreover, Khrushchev claimed that, in unleashing massive state terror,
Stalin was guided by defending "the interests of the working class, the interests of the laboring people, the interests of the victory of socialism and communism. It cannot be said that these were actions of a bully. He felt that he had
to do this in the interests of the party and the workers, in the interests of defending the gains of the revolution. Herein lies the real tragedy!"[4] From these
words one must conclude that the Stalinist terror was a tragedy not for the
Soviet people and the Bolshevik Party, but a tragedy ... for Stalin himself. This
idea was even more clearly expressed in the resolution from the Central Committee of the CPSU on 30 June 1956, "On Overcoming the Personality Cult and
its Consequences," in which it was openly stated that "Stalin's tragedy" consisted in applying illegal and "unworthy methods."[5]

This false version, which bored into the consciousness of the Soviet people
during the years of "the thaw," was renounced by Khrushchev only in his memoirs at the end of the 1960s, where he repeatedly returned to an assessment of
Stalin. Here he called Stalin a murderer who had performed "criminal acts which
are punished in any state except for those which are not guided by any laws."[6]
Khrushchev correctly referred to the "rather wooden logic" of those who feel
that Stalin committed his evil deeds "not for personal gains, but out of concern
for his people. What savagery! Out of concern for the people to kill its best
sons."[7] Here we might add that Khrushchev's judgments about "savagery" and

"wooden logic" could well be applied to several of his own statements in his report at the Twentieth Congress and in a number of subsequent speeches which "softened" the sharper passages of this report.

In the chapter of his memoirs called "My Reflections on Stalin," Khrushchev adopted a fundamentally different approach than in his earlier official speeches in evaluating the reasons for the "great purge" and Stalin's "uprooting" of the bearers of oppositional moods in the party and in the country. "After destroying the outstanding core of people who had been tempered in the tsarist underground under Lenin's leadership," he wrote, "there then followed the wanton extermination of leading party, soviet, state, academic and military cadres, as well as millions of rank-and-file people whose way of life and whose thoughts Stalin didn't like.... Some of them, of course, had stopped supporting him when they saw where he was taking us. Stalin understood that there was a large group of people opposed to him. Opposition moods, however, still do not mean anti-Soviet, anti-Marxist or anti-Party moods."[8] Thus Khrushchev, who thought deeply about the material produced by investigations into Stalin's crimes, arrived at two important conclusions: (1) The inner-party oppositions were by no means some kind of mortal evil (which the Soviet people were taught for several decades); (2) The anti-Stalinist opposition forces in the 1930s were rather numerous.

In drawing close to an adequate understanding of the political meaning of the Great Purges, Khrushchev explained it by referring to Stalin's break with the fundamentals of Marxist theory and Bolshevik political practice. He openly stated that the terror was unleashed by Stalin "in order to preclude the possibility of any people or groups appearing in the party who wanted to return the party to Lenin's inner-party democracy, and to redirect the nation toward a democratic social structure.... Stalin said that the people are manure, an amorphous mass which will follow a strong leader. And so he demonstrated such strength, destroying everything which might contribute to a true understanding of events or to sound reasoning which would have contradicted his point of view. Herein lies the tragedy of the USSR."[9] Here, for the first time, Khrushchev called the Great Terror a tragedy not for Stalin, but for the nation and its people.

It was very difficult for Khrushchev to part with Stalinist mythology. The difficulty can be seen even on the pages of his memoirs, where he repeated certain fictions contained earlier in his report to the Twentieth Party Congress. As before, he called Stalin's activity "positive in the sense that he remained a

Marxist in his basic approach to history; he was a man devoted to the Marxist idea." Having poorly mastered Marxist theory, Khrushchev decided to introduce only hypothetically the "Trotskyist" thesis: "Perhaps Stalin had degenerated and was acting as a whole against the ideas of socialism, and for this reason killed its adherents?"—only to decisively reject the very possibility of raising such a question: "Absolutely not. Stalin remained faithful in principle to the ideas of socialism."[10] As a result, Khrushchev was simply incapable of drawing the balance of his own evaluations, remaining prisoner of a purely psychological, if not clinical, explanation of Stalin's terrorist actions: "Could these be the actions of a genuine Marxist? These are the deeds of a despot or a sick man.... There can be no justification for such actions.... On the other hand, Stalin remained a Marxist in principle (but not in concrete deeds). And, if one excludes his pathological suspiciousness, cruelty, and treachery, then he assessed the situation soberly and correctly."[11] This is how the Stalinist past continued to weigh upon the most active initiator and executor of destalinization. Is it any wonder that after the Brezhnev and Suslov leadership had forbidden for many years any mention of the theme of Stalinism, and after the chaos of "Perestroika" in "investigating" our historical past, that it was precisely these ideas expounded by Khrushchev (and by Stalinists in general) that were taken in the former republics of the Soviet Union during the 1990s as armament by many parties and groupings calling themselves "Communist"?

The version that Stalin's mistrustfulness, "evolving into a persecution complex," served as the main cause of the Great Purges, was repeated in historical works during the second half of the 1950s and first half of the 1960s.[12]

Explaining the "Yezhov period" by Stalin's personal pathological traits was characteristic even of several insightful experts on Soviet history from the milieu of Western Sovietologists and the first Russian emigration. This version was discussed in detail in letters between the former Mensheviks N. Valentinov and B. Nikolaevsky. The discussion of this topic unfolded in correspondence in 1954–1956, when it became obvious that state terror and mass persecutions on the basis of false accusations were by no means a necessary and inevitable attribute of the "Communist system." Literally in the days following Stalin's death, his successors put a halt to a new wave of terror which threatened to surpass even the terror of the 1930s in its scope. A month later, they declared that the "Doctors' Plot"—one of Stalin's last crimes—was a frame-up. Then it came to light that Stalin's successors had begun to free and rehabilitate those unjustly convicted in the previous years and decades. Under these conditions, Valentinov tried to convince Nikolaevsky that the "Yezhov period" was wholly a product of Stalin's paranoia, i.e., of a chronic mental illness expressed in the pursuit of maniacal obsessions. In support of this thesis, Valentinov referred to evidence supposedly originating from V. I. Mezhlauk, a member of the Central Committee, who allegedly transmitted a message abroad, through his brother who had traveled in 1937 to an international exhibition in Paris. The message dealt with Stain's illness (paranoia), "with a mass of important details."[13]

In answering Valentinov, Nikolaevsky agreed that in the last years of his life Stalin "lost the sense of moderation and, from the 'brilliant man who measured things out in doses,' as Bukharin had called him, he turned into a man who had lost his grasp of reality." Nikolaevsky objected only to attempts "to extend this line into the past in order to explain the 'Yezhov period,' which was a criminal, but carefully calculated and correctly (from his standpoint) measured act of destroying his opponents, who otherwise would have gotten rid of him."[14]

In order to support his version of resistance to Stalinism within the Bolshevik milieu, Nikolaevsky referred either to insignificant facts (Bukharin's appointment in 1934 as editor of *Izvestiia* and his propaganda of a course toward "proletarian humanism"), or to information of a clearly apocryphal nature ("beginning in 1932, Stalin did not have a majority in the Politburo or Central Committee Plenums"). However, Nikolaevsky's idea that "the entire 'Yezhov period' was a diabolically calculated game, a crime, but not madness,"[15] is profoundly justified. In developing this idea, Nikolaevsky noted: "To people like Mezhlauk, it seemed that the purge was completely senseless and that Stalin had gone mad. In actuality, Stalin was not mad, and he conducted a precisely determined line. He arrived at the conclusion about the need to destroy the layer of old Bolsheviks not later than the summer of 1934, and then he began to prepare this operation."[16]

Nikolaevsky wrote that he would agree to acknowledge Stalin a paranoiac if the latter had acted against his own interests. At first glance, such a contradiction did actually exist. On the eve of a war that was relentlessly approaching, Stalin destroyed not only the overwhelming majority of party and governmental leaders, thousands of leaders of enterprises, engineers and scientists working on defense, but also almost the entire commanding personnel of the army, people who were needed for defending the country against foreign invasion. However, a deeper analysis shows that the Great Purges fully corresponded to the task of preserving Stalin's unlimited control over the party, the nation, and the international communist movement. As Nikolaevsky correctly noted, Stalin carried out "a criminal policy, but the only one which would insure the continuation of his dictatorship. His actions were determined by this policy. He launched the terror not because he was mad like Caligula, but because he had made it a factor of his active sociology.... He killed millions and, in particular, exterminated the entire layer of old Bolsheviks because he understood that this layer was opposed to his 'communism'.... Stalin destroyed the Central Committee of the Seventeenth Congress and the members of this congress not because he was insane, but because he had guessed the plans of his opponents.... Khrushchev now wants to declare him insane because it would be more favorable to attribute everything to the insanity of one man than to acknowledge his own participation in the criminal activities of this gang."[17]

Of special interest in Nikolaevsky's arguments are his thoughts about the differences between Stalin's mental state at the end of the 1930s and the beginning of the 1950s. Stalin's persecution complex and other pathological symptoms during the last years of his life have been described not only by Khrushchev, but by people who were the closest to Stalin and who were by no means inclined to discredit him. In no uncertain terms Molotov declared to the writer F. Chuyev that "in the last period, he [Stalin] had a persecution complex."[18] "He did not enjoy his harvest," wrote S. Alliluyeva. "He was spiritually empty, had forgotten all human affections, and was tormented by a fear which in the last years turned into a genuine persecution complex—in the end, his strong nerves finally cracked."[19]

In sharp contrast, in 1937 Stalin held the entire grandiose mechanism of state terror under his unwavering and effective control. Without weakening or losing this control for even a minute, he displayed in his actions not the nervousness and alarm of a paranoiac, but, on the contrary, a surprising, almost superhuman self-control and the most refined calculation. "During the 1930s, he conducted the 'Yezhov' operation very precisely (from his point of view), since he prepared everything and seized his enemies unawares; they didn't understand him," Nikolaevsky noted correctly. "Even many of his supporters didn't understand him."[20]

The mystery of the Great Terror has also sparked the intense interest of many prominent people who stood far from politics. In the novel *Doctor*

Zhivago, Boris Pasternak used his hero to express the following thoughts: "I think that collectivization was a mistaken and unsuccessful measure, but it was impossible to admit the mistake. In order to hide the failure, it was necessary to use all means of terror to make people forget how to think and to force them to see what didn't exist, or to prove the opposite of what was obvious. Hence the unbridled cruelty of the Yezhov period, the declaration of a constitution never intended to be applied, and the introduction of elections not based on elective principles."[21]

These statements display what is at first glance an unusual resemblance to the ideas of Trotsky, who repeatedly pointed to the connection between the Great Terror and the mass discontent which had arisen in the country as a result of forced collectivization. He also stressed the camouflaging of the barbaric purges with the liberal decorum of "Stalin's most democratic constitution in the world," which served as a disguise and performed purely propagandistic functions.

Pasternak's explanation of the tragedy during the "Yezhov period" also displays unmistakable proximity to Lenin's prognoses made in 1921. In referring to the alternatives Soviet Russia faced at that time, Lenin saw two outcomes from the contradictions which had accumulated by then: "ten to twenty years of correct relations with the peasantry and victory is guaranteed on a world scale (even given delays in the proletarian revolutions which are growing), or else twenty to forty years of torment from White-Guard terror. Aut-Aut. Tertium non datur [Either/or. A third is not given]."[22]

Because it was not able to secure correct relations with the peasantry, and turned, in search of a way out, to forced collectivization, the Stalinist clique provoked the most acute economic and political crisis from 1928–1933. Instead of demonstrating the power associated with setting an example as the first country in the world to take the path of socialism, an example which Lenin felt would be one of the main conditions for the upsurge of the world revolution, the Soviet Union set a negative example in the economic, social, political and intellectual spheres—showing a sharp fall in agricultural productivity and commodity production, the growth of poverty and inequality, the consolidation of a totalitarian regime and the stifling of dissident thought, criticism and ideological inquiry. All of these factors, along with the incorrect policies of the Stalinized Comintern, served as a brake on the socialist revolutions in other lands—just at the historical moment when, as a result of the all-embracing worldwide crisis of the capitalist system, the most propitious conditions in all history arose for the upsurge of the revolutionary workers' movement.

What was essentially a White-Guard terror fit approximately within the chronological framework suggested by Lenin—twenty-five years (1928–1953). However this terror, which destroyed many more communists than even the fascist regimes in Germany and Italy, was realized in a specific political form which had not been foreseen by Marxists: it unfolded from within the Bolshevik Party, in its name and under the direction of its leaders.

To the extent that the party was purged of genuine opposition elements, the thrust of the terror was then directed at that part of the bureaucracy which had helped Stalin rise to the summit of power. Trotsky explained the social meaning of this stage of the Great Purges in the following way: "The ruling stratum is expelling from its midst all those who remind it of the revolutionary past, of the principles of socialism, of liberty, equality and fraternity, of the unresolved problems of the world revolution.... In this sense, the purges increase the uniformity of the ruling stratum and seemingly strengthen Stalin's position."[23] The brutal purging of foreign elements from the ruling stratum, i.e., of those people whose consciousness still retained a fidelity to the traditions of Bolshevism, had as its consequence an ever-increasing breach between the bureaucracy and the masses, as well as an ever-increasing decline of the intellectual and moral level of party members, military leaders, scholars, and so forth. "All the advanced and creative elements who are genuinely devoted to the interests of the economy, to the people's education or defense, are inevitably coming into a collision with the ruling oligarchy," Trotsky wrote. "That's the way it was in its time under tsarism; that's what is happening now, at an incomparably faster rate, under Stalin's regime. The economy, cultural life and the army need innovators, builders, creators; the Kremlin needs faithful executors, reliable and ruthless agents. These human types—agent and creator—are irreconcilably hostile to each other."[24]

Such a shift in social types during the course of the Great Purges of 1936–1938 was noted even by anticommunist writers who were able to observe the consequences of Stalin's "cadre revolution." Thus, M. Voslensky, a former Soviet apparatchik who fled to the West and became a specialist on problems of the Soviet elite, stressed that in the process of the Great Purges "those who were inevitably cast aside and who perished in the bitter struggle were those who still believed in the correctness of Marxism and in the construction of

communist society; in the ruling layer of society the communists by conviction were replaced by communists in name." For the apparatchiks coming to
power in 1937 and later years, "the question of the correctness of Marxism ...
was of little interest, and they replaced a belief in such correctness with Marxist phraseology and quotations. In reality, despite their loud affirmations that
communism was the radiant future for all mankind, Stalin's protégés who had
climbed their way to high posts least of all would want to create a society where
not in words, but in deeds, everyone worked according to his abilities and received according to his needs."[25]

In the next generation, this social milieu inexorably fostered and promoted
people who at the appropriate moment turned into open renegades from communism—Gorbachev, Yeltsin, and Yakovlev, as well as the majority of presi-
dents of the new states which have been formed on the ruins of the Soviet
Union.

The political meaning and political results of the Great Purges had already
been adequately understood by the more serious Western analysts by the end
of the 1930s. In a report of the British Royal Institute of Foreign Relations, published in March 1939, it states: "The inner development of Russia is headed
toward the formation of a 'bourgeoisie' of directors and officials who have
enough privileges to be greatly satisfied with the status quo.... In the various
purges one can discern a device through which all are exterminated who wish
to change the current state of affairs. Such an interpretation lends weight to
the view that the revolutionary period in Russia has come to an end, and that
henceforth the rulers will try only to maintain those benefits which the revolution has granted them."[26] In many ways these words explain the reasons for the
tenacity of the Stalinist and post-Stalinist regimes over the course of fifty years
after the Great Purges, which bled the country dry and deprived it of the gigantic intellectual potential which had accumulated over many years.

In light of all that has been said, it is easy to determine the true value of the
ideological manipulations of today's "democrats" who call Bolsheviks or
Leninists anyone who at any time occupied a leading post in the ruling party of
the USSR—right up to Brezhnev, Chernenko and Gorbachev. Indulgence is
shown only to those party bosses who have burned everything they worshiped
in the past, and have begun to worship everything that they once burned, i.e.,
zoological anticommunism.

In the Soviet Union the topic of the Great Terror was forbidden as an area of research that was the least bit objective right up until the end of the 1980s. The absence of Marxist works on these problems, as well as on the problem of Stalinism in general, finally led to the fulfillment of the prognosis outlined by J. Becher in the 1950s: the inability to give a Marxist explanation of the acute problems in recent history will foster attempts to use the exposure of Stalin in order to "strike a blow against the new social structure and even liquidate it gradually, in pieces."[27] That, essentially, is what happened at the end of the 1980s and beginning of the 1990s, when these attempts were crowned with complete success.

While in official Soviet scholarship these themes were taboo, they were thoroughly worked over—in their own way—by Western Sovietologists and Russian dissidents. With any of these authors, it is not difficult to find many factual errors, inexact formulations, juggling of facts and outright distortions. This can be explained on the whole by two reasons. The first is the limited nature of the historical sources which these authors had at their disposal. Thus, the basic research for R. Conquest's *Great Terror* consists of an analysis of Soviet newspapers and other official publications, to which are added references to the memoir accounts of several people who managed to escape from the USSR. The second reason is that the majority of Sovietologists and dissidents served a definite social and political purpose—they used this enormous historical tragedy to show that its fatal premise was the "utopian" communist idea and revolutionary practice of Bolshevism. This prompted the researchers concerned to ignore those historical sources which contradict their conceptual schemes and paradigms. Not one of the anticommunists who analyzed the Moscow Trials of 1936–1938 bothered to turn to the "testimony" of the man who was the main accused in all these trials, even though he wasn't sitting in the courtroom. Thus, A. Solzhenitsyn's book, *Gulag Archipelago*, contains no references whatsoever to Trotsky's works. Solzhenitsyn's work, much like the more objective works of R. Medvedev, belongs to the genre which the West calls "oral history," i.e., research which is based almost exclusively on eyewitness accounts of participants in the events being described. Moreover, using the circumstance that the memoirs from prisoners in Stalin's camps which had been given to him to read had never been published, Solzhenitsyn took plenty of license in outlining their contents and interpreting them.

Besides the myths circulated by open anticommunists, there are myths which issue from the camp of the so-called "national-patriots." They amount to a rejection of the October Revolution and Bolshevism, coupled with admiration for Stalin and the justification of his terrorist actions. This kind of "world outlook," which was widely disseminated on the pages of the Soviet press during the years of "perestroika" and the Yeltsin regime, developed in certain circles among the Soviet intelligentsia around the end of the 1960s. S. Semanov's article, "On Relative and Eternal Values," published in 1970 in the journal *Molodaia gvardiia* [Young Guard], became a kind of ideological manifesto for this tendency. Its author, who was still unable to openly declare his fidelity to the ideals of "autocracy, orthodoxy and nationalism" (considered by the "national-patriots" to be "eternal" and "truly Russian" values), limited himself to comparing the "nihilistic" 1920s to the "patriotic" 1930s.

"Today it is clear," wrote Semanov, "that in the struggle against destructive and nihilistic forces, a major turning point came in the middle of the 1930s. How many derogatory words were later hurled at this historical epoch!... It seems to me that we have not yet recognized the full significance of the gigantic changes which occurred at this time. These changes exerted an extremely beneficial influence on the development of our culture." Without a shade of restraint, Semanov declared that "precisely after the adoption of our Constitution, which legally reinforced the enormous social shifts taking place in our nation and society, Soviet citizens enjoyed general equality before the law. And this was our gigantic achievement.... All honest workers in our country henceforth and for all time became united together into a single, monolithic whole."[28]

Semanov's article advanced "the most important evaluative criterion with regard to the social phenomena now occurring." This criterion, in the opinion of its author, was the following: "Does a given phenomenon assist in strengthening our state or not?"[29]

The ideology based on this "evaluative criterion" was widely disseminated during the years of "perestroika" and "reforms" on the pages of *Nash sovremennik* [Our Contemporary], *Moskva* [Moscow] and *Molodaia gvardiia* [Young Guard], journals whose authors began to call themselves "gosudarstvenniki" [statists]. Their historical and polemical articles organically joined together a hatred for Bolshevism and the glorification of Stalin. As it developed further, this system of views organically flowed into the ideology of the national bourgeoisie which counterposed itself to the comprador bourgeoisie and its political representatives. The battle between these two factions of the nascent Russian bourgeoisie during the 1990s shoved all other ideological tendencies into the background.

Semanov, as well as today's members of the "irreconcilable opposition" who have carried on his ideological tradition a quarter of a century later, correctly pinpointed the social, political and ideological turning point in the development of Soviet society. However, their assessment of this turning point was quite specific in nature. According to the logic of Semanov's article, the first "happy" year in Soviet history was 1937, when "Soviet citizens enjoyed general equality before the law," and along with this "equality," all society was consolidated "into a single monolithic whole." However, at that time such "equality" could be observed only in the Gulag, where, in A. Tvardovsky's words:

> *And behind one side of the law*
> *Fate made everyone equal:*
> *Son of kulak or narkom,*
> *Son of army commander or village priest.*[30]

If we leave aside the relatively few representatives of the "statist" tendency, then right up until the appearance of the dissident movement in the 1970s the majority of Soviet intellectuals thought that the tragedy that befell the nation and the people was what was referred to as "1937" or the "Yezhovshchina" [the Yezhov period], but by no means the October Revolution.

There was hardly anyone in the Soviet Union for whom the exposures made at the Twentieth Party Congress came as a complete revelation. Both the scale and the character of Stalin's brutality were known to millions of Soviet people. During the years of Stalinism, many of them saved themselves through self-deception, which was necessary to keep going; in their minds they built a chain of rationalizations, i.e., a justification, if not fully then partially, of Stalin's terror as something which made sense politically. In this regard we must stress that one of the goals (and therefore one of the results or consequences) of the "Yezhov period" was the destruction of the social and historical memory of the people, which is passed from generation to generation through its living bearers. A wasteland of scorched earth was formed around the murdered leaders of Bolshevism, insofar as their wives, children and closest comrades were eliminated after them. The fear evoked by the Stalinist terror left its mark on the consciousness and behavior of several generations of Soviet people; for many it eradicated the readiness, desire and ability to engage in honest ideological thought. At the same time, the executioners and informers from Stalin's time continued to thrive; they had secured their own well-being and the prosperity of their children through active participation in frame-ups, expulsions, torture, and so forth.

Meanwhile it is difficult to overemphasize the shifts in mass consciousness which were engendered by two waves of exposures of Stalinism: both during and after the Twentieth Congress, and then during and after the Twenty-second Congress. The second wave was halted by the Brezhnev-Suslov leadership soon after Khrushchev's overthrow. The last works of art, scholarly investigations and investigatory articles which were devoted to the theme of the Great Terror appeared in the USSR in 1965–1966.

The brief historical period separating the Twenty-second Congress of the CPSU from Khrushchev's removal from power witnessed the final formation of the so-called generation of "the people of the '60s." The main spokesmen for this generation included not only Solzhenitsyn, but also a young generation of poets who recited their poems at the famous evenings held at the Polytechnical Museum. In later years, the majority of the "people of the 60s" passed through a number of stages of ideological degeneration. They reoriented in the direction of anticommunism and renounced their earlier works as the "sins of youth." This reorientation, which produced nothing but malicious and vulgar anti-Bolshevik slander, cannot, however, erase the undying significance of their early works. Here, the ideological dominant was a reassertion of their devotion to the ideas of the October Revolution and Bolshevism. It was precisely at the beginning of the '60s that A. Voznesensky wrote his poem, "Longjumeau," in which the whole text is permeated with a counterposing of Leninism to Stalinism. In addition, B. Okudzhava concluded one his best songs with the moving lines:

> But if suddenly, sometime,
>   I can't manage to protect myself—
> No matter what new battle
>   may shake the earthly globe,
> I will nonetheless fall in that war,
>   in that distant civil war,
> And commissars in dusty helmets
>   Will bend silently over me.[31]

In the 1960s even Solzhenitsyn wrote the anti-Stalinist, but by no means anticommunist novels, *Cancer Ward* and *The First Circle* (although it is true that the variant of the second novel published abroad differs significantly in its ideological orientation from the variant which made its rounds in Samizdat and was submitted for publication to the journal *Novyi mir.*).

Even in the best years of "the thaw," thoughtful people kept in mind the incomplete nature of the truth about Stalinism's crimes which had been allowed to be made public. In the 1950s, the author of this book had occasion to hear many times in private conversations that the full truth about the Great Terror would not become known until 100 years had passed.

To the Brezhnev clique which replaced Khrushchev, even the explanation of the Great Terror which had prevailed in the years of "the thaw" seemed dangerous. Therefore it simply placed a taboo on discussing this topic and on developing the related subjects in works of art or in historical literature.

Of course, even during the Brezhnev years (known as the "time of stagnation") witnesses of the events of the 1930s continued to write memoirs, and writers, scholars and journalists continued to write works on these themes. The wound inflicted by 1937 had healed so little, and the pain from memories about the Stalinist terror was so great, that many outstanding writers and memoirists devoted years to such works, which were written "for the desk drawer," i.e., without any hope of seeing them published in the foreseeable future. Meanwhile, by the end of the 1960s, memoirs and literary works began to circulate widely in Samizdat even though an official ban had been placed on their publication in the USSR. Then many Soviet authors began to send their works abroad to be published there.

In the official Soviet press, a return to the theme of Stalinist repressions began only in 1986. However, much as in the 1950s and 1960s, official approval of turning to this theme was hardly dictated only by a desire to restore historical truth and overcome the damage done by Stalinism. If both of the "Khrushchev" waves of exposures had been evoked largely by considerations in the struggle against the so-called "anti-Party group" of Molotov, Kaganovich and Malenkov, then the "perestroika" wave, too, was initially prompted by other conjunctural considerations: by a desire to redirect the attention of public opinion away from the obvious failures of the broadly promoted "perestroika" to the tragic events of the past, for which the new generation of party leaders bore no responsibility.

The flood of exposures which broke out under the flag of "glasnost" [openness] was so powerful at first, that in 1987–1989, public opinion was almost completely consumed by questions of the country's history during the Stalinist years. This interest largely explains the sharp increase during those years of subscriptions and subsequently the press runs of the mass-circulation newspapers, as well as literary and political journals which tirelessly published ever newer works about Stalin's crimes.

However, very soon it became clear that the themes of the Great Terror and Stalinism were being used by many authors and organs of the press in order to compromise or discredit the idea of socialism. This anticommunist and anti-Bolshevik approach had largely been prepared by the activity of Western Sovietologists and Soviet dissidents from the 1960s through the 1980s, who had put into circulation a whole number of historical myths.

Historical myth-making has always been one of the main ideological weapons of reactionary forces. But in the modern epoch historical myths can't help but disguise themselves as science, and in search of support they are always looking for pseudoscientific arguments. At the end of the 1980s, myths created during the first decades of Soviet power were given a second life in the pages of the Soviet press. One of these myths amounted to a virtual repetition of the Stalinist version from 1936 in which the struggle of Trotsky and the "Trotskyists" against Stalinism had allegedly been determined by a naked yearning for power. According to this myth, the political doctrine of "Trotskyism" did not differ in any substantial way from the Stalinist "general line," and if the opposition had triumphed in the inner-party struggle, it would have pursued policies differing in no significant way from Stalin's.

Other myths, which originated in the works of the ideologues among the first Russian emigration and the renegades from communism in the 1920s and 1930s, were aimed at discrediting and denigrating the historical period of the Russian Revolution. In order to ideologically clear the way for the restoration of capitalism in the USSR, what was required was the destruction of a significant stratum in the consciousness of the masses; pluses had to be changed into minuses in the interpretation of the October Revolution and Civil War, events which were surrounded with an aura of grandeur and heroism in the minds of millions of Soviet citizens. It is no accident that from approximately 1990 on, the center of attention in criticizing our historical past was shifted from an exposé of the Stalinist epoch to the first years of post-October history.

The most derogatory term in the works both of the "democrats" and of the "national-patriots" suddenly became the half-forgotten concept of the "Bolshevik," which can be applied correctly only to Lenin's generation of the party and to its elements who didn't degenerate in subsequent years.

In the formation of this myth, no small contribution was made by Solzhenitsyn, who claimed in his book *The Gulag Archipelago* that the "Yezhov period" was simply one of the waves of "Bolshevik terror," and that the civil war, collectivization and repressions of the postwar period were no less horrific waves of the same essential type.

But it is clear that a popular struggle against an open class enemy and well-armed conspiracies—which are inevitable in a civil war when it is hard to distinguish between the front and the rear—is something quite different from the struggle of a ruling bureaucracy against a peasantry which comprised a majority of the country's population (and precisely this kind of struggle was provoked by "rapid collectivization" and the "liquidation of the kulaks as a class"). In turn, the struggle against peasants who frequently responded to forced collectivization with armed uprisings (such uprisings never ceased during the entire period of 1928–1933) is something quite different from the extermination of unarmed people, the majority of whom were devoted to the idea and cause of socialism. And when it comes to the repressions during the last years of the war, they were directed not only at innocent people, but also against thousands of collaborationists and participants in roving bands (strict retribution against accomplices of Hitler's forces was meted out in all the countries of Western Europe at that time which had been liberated from fascist occupation).

If the October Revolution and Civil War of 1918–1920 had achieved their goals, their victims would seem justified to any unbiased person—much like today's Americans feel that the victims lost in the revolutionary wars of the eighteenth and nineteenth centuries are justified. However, in the USSR, only a few years after the close of the civil war which had led to the victory of the Soviet regime, what began was virtually a new civil war against the peasantry, caused not so much by objective class contradictions as by the mistaken policy of the Stalinist leadership. At the same time, the ruling bureaucracy unleashed a number of small civil wars against the communist opposition, which swelled into the Great Terror of 1936–1938.

Thus in the history of Soviet society we can count not one, but at least three civil wars, which differ substantially according to their character and consequences. The civil war of 1918–1920 led the country out of a state of collapse, anarchy and chaos which had grown ever more acute after the February Revolution (this fact is acknowledged even by such opponents of the Bolsheviks as Berdyaev and Denikin). The civil war of 1928–1933 was a war which significantly weakened the USSR, although it did accomplish the "pacification" of the peasantry. The "Yezhov terror" was a preventive civil war against Bolshevik-Leninists who had fought for the preservation and strengthening of the gains of the October Revolution. This last civil war in the USSR (until the "low intensity civil war" launched by "perestroika" and continuing to this very day) resulted in more victims than the Civil War of 1918–1920 or all the Stalinist acts of repression before and after it.

Historical analogies usually help us to understand the essence of great historical events. The civil war of 1918–1920 can be compared to civil wars in other countries, especially to the civil war during the 1860s in the United States. Trotsky found so much in common between these wars that he even intended to write a book devoted to their comparison. In addition, the struggle against the rebellious peasants during the years of forced collectivization reminds us of the battle of France's revolutionary armies against the "Vendée."

But it is impossible to find analogies in previous history to the phenomenon which is referred to variously as "1937," "the Yezhov Terror," "the Great Terror" or "the Great Purges." Similar events have been observed only after the Second World War in other countries which are called socialist. This applies first of all to the purges of the ruling communist parties, incited from Moscow, which were not avoided by a single one of the "People's Democratic" countries. Secondly it applies to the so-called "Cultural Revolution" in China, which occurred without the slightest pressure on the part of the Soviet Union. The "Cultural Revolution," which, like the "Yezhov Terror," began almost twenty years after the victory of the socialist revolution, gave rise to the conception that every socialist country will inevitably pass through a period of mass state terror.

"The Great Purges" in the USSR and the "Cultural Revolution" in China differed from each other in substantial ways regarding the way the terror was carried out. In China it was presented as an outburst of the spontaneous indignation of the masses, and especially the youth, over the behavior of "those invested with power and following the capitalist road." Public mockery, beatings and other forms of violence employed against the victims of the "Cultural Revolution," including leading members of the party and state, were applied openly, before large crowds, by "Red Guards" who were allowed to do as they pleased and who became intoxicated by the power they had over helpless people. However, it would be more appropriate to compare the Red Guards to Hitler's storm-troopers than to Stalin's inquisitors who conducted their bloody affairs in prison torture chambers.

Feeling that it was possible to implement the Great Terror by crudely victimizing "enemies of the people," Trotsky pointed out that Stalin preferred, over this "Asiatic" variant, to annihilate his victims while concealing from the people both the scale and the brutal forms of the repression being carried out. "It would require little effort for the Stalinist bureaucracy," Trotsky wrote, " to organize the wrath of the people. But it had no use for this; on the contrary, it saw in such unauthorized actions, even if they were actually ordered from above, a threat to the existing order. Beatings in prison, murders—all this the Kremlin Thermidorians could accomplish in a strictly planned fashion, through the GPU and its detachments.... This was possible due to the totalitarian character of the regime, which had at its disposal all the material means and forces of the nation."[32]

1937 determined the development of historical events for many years and decades ahead. We can call this year "historically crucial" (a justifiable epithet, although it was thoroughly vulgarized by Gorbachev, who called his confused and unsystematic actions "historically crucial" during the "perestroika" period) even more than the October Revolution. If the October Revolution had not occurred,* socialist revolutions would have erupted somewhat later in Russia or in other, more developed, countries, due to the extremely tense contradictions of capitalism in the 1920s–1940s. In this case, the revolutionary process would have developed more auspiciously than it did in reality, insofar as the revolutionary forces would not have been fettered, demoralized and weakened by the Stalinized communist parties.

1937 became crucial in a profoundly tragic sense. It caused losses to the communist movement both in the USSR and throughout the world from which the movement has not recovered to this very day.

---

* Such an historical variant, as Trotsky noted, could have been possible due to fortuitous causes: for instance, if Lenin had been absent from Petrograd in 1917. It was thanks to Lenin's authority that the opposition from many party leaders to adopting a course toward the socialist revolution was successfully overcome.

The tragedy of 1937 cannot be explained by the popular aphorism "every revolution devours its own children," which by no means possesses the profound meaning which is usually ascribed to it. Thus, the bourgeois revolutions in America by no means devoured their children, and they achieved the goals set by their leaders. Nor did the October Revolution and the accompanying civil war devour its children. All its organizers, with the exception of those who were killed by declared enemies, survived this heroic epoch. The destruction of the Bolshevik generation which headed the popular revolution occurred only twenty years after its triumph.

In this book I will not deal in detail with subjects which have been thoroughly examined in other works: the application of physical torture during interrogation, the general conditions of life in the Stalinist camps, and so forth. Its main attention will be focused on those aspects of the Great Terror which in many ways continue to remain enigmatic even today: How was it possible to annihilate in peacetime such an enormous number of people? Why did the ruling stratum allow itself to be almost completely exterminated in the flames of the Great Purges? Were there forces in the party who tried to prevent the terror?

In accordance with these objectives, the book will examine the period which opens with the first show trial (in August 1936) and ends with the June Plenum of the Central Committee in 1937.

It is appropriate to preface a concrete account of historical material with a concise outline of the book's conception, the correctness of which the reader will be able to verify as he thinks over and evaluates the historical facts contained within it.

The October Revolution, which was an integral part of the world socialist revolution, was such a powerful historical event that the bureaucratic reaction to it (Stalinism) also assumed grandiose proportions, demanding an accumulation of lies and repressions never before seen in history. In turn, Stalinism's desecration of the principles and ideals of the October Revolution evoked in the USSR and beyond its borders a powerful and heroic resistance on the part of political forces retaining their belief in the Marxist theoretical doctrine and their loyalty to the revolutionary traditions of Bolshevism. To overcome this resistance required a terror which, in its scale or brutality, has no analogies in history.

The ignoring of this tragic dialectic of history leads anticommunists to an interpretation of the Great Terror as something irrational, engendered by the "Satanic" nature of the Bolsheviks who were allegedly driven by a thirst for senseless violence, including in turn their own self-annihilation.

Material from the Soviet archives which has become available in recent years (although far from all the archives are open), as well as the publication of many new memoirs, has helped the author accomplish the tasks set by this book: to investigate the mechanism of the origin and relentless spread of the Great Terror, and to discover the reasons why this mass terrorist action became not only possible but also so successful.

The author is fully aware that the goals of this research have by no means been fully accomplished. Despite the enormous and ever-increasing flood of publications containing archival material, there are significant gaps in our treatment of many events in 1937. The author did not have access to the investigatory dossiers, a careful analysis of which could untangle the Stalinist amalgams—a combination of what actually occurred with what was invented by Stalin and his inquisitors. In light of the shortage of source material, some of the author's arguments are historical hypotheses which he hopes to ground more fully in his future works. The author would be grateful to any readers who help him refine, concretize or refute these hypotheses on the basis of new ideas or material.

1. Preparations for the First Show Trial

STALIN FELL FAR SHORT of achieving his goals with the trials that followed Kirov's murder. The immediate organizers of the murder were declared to be a group of thirteen young "Zinovievists," shot in December 1934 during the case of the so-called "Leningrad Center." Zinoviev, Kamenev and other leaders of the former Leningrad Opposition, who had been convicted in January 1935 during the case of the "Moscow Center," were declared guilty of only the following: with their "counterrevolutionary" discussions they "objectively" contributed to inflaming terrorist moods among their Leningrad cothinkers.

The "post-Kirov" trials of 1934–35 were unable to establish ties leading from the "Zinovievists" to the "Trotskyists," let alone to Trotsky himself. Meanwhile Stalin needed at all costs to accuse Trotsky and the Trotskyists of terrorist activity. This version was outlined in Yezhov's manuscript, "From Fractional Activity to Open Counterrevolution," where he claimed: "There is no doubt that the Trotskyists were also informed about the terrorist side of the activity conducted by the Zinoviev organization. Moreover, from the testimony given by separate Zinovievists during the investigation of the murder of Comrade Kirov, and during the subsequent arrests of Zinovievists and Trotskyists, we have established that the latter had also embarked on the path of terrorist groups."[1]

Yezhov's "opus," which was presented to Stalin in May 1935 and edited by the latter, never saw the light of day. However, its basic conceptions turned into the fundamental points of directives issued to the organs of the NKVD. In the middle of 1935, Yezhov told the deputy Narkom of Internal Affairs, Agranov, that "in his opinion and in the opinion of the party's central committee, there existed in the Soviet Union an undisclosed center of Trotskyists," and "he sanctioned the carrying out of operations against Trotskyists in Moscow." According to Agranov, Molchanov, the head of the secret-political department of the NKVD, who had been entrusted with conducting this operation, acted without the operative effectiveness characteristic of the "organs," insofar as he felt that "there was no serious Trotskyist underground in Moscow."[2]

On 9 February, the deputy Narkom of Internal Affairs, Prokofiev, sent a directive to the local bodies of the NKVD which spoke of the "increased activity of the Trotsky-Zinoviev counterrevolutionary underground and the presence of underground terrorist formations among them." The directive demanded the "total liquidation of the entire Trotsky-Zinoviev underground" and the uncovering of "all organizational ties between the Trotskyists and Zinovievists."[3]

On 23 February, Stalin received a report from Prokofiev about a new series of arrests and about the seizure of Trotsky's archives from the 1927 period from one of those arrested. He then arranged by means of a Politburo resolution for Yezhov to be added to the investigation. As Yezhov declared at the February-March Plenum of the Central Committee in 1937, "the person responsible for opening the case (of the "Trotsky-Zinoviev Center") was essentially Comrade Stalin, who, upon receiving ... the material, wrote in a resolution: 'This is an extremely important case; I propose handing over the Trotskyist archive to Yezhov. Second, to appoint Yezhov to supervise the investigation, so that the investigation be carried out by the Cheka and Yezhov.'" "I understood this directive in the following way," added Yezhov, "that I had to implement it no matter what, and to the extent that it was in my power, I applied pressure. And here I must say that I met not only loyal resistance [sic—V. R.], but sometimes open opposition."[4]

This "opposition" came most of all from Yagoda who was disturbed by the fact that Yezhov's efforts were directed at "proving" the existence of a Trotskyist conspiracy from the beginning of the 1930s, and, consequently, of "failures" in the work of Yagoda's apparatus. Understanding Yezhov's inclusion in the investigation to be an expression of Stalin's lack of confidence in the leadership of the NKVD, Yagoda sent a directive to the organs of state security about increasing the repression directed against "Trotskyists." At this time, however, Stalin's idea of organizing a trial of the "Trotsky-Zinoviev Center" apparently remained a secret not only for members of the Politburo, but for Yagoda as well.

The first to be arrested among the participants in the future trial was the political emigré Valentin Olberg. Unlike the other emigrés who were brought to trial, he actually did meet with Sedov and conduct a correspondence with Trotsky. The Harvard archives contain the correspondence between Trotsky,

Sedov and Olberg, which discusses distributing the *Bulletin of the Opposition* in various countries, including the USSR, and deals with the activity of the German group of the Left Opposition.[5] However, by 1930 Trotsky had already rejected Olberg's proposal to come to Prinkipo in order to serve as his secretary. This occurred because Trotsky's friends in Berlin who knew Olberg well considered him "if not an agent of the GPU, then a candidate-agent."[6]

According to A. Orlov, at the end of the 1920s Olberg had been recruited by the OGPU and acted as an agent among foreign groups of the Left Opposition. Then he was recalled to the Soviet Union and in 1935 sent into the Gorky Pedagogical Institute, where "the organs" had found traces of an illegal circle studying the works of Lenin and Trotsky.

In 1937, the Paris Commission to Counter-Investigate the Moscow Trials received testimony from Olberg's mother. From her testimony it became clear that, besides V. Olberg, his brother Pavel had also emigrated to the USSR and was working as an engineer in Gorky. In his letters to his mother, P. Olberg enthusiastically told about receiving Soviet citizenship and relayed his impressions of the USSR.[7] On 5 January 1936 (on the same day as his brother) he was arrested, and in October shot along with a large group of "Trotskyists" from Moscow, Gorky and other cities (included in this group was Trotsky's son-in-law, Platon Volkov, who at the moment of his arrest was a worker in Omsk).[8]

Valentin Olberg, it was said at the February-March Plenum, "was known to the organs of the NKVD in 1931." Moreover, the "organs" had at their disposal letters from Trotsky to Olberg which had been handed over in the same year by a foreign agent of the GPU.[9] Only one thing could explain the fact that after all this Olberg had not been arrested: the OGPU considered him to be an extremely valuable agent and hoped that he would penetrate more deeply into Trotsky's entourage.

After the first round of interrogations, V. Olberg sent a declaration to the investigator in which he wrote: "I can, it seems, slander myself and do everything if only to put an end to my suffering. But I clearly cannot cast aspersions on myself and state an obvious lie, i.e., that I am a Trotskyist, Trotsky's emissary, and so forth."[10] A month later, however, Olberg "confessed" that he had come from abroad on assignment from Trotsky, and that he had recruited into a terrorist organization many teachers and students at the Gorky Ped-Institute. All the people he named were brought to Moscow and shot on 3 October 1936.

At the February-March Plenum, Yezhov placed the date of the beginning of the investigation into the case of the "United Trotsky-Zinoviev center" in December 1935. In the beginning of 1936 this case "began gradually to expand, and then the first material was sent to the Central Committee (from the NKVD)." However Molchanov, who had been directly responsible for handling cases against Trotskyists, considered Olberg to be a "solitary emissary." He therefore intended to bring Olberg to trial and close the given case with his conviction.[11]

A bit later, Yagoda and Molchanov felt that it would be enough to "link" Olberg to I. N. Smirnov, who had been brought in April 1936 from a political isolator to the GPU's internal prison. According to Agranov, Molchanov wanted "to close the investigation in April 1936, showing that the uncovered terrorist group of Shemelev-Olberg-Safonova, with ties to I. N. Smirnov, was the All-Union Trotskyist Center, and that with the discovery of the center, all the active Trotskyists had already been liquidated. Yagoda, and then Molchanov, added that, without any doubt, Trotsky personally had no immediate ties with representatives of the Trotskyist Center in the USSR."[12]

When he learned of Molchanov's and Yagoda's position, Stalin "sensed that something wasn't right in this [case] and gave instructions to continue the investigation." To carry out these instructions, Yezhov arranged a meeting with Agranov which was conducted unbeknownst to Yagoda and Molchanov. ("I invited Agranov to my dacha on a day off, pretending that we would be going for a walk"). During this meeting, Yezhov gave Agranov "Comrade Stalin's indications of mistakes that had been made by the investigation into the case of the Trotskyists; he ordered him to take measures to uncover the actual Trotskyist Center, thoroughly exposing the still concealed terrorist band and Trotsky's personal role in the entire affair." Yezhov told Agranov the names of "Trotsky's direct cadres," placing emphasis on Dreitser most of all. "After a long conversation, which was rather concrete, we came to a decision—he [Agranov] went to the Moscow region [that is, to the UNKVD of the Moscow region—V. R.] and joined the Muscovites in arresting Dreitser, thereby making an immediate breakthrough."[13]

Dreitser was brought in May to the internal prison of the NKVD from the Cheliabinsk region where he worked as the deputy director of the factory "Magnezit." Then the former head of Zinoviev's secretariat, Pikel, was arrested. They were handed over to the investigator Radzivilovsky who would later say: "extraordinarily difficult work over the course of three weeks on Dreitser and

Pikel resulted in the fact that they began to give testimony."[14] Yagoda, however, felt that their testimony was a complete fabrication. On the record of Dreitser's interrogations, which contained passages speaking of receiving terrorist directives from Trotsky, Yagoda wrote: "untrue," "nonsense," "rubbish," and "this cannot be."[15]

It was with these preconceptions that Yagoda proceeded in his report on the "Trotskyist conspiracy" at the June (1936) Plenum of the Central Committee, where he categorically denied any link between the "terrorist center" and Trotsky. When Stalin spoke at the plenum, however, he "filled in" these "gaps" in Yagoda's report. When he recalled this speech at the February-March Plenum, Yezhov said: "I sensed that in the apparatus [of the NKVD] something was going on with Trotsky, but to Comrade Stalin this was as clear as day. With his speech Comrade Stalin directly posed the question that here was Trotsky's hand, and that we had to catch him by the hand."[16]

On 19 June Yagoda and Vyshinsky presented Stalin with a list of eighty-two Trotskyists who they felt could be brought to trial as participants in terrorist activity. However Stalin demanded that they unite the Trotskyists with the Zinovievists and prepare the corresponding open trial.

After this, the investigation into the Olberg case which had been finished in May was reopened; by now Olberg was giving testimony that he had links with the Gestapo. Analogous confessions were received from the four other political emigrants who had been arrested in June.

In the middle of July, Zinoviev and Kamenev were brought from a political isolator to Moscow for further investigation. By this time Zinoviev, who had spent a year and a half in prison, was in a state of deep depression and demoralization. Beginning with the spring of 1935, he had repeatedly sent letters to Stalin in which, among other things, he said: "My soul burns with one desire: to prove to you that I am no longer an enemy. There is no demand which I would not fullfil in order to prove this.... I have come to the point where I stare for long stretches at your portrait and those of the other members of the Politburo in the newspapers, and think to myself: my friends, look into my soul—can it possibly be that you fail to see that I am no longer your enemy, that I am yours body and soul, that I understand everything, that I am ready to do anything to be worthy of your forgiveness and leniency." On 10 July 1935 Zinoviev turned to the leadership of the NKVD with a request that he be transferred to a concentration camp "with the possibility of working and moving about," insofar as it seemed that only there he "would be able to last if only for a while."

Zinoviev's letter to Stalin, sent on 12 July 1936 from a Moscow prison, shows how little Zinoviev understood what was happening. In it he presented an "urgent request" to publish the book of memoirs he had written in the political isolator, and to help his family, especially his son, whom he called "a talented Marxist with a scholarly bent."[17]

Since 1935, Stalin had managed to sow mutual discord between Zinoviev and Kamenev. Kamenev's staunchly ill-disposed attitude toward Zinoviev can be seen in his correspondence with his wife, T. Glebova, who remained at liberty. In a letter written on 12 November 1935, Glebova, who had been expelled from the party for "loss of party vigilance," reproached her husband, who was located in a political isolator, for the fact that she had "been deceived before the party." Before the trial of the "Moscow Center" she had put "her party life and honor" on the line by vouching for Kamenev's "complete lack of participation" in any "political and anti-party ties with the Zinovievists." In this letter, which would undoubtedly be read by the authorities, Glebova included an indirect denunciation of Zinoviev. She expressed her regret that, "after hearing Zinoviev's whining in the summer of 1932 and even his counterrevolutionary statement about the ineptitude of the leadership of the kolkhoz movement, she had not acted in a party way [that is, she had not denounced Zinoviev— V. R.], but had expressed her indignation only to you." In her letter, Glebova told how their seven-year-old son happened upon a toy that Zinoviev had given him. "He literally began trembling and grew pale: 'I will throw it out, for I hate the man who gave it to me.' Yet during the summer he saw much more of them (Zinoviev and his wife) than us, and had always loved them."

In a reply letter, Kamenev wrote that Zinoviev and his wife "no longer exist for me; like Volik, I 'hate' them, and probably have good reasons to do so."[18]

In the course of the renewed investigation, Zinoviev and Kamenev were once again joined together by Stalin and forced to make joint decisions. At first they firmly denied the charges made against them. Kamenev bore himself with particular courage. He declared to Mironov, the head of the economic department of the NKVD's GUGB [The Chief Directorate of State Security] who was interrogating him: "You are now observing Thermidor in a pure form. The French Revolution taught us a good lesson, but we weren't able to put it to use. We didn't know how to protect our revolution from Thermidor. That is our greatest mistake, and history will condemn us for it." When Kamenev was presented with testimony about a conspiratorial meeting with Reingold at his apartment, he declared that from the diary of the round-the-clock surveillance which was conducted outside his apartment, and from interrogation of the OGPU operative who was always present inside the apartment in the guise of a bodyguard, it would be easy to establish that Reingold had never once visited him. Finally, Kamenev threatened Mironov: if there were any further provocations he would demand that Medvedev and other former leaders of the Leningrad UNKVD be put on trial. He personally would ask them questions about the circumstances of Kirov's murder."[19]

It is understandable that reports about Kamenev's behavior during the investigation would have had to drive Stalin into a paroxysm of enraged cruelty. As Orlov recalled, "even the heads of the NKVD, who knew Stalin's insidious and merciless character, were struck by the savage hatred which he displayed with regard to the Old Bolsheviks, Kamenev, Zinoviev and Smirnov." Although Yagoda and his underlings had gone a long way in their own degeneration and had rich experience in persecuting Oppositionists, "the names of Zinoviev, Kamenev, Smirnov and especially Trotsky still retained their magical power over them."[20] They felt that Stalin would not dare to shoot the Old Bolsheviks and would limit himself to publicly disgracing them.

Prokofiev's wife told A. M. Larina in the camps that Stalin had said to Yagoda: "You work poorly, Genrikh Grigorievich. I already have reliable information that Kirov was killed on orders from Zinoviev and Kamenev, yet you still haven't been able to prove it! You have to torture them so that they finally tell the truth and reveal all their ties." When he recounted those words to Prokofiev, Yagoda began to sob.[21]

When he received information about Kamenev's and Zinoviev's "refusal to cooperate," Stalin ordered Yezhov to conduct their further interrogations, and the latter made it very clear to the accused that they would have to take part in a judicial frame-up. Yezhov explained to Zinoviev the political necessity of this step in the following way: Soviet intelligence had seized documents of the German general staff which showed the intentions of Germany and Japan to attack the Soviet Union the following spring. Therefore, what was now needed more than ever was the support of the international proletariat for the "fatherland of all laborers." Trotsky was impeding this support with his "anti-Soviet propaganda." Zinoviev must "help the party strike a shattering blow against Trotsky and his band, in order to drive the workers away from his counterrevolutionary organization under an artillery barrage."[22]

Following this, Yezhov told Zinoviev that the lives of thousands of former Oppositionists depended on his conduct at the trial. Repeating the same arguments to Kamenev, Yezhov issued an additional threat by announcing the possibility of dealing with the latter's oldest son, who had been in prison since March 1935. He showed Kamenev Reingold's testimony that he and Kamenev's son had conducted surveillance of automobiles containing Stalin and Voroshilov in order to organize terrorist acts against them. The promise to preserve the life of his oldest son was one of the main reasons which prompted Kamenev to "confess." Nevertheless, not only Kamenev's oldest son, but his middle son as well, the sixteen-year-old Yurii, was shot in 1938–39.

In his memoirs Orlov describes in detail the entire course of the investigation, its methods and mechanisms, but he doesn't mention the application of direct torture with regard to Kamenev and Zinoviev. In their case, the application of "methods of physical coercion" was limited to placing them in a cell where the central heating was turned on during the hot summer days. The unbearable heat and humidity were particularly painful to Zinoviev, who suffered from severe asthma and attacks of colic in the liver; moreover the "treatment" which he received only increased his suffering.

Zinoviev was the first to indicate that he was ready to make a deal with Stalin. After an interrogation conducted by Yezhov and Molchanov which had lasted a whole night, Zinoviev asked them to arrange a meeting where he and Kamenev could be alone. In their conversation, which was of course monitored, Zinoviev convinced Kamenev to provide the testimony demanded at the trial, on the condition that the promise made by Yezhov in Stalin's name to preserve their lives and the lives of other oppositionists be confirmed by Stalin personally in the presence of all the members of the Politburo.

Soon after this meeting, Zinoviev and Kamenev were taken to the Kremlin where they were received by Stalin and Voroshilov. When Kamenev said that they had been promised a meeting with the full membership of the Politburo, Stalin replied that he and Voroshilov were a "commission" appointed by the Politburo to negotiate with them.

Zinoviev recalled that before the trial in 1935 Yezhov had spoken on Stalin's behalf in assuring them that this trial would be the last sacrifice which they would have to make "for the sake of the party." With tears in his eyes he tried to convince Stalin that a new trial would cast a permanent shadow on the Soviet Union and the Bolshevik Party: "You want to depict members of Lenin's Politburo and Lenin's personal friends to be unprincipled bandits, and present the party as a snake's nest of intrigue, treachery and murders" [the main defendants at the impending trial were the embodiment of Bolshevism in the eyes of world public opinion—V. R.]. To this Stalin replied that the upcoming trial was directed not against Zinoviev and Kamenev, but against Trotsky, "the sworn enemy of the party." "If we didn't shoot them," he continued, referring to Zinoviev and Kamenev in the third person, "when they actively fought against the Central Committee, then why should we shoot them after they have been helping the Central Committee in its struggle against Trotsky? The comrades also are forgetting that we Bolsheviks are the followers and disciples of Lenin, and that we don't want to spill the blood of old party members, no matter how serious the sins that can be attributed to them."

Mironov, who had been present during the negotiations, told Orlov that this performance, in which Stalin called Zinoviev and Kamenev comrades, was delivered with deep feeling and sounded both sincere and convincing. Even Mironov, who knew better than others about Stalin's fierce hatred for Zinoviev and Kamenev, believed after these words that Stalin would not allow their execution.

Having listened to Stalin, Kamenev said that they would agree to give testimony at the trial under the condition that none of the defendants would be shot, that their families would not be persecuted, and that no one would receive the death penalty for past oppositional activity. Stalin vowed that all this "goes without saying."[23]

Until recently, Orlov's memoirs were the only evidence about the meeting of the "Politburo commission" with Zinoviev and Kamenev. Only at the end of the 1980s was this fact confirmed by Kaganovich, who declared in a confidential conversation with the writer Chuyev: "I know that Zinoviev and Kamenev were received.... Stalin and Voroshilov were there. I wasn't at this reception. I know that Zinoviev and Kamenev asked for mercy. They had already been arrested.... Evidently, the conversation proceeded along the lines that they had to acknowledge their guilt...."[24]

After this "reception," Zinoviev and Kamenev were moved to comfortable cells. The authorities began to give them serious medical treatment, feed them well and allow them to read books, but not, of course, newspapers, where after the announcement of the upcoming trial, the editors began to publish "demands from the workers" that they receive the death penalty.

A more complicated task turned out to be the obtaining of confessions from Smirnov and Mrachkovsky, who were widely known throughout the party for their heroic biographies. Mrachkovsky had grown up in a family which belonged to Narodnaya Volya [The People's Will], and from his earliest years he took an active part in the revolutionary movement. I. N. Smirnov, a member of the party since it was founded, led the army which defeated Kolchak during the Civil War.

For several months Smirnov and Mrachkovsky stubbornly refused to make any confessions. According to Vyshinsky, Smirnov's entire interrogation on 20 May consisted of the words: "I deny this, I deny it once again, I deny it."[25]

Twice Mrachkovsky was taken to Stalin, who promised to send him to direct industry in the Urals if he behaved "properly" at the trial.* Both times Mrachkovsky replied with a firm refusal. Then they appointed as the investigator in his case the head of the NKVD's foreign department, Slutsky, who soon told V. Krivitsky "about his experience as an inquisitor." According to Slutsky, he interrogated Mrachkovsky nonstop for ninety hours. During the interrogation, every two hours the phone rang from Stalin's secretary who asked him whether he had managed to "break" Mrachkovsky.[26]

Analogous information ("Interrogations for ninety hours. Slutsky's remarks about Mrachkovsky") is contained in Ignace Reiss's "Notes" (Cf. Chapter 40), which were published in the *Bulletin of the Opposition*. In the comments to these notes, the editors of the *Bulletin* referred to the way Reiss orally deciphered the material and then reported: "In order to break Mrachkovsky, the GPU subjected him to unbroken interrogations, lasting up to ninety hours straight! The same 'method' was applied to I. N. Smirnov, who offered greater resistance."[27]

At the beginning of the interrogation, Mrachkovsky told Slutsky: "You can tell Stalin that I hate him. He is a traitor. They took me to Molotov, who also wanted to buy me off. I spit in his face." During the remaining interrogation, which turned into a political dialogue between the arrested and the investigator, Slutsky showed Mrachkovsky the testimony given by others who had been accused in order to prove how "low they had fallen by being in opposition to

---

* According to Orlov, when Stalin was trying to tear Mrachkovsky away from the opposition in 1932, he said to him: "Break with them, what binds you, a famous worker, with this Jewish Sanhedrin?" (A. Orlov, *The Secret History of Stalin's Crimes*, p. 110).

the Soviet regime." Days and nights passed in debates on the political situation in the Soviet Union. In the end, Mrachkovsky agreed with Slutsky that great discontent existed in the land which could not be controlled from within the party and might therefore lead the Soviet regime to destruction; at the same time there was no party grouping strong enough to be able to change the regime which had developed and overthrow Stalin. "I led him to the point where he began to sob," Slutsky later told Krivitsky. "I sobbed with him when we came to the conclusion that everything was lost, that the only thing we could do was to make a desperate effort to prevent the doomed struggle of opposition leaders who were dissatisfied with their 'confessions.'"

After this session Mrachkovsky asked that he be allowed to meet with Smirnov, his close friend and comrade-in-arms on many fronts of the Civil War. During this meeting Mrachkovsky said: "Ivan Nikitich, let's give them what they want. We have to." After Smirnov sharply refused to make such a deal, Mrachkovsky "once again became angry and uncooperative. He began once more to call Stalin a traitor. However at the end of the fourth day he signed a full confession." Slutsky ended his account about Mrachkovsky's interrogation with the words: for a whole week after the interrogation "I couldn't work, and I felt that I couldn't go on living."[28]

Krivitsky's story finds a certain degree of confirmation in the material contained in Mrachkovsky's dossier, where there are seven protocols of the interrogation, of which six were prepared beforehand and typed up.* Mrachkovsky signed all of these protocols without making any changes, with one exception. Opposite the sentence about ties with the foreign Trotskyist center he wrote: "Please show me your evidence concerning the existence of ties between our organization and L. Trotsky."[29] We can assume that, although he had agreed to smear himself, Mrachkovsky continued for a long time to refuse to smear Trotsky with accusations about directing any terrorist activity.

Smirnov's former wife, Safonova, was used to put pressure on him. In face-to-face confrontations she begged him to save both their lives, "by bowing to the demands of the Politburo." Safonova continued to play the role of provoca-

---

* In his speech at the February-March Plenum, Yezhov said: "I must openly say that we observed the following practice: before giving the protocol to the accused for his signature, it was first reviewed by the investigator, then handed to his superiors; important protocols even made it to the Narkom [i.e., Yagoda—V. R.]. The Narkom would make corrections, saying that we had to record this, and not this, and then the protocol would be given to the accused to sign" (*Voprosy istorii*, 1995, no. 2, p. 16).

teur at the trial, too, where she served as a witness. As a result, she turned out to be the only person among dozens mentioned at the trial who not only avoided being shot, but was set free. At the end of the 1930s she worked in Grozny as a professor at the Chechen-Ingush Pedagogical Institute. There, according to A. Avtorkhanov, she continued to carry out assignments for the NKVD, providing, among other things, "scholarly expertise" with regard to books which supposedly contained "ideological sabotage."[30]

Unlike Safonova, many of the 160 people convicted of terrorist acts carried out on orders from the "center" who were shot after the trial never confessed to being guilty. According to Orlov, the young political emigrant, Z. Fridman, conducted himself with extraordinary courage. His name was mentioned at the trial among the "terrorists." He was shot in October 1936 along with several teachers from the Gorky Ped-Institute as part of the group case against the "terrorist organization."[31]

Judging from the numbers on the dossiers indicated in the court records, and the number of pages contained in them, the ones who most actively "collaborated" with the investigation were the five young emigrants being tried; the testimony of each one went on for hundreds of pages. The testimony of the main defendants, however—the Old Bolsheviks—was limited to a few pages and was obtained only at the end of July and the beginning of August.

On 7 August Vyshinsky presented Stalin with the first variant of the indictment, according to which twelve people were to be tried. Stalin added the names of M. I. Lurie and N. L. Lurie to this list, and crossed out from the text all references to the testimony of the Old Bolsheviks in which they evaluated the situation in the party and country which had prompted them to continue their oppositional activity.

Three days later, Stalin was presented with a new variant of the indictment which now named fourteen defendants. Stalin changed this text as well and once again extended the list of the accused—this time with the names of Yevdokimov and Ter-Vaganian.[32]

Stalin made a few additions to the defendants' testimony which they were supposed to give at the trial. He demanded that Reingold formulate the alleged terrorist instructions he received from Zinoviev in the following way: "It is not enough to cut down the oak tree [i.e., Stalin—V. R.], you have to cut down all the young oaks which grow around it." Another "imaginative" addition placed the following expression in Kamenev's mouth: "Stalin's leadership has become as solid as granite, and it would be foolish to hope that this granite will begin to crack. That means that we will have to shatter it."[33]

Before publishing any kind of announcement about the impending trial, Stalin decided to prepare the party. On 29 July a secret letter from the Central Committee "On the Terrorist Activity of the Trotsky-Zinoviev Counterrevolutionary Bloc" was sent to every party organization to be read aloud. To the draft of the letter which had been prepared by Yezhov, Stalin introduced many corrections and additions. On the first page he wrote that earlier "the role of the Trotskyists in the murder of Comrade Kirov had not been uncovered" and that now "it has been established that the Zinovievists carried out their terrorist practice in a direct bloc with Trotsky and the Trotskyists." To develop this thought the letter stated that after Kirov's murder and "the subsequent smashing of the Trotsky-Zinoviev Center, Trotsky took upon himself all direction of terrorist activity in the USSR."[34]

Whereas Yezhov reduced the "main and principal task of the 'center'" to the assassination of Stalin, Stalin formulated it as the "assassination of Comrades Stalin, Voroshilov, Kaganovich, Kirov, Ordzhonikidze, Zhdanov, Kosior and Postyshev."[35] We can assume that Stalin deliberately shifted the emphasis from himself personally to a whole group of party leaders which included those who enjoyed the genuine sympathy of the party and working-class masses.

The letter, which was intended to create an impression of the special trust with which the given information was transmitted only to members of the party, ended with the demand that "every Bolshevik" "recognize an enemy of the party no matter how well he may be disguised."[36]

After he had finished the trial's preparation, Stalin was so confident of its results that he left for vacation in Sochi before the trial opened. Control of the course of the trial was entrusted to Kaganovich, to whom Ulrich presented several variants of the sentence for approval. After Kaganovich had reviewed the last variant, he made the final corrections. In doing so, Kaganovich included his own name on one of the pages of text which contained a list of people against whom terrorist acts had been prepared. Even before the trial ended, Kaganovich sent the sentence to Stalin in Sochi for his information.

2. THE TRIAL OF THE SIXTEEN

On 15 August 1936 an announcement appeared in the newspapers from the Procurator of the USSR about transferring the case of "the United Trotsky-Zinoviev Center" for review to the Military Collegium of the Supreme Court of the USSR. The announcement stated: "An investigation has established that the Trotsky-Zinoviev Center was organized in 1932 on the orders of L. Trotsky and Zinoviev.... And that the perfidious assassination of Comrade S. M. Kirov on 1 December 1934 was prepared and carried out also on the orders of L. Trotsky and Zinoviev and this united center."

From that day on, the press began to publish numerous articles and resolutions from "workers' meetings," which spoke not only about the guilt of the defendants as an undisputed fact, but virtually decided the sentence in advance. "The case of Trotsky-Zinoviev-Kamenev breathes its stench upon us from the bandits' underground," wrote *Pravda*. "The snakes slither up to what we hold dearest of all.... We have uncovered ties between the Zinovievists with Trotsky's foreign counterrevolutionary organization, and systematic ties with the German fascist secret police (Gestapo).... No mercy, no leniency for enemies of the people who have tried to deprive the people of its leaders. We now await the word of the law, which knows only one measure of punishment for the crimes committed by the Trotsky-Zinoviev band."[1] Similar phrases appeared in the "responses" to the announcement about the upcoming trial given by well-known writers, scientists, actors and "celebrities from among the people."

The defendants at the Trial of the Sixteen included two completely disparate groups. The first consisted of eleven prominent Bolsheviks who had participated in 1926–27 in the "united opposition bloc." The second group consisted of young members of the German Communist Party who had emigrated to the USSR. At the beginning of the 1930s, three of them had belonged to the German Left Opposition, they had been expelled from the KPD, and then they had been readmitted to the party after ritual recantations. After arriving in the USSR, all five of these emigrants worked in Soviet establishments or in the

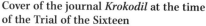

Cover of the journal *Krokodil* at the time of the Trial of the Sixteen

Cartoon about the Trial of the Sixteen

Comintern apparatus, publishing fervently anti-Trotskyist articles.

Summarizing the observations contained in articles written by foreign journalists at the trial, L. Sedov wrote: "The old men sat there, completely crushed and broken; they answer in muffled voices, and even cry. Zinoviev is thin, hunched over, grey, with sunken cheeks. Mrachkovsky coughs up blood, loses consciousness, and they carry him out in their arms. They all look like people who have been hounded and completely worn out. The young people, on the other hand ... conduct themselves in a self-confident and free-and-easy manner; they have fresh, almost joyful faces; they feel almost as if they are at a birthday party. With unconcealed pleasure they tell about their ties with the Gestapo and all kinds of other fantastic tales."[2]

The indictment stressed that the trial of 1935 had not established facts which showed that the leaders of the Zinoviev opposition had given directives about organizing Kirov's murder or had even known about its preparation. This could be explained by the fact that the defendants who had taken a direct part in preparing the assassination, not only of Kirov but also of other party leaders, maliciously concealed all such information.

Apart from this detail, there was no continuity between the "Zinoviev" trial of 1935 and the trial of the sixteen. From among the nineteen people condemned at the first trial, only four were called to the new trial; the remaining figures were not even summoned as witnesses. At the Trial in 1936, besides the "United Trotsky-Zinoviev Center," reference was made to a certain "Moscow Center," but its composition had nothing in common with the composition of the "Moscow Center" whose activity had been the subject of the trial in January 1935. As the trial established, the new "Moscow Center" busied itself with preparing terrorist acts against Stalin and Voroshilov on the basis of a directive contained in a letter from Trotsky, written in invisible ink and brought in October 1934 from abroad by Dreitser's sister. After developing the letter, Dreitser immediately sent it to Mrachkovsky in Kazakhstan; he in turn recognized Trotsky's handwriting, and, having thereby vouched for the authenticity of the letter, "burned it out of conspiratorial considerations." Vyshinsky imposed the guilt for receiving this directive on Smirnov, too. Without introducing the slightest bit of evidence, he declared: "*I am deeply convinced* that you knew about it even though you were imprisoned in a political isolator [my emphasis—V. R.]."[3]

According to the version produced by the investigation, Trotsky's terrorist activity was conducted under conditions of the utmost secrecy. However Vyshinsky in his indictment speech could not refrain from discovering terrorist propaganda even in Trotsky's public literary and political articles. He declared that "in March 1932, Trotsky burst into a counterrevolutionary frenzy when he published an open letter calling to 'remove Stalin.'"[4]

Vyshinsky was referring to a letter to the Presidium of the Central Executive Committee which Trotsky had published in the *Bulletin of the Opposition* in connection with being deprived of his Soviet citizenship. Vyshinsky limited himself to introducing a total of two words from this letter, without indicating in what context they had been written. Trotsky's appeal, however, had been addressed not to his cothinkers, but to the highest body of the Soviet state. "Stalin has led you into a blind alley," wrote Trotsky. "You cannot find your way back to the main road without liquidating Stalinism. You must trust in the working class; you must give the proletarian vanguard the chance, by means of free criticism from top to bottom, to review the entire Soviet system and mercilessly cleanse it of all the accumulated garbage. And you must finally carry out Lenin's last insistent advice: *remove Stalin*."[5]

The expression, "remove Stalin," was widely used by the opposition groups which arose at the beginning of the 1930s around Riutin and A. P. Smirnov-

Eismont. The delegates to the Seventeenth Party Congress who crossed Stalin's name off the ballot during the secret elections also acted in the spirit of this appeal by Trotsky. The fact that the advice to "remove Stalin" envisioned the use of statutory and constitutional means was addressed by Trotsky when he explained in an article published at the end of 1932 that the slogan, "remove Stalin," did not mean a call for his physical elimination.

In order to give weight to his version identifying the terms "remove" and "kill," Vyshinsky forced Goltsman to declare at the trial that in a conversation with him Trotsky repeated the expression, "Remove Stalin." Then Vyshinsky demanded that Goltsman explain what the word "remove" meant. Goltsman obediently declared: "the only way to remove Stalin was terror."[6]

A week after the trial was over, the whole world learned that the meeting at which these sacramental words had been spoken had never taken place. According to the trial material, Goltsman was the only one among the Old Bolsheviks who met with Trotsky abroad. The location of this meeting was alleged to be Copenhagen, where Trotsky was spending a week in 1932 in order to give a lecture. As Goltsman testified, Sedov accompanied him to the Hotel Bristol where he met with Trotsky. A few days after the publication of this part of the court transcripts, the Danish Social-Democratic newspaper published an article which was reprinted in the entire world press: the Hotel Bristol had been torn down in Copenhagen in 1917.

According to Orlov, this "slipup" could be explained by the confusion allowed by the slow-moving investigators. When they first began to work out the version of Goltsman's meeting with Trotsky, the decision had still not been made where this meeting was to have taken place: in Denmark or in Norway, where Trotsky moved in the middle of 1935. Molchanov therefore ordered them to ask the Commissariat of Foreign Affairs for information about the names of hotels both in Copenhagen and in Oslo, where there actually was a Hotel Bristol. When the decision was made to move the meeting up in time, and consequently to Copenhagen, one of Molchanov's assistants mistakenly retained the name of the hotel which had figured in the "Norwegian" variant.[7]

Not one document, not one piece of material evidence was introduced at the Trial of the Sixteen. All the convictions were constructed exclusively on the slander and self-slander of the accused and the witnesses. G. S. Liushkov, one of the trial investigators, fled abroad in 1938 and released a declaration which stated: "At the trial which occurred in August 1936, accusations that Trotsky, via Olberg, was connected with the German Gestapo; accusations against Zinoviev and Kamenev for espionage; accusations that Zinoviev and Kamenev were linked to the so-called "Right Center" via Tomsky, Rykov and Bukharin— all these accusations were completely fabricated. Zinoviev, Kamenev, Tomsky, Rykov, Bukharin and many others were executed as enemies of Stalin who were impeding his destructive policies. Stalin took advantage of the favorable opportunity presented by the Kirov affair in order to rid himself of these people by fabricating broad anti-Stalinist conspiracies, espionage trials and terrorist organizations. Thus Stalin was using all measures to eliminate his political opponents and all those who might become his opponents in the future. Stalin's diabolical methods led to the downfall of even the strongest and most experienced people."[8]

In the explanations she gave to the Party Control Commission in 1956, Safonova described these "diabolical methods" and stressed that the investigators were motivated in their extortion of false testimony by the fact that such testimony was necessary in the interests of the party. "Yes, it was with this understanding—that the party demands this and we were obligated to pay with our heads for Kirov's murder—that we arrived at giving false testimony, not only I, but all the other accused.... That's what happened during the pretrial investigation, and at the trial this was aggravated by the presence of foreign correspondents; knowing that they could use our testimony to harm the Soviet state, none of us could tell the truth."[9]

In the given instance, Safonova, who played one of the most unseemly roles at the trial, was arbitrarily extending her own conduct and its "patriotic" motivation to all the accused. In actuality, the Old Bolsheviks couldn't help but understand that the accusations with which they were incriminated wouldn't raise, but lower the prestige of the USSR, Bolshevism and the October Revolution. It is worth noting that not one of the main defendants acknowledged links to the Gestapo. Commenting on this part of the trial, Trotsky wrote: "From their dialogue with the procurator regarding the Gestapo, it is not difficult to reconstruct the haggling that went on behind the scenes during the trial session. 'You want to vilify and destroy Trotsky?' Kamenev, for instance, probably said. 'We will help you. We are prepared to present Trotsky as the organizer of terrorist acts. The bourgeoisie doesn't understand these issues very well, and not only the bourgeoisie: Bolsheviks ... terror ... murders ... thirst for power ... yearning for revenge ... This they might believe.... But no one can believe that either Trotsky or we (Kamenev, Zinoviev, Smirnov and others) were linked to Hitler. By passing beyond the bounds of believability, we risk compromising the charge of terror, which, as you yourself well know is also not built on granite foundations. In addition, the charge of ties to the Gestapo reminds everyone all too well of the slander against Lenin and the very same Trotsky in 1917...."[10]

Another point which all the defendants with famous political names categorically refused to acknowledge was the charge that the "center" intended after coming to power to destroy all those who had carried out terrorist acts. When Vyshinsky proposed that Zinoviev confirm Reingold's testimony to that effect, Zinoviev replied: "That's from Jules Verne.... Those are Arabian fairy tales." When he repeated these words in his indictment speech, Vyshinsky declared: "And the murder of Zinoviev's secretary, Bogdan, what is that?! A fairy tale?"[11]

Here Vyshinsky was referring to one of the foulest aspects of the trial. After he had been expelled from the party during the purge of 1933, Bogdan, who was Zinoviev's former secretary, committed suicide. His suicide made a big impression on the party. Now it was being presented, in essence, as a murder committed by Bogdan's cothinkers. Basing his accusation on Pikel's testimony, Vyshinsky declared: Zinoviev and Kamenev "led Bogdan to suicide by placing him before a dilemma: either agree to a terrorist act, or kill himself."[12]

Such charges and "confessions" could be accepted as true only by those who had been led, as Trotsky said, to a state of "totalitarian idiotism." And only such people could believe the hysterical outbursts of Vyshinsky when he cried: "In the dark underground, Trotsky, Zinoviev and Kamenev issue their wretched call: remove him, murder him! The underground machine begins to do its work, knives are sharpened, revolvers are loaded, bombs are armed, false documents are written or forged, secret ties with the German political police are established, sentries are posted, people are trained to shoot, and finally, they shoot and kill.... They not only talk about shooting, they shoot; they shoot and kill!"[13] Meanwhile, the only shooting which was mentioned at the trial was Nikolaev's, after which dozens of people had already been executed, but the trial wasn't presented with a single document. The only revolver mentioned at the trial belonged to Lurie, but it, according to Lurie's own testimony, had been stolen from him along with a suitcase which had been left in the baggage room at the train station.

The "young" defendants among the political emigrants tried to fill in all these "gaps" in the investigation and charges. They were declared Trotsky's immediate emissaries, sent by him into the USSR with orders to kill as many leaders as possible. Fritz David and Berman-Yurin testified that they had received such directives from Trotsky personally. Olberg and both Luries, according to their testimony, were sent by Trotsky for terrorist activity although he had never once laid eyes on them.

The "young" defendants readily told about murders they had planned which inevitably miscarried. Thus, Berman-Yurin and Fritz David testified that they intended to arrange an attack on Stalin during the work of the Eighth Plenum of the Executive Committee of the Comintern, but this "plan failed" insofar as Fritz David didn't manage to obtain a guest pass to the plenum for Berman-Yurin, who was supposed to have shot Stalin. Fritz David gave another explanation for this "failure." "These plans collapsed because Stalin didn't attend the Eighth Plenum."

After this, both conspirators decided—following Trotsky's directive to carry out the attack "before an international forum"—to shoot Stalin at the Seventh Congress of the Comintern. However this plan failed as well, insofar as Berman-Yurin once again didn't manage to obtain a pass, and Fritz David couldn't execute the terrorist act because he was sitting far from the table of the presidium.[14]

The same "credibility" was a feature of Olberg's testimony, who announced that even before his arrival in Gorky, the director of the pedagogical institute there had already organized "armed detachments"; therefore all that remained for Olberg was to work out the "plan of the attack." According to this plan, the teachers and students at the institute were supposed to carry out a terrorist act during their participation in the May Day demonstration in Moscow, but Olberg's arrest prevented this attack.

Details of "terrorist preparations" which had not been mentioned at the trial were filled by obliging journalists (in such cases, nothing was too fantastic). Thus, in Rovinsky's article with the pretentious title, "A Thousand and One Nights and the Spies of Trotsky and the Gestapo," it said that Olberg not only organized terrorist groups, but that he also "trained terrorist snipers and bomb throwers, in short, did everything that was demanded of him by his masters—Trotsky and the Gestapo, whose activity was so closely and inextricably interwoven."[15]

According to the trial material, uninterrupted failures also accompanied the activity of the like-named Luries. N. Lurie formed a group of three people for an attack on Voroshilov. This troika carefully monitored the travels of the "first marshal," but his car always "passed by too quickly. It was useless to shoot at a fast-moving automobile." In July 1933, N. Lurie left for Cheliabinsk, where he worked as a physician. There he prepared terrorist acts against Ordzhonikidze and Kaganovich in case they visited the tractor factory. Although neither of them came to Cheliabinsk, the sentence indicated that N. Lurie "tried to carry out an attack on the life of Comrades Kaganovich and Ordzhonikidze."[16] Finally, N. Lurie, on orders from M. Lurie, traveled to Leningrad in 1936 where he prepared to shoot Zhdanov during the May Day demonstration; this plan, too, was unsuccessful, however, since his column marched by far from the tribune.

The attempts to use the aid of the German special services by the terrorists sent to the USSR also failed without exception. A secret letter from the Central Committee on 29 July stated that these terrorists "had access to the German embassy in Moscow and undoubtedly used its services." Only N. Lurie's testimony was introduced as confirmation, however; he claimed that his group was supposed to receive "explosive devices" at the German embassy, but that the group never made it once to the embassy because his trip to Cheliabinsk prevented them from doing so.

The spirit of "totalitarian idiotism" also permeated the accounts of how the terrorists obtained resources for their activity by "stealing the people's money." As an example, "facts" were introduced concerning the transfer of thirty thousand rubles by the "hidden double-dealer" Arkus, the deputy chairman of the USSR State Bank, to trusts headed by Yevdokimov and Fedorov (the latter was one more prominent "Zinovievist" whose name was mentioned at the trial). In addition, as the Central Committee's secret letter indicated, the terrorists planned to carry out plain robberies. With regard to this claim, the letter introduced the testimony of a certain "Trotskyist Lavrentiev," who confessed that four members of his group were fired from work in order "to fully devote themselves to terrorist activity" and raise the necessary resources for it. To do this they first decided to rob the funds of the village council. After this robbery fell through, they traveled to Arzamas to attack cashiers who were receiving money from the bank. However, this "robbery never took place because the right circumstances were absent."[17]

The secret letter from the Central Committee and the final indictment named dozens of members of underground groups who acted on orders from the "unified center" in various cities around the country. Although the preparation of attacks on Kosior and Postyshev was not mentioned during the trial, the sentence indicated that the "center" also prepared terrorist acts against them through a conspiratorial group subordinate to it.

Not all of the defendants at the trial confessed to participating in terrorist activity. These charges were categorically denied by Goltsman and Smirnov—the only defendants who had actually been in contact with Trotsky (through Sedov) at the beginning of the 1930s (see Chapter 9).

It was only on 13 August, i.e., a day before the indictment was signed, that the pretrial investigation managed to obtain a confession from Goltsman that Sedov had given him "a directive" to kill Stalin as the only way to change the situation in the Soviet Union.

Smirnov declared at the trial that Sedov had also given him "a terrorist directive," which, however, only expressed Sedov's personal opinion and was not a command from Trotsky. This testimony undercut the version outlined in the indictment: one of the oldest Bolsheviks clearly could not have accepted "a directive" coming from a young man who could hardly have served as an authority for him.

Despite all the efforts of both the prosecutor and Safonova, who furiously defamed Smirnov at the trial, the latter refused during the entire trial to conduct himself in a manner which would please Vyshinsky. For this reason, his answers to the prosecutor in the trial transcript are given not in a full, but in an abridged form. As we can tell from the transcript, they managed to pry less than they wanted from Smirnov: he only called Trotsky an enemy "standing on the other side of the barricades," and confessed to having met with Sedov in Berlin in 1931. As the transcript states in summary, "during a nearly three-hour-long interrogation, Smirnov tried in every way possible to avoid the questions posed directly by the prosecutor, Comrade Vyshinsky; he attempted to diminish his role and denied his terrorist activity against the party and government leaders."

The account of Smirnov's interrogation regarding the existence of the "center" was published in the following form:

> Smirnov once again tries to deflect responsibility from himself for the work of the Trotsky-Zinoviev center.

A. Y. Vyshinsky

Vyshinsky: When was it that you left the center?
Smirnov: I never even intended to leave, there was nothing to leave from.
Vyshinsky: Didn't the center exist?
Smirnov: What center are you talking about?...

After this statement from Smirnov, which threatened to destroy the entire conception of the indictment, Vyshinsky asked several defendants to rise, one after the other. He asked Mrachkovsky, Zinoviev, Yevdokimov and Bakaev the same question: "Did the center exist?", and the defendants all responded with the same monosyllabic reply: "Yes." Then Vyshinsky felt that he could return to Smirnov's interrogation, declaring: "How is it that you, Smirnov, permit yourself to claim that there was no center?" In response, as the court transcript notes, "Smirnov once again tried to prevaricate, claiming that the center never met, but the testimony from Zinoviev, Ter-Vaganian and Mrachkovsky once again exposed his lies."[18]

When other defendants "confirmed" that Smirnov headed the Trotskyist part of the conspiracy and named him "Trotsky's deputy in the USSR," Smirnov turned to them with the bitter rejoinder: "You want a leader? Well, then, take me." Finally, in his concluding remarks, Smirnov "just as he had done at the pretrial and trial investigations, continued to deny responsibility for the crimes committed by the Trotsky-Zinoviev center after his arrest"[19] (even though Smirnov had been in prison since 1 January 1933, Vyshinsky stubbornly insisted that he had been in communication from there with his cothinkers and that he had given them directives).

The remaining defendants from among the Old Bolsheviks conducted themselves in a much more compliant manner, but only in the part of the trial which was concerned with vilifying Trotsky. Zinoviev and Kamenev obediently repeated all the most horrific characterizations of "Trotskyism" which Stalin had invented, right up to declaring Trotskyism a variety of fascism. This testimony was all the more easy to extract from them since they had joined with Stalin in 1923 in fabricating the myth about "Trotskyism," and, after a brief collaboration with Trotsky in the ranks of the "United Opposition" (1926–1927) had once again resurrected this myth.

If Stalin had managed to sow hostility between Kamenev and Zinoviev as the trial approached, then it was even easier to stir them up against Trotsky. No small role in fanning this hatred was played by an episode from 1932. After the foreign communist press reported the preparation of a terrorist act against Trotsky by White-Guardists led by General Turkul, Trotsky sent a secret letter to the Politburo of the Central Committee and the Presidium of the Central Control Commission in which he expressed his certainty that these actions on the part of White emigrants had been incited by Stalin. In this regard, Trotsky wrote: "The question of terrorist reprisal against the author of this letter was posed by Stalin long before Turkul: in 1924–25, at a small meeting, Stalin weighed the arguments *for* and *against*. The arguments *for* were clear and obvious. The main argument *against* was the following: there are too many young and selfless Trotskyists who might respond with counterterrorist acts. I received this information at one time from Zinoviev and Kamenev"[20] (in 1935 Trotsky described in greater detail the accounts from Kamenev and Zinoviev about their negotiations with Stalin over the expediency of such an attack).[21]

After receiving this letter, Stalin instructed Shkiriatov and Yaroslavsky to show it to Zinoviev and Kamenev. The latter two immediately sent a declaration to the Central Committee in which they called Trotsky's account a "foul invention" and "repulsive slander aimed at compromising our party."[22] It is understandable that at the trial they confirmed all the charges made against Trotsky.

As far as their own terrorist activity is concerned, the testimony from Zinoviev and Kamenev is distinguished by its extreme brevity. In reply to Vyshinsky's questions, "Didn't you all kill Comrade Kirov?", and "Didn't Kirov's murder immediately involve your own hands?", they answered with one syllable: "Yes."

On a number of occasions, however, even these defendants uttered equivocal formulations which suggested that their confessions were forced. Thus, during Bakaev's interrogation, Zinoviev declared: "*In my opinion*, Bakaev is right when he says that the actual main perpetrators of Kirov's villainous murder were myself—Zinoviev, Trotsky and Kamenev [my emphasis—V. R.]."[23]

The fact that the "terrorist center" which had existed since 1932 had not been discovered earlier was explained at the investigation and trial by the assiduous precautions followed by the conspirators. However, from the trial material it became clear that the "terrorist activity" of the defendants amounted to incessant discussions among themselves and with dozens of other people about terror, the arranging of meetings and of trips for the transmission of Trotsky's directives, and so forth. The indictment and sentence describe in detail how the defendants created large groups for the preparation of terrorist acts, how they "inspired" and "egged on" these groups, gave each other assignments and reported about their execution. But the "active preparation" of the terrorist act was limited to observing the movements of the "leaders" and to the interruption at the last moment of carefully prepared attacks because of some "unforeseen circumstances."

Behind all this, however, one important question remained: What motives prompted the defendants to undertake their treacherous crimes?

3. "Thirst for Power" or "Restoration of Capitalism"?

A T THE TRIAL of the "Moscow Center" (January 1935), Zinoviev and Kamenev confessed only to their "moral and political responsibility" for terrorist moods among their former supporters. In the newspaper commentaries accompanying the trial transcript, the desire to restore capitalist society in the USSR was given as the incentive for these terrorist moods and for oppositional inclinations in general.

The Stalinist and post-Stalinist regimes would have to discredit the socialist idea for decades in order for the desire to restore capitalism to be openly announced in the USSR, and then to be declared praiseworthy in its disintegrating republics. For the modern reader who is disoriented by the mass anticommunist propaganda, it is difficult to imagine what the accusation of wanting to restore capitalist relations would mean to a bearer of the Bolshevik type of social consciousness. In any case, it was no less insulting and shameful than charges of treachery, espionage, sabotage or the preparation of the USSR's defeat in the impending war.

We can assume that when Zinoviev and Kamenev met with Stalin and agreed to confess to the charge of terrorist activity, they asked in return to remove the charge of preparing to restore capitalist relations in the country after they had come to power. In a certain sense, this request would also answer Stalin's needs, because he wanted to declare through the mouths of his opponents that they could imagine no other model of socialism than Stalin's.

With casuistic refinement, this version was first presented in the Central Committee's secret letter of 29 July 1936. The letter referred to the extensive testimony of those under investigation and claimed that the Trotskyists and Zinovievists no longer had any political incentives for "fighting against the party," and that in the 1930s they hadn't even tried to develop "any kind of a somewhat coherent and all-embracing political program," insofar as they were in no position to counterpose any positive program to the "policies of the

26

VKP(b)." Therefore, after coming to power, they intended to continue Stalin's policies.

The letter indicated that, after they had killed "the main leaders of the party and the government," the Trotskyists and Zinovievists counted on coming to power because "in the eyes of the party and the broad masses of workers they will look like fully repentant supporters of Leninist-Stalinist politics who had acknowledged their mistakes and crimes." A more concrete description of these intentions was contained in Kamenev's testimony when he said that the "center" had outlined two variants of seizing power. The first variant amounted to the following: "after they had completed their terrorist act against Stalin, the leadership of the party and government would be bewildered" and the remaining "leaders" would enter into negotiations with the leaders of the Trotsky-Zinoviev bloc, especially with Zinoviev, Kamenev and Trotsky. This variant, which was undoubtedly placed in Kamenev's mouth by Stalin-Yezhov, aimed to create an impression of the "unreliability" of the members of the Politburo, who, if left without Stalin, would find nothing better to do than transfer the "leading position" in the party and nation to their political opponents.

The second variant looked no less absurd. According to this version, after the terrorist act on Stalin, "uncertainty and disorganization" would arise in the party leadership. The oppositionists would then hurry to use the chance "to compel the remaining party leaders to allow us to come to power, or else force them to yield their places to us." This version, too, implicitly suggested both Stalin's exclusivity and the pitiful role of his comrades, who, if they ended up without him, would allow the leaders of the opposition to strip the power from their hands.

The usefulness of both these variants for Stalin consisted in what they confirmed: "In the face of the absolutely indisputable successes of socialist construction," the oppositionists had lost any kind of political alternative and were experiencing only bitterness and a desire to exact revenge for "their complete political bankruptcy."[1]

Stalin's version was underscored in the final indictment, which stated: "It has been established beyond any doubt that the sole motive for the organization of the Trotsky-Zinoviev bloc was the desire to seize power at any cost."[2] Taking his lead from this version, Vyshinsky declared in his indictment speech: "Without the masses, and against the masses, but for power, power at any cost, the thirst for personal power—that is the entire ideology of the company sitting on the defendants' bench."[3]

Referring to the shift from the version about wanting to restore capitalism to the one about the naked thirst for power, Trotsky wrote: "The indictment rejects one version in favor of the other, as if we were dealing with various solutions to a chess problem." However even the second version (the leaders of the opposition had lost all political principles, rejected their own program and wanted only their own return to power) seemed no less fantastic that the first. "In what way could the murder of 'leaders'" Trotsky asked in this regard, "transfer power to people who in a number of confessions have succeeded in undermining confidence in themselves, humiliating themselves, dragging themselves through the mud and thereby depriving themselves of any possibility of playing a leading political role at any time in the future?"

The judicial frame-up, Trotsky demonstrated, misses the mark in its statements both about the goals which the defendants had set, and the methods which they intended to use for achieving these goals. The version of terror, chosen as a means in the unprincipled struggle for power, was useful to Stalin when it came to destroying the opposition, but absolutely useless when it came to explaining how the "center" could attract people to carry out the plans. Even if we allow for a minute that the leaders who had been hiding behind the scenes were actually ready to resort to terror, then what incentives could move people who "inevitably should pay for someone else's head with their own? With neither ideals nor deep faith in their banner, a hired killer who had been guaranteed impunity ahead of time is conceivable; what is not conceivable is a terrorist who is going to sacrifice himself."[4]

The absurdity of the explanation of the aims and methods of the political struggle supposedly chosen by the conspirators was so obvious that three weeks after the trial, an article in *Pravda* suddenly announced that the defendants "had tried to conceal the true goal of their struggle" and therefore had claimed that "the Trotsky-Zinoviev unified bloc had no new political program." In actual fact, they had been guided by the program "of returning the USSR to bourgeois tracks."[5]

Commenting on this new and sudden exchange of versions about the goals of the defendants, Trotsky wrote: "Neither the workers nor peasants could have had any particular grounds for being upset at fake 'Trotskyists' who wish to seize power: in any case, they wouldn't be any worse than the ruling clique. To frighten the people it was necessary to add that the 'Trotskyists' want to return the land to the landowners and the factories to the capitalists."[6]

Trotsky felt that the outlines of this charge had unwittingly been suggested to Stalin by Radek, who was trying to dig a trench that was as deep as possible between himself and the defendants at the trial of the Sixteen. With this aim, Radek widened the circle of crimes in comparison to those officially attributed to Stalin's victims. In an article appearing during the trial, Radek wrote: the defendants knew that "the murder of Comrade Stalin, the brilliant leader of the Soviet people, meant to work directly for fascism"; they tried to "expedite the victory of fascism in order to receive from its hands at least the semblance of power."[7] Thus, if the act of indictment was limited to the version of the defendants' collaboration with the Gestapo for the sake of carrying out terrorist acts, then Radek was ascribing to his former comrades and cothinkers the desire for the USSR's defeat in a war with fascism, which inevitably would have led to the restoration of capitalism and the national subjugation of the USSR. Radek "perfected" this schema at the second show trial, where he figured as a defendant (see Chapter 15).

After the second Moscow Trial, which "confirmed" the version about wanting to restore capitalism and used hindsight to ascribe this desire to the Old Bolsheviks executed six months earlier, Stalin felt that it would make sense to personally establish the "masked" nature of the version about the naked thirst for power. In his report to the February-March Plenum he said: "At the trial of 1936, if you remember, Kamenev and Zinoviev sharply denied that they had any political platform.... There can be no doubt that they both lied.... They were afraid of demonstrating their actual platform of restoring capitalism in the USSR, since they feared that such a platform would provoke disgust in the working class."[8]

The second Moscow Trial broadened the framework of the crimes committed by the "Unified Trotsky-Zinoviev Center" in one more significant sense— it added to the circle of people whom this center planned to attack.

4. "The Molotov Affair"

A sensational moment during the Trial of the Sixteen was the listing of people marked by "the center" as targets for terrorist acts. Among them, besides Stalin, were five members of the Politburo (out of ten elected at the Seventeenth Congress) and two candidate members of the Politburo (out of five). It was particularly noteworthy that the defendants, according to the material from the investigation and the trial, passed over in their criminal plans the second person in the party and the country—the Chairman of the Council of People's Commissars, Molotov. Moreover, this fact was not concealed, but, on the contrary, indirectly emphasized by Vyshinsky.

While interrogating Zinoviev, Vyshinsky was not satisfied with the confession that the conspirators intended to kill "the leaders of the party and government." He felt that it was necessary to concretize these words, and asked Zinoviev: "That is, Stalin, Voroshilov and Kaganovich?" Zinoviev obediently confirmed this, thereby showing that the terrorists did not consider Molotov "a leader of the party and government."[1]

Vyshinsky's entire indictment speech was filled with high-flown and bombastic sentences like the following; "The despised and insignificant band of adventurists have tried with their muddy feet to trample the most fragrant flowers in our socialist garden," or "These mad dogs of capitalism have tried to tear to pieces the very best of the best people of our Soviet land."[2] In his repeated enumeration of "the very best people," and of "marvelous Bolsheviks, talented and tireless architects of our state," however, Molotov's name was never mentioned.

In *The Red Book* (see Chapter 8), L. Sedov turned attention to the fact that "the list of leaders whom the terrorists were allegedly preparing to kill contained not only the leaders of first magnitude, but even the Zhdanovs, Kosiors and Postyshevs. *But it did not contain Molotov.* In such matters, Stalin allows nothing which is accidental."[3]

Trotsky felt that the question about Molotov's absence from the given list was so important when it came to understanding the mechanism of the Moscow Trials that he devoted a special chapter to it in his book, *Stalin's Crimes*. Here he emphasized that, at the time of the Trial of the Sixteen, "Those who are uninitiated into the secrets of the upper echelons simply couldn't understand: why did the terrorists feel that it was necessary to kill ... 'leaders' of a provincial scale while leaving unnoticed Molotov, who is generally recognized as being a head, if not two, taller than these candidates for victimization." From the defendants' testimony it follows that "the plans of the 'center' as well as my directives contained all conceivable and inconceivable candidates for martyrdom—except Molotov." Meanwhile, "no one ever considered Molotov a decorative figure like Kalinin. On the contrary, if one raises the question of who might replace Stalin, then one can't fail to answer that Molotov has incomparably more chances than all the others."[4]

Trotsky found an explanation for Molotov's ostracism in the stubborn rumors about Molotov's disagreement with Stalin's rejection of the theory of "social fascism" and the adoption in 1935 of the policy of the Popular Front. These rumors found indirect confirmation in the Soviet press, where Molotov was neither quoted nor praised for a while, nor was his photograph published. During this period Trotsky not only wrote in his articles about "Molotov's disgrace," but in his diary entries expressed the view that Molotov's impending fall was likely.

Trotsky assumed that Stalin's reconciliation with Molotov had occurred before the Trial of the Sixteen. This immediately found reflection in the pages of the Soviet press, which, "on a signal from above, restored Molotov's previous rights. It would be possible, by studying *Pravda*, to paint a very clear and convincing picture of Molotov's steady rehabilitation during 1936."[5]

In May of 1936, Trotsky published a note called "The Columns of *Pravda*," in which he commented on the "successful turnaround" in Molotov's fate, insofar as the latter "had decisively evened out the front." Before this, Molotov "had been named, it is true, among the innate leaders, but not always, usually after Kaganovich and Voroshilov, and often without his initials. In the Soviet rituals, all these are signs of great political importance.... On his part, Molotov has given the necessary praise to the leader, but only two or three times per speech, which in the atmosphere of the Kremlin sounds almost like a call to overthrow Stalin." Only during the last weeks, Trotsky continued sarcastically, has Molotov "uttered a few panegyrics to Stalin, which forced Mikoyan himself to turn green with envy. As compensation Molotov has received his initials, his name has moved to second place and he is now called 'the closest comrade-in-arms.'"[6]

In his book, *Stalin's Crimes*, Trotsky wrote that the Trial of the Sixteen revealed Stalin's intention not to hurry with a full amnesty for Molotov but to teach him a lesson. These arguments of Trotsky, based on circumstantial evidence, are supplemented by the testimony of Orlov, who was well initiated in the ways of the first Moscow Trial. In his words, at the beginning of the investigation in the case of the "Trotsky-Zinoviev Center" the investigators were instructed to obtain confessions from the defendants regarding the preparation of terrorist acts against all members of the Politburo. When, however, Stalin was presented with the first transcripts of the interrogations, he significantly shortened this list. Nor did the names of such Politburo members as Kalinin, Mikoyan, Andreev, or Chubar figure among the intended victims of terrorist acts named by the conspirators at the subsequent trials. This omission didn't cause much confusion insofar as everyone knew the secondary political role which these people played. The decision, however, to strike Molotov's name from the material of the impending trial was taken by the investigators to be an event of extraordinary importance. "Stubborn rumors circulated in the NKVD that Stalin had become angry at Molotov's attempts to talk him out of arranging the shameful frame-ups of the Old Bolsheviks.... From day to day the NKVD awaited orders to arrest Molotov."[7]

After the Trial of the Sixteen, the preparation of the subsequent trial reflected Stalin's new directives regarding Molotov, who had turned into his main assistant in the organization of the anti-Bolshevik terror. Already by September 1936, an investigator would say to Arnold, a petty functionary arrested in Siberia: "We have sufficient material to charge you with espionage [at the time of the first World War Arnold had deserted from the tsarist army and served from 1917 to 1923 in the American armed forces—V. R.], but right now we are charging you as a participant in a terrorist organization, and we don't demand any other confessions; choose what you would rather be—a spy or a terrorist."[8] Arnold chose the second variant which then was utilized at the Kemerovo Trial in November 1936 (see Chapter 8). Here the court said that Arnold, on assignment from the "Western Siberian Trotskyist Center," tried to arrange an automobile accident involving the car in which Molotov was riding.

The article, "A Just Sentence," which was devoted to the results of the

Kemerovo Trial, stressed that "fortunately for the Motherland, for the people," the assault on Molotov had failed, but "the thought alone that it was possible is capable of making every citizen of the Soviet Union shudder."[9]

The basis of this version was taken from an actual incident which occurred in September 1934 in the city of Prokopievsk. When Molotov arrived there, he was driven from the train station in a car chauffeured by Arnold, who had been assigned by the city department of the NKVD; Arnold at that time headed the Kuzbasstroi Garage (the chauffeur of the party's City Committee was considered to have not been "tested" enough to fulfill such an important mission). Along the road into the city, the car's right wheels went into a ditch by the side of the road, the car tilted and came to a halt. No one was injured in this automobile mishap. Arnold was given a party reprimand for negligence. Although for those times such a punishment was trivial, Arnold wrote a letter to Molotov complaining about the local party functionaries. Molotov wrote to the party's regional committee, asking for a review of Arnold's case and indicating that he didn't deserve a reprimand. As a result of Molotov's intervention, the party reprimand was removed from Arnold's personal dossier.[10]

However at the Kemerovo Trial, and then at the Trial of the "Anti-Soviet Trotskyist Center," this event figured as the only actual terrorist act, although it had failed at the last moment. At the second Moscow Trial, Piatakov, Shestov and Arnold himself spoke about the attack on Molotov. Shestov explained the failure of the attack by the fact that Arnold had driven the car into the ravine "not decisively enough, and the bodyguards which were traveling behind were able to literally lift up this car in their hands. Molotov and the others sitting in the vehicle, including Arnold, crawled out of the overturned car."[11]

Arnold described the circumstances of the attack somewhat differently, but also confessed his criminal intentions and readiness to die together with Molotov. He turned out to be one of only a few defendants at the trial who avoided the death penalty. In 1938, when he was located in the Verkhneuralsk Prison, Arnold called the charge of attacking Molotov "a soap bubble," and the entire trial of the "Trotskyist center"—a "political comedy."[12]

At the Twenty-second Congress of the CPSU, Shvernik, the chairman of the commission to investigate Stalinist repression, described the automobile mishap in Prokopievsk and declared: "here is another example of Molotov's extreme cynicism.... This episode (in Prokopievsk) served as the basis for the version of the 'attack' on Molotov's life, and a group of innocent people was

Chubar,
Voroshilov,
Molotov and
Yezhov on the
tribune of the
Mausoleum,
1 May 1937

Voroshilov,
Molotov, Stalin
and Yezhov
visit the Moscow-
Volga Canal,
May 1937

convicted for this incident. Who better than Molotov knew that in actual fact there had been no attack, but he didn't say a single word in defense of innocent people. That is the true face of Molotov."[13]

In the 1970s–1980s, F. Chuyev stubbornly tried to wrest from Molotov an answer to the question of how he assessed Shvernik's statement. Each time, Molotov answered very unintelligibly:

"There was an attack.... It is hard to believe, but I would allow that there had been talk and chatter about it."

"But was there actually an attack?" (Chuyev asks once again).

"I can't judge. There was testimony.... At the trial people said that they were preparing an attack. I read Trotsky at that time. He writes—I am trying to repeat his ideas precisely—it is suspicious, here they say about Molotov that he is second after Stalin. That is true. But it is strange that there have been no attacks upon him. That means, it's a frame-up—that's the conclusion he draws."[14]

The sudden mention of Trotsky in this context is eloquent testimony that Molotov not only carefully studied Trotsky's exposés at the time, but that the latter's sarcastic comments about his "affair" were engraved on Molotov's memory for the rest of his life.

In his book, *Stalin's Crimes*, Trotsky focused attention on the fact that at the second Moscow Trial, matters were not limited to merely mentioning the Prokopievsk episode. The main defendants named Molotov among the victims who had been marked by the "Trotsky-Zinoviev Center." Thus Radek declared that Mrachkovsky had told him the terrorist acts "must be directed against Stalin and his closest comrades: Kirov, Molotov, Voroshilov and Kaganovich." In this regard, Trotsky wrote: "It turns out that even in 1932 the Trotskyists were trying to kill Molotov: they only 'forgot' to tell about this in August 1936, and the prosecutor 'forgot' to remind them. But as soon as Molotov received his political amnesty from Stalin, the memory of both the prosecutor and the defendants suddenly brightens. We then become witnesses to a miracle: despite the fact that Mrachkovsky himself in his testimony spoke about preparing terrorist acts only against Stalin, Kirov, Voroshilov and Kaganovich, Radek, on the basis of a conversation with Mrachkovsky in 1932, retroactively includes Molotov on this list." Thus, the list of victims changes "not only with regard to the future, but also with regard to the past." Absolutely clear conclusions flow from this: "the defendants had as little freedom in choosing their 'victims' as they had in all other matters. The list of the objects of terror was in actual fact a list of leaders officially recommended to the masses. It changed depending on combinations in the upper echelons of power. The defendants, as well as the prosecutor Vyshinsky, simply had to adapt themselves to the totalitarian instructions."

In response to the question, "Don't all these machinations appear too crude?", Trotsky wrote: "They are no cruder than all the other machinations of these shameful trials. The director is not appealing to reason or to criticism. He wants to crush the rights of reason with the massive scale of the frame-up, reinforced with executions."[15]

5. Results of a "Rotten Compromise"

IN THE PAGES of this book, we will return more than once to the question of the reasons behind the "confessions" of the defendants at the Moscow Trials. In speaking in this regard about the Trial of the Sixteen, we must note that this was the first open trial of Old Bolsheviks. Prior to this trial, the death penalty had not been applied to the defendants at other show trials (of the "Promparty" [The Industrial Party], "The Union Bureau of Mensheviks," and others). It would be even more natural to assume that not a single one of the Old Bolsheviks would be sentenced to death. After all, in 1932 even Stalin's most consistent and open opponent—Riutin—was sentenced to "only" ten years of prison.

Stalin's promises to spare the lives of the defendants may have been given weight by a decree published in February 1936 by the Central Executive Committee freeing the defendants of the "Promparty" Trial from further time in prison. This amnesty was linked to their "full repentance ... with regard to their earlier crimes against the Soviet regime" and their successful work performed in prison.[1] It was also well known that the Academician Tarle, who, according to the material of the same trial had been marked by the "Promparty" for the post of Foreign Minister, was living at liberty, pursuing scientific studies, and completing the preparations for the publication of his book, *Napoleon*.

The Trial of the Sixteen was supposed to be conducted in accordance with the law of 1 December 1934, which established extraordinary procedures for reviewing all cases involving terror: these cases were to be held behind closed doors and the defendants were to be deprived of the right to appeal for clemency. However, as an exception to this law, the court session lasting from 19 to 24 August 1936 was open, and besides "representatives of Soviet society," foreign journalists and diplomats were in the courtroom. Of course, this "liberalization" of the court procedures was highly relative. The trial was held in the October Hall of the House of the Trade Unions, a room which held only three hundred fifty people. As would be the case at all the subsequent open trials, not a single relative of the defendants was present. The few foreign journalists who were admitted to the trial were lost among the specially selected audience which, judging from the trial transcript, often laughed at the vulgar witticisms Vyshinsky directed at the defendants. An announcement was made that all the defendants had refused the services of defense lawyers.

Five days before the trial began, the Central Executive Committee passed a decree which restored the right of those condemned on charges of terror to appeal for clemency. This decree was an important part of the game which Stalin was playing with the defendants. It was perceived by many as a sign that the defendants' lives would be spared. Immediately after the trial, the Moscow correspondent of the English newspaper, *Daily Herald*, wrote: "Right up until the last moment, the sixteen who were shot hoped for mercy.... It was assumed in broad circles that the special decree passed five days ago and giving them the right to appeal was published in order to spare them."[2]

It is true that Vyshinsky concluded his speech for the prosecution with the exclamation: "I demand that we shoot the mad dogs—every single one of them!"[3] The expression, "mad (or crazed) dogs," entered widely into the lexicon of Soviet propaganda and was often repeated in the responses to the trials which were published in the press.

However even this frenzied demand was perceived by the defendants as a necessary part of the staging of the trial. According to eyewitness accounts of foreign journalists, the accused met their death sentence relatively calmly, as something that was entirely natural. Resting on these accounts of the defendants' behavior, Trotsky noted: "They understood that only the death penalty could lend credence to their theatrical confessions. They did not understand, i.e., they tried not to understand, that real credence could be given to the death penalty only by carrying it out. Kamenev, who was the most calculating and thoughtful among the accused, was evidently filled with the greatest doubts about the outcome of this uneven deal-making. But even he must have repeated to himself hundreds of times: can it really be that Stalin will decide [on execution—V. R.]? Well, Stalin decided."[4]

Trotsky's ideas that the defendants hoped for mercy until the very last minute are confirmed by the recent publication of their appeals to the Presidium of the Central Executive Committee (fifteen of the defendants submitted appeals—all, with the exception of Goltsman). The defendants evidently hoped that Stalin was satisfied with their last act of self-abasement, and that he would grant them their lives as a reward.

"Deeply repenting my extremely grave crimes before the proletarian revolution," wrote Kamenev, " if the Presidium doesn't find my request to be in contradiction to the future cause of socialism, the cause of Lenin and Stalin, I ask that my life be spared." In similarly abject tones, I. N. Smirnov, the most steadfast of the defendants, submitted his appeal. "At the end of my life I made an enormous mistake: I followed Trotsky and for a number of years waged a struggle against the party as a Trotskyist," wrote Smirnov, as he strung together the ritual formulas. "What was in the beginning an oppositional struggle turned into a counterrevolutionary one, and ended in the shame which I am now suffering.... Many times I looked death in the eye, but that was when I fought for my native class and my party, and I never experienced the fear of death then. Now the sword of proletarian justice is raised above me, and it is terrible to die at the hands of my own state."[5]

All these statements were written immediately after the sentence was read by Ulrich at two thirty in the morning. The most precise time is indicated on Zinoviev's appeal—four thirty in the morning. The defendants evidently expected that they would be able to live at least another seventy-two hours, which is the amount of time that the decree from the Central Executive Committee allotted for the submission and review of appeals for mercy. However, immediately after their appeals were received, they were led away to be shot. On 24 August the newspapers published the text of the sentence, and on 25 August, an announcement that the sentence had been carried out. Thus Stalin not only shamelessly committed an outrage against the defendants in their last hour of life, but then subsequently made a complete mockery of his own laws.

Nor did Stalin deny himself the pleasure of desecrating the memory of the defendants after their death. On 20 December 1936, a blasphemous spectacle unfolded in the Kremlin. Stalin arranged a reception for the leadership of the NKVD on the occasion of the anniversary of the founding of the Cheka. He paid special tribute to the "merits" of the organizers of the trial. When the banquet's participants had become intoxicated, Pauker, the head of Stalin's personal bodyguards and a person known for his inclination for playing tricks, staged an impromptu display of clownishness. He mockingly imitated Zinoviev's behavior as the latter was unexpectedly dragged off to be shot. Held up under his arms by two colleagues who played the role of guards, Pauker fell onto his knees and, wrapping his arms around the boots of a "guard," began to wail: "Please....

For God's sake, comrade ... call Iosif Vissarionovich." Watching this scene, Stalin broke into wild laughter. Egged on by the laughter, Pauker, who knew very well Stalin's anti-Semitic propensities, added one more episode to the spectacle. He raised his hands toward the ceiling and cried out: "Oh, hear me, Israel, our God is the only God." Only at this point did Stalin, choking with laughter, begin to signal Pauker to put a stop to his performance.[6]

Commenting on the behavior of the defendants who had agreed to sacrifice their honor for the sake of saving their lives, Trotsky recalled Lenin's words which had been passed to him in March 1923 by Lenin's secretaries. Lenin was preparing to open a decisive battle against Stalin and viewed Trotsky as an ally in the impending struggle. He advised Trotsky not to make any concessions to Stalin, insofar as the latter would "make a rotten compromise, and then deceive [you.]" "This formula," wrote Trotsky, "embraces better than anything else Stalin's political methodology, including its application to the sixteen defendants: he made a compromise with them through the GPU investigator, and then deceived them—through the executioner." (Trotsky, of course, could not know that "the rotten compromise" with Zinoviev and Kamenev had been made by Stalin personally).

Trotsky noted that Stalin's methods were no secret for the defendants. In this regard he recalled that in the beginning of 1926, when the rift took place between Kamenev and Zinoviev on one side and Stalin on the other, the ranks of the Left Opposition discussed the question: with which part of the divided ruling faction should they form a bloc? In the discussion Mrachkovsky said: "With neither one: Zinoviev will run away, and Stalin will deceive." "This phrase soon became an aphorism," Trotsky added. "Zinoviev soon formed a bloc with us, and then indeed 'ran away.' Following him, among many others, by the way, was Mrachkovsky, who also 'ran away.' 'Those who ran' tried to form a bloc with Stalin. He chose to make a 'rotten compromise,' and then deceived them. The accused drank the cup of humiliation to the dregs. After this, they were executed."[7]

6. POLITICAL REPERCUSSIONS OF THE TRIAL OF THE SIXTEEN

THE FALSIFIED CHARACTER of the Trial of the Sixteen was clear to everyone familiar with Stalin's politics. During the first days of the trial, Raskolnikov, who was then living abroad, said to his wife: "I don't believe one word of the charges. It's all a blatant lie, needed by Stalin for his personal aims. I will never believe that the defendants did what they are accused of or what they are confessing to."[1]

Many Western Social-Democrats also saw the Moscow judicial dramatization as a "witch trial." O. Bauer, one of the leaders of the Second International, wrote with horror about the painful impression which the execution of the defendants made on sincere liberal and socialist friends of the USSR.

Before the trial began, four leaders of the Second International and the International Federation of Trade Unions sent a telegram to Molotov. It said that, despite the fact that the defendants were "sworn enemies of the Second International," its leaders were asking the Soviet government to give them all judicial guarantees and allow them to have defense lawyers who were independent of the government. The leaders of the Second International also asked that the accused "not be given death sentences, and, in any case, that no procedures be employed which excluded the possibility of appeal."[2]

This telegram was published in *Pravda* with an accompanying malicious editorial commentary entitled, "Despicable Defenders of Murderers and Gestapo Agents." On the next day, in an article called "The Trial's Sentence is the People's Sentence," *Pravda* wrote: "These scum have found their lawyers. The heads of the Second International have taken on the mission of being advocates for fascism."[3] Two weeks later, an article was exacted from N. K. Krupskaya, who had not spoken earlier about the trial. In an article entitled, "Why the Second International Defends Trotsky," Krupskaya wrote: "It is also no accident that the Second International rants and raves, raises the Trotsky-Zinoviev gang of killers on its shield, and tries to break up the Popular Front. The De

Brouckères and Citrines [two who signed the telegram—V. R.] support any foul deeds which enemies perform against the working class of the USSR."[4]

Pravda felt that it was necessary to stigmatize the leaders of the Second International in poetic form, too, by publishing D. Bedny's crude lines:

> Traitors! Arch-operators,
> Sharp-witted agents of the bankers who have bought you!
> Where were you when Trotsky's couriers
> Rushed to the bandit center, and these scoundrels
> Prepared murders and covered up their tracks?
> Where were you when honest Kirov was struck down?
> Did we read your indignant protest?
> Did you even lift a finger then?
> And now you've brought yourselves to write—o gesture foul!—
> A letter, a manifesto in defense!
> How do you expect to extract a tidy sum?
> Our scorn is your reply!
> There is no other.[5]

In unleashing such unbridled slander against everyone who had any doubts about the Moscow Trial, Stalin was not worried that this might threaten the unity of the antifascist front in Europe. The Trial of the Sixteen was evidently timed to coincide with such dramatic events as Hitler sending troops into the Rhine district, the formation of a Popular Front government in France, and the beginning of the Civil War in Spain. With his executioners' consistency in carrying out the anti-Trotskyist terror, Stalin was showing unequivocally to the socialist parties of the West that if they made any further protests against his domestic policies, he would break up the Popular Front and leave Europe face to face with the Third Reich, which was arming itself and growing ever stronger.

The Moscow Trial seriously undermined the prestige of the USSR in the eyes of the democratic intelligentsia of the West. As Leon Feuchtwanger noted: "Many, who saw in the social structure of the Soviet Union the ideal of socialist humanism, have simply been driven into an impasse by this trial; it seemed that the bullets which tore into Zinoviev and Kamenev killed not only them, but the new world."[6] These words are confirmed in the published diaries and letters of several major foreign writers. During the trial, Thomas Mann made the following diary entry: "What to think about all these repentant confessions, followed by a common death penalty?... Perhaps the transcripts are simply falsified? Or the accused were promised clemency if they were to give testimony which benefited the government? But their characters are such that it is difficult to believe it. For we are talking about the last Leninists.... After dinner the newspapers arrived. Sixteen Leninists, who received a death sentence after giving grotesque confessional speeches, have actually been executed. Terrible." After a few days, Mann made a new entry that is noteworthy: "I am worried—what to think of Russia after a trial which is an even greater stupidity than the crime?"[7]

During the same period, Romain Rolland, who felt that the existence of an anti-Stalinist conspiracy in the USSR was possible, wrote anxiously in his diary: "Even someone who has never respected the heads of the conspiracy, even someone who accepts the charges against them ... cannot help but feel concern much like that which seized the best members of the Convention in 1794.... I fear that the instincts of malice and pride gained the upper hand over political reason in this affair."[8]

Soon Rolland received a letter from Stefan Zweig, in which similar thoughts were expressed but more sharply: "Some kind of fate, some kind of metaphysical will is leading people to blindness. Thus, in your Russia, Zinoviev and Kamenev, veterans of the Revolution and Lenin's first comrades-in-arms, are shot like mad dogs.... As always, the same technique shared by Hitler and Robespierre: ideological differences are called a conspiracy.[9]

None of these "influential friends of the USSR," however, felt that they could publicly express their depressing impressions from the trial—because they feared damaging the Soviet Union. Against the background of this "conspiracy of silence," what stood out were the voices of Stalin's minions who obediently circulated throughout the entire world the slander that had been expressed at the trial. Special zeal was evinced by the English jurist and member of the Labour Party, D. N. Pritt, who called the "procedures" of the Trial of the Sixteen "an example for the whole world." After the official exposure of Stalin's crimes at the Twentieth and Twenty-second Party Congresses, Pritt didn't breathe a word in refutation of his earlier pronouncements. He continued to be among the "friends of the USSR," was awarded the International Lenin Peace Prize in 1954, and, until the end of the 1960s, headed the International Association of Jurist-Democrats and the English Society of Cultural Relations with the USSR.

However paradoxical it may be, the opinions of the most reactionary circles in the West joined in with the voices of such "friends of the USSR." In the foreign responses to the trial, the following law could be observed: the more right-wing the political forces, the more insistently they acknowledged the "reasonableness" of the charges pronounced at the trial.

In the bourgeois-democratic countries, the right-wing press inflated the charges that Trotsky and his supporters were collaborating with Hitler. The reactionary French newspaper, *Echo de Paris*, hastened to declare that the Trotskyists in France were serving the interests of Germany. This statement was quickly reprinted in the organ of the French Communist Party, *L'Humanité*.

The frenzy whipped up by such statements was aided by the fascist press in Germany and Italy, which published provocative articles naming even more, as yet unarrested, Old Bolsheviks and military leaders allegedly involved in the antigovernmental conspiracy.

A week after the trial, the Italian fascist newspaper, *Il Messaggero*, wrote with unconcealed delight that the Moscow executions were a justified reaction by Stalin, who had rolled up the banner of world revolution, to criticism from the opponents of his new "realistic policies": "Lenin's Old Guard has been shot.... Stalin was a realist, and what his opponents felt was a betrayal of the ideal, was only a necessary and inevitable concession to logic and life.... To the abstract program of universal revolution he juxtaposes a five-year-plan, the creation of an army, and economics which do not reject the individual.... The demon of revolution for the sake of revolution [i.e., Trotsky—V. R.] rises up against this positive creativity.... It was inevitable—the police uncovered the conspiracy and acted with force which is demanded by public security."[10]

The commentaries of the German newspapers were different. They tried to confuse public opinion in the West, which was already disoriented by the sensational news coming from Moscow. The German official press stated that "Trotsky is whatever you might like, but he is not an enemy of Moscow as they are trying to depict him.... On the contrary, he is one of the most active and ... most energetic agents of the world revolution"; "in Moscow they are trying to use a great theatrical trial to camouflage once again the activity of Mister Trotsky"; "wherever Trotsky has gone ... revolutionary flames break out." These excerpts were immediately reprinted by *Pravda* in a note called "German Fascists Shield Trotsky."[11]

The Trial of the Sixteen caused a sharp polarization between the right and left wings of the Russian emigration. The Menshevik journal, *Socialist Herald*, published an article, "Who is Applauding?", which stressed that Stalin had brought "outright and tumultuous joy" to the reactionary emigrant press with the trial. As an example, the journal printed an "Ode" written by a certain Goriansky which had been published in the White-Guard newspaper, "Vozrozhdenie [Rebirth]." "We ask our readers to forgive us for citing these cynical and bloodthirsty lines," wrote the author of *Socialist Herald*, "but the deep feelings and hidden dreams of the reactionaries are best related by an exact quotation:"

> Thank you Stalin;
> Sixteen scoundrels
> Have been sent to the land of our fathers—
> Sixteen executioners of our native land ...
> We send you greetings.
> Today the heavenly vault is blue and clear.
> You have rewarded us
> For many years of sorrow.
> We thank you for your generous gift!
> We thank you!

But the Black Hundreds were not satisfied; they were waiting for Stalin to give them more joy and new executions.

> Sixteen is not enough!
> Give us forty more,
> Give us hundreds,
> Give us thousands,
> Span the Moscow River
> With a bridge, not of boards or moorings,
> But of Soviet carrion.

In quoting this ungifted doggerel, which repeated the traditional White-Guard ravings against the Bolsheviks, the author noted: "The spectacle of Christians by passport enthusiastically applauding the executioner standing by the fresh grave of victims who were morally tortured and then shot—is loathsome...."

A new distinguishing feature of the latest executions is that, while they evoked open or concealed horror among those who hold the Russian Revolution dear, they caused an enthusiastic reaction among the most fervent enemies of the working class."[12]

More respectable and prominent adherents of centrist political tendencies did not descend to such depths of mockery and blasphemy as the monarchist Black Hundreds. However, some of them saw the trial as a good reason to revive old anti-Bolshevik slander. Kerensky did not fail to declare that he saw nothing surprising in Trotsky's collaboration with the Gestapo, for Lenin and Trotsky in 1917 already had ties to the German general staff. The slander of Trotsky as an agent of Hitler was readily embraced by Miliukov as well.

Under these conditions, thousands of people in the capitalist countries wanted to hear what Trotsky thought of the charges smearing himself and his cothinkers. However the Norwegian "labor" government, on orders from Moscow, deprived Trotsky of the chance to publicly respond to the Stalinist slanders.

7. TROTSKY INTERNED

O N 5 AUGUST 1936, Trotsky sent off the manuscript of his completed book, *The Revolution Betrayed*, to be translated into foreign languages. On the same day, he and the journalist Knudsen, who owned the house in which he was living, left for two weeks' rest by the sea. On the night after they departed, a group of Norwegian fascists attacked Knudsen's house in order to steal Trotsky's documents. The attackers showed Knudsen's family members some fake police badges and tried to start a "search." After Knudsen's son and daughter sounded an alarm, the fascists seized a few documents and ran off. On the next day, the police established the identity of the participants in the raid.

During his rest, Trotsky learned from radio announcements about the Moscow Trial. He immediately returned to Oslo and gave a statement for the world press to the many journalists who were asking him for explanations. In it he called for the workers' organizations of all countries to create an international commission to investigate the charges made at the trial, which Trotsky called "the greatest frame-up in the political history of the world."

At first, the Norwegian press published Trotsky's exposés, which were then reprinted in the press of other countries. On 21 August, the newspaper of the ruling Labor Party, *Arbeiderbladet*, published on the front page an interview with Trotsky under the heading, "Trotsky declares that the Moscow charges are invented and fabricated." Very soon, however, the campaign begun by Trotsky was blocked by the Norwegian government. The reason was an official note from the Soviet government directed to the Norwegian government, demanding that Trotsky be denied political asylum insofar as he had been "found guilty" of terrorist crimes. Otherwise, the note said, friendly relations between the USSR and Norway would be undermined. Making this threat more concrete, the Soviet ambassador Yakubovich declared that the Soviet Union might stop importing Norwegian herring. In connection with this possibility, the fish processing and shipping industries began to demand that the government "regulate the Trotsky question" in order to prevent the growth of unemployment in Norway.

Fearing defeat in the upcoming elections because of Trotsky's presence in the country, the leaders of the ruling party were inclined to deport him. However, not a single other government was prepared to admit Trotsky into its country. Then the plan to intern Trotsky began to be implemented. On 26 August the head of the Norwegian police proposed that he sign a statement agreeing to new conditions for remaining in Norway, including the cessation of articles and interviews on political topics and the granting of permission to the police to examine all his correspondence. After Trotsky categorically refused these conditions, the decision was made to apply them by force. Inasmuch as the Norwegian constitution did not allow such restrictions without a court decision, the Minister of Justice, Trygve Lie (the future secretary general of the United Nations), obtained a special decree from the Norwegian king which granted the Minister of Justice extraordinary powers for resolving "this concrete and exceptional case." On the basis of this decree, Lie did not allow journalists to visit Trotsky, had the police monitor his mail, turned off the telephone in his apartment, deported his secretary, and denied him the possibility of communicating even with Knudsen. On September 2, Trotsky was transferred to a more distant village, where he was held for about four months under house arrest and under surveillance by thirteen policemen. The official reason for this internment was declared to be the manuscript of an article Trotsky had written about the revolutionary events in France. The manuscript had been taken by the fascists and presented by them to the authorities as evidence of Trotsky's interference in the internal affairs of other states. Thus the "workers'" government, which not long before had prided itself on giving Trotsky political asylum and had called him a "great workers' leader," acted as an accomplice to Stalin and the Norwegian fascists who had carried out the illegal raid.

On September 12, the Soviet press published an article: "An Exchange of Declarations between the Soviet and Norwegian governments." The article said that in answer to the presentation made by the ambassador from the USSR to the government of Norway, the Norwegian minister of justice had declared: "on the basis of Trotsky's own statements, various newspaper articles and other material, the Central Passport Bureau has found that he has violated the conditions of residing in the country which had been presented to him by the government. The Norwegian government therefore directed the elaboration of more

precise conditions for remaining in the country.... On 28 August ... in the afternoon he was completely isolated from the outside world and taken under police observation...." Mr. Lie announced that "the Norwegian government has
placed Trotsky (and his wife) under such control that it must be excluded that
he would be able in the future to undertake any activity that would harm or
threaten the interests of the USSR."

Further on the article stated: "Because the aforementioned measures can
not be considered a genuine revocation of the right to asylum, Comrade
Yakubovich declared to the Norwegian Minister of Foreign Affairs that ... the
Soviet government unfortunately does not find that it is possible to consider
this declaration satisfactory and corresponding to the cordial relations between
the USSR and Norway, and that, in the opinion of the Soviet government, with
its response the Norwegian government has assumed full responsibility for the
efficacy of the measures it has taken and for the consequences of Trotsky's
continued presence in Norway."[1]

The very fact of Trotsky's internment by his "friends," the Norwegian socialists, was perceived by many people in the West to be confirmation that the
accusations made against him were justified. Taking advantage of Trotsky's
inability to respond to their slander, the Soviet and Comintern press inundated
world public opinion with ever newer provocative articles about Trotsky's desire to destroy the Popular Front in France, bring about the victory of Franco in
Spain and guarantee Hitler's victory in the coming war against the USSR and
its allies. At the high-point of this slander campaign, Vyshinsky published an
article which said: "Trotsky, it is true, has been threatening to disprove these
accusations, but, as we can see, he is in no hurry with the refutation; since the
day the trial ended, enough time has passed for him to gather his strength and
try to refute at least one point of the trial's sentence."[2]

L'Humanité went even farther by publishing a telegram from Oslo which
stated that the Norwegian authorities had begun an investigation against
Trotsky because they had established his ties with local fascists who "paid him
a friendly visit one night" (such was the way the raid on Trotsky's apartment
when he was away was interpreted).

Characterizing the position in which Trotsky found himself after the Moscow Trial, F. Adler, the secretary of the Second International, wrote: "We are
dealing with an attempt to deprive Trotsky of the right to asylum in Norway
and to arouse such a slander campaign against him that he would be denied

the possibility of existing anywhere on the globe."[3]

In trying to break through the information blockade, Trotsky brought a suit for defamation against two Norwegian journalists—a Stalinist and a fascist—who repeated in their articles insinuations made by the Soviet press. The Norwegian court took the case under review. Then Trygve Lie arranged the publication of a new extraordinary decree, granting the Minister of Justice the right to prevent "an interned foreigner" from taking part in any trials. Using this decree, Lie impeded Trotsky's attempts to bring to trial slanderers even from other countries. As N. I. Sedova was to recall, "The Minister of Justice informed [Trotsky] that he must not engage in litigation anywhere in the world while he remained in Norway. It seemed that he had no more rights at all. We began to fear that, though we had 'forfeited' Soviet nationality, the Norwegians might hand us over to the GPU."[4]

Anticipating new provocations, Trotsky managed to send Sedov instructions to transfer his archives to the Paris branch of the Dutch Institute for Social History—in order to prevent theft of the archives by NKVD agents. The director of this branch was the emigré Menshevik, Nikolaevsky; Trotsky did not doubt his honesty. Sedov's closest colleagues, Zborowski and Lola Estrine, took the first part of the archives to the institute. A few days later, a break-in occurred at the institute, in the course of which 85 kilograms of documents were stolen. Everything else, including money that was on site, remained untouched. In describing the crime, the Paris emigré newspaper *Poslednie novosti* declared that the French "police inspectors announced that the technique of the entire operation ... was absolutely unknown in France until today. Only foreign 'professionals,' equipped with special tools, could perform such a job."[5]

In the mid-1950s, Zborowski, who was then living in the United States, was exposed as an agent of the NKVD and was forced to give testimony to the American authorities. In 1955, Nikolaevsky wrote to Souvarine about this investigation: "Have you heard about the provocation by 'Etienne' [Zborowski's nickname—V. R.], the late Sedov's secretary? It is he ... who brought the so-called 'Trotsky Archive' to the institute at Rue Michelet, and he was the one who informed his superiors so that the material could be stolen. Now he has confessed, although he claims that he had no direct part in the theft. He says that his bosses were disappointed: the archives turned out to be just newspapers (of Trotskyist groups) from all around the world."[6]

At hearings before the Senate Subcommittee on Internal Security, Lola

Mark Zborowski

Bulletin of the Opposition, no. 52-53, October 1936;
"The Moscow Trial is a Trial Against October"

Estrine (who changed her name after her second marriage to Dallin) testified:
in 1955 Zborowski told her about his conversation with an NKVD agent after
the archives had been stolen. Zborowski expressed his concern that he might
be exposed insofar as the theft was carried out only a few days after the archives had been transferred to the institute. Besides himself, only Sedov,
Nikolaevsky and Estrine knew about this, and they could not fall under suspicion as NKVD informers. In response to Zborowski's objection, the agent said
that the theft was performed during the night before 7 November because the
Paris NKVD "wanted to present a gift to Stalin on the anniversary of the October Revolution."[7]

    When reflecting on the possibility of further provocations by the Stalinists,
Trotsky turned attention to the formulation contained in the sentence of the

Moscow Trial: "Trotsky, Lev Davidovich and his son, Sedov, Lev Lvovich ... are shown to have taken part in the direct preparation and personal leadership of the organization of terrorist acts in the USSR; ... if they are found on the territory of the Soviet Union they are subject to immediate arrest and will be tried before the Military Collegium of the Supreme Court of the Union of Soviet Socialist Republics."[8] With this statement in mind, Trotsky asked a reasonable question: "With what technical aids does Stalin hope to find me and my son on the territory of the USSR?"[9] He felt that this formulation revealed not only Stalin's intention to obtain his extradition by the Norwegian authorities, but plans to kidnap himself and Sedov.

It was practically impossible to kidnap Trotsky in Norway. Another situation prevailed in France, where the NKVD possessed a wide network of agents. As Zborowski testified in 1956 before the hearings of the Senate Commission, he was ordered to lure Sedov to a certain place, where the latter was supposed to be kidnaped, in order to then be forcibly repatriated to the Soviet Union. Zborowski explained the failure of this plan by his sabotage of the order, because it "contradicted his convictions."[10]

Right until the end of 1936, the Norwegian government continued to withhold letters which Trotsky sent to his son, lawyer and friends. Trotsky's addressees received only a few letters which had been written in invisible ink and illegally passed on.

The October issue of the *Bulletin of the Opposition* contained a short note from Trotsky: "Forgive me for not being able to send you the article on the trial that I had promised for the next issue of the *Bulletin of the Opposition* ... but I am sure that you yourselves will say everything that needs to be said about this foul amalgam."[11]

The same issue of the journal contained Leon Sedov's long article, "The Moscow Trial—October on Trial," soon to be published as a separate pamphlet under the title, "The Red Book on the Moscow Trial."

8. Leon Sedov's *Red Book*

Sedov opened *The Red Book* with an analysis of the political reasons behind the judicial frame-up undertaken by Stalin. Basing himself on the ideas outlined in the manuscript of Trotsky's book, *The Revolution Betrayed*, which he had just received, Sedov wrote that the social gains of the October Revolution were being liquidated in the USSR. Bitter contradictions were ripping apart Soviet society. With every day social inequality was growing throughout the country. Revolutionary internationalism had been replaced by a cult of national statehood. Abortions had been banned, which in difficult material conditions, given both primitive culture and hygiene, meant the enslavement of women. The pursuit of such social policies was incompatible with Soviet democracy; it imperiously demanded bloody reprisals, falsifications and slander.

In addition, as Sedov stressed, the gradual improvement of the material conditions of the masses after the cruel poverty during the first Five Year Plan was raising the consciousness of the workers, inducing a desire to defend their interests and actively participate in political life. Stalin was attempting to smother their growing social protest with political repression. In order to lend it a ruthless character, he invented "terrorism." If in the past he had called any social dissatisfaction "Trotskyism," now he was identifying "Trotskyism" with "terrorism." Any person who was critical of the Stalinist regime was no longer threatened with a concentration camp or prison, but with immediate execution.

Having decided to physically exterminate all opponents of his regime, Stalin was terrorizing his own apparatus even more. A broad but concealed discontent had arisen in this milieu because "the former revolutionary who had turned into a blind executor of commands from his Stalinist superiors loses all perspective; his rights are reduced to the right of exalting the 'father of the people,' and he better than others knows Borgia-Stalin."[1] Therefore the main assignment of the NKVD, which had become Stalin's personal instrument, was the defense of his personal power from this very same bureaucracy.

In addition, the Moscow Trial demonstrated the insecure position of the ruling clique. "People don't engage in such bloody affairs from a surfeit of power."[2] In order to strengthen his position, Stalin was trying to drive an already terrorized country to new, as yet unknown forms of arbitrary rule.

Besides domestic causes, the Moscow Trial had no less serious foreign policy causes. In place of sincere socialist friends, whom Stalin had only recently summoned to join the united antifascist front, "he was seeking more 'solid' friends and allies in the event of war: French, English, American and other bourgeois forces.... Without any hesitation Stalin would make an agreement even with Hitler, at the expense of the German and international working class. It would only depend on Hitler!"[3]

By shooting people who had gone down in history as the leaders of revolutionary Bolshevism, Stalin wanted to present the world bourgeoisie with a "symbol of the new times," evidence of his break with the idea of world revolution, and proof of "nation-state maturity." Such policies were driving the working class of the capitalist countries away from the official communist parties. This would not have worried Stalin very much if he had not feared that Western workers would find their way to the Fourth International. Therefore he "wanted to use blood and filth to block the way for advanced workers into the ranks of the Fourth International. This was one more goal of the Moscow Trial."[4]

In describing the history of political trials in recent years, Sedov stressed that they were all constructed on Kirov's corpse, around which the fourth case was already being fabricated. The reality of Kirov's murder was supposed to lend credibility to the reality of the preparation of other assassination attempts.

Relying on official Soviet sources, Sedov provided figures associated with the Kirov assassination according to which 104 White-Guardists had been condemned; 14 people had been shot in the case of the "Leningrad Center"; 19 were victims of the trial of the "Moscow Center"; 12 members of the Leningrad NKVD had fallen victim; 78 people had been included in the case of "the Safarov-Zalutsky counterrevolutionary group"; 16 had been shot in the last trial; the cases of 12 people had been singled out for special prosecution by this trial; and 40 people had been named as terrorists during the trial. The overwhelming majority of this almost 300 people had absolutely nothing to do with the Kirov assassination. Nevertheless, they were all "implicated by Stalin in this murder, and it is not known how many times Stalin will again drag out Kirov's corpse or how many people will yet be accused of responsibility or participation in this murder." Apart from the White-Guardists, Chekists and persons shot along with Nikolaev, there remained more than 150 people, predominantly Old Bolsheviks. "If someone had to compile a list of the 20–25 most prominent representatives of Bolshevism who had played the greatest role in the history of the party and the revolution, he could confidently take this list as a starting point."[5]

Noting that in the West no one understood how old revolutionaries could offer false testimony on the stand, Sedov wrote: "People are thinking of Zinoviev or Smirnov not of the recent period, but during the heroic years of the Russian Revolution. But since then almost twenty years have passed, more than half of which fell on the rotten, Thermidorian Stalinist regime. No, on the defendants' bench sat only the shades of Smirnov during the civil war or Zinoviev during the first years of the Comintern. On the defendants' bench sat broken, cowed and finished people. Before killing them physically, Stalin slashed away and murdered them morally." The behavior of the defendants during the trial had been prepared by the logic of their political evolution after they had renounced their views. Long before the trial they had lost any urge to do battle, thereby helping Stalin to trample them in the mud. "The Stalinist 'art' of breaking revolutionary characters consisted of going slowly, gradually pushing these people step by step, lower and lower."[6]

Sedov felt that stark confirmation of this statement was the behavior of Rakovsky, who had refused to capitulate longer than the others. After his capitulation in 1934, he went so far as to write an article during the Trial of the Sixteen demanding the execution of "these agents of the German Gestapo, the organizers of the attempt on the life of our dear leader, Comrade Stalin."[7] This shameful article evoked particular bewilderment among the Western socialist intelligentsia, where Rakovsky was well known and highly appreciated as one of the oldest participants of the international workers' movement, a leading diplomat and a morally irreproachable man. In explaining Rakovsky's act, Sedov wrote: "Capitulation is a steep slope.... Once you've stood on it, you can't help but slide further, to the very end.... Stalinist absolutism doesn't recognize half-hearted capitulation: all or nothing, there is no middle ground."[8]

In these assessments of the behavior of capitulationists who had already stood trial or were at liberty for the time being, some might detect the self-confidence of youth, or the excessive cruelty of a young man who had no moral right to judge, to pass a moral sentence or to place a cross over these persecuted people. Using this approach one might draw a sharp line between Trotsky, who had the right to make severe and oftentimes merciless criticisms of the behavior of his former comrades because he himself had experienced much in his forty years of revolutionary activity, and Sedov, who had not participated as directly in such cruel political skirmishes. In actual fact, in his letters to Sedov, Trotsky warned the latter about judging too sharply the behavior of the defendants in the Moscow Trials. We must not forget, however, that under conditions in which the interned Trotsky had no chance to answer the many questions which arose regarding the Trial of the Sixteen, Sedov was compelled to speak (proceeding from the psychological schema proposed by his father in articles about the trials of 1934–35) on behalf of the thousands of Soviet oppositionists who had endured the most terrible torments and who nevertheless had not placed themselves under the thumb of their executioners.

Of course, neither Trotsky nor Sedov had been imprisoned in a heated cell, like Zinoviev, or put through a ninety-hour conveyor belt interrogation, like Mrachkovsky; nor had they been toyed with, like Bukharin (although the latter, as will be evident later on, virtually asked for such treatment). But the fate of both Trotsky and his son, who were subjected to relentless surveillance and the danger of terrorist attacks on their lives, can by no means be called a happy one. The logical end of the prolonged hunt for them turned out to be the tragic deaths of Sedov in 1938 and of Trotsky in 1940.

In speaking of the defendants' behavior, Sedov noted the superficiality of comparing it with the conduct of Dimitrov at the Leipzig Trial. Neither Dimitrov nor other opponents of Hitlerism were isolated from the revolutionary movement; he could feel the sharp political demarcation (fascism—communism) and the mass support of progressive forces throughout the world. As for the Moscow defendants, "even though they stood before a Thermidorian court of Stalinist usurpers, nevertheless it was a court which in its phraseology appealed ... to the October Revolution and socialism. Along with monstrous moral tortures the inquisitors from the GPU naturally used both this phraseology, in particular, and the threat of war. This danger couldn't help but assist them in breaking these unfortunate defendants."[9]

In recalling that, according to the testimony of Stalinist prisoners who managed to escape from the USSR, the GPU broadly resorted to threats of dealing with families of the accused and to cruel conveyor belt interrogations ("the same question would be asked from morning to night while the person being investigated would be standing for weeks"), Sedov expressed certainty that in preparing the Trial of the Sixteen, the GPU employed "tortures from the arsenal of the blackest and most terrible inquisition." However, despite all this horror, all the defendants who were Old Bolsheviks, as Sedov wrote with profound sympathy toward their fate, "found the last remnant of strength, the last drop of personal dignity. No matter how broken they were, not *one* of the old men took upon himself—simply physically could not take upon himself—'ties to the Gestapo.' We feel, and this might appear to be paradoxical at first glance, that the inner moral strength of Zinoviev and Kamenev very significantly surpassed the average level, although it turned out to be insufficient under absolutely extraordinary conditions."[10]

Sedov was able to show that the defendants were chosen "by means of a long and terrible investigation from among fifty or even more other prisoner-candidates." To prove this hypothesis he used a significant blunder committed by the organizers of the trial. The trial transcript indicates with bureaucratic accuracy the case numbers of each defendant. Arranging the names of eleven defendants in alphabetical order, Sedov discovered that their cases included numbers from 1 to 29. "Who are the remaining eighteen? It seems very likely to us that with a few exceptions such as Safonova ... these 'missing' defendants are those whom Stalin didn't manage to break and whom he probably shot without trial."[11]

Sedov directed attention to the fact that the cases of four defendants were numbered from 32 to 38 and that, according to the trial transcript, Yevdokimov's testimony was received only on August 10, and Ter-Vaganian's on August 14, the day that the concluding indictment was signed. In this he saw one of the secrets of the pretrial investigation, tied to the intervention of Stalin himself. "The list of defendants," wrote Sedov, "undoubtedly changed more than once and was finally determined only on the day that the procurator signed the act of indictment.... The fact that Yevdokimov and Ter-Vaganian come in at the very end indicates, apparently, that at the beginning Stalin did not intend to include them in the trial.... Both Luries, probably, were not intended initially to be included in this trial and were added only later."[12]

Sedov was firmly convinced that the investigation tried to bring to trial genuine Trotskyists who had never renounced their convictions. However these people, who were free from the fetish of Stalinist "party-mindedness," could not yield to sophisms about the need to "help the party" in the struggle against

Trotsky, nor to the most inhuman tortures. Such unwavering revolutionaries "Stalin could not drag into his trials, although he was in a position to exterminate them one by one; exterminate—but not break. These revolutionary fighters did not take and will not take the fatal path of capitulation—for they believe in the correctness of their cause. They prefer to perish in the cellars of the GPU in obscurity, without support or sympathy."[13]

In exposing the many falsifications contained in the trial transcript, Sedov wrote with special indignation about the more abject products of Stalin's imagination or of the imagination of his satraps, like the explanation of the causes of the persecuted Bogdan's suicide. Around this tragic fact "Stalin weaves a web of some kind of pathological and delirious lies. At times it seems that you are reading *The Possessed*." Sedov detected the same delirium from Dostoevsky's novel in Reingold's testimony about the "center's" decision to annihilate the executors of terrorist acts after they had come to power. "This testimony is a product of the creativity of Stalin 'himself!' No one who knows Stalin even a little can have any doubt. These methods—shooting one's own agents who are dangerous because they know too much—are his methods, the methods of a man who will stop at nothing, of a man who is unscrupulous and capable of *anything*.... Psychologically Stalin gives himself away here. Stalin ascribes his own foul deeds to his victims!" Reingold's version looked absurd also because it would mean Zinoviev and Kamenev had announced their plans ahead of time, "seemingly warning their allies about what awaited them if their activity was successful. Apparently the (Stalin) GPU deliberately was supposed to leave alive the terrorists who carried out assassinations in order that they and all their comrades could be shot by the (Zinoviev) GPU after Zinoviev had come to power!"[14]

Summarizing the impressions from the judicial frame-ups, Sedov wrote: "Your hair stands on end when you read this Stalinist edition of *The Possessed*." And he found it far from accidental that the main creators of this demonic atmosphere were people who before the October Revolution had fought furiously against the Bolsheviks. Recalling that in 1917 Vyshinsky had been a right Menshevik and had signed an order to arrest Lenin, Sedov noted: "An enemy of Bolshevism and October, demanding the heads of the leaders of Bolshevism and the October Revolution. Isn't this symbolic!" The very fact that Vyshinsky was named prosecutor was the gravest insult for the defendants.

No less characteristic was the example of Zaslavsky, who in 1917 had shown himself to be a venal journalist. With particular frenzy he had spread the slander about Lenin and Trotsky as German agents. Lenin's articles of this period contain dozens of characterizations of Zaslavsky as a "slanderer" and a "blackmailing scoundrel." "And who today is writing articles in *Pravda* slandering Trotsky as an agent of the Gestapo? The same Zaslavsky! Isn't that once again symbolic?"[15]

Sedov saw the atmosphere of *The Possessed* in the fact that Piatakov and Radek, who demanded the execution of the defendants during the trial, were a month later facing the preparations of a trial in which they would be accused of the same crimes. "The ink had still not been able to dry on the draft of the new Stalinist constitution when one of its main editors—Radek—was handed over for reprisals to another of its editors—Vyshinsky. After creating 'the most democratic constitution in the world,' its authors were sending each other to the guillotine."[16]

In unmasking the illusoriness and futility of expecting democratic changes after the adoption of the new constitution, Sedov wrote: "It is as if Stalin is saying, 'Let those who have illusions know that the democratism of the constitution means that voters and congresses are given the right to vote for me. And whoever is not for Stalin, i.e., not for the bureaucracy with its privileges, is a Trotskyist, or in other words a terrorist whom we will shoot within twenty-four hours.'"[17]

While describing the political evolution of Stalin's regime, Sedov recalled that ten years earlier Stalin had publicly declared to his opponents from the opposition: "These cadres [i.e., the ruling elite—V. R.] can be removed only by civil war." With these words he clearly showed that he rejected any statutory or constitutional methods of removing his clique, and that he placed it above the party and the working class. Now he had shifted to a preventive civil war against all those who were dissatisfied with his rule. Along the way he was uniting methods of the Middle Ages with methods of political provocation and frame-ups practiced by reactionary forces over the previous decades. "Soon it will be one hundred years since police around the world excelled at affairs of this type—even before Bismarck and Napoleon III—but each time they have only burned their fingers! Police falsifications and Stalin's machinations hardly surpass other examples of the same creativity; but he has supplemented them—and how he supplemented them!—with 'confessions' exacted from the defendants by infinitely perfected methods of the inquisition."[18]

Sedov insisted that the Moscow Trial had not ended, and that it would continue in new forms. As could be ascertained from articles in the Soviet press, tens and hundreds of writers, economists, military figures and journalists were being arrested under charges of terror. "It is not difficult to imagine what a nightmarish atmosphere now reigns in the USSR. No one is certain of what tomorrow will bring, least of all the Old Bolsheviks ... who cannot help but ask themselves the anguished question: 'Who is next in line?'"[19]

Warning that Stalin, "in pursuing the liquidation of the revolution, is preparing something new, something incomparable to all that has already been done," Sedov wrote of the inevitability of new trials in which the slander of "terror" would be supplemented with slander about "military conspiracies" and "espionage." "A number of symptoms indicate that the new trial will be built around just such accusations.... It is our duty to warn the Western public about this. There can be no illusions in the Moscow Borgia, armed with modern technology!"[20]

Without a careful review of one more aspect contained in *The Red Book*, it is impossible to understand the causes and mechanism lying behind the organization of the Trial of the Sixteen, as well as the other Moscow show trials.

As he exposed the Stalinist amalgams, Sedov simultaneously indicated that, along with a mountain of false accusations, there were particles of the truth. In this regard, let us examine the actual underground activity of the Oppositionists, certain aspects of which found their reflection in the Trial of the Sixteen.

9. Ten Percent of the Truth, or What Really Happened

In her explanation given in 1956 to the Procurator of the USSR, Safonova wrote that her testimony, just like the testimony of Zinoviev, Mrachkovsky, Yevdokimov and Ter-Vaganian which had been given at the pretrial investigation and trial, "did not correspond to reality 90 percent of the time."[1]

The rehabilitation notes concerning the case of the "United Trotsky-Zinoviev Center" do not provide an answer to what the "ten percent of the truth" was which was contained in the defendants' testimony (of course, this number is approximate, since the relationship between truth and falsehood cannot be measured in percentages).

We find a partial answer to this question in the chapter of *The Red Book*, "What Actually Happened?" Here Sedov referred, although in a very cautious and hypothetical form, to the attempt by opposition groups to form an anti-Stalinist bloc in 1932. In this regard he described the situation in the country which had developed by this time: "The administrative abolition of classes in the countryside and the forced 'complete' collectivization had radically undermined agriculture. Disproportions in the Soviet economy had assumed extraordinary dimensions, both between industry and agriculture, and within industry; there was a catastrophic level of quality, an absence of consumer goods, inflation, and the complete disruption of transportation. The material situation of the masses worsened continuously, and malnutrition turned into actual starvation. Millions of new workers lacked housing and languished in barracks, often without light, in the cold and filth. Across the country people suffered from an epidemic of spotted fever, the likes of which had not been seen since the Civil War. A general feeling of exhaustion and discontent began to surface. Workers began to resort to strikes ever more frequently; in Ivanovo-Voznesensk there were major working class upheavals.... In the Caucasus and the Kuban a minor civil war was actually under way. The demoralization which was growing ever stronger in the party, the discontent and the distrust of the leadership had even spread into the apparatus. Conversations about how Stalin was leading the country to its destruction could be heard everywhere: among Old Bolsheviks, workers, and young Komsomol members."[2]

Under these conditions, Sedov continued, a certain rejuvenation occurred among groups of the Trotskyist opposition which had capitulated earlier, as well as groups of Zinovievists, rightists and others. "Probably, people from the various groups and circles sought ties with each other and ways of coming together personally. The most audacious, perhaps, began to say that it would be good to create a 'bloc.'"

In declaring that the unbroken Trotskyists had never formed a bloc with any of these groups, Sedov added that their "politically irreconcilable attitude toward capitulation did not exclude individual personal gatherings or the exchange of information—but nothing more than that."[3]

In discussing the testimony given at the trial by Smirnov and Goltsman, Sedov wrote that he and Smirnov had actually talked in July 1931 during their chance meeting at a Berlin department store. During this meeting Smirnov declared that "today's conditions in the USSR do not allow the conduct of any oppositional work, and that in any case one had to wait for changes in these conditions"... On political questions the two found that their views were rather close. At the end of the conversation, they agreed that, "if the possibility arose, I. N. Smirnov would send information about the economic and political situation in the USSR, so that it would help them here, abroad, to more correctly find an orientation on Russian questions."

Sedov recounted that for a long time after this meeting, there was no news from Smirnov. Only in the fall of 1932 did Goltsman come to Berlin on business matters. He gave Sedov Smirnov's article on the economic situation in the USSR. This article was printed under a pseudonym in the November 1932 issue of the *Bulletin of the Opposition*. The same issue contained anonymous correspondence from Moscow, compiled by the editors of the *Bulletin* on the basis of Goltsman's accounts of the political situation in the USSR.

On his part Sedov told Goltsman (to be passed on to Smirnov) about Trotsky's views concerning events taking place in the Soviet Union. "These two facts," Sedov emphasized, "i.e., that the meetings of Smirnov and Goltsman with Sedov actually took place, were the *only* grains of truth in the sea of lies at the Moscow Trial."[4]

And these facts were told by Trotsky and Sedov in 1937 to the International Commission created to investigate the accusations of the Moscow Trials.

A study of documents held in foreign archives has shown that Sedov did not tell everything he knew about the facts which at the Trial of the Sixteen had been combined with lies concerning terrorist activity by oppositionists, their ties to the Gestapo, and so forth.

While working on the portion of Trotsky's archive which opened in 1980, the American historian J. Arch Getty and the French historian Pierre Broué, independently of each other, discovered documents which indicate that Trotsky and Sedov entered into contact with participants in an anti-Stalinist bloc which was being formed.[5] Thus, in a report to the International Secretariat of the Left Opposition written in 1934, Sedov stated that members of Smirnov's group, who had broken in 1929 with the Left Opposition, three years later had once again rejoined it and conducted negotiations with members of other former opposition groups about creating an anti-Stalinist bloc.[6]

In a letter of 1 November 1932, Sedov told Trotsky that the Smirnov group had entered into a bloc with Zinovievists and with the Sten-Lominadze group. In the course of negotiations about the bloc which occurred not long before Zinoviev and Kamenev were exiled from Moscow (in connection with the "Riutin affair"), the latter acknowledged that the most serious political mistake of their lives had been to renounce the Left Opposition in 1927. Sedov also wrote that arrests of the Smirnov group had begun and that Smirnov himself, who had been informed about the course of the investigation by a member of the GPU sympathetic to the Opposition, "a few days before his arrest told our informer: 'I await my arrest any day now.'" In the letter's conclusion, Sedov wrote: "the downfall of the 'formers' [capitulators—V. R.] is a great blow, but our ties to the factories have been preserved."[7]

In a reply to Sedov, Trotsky indicated that he felt it was possible to collaborate with the bloc. This collaboration might at first take the form of exchanging information. He proposed that their "allies" send correspondence for the *Bulletin of the Opposition*, which the editors would publish while retaining the right to provide commentary on this material. Further Trotsky asked Sedov to answer the following questions: what was the opinion of their "allies" on the draft of the Opposition Platform which had been published not long before in the *Bulletin*; what was the position of the "ultra-left" groups (the Democratic Centralists, the Workers Opposition); what was the content of the Declaration of the Eighteen (this was the title given to the "Manifesto" of the Riutin Group in the Menshevik journal, *Socialist Herald*)?[8]

After studying archival documents, P. Broué came to the conclusion that the Trial of the Sixteen used certain facts which were actually true. "If we decide to treat the official minutes of the first Moscow Trial as a palimpsest, suppressing from them all mention of terrorism," he writes, " we find the story of a political evolution of political people in a changing but dramatic situation."[9] The French historian considers the following facts which were mentioned at the trial to be real. After his return from exile Safarov proposed to his comrades in the opposition that they return to a discussion of ways to fight against Stalin (Kamenev's testimony); in 1931–1932 Zinoviev entered into oppositional contact with Smirnov, Sokolnikov, leaders of the former "Workers Opposition" Shliapnikov and Medvedev and members of the Sten-Lominadze Group (Zinoviev's testimony); during this period Zinoviev and Kamenev thought that it was possible and necessary "to remove Stalin" (that is, to remove him from the post of general secretary), and also to establish contact with Trotsky (testimony of Zinoviev and Kamenev); during a meeting at Zinoviev's dacha in 1932, members of the former "Leningrad opposition" came to the conclusion that it was necessary to reestablish the bloc with the Trotskyists which they had broken up five years earlier (Reingold's testimony). They delegated Yevdokimov to meet with the "Smirnovists," and this meeting took place at one of the Moscow train stations in Mrachkovsky's official railway car. Mrachkovsky was then working as head of the construction of BAM (the Baikal-Amur line). There Smirnov told representatives of other opposition groups about his meetings with Sedov.

The anti-Stalinist bloc finally took form in June 1932. After a few months, Goltsman passed information to Sedov about the bloc, and then brought back to Moscow Trotsky's reply about agreeing to collaborate with the bloc.

In relations between Trotsky and Sedov and their cothinkers in the USSR, the conspiracy was outstandingly maintained. Although the GPU conducted careful surveillance of them, it was unable to uncover any meetings, correspondence or other forms of their contact with Soviet oppositionists. And far from all of the opposition contacts inside the Soviet Union were tracked down. Although there was a series of arrests of participants in illegal opposition groups at the end of 1932 and the beginning of 1933, not a single one of those arrested mentioned negotiations about the creation of a bloc. For this reason several of the participants in these negotiations (Lominadze, Shatskin, Goltsman and others) remained at liberty until 1935–36. Only after a new wave of arrests following Kirov's assassination, after interrogations and reinterrogations of dozens of Oppositionists, did Stalin receive information about the 1932 bloc, which served as one of the main reasons for organizing the Great Purge. It is not excluded that this information might have been received from Zborowski, too, who by 1935 had penetrated into Sedov's closest circle and who enjoyed his full confidence.

At the February-March Plenum of the Central Committee, Yezhov said that the secret political department of the OGPU in 1931–1932 had material from agents about the existence "of a Trotskyist center headed by Smirnov," about how the latter arranged contacts with Trotsky and Sedov, and about the creation of a bloc "of Trotskyists and Zinovievists, rightists and leftists." On the basis of this material, Smirnov and his group, consisting of eighty-seven people, were arrested in 1933. However, the investigation into their case "was conducted in such a way that this material from the agents had not been used."[10]

The majority of the bloc's participants were shot in 1936–37. Evidently, only two of them—Safarov and Konstantinov—lived until the beginning of the 1940s, when they were killed in the course of systematically liquidating all the former active oppositionists who still remained in the camps.

In the Harvard archives I found a number of new documents showing that Trotsky and Sedov entered into contact with participants in the anti-Stalinist bloc as it was forming. In 1936, Sedov wrote to Victor Serge about the NKVD's uncovering of foreign "Trotskyist" ties: "I personally feel that the source of the provocations lies in Russia and not here. *No one* besides L. D. and I has ever known anything about the Russian comrades whom I see abroad. A number of disasters I know about occurred many months later, without anything to do with meetings abroad.... For me there is no doubt that the charge of foreign ties was issued on the basis of information gathered in Moscow and not on the basis of information received abroad."[11]

After the appearance of the first announcements about the Trial of the Sixteen, Sedov sent a letter by special courier to Trotsky. Fear that it might somehow be seized explains some of the peculiarities of this letter (using the formal "vy", etc.). In it, Sedov recalled that at the end of 1932 Kolokoltsev (the conspiratorial name for I. N. Smirnov—V. R.) delegated Orlov (Goltsman—V. R.), who brought to Berlin the letter and economic article which was published in the *Bulletin*. At that time "Orlov told how Kolokoltsev awaited his arrest any day, for a provocateur had been uncovered close to him." "From what he has said [Orlov, at the trial—V. R.] so far," added Sedov, "there has been nothing mentioned about all this. He names another city and another person whom he supposedly saw (Copenhagen and Trotsky—V. R.)." Recalling that I. N. Smirnov had been arrested at the end of 1932 and sentenced to ten years in a political prison "for foreign ties," Sedov wrote: "Insofar as he himself feels that it is necessary to hide nothing [at the trial—V. R.], and moreover, since he is telling the most fantastic tales, I think that I have to say exactly what did happen. Observing this principle *in general*, we must make sure that we don't harm anyone."

In the same letter, Sedov asked Trotsky to reply "whether there had been any provocative attempts to see you at the time of your trip several years ago, when you gave lectures. As far as I know, there weren't even any attempts."[12]

Trotsky and Sedov felt that the Trial of the Sixteen was a provocation or complex amalgam (i.e., a maliciously deliberate weaving together of the truth and false versions) rather than a simple falsification.

Since, relatively speaking, the organizers of the trial had created an amalgam consisting of 90 percent lies and 10 percent truth, Trotsky and Sedov denied several facts which they knew to be true. For instance, at the trial it was said that the Old Bolshevik Yuri Gaven had passed Trotsky's "instructions" to Smirnov. Gaven's name had figured in the testimony given by Smirnov, Mrachkovsky, and Safonova, and had been mentioned several times in Vyshinsky's indictment speech. However, Gaven had not appeared at the trial even as a witness, and his case had been "set aside for special treatment." In the trial's sentence, Gaven's name was not mentioned, and Goltsman was designated as the transmitter of Trotsky's "instructions." From all this, Trotsky and Sedov concluded that Gaven had not been broken and during the investigation he had refused to confess to the charges made against him. In a letter to Trotsky, Sedov stressed that "Sorokin [Gaven's conspiratorial name—V. R.], whom you also know, has not been included in the case. It seems to me that the only explanation for this is that he stubbornly held out, didn't agree to any foul behavior, and therefore remained outside the case." At this point Sedov wrote about the necessity of "remaining silent only about those matters which might harm various people."[13] Proceeding from this principle, Trotsky and Sedov denied their contacts with Gaven, who had acted as one of the intermediaries between Trotsky and the anti-Stalinist bloc. Similar facts convince us that Trotsky and Sedov decided to deny everything except what the Stalinist inquisitors knew for certain.

This total denial was dictated by the need to defend the Old Bolsheviks. "To acknowledge the existence of a 'Trotsky-Zinoviev bloc,' falsely accused of terrorism at the trial," writes P. Broué, "would have meant that Trotsky and Sedov were giving away their friends and allies.... Trotsky and Sedov were fighting for their own lives and honor, for the lives and honor of their comrades-in-arms, and they were not inclined to give them away."[14]

P. Broué feels that the time has come for a new investigation which will allow us to determine what aspects of the genuine struggle of Old Bolsheviks against Stalin and Stalinism found their reflection at the trials of 1936–1938 and were amalgamated with invented charges. He stresses that the facts about the organization of a bloc of communist opposition demolishes the legend about the absence of any resistance to Stalinism in the Bolshevik milieu. The creation of this bloc reflected the attempt by the best forces of the party to unite in order to lead the country out of the bitter economic and political crisis which the adventurist policies of the Stalinist clique had produced.

As Broué correctly indicates, the version about the absolutely whimsical nature of the Stalinist repressions is shared by those who refuse to acknowledge the degeneration of the political regime established by the October Revolution. They assert that this regime from the very beginning set the goal of securing the absolute "monolithism" of the party, excluding any possibility of criticism, discussion or opposition. Falsifiers of this type try to convince public opinion that all Soviet history is subject to a strict and fatal predetermination, and that Stalinism was the logical continuation of Leninism. "Virtually proceeding from the position that scientific approaches to history are inapplicable in the study of the evolution of Soviet society, they explain the Moscow Trials not as a political crisis of the Stalinist regime, but as the essence of what they call 'communism.' "[15]

In actual fact, the Moscow Trials were not a senseless and cold-blooded crime, but Stalin's counterblow in the sharpest of political battles.

10. CANDIDATE DEFENDANTS AT FUTURE TRIALS

PERHAPS THE MOST repulsive side of the political hysteria unleashed during the days of the trial was the activity of former oppositionists who demanded bloody reprisals against their recent friends and cothinkers.

Particularly shameful were the articles by Piatakov and Radek. "After the pure, fresh air which our beautiful, flourishing socialist country has been breathing," Piatakov wrote bombastically, "suddenly we are enveloped by the overwhelming stench emanating from this political morgue. People who long ago became political corpses are rotting and decomposing, poisoning the air around themselves. And it is precisely in this final stage of decomposition that they have become not only loathsome, but socially dangerous.... There are no words which can fully express one's indignation and loathing. These are people who have lost their last human characteristics. They must be destroyed like carrion which infects the pure and refreshing air of our Soviet land, like dangerous carrion which is capable of bringing death to our leaders and which has already brought death to one of the best people in our land—such a wonderful comrade and leader as S. M. Kirov."[1]

Radek used similar expressions to state his attitude toward the trial. "From the trial room in which the Military Collegium of the Supreme Court of the USSR is investigating the case of Zinoviev, Kamenev, Mrachkovsky, and Smirnov, the case of the absent Trotsky," he wrote, "a corpse-like stench engulfs the whole world. The people who raised their weapons against the lives of the favorite leaders of the proletariat must pay with their heads for their boundless guilt."[2]

A few months later at the trial of the "anti-Soviet Trotskyist Center," Vyshinsky mockingly introduced excerpts from these articles as proof of "double-dealing" on the part of Piatakov and Radek.

On the day that these articles appeared, the defendants obeyed Vyshinsky's conductor's baton and began to reveal new names of people with whom the "center" had maintained conspiratorial ties. After this, Vyshinsky made the following

Yu. L. Piatakov

announcement: "I find it necessary to report to the court that yesterday I issued instructions about initiating an investigation ... into Bukharin, Rykov, Tomsky, Uglanov, Radek and Piatakov, and depending on the results of this investigation, the Procuracy will take appropriate steps in this case. As far as Serebriakov and Sokolnikov are concerned, evidence already at the disposal of the investigative organs demonstrates that these persons have engaged in counterrevolutionary crimes, in connection with which criminal proceedings are being initiated against Sokolnikov and Serebriakov."[3]

Among the "conspirators" named at the trial, there were eighteen members of the Central Committee who had been elected under Lenin, six members of Lenin's Politburo (everyone except Stalin) and five people mentioned in Lenin's "Testament" (once again, everyone except Stalin).

Whereas the main defendants at the Trial of the Sixteen had long since been removed from leadership activity, among the other "conspirators" they named were five members and candidate members of the present Central Committee of the VKP(b). This included former participants in the Bukharin "troika," Sokolnikov, who had announced his break with the united opposition at the Fifteenth Party Congress and had been chosen a member of the CC (at the Sixteenth and Seventeenth Congresses he was chosen a candidate member of the CC), and Piatakov, who had been elected a member of the CC at the Sixteenth and Seventeenth Congresses.

Sokolnikov was arrested on 26 July, after a resolution had been passed by referendum within the CC calling for his expulsion from the CC and the party.

At first, Piatakov did not feel any similar threat hanging over him. At the end of July he was even selected as public prosecutor at the trial of the "Trotsky-Zinoviev Center." In his own words, he saw this appointment "as an act of the most enormous confidence on the part of the CC," and he prepared to fulfill this mission "heart and soul." However, on the night of 28 July, Piatakov's former wife was arrested. At her apartment correspondence was seized belonging to Piatakov, including material relating to the period when he was in the Opposition.

On 10 August, Yezhov acquainted Piatakov with the testimony given against him and informed him about the cancellation of his "honorary" appointment as prosecutor at the trial, his removal from the post of Deputy Narkom for Heavy Industry and his appointment as head of the Chirchik Construction Project. Piatakov's reaction to this news surprised and perplexed even Yezhov, who had seen quite a lot. In a report to Stalin about his conversation with Piatakov, Yezhov wrote that Piatakov declared that "the Trotskyists" were spreading slanders out of hatred toward him, but that he was incapable of opposing their testimony "except with naked refutations in words," and therefore "he understands that the CC's trust in him had been undermined." Calling himself guilty of "not paying attention to the counterrevolutionary work of his former wife, and of being indifferent to meetings with her acquaintances," Piatakov said that he should be punished more severely, and asked "that he be granted any form (as the CC saw fit) of rehabilitation." With this in mind, he asked that "they allow him personally to shoot all those sentenced to be shot in the (upcoming) trial, including his former wife," and to publish a statement about this in the press. "Despite the fact that I pointed out to him the absurdity of this proposal," Yezhov added, "he nevertheless insisted that I tell the CC about it."[4]

In reporting these events at the December Plenum of the Central Committee in 1936, Stalin stated that Piatakov had prepared "with pleasure" to play the role of prosecutor. "But then we thought things over and decided that this wouldn't work. What would it mean to present him as public prosecutor? He would say one thing, and the accused would object by saying: 'Look where you've managed to crawl, into the prosecutor's chair. But didn't you used to work with us?' And what would that lead to? It would turn the trial into a comedy and disrupt the trial."

Then Stalin discussed the reasons Piatakov was refused his request to personally shoot the defendants: "If we announced it, no one would believe that we hadn't forced him to do it. We said that this wouldn't work, no one would believe that you voluntarily decided to do this, without being coerced. Yes, and besides, we never have announced the names of the people who carry out sentences."[5]

After his conversation with Yezhov, Piatakov sent a letter to Stalin in which he assured him that he had long ago unconditionally broken from his "Trotskyist past," and that he was ready to die for Stalin. After receiving this letter, Stalin left Piatakov at liberty for one more month, and then as an example of typical bureaucratic routine, passed a resolution by referendum in the CC expelling him from the CC and the party, after which Piatakov was arrested.

The former leaders of the "rightists" learned about the charges against them only from the trial transcript. During the trial, the Combined State Publishing House (OGIZ), which Tomsky headed, held a party meeting. The only "confession" which was extracted from Tomsky at the meeting was the statement that he "had concealed from the party his meetings and counterrevolutionary negotiations in 1929 with Kamenev about creating a joint bloc," letting only Bukharin and Rykov know about these matters.

On the morning of 22 August, a car came to Tomsky's dacha to take him to work as usual. The chauffeur brought a fresh issue of *Pravda*, the front page of which contained a headline in large letters: "Investigate the Ties of Tomsky-Bukharin-Rykov and Piatakov-Radek with the Trotsky-Zinoviev Gang." The same issue published a notice about the party meeting at OGIZ which had uncovered the "wretched double-dealing" by Tomsky (this conclusion was made because Tomsky had said that in 1929 he "only generally accepted the party line" rather than seeing it as "completely correct." The note drew an unmistakable conclusion: "For the meeting, Tomsky's treacherous behavior became absolutely clear. There can be no doubt that even today Tomsky is hiding his ties to the bloc's participants."[6] A few minutes after reading the newspaper, Tomsky shot himself. He left a letter to Stalin in which he said: "I turn to you not only as leader of the party, but as an old, militant comrade, and this is my last request—do not believe Zinoviev's brazen slander, I never entered into any blocs with him, and I never joined any conspiracy against the party."[7]

The next day, *Pravda* carried a statement from the Central Committee of the VKP(b) about how Tomsky had committed suicide "after getting tangled up in his ties with counterrevolutionary Trotsky-Zinoviev terrorists."[8] The authorship of this formulation belonged to Kaganovich. Before publishing this statement he conveyed its contents to Stalin, who was vacationing in Sochi.

In an article about Tomsky written soon after his death, Trotsky described the last years in the life of this "most outstanding worker whom the Bolshevik Party produced, and perhaps even the Russian Revolution as a whole." "When he was appointed head of the State Publishing House, Tomsky became a shadow of his former self. Much like other members of the Right Opposition (Rykov and Bukharin), Tomsky had to 'repent' more than once. He carried out this ritual with greater dignity than the others. The ruling clique was not mistaken when it detected a restrained hatred among the notes of repentance. In the State Publishing House, Tomsky was surrounded on all sides by carefully chosen enemies. Not only his assistants, but even his personal secretaries were undoubtedly agents of the GPU. During the so-called purges of the party, the party cell at the State Publishing House, on instructions from above, would without fail subject Tomsky to a thorough political checkup. This firm and proud proletarian endured no few bitter and humiliating hours. But there was no salvation: like an alien body he would have to be rejected in the end by the Bonapartist bureaucracy. The defendants at the Trial of the Sixteen mentioned Tomsky's name together with the names of Bukharin and Rykov as persons involved in terror. Before Tomsky's case made it to the trial investigators, the party cell at the State Publishing House began to work him over. Every type of careerist, every old or young scoundrel ... asked Tomsky brazen and insulting questions; they gave him no respite and demanded ever newer confessions, acts of contrition and denunciations. The torment lasted several hours. Its continuation was set for a new session. In the interval between these two sessions, Tomsky put a bullet into his head."[9]

During the days of the trial, Bukharin and Rykov were far from Moscow. Rykov was on a business trip to the Far East (later, all the people with whom he met on official matters of his Commissariat during this trip were arrested on charges of having received from him instructions to engage in sabotage). As he traveled past Baikal, Rykov showed his twenty-year-old daughter, whom he had taken on the trip as a secretary, some derailed railway cars and said: "Look what hatred brings" (having in mind that the accident which had occurred here was the result of sabotage).[10]

On 10 July the Politburo passed a resolution allowing Bukharin to go on vacation. At the beginning of August Bukharin left for a trip in Central Asia.

His plans were not changed by news of the arrest of Sokolnikov, who had been his friend since their years in school. A. M. Larina writes about these matters: "N. I. failed so completely to foresee the impending mass terror and rapidly approaching trials that he absolutely excluded political motives in Sokolnikov's arrest. He reckoned that his arrest was connected with overspending government funds when he was ambassador in London ... and hoped for Sokolnikov's quick release."[11] Here Larina is clearly mistaken. As a candidate member of the Central Committee, Bukharin couldn't help but know about the official motive for Sokolnikov's arrest (which was also announced in the press). He evidently told the version mentioned by Larina to his young wife, who had just given birth to a child, in order to keep her from becoming upset.

While traveling throughout the Central Asian republics, Bukharin sent two letters to Stalin in which he shared his impressions about what he had seen and made businesslike proposals about building new factories in Uzbekistan, improving supplies in Pamir, and so forth. In the second letter he excitedly told about visiting "the flourishing and well-to-do" Fergana District, where he "was in a collective farm named after you, saw a collective farm theater, and promised to tell you how people there know both how to work and to have a good time."[12]

After spending a few days in remote areas in Pamir, Bukharin descended from the mountains and traveled into Frunze, where he learned about the trial that was taking place. He was struck not by the very fact of the trial (whose preparations he apparently had known about before his trip), but by the mention of his name at the trial along with the names of conspirators and collaborators with the "Trotsky-Zinoviev Center." On the day the trial ended, he sent Stalin a coded telegram in which he said: "I have just read the bastards' slanderous testimony. Am deeply upset. Leaving Tashkent by plane the morning of the twenty-fifth. Please forgive me for the violation."*[13]

The next shock for Bukharin and Rykov was the announcement of Tomsky's suicide, to which they reacted in a similar manner. Rykov said to members of his family: "The fool. Now he's cast a shadow on us, too."[14]

After reading the official version of the reasons for Tomsky's suicide,

---

* In the Politburo resolution, "On Airplane Flights of Responsible Cadres," passed in 1933, a ban was placed, "under threat of expulsion from the party, on airplane flights without special permission of the CC in each separate instance" (*Stalinskoe politburo v 30-e gody*, Moscow, 1995, p. 40).

Bukharin exclaimed: "Nonsense!" As A. M. Larina recalls, he "was shaken more by the formulation of the article about M. P. Tomsky's suicide, than by the loss of a dear friend and morally pure comrade—that's how he characterized Mikhail Pavlovich."[15] In Tomsky's suicide he saw most of all "a threat to *himself,* and the hopelessness of his position,"[16] insofar as the official version confirmed the guilt of the "Rightists," once again united by Stalin, but this time as participants in conspiratorial activity.

When he landed at the Moscow airport, Bukharin expected to be immediately arrested. However, without any difficulties he was allowed into the Kremlin, where his apartment was located. When he then called Stalin, Bukharin was surprised to learn that, before the trial began, Stalin had left for a vacation in Sochi. Then he wrote a letter to members of the Politburo and asked Stalin's secretariat to send it immediately to Stalin. The letter bore the signatures of the following people who had read it: Molotov, Voroshilov, Ordzhonikidze, Andreev, Chubar and Yezhov.

Using the lexicon of the current newspapers, Bukharin expressed in his letter his enthusiastic satisfaction with the trial's results: "That the bastards have been shot—wonderful: the air immediately became fresher. The trial will have the most enormous international significance. This is an aspen stake—a real one—driven into the grave of the bloody turkey, filled with arrogance which led him into the fascist secret police [i.e., Trotsky—V. R.]."[17] Bukharin did not call into question a single charge made at the trial, with the exception of the charges concerning himself. He explained the testimony directed against him by the special craftiness of the defendants who had thereby pursued—to use his words—the following goals: "a) to show (on a world scale) that 'they' *are not alone*; b) to use even the smallest chance for clemency by demonstrating what is supposedly their utmost sincerity ('to expose' *even* others, which doesn't exclude covering *their own* tracks); c) a secondary goal: revenge over anyone who in some way leads an active political life. Kamenev therefore joined Reingold in trying to poison all the wells—a gesture that was clever, calculated and very deliberate."

Thus, in his attempts at self-defense, Bukharin from the very beginning accepted the rules of the game established by Stalin: to defend only himself, without expressing even a shadow of doubt regarding the crimes of the others who had already been condemned. To his timid comment that after the trial "any member of the party is afraid of believing the word of anyone who had formerly been at any time in any opposition," Bukharin added the qualification that the defendants who had been shot were to blame for the creation of such an atmosphere. In order to prove his own exclusive innocence (such was Bukharin's tactic right up until his arrest), he referred to the lead article in *Pravda*, where it stated: we must clarify who among the people being investigated is "honest, and who harbors a grudge." While endorsing these words, Bukharin stressed that he was not only innocent of the crimes ascribed to him, but that he could "say with pride, that during all the recent years he had defended the line of the party, the line of the Central Committee and the leadership of Stalin. Moreover he had done so with passion and conviction."

Clearly understanding the weakness of the version about "yearning for power," Bukharin reasonably pointed to the contradictions in the testimony of the defendants: "on the one hand, Bukharin, they say, does not agree with the general line; on the other hand, they do agree with the general line, but they want naked power; at the same time, Bukharin supposedly agrees with them." In this regard he vowed: "after recognizing and confessing my mistakes ... I considered and consider that only *fools* (if they generally want socialism, and not something else) can propose 'another line.' For only a fool (or a traitor) does not understand the kind of lion bounds which have been made by our country as it is inspired and guided by Stalin's iron hand."

Thus Bukharin fully accepted the "logic" of the Stalinist amalgams: rejection or criticism of Stalinist "socialism" and Stalin's "iron hand" ineluctably leads to betrayal of one's country and socialism. Proceeding from these postulates, he virtually prompted Stalin to "correct" the version about the defendants' lack of a political program. Affirming that the "bastards" were afraid of talking about their "line," Bukharin wrote: "Trotsky has his own, profoundly insidious, and, from the standpoint of socialism, profoundly stupid line: they *were afraid* of talking about it; it is the thesis about the enslavement of the proletariat by the 'Stalinist bureaucracy,' it is spitting at the Stakhanovists, it is the question of our state, and it is spitting at the draft of our new Constitution, at our foreign policy, etc."[18]

To prove his boundless loyalty to the "general line," Bukharin described in detail his conversations over recent years with Zinoviev, Kamenev and other former Oppositionists, stressing that in each of them he inevitably spoke about the "brilliant qualities" of "the leadership" and of Stalin personally. Stating that he had three years earlier severed all personal relations with Rykov and Tomsky, in order to "dispel, as much as possible, even superficial reasons for gossiping about a 'group,' " he proposed to verify the correctness of this statement "by asking my chauffeurs, by analyzing their schedules, by questioning guards, agents of the NKVD, servants and so forth."[19] Thus Bukharin himself requested the use of police methods in order to verify how obediently he had met Stalin's decree about separating former Oppositionists.

Not having received a reply to his letter from a single member of the Politburo, Bukharin sent a letter to Voroshilov, in which he used Vyshinsky's terminology: "I am terribly happy that they shot the dogs. Trotsky has been politically destroyed by the trial, and this will soon become absolutely clear." Trying to find arguments able to convince Voroshilov of his innocence, Bukharin confirmed that "from an international point of view it would be *stupid* to widen the base of the swinishness (this would mean going halfway to meet the wishes of the scoundrel Kamenev! They would then only have to show that they were not alone)."

Clearly sensing the "laws" of Stalinist justice, Bukharin wrote that the published resolutions of party organizations indicated that Bukharin knew about the plans of the "terrorists." In connection with this, he correctly noted that in such conditions an objective investigation becomes impossible "After all, for instance, if the Kiev party activists *decide*: he knew, then how could the investigator say: 'he *did not* know,' if 'the *party* said': 'he knew.'"

Finally, in despair, Bukharin resorted to one more argument which, despite his intentions, provoked Voroshilov's wrath. He declared: if the members of the Politburo believed what "lies were told about him by the cynic-assassin Kamenev, that most wretched of people, that human carrion," and they still left him, Bukharin, at liberty, then they were "cowards who deserved no respect."[20]

In writing his confused letter, Bukharin did not imagine how insecure the members of the Politburo felt themselves to be after being thoroughly frightened by the "Molotov affair." Disturbed by the very fact that he had received a letter from Bukharin, Voroshilov immediately showed it to Kaganovich, Ordzhonikidze and Yezhov. As Voroshilov related at the February-March Plenum, they all "somehow overlooked the disgusting attacks on the CC"; only Molotov, who soon returned from vacation, declared that "this is simply a vile letter."[21]

On the next day after receiving the letter, Voroshilov sent a copy to Stalin, and a few days later sent to the same address a copy of his reply to Bukharin. In this reply, Voroshilov expressed his anger over Bukharin's words about the "stupidity" and "cowardice" of the Kremlin leaders. "I am returning your letter, in which you allowed yourself to make vile attacks with regard to the party leadership," wrote Voroshilov. "If you wanted to convince me with your letter about your complete innocence, then you have convinced me of only one thing—to stay a bit further away from you regardless of the results of the investigation into your case, and if you do not renounce in written form the detestable epithets directed at the party leadership, then I will consider you a scoundrel."

Stalin assessed favorably the character of Voroshilov's reply. He sent it to Molotov along with a resolution which cited Voroshilov's behavior as an example for Ordzhonikidze: "Voroshilov's reply is good. If Sergo had just as soundly rebuked Mister Lominadze, who wrote him even more libelous letters against the CC VKP,* Lominadze would be alive today, and perhaps he would have become a man."[22]

After he received Voroshilov's harsh rebuke, Bukharin sent him a new letter filled with humble apologies and the assurance that: "I by no means wanted to say what you thought I did." He tried to persuade Voroshilov that he had the highest regard for the "party leadership," and that he considered it capable of making "mistakes only in personal cases," much like the mistake being allowed with regard to Bukharin himself.[23]

The ritual abuse directed against the victims of the Trial of the Sixteen in Bukharin's letters was not only out of his desire to please Stalin. As Larina recalls, Bukharin "was tormented by unbelievable animosity toward the 'slanderers' Zinoviev and Kamenev, but not at all toward Stalin." In Larina's opinion, by that time Bukharin had changed his former attitude toward Stalin as Genghis Khan, "attributing to him only a painfully crude sense of suspicion. And he felt that the only salvation lay in dispelling this suspiciousness."[24]

When his wife once turned to him with the question: could he really believe that Zinoviev and Kamenev were involved in Kirov's assassination?—Bukharin replied: "But these bastards and slandering scoundrels are killing me

---

* Evidently it was in this period that Ordzhonikidze first told Stalin how Lominadze (who committed suicide in 1935) had sent him letters over a number of years expressing oppositional sentiments. Stalin spoke angrily at the February-March Plenum of the Central Committee (see Chapter 22) about the fact that Ordzhonikidze had hidden the content of these letters.

and Aleksei! They already killed Tomsky, so that means they are capable of anything!"[25] This reply, which is devoid of logic, more fully reflects the confusion which had seized Bukharin during the days of the investigation being carried on behind his back.

Meanwhile the newspapers continued to print articles about meetings and party activists who passed resolutions: "Fully investigate the ties of Bukharin and Rykov with the despicable terrorists!", "Put Bukharin and Rykov on the defendants' bench!", and so forth. Languishing in total isolation, Bukharin anxiously awaited Stalin's return to Moscow in order to personally explain everything to him. When Radek called at this time and on behalf of the Party bureau of *Izvestiia*'s editorial board invited him to a party meeting, Bukharin answered that he would not appear at the editorial offices "as long as a refutation of the foul slander has not been published in the press." Radek then expressed the desire to meet personally with Bukharin. Bukharin refused such a meeting in order "not to complicate the investigation," and said that for the same reasons he had not even called Rykov, whom he very much wanted to see.[26]

A few days after this conversation, Bukharin was finally summoned to appear before the Central Committee. There, on 8 September, Bukharin and Rykov had face-to-face confrontations with Sokolnikov, proceedings which were conducted by Vyshinsky in the presence of Kaganovich and Yezhov. Sokolnikov announced that he had no direct evidence of the participation of Rykov and Bukharin in a bloc with the Trotskyists, but that he had heard about this from other conspirators in 1932–1933. In Sokolnikov's words, Kamenev told him about the intention of the "Trotskyists" to form a government with Rykov's participation.[27] Rykov categorically denied this testimony, saying that in those years he had no meetings with Kamenev. In a letter to Stalin reporting the results of the confrontations, Kaganovich wrote that they had managed to obtain only one "confession" from Rykov: in 1934 Tomsky had sought his advice about whether he should accept Zinoviev's invitation to visit him at his dacha; "Rykov limited himself to saying that he had advised Tomsky against accepting, but that he had told no one about the incident."[28]

Bukharin was just as categorical in denying Sokolnikov's testimony, calling it a "vicious fabrication." When Sokolnikov was led away, Kaganovich confided to Bukharin: "He's lying, the whore, from beginning to end! Go to the editorial board, Nikolai Ivanovich, and work there in peace."

"But why is he lying, Lazar Moiseevich," asked Bukharin, "that's the question that has to be answered."

Kaganovich assured Bukharin that everything would be done to find such an "answer."

After this, Bukharin told Kaganovich that he wouldn't return to work until an announcement had been printed in the press about the closing of his case.[29]

On the day after the face-to-face confrontations, the newspapers published an announcement from the Procuracy of the USSR which stated: "the investigation did not establish probative evidence for the bringing of charges against N. I. Bukharin and A. I. Rykov, as a consequence of which the present case is closed pending further investigation."[30]

The genuine meaning of this casuistic document couldn't help but be clear to every politically farsighted person. "How familiar to us is this vile formulation!" wrote Sedov in *The Red Book*. "It repeats verbatim the first 'rehabilitation' of Zinoviev [in 1935—V. R.]. With this purely Stalinist formulation, the 'father of the people' leaves his hands free for future abominations.... The mention of the names of Bukharin and Rykov at the trial is a 'hint' from Stalin: 'I have you in my hands, all I have to do is give the word and it's the end of you.' In the language of criminal law this 'method' is called blackmail (in cruder form: life or death)."

Sedov noted that the "rehabilitation" of Bukharin and Rykov indirectly provided an unequivocal assessment of all the other testimony given by the defendants at the Trial of the Sixteen: they said, after all, that Bukharin and Rykov knew about their terrorist activity and had found a "common language" with them. It was also characteristic that the "rehabilitation" did not extend to Tomsky, who had chosen suicide in order to avoid the humiliations, confessions and then—execution. For this "Stalin took revenge on Tomsky in the Stalinist way. Having half-executed and half-rehabilitated Rykov and Bukharin, he didn't mention a word about Tomsky."

Warning that the "semirehabilitation" of Rykov and Bukharin meant only a delay for them, Sedov made a strikingly precise prognosis for Stalin's further actions: "The time will come when we will learn that the united center was nothing in comparison with the other, 'Bukharin-Rykov' center, the existence of which was concealed by those executed."[31]

Thoughts about a similar turn of events undoubtedly visited Bukharin. After his "semirehabilitation" he went to the editorial offices of *Izvestiia*, where he found in his office the head of the Press department of the CC, Tal, who was simultaneously filling in as chief editor of the newspaper. Bukharin announced that he refused to work with a political commissar and never again visited the editorial board. During this period he spoke to his wife about the guiding role of Stalin in the organization of the terror; "however, once again, on the same day or on the next day he might prefer the idea about Stalin's abnormal suspiciousness, shielding himself against recognizing the hopelessness of his position."

A few days after Bukharin's "semirehabilitation," Radek came to see him at his dacha, explaining his visit by the fact that he expected his arrest any day now. Feeling that his letters from prison would not reach Stalin, Radek asked Bukharin to write to Stalin so that the latter would take his (Radek's) case into his own hands. In parting, Radek once again repeated: "Nikolai! Believe me, yes, believe you me, no matter what happens to me, I am guilty of nothing."

On 16 September Radek was arrested. On the same day, his wife came to see Bukharin and conveyed the words Radek uttered when they were leading him away: "Don't let Nikolai believe any slanders: I am as pure before the party as a tear drop." Only after this visit did Bukharin decide to write Stalin about his conversation with Radek. Adding on his own part that he didn't believe in Radek's ties to Trotsky, Bukharin nevertheless ended his letter with the words: "But, after all, who knows what he is?"[32]

During the following months, Bukharin as before saw no one except members of his own family. In order to distract himself from depressing thoughts, he tried to work on a book about the ideology of fascism. On 16 October he sent Ordzhonikidze a letter of congratulations on his fiftieth birthday. "Don't be surprised if there is no article from me about your birthday, " he wrote. "Although I am listed as the chief editor, the new personnel have deliberately and demonstratively not asked me to write about you (or about anything in general).... Slanderers have tried to devour me. But even now there are people who are tormenting me and tearing me to pieces.... My soul trembles as I write you this letter."[33]

As one immerses oneself in the suffering of the people condemned to death who are the subject of this chapter, it is difficult to remain within the framework of rational conceptions. Involuntarily the impression of irrationality arises —of frantic behavior, delirium, absurd squabbles and the absolute power that Stalin had over these people. On this plane of the absurd, isolated and torn away from the reality of those years, it is impossible to understand the behavior of the "candidate defendants" at future trials. Neither amateur psychoanalysis, expressed in assigning them primitive motives which amount only to the urge to survive at any price, nor the reminiscences of wives and children (and there is no shortage of these today) can help here. Stories of the latter about their impressions of that period not only remain on the same level, but even add the irrationality of unintentional partiality to the irrationality of being doomed.

In order to understand what actually happened sixty years ago with these people, we must try to see their lives as a whole. If that is impossible, then we must add at least a second, fundamental plane of their lives—the real management activity in which they took an active part. After renouncing their oppositional views, the majority of them directed whole branches of the national economy, large collectives and important structures in the economy and culture of the nation. On the same days when fear, hatred and despair ate away at their souls, they participated in making important decisions about the structure of investments (like Piatakov), about the publishing plans of an enormous complex (like Tomsky), or about the most crucial diplomatic actions (like Radek).

We must juxtapose these two currents of political life—the dynamic of far-reaching decisions and their real consequences for the development of society, and, let us say, the dynamic of the inner life of power structures, or of the inner struggle which flowed within them.

These two currents were tightly and dramatically bound together. Whether politicians themselves recognize it or not, it is precisely this relationship which determines their conduct, and often their fate.

In conditions of the totalitarian regime which became established in the 1930s, the arguments and debates in the structures of power lost their real, businesslike and constructive content. They took on new meaning and produced a different result—the crushing of people who thought differently by more powerful and cynical opponents, and the humiliation of those who proved to be weaker, who could be deceived and who could be forced to assume the guilt for the mistakes and miscalculations of an all-powerful leadership.

Such ruthless pressure in the corridors of power, as well as the reaction to it by various politicians, assumes different forms depending on concrete social and historical circumstances.

In the 1930s this was expressed in the form of relentlessly verifying the ideological purity, loyalty to the "general line," and essentially personal devotion of the political elite toward the supreme leader, or, in the terminology of those years, the "vozhd" [chief, leader, Führer]. The vacillating, relative and arbitrary nature of such criteria, under conditions of unceasing political zigzags, gave birth to chaotic feelings among the future victims of the political trials, which shaped what Stalin called their "double-dealing." These feelings, about which we have been learning more and more in recent years, became genuinely irrational because, in the life and consciousness of the capitulators who had returned to political activity, two morally and psychologically incompatible layers coexisted inseparably. On the one hand there was real collaborative work (with their future executioners), active participation in economic, military, and cultural endeavors. On the other hand, there was just as real ideological and psychological opposition, which remained concealed because of the lack of any opportunity to make political decisions which were collective, optimal and based on mutual trust. In such circumstances, rational political behavior is rendered difficult if not impossible.

We must not forget that the results of the activity of both the capitulators and the orthodox bearers of the "general line" were not only the indicators of undisputed successes achieved in the realm of economic and cultural construction. A fundamental corrective must be factored into these indicators by calculating, as much as it is possible, the social and human cost of their increase, i.e., the toll it placed on millions of people, their lives, their health and personal development. For it is precisely the social cost of economic growth that is the basic criterion by which people evaluate a regime.

The greater the social cost of the transformations being carried out by a regime, the more powerfully the fear of paying for mistakes will weigh upon its bearers and the more powerfully will grow the desire to shift this retribution onto others. In this we must search for the key to the conduct of both the "victors" and the "vanquished" in the bureaucratic upper echelons of that period.

Apropos of this observation, it would be useful to compare the political situation of the 1930s with today's political situation. Today's struggles within the corridors of power do not take ideological form, insofar as the ruling structures do not have an ideology as such. Therefore the second criterion—personal devotion—is becoming, no matter how wild this sounds, even more powerful than in the 1930s. But the greatest difference is bound up with the character of the reform activity which is being undertaken by the regime. Insofar as its fundamental direction is now the destruction of the old economic, social and cultural structures, the indicators of economic and social development are steadily declining. This means that the social cost of the reforms would have increased even given stable indicators of mortality, illness, crime, poverty and impoverishment. But in the present situation, when these figures are growing relentlessly, the social cost of the reforms is growing exponentially.

Thus what is happening is, on the one hand, the uncontrolled growth of the social cost which has escaped the control of the regime, and on the other— sharp struggles within the power structures. In these conditions, the behavior of the ruling elite assumes, not an irrational character (as might appear at first glance), but, on the contrary, a strictly rational one. The piling up of contradictions and lies, the shifting from one "camp" into another, and the obvious lack of morality which many people perceive to be irrationality—all this in actual fact is the result of the interaction and collision of extremely rational decisions and actions on the part of modern political figures. They are continually making cruel and absurd blunders, but the frantic behavior of Bukharin or Radek cannot help but appear to be amusing and inexplicable to them.

If the experiences and conduct of the defendants at the political trials of the 1930s have attracted and will continue to attract for many years to come the attention of millions of people and yet will remain a mystery for many of them, there is no room for mystery in the conduct of today's politicians. This behavior is based on rational schemas, selfish calculation and individual interest. Only one thing is striking here: how people who have freed themselves, as they put it, from "communist utopianism" and who have acquired the "rationalistic mentality of modern civilization," could have committed so many blunders and crimes in such a short time.

11. FROM CHARGES OF TERROR TO NEW AMALGAMS

WHILE BUKHARIN and other capitulators who remained at liberty languished in uncertainty over their impending fate, the press launched a clamorous campaign which was intended to broaden the circle of crimes being attributed to the "Trotskyists" and "Rightists."

At the first Moscow Trial, the defendants were charged only with terrorist activity. Stalin assumed that such an indictment would be fully adequate to produce death sentences, and that it would seem completely reasonable in the eyes of public opinion. People would see nothing improbable about political leaders who had suffered defeat and then decided to use such extreme means as terror in order to regain the power they had lost.

However, after he returned from vacation, Stalin learned that among many Soviet people the trial evoked not only sympathy for those executed, but even regrets that the old revolutionaries had not managed to overthrow his tyrannical power. "Having dreamt up the legend about how the Old Bolsheviks felt it was necessary to assassinate him," wrote Orlov, "Stalin was the one who gave the idea of revolutionary terror to the masses; he allowed to be born in the minds of people the most dangerous thought, that even Lenin's closest comrades-in-arms saw terror as the only way to rid the land of Stalin's despotism." As confirmation of this, Orlov recalled that in Yagoda's reports, Stalin was told that soon after the trial, the walls of several Moscow factories carried the messages: "Down with the murderers of the leaders of October!", and "Too bad they didn't finish off the Georgian snake."[1]

In addition we should note that for many people, terrorist activity against Stalin might suggest associations with the activity of the organization Narodnaya Volya [The People's Will], which had long since been surrounded with an aureole of heroism and martyrdom in the struggle for a just cause. It is no accident that at the Trial of the Sixteen Vyshinsky felt that it was necessary to "erase the blasphemous parallel," "the shameless comparison to the epoch of People's Will terrorism."[2] A year and a half before, Stalin himself had issued a stern edict: "If we educate our people on the example of the People's Will, then we will be raising terrorists."[3] To carry out this edict, a ban was placed on historical publications about the heroes of "The People's Will."

This was, however, insufficient to achieve the goal set by Stalin—to instill in the consciousness of the masses a bitter hatred for the Opposition. Trotsky wrote very expressively in his book, *The Crimes of Stalin*, about how limiting the crimes of the oppositionists to terror alone might bring consequences which were unpleasant for Stalin: "The bourgeoisie will think: 'The Bolsheviks are destroying each other; let us see what comes of this.' As for the workers, a significant section of them might say: 'The Soviet bureaucracy has grabbed all the wealth and all the power and is suppressing every word of criticism; perhaps Trotsky is right in calling for terror.' The most passionate section of the Soviet youth, upon learning that the authority of names well known to them stands for terror, might actually set out upon this as yet unexplored path."[4]

Trotsky returned more than once to the idea that accepting on faith the false charges of terrorist activity by the oppositionists might create an effect directly opposed to what Stalin was trying to achieve. In the article, "A New Stalinist Amalgam," he wrote: "'Terror?' unsatisfied and politically unsophisticated layers of workers might ask themselves: 'Maybe it is true after all that against this violent bureaucracy there is no other means of fighting except with the revolver and bombs.'"[5]

It is true that, seeing the dangerous consequences of playing with the bugbear of "terror," at the Trial of the Sixteen Stalin supplemented the charge of terror with another one, designed to sink his opponents in the mud. "He could think of nothing more effective than ties to the Gestapo," Trotsky wrote. "Terror in a union with Hitler! Any worker who believed this amalgam would receive an inoculation for all time against 'Trotskyism.' The difficulty lies only in forcing him to believe...."[6]

The first Moscow Trial of the Old Bolsheviks could not overcome this difficulty insofar as the main defendants vigorously denied the charges that they had ties to the Gestapo. Moreover, the act of indictment linked the collaboration of the "Trotskyists" and the Gestapo only to the means of struggle (this collaboration supposedly only served to facilitate the preparation of terrorist acts), but not to its goals.

It was therefore necessary to expand the circle of crimes committed by the "Trotskyists," supplementing them with espionage and direct complicity with foreign governments and special services in preparing the defeat of the USSR in an impending war (a charge designed to arouse the patriotic feelings of the Soviet people). Moreover, it was necessary to charge the "Trotskyists" not only with terror against political leaders, but with crimes directly aimed at ordinary citizens: with the organization of railroad catastrophes, industrial accidents and fires, all of which would bring death or mutilation to the common people. Such accusations had not figured even at the "sabotage" trials at the end of the 1920s and beginning of the 1930s, involving nonparty specialists, many of whom were hostile to the Soviet regime. Now, however, charges of the conscious extermination of Soviet people were being lodged against the builders of the Soviet regime or against people raised by this regime, but the absurdity of the charges was concealed by massive propaganda and wide-scale repressions.

The forcing of ever newer and more terrible charges, designed to morally destroy the Opposition and arouse hatred toward it among the broadest masses, presupposed the construction of a much more gigantic conspiracy than the one which, according to material from the Trial of the Sixteen, the "Trotsky-Zinoviev center" had dreamt up.

In *The Red Book,* Sedov stressed: The Trial of the Sixteen clearly showed that "Stalin needs Trotsky's head—this is his main goal. To achieve it he will launch the most extreme and even more insidious cases."[7] While Trotsky was isolated, Stalin prepared not only the intrigue in Norway, but another intrigue involving the League of Nations. In 1934, after the murder of the Yugoslav king by Croatian nationalists and of the French Minister of Foreign Affairs, the Soviet government had launched a campaign to create an international court for the struggle against terrorism. However, Trotsky took the initiative into his own hands in this instance as well. On 22 October 1936 he had his attorney contact the Geneva Commission of Lawyers, which had been working on the status of the future tribunal. Trotsky declared that as soon as the tribunal was created, he demanded that his case be reviewed before it. Of course, Trotsky's appearance before an international court containing impartial legal experts from foreign countries was unacceptable for Stalin. The creation of a tribunal against terrorists was gradually brought to a halt.

More important proved to be the organization of new trials, expanding the circle of crimes inspired by Trotsky. This was necessary primarily in order to undermine the influence of the Fourth International in the West. As Sedov stressed, "Stalin wants to reduce political disagreements in the workers' movement to the formula: with the GPU or the Gestapo. Whoever is not with the GPU is an agent of the Gestapo."[8]

From the standpoint of domestic policy, as Sedov noted, Stalin needed new trials first of all in order to blame the economic disasters, disproportions, and miscalculations caused by his policies on the "sabotage" of Trotskyists.

Secondly, at the Trial of the Sixteen, the beginning of the "counterrevolutionary activity" of the Trotskyists was placed in 1932. This "makes unassailable for the executioner all Trotskyists who had been in prison since 1928. Many things compel us to think that the accused at a new trial will be called upon to confess to crimes or intentions which relate to the period when they still had not managed to repent."[9]

Having correctly defined the trajectory of Stalin's next repressions and frame-ups, Trotsky and Sedov did not foresee only their scale. However they indicated with unerring exactitude that the Trial of the Sixteen signified the beginning of a new and even more terrible chapter in the history of the USSR. This chapter became widely known as "the Yezhov period."

12. THE BEGINNING OF THE YEZHOV PERIOD

THE FIRST MEASURES directed at widening and intensifying the repressions were taken in July 1936, following Yezhov's report on the case of the "Trotsky-Zinoviev Center" at a session of the Politburo. Stalin proposed to give the People's Commissar of Internal Affairs extraordinary powers for one year. Accompanying this decision was the formation of a Politburo commission to monitor the activity of the NKVD.

Nevertheless, at that time even the majority of the members of the Politburo apparently expected that after the trial the repressions would subside. This can be seen in the appearance of several decrees from the Central Committee which were aimed at halting reprisals against communists who had been labeled "accomplices of the Trotskyists." These decrees were adopted not at CC plenums (which were not called from June to December 1936), but in what had become the usual apparatus procedure, whereby it was sufficient for them to be approved by the Politburo, sometimes even by means of referendum.

On 29 August, *Izvestiia* carried a notice, "Unmasked Enemy," which was typical for the "anti-Trotskyist" hysteria of the time. Tabakov, the director of the factory "Magnezit" (in the Cheliabinsk area), had been expelled from the party for "abetting and concealing the Trotskyist terrorist, Dreitser, who had been shot," and who had worked as Tabakov's deputy before his arrest. Two days later, the Central Committee overturned the decision of the party organization at the factory regarding Tabakov's expulsion, and approved the decision of *Izvestiia*'s editorial board to fire its Cheliabinsk correspondent "for printing without verification information about Comrade Tabakov which was taken from the local newspaper."[1]

However, even the "protection" of a higher party body did not save Tabakov from subsequent reprisals. At the end of 1937, B. N. Lesniak happened to end up in the same cell of the NKVD's inner prison with Tabakov. As Lesniak recalls, there he learned that Tabakov—a member of the party since before the revolution, a Red Partisan, and a graduate of a communist institute of higher learning—had been charged with espionage on behalf of Germany, where he had been sent at the beginning of the 1930s in order to obtain equipment for his factory.[2]

On 31 August the Politburo issued an edict on the work of the Dnepropetrovsk Regional Committee of the VKP(b), in which, among other things, Vesnik, the director of the Krivorog Metallurgical Complex, and Ildrym, his deputy, were defended against "ungrounded inclusion among accomplices of the Trotskyists." As Molotov explained at the February-March Plenum, the Politburo sent a "special telegram, putting the Dnepropetrovsk Regional Committee in its place regarding ... Comrade Vesnik, whom they almost shot in August."[3] On 5 August, *Pravda* published information about a plenum of the Dnepropetrovsk Regional Committee at which party organizations were criticized for allowing "elements of overly severe behavior, for excesses, for petty-bourgeois, self-insuring alarmism, and for self-deprecation." Rescinding the expulsion from the party of Vesnik and Ildryn by the Krivorog City Committee, the Plenum recognized as "absolutely correct" the decision of the CC to remove from his post in connection with this incident the secretary of the Krivorog City Committee and "decisively warned" the region's party organizations against allowing future "excesses expressed in the indiscriminate inclusion of party members in the ranks of the Trotskyists and their accomplices without sufficient, and moreover serious, grounds."[4]

On the wave of the "anti-Trotskyist" hysteria, *Pravda* repeatedly "called to order" local party organizations and organs of the press with regard to the more odious examples of "vigilance." Thus, the article "On a Cowardly Secretary and an Irresponsible Journalist," told about charges of Trotskyism being lodged against the journalist Voitinskaya. This accusation had appeared in a comment by the *Izvestiia* correspondent, Beliavsky, "On Enemies and Rotten Liberals in Several Writers Organizations."[5] "Where did Beliavsky learn that Voitinskaya is a Trotskyist?" *Pravda* angrily wrote. "... He had no grounds whatsoever. He simply took it into his head to write ... and did so without a twinge of conscience, slandering and defaming a person in the press." After the appearance of the *Izvestiia* article, the party organization where Voitinskaya was registered immediately expelled her from the party, declaring her guilty of several times visiting the home "of the Trotskyist Serebriakova." In discussing the affair, *Pravda* pointed out that "the only people who could act like that were those ... trying to over-insure themselves."[6]

Even more monstrous were the facts about events in Rostov which *Pravda* made public. There, a trade union member, Grober, was expelled from the party as an "undisarmed Trotskyist" and enemy of the party. The grounds for these actions were the fact that, in 1927, when he was a seventeen-year-old Komsomol member, Grober "spoke in an unclear and confused way at a meeting." After he had been given an explanation of the "harmful nature of his vacillating position," he "voted for the theses of the party's Central Committee." "He never uttered the truth about his vacillations," the article stipulated, " ... either at a purge, or during verification (of party documents), or during the exchange of party documents."

Grober's expulsion from the party was followed by the expulsion from the Komsomol of his nineteen-year-old brother and seventeen-year-old sister—"both Stakhanovites, and exemplary Komsomol members." The newspaper published by the factory where they worked spoke about how the Komsomol organization had driven out of its ranks "the remnants of the counterrevolutionary Grober riffraff."

Following these steps, three people were then expelled from two other organizations because they had been in the same Komsomol cell with Grober in 1927 and had not "unmasked" him. In yet another organization, Grober's second brother was expelled, because, "in the opinion of the regional committee, he was obliged to know about his brother's speech in 1927 and unmask him." Expelled also was the leader of the place where Grober worked; an older woman, a worker and communist since 1920 who had given Grober a recommendation when he joined the party; and one more communist—simply because he was Grober's comrade. As he reported these facts, the *Pravda* correspondent added: "The matter is not confined to the expulsion from the party and Komsomol of innocent people. In order to avoid being accused of aiding and abetting enemies, the leaders of trade union and economic organizations expel such people from the trade unions and remove them from work."[7]

The last maneuver, bound up with criticizing "local excesses," was performed by Stalin himself, who sent a telegram on 25 December 1936 to the Perm District Committee. It said the Central Committee had received information about the persecution and defamation of the director of the motor factory, Poberezhsky, and his coworkers "for the past sins of Trotskyism." "In view of the fact that both Poberezhsky and his workers are now functioning conscientiously and enjoy the full confidence of the CC VKP(b)," the telegram stated, "we ask you to protect Comrade Poberezhsky and his workers from slander and to create around them an atmosphere of full confidence. Send immediate information about measures taken to the CC VKP(b)."[8] Thus, on the very eve of 1937, Stalin let it be known that people with "the past sins of Trotskyism" could enjoy "full confidence." This playful formula, by the way, left party organizations in the dark with regard to what precisely Stalin considered to be the "past sins" which would allow communists to remain in the party and at their posts.

At first, such edicts allowed for a partial containment of the widely spread repressions. Thus, in the beginning of September Ordzhonikidze sent Vyshinsky a letter from Zaveniagin, the director of the Magnitogorsk Metallurgical Combine. The latter said that after a major accident in the coke/chemical department, resulting in human victims, the leaders of the department and the engineers, who were not to blame for the accident, had been arrested. After receiving this letter with Ordzhonikidze's resolution, "I support Comrade Zaveniagin's request," Vyshinsky told Ordzhonikidze that he had ordered an end to the criminal case against the workers named by Zaveniagin. He had also ordered that the others arrested in connection with the accident be given a light punishment—several months of corrective labor at their previous place of work."[9]

The situation changed sharply after 25 September, when Stalin and Zhdanov, who were vacationing in Sochi, sent a telegram to the members of the Politburo in Moscow: "We consider the appointment of Comrade Yezhov to the post of People's Commissar of Internal Affairs to be an absolutely necessary and urgent matter. Yagoda has clearly proven not to be up to the task of exposing the Trotsky-Zinoviev bloc. The OGPU has been four years late in this matter. That is what all the party workers and the majority of the regional representatives of the NKVD are saying." When he read this secret telegram at the 20th Party Congress, Khrushchev declared, "Stalin never met with party workers and therefore could not have known their opinion."[10]

The phrase about being late by four years was prompted by Stalin's demand to henceforth place the date of the terrorism and sabotage by the Oppositionists from 1932, when the bloc of opposition inner-party groupings was formed. This sentence directly spurred the NKVD to "make up for lost time" by carrying out new mass arrests.

The day after receiving the telegram, the Politburo passed by referendum a resolution to free Yagoda from his responsibilities as People's Commissar of Internal Affairs and to appoint Yezhov to this post, "so that he could give ten-tenths of his time to the NKVD."[11] Yezhov had been working at two jobs simultaneously, secretary of the Central Committee of the VKP(b) and chairman of the Party Control Commission. Henceforth Yezhov not only combined more prominent party and state posts than any other of the party leadership, but as secretary of the Central Committee, which oversaw the organs of state security, he was, so to speak, keeping tabs on himself, while remaining subordinate only to Stalin.

On the same day, the decision about Yezhov's new appointment was rubber-stamped at a session of the Council of People's Commissars, chaired by Molotov, who had by then drawn the lessons from Stalin's "warning" during the Trial of the Sixteen. Consequently he became one of the main organizers of the repressions.

On 30 September Kaganovich, who had always been the most fervent Stalinist toady, wrote to Ordzhonikidze, who was staying at Kislovodsk: "Our main news of late has been the appointment of Yezhov. This remarkably wise decision of our parent [Kaganovich repeatedly referred to Stalin this way in his personal correspondence—V. R.] ripened and was warmly received both in the party and in the nation."[12]

Yagoda was transferred to the post of People's Commissar for Communications, which signified a new blow directed against Rykov; after losing this post he remained without work right up until his arrest.

On 29 September the Politburo adopted by referendum a resolution prepared by Kaganovich entitled "On the Relationship to Counterrevolutionary Trotsky-Zinoviev Elements," which contained the following directives:

"a) Until recent times the Central Committee of the VKP(b) viewed the Trotsky-Zinoviev scoundrels as the advance political and organizational detachment of the international bourgeoisie. Recent facts say that these men have descended even further and that they now must be seen as intelligence agents, spies, saboteurs and wreckers of the fascist bourgeoisie in Europe.

"b) In connection with this, reprisals are needed against the Trotsky-Zinoviev scoundrels, including not only the consistent ones such as Muralov, Piatakov, Beloborodov and others, whose cases are still not concluded, but against those who earlier had been exiled."[13]

The directives adding sabotage to the crimes of the "Trotskyists" produced the corresponding wave of clamorous anti-Trotskyist propaganda. On 8 October, the lead article in *Pravda* many times repeated that the Trotskyists "were serving as spies and saboteurs in the Soviet Union." In presenting a new "list of malicious deeds," *Pravda* stated that "the counterrevolutionary sabotage of the Trotskyists in our industry, in the factories and mines, on the railways, on construction sites and in agriculture had been proven and even acknowledged by a whole number of the most prominent Trotskyists."

In order to create a factual basis for such charges, on 29 November 1936 Vyshinsky signed a directive for prosecutors to obtain within one month and reexamine all criminal cases from previous years dealing with major fires, accidents, the production of poor quality goods, and so forth, "in order to expose the counterrevolutionary, saboteurs' underpinnings of these cases and to bring those guilty to a more severe form of justice."[14] In fulfilling these directives, various localities began the work of reclassifying charges of negligence, lack of caution, etc., as state crimes. Throughout the country, economic leaders began to be charged with sabotage and arrested.

Parallel to these developments were the arrests of former members of the "Right Opposition," as part of the preparations for the Bukharin-Rykov "case." Not long before he was removed as People's Commissar of Internal Affairs, Yagoda sent Stalin the transcripts of the interrogations of Kulikov (a former member of the Central Committee who voted with the leaders of the "rightists" at the April 1929 Plenum) and Lugovoi, with testimony against Bukharin, Rykov and Tomsky. In an accompanying letter, Yagoda said that the "accomplices" named by these people had been arrested, "are being arrested" or "have been designated for arrest," and requested permission to arrest the prominent "Bukharinists," Kotov and Rovinsky.

At about the same time, Yezhov informed Stalin that he had become acquainted with the material of recent years regarding the cases of the "Rightists," and had come to the conclusion: "At that time we didn't get to the bottom of things.... In any case, there are all the grounds to assume that it will be possible to uncover much that is new and that the Rightists will be seen in another light, particularly Rykov, Bukharin, Uglanov, Shmidt and others."

A week after becoming People's Commissar of Internal Affairs, Yezhov sent Stalin the transcript of the interrogation of Stankin, Tomsky's former secretary. According to this document, Stankin and other former secretaries for Tomsky joined a "militant terrorist group," which prepared an attack on Stalin which was to have taken place during the triumphant celebration in the Bolshoi Theater dedicated to the anniversary of the October Revolution.[15]

Stalin did not acquaint Bukharin and Rykov with such testimony, since he was preparing to deal them a shattering blow at the next Plenum of the CC. In order to keep them in a constant state of tension, he inspired a slander campaign in the press about their past political activity. Thus, *Pravda* printed an article with the false accusation that Rykov in 1917 had called for Lenin to appear in court under the Provisional Government.[16] Rykov appealed to Stalin with a letter in which he protested against this insinuation. The letter was left unanswered by the addressee.

As far as we can judge according to the documents and eyewitness accounts we have, in 1936 the people under investigation were still not subjected to inhuman physical torture. The investigators limited themselves to such devices as sleep deprivation, conveyor belt interrogations lasting many hours, and threats to shoot or arrest relatives. In writing to Stalin about the character of the investigation of his case, Shatskin noted: "Twice they didn't allow me to sleep at night 'as long as you have not signed.' Moreover, during one twelve-hour interrogation at night the investigator ordered: 'Get up, take off your glasses!' and, shaking his fist before my face: 'Get up! Take this pen! Sign!' and so forth."[17] Riutin wrote a letter to the Presidium of the Central Executive Committee, describing the "absolutely illegal and inadmissible" methods of investigation: "At each interrogation they threaten me, they shout at me as if I were an animal, they insult me, and finally, they don't even allow me to give an explanatory, written refusal to provide testimony."[18]

The behavior of the arrested during the period of investigation depended on their attitude toward the fetish of "party-mindedness" and on their belief or disbelief in Stalin's desire to get to the truth. Thus Shatskin, who retained illusions regarding Stalin, wrote in a letter to him: "While not disputing the legitimacy of the investigation's suspicions and understanding that the investigation cannot take people at their word, I nevertheless feel that the investigation must carefully and objectively verify what they call the corresponding testimony at their disposal. In actual fact, the investigation denied me of the most elementary means of refuting false testimony against me. The leitmotif of the investigation was: 'We will force you to confess to terror, and you can refute it in the afterworld.'" Shatskin stressed that he was providing facts about the mockery coming at the hands of the investigators not in order to "protest against

I. T. Smilga, Moscow, 1923

them from the standpoint of abstract humanism," but only in order to say, "after several dozen interrogations, the major part of which are devoted to verbal abuse, such devices might lead a person to such a state that false testimony might be the outcome. More important, however, than the interrogations: the investigator demands that you sign the confession in the name of the party and in the interests of the party."[19]

The behavior was quite different with those who renounced the dogma of "party-mindedness," understood as Stalin understood it, and who harbored no illusions about the investigation's outcome. Characteristic in this sense was the conduct of Riutin, whom Stalin particularly wanted to put in the dock at one of the show trials because the "Riutin Platform" was declared to be the programmatic document of the "Rightists" and the ideological justification for terror. Riutin, however, who was brought to Moscow in October 1936 from a Suzdal political prison, from the very beginning of the reinvestigation of his case categorically refused to give any testimony. In a letter to the Presidium of the Central Executive Committee (but not to Stalin!), he sharply protested against the violation of "the most elementary rights of a person under investigation," and against the extortion of false testimony. Calling the charges made against him of terrorist intentions "absolutely illegal, arbitrary and biased, dictated solely by malice and the yearning for new, and this time bloody, reprisals against me," he wrote that he was not afraid of death and that he would not ask for mercy in the event that he received a death sentence.[20]

Having no doubts about the results of the investigation and trial, while he was in the NKVD's internal prison Riutin repeatedly resorted to hunger strikes and attempted suicide. Once he was pulled out of a noose by the guards.

After encountering Riutin's refusal to submit, Stalin abandoned the attempts to prepare him for an open trial. Riutin's solitary case was reviewed on 10 January 1937 at a closed court session. When the chairman of the court, Ulrich, asked: "Does the accused acknowledge his guilt?", Riutin replied that he "did not wish to answer that question and in general that he refused to give any testimony regarding the charges made against him."[21] Half an hour after the sentence had been passed, Riutin was shot.

Finally, some of the people being investigated openly declared their hostility to Stalin and their renunciation of Stalin's "socialism." At the February-March Plenum, Molotov told how one of Bukharin's former disciples, Kuzmin, declared at the investigation: "I am your political enemy, an enemy of the existing order which you call the dictatorship of the proletariat. I believe that the USSR is an All-Russian concentration camp, directed against the revolution.... I am against your socialism." One of the former leaders of the Left Opposition, I. T. Smilga, proved to be just as "undisarmed." He had been elected a member of the CC at the April Conference of 1917, and at several subsequent party congresses. In Molotov's words, Smilga also said at the investigation: "I am your enemy."[22] This was the reason that Smilga was not a defendant at one of the public trials, but was shot on 10 January 1937, the same day that Riutin was executed.

By then, the more submissive people under investigation were being prepared for a new trial—the case of the "Anti-Soviet Trotskyist Center." The so-called "Kemerovo Trial," which was held 19–22 November 1936 in Novosibirsk, served as a rehearsal of sorts for this more prominent case. The Kemerovo Trial was the first "Trotskyist" frame-up at which the defendants were charged with sabotage.

13. THE KEMEROVO TRIAL

THE KUZBASS was chosen as the object of sabotage because several formerly prominent Trotskyists worked there who had been sent to Western Siberia at the end of the 1920s. The labor of exiles who had been "de-kulakized" was widely used at the mines of the Kuzbass. Accidents and fires often occurred due to the inexperience of the workers and the abysmal organization of labor. The archives contain no small number of accounts by the defendants at the Kemerovo Trial in which attention is directed to the intolerable work conditions at the mines, which could not help but lead to industrial accidents. However, much as at many other enterprises, not enough resources were allocated here for the safety needs of labor.

The main charge at the trial was that "Trotskyists" organized an explosion which occurred on 23 September 1936 at the "Central" mine, as a result of which twelve miners died and fourteen were severely injured. Workers who spoke as witnesses at the trial told how the mine's administration had ignored elementary rules of safety technique and had accused miners who protested against the difficult working conditions of loafing and of disrupting coal production plans. This was followed by the outlining of the results of the investigation by a commission of experts, which, as would be shown by a reexamination in the 1950s, was conducted with the crudest violations of the law. For two weeks, members of the commission of experts did not leave the building which housed the Kemerovo branch of the NKVD; nor did they meet with a single one of the accused or officials at the mine sites. The conclusion of the experts was repeatedly reworked under the direction of NKVD officials.

The Kemerovo Trial fabricated a "Trotskyist sabotage group," which was formed by combining Trotskyists with "engineers and technicians who were hostile to Soviet power," headed by the engineer Peshekhonov, who had been condemned at the Shakhty Trial to three years of exile. Besides eight Soviet engineers, those on trial included a German specialist, Stikling, who was charged with ties to the Gestapo and with "an official from a foreign state who was living in

Novosibirsk." Stikling's role amounted to passing directives about sabotage to other defendants "on assignment from the intelligence organs of a foreign state."

Witnesses at the trial included Stroilov, a nonparty engineer, as well as the former oppositionists Drobnis and Shestov, whose cases had been "designated for special treatment." They testified that the sabotage group at the "Central" mine acted under the immediate leadership of the underground Trotskyist center of Western Siberia headed by Muralov—"one of Trotsky's most trusted agents." In turn, the Western Siberian Center "received orders for sabotage, wrecking and terrorism from Piatakov, a member of the All-Union Trotskyist Center and Trotsky's closest assistant."

Shestov and Drobnis, who were declared to be "the leaders of the sabotage activity of Trotskyists in the Kuzbass," testified that they received directives from Piatakov "to knock enterprises out of commission and to weaken the country's defense capabilities," by organizing explosions and fires in the mines. In addition to these accusations, the trial stated that Piatakov gave Shestov the assignment of organizing terrorist acts against members of the Politburo in case they came to the West Siberian region, as well as against the secretary of the West Siberian Regional Committee, Eikhe.

The prosecutor Roginsky stressed at the trial that "the interests of the Trotskyists coincided with the interests of the international bourgeoisie and fascism. Sabotage and wrecking was the long-term task of the foreign center of the opposition, which fully corresponded to the desires of international financial circles and fascist governments." In developing this statement in an article entitled, "A Just Sentence," *Pravda* indicated that "the threads from the bandits who carried out the Kemerovo crime lead ... abroad, to Trotsky and his son."[1]

Noting that what was "new" at the Kemerovo Trial was the charge that "Trotskyists" committed wrecking and sabotage, L. Sedov wrote: "This new element is in actual fact a return to what is very old: to the wrecking trials which were once so fashionable in the USSR, with one difference, that the wreckers in the past were engineers and specialists, now, however, they are Old Bolsheviks, former leaders of the party, the state, and the economy."[2]

All nine of the defendants at the "Kemerovo Trial" were sentenced to be shot. Besides them, eight people were named as "Trotskyist saboteurs" at the trial: Piatakov, Muralov, Drobnis, Shestov, Boguslavsky, Norkin, Stroilov and Arnold. Two months later they would be included in the trial of the "Anti-Soviet Trotskyist Center."

14. The December Plenum of the Central Committee

THE DECEMBER 1936 Plenum of the Central Committee became a new milestone in the unfolding terror. One of its main tasks was the creation of the "Bukharin-Rykov case."

On the threshold of this plenum, Rykov had a more realistic attitude to what was taking place than Bukharin, who still retained illusions about a possible ray of hope in his fate. As Larina recalls, he sincerely rejoiced when he learned that Yezhov had replaced Yagoda. "Bukharin then thought, no matter how paradoxical this might now seem, that Yezhov, despite being a limited man, had a kind heart and a pure conscience. 'He won't engage in falsification,' N. I. naively believed before the December Plenum."[1]

Bukharin also saw a favorable change in an event which happened on the day celebrating the anniversary of the October Revolution. Soon after he had taken his place in the guest section located next to the Mausoleum, a Red Army soldier approached him and said: "Comrade Stalin asked me to say that you are standing in the wrong place. You should go up onto the Mausoleum." Bukharin was flattered by this sign of Stalin's good will and hoped that he would finally be able to speak with him. However Stalin stood at a distance from him and left the tribune before the demonstration had ended.

The same day of celebration proved to be highly disturbing for Rykov. Before leaving for the triumphal session at the Bolshoi Theater, he discovered that he had lost the ticket of invitation sent to him. Rykov reacted to this circumstance very nervously, telling his relatives that his absence at the session might be interpreted as a demonstration of protest; they might blow this fact out of proportion and lodge new charges against him.[2]

There were no immediate changes in the fate of Bukharin and Rykov after the October Jubilee. At first Bukharin assumed that they might let him "quietly work," but no news emerged from either the editorial board or from the Central Committee. "The more time passed from that memorable day, the greater the consternation which engulfed him. Toward the end of November the nervous tension was so great that he was completely unable to work."[3] In a letter to Stalin, written a day before the plenum opened, Bukharin recalled his letter to Yezhov, which had remained unanswered. He also wrote of his extreme exhaustion: "I am now ill, and my nerves are in very bad shape; for more than ten days I have not gone to the editorial offices. I lie in bed, completely shattered. I attended only your report [at the All-Union Congress of Soviets— V. R.]. Of course, I will drag myself wherever I am told for any form of explanations."[4] It was in such a state that Bukharin showed up at the December Plenum.

This plenum, the work of which was not announced in the press, took place on the fourth and seventh of December 1936. In the interval between these two days, the last session of the Eighth Extraordinary Congress of Soviets was held in order to adopt the constitution. After the congress a demonstration celebrated the event. However the mood of the majority of the participants in the plenum was hardly a mood of celebration. The agenda proposed to discuss two questions: 1. Review of the final text of the Constitution of the USSR, and 2. Comrade Yezhov's report on anti-Soviet Trotskyist and Rightist organizations.

The discussion of the first point on the agenda lasted less than an hour. Those in attendance were asked to make comments on the text of the constitution which would be confirmed by the Congress of Soviets on the next day. Several proposed amendments met the disapproval of Stalin and other members of the Politburo and were rejected without a vote. Following this, Stalin made one editorial change which was adopted, also without a vote. With this, the review of the first question came to an end and Yezhov was given the floor.

Yezhov cited figures which represented the number of arrested "Trotskyists" in several regions: more than two hundred in the Azov-Black Sea region, more than three hundred in Georgia, more than four hundred in Leningrad, etc. In all of these regions, according to Yezhov's report, conspiratorial groups headed by major party figures had been uncovered.

Yezhov's report shows that by the time of the plenum his department had already basically "worked out" the subsequent open trial. Yezhov listed the names of almost all of its future defendants and announced that Sokolnikov, Piatakov, Radek and Serebriakov were members of a "reserve center," and simultaneously "reserve members" of the main center, "in case the main center was arrested and destroyed." Filling in the "gaps" of the previous trial, Yezhov claimed that "the Trotskyist-Zinovievist bloc" had not managed to carry out wrecking activity, whereas the "reserve center" had begun in 1931 "the main work of wrecking, which ruined much in our economy." Giving examples of wrecking and sabotage activity, Yezhov liberally cited the testimony given by the arrested directors of military factories and enterprises in the chemical industry, by heads of the railways, etc. Stirring up hatred for the "wreckers," he mentioned that, when Piatakov was giving out sabotage assignments, he was asked about possible victims among the workers. Piatakov told the future saboteur: "So you've found someone to feel sorry for."[5]

Another "gap" filled in from the previous trial was expressed in information about spying activity carried out by the "Trotskyists" and about their pact with foreign governments. Not only Sokolnikov and Radek were charged with negotiations of this kind, but also Kamenev, who had supposedly conducted negotiations with the French ambassador.[6]

Not having yet become skilled at falsification, Yezhov was often interrupted by Stalin and Molotov, who "corrected" his statements. When Yezhov first mentioned espionage, Stalin felt compelled to "add" that Shestov and Rataichak "received money from German intelligence for information." Interrupting the report once more, Stalin declared: the Trotskyists had a platform which they concealed out of fear that if it were made public, "the people would become indignant." According to Stalin, this platform amounted to restoring private initiative and "opening the gates to English capital and to foreign capital as a whole."

The degree to which the "leaders" still had not come to an agreement even among themselves over what charges were to be lodged against the defendants at the future trial can be seen from their "additions" to the list of foreign governments with which the Trotskyists were working. After Stalin had made the remark that the "Trotskyists" "had ties with England, France and America," Yezhov immediately referred to negotiations between "Trotskyists" and the "American government," "the French ambassador," and so forth. Then an obvious confusion arose:

"*Yezhov*: ... They tried to conduct negotiations with English governmental circles, for which they established contact *(Molotov*: with the French ...) ...with major French industrialists *(Stalin*: You said, with the English.) Excuse me, with the French."[7] By the way, a month and a half later at the trial of the "Anti-Soviet Trotskyist Center," references to espionage contacts with the USA, England and France were discarded, insofar as the decision had been made to lend an exclusively fascist coloring to these "contacts."

Shifting from the "Trotskyists" to the "Rightists," Yezhov reported on the September face-to-face confrontations between Bukharin, Rykov and Sokolnikov. Although Bukharin and Rykov were rehabilitated after these confrontations, Yezhov declared that he and Kaganovich "had no doubt whatsoever" that they "were informed about all the terrorist and other plans of the Trotskyist-Zinovievist bloc." Now, Yezhov related, those newly arrested had named the members of a "Right Center," and of the terrorist groups it had formed. Yezhov noted that "despite my peaceable nature, it seems I arrested about ten people" in *Izvestiia*, hinting that Bukharin had "littered" his editorial board with "enemies." In conclusion, Yezhov vowed that "the CC's directive, dictated by Comrade Stalin, will be carried out by us to the end, we will root out all this Trotskyist-Zinovievist filth and destroy them physically."[8]

Unlike the following February-March Plenum, during Yezhov's speech the "rank-and-file" participants at the December Plenum almost never interjected comments "encouraging" the speaker. Such zeal was displayed only in the conduct of Beria, who throughout the work of the plenum kept shouting: "There's a swine!", "What a wretch!", "What a monstrosity!", "Ah, what a scoundrel!", "Well, what bastards they are, words simply can't describe them!"

After Yezhov finished speaking, the floor was given to Bukharin, who began by expressing his agreement with the fact that "now, all members of the party, from the bottom to the top, are filled with vigilance and have assisted the corresponding organs in exterminating the scum that is carrying out wrecking acts and everything else.... I am happy that this entire record is being uncovered before the war ... so that we shall emerge from the war as victors."

Calling the charges made against him "a type of political sabotage" on the part of the Trotskyists, Bukharin tried to persuade his listeners that he had nothing in common "with these saboteurs, these wreckers, these scoundrels." Denying the very possibility that he could draw close to the Trotskyists, he recounted how in a meeting with Romain Rolland at Gorky's residence, he had dispelled any doubts the foreigner had regarding the criminal behavior of the Trotskyists. As a result, "Romain Rolland has yet to conduct himself as André Gide was doing." Appealing personally to Ordzhonikidze, Bukharin recalled that in one of his conversations with the latter he had spoken in a negative vein about Piatakov.

Expressing his interest in "untangling this knot," Bukharin reiterated that "he cursed this filthy affair [i.e., the "crimes" of the Trotskyists]." After declaring: "In all that has been said here there is not a single word of truth," he repeated his ritual vow of fidelity: "I assure you that no matter what you have confessed, no matter what you have stated, no matter what you believe or do not believe, I always, till the last minute of my life, I always will stand for our party, for our leadership, for Stalin. I am not saying that I loved Stalin in 1928. But I am saying that now I love him with all my soul. Why? Because ... I understand the significance of this fortress and centralized essence of our dictatorship."

In concluding his speech, Bukharin declared: "I am not worried about myself, about the conditions of my life or death, but I am concerned about my political honor. I have said and I will continue to say that I will fight for my honor as long as I shall exist."[9]

In order to destroy any impression of Bukharin's innocence which might have been created among the plenum's participants after this speech, Stalin took the floor immediately after Bukharin. He began by stating that "Bukharin absolutely has failed to understood what is taking place here.... He strives for sincerity, and demands trust. Well, all right, let us talk about sincerity and about trust." In this regard, Stalin recalled how Zinoviev, Kamenev, Piatakov and other "Trotskyists" had renounced their "errors." When he then asked: "Isn't that true, Comrade Bukharin?", he received the reply: "That's true, that's true, I have been saying the same thing."

After he then told about testimony recently received from Piatakov, Radek and Sosnovsky, Stalin declared: "Believe after this in people's sincerity!... We came to the conclusions: you cannot take a single former oppositionist at his word.... And the events of the last two years have shown this clearly, because it has been shown in deed that sincerity is a relative concept. And when it comes to trusting former oppositionists, then we have shown them so much trust.... (*Noise in the hall, voices from the audience:* That's right!). We should be punished for the maximum trust, for the unbounded trust, that we offered them."

Stalin then proceeded to allow himself to say things which could be met without objection only in the poisoned atmosphere of "totalitarian idiotism" which permeated the whole work of the plenum. He declared that "former oppositionists had taken an even more severe step in order to preserve at least a particle of trust on our part and to once more demonstrate their sincerity—people have begun to commit suicide." Enumerating what by then had become an imposing list of suicides among leading members of the party (Skrypnik, Lominadze, Tomsky, Khandzhian, Furer), Stalin claimed that all these people had resorted to suicide in order to "cover their tracks, ... distract the party, undermine its vigilance, deceive it one last time before they died by committing suicide, and to place it in a stupid situation.... A person would turn to suicide because he feared that everything would be discovered, he did not want to witness his own worldwide shame.... Here you have one of the sharpest and easiest [*sic!*—V. R.] ways before dying, as one leaves this world, that one can spit on the party for the last time, and deceive the party." Thus, Stalin unequivocally was warning the candidate-defendants at future trials that their possible suicide would be interpreted as new proof of their double-dealing.

Having uttered these "arguments," Stalin said to Bukharin: "I am not saying anything personally about you. Perhaps you are right, and perhaps you are not. But you can't come here and say that you have not been trusted, that there is no belief in my, Bukharin's, sincerity. And do you want, Comrade Bukharin, that we take you at your word? (*Bukharin:* No, I don't want that.) And if you don't want that, then don't get upset because we have raised this question at a plenum of the CC.... And you cannot frighten us with your tears or with suicide. (*Voices from the audience:* That's right! *Prolonged applause.*)"[10]

After Stalin had spoken, the floor was given to Rykov, who announced that he "must fully and completely acknowledge the correctness of the points" made in Stalin's speech, "correctness in the sense that we live in a period when double-dealing and deception of the party have reached such dimensions and have assumed such a sophisticated and pathological character, that, of course, it would be absolutely baffling if you took Bukharin or me at our word."

Like Bukharin, Rykov denied only the charges which concerned him personally. He said that after Kamenev's testimony had surfaced, he asked Yezhov to "find out from Kamenev where and when I had met with him, in order that I can somehow refute this lie. I was told that Kamenev had not been questioned about this, and that now he could not be questioned—he had been shot."

Refuting the version about the existence of a "center of Rightists," Rykov declared that the last time he had met with Bukharin in a nonofficial capacity was in 1934, that he had met with Tomsky very rarely over the last two years, and that when he had, he had not discussed any political questions with him. The only "confession" coming from Rykov was the following: Tomsky told him that in 1934 Zinoviev "had complained of his isolation, of his lack of friends, and had invited him to come over to his dacha." According to Rykov, he tried to persuade Tomsky not to go, because he said that "any meeting is already the preparation to form a group." Now, however, Rykov added, "this inspires in me the conviction that Tomsky participated in some way in this affair." Then Rykov expressed his agreement with Stalin that "suicide is one of the ways to tarnish the cause," and Tomsky's suicide "is a very strong piece of evidence against him."

At the end of his speech, Rykov declared: "I will show, and I will shout that here [in the testimony against him—V. R.] there is defamation, lying and black slander from beginning to end. I never was a fascist, I never will be one; I never covered for them, and I never will. And I will prove this."[11]

While Rykov was speaking, Stalin felt compelled to interrupt in order to explain why it was that a month and a half earlier he had agreed to "rehabilitate" Bukharin and Rykov. In this connection, the following exchange took place:

Stalin. You see, after Bukharin's face-to-face confrontation with Sokolnikov, we formed the opinion that there were no grounds for bringing you and Bukharin to trial. But doubts of a party character remained in our minds. It seemed to us that both you and Tomsky, without doubt, and perhaps, Bukharin, too, could not help but know that these scum were preparing some foul deed, but that you didn't tell us.
Voices from the audience. Fact.
Bukharin. What are you saying, comrades? You have no conscience.
Stalin. I am saying that this was only because it seemed to us that it wasn't enough to bring you to trial.... I said, don't touch Bukharin, wait a bit.... We didn't want to put you on trial, we showed mercy, I must confess, we showed mercy.[12]

After Rykov's comments, five people spoke, each of whom tried to make his own contribution to further whipping up the political hysteria. Eikhe stated that "the facts uncovered by the investigation have revealed the bestial face of the Trotskyists before the whole world. What has been recently uncovered cannot be compared to the wrecking ... which we uncovered (earlier)." Eikhe added to the "facts" provided by Yezhov by adding an account of the behavior of Trotskyists while they were being sent in several groups from exile in Western Siberia to the concentration camps in Kolyma. It is well known that when they

R. I. Eikhe

were put in groups, the Trotskyists shouted anti-Stalinist slogans (see Chapter 44). Eikhe, however, preferred to conceal the actual content of these slogans. Instead, he provocatively ascribed to the Trotskyists an appeal they supposedly made to the Red Army guards accompanying the convoy: "The Japanese and fascists will cut your throats, and we will help them." Proceeding from this appeal, which he had thought up himself, Eikhe found a fitting opportunity to demonstrate his bloodthirstiness: "Comrade Stalin, we are acting too leniently. We only have to read these guileless reports from nonparty Red Army soldiers, ... to shoot any one of them [the Trotskyists—V. R.]."[13]

Molotov "developed" Stalin's conception of suicide as a mean of "fighting against the party" in the following way: "Tomsky's suicide is a conspiracy which was a preconceived act, moreover Tomsky arranged to commit suicide not with just one, but with several people, thereby once more delivering one blow or another to the Central Committee."[14]

A spirit of fanaticism infused the speech of Sarkisov, the secretary of the Donetsk Regional Committee, who described in detail how he tried to "remove the stain" of participating in the 1920s in the Left Opposition. "Although I broke from this scum ten years ago," he said, "it is still hard even to recall that I had contact with these fascist bastards." Listing the names of many "Trotskyists" whom he had "unmasked" in recent years, Sarkisov declared: "I always have felt that this is a triple duty of every former oppositionist ... to try to be as vigilant as possible and to unmask Trotskyists and Zinovievists. Moreover, as a rule I chose not to hire for any work, much less for party work, any person who once was an oppositionist. This is how I thought: if the party trusts me, then I cannot transfer this trust to others. Therefore, proceeding from this, I always was systematic and consistent in driving away people with an oppositional past, driving them away particularly from party work.... If I, a responsible party cadre who enjoys the trust of the CC, conceal even a single person who in the past was a Trotskyist, then I would be in the camp of these fascists."[15]

Kaganovich conducted himself even more shamelessly on the tribune. Together with Stalin he played a game which could be called the "affair with the dog," thereby mocking the still fresh graves of Zinoviev and Tomsky. While telling of the results of an "investigation" he conducted (in the spring of 1936 Tomsky had been asked for "testimony" about his "ties" with Zinoviev), Kaganovich said: " ... And, finally, in 1934, Zinoviev invited Tomsky to visit him at his dacha for tea.... After they finished their tea, Tomsky and Zinoviev traveled in Tomsky's automobile to choose a dog for Zinoviev. You see what kind of friendship they had, they even travel to pick out a dog, and Tomsky helps out. (*Stalin:* What kind of a dog: a hunting dog or guard dog?) We weren't able to establish that.... (*Stalin:* nevertheless, did they get a dog?) They did. They looked for a four-legged companion, since they were no different, they were the same kind of dogs.... (*Stalin:* Was it a good dog, or a bad one? Does anyone know? *Laughter.*) During the face-to-face confrontation, this was hard to determine.... Tomsky was supposed to confess that he and Zinoviev had ties, and that he helped Zinoviev even to the point of traveling with him to pick out a dog."[16]

Another example of Kaganovich's cynicism was the motivation he gave for a more terrible accusation made against Bukharin:

> *Kaganovich:* ... You didn't manage to carry out the foul assassination of Comrade Kirov, since the killers turned out to be Trotskyists and Zinovievists. You knew, however, that they were preparing the assassination.
> *Bukharin:* That is amazing slander, bloody slander.
> *Kaganovich:* ... Tomsky testifies that he was at Zinoviev's in 1934; would it be possible for Tomsky not to know about their plans?[17]

When reading the transcript of the December Plenum, one cannot help but get the impression that something infernal or improbable was taking place.

"Leaders" who were completely unrestrained utter obvious absurdities as proof of "conspiratorial ties," and the plenum participants sit there silently listening. "The accused" defend only themselves, not only refusing to even hint at their doubt regarding the guilt of their comrades of not long ago who have been either shot or arrested, but repeating the most outlandish abuse about them. This monstrous "logic" can only be understood if one remembers that this entire frame-up was only the final link in a chain of conscious falsifications concerning the intentions and deeds of their political opponents, which both the accusers and the accused engaged in over the previous decade. All those attending the plenum had already approved more than once the police persecution of participants in various oppositions on false grounds. To call into question the new and more monstrous charges made against the former oppositionists would mean to call into question the truthfulness of the entire preceding struggle against the oppositions, carried out with barbaric methods. Not a single one of the plenum's participants, who in one way or another had participated in this struggle, could decide to take such a step.

All that has been said does not mean, however, that at this stage Stalin had achieved his goal—of securing the full and unhesitating support from the plenum for his provocations. This explains his further maneuvering, especially after Bukharin's new attempt to protest on the morning of 7 December when Stalin was given a statement to all members and candidate members of the CC. In this document, Bukharin adhered to his previous tactic: he unreservedly agreed with the charges against the "Trotskyists" and even supplied additional "grounds" for their correctness; at the same time he defended himself as an exemplary and dedicated Stalinist who was being slandered by the "Trotskyists." Vowing that he did not have "an atom of disagreement with the party line ... and that I have defended this line all the recent years with passion and conviction," Bukharin endorsed the "statements regarding the general misfortune flowing from the particular virtuosity with which the 'Trotskyists' masked themselves." Moreover, he developed his criticism of the version that the Trotskyists and Zinovievists lacked a platform and were striving for "naked power." As if he were helping Stalin correct this absurd version which lay at the foundations of the Trial of the Sixteen, Bukharin wrote: "As for the Trotskyists, they do have their own press, their own documents, and their own, if I may be allowed to say, so-called Fourth International. Their platform, from beginning to end seething with counterrevolutionary malice toward the USSR and our party, is completely contemporary, and it explains both their defeatist tactics and their terror. It proceeds from the thesis that the 'bureaucracy' in the USSR has turned into a new class exploiter (with the completion of Thermidor). It furiously rejects our foreign policy (regarding both the USSR and the Comintern), rejects the tactic of the popular front as betrayal, rejects our entire position regarding the defense of the fatherland, and so forth.... Given such a frenzied malice toward the very foundations of our policies (and even more so to the personal bearers of this policy) and given the centralization of our regime, they have placed the question of terror on the agenda. They are out-and-out traitors, but with a thoroughly contemporary program." For the same reasons, Bukharin also distanced himself from the Riutin Platform, calling it "a filthy counterrevolutionary concoction."[18]

Given his strong desire to make a powerful contribution to "unmasking Trotskyism," Bukharin did not understand that even a crudely tendentious exposition of Trotsky's views at this stage was unacceptable for Stalin. After all, genuine ideas which terrified Stalin might have reached the reader even through the most distorted presentation. Consequently the "Trotskyist platform" now had to be presented—contrary to all logic and common sense—as advocating defeatism, sabotage, espionage and "the restoration of capitalism."

Also unacceptable to Stalin was Bukharin's refusal to endorse Kaganovich's thesis that all former opposition groups had turned into "counterrevolutionary bands." Bukharin, by the way, was not far from this thesis when he claimed that "all forms of opposition, if they are not halted in their development in time, turn into counterrevolution, which leads to the restoration of capitalism." Proceeding from this premise, he admitted the possibility of "the independent evolution of Uglanov and Co., but without any relationship or any connection with me: they had grown disillusioned with Bukharin's 'betrayal,' and had begun to seek out other people." "If Uglanov testified that he prepared Kirov's assassination," added Bukharin, "then that terrible fact proves how low Uglanov had stooped in continuing his struggle and refusing to stop."

While indignant at the charges of his own "criminal ties" with those arrested, Bukharin didn't express even a shadow of a doubt with regard to the accusations made against his former friends and colleagues. In response to the charge that he maintained his friendship with Radek, he wrote: "I find it very difficult to confess that I swallowed the bait of this extraordinarily refined and corrupt double-dealer." The sole step that Bukharin decided to take in this regard was to say cautiously that even the most orthodox Stalinists had "ties" with "the criminals." By this time, no small number of "enemies" had been arrested at the Academy; acting offended that "people were trying to shift all responsibility for virtually the entire Academy" onto him, he declared that "this sector of the front is very cluttered in general. Therefore, for example, in the Zhdanov historical commission [he had in mind the panel of judges in the competition for a school history textbook, the chairman of which was Zhdanov—V. R.], there turned out to be a significant number of *displaced people*, and the entire historical front of young historians no longer *existed* [with these euphemisms Bukharin was referring to the mass arrests of historians at the end of 1936—V. R.]." Bukharin concluded this portion of explanations with the statement that if he were to be declared responsible for his former students and supporters, then those former participants in the Left Opposition who were sitting at the plenum should answer for Trotsky, Zinoviev and other "terrorists."

Referring to the charges against other people, Bukharin called into question only "obvious exaggerations," for example, Kaganovich's assertion about ties between Tomsky and Zinoviev before 1936, when "Zinoviev, as we all know, had been sitting under lock and key since the end of 1934."

Admitting only to insufficient vigilance, Bukharin protested that "this is being made into the conclusion of participating in Trotskyist banditry." He asked the plenum to arrive at "party and organizational conclusions after a careful analysis of the facts, and not on the basis of political intuition alone." While understanding and even sharing the "logic" of Stalinist "justice," he noted that after the plenum had made a decision in his case, the legal investigation could only ratify this decision, "obligatory for the trial investigator, obligatory for the judge (if the case went to trial), and obligatory, no matter how strange it might sound, even for the defendant, if he was still a member of the party. The investigation could not whitewash a person who had been politically blackened by a higher party body."

Arguing from these premises, Bukharin then tried to appeal to the conscience and common sense of the plenum's participants. Characterizing the atmosphere which had developed at the plenum, he wrote: "Everyone has material (not verified by confrontations), but the accused do not; the defendant faces the stupefaction brought on by sudden and extraordinarily monstrous charges which have been placed before him for the first time. Given the mood which had been conjured up beforehand (the very fact that the question is posed, the unverified material, the tendentiousness of the reporter, the press, the slogans directed from above, such as Molotov's reference to "accomplices and yes-men"*), everyone says: 'I am convinced,' 'there is no doubt,' and so forth. People look the defendant right in the eye and say: we do not believe you, every word you say has to be verified. On the other hand, the words of the accusers are taken for good coin. It means that any defense here is truly difficult. Of course, in the general atmosphere today no one is prepared to speak in favor of the accused. And later on? At further stages, after the obligatory party decision, and so forth, this defense becomes almost impossible."[19]

Such a statement might have caused many of the plenum's participants to vacillate. Stalin therefore had prepared a new and timely countermaneuver. When they had been contesting the good faith of Yezhov's investigation, Bukharin and Rykov noted in their contributions at the plenum that they had been allowed only one face-to-face confrontation with the "slanderer" Sokolnikov, and asked that additional confrontations be arranged with other people who had vilified them. Therefore, on 7 December, the plenary session was recessed for four hours. During this time, Bukharin and Rykov confronted Piatakov, Sosnovsky and Kulikov, who had been brought from prison. Stalin, Molotov, Voroshilov, Kaganovich, Ordzhonikidze, Mikoyan, Andreev and Zhdanov were also present.

Sosnovsky stated at the confrontation that he had held "a political conversation" with Bukharin, in the course of which "they agreed that the practice of terror was correct."

Piatakov recounted that in 1928 Bukharin had read him his platform, about which he, Piatakov, had then informed the members of the Stalinist grouping in the Politburo. To this solitary real fact Piatakov added that at the beginning of the 1930s he had told Bukharin about Trotsky's directives for terror and sabotage; after Bukharin, Rykov and Tomsky had exchanged opinions on this question, they told Piatakov that they shared Trotsky's position and that the center of rightists had itself come to analogous conclusions.[20]

During the confrontation, Stalin and Ordzhonikidze asked Piatakov

---

* Here Bukharin had in mind Molotov's statement at the Eighth All-Union Congress of Soviets: "In the wolf pack of the enemies of communism, by no means the last place is occupied now by the Trotskyist gentlemen, who share the same goals as the bourgeoisie.... We know that they also have yes-men and accomplices among the rightist renegades." (*Pravda*, 30 November 1936).

whether he was giving his testimony freely or under pressure. Piatakov replied that no pressure had been applied. When he recounted this episode at the February-March Plenum, Voroshilov added: during the face-to-face confrontation, "Piatakov knew that he would be shot.... When Sergo asked him this question, he waved his hand and said: 'I know the position I am in.'"[21]

Particularly dangerous for Bukharin was the confrontation with Kulikov, who said that the "center" of rightists had participated in the preparation of the Riutin Platform. When Bukharin stated that he had become acquainted with this platform only in the Central Committee, Kulikov declared: "But it was the basis of our work."

Only one real fact figured in Kulikov's testimony: a conversation with Bukharin in 1932 when they accidentally met on the street. In the course of this discussion, Kulikov reproached Bukharin for refusing to continue to struggle against Stalin. However, in Kulikov's account, this conversation assumed just the opposite character. According to Kulikov, Bukharin gave him a directive from the "Rightist Center" about shifting over to terror and then gave him a concrete assignment—to organize a terrorist act against Kaganovich.[22]

This face-to-face confrontation became deeply engraved on Kaganovich's memory insofar as it contained information about an attack on him personally. In conversations with Chuyev, the elderly Kaganovich related its contents in the following way: "Kulikov says to Bukharin: 'And do you remember, Nikolai Ivanovich, how you took my arm and we walked along Vozdvizhenka, and I said to you: "Why are you wasting your time, talking nonsense. We have to act, we have to act in a real way!" Bukharin replied: "And where are your people? Who will act?"—"We'll find the people."— "And why can't you do something yourself? Engage in terror?"'"

According to Kaganovich, after Kulikov said these words, Bukharin cried out: "I never said that." "What do you mean, never said that," Kulikov replied, "when you began asking me the names of people so that I would name whom I had in mind."[23]

On another occasion, Kaganovich added to his tale about the confrontation: "Kulikov asked: 'You testify that you wanted to kill Kaganovich.... But why was it that you wanted to kill him?'—'Because he is the transmitter of incorrect policy, because he is one of the main transmitters of Stalinist policy.'"[24] Even half a century later, this characterization coming from an "enemy" gave Kaganovich undoubted pleasure.

Immediately after the confrontations were finished, a second session of the plenum began which lasted no more than half an hour. Stalin spoke "on behalf of the members of the Politburo" with a statement about the confrontations. Noting that Bukharin categorically denied the testimony of the arrested, Stalin said that the following impression had been formed among the Politburo members: the testimony could not be "fully accepted," and they "did not completely deserve to be trusted." Moreover, the arrested people, according to Stalin, had made such "general statements" about contacts between the Trotskyists and former leaders of the Rightists, that they "could have been made up." In all the testimony heard by the members of the Politburo, there was reference only to "terrorist conversations," but there was no indication that Bukharin and Rykov were tied with any terrorist group, of which "there had been quite a few among intermediate and advanced students, and among the peasants."

Stalin summarized the general opinion which arose among Politburo members after the confrontations in the following casuistic formulations: "While not trusting Bukharin and Rykov with regard to what has recently happened, perhaps they should be removed from membership in the Central Committee. It is possible that this measure will prove to be insufficient, and it is possible that this measure will prove to be too severe. Therefore the opinion of the members of the Politburo amounts to the following—to consider the question of Rykov and Bukharin unresolved." Stalin reinforced this conclusion with an announcement that five or six confrontations had to be set up with people who had "vilified" Bukharin and Rykov to a greater degree than the three who had just been interrogated by members of the Politburo.[25]

After Stalin's proposal had been passed, Stalin ordered: "Do not report on the Plenum in the newspapers." Someone in the audience asked: "Can we tell about it?" To the accompaniment of "general laughter," Stalin replied: "What, you want to shut people up? Different people will say different things."[26]

The plenum's resolution stated: "(a) To take under consideration Comrade Yezhov's report. (b) To accept Comrade Stalin's proposal to consider the question of Rykov and Bukharin unresolved. To continue further verification and to set aside case until it can be resolved at the next plenum of the Central Committee."[27] "Further verification" was entrusted, of course, to the People's Commissar of Internal Affairs, i.e., to Yezhov, at whose unlimited disposal the fate of all the arrested "accused" remained.

15. The Trial of the "Anti-Soviet Trotskyist Center"

In the interim between the two plenums of the Central Committee (December and February-March), a second show trial was held which lasted for eight days (23–30 January 1937).

The first of the defendants at this trial to be arrested was Muralov (in April 1936). It is possible that he was designated to be placed on the stand at the previous trial, but in the course of seven and one-half months they had not managed to obtain a confession.

The first of the defendants who agreed to collaborate with the investigation was Sokolnikov. A. M. Larina recounts that in the camps the wife of the Deputy People's Commissar of Internal Affairs, Prokofiev, told her what her husband had said. Immediately after he was arrested and informed of the charges against him, Sokolnikov declared: "As soon as you demand that I give outlandish confessions, I will agree to give them. The greater the number of people who will be drawn into the spectacle you are staging, the sooner people will wake up in the CC and the sooner you will be sitting in my place."[1]

This fact is one of the examples demonstrating that in 1936, not only people who were uninformed about Stalin's political intrigues but also sophisticated political figures who had fallen under the steamroller of repression had no conception of how cruel the political strategy would be which had been formulated by combining a complex mixture of domestic and geopolitical circumstances together with Stalin's personal qualities.

Even leaders of such stature as Sokolnikov were captive to a psychological dictum which is natural in such extreme situations: "This cannot be." They believed in the "common sense" of the ruling elite. As today's experience now shows, similar ineradicable mass illusions are born in conditions of cruel historical changes. They often prove to be fatal, since they form for many people an absolutely inadequate conception of what is taking place and in the final analysis they prompt people to arrive at false historical conclusions.

Karl B. Radek

Stalin, who carefully followed the course of the investigation in Sokolnikov's case, made comments on the transcript of his interrogation which directly indicated what testimony should be obtained from him. Next to the record of Sokolnikov's account of his meeting with the English journalist, Talbot, Stalin wrote a question and then provided the necessary answer to his own question: "But nevertheless did he tell of the plan to kill leaders of the VKP? Of course he did." On the next page of the transcript, where Sokolnikov testifies that he did not know of Talbot's links with English intelligence, Stalin wrote in: "Sokolnikov, of course, gave information to Talbot about the USSR, CC, PB, GPU, about everything. Sokolnikov—consequently—was an informer (spy-intelligence agent) for British intelligence."[2]

It proved to be more complicated to obtain testimony from Radek—the only prominent Trotskyist who was allowed after capitulation to occupy a responsible position in the party apparatus (before his arrest he had headed the international information bureau of the CC VKP[b]). After giving a declaration of repentance, Radek promised Stalin to wage active propaganda against the

Left Opposition and became one of his main assistants in the slander campaigns against "Trotskyism." "From his pen now flowed the most unprincipled accusations and poisonous invectives directed against Trotsky," wrote A. Orlov. "Even in 1929, seven years before the beginning of the Moscow Trials, Radek publicly called Trotsky Judas and accused him of becoming 'Lord Beaverbrook's stooge.' The flood of this abuse and slander literally increased over the years in geometrical proportions."[3]

Radek's most filthy deed—the betrayal of Bliumkin in 1929, when the latter brought Radek a letter from Trotsky after an illegal visit to Trotsky in Prinkipo—was related to the oppositionists by Rabinovich, a member of the secret political sector of the OGPU who secretly shared the views of the opposition. Rabinovich, like Bliumkin, was shot without a trial. "Radek's guilt was as severe as if he had become an agent-provocateur of the Soviet punitive organs.... Old Bolsheviks—even those who never had anything to do with the Opposition—began to boycott Radek and stopped greeting him."[4]

In an article published during the Trial of the Sixteen, Radek boasted of his role as informer in the Bliumkin case, and introduced a new nuance in his story about Bliumkin's meeting with Trotsky. According to Radek, Trotsky persuaded Bliumkin to organize the transport of illegal literature into the USSR. Radek also told how in 1928 Trotsky prepared to flee abroad, "and tried to persuade me and others to do the same, for without a foreign center, nothing would work." "I was horrified," Radek added, "by the thought of actions against the USSR under the aegis of bourgeois states and sabotaged the attempt to escape."[5]

On the eve of his own arrest, Radek often sent letters to Stalin in which he reiterated his own innocence. He evidently assumed that he would have to play a shameful role in the upcoming trial. When he was being led away to prison, he said in farewell to his daughter: "Whatever you learn and whatever you hear about me, be assured that I am guilty of nothing."[6]

For two and a half months after his arrest, Radek gave no confessional testimony, although a whole brigade of investigators worked on him, resorting to the conveyor system of interrogation.* At the December Plenum of the Central Committee, Stalin announced that he had received long letters from Radek

---

* The wide use of exhausting "conveyor" interrogations of the accused and of standing for many hours was reported in 1961 by the surviving investigators who had taken part in the fabrication of this "case."

in prison in which he said that "a terrible crime" was being committed. " ... People want to put him—a sincere man, devoted to the party, who loves the party, loves the CC, and so on, and so forth—on the spot.... You can shoot him or not, that is up to you. But he would like his honor to remain untarnished."[7]

According to Orlov, Radek began to confess only after a long conversation with Stalin. Renouncing the testimony that had been written for him by the investigators, he offered his own version about the activity of the "center" which supposedly had authorized Trotsky to carry on negotiations with the German government."[8]

Like Muralov and Radek, the majority of the other defendants gave confessional testimony far from immediately. Such testimony was received from Drobnis forty days after his arrest, from Piatakov and Shestov after thirty-three days, from Serebriakov after three and a half months, from Turok after fifty-eight days, and from Norkin and Livshits after fifty-one days.

The preparation of this trial, like the preceding, Stalin placed under his personal control. Notes which survive in Vyshinsky's personal archive, which were made during a discussion with Stalin, show that Stalin evidently feared that the defendants would slip up during concrete descriptions of wrecking acts. He ordered Vyshinsky: "Don't allow them to talk much about disasters. Shut them up. They caused so many disasters, don't let them blab too much."[9]

Yezhov and Vyshinsky presented Stalin with three variants of the final indictment. Stalin gave instructions about reworking the first variant and personally edited the second variant, striking out the name of one defendant (Chlenov) and writing in another in his place (Turok).

Besides well-known political figures (Sokolnikov, Radek, Piatakov, Serebriakov, Muralov and Boguslavsky), the trial included five men who had worked at Kuzbass enterprises and who had passed through the rehearsal of the "Kemerovo Trial" (Drobnis, Norkin, Shestov, Stroilov and Arnold), four highly-placed officials in economic Commissariats (Livshits, Rataichak, Kniazev and Grashe) and two provincial economic specialists (Turok and Pushin). The last six were chosen from a larger number of economists and engineers who had been arrested by that time.

In order to invest the trial with greater credibility, the court transcript contained not one hundred fifty pages, like the transcript of the Trial of the Sixteen, but four hundred pages. The entire transcript was presented in the form of a dialogue between the prosecutor and the defendants, and was free of anonymous commentary about the behavior of the defendants.

The trial transcript mentioned Trotsky's name hundreds of times. Piatakov and Radek said that the defendants at the previous trial had concealed the most important point: they had received directives from Trotsky about sabotage, a pact with the fascist powers and preparation of the defeat of the USSR in a future war. Such directives, according to Radek's testimony, were also contained in letters to him from Trotsky which were brought by the "center's" emissaries from Sedov. Piatakov testified that he personally met with Sedov (in 1931) and with Trotsky (in 1935).

Among the tasks of the "Trotskyist center," terror was named as before. The list of the seven names designated as victims of terrorist acts at the previous trial was supplemented by the names of Molotov, Eikhe, Yezhov and Beria. The defendants introduced the names of dozens of new people who belonged to the groups preparing the attacks on the "leaders."

Victor Serge, who personally knew several of the "terrorists" mentioned at the trials, told how one of them was Zaks-Gladnev, an erudite old Marxist and wonderful orator who led a solitary life and was completely incapable of any practical actions; another was the young journalist and scholar, Tivel, who studied Hinduism. One other group of "terrorists" included the young historians Zaidel, Fridliand, Vanag and Piontkovsky, whose works were not lacking in merit, but which were permeated with a thoroughly Stalinist spirit.[10]

After Kirov's assassination, not a single terrorist act occurred. And this is in a country where under the tsarist regime, dozens of attacks were carried out against the tsars, their officials and gendarmes. "It is impossible to endlessly use Kirov's corpse in order to annihilate the entire opposition," Trotsky wrote. " ... The new trial therefore advances new charges: economic sabotage, military espionage, assisting the restoration of capitalism, and even attempts at 'the mass extermination of workers.'"[11]

Noting that nothing had been said at the previous trial about these vicious crimes, Trotsky wrote: "No one has been able to understand as yet how and why Radek and Piatakov, who had already been named as 'accomplices' of the accused in the case of the sixteen at the pretrial investigation, had not been brought to trial in a timely fashion. No one could understand how it was that Zinoviev, Kamenev, Smirnov and Mrachkovsky knew nothing about the international plans of Radek and Piatakov (to expedite war, dismember the USSR, and so forth). People who were not lacking in powers of insight felt that these grandiose plans, as well as the very idea of a 'parallel center' arose with the GPU after the execution of the sixteen, in order to reinforce one falsification with another. It turns out that this is not the case. In the fall of 1932, Radek told Romm* in good time that the Trotskyist-Zinovievist Center had already come into being, but that he, Radek, and Piatakov had not joined this center; they were saving themselves instead for a 'parallel center dominated by Trotskyists.' In this sense, Radek's sociability was providential. This must not be understood, however, in the sense that Radek in 1932 actually told Romm about a parallel center, as if he had foreseen Vyshinsky's future concerns in 1937. No, the matter is simpler: under the guidance of the GPU, Radek and Romm retrospectively created a scheme of events in 1932. And we must state the truth: they did so poorly."[12]

Trotsky saw an even more absurd judicial blunder in Romm's statement that he had given Sedov "detailed reports" from Radek "about both the main and parallel centers." "Let us note this priceless circumstance!" wrote Trotsky. "Not one of the sixteen accused, beginning with Zinoviev and ending with Reingold, who knew everything and informed on everyone, knew anything at all in August 1936 about the existence of a parallel center. However Romm, already in the fall of 1932, was fully informed of the idea of a parallel center and of its subsequent realization. No less remarkable is the fact that Radek, who did not belong to the main center, nevertheless sent him "detailed reports about both the main and parallel centers."[13]

Noting that, according to the testimony of the defendants, the "Trotskyists" unquestioningly executed all of Trotsky's directives, Victor Serge wrote: "The Left Opposition included devoted fighters, but it has never had a 'leader' and has stood against the very idea of leader-worship. The genuine Trotskyists in Stalin's prisons, even if they accepted this label out of respect for "The Old Man" (that is how they referred to Trotsky—V. R.), nevertheless have never taken a single one of his ideas on faith, but have critically examined them. The very idea of authoritarian 'directives' was a product of the twisted imagination (of the Stalinists)."[14]

The testimony of Radek, Sokolnikov, and Piatakov outlined the following version. Trotsky conducted negotiations with Hess, the deputy chairman of

---

* V. G. Romm was a Soviet intelligence officer who acted abroad under the guise of a correspondent from TASS and *Izvestiia*. He served as a witness at the trial of the "Trotskyist Center."

the Nazi Party. Referring to these negotiations, Trotsky told the "center" that in 1937 Germany was planning to attack the USSR.* In this war, Trotsky felt, the Soviet Union would inevitably suffer a defeat in which "all the Trotskyist cadres would also perish in the ruins of the Soviet state." In order to save these cadres from destruction, Trotsky obtained a promise from the leaders of the Third Reich to allow the Trotskyists to come to power, promising them "compensation" in turn: they would be granted concessions and Germany would be sold important economic objects of the USSR; she would be provided with raw materials and produce at prices below the world market, as well as territorial concessions in the form of satisfying German wishes for expansion in the Ukraine. Analogous concessions would be made to Japan, to whom Trotsky promised to give the Priamur and Primore regions in the Far East; he also pledged to guarantee oil "in case of war with the USA." In order to expedite the defeat of the USSR, Trotsky ordered the "center" to prepare a series of the most important industrial enterprises to be taken out of commission at the start of the war. Radek and Sokolnikov "confirmed Trotsky's right to speak in the name of Soviet Trotskyists" in negotiations with the fascist powers, and in conversations with German and Japanese diplomatic representatives they promised the support of "realistic politicians" in the USSR for Trotsky's position.[15]

Radek was particularly loquacious as he outlined this version; Vyshinsky called him the "holder in the anti-Soviet Trotskyist Center of the foreign affairs portfolio" and "one of the most prominent, and, we must give him his due, most talented and obstinate Trotskyists.... He is one of the most trusted and closest people to the main ataman of this gang, Trotsky"[16] (Vyshinsky borrowed the expression, "ataman of this gang," from an article by Radek which had been published during the Trial of the Sixteen).

As he concluded, Radek was generous in his warnings to not only Trotskyists, but, as he expressed himself, to "semi-Trotskyists, quarter-Trotskyists, and one-eighth Trotskyists," to people who "helped us, without knowing about the terrorist organization, but who sympathized with us, and to people who, out of liberalism or because of discontent with the party, gave us assistance.... To all these elements we say before the court and before the fact of retribution: whoever has the slightest fissure with regard to the party,

---

* During the Nuremberg Trial (1946), several Western figures appealed to the members of the tribunal and to the prosecutors to question Hess about these negotiations. However the Soviet side refused "to burden the court" with these "embarrassing" questions.

let him know that tomorrow he might be a saboteur, he might be a traitor if this fissure is not painstakingly closed up with absolute openness before the party." Radek's words directed at "Trotskyist elements" abroad sounded even more threatening; he warned that "they would pay with their heads if they do not learn from our experience."[17] These words were soon confirmed by bloody actions performed by the Stalinists in Spain (see Chapter 43).

Meanwhile, in response to insults from the prosecutor, Radek twice said more than Vyshinsky demanded. After Radek's words about the tortuous doubts which he experienced when he received Trotsky's directives, the prosecutor asked him: "Can we ... seriously take what you have said here about your doubts and vacillations?" In response, Radek allowed himself to snap back: "Yes, if you ignore the fact that you learned about the program of the conspirators and about Trotsky's directives only from me, then of course, you cannot take me seriously."[18]

Even more ambiguous was Radek's statement in his concluding remarks, when he touched on Vyshinsky's characterization of the defendants as a "gang of criminals, differing in no way, or in the best case, differing little from bandits who operate with bludgeons and daggers in the dark of night along the highway."[19] Apropos of this comment, Radek declared: "The trial has shown the forge of war, and it has shown that the Trotskyist organization became an agent of those forces which are preparing a new world war. What evidence is there of this fact? There is the testimony of two people—my testimony, about how I received directives and letters from Trotsky (which, unfortunately, I burned) and the testimony of Piatakov, who spoke with Trotsky. All the other testimony from the other defendants rests on our testimony. If you are dealing with simple criminals, or secret agents, then on what can you base your certainty that what we have said is the truth, the unshakable truth?"[20]

There were a few "shortcomings" in the testimony of the other defendants, too. Thus Muralov, who confessed his participation in the preparation of attacks on Molotov and Eikhe, stubbornly denied Shestov's testimony, according to which he, Muralov, had given directives about preparing a terrorist act against Ordzhonikidze.[21]

Piatakov, who was the actual leader of heavy industry (he far surpassed Ordzhonikidze in technical and economic knowledge), was entrusted with developing a detailed version about wrecking at the industrial enterprises. Although he was rather compliant during the trial, it was in connection with his testimony that the investigators made a blunder that was even more signifi-cant than the episode with the Hotel "Bristol" at the previous trial.

On 15 September 1936, Trotsky appealed to world public opinion with a warning: after the political disaster of the first trial, Stalin would be compelled to stage a second, at which the GPU would try to transfer the operational base of the conspiracy to Oslo.[22] As if proving this hypothesis, Piatakov testified that in December 1935, during a business trip, he was sent from Berlin to Oslo on an airplane provided by the German special services. That this version was invented from beginning to end could be seen not only from the exposés widely circulated in the world press, but in the secret report filed by Zborowski, who said that in a cautious conversation with Sedov, he was able to establish that after Trotsky had left the USSR, he had never met with Piatakov.[23]

The first commentary for the world press on this question was given by Trotsky on 24 January, immediately after the publication of Piatakov's testi-mony. Within three days, he addressed thirteen questions to the Moscow Trial through the various telegraph agencies. He asked that these questions be sub-mitted to Piatakov to clarify the circumstances of his pretended meeting with him. By this time, the Norwegian newspaper *Aftenposten* had published a state-ment that in December 1935 the airport in Oslo had not received a single for-eign airplane. On 29 January, the newspaper of the government party announced that the director of the aerodrome in Oslo confirmed that from 19 September 1935 until 1 May 1936, not a single foreign airplane had landed at this airport. On the same day, Trotsky released a new statement in which he said: "I greatly fear that the GPU will rush to shoot Piatakov in order to forestall any further uncomfortable questions and to prevent an international commission of in-quiry from demanding precise explanations from Piatakov."[24] On the next day, in his final statement Piatakov declared that Trotsky will accuse the defen-dants of lying "instead of coming here to the trial to deny the charges to my face or turn them against me; he is avoiding a face-to-face confrontation with us."[25] However, even this absurd declaration, which was clearly placed in Piatakov's mouth by Vyshinsky, did not save Piatakov from being shot.

As they told of their wrecking activities, Piatakov and other defendants cited actual facts of accidents, disasters and fires which had previously been investigated by numerous commissions. They had always come to the conclu-sions that these tragic events were the result of the violation of manufacturing and technological discipline, of negligence and poor work quality. Now, however, all these events were being declared the result of sabotage. Romm, who was presented as an intermediary between Trotsky and the "center," testified that in a conversation with him in the Bois de Boulogne,* Trotsky spoke about the necessity of carrying out wrecking acts without any concern for human victims.[26] Following Romm's example, the defendants insisted that, in preparing the fires, explosions and train accidents, they were consciously trying to cause human suffering in order to "strike separate blows against the population and at the same time to provoke animosity toward Stalin and the government."[27] The defendants "confessed" that they carried out sabotage and espionage under orders not only from Trotsky-Piatakov, but also the German and Japanese intelligence services.

Trying to produce a feeling of horror, Vyshinsky exclaimed during his indictment speech: "It is not I alone who make the charges! Alongside me, comrade judges, I feel as if right here are standing the victims of these crimes and these criminals—crippled, on crutches, half-alive, and, perhaps even without legs, like Comrade Nagovitsyna, switchman at the Chusovskaya station, who appealed to me today through the pages of *Pravda*, and who at age twenty lost both her legs while thwarting the derailment organized by these people!... Perhaps the victims have been buried, but they are standing here beside me, pointing at the defendants' bench, at you, the defendants, with their terrible hands which have rotted in the graves where you sent them!"[28]

Vyshinsky's indictment speech contained a number of innovations in comparison to the previous trial. Declaring that "Trotsky and the Trotskyists had long been capitalist agents in the workers' movement," Vyshinsky asserted that Trotskyism, "the age-old enemy of socialism," in accordance with "Comrade Stalin's predictions," "had actually turned into the main gathering point of all forces hostile to socialism, into a detachment of common bandits, spies and murderers," into "a vanguard fascist detachment, into the storm-troop battalion of fascism," into "one of the branches of the SS and the Gestapo."[29]

Without a hint of shame, Vyshinsky made statements from which it became clear that the concrete guilt of the defendants had not even been demonstrated at the trial. Thus, in comments about the former head of the Main Chemical Industry, Rataichak, he made the insulting and mocking remark: "He is ... either a German, this has still yet to be finally clarified, or a Polish spy, of

---

* Trotsky presented documents to the commission to investigate the Moscow Trials which showed that at the time designated by Romm, he was not in Paris.

this there can be no doubt; and he deserves to be called a liar, deceiver and swindler."[30]

Touching upon the trial's main weak spot—the absence of even the slightest material evidence of the defendants' criminal activity—Vyshinsky declared: "May I be so bold as to state that, in accordance with the fundamental demands of the science of criminal procedure, in cases of conspiracy such demands cannot be presented."[31]

In conclusion, Vyshinsky saw only one shortcoming in the given trial. "I am convinced," he said, "that the accused have not stated even one-half of the truth which comprises the nightmarish tale of their terrible crimes against our country, against our great motherland."[32]

Once again calling Trotsky's open letter from 1932 a terrorist directive, Vyshinsky added a reference to one more article written by Trotsky which contained, in his words, "in rather open, uncamouflaged form ... directives for terror." This time, Vyshinsky quoted not two words, but several sentences from Trotsky's article: "It would be childish to think that the Stalinist bureaucracy can be removed by means of a party or Soviet congress.... For removing the ruling clique there remain no normal, 'constitutional' means. The bureaucracy can be forced to transfer power to the proletarian vanguard only *by force.*"[33] "What can this be called," Vyshinsky declared, "if not a direct call ... for terror? I can assign no other name to this." Identifying terror with any force, Vyshinsky stated: "An opponent of terror, of violence, would have to say: yes, it is possible [the reorganization of the Soviet state—V. R.] by peaceful means, let us say, on the basis of the constitution."[34]

Commenting on the prosecutor's arguments, Trotsky wrote: "Serious revolutionaries don't play games with violence. But they never refuse to resort to revolutionary violence if history denies them other means.... I think that the system of Stalinist Bonapartism can only be liquidated by means of a new political revolution. However, revolutions are not made on order. Revolutions grow out of the development of society. They cannot be summoned forth artificially. Even less so can a revolution be replaced by the adventurism of terrorist attacks. When, instead of counterposing these two methods—individual terror and the uprising of the masses—Vyshinsky identifies them, he is striking out the entire history of the Russian Revolution and the entire philosophy of Marxism. What does he put in their place? Forgery."[35] Trotsky also labeled a forgery Vyshinsky's statement about the possibility of replacing the Stalinist totalitarian regime "on the basis of the Constitution," which was a fiction and a false foundation for the democracy which supposedly existed in the USSR.

Unlike the previous trial, in the trial of the "parallel center" famous Soviet lawyers participated in defending three of the secondary defendants. They all saw their main assignment as assisting the prosecutor as much as they could. The lawyer Braude, who was defending Kniazev, turned to the judges and openly stated: "I will not conceal from you the exceedingly difficult, incredibly difficult position in which a defender finds himself in this case.... The feelings of great indignation, rage and horror which now seize our entire country, young and old, the feeling which the prosecutor so clearly reflected in his speech, these feelings cannot be foreign to the defense lawyers." Acknowledging that it had been proven beyond any doubt that Kniazev "derailed trainloads of workers and Red Army troops at the service of Japanese intelligence," Braude detected mitigating circumstances in the fact that Kniazev was only the indirect executor of "the most troubling crimes," the main guilt for which was borne by "the despicable Trotsky."[36]

It was announced at the trial that fourteen of the defendants not only refused to have defense lawyers, but also refused the right to make a speech in their own defense, deciding to combine it instead with their concluding remarks. However even these speeches resembled not so much a defense as degrading self-condemnation.

In their concluding remarks several of the defendants tried to explain indirectly the reasons for their false confessions. In this regard, Muralov's speech was particularly characteristic, and it later served as one of the main arguments for advocates of the "Koestler complex" (see Chapter 20). Muralov stated that in prison he had come to the conclusion: "If I continue to remain a Trotskyist, then I might become a banner for the counterrevolution. This terrified me. If I refused to speak out, I would become a banner for the counterrevolutionary elements which still existed, unfortunately, on the territory of the Soviet republic. I did not want to be the root from which these poisonous shoots would sprout.... And I then said to myself, after almost eight months [in which Muralov had not confessed—V. R.], let me subordinate my personal interest to the interests of the state for which I had actively fought in three revolutions, when dozens of times my life had hung by a thread."[37]

At the prosecutor's bidding, the defendants denied even the suggestion that they had given their testimony under "external pressure." Thus, Vyshinsky ques-

N. I. Muralov, Moscow, 1926.

tioned Norkin in detail about whether the investigators had "pressured" him. Such "pressure," Vyshinsky said in concretizing his questions, could be expressed in depriving the accused of good food or sleep: "We know this from the history of capitalist prisons. They might take away cigarettes." In response to these cynical questions, Norkin meekly replied that "there had been nothing of the sort."[38]

Radek went even further in his concluding remarks when he himself raised this risky theme: "If the question is posed here, did they torture us during the investigation, then I must say that they did not torture me, but I tortured the investigators by forcing them to perform unnecessary work [i.e., by refusing for two and a half months to confess—V. R.]."[39]

The sentence of the court indicated that "Piatakov, Serebriakov, Radek and Sokolnikov were members of the anti-Soviet Trotskyist center and on direct orders from L. Trotsky, the enemy of the people who was living abroad ... directed the sabotage-wrecking, espionage and terrorist activity of the anti-Soviet Trotskyist organization in the Soviet Union." The remaining defendants were found guilty of participating in this organization and of fulfilling the assignments of the "center."[40]

On 28 January, Ulrich sent the draft of the sentence he had written to Yezhov "for approval." Only one measure of punishment figured in this sentence for all the defendants—shooting. Yezhov, on orders from Stalin, of course, amended the sentence by softening the punishment for four of the defendants, including two members of the "center"—Sokolnikov and Radek. This maneuver was supposed to serve as a source of hope for the defendants at future trials.

After the sentence had been pronounced, the men who had been condemned to death by shooting submitted appeals for clemency to the Central Executive Committee. Trying to choose words that would be the most convincing for the Stalinists, Piatakov wrote: "During all these months of imprisonment and the extremely difficult days of the trial, many times I have checked myself to see if a single, even the most minuscule remnant of Trotskyism remained within me." "I am sixty years old," wrote Muralov. "I want to devote the remainder of my life fully to the good of constructing our great Motherland. I take the liberty of beseeching the Central Executive Committee of the USSR to spare me my life."[41]

This time as well, despite the seventy-two hours that were provided for reviewing appeals for mercy, the defendants were shot on the day after the sentence was read.

The four defendants who were spared did not outlive their codefendants for long. Radek and Sokolnikov were murdered in 1939 by criminals who were prison cellmates, apparently on orders from the "organs." Arnold and Stroilov were shot in October 1941 in the Orlov prison, according to a new sentence passed in absentia. They were executed along with the defendants in the case of the "Right-Trotskyist Bloc" who avoided death in 1938, and with other political prisoners (for instance, Maria Spiridonova).

On the day the trial ended, a meeting was held on Red Square in temperatures of thirty degrees below zero. Speeches condemning the defendants were given by Khrushchev, Shvernik and Komarov, the president of the Academy of Sciences.

The case of the "Anti-Soviet Trotskyist Center" contained even fewer actual facts than the material of the previous trial. Sedov wrote about this very explicitly to Victor Serge, who had assumed that behind the second trial might lie the provocative use of attempts or at least the readiness on the part of some of the defendants to fight against Stalinism. "If this trial is constructed more successfully [than the Trial of the Sixteen—V. R.]," Sedov emphasized, "then that is chiefly because the defendants themselves, especially Radek, actively participated in the work of falsification, and, without any doubt, Radek in particular personally 'edited' L. D.'s letters; Piatakov's conversation with L. D. was worked out by Piatakov with Radek's collaboration, otherwise such idiots as Yezhov never would have managed to carry out this refined and sophisticated falsification. Moreover, Radek's amorality, his cynicism, and other qualities made him the most appropriate candidate, in essence the leader, of the GPU's investigatory kitchen.... If we had tried to draw such people as Piatakov and Radek into some kind of 'conspiracy,' by sending them some kind of provocative letters, they immediately would have informed the GPU about this. There can be no doubt about this fact for anyone who knows these people and the situation in Soviet Russia.... Your hypothesis cannot help but be of use to all well-wishers of Stalinism who readily speak out in these or other questions of form, and who acknowledge that there was much that was untrue or exaggerated at the trial, but that something real lay at the heart of the trial.... At the trial of Radek and Piatakov, insofar as we are talking about the political formulations of this trial, there is even less truth than at the trial of Zinoviev-Kamenev. There are not even the pitiful crumbs such as my meeting with I. N. Smirnov. Everything here is a lie, perhaps less vulgar, but even more despicable and demoralizing."[42]

Immediately after the trial ended, foreign communist parties unleashed a loud campaign to discredit "the Trotskyist counterrevolutionaries and servants of the Gestapo." A few days after the defendants had been shot, *Pravda* reprinted an article by Dolores Ibarruri, which had been published in the Spanish communist newspaper, *Frente Rojo*. "After the trial," the article said, " ... every worker and peasant, every fighter for the cause of freedom and progress could clearly see the wretched role which the Trotskyists have played in the international revolutionary movement.... In the face of irrefutable facts and proof, what has been unmasked is the genuine meaning of the theory, camouflaged with ultrarevolutionary phrases, which concealed the rot, ambition and egoism of the renegade Trotsky." Asserting that in every country the goal of the Trotskyists was to undermine the revolution from within, Ibarruri declared that "as a result of the trial of the anti-Soviet Trotskyist Center, those people who until now, perhaps, had still believed the Trotskyists, must now acknowledge the correctness of the policy of the Spanish Communist Party, which does not wish to collaborate with Trotskyists in a single communist organization."[43]

Abroad, the trial was also justified by liberal "friends of the USSR," particularly by Pritt, who wrote about the trial's juridical irreproachability. At the beginning of March, the famous Danish writer, Andersen-Nexø, who had attended the trial, arrived in Oslo and declared that he had no doubts about the veracity of Piatakov's testimony concerning his meeting with Trotsky.

Among Western liberals, first place in disorienting the Western public fell inarguably to Feuchtwanger, who before the trial had even finished appeared in *Pravda* with the article, "First Impressions about the Trial." In it he "stated with satisfaction" that "the Trial of the Anti-Soviet Trotskyist Center has shed light on the motives which have forced the defendants to confess their guilt. For those who are honestly trying to establish the truth it thus becomes easier to evaluate these confessions as evidence." Understanding the unconvincing nature of such an explanation for world public opinion, Feuchtwanger called for help from "the pen of a great Soviet writer," which "alone ... might explain to Western European people the crimes and punishment of the defendants."[44]

In his book *Moscow 1937*, as a counterweight to those "doubters" who felt that the behavior of the defendants was psychologically inexplicable, Feuchtwanger referred to the opinion of "Soviet citizens," who gave "a very simple" explanation of the reasons for the confessions by the accused: "During the pre-trial investigation, they were so thoroughly exposed by the testimony of witnesses and by documents, that their denial would be pointless." "The pathetic character of the confessions," Feuchtwanger wrote further, "must be attributed fundamentally to the translation. Russian intonation can be transmitted only with difficulty, and the Russian language in translation sounds somewhat strange and exaggerated, as if its basic tone is one of the superlative degree."[45]

Feuchtwanger accompanied these linguistic excursions with an exposition of his "immediate impressions" of the trial, which he attended every day. Addressing the fact that many people who had earlier been friends of the Soviet Union had changed their positions after the first Moscow Trial, Feuchtwanger wrote: "For me, too ... the charges made at the Zinoviev trial seemed to be unworthy of trust. It seemed to me that the hysterical confessions of the accused had been obtained by some form of secret methods. The entire trial seemed to me to be some kind of theatrical spectacle which had been staged with unusually outlandish and unrestrained artifice. But when I attended the second trial in Moscow, when I saw and heard Piatakov, Radek and their friends, I felt that my doubts had dissolved like salt in water.... If all this had been invented or contrived, then I do not know what truth would then mean."[46]

Feuchtwanger added that the trial was to a certain degree a party trial at which the accused felt themselves still bound to the party. "Therefore it is not accidental that the trial from the very beginning bore the character of a discussion, which is strange for foreigners. The judges, prosecutor and accused—and it did not just seem this way—were bound together by the bonds of a common goal. They were like engineers who were testing an absolutely new and complex machine. Some of them had ruined something in the machine, they had ruined it not out of malice but simply because they capriciously wanted to test out their theories about improving the machine [that is how Feuchtwanger interpreted charges of terror, espionage, wrecking, defeatism, and so forth!— V. R.]. Their methods proved to be wrong, but this machine is close to their hearts no less than for others, and therefore they discuss their mistakes in open conversation with others. They are all united by their interest in the machine and by their love for it. And it is this feeling that prompts the judges and the accused to collaborate so cordially with each other."[47]

Feuchtwanger supplemented this string of sophisms by repeating Socrates' words, who "with regard to some of Heraclitus' unclear propositions said the following: 'What I understood is beautiful. Therefore I conclude that the rest which I did not understand is also beautiful.'"[48]

Feuchtwanger's sophistry to no small degree was evoked by "arguments" which he borrowed from Stalin, who devoted several hours to a "sincere" discussion with him. The writer recalled that he told Stalin "about the poor impression which was made abroad, even on people favorably disposed to the USSR, by the overly simple devices in the Zinoviev trial. Stalin laughed a bit at those who, before agreeing to believe in a conspiracy, demand to see a large number of written documents; experienced conspirators, he noted, rarely are accustomed to keeping their documents in an open place." Stalin aroused particular trust in Feuchtwanger by the fact that he spoke "with sorrow and consternation" about his friendly attitude toward Radek, who nevertheless had betrayed him.[49]

This time, the "explanations" given by "friends of the USSR" such as Feuchtwanger did not sound as convincing for foreign public opinion as they had after the first trial—primarily because now the whole world could hear Trotsky's own voice as he exposed them.

16. Trotsky Returns to Battle

UNTIL THE MIDDLE of December 1936, Trotsky lived in conditions of strict isolation. On 11 December he was called as a witness in the trial of the fascists who carried out the raid on his apartment. Inasmuch as the court was interested in Trotsky's political activity, he gave a four-hour speech which ended with the words: "It is hardly possible to find throughout human history a more grandiose apparatus of slander than that which has been set in motion against me. The budget of this international slander campaign reaches into the millions of pure gold."[1] While Trotsky remained in Norway, this speech, which had been given at a trial taking place behind closed doors, was never published. Later Trotsky restored its contents by using the outline in his possession and included it in his book, *The Crimes of Stalin*.

At about the same time, Trotsky was visited by Trygve Lie, for whom the prisoner recalled the words spoken by Doctor Stockman, the hero of Ibsen's play, *Enemy of the People*: "We shall yet see if baseness and cowardice are strong enough to close the mouth of a free and honest man!" When the minister declared that his government had committed a stupid mistake by offering Trotsky political asylum, Trotsky said: "And you want to correct this stupidity by committing a crime? You are acting toward me like the Noskes and Scheidemanns acted in relation to Karl Liebknecht and Rosa Luxemburg. You are paving the way for fascism. If the workers of Spain and France do not save you, you and your colleagues in a few years will become emigrants, much like your predecessors, the German Social-Democrats."[2] In 1940, before fleeing to England after German troops had invaded Norway, the Norwegian king reminded Trygve Lie of "Trotsky's curse." In his memoirs about the war Koht, the former chairman of the Norwegian parliament, wrote mournfully that the leaders of his party in 1936 ignored Trotsky's words, considering his prognosis to be absolutely unrealistic.[3]

In the middle of December, news reached Norway of the Mexican government's offer to give Trotsky political asylum. This decision was made by

Trotsky waiting to give a deposition
concerning the raid of the fascists

the President of Mexico, Lazaro Cardenas, an active participant in the popular revolution of 1910–1917. After being elected president in 1934, Cardenas enacted social and anti-imperialist reforms—giving the peasants the landowners' latifundia and nationalizing the oil and railway companies which were owned by American and British capitalists. Only after Stalin's death did the Soviet authorities recognize Cardenas as an outstanding political and social activist. In 1955, he was awarded the International Lenin Prize for strengthening peace and friendship between nations. In 1961, Cardenas was elected chairman of the International Peace Council.

When he learned of the Mexican government's decision, Trotsky asked Lie to allow him to travel to Mexico via France, where he wanted to meet with his son and friends. Although a French transit visa did arrive, Lie forbade Trotsky to follow this route. In order to send Trotsky and his wife to Mexico, the Norwegian government chartered a tanker; preparations for sailing were completed in deep secrecy, out of fear that Stalinist agents might place explosives in it or carry out an attack at sea. Not ruling out his tragic death during the journey, Trotsky secretly sent his son a letter and testament. He also managed to send to Paris an article, "Shame," written in invisible ink and addressing the Trial of the Sixteen. In publishing this article, the editors of the *Bulletin of the Opposition* indicated that they had been forced to omit several words which they had not been able to decipher in the text which had been received. The article ended with the words: "A final response to the accusers and their lackeys.... I will give in Mexico, if I arrive there.... I do not know if this letter will reach you. In any case, I cast this 'bottle' into the sea."[4]

A few months after arriving in Mexico, Trotsky wrote: "I left a Europe torn by horrific contradictions and shaken by the foreboding of a new war. This general anxiety explains the origin of the innumerable panic-stricken and false rumors which are circulated about many subjects, including myself. My enemies are skillfully using this atmosphere of general disquiet against me. They will undoubtedly continue their efforts in the New World as well. On this account I am not creating any illusions for myself."[5]

During his trip, Trotsky entered into his diary preparatory notes for the counterinvestigation of the Trial of the Sixteen. In Mexico he supplemented these with commentaries on the second show trial. This material made up the book *The Crimes of Stalin*, which was published in 1937 in the main languages of Europe except Russian (it was first printed in Russian only in 1994). "This book," wrote Trotsky, "will make it easier, I hope, for wide circles of readers to understand where it is they must look for criminals, on the benches of the accused or on the benches of the accusers."[6]

Viewing the Moscow Trials as the logical conclusion of many years' struggle of the Stalinist clique with "Trotskyism," Trotsky noted, "in the West, people do not have even an approximate idea of the quantity of literature which was published in the USSR over the last thirteen years against the Left Opposition in general, and the author of these lines in particular. Tens of thousands of newspaper articles in tens of millions of copies, stenographic reports of innumerable indictment speeches, popular pamphlets in runs of millions, thick books have distributed and continue to this day to distribute the most despicable lies which can be prepared by thousands of hired writers lacking conscience, ideas and imagination."[7]

These lies, as Trotsky emphasized, changed their coloration depending on Stalin's various foreign policy maneuverings. In 1933, the entire Soviet and Comintern press wrote that Trotsky had arrived in France with the goal of helping Daladier and Blum organize a military campaign against the USSR.

Trotsky and
Sedova before
disembarking
in Mexico

After Blum and Daladier became heads of the Popular Front government, sup-ported by the Comintern and Soviet diplomacy, the same press with an even greater frenzy began to accuse Trotsky of collaborating with Hitler and trying to break up the Popular Front in France. Apropos of such shifts Trotsky wrote: "The times change and the GPU forgeries change along with them."[8]

As he unmasked the political meaning of these changes, Trotsky noted: "During the period when I, according to the latest retrospective version, was engaged in organizing collaboration with Hitler, the press of Moscow and the Comintern depicted me as an agent of France and Anglo-Saxon imperialism. I was transferred to the German-Japanese camp only after Hitler refused Stalin's extended hand and forced him, despite his initial plans and calculations, to seek the friendship of the 'Western democracies.' The charges against me were and remain only a negative supplement to the diplomatic reversals of Mos-cow."[9]

On 9 January 1937, Trotsky arrived in Mexico City. From there he was ac-companied by his supporters as they headed for the villa of Diego Rivera, from whom he had received an invitation. Rivera was not only a world-famous art-ist, but one of the founders of the Mexican Communist Party, and a member of its Central Committee in the 1920s. In 1927 he visited Moscow, where he be-came a witness to the first reprisals against the Left Opposition. Under the influence of these events, Rivera left the party and severed his friendship with

Trotsky and Diego Rivera

Trotsky being met in Mexico,
9 January 1937

another outstanding Mexican artist, David Siquieros, who had turned into a fervent Stalinist.

One of Rivera's best works was a panel of frescoes created for Rockefeller Center in New York. This work, to the horror of bourgeois America, turned out to be dedicated to the themes of class struggle and proletarian revolution; in the center of the panel Rivera sketched the portraits of Lenin and Trotsky.

From the first days of Trotsky's presence in Mexico, the local Communist Party and the leadership of the Confederation of Mexican Trade Unions headed by the Stalinist Lombardo Toledano raised a slander campaign hoping to achieve Trotsky's exile from the country. Stalin hoped that Trotsky, who was in a distant and unknown land, lacking his own press and means for conducting counterpropaganda, would not be in any position to effectively resist this massive campaign.

In the failure of the relentless provocations directed against Trotsky to achieve their goal, a decisive role was played by the firm position of Cardenas, who declared that Trotsky was a guest of the Mexican government. In a letter sent to Cardenas after Trotsky's death, N. I. Sedova wrote: "In Norway we lived under the constant threat of death, and almost none of the countries of the world were brave enough to accept us. The only exception was legendary Mexico and its courageous, independent and all-knowing people. You prolonged the life of Leon Trotsky by forty-three months."[10]

Immediately after coming to Mexico, Trotsky resumed his active political life. Whereas Stalin was trying to put him in a position of self-defense or retreat, Trotsky chose the tactic of going on the offensive, exposing not only the judicial frame-ups, but the entire Stalinist regime which had spawned these frame-ups. In his many articles he defended primarily not himself, but the cause of socialism, across which the crimes of the Stalinist clique had cast a dark shadow.

On 9 February 1937, a meeting organized by the American Committee for the Defense of Trotsky was attended by several thousand in New York. The organizers planned that Trotsky would personally read his speech over the telephone. However, at the last moment, the telephone connection between Mexico City and New York was broken (later it was discovered that this was deliberately done by a Stalinist telephone operator); therefore Trotsky's speech was read by a member of the meeting's presidium, Max Shachtman.

Trotsky's secretary, Sarah Weber, who was then in the United States, described the New York meeting in a letter to Trotsky: "Before midnight, the entire theater was overflowing with people (around seven thousand people) who were waiting for your speech. They waited anxiously, in an absolutely unbelievable silence. At 10:40, Shachtman proposed to begin reading your speech. 'No, no,' people shouted from all sides, 'we will wait,' and again a strained silence, broken from time to time by announcements from the telephone company. No one left the hall. Only at 11:30 was Shachtman allowed to read your speech. The resolution to organize a commission of inquiry was carried almost

unanimously—only a few solitary voices hesitatingly said 'no.' Despite the sharp disappointment that we were not able to hear your voice (especially for those who know Russian), or establish a connection between the audience in New York and you in Mexico City, your speech had an astounding impact. The fact alone that the Stalinists (there were quite a few, and they came with the intention to act like hooligans) didn't dare to disrupt it and sat in the same strained silence as the rest of the audience is testimony of this."[11]

In his speech, Trotsky demanded the creation of an authoritative, open and impartial commission to investigate the charges made by the Moscow Trials. He declared his readiness to appear before this international commission with a variety of documents and testimony of his political activity. "If this commission finds," he said, "that I am guilty even to a minor degree of the crimes which Stalin has heaped upon me, I pledge beforehand to voluntarily place myself in the hands of the executioners from the GPU.... But if the commission establishes that the Moscow Trials are a conscious and deliberate forgery, constructed of human nerves and bones, I will not demand of my accusers that they voluntarily place themselves before the gun. No, it will be enough for them to face eternal shame in the memory of human generations! Do the accusers in the Kremlin hear me? I hurl my challenge at their faces. And I await from them an answer!... We are not dealing here with personal *trust*. We are dealing with *verification!* I propose verification! I demand verification!"[12]

In speaking about the absurdity of the charges made at the Moscow Trials, Trotsky emphasized that the crimes which implicated the defendants "make no sense from the standpoint of the accused, even if they do for the accusers.... In no other regime would Piatakov and Radek be able to hope for a higher position than the ones which they occupied before their arrest."[13] Trotsky called even wilder and more absurd the version presented at the trials, as if "the way to power in the USSR could pass through ... the Gestapo."[14]

In exposing the falsifications of the Moscow Trials, Trotsky stressed that they had painted a picture of a grandiose conspiracy which had drawn into its orbit a multitude of people. However, the accusers ignored the fact that over the course of the previous decade thousands of oppositionists had been arrested, exiled, driven to their deaths in prisons and concentration camps, and shot. During the innumerable arrests, searches, opening of letters, and so forth, the GPU should have been able to "assemble an enormous museum of material evidence. Meanwhile, at not one of the trials had a single genuine letter, a single document, or a single irreproachable piece of evidence been presented."[15]

Whereas one might stretch things by explaining this circumstance with references to the caution shown by professional revolutionaries, even more surprising is the fact that among the conspirators, according to the trial transcripts, over the course of many years there were no disagreements, failures, splits or denunciations. Only at the trials themselves was this unprecedented unanimity of "criminals" replaced by an equally striking unanimity of an opposite character: "the hour had come for general repentance," and "a new miracle unfolded. People who had been organizing murders, preparing war and dismembering the Soviet Union, these well-tempered criminals suddenly repented ... not under the weight of evidence, no, for there was not one piece of evidence, but for some kind of mystical reasons.... Yesterday they were derailing trains and poisoning workers at the invisible command of Trotsky. Today they have come to hate Trotsky and are heaping on him their imaginary crimes. Yesterday they could only think about one thing—how to murder Stalin. Today they are all singing hymns of praise to him." Noting that Western "psychologists" explain these fantastic transformations by the infamously enigmatic character of the "Russian soul," Trotsky angrily declared: "You are slandering, my dear sirs, the Russian soul. You are slandering the human soul in general."[16]

In the responses to the Moscow Trials which appeared abroad, Trotsky saw two equally dangerous extremes. On the one hand, "the friends of the USSR" maintained "a conspiracy of silence" concerning the obvious judicial frame-ups—out of fear that their exposure might weaken the Soviet Union and thereby render a service to fascism. In this regard Trotsky pointed out that in actual fact the Stalinist bureaucracy, containing the "most repulsive traits of a totali-tarian regime," was facilitating the strengthening of the positions held by fas-cism.[17] (Later, long before the signing of the "Molotov-Ribbentrop" Pact, Trotsky repeatedly warned that, by purging the party of all consistent bearers of the Bolshevik type of social consciousness, Stalin was preparing a shameful deal with Hitler).

On the other hand, the anticommunist press saw the Moscow Trials as the logical outcome of the October Revolution and the ideology of Bolshevism. In response to this view, Trotsky replied: "The Moscow Trials do not dishonor the revolution, for they are the offspring of reaction. The Moscow Trials do not dishonor the old generation of Bolsheviks; they only show that Bolsheviks, too, are made of flesh and blood and that they cannot hold out endlessly when the pendulum of death swings above them for years. The Moscow Trials dishonor the political regime which fostered them: the regime of Bonapartism that is lacking both honor and conscience."[18]

Trotsky clearly understood what long-term detriment was being done to the cause of socialism by the Stalinist crimes committed supposedly under a revolutionary banner: "We will not hand this banner to the masters of falsifica-tion. If our generation has proven to be too weak to establish socialism on this earth, we will give its unstained banner to our children. The struggle which looms ahead by far supersedes the significance of individual people, factions and parties. It is a struggle for the future of all humanity. It will be severe. It will be long. Whoever seeks physical repose and spiritual comfort—let him step aside. During times of reaction it is easier to lean on the bureaucracy than on the truth. But for all those for whom socialism is not an empty phrase but the content of their moral life—forward! Neither threats, nor persecution, nor vio-lence will stop us. Perhaps it will be on our bones, but the truth will triumph. We are paving the way for it, and the truth will be victorious. Under the terrible blows of fate I will feel as happy as during the best days of my youth if I can join you in facilitating its victory. For, my friends, the highest human happiness lies not in the exploitation of the present, but in the preparation of the future."[19]

17. Trotsky on the Goals of the Moscow Trials

In analyzing the reasons for the Moscow Trials, Trotsky swept aside any explanation which relied on purely personal motives. While agreeing that such motives always played an important role in Stalin's political psychology, he stressed that in organizing as grandiose an action as the Great Purges, Stalin was guided by serious political considerations in which one must distinguish between the individual and social aspects.

The individual aspect was connected most of all with Stalin's fear regarding the possibility of counterterrorist acts being organized against him. The memoirs of Admiral Isakov, in particular, show how much Stalin was seized by such fear. They tell how, soon after Kirov's assassination, Stalin was speaking to Isakov about the officers on duty who stood at every passage in the Kremlin and who, of course, had repeatedly been checked "by the organs": "Every time you walk along a corridor you think: which one of them? If it is that one, then he will shoot you in the back, and if you turn the corner, then the next one will shoot you in the face."[1]

However, these considerations alone could not play the determining role in Stalin's organization of the monstrous auto-da-fé which produced millions of victims. Just as unconvincing was the version which explained the reprisals against the "Trotskyists" as well as Trotsky's continuation of the struggle by the personal hostility between Stalin and Trotsky. This version by the reactionary press of the 1930s has been reanimated in recent years by Russian "democrats." Thus Volkogonov, who measures the struggle of the Left Opposition against Stalinism by the yardstick of the unprincipled squabbles between Gorbachev and Yeltsin, endlessly repeats that Trotsky's "absolute rejection of Stalinism" was to be explained by his personal hatred for Stalin.[2]

However, Trotsky in 1937 provided rather convincing arguments which destroy this version. Feeling that it was superficial, ridiculous and absurd to reduce the struggle of the opposition against bureaucratic absolutism to the struggle for personal power between Stalin and Trotsky, he viewed this problem not from the side of Stalin, but from the side of Stalin's many opponents from the ranks of the Left Opposition. "Many tens of thousands of so-called 'Trotskyists,'" he wrote, "have been subjected to cruel persecution in the USSR over the last thirteen years; they have been torn from their families, their friends and from work, deprived of hearth and home, and not infrequently of their lives—can it really be that all of this was for the sake of a personal struggle between Trotsky and Stalin?"[3]

One of the main motives which prompted Stalin to organize the Moscow Trials was the desire to remove Trotsky from the political arena. "If Stalin assumed the work of Cain with regard to Zinoviev, Kamenev and others, then it is not because their deaths were needed by him as such.... For Stalin, the corpses of Zinoviev and Kamenev were primarily steps leading to Trotsky."[4] A similar role was played by the main defendants of the second trial—Radek and Piatakov. Unlike the leaders of the Zinoviev opposition, who took a political back seat after 1927, they were brought closer to the echelons of power by Stalin. Piatakov and Radek "were faithful weapons in Stalin's hands; he valued them highly because they were more intelligent and more educated than all his closest collaborators. But he had no other prominent and famous ex-Trotskyists whom he could set in motion for a new show trial. He was forced to sacrifice Piatakov and Radek."[5]

A two-way connection existed between the reprisals against "ex-Trotskyists" and the task of politically discrediting Trotsky. "Stalin had to sacrifice tens of his former comrades in order to create the fantastic figure of the counterrevolutionary superconspirator Trotsky. And then he used this figure to launch reprisals against all his opponents."[6] This "dialectic of falsification" grew out of Stalin's fear of the growing influence of Trotsky abroad and the growth of oppositional, "Trotskyist" moods in the USSR. In both instances, Stalin was guided not only by personal hatred for "disarmed" and "undisarmed" members of the Left Opposition, who had dealt him no small number of shattering ideological blows in the past, but primarily by the interests of the class struggle, of the political struggle. The Great Terror and its necessary component—the show trials of former leaders of the opposition—had profound social and political causes.

The first and most important of these causes—and correspondingly the first and most important of Stalin's goals—flowed from the irreconcilable contradictions of social interests. These contradictions, which had torn through all social life in the Soviet Union, were fostered by the creation of a "new privileged layer, yearning for power, thirsting for good things in life, fearful of their positions, fearing the masses and mortally filled with hatred toward any opposition."[7] This layer turned the regime of the Soviets into a bureaucratic tyranny. The result of the degeneration of the political regime was a change in the social structure of society and the regime, which came into contradiction with the goals of the October Revolution: "to establish a society without classes, i.e., without those who are privileged or destitute. Such a society has no need for state violence. The founders of the (Bolshevik) regime assumed that all social functions would be performed by means of the self-rule of citizens, without a professional bureaucracy rising above society."[8] The real development of Soviet society, however, followed just the opposite course: the bureaucracy usurped the power of the people, concentrated in its hands the control over the country's entire wealth and established for itself privileges which grew from year to year.

Even in the first stages of this process the bureaucracy had encountered the resistance of the Left Opposition (in Stalinist terminology, of the "Trotskyists"), the sole political force in the land which possessed a program expressing the interest of the popular masses. As the Thermidorian degeneration of the regime proceeded, reality revealed to an ever greater degree the official lies and confirmed the correctness of the Opposition's criticism and program. This forced the bureaucracy, in order to preserve the reputation of its own innocence, to resort to ever sharper forms of struggle against the opposition. At first the oppositionists were removed from responsible positions and expelled from the party, then they began to be denied any work and were sent into exile. Ever more poisonous slander was circulated about them. "In all the articles of condemnation against 'Trotskyism' there never was a single honest citation, just as in all the trials against it there never was a single substantive piece of evidence."[9]

Gradually, Stalin's assistants in this struggle became the capitulators who had broken from the opposition and turned into professional false witnesses against the Opposition and themselves. In all the capitulators' declarations, beginning with 1929, Trotsky's name inevitably figured as the main enemy of the USSR; without this, repentance would have no force. At first people spoke of Trotsky's "deviations" in the direction of Social-Democracy; at the next stage, about the "objectively" counterrevolutionary consequences of his activity; then, about his alliance with the world bourgeoisie against the USSR. These slander campaigns logically ended by ascribing to Trotsky a desire not only to split the party, but to break up the army, overthrow Soviet power and restore capitalism. In order to make these charges convincing in the eyes of Soviet people and world public opinion, prominent former oppositionists had to be brought to trial and turned into Trotsky's accusers.

Before these trials, the main method of rooting out "Trotskyism" was the party purge, during which the label of "Trotskyist" was placed not only on workers who were dissatisfied with the country's situation, but on all scientists and journalists who conscientiously cited historical facts and references contradicting the official lies. As a result, the intellectual atmosphere of the country became thoroughly permeated with the poison of deception, falsehood and out-and-out ideological and historical falsifications. However, the falsification of the theory and history of Bolshevism, which assumed an ever more vulgar character, did not achieve its goal—discrediting Trotsky and "Trotskyism" in the consciousness of the masses. "It was necessary to find a more massive justification for the bureaucratic repressions. Charges of a criminal character came to the assistance of the literary falsifications."[10]

Both the ideological and judicial frame-ups flowed necessarily from the position of the ruling caste, which was "false in its foundations. It is forced to conceal its privileges, lie to the people, and to camouflage with communist formulas such relations and activities which have nothing in common with communism. The bureaucratic apparatus does not allow anyone to call things by their real names. On the contrary, it demands from each and everyone the use of a conventional 'communist' language, which serves to mask the truth.... Mandatory lying permeates the entire official ideology. People think one thing, but say and write another. Since the difference between word and deed grows without respite, then most sacred formulas must be reviewed virtually every year.... Under the bureaucracy's knout, thousands of people carry out the systematic work of 'scientific' falsification. Any attempt at criticism or objection, the slightest note of dissonance, is seen as the most serious crime."[11]

As the reader can easily see, the situation described above characterizes the intellectual and ideological atmosphere of Soviet society not only during the period of Stalinism, but also in the following years—with two, however, substantial exceptions. First, after Stalin's death, the measures of punishment for dissident thought were significantly softened. Second, the oppositional moods in the post-Stalinist period (the further along, the greater this became)

assumed a predominantly anticommunist character. In addition, the bearers
of such moods did not possess a clearly formulated, cohesive program of rebuilding social relations. In contrast, during the 1930s, the traditions and ideals of the October Revolution were still alive in the masses. These unextin-
guished traditions threatened the very existence of the bureaucracy, which
feared the masses who had shown their true force and capacity for action during the years of the revolution and Civil War.

In a country where the lava of socialist revolution had not yet cooled, in
order to reinforce the social, political and ideological relations created by
Stalinism, which were still highly unstable, it was necessary to physically exterminate the communist opposition. However the ruling caste, which had concealed its selfish social interests under the flag of Bolshevism, could not "punish the opposition for its actual ideas and deeds: the relentless repression fully
intends to prevent the masses from learning the genuine program of
'Trotskyism,' which demands first of all greater *equality* and more *freedom* for
the masses."[12] The bureaucracy did not dare to inflict bloody repressions upon
the heads of the dissatisfied and critical while accusing them of demanding
the liquidation of its own power and its privileges. "To accuse the oppositionists of criticizing the autocracy of the bureaucracy would mean only to help
the opposition. Nothing else remained but to charge it with crimes directed
not against the privileges of the new aristocracy, but against the interests of
the people. At each new stage these charges assumed an ever more monstrous
character. Such was the general political atmosphere and social psychology
which made possible the Moscow judicial phantasmagoria."[13]

Of course, in the 1930s there still remained oppositional elements in the
Soviet Union whose inclinations bore an anti-communist character and who
were prepared at the appropriate moment to wage a battle against Stalinism
"from the right," even at the cost of collaborating with fascist interventionists.
The continued existence of such elements was clearly seen during the years of
World War II. But the thrust of the Great Terror was not directed against these
potential participants in a "fifth column." However, in the struggle against his
most dangerous political opponents from among the Bolshevik-Leninists, Stalin
widely employed his favorite method—the political amalgam, which included
identifying opponents "from the left" and "from the right," attributing to the
first the inclinations of the second. Here his political "methodology" closely
bordered on the methodology of Hitler, who, with his characteristically boast-

ful cynicism, once blurted out one of the main "secrets" of his political strategy. "The genius of a great leader," declared Hitler, "also consists in depicting
even widely differing opponents as always belonging to the same category, for
the understanding of differences between enemies too easily becomes the starting point with weak and unstable characters for doubts about their own correctness."

Of course, with Stalin, who was forced to resort to political mimicry and
therefore was much less sincere in his official declarations than Hitler, we will
not find anything resembling these statements. However in his political practice, Stalin in actual fact armed himself with the principle formulated by Hitler,
which, as Trotsky stressed, "is directly opposed to the principle of Marxist politics, as well as scientific thought in general, for the latter begins with separation, counterposition, and the discovery of not only basic differences, but even
transitional shades. Marxism, in particular, has always been opposed to treat-
ing all political opponents as 'one reactionary mass.'" At the ideological foundations of his terror, Stalin, however, used the methods not of Marxist, but of
fascist, agitation. The difference between these methods, according to Trotsky,
was the "difference between scientific education and demagogic hypnosis. The
method of Stalinist politics, which has found its most refined expression in
judicial frame-ups, completely coincides with Hitler's recipe, but in its scale
leaves Hitler far behind. Everyone who does not bow down to the ruling Moscow clique is now presented as part of a 'general fascist mass.' "[14]

Thus, Trotsky showed that Stalin's crimes were the only method of political struggle available to Stalin. The falsified charges against the Opposition,
which reached their culmination at the sensational trials, served as a means of
crushing the social protest which had accumulated among the people against
growing inequality and the political disenfranchisement of the masses.

"When the Stalinists call us 'traitors,'" wrote Trotsky, "in this accusation
one can detect not only hatred, but a peculiar sincerity. They feel that we have
betrayed the interests of a sacred caste ... which alone is capable of 'building
socialism,' but which in fact is compromising the very idea of socialism. We,
on our part, feel that the Stalinists are traitors to the interests of the Soviet
popular masses and of the world proletariat. It would be absurd to explain such
a ferocious struggle by referring to personal motives. We are dealing not only
with *different programs*, but also with different *social interests* which are coming into ever more hostile collision with each other."[15]

The main goal of the Moscow Trials was to create the conditions for politically discrediting and physically exterminating the entire communist opposition in order to behead the population, to deprive it for many years of a political avant-garde and therefore of the ability to resist the totalitarian regime. The class struggle in the USSR assumed, essentially, its sharpest form—civil war. This civil war, unlike the Civil War of 1918–1920, took the specific form of state terror directed at precluding any political activity by the masses. "In the masses, without any doubt, the traditions of the October Revolution are alive," emphasized Trotsky. "Hostility toward the bureaucracy is growing. But the workers and peasants who even formally belong to the so-called party, have no channels or levers for influencing the politics of the country. The present trials, arrests, exiles, judicial and extra-judicial reprisals are a form of preventive civil war which the bureaucracy as a whole is waging against the workers."[16]

An important feature of this civil war was that, despite Stalin's intentions, it inevitably led to the growth in the numbers of his opponents within the country. As a result of the reprisals against clearly innocent people, the builders of the Bolshevik Party, there proved to be significantly more of such opponents than Stalin had assumed. The reprisals "could not help but send a shudder though the ranks of the bureaucracy itself." It was possible to overcome the centrifugal tendencies within the ruling stratum, which retained no small number of people who were subjectively devoted to communist ideals, only by destroying the basic core of this stratum. Therefore the Great Terror developed into a struggle which the "most consistent Bonapartist wing wages against the rest of the less hardened or less reliable of its groups."[17]

The scale of the preventive civil war unleashed by Stalin was determined by the strength of the ideas and traditions of the October Revolution, which preserved their vitality not only among the popular masses, but among the party apparatchiks, economists, military leaders, and so forth. What was needed in order to overcome this force, which had no precedent in history, was state terror which was just as unprecedented in its scale and cruelty. In turn, this terror proved to be possible and effective because it superficially acted not in its genuine counterrevolutionary form, but in a form of social mimicry, under the mask of defending the gains of the October Revolution. The Stalinist Bonapartist regime could persevere only with the help of repressions and falsifications which were inseparably linked to one another. These falsifications— philosophical, historical, political and literary—"the inevitable ideological superstructure above the material foundations consisting of the usurpation of state power by the new aristocracy and the exploitation of the revolution's gains by it,"[18] necessarily were supposed to be crowned with historically unprecedented judicial frame-ups. A secondary goal of these frame-ups was the desire of the ruling clique and the more lowly and inferior portion of the bureaucracy standing behind it to "heap their economic failures, miscalculations, disproportions, misappropriations and other abuses on ... the Trotskyists, who were now playing in the USSR the exact same role which the Jews and Communists were playing in Germany."[19]

One more important goal of the Moscow Trials was related to foreign policy. The Stalinist clique needed to have millions of people throughout the world identify the Soviet Union with themselves. "The moral authority of the leaders of the bureaucracy and most of all, of Stalin, rests upon, to a significant degree, a Babylonian tower of slander and falsification.... This Babylonian tower, which frightens its own architects, is maintained ... outside the USSR—with the assistance of a gigantic apparatus, which uses the resources of the Soviet workers and peasants to poison world public opnion with the microbes of lying, falsification and blackmail." This apparatus of the Comintern, which was throughly demoralized, could enjoy influence among the masses only as long as the latter identified it with the revolutionary workers' movement. The obvious bankruptcy of the Comintern, whose strategy revealed its impotence during every revolutionary crisis, created a space for the new International. "If Stalin is terrified by the tiny *Bulletin of the Opposition* and shoots those who receive it in the USSR, then it is not difficult to understand how desperately the bureaucracy fears that news of the self-sacrificing work of the Fourth International will penetrate into the USSR.... That is why for Stalin a question of life or death is to kill the Fourth International in embryo!"[20]

18. A Tyrant's Revenge

IN RESPONSE TO Trotsky's exposés, Stalin resorted to ever newer slander, the public avowal of which became the duty of every Soviet citizen. The higher the post occupied by a given bureaucrat, the greater the demands placed upon him when it came to initiative and independence in the selection of the most abusive expressions and epithets. N. V. Krylenko, the People's Commissar of Justice, was able to outdo many of his colleagues in these endeavors. His particular zeal can be explained by the fear which arose from his personal "ties": his sister not only lived abroad, but was married to a famous American "Trotskyist," Max Eastman.

In an article, "Enemy of the People—Trotsky," Krylenko seemed to be trying to surpass Vyshinsky in his declamations. He wrote: "Trotsky will go down in history as the monstrous combination in one person of the entire sum of crimes known by the criminal code and which can be created by the human conception of 'the criminal,' for in actual fact, he has concentrated in his affairs the most severe and ignoble of all the crimes which have been discovered in the history of human relations."[1]

Besides the low-grade slander circulated by his satraps, Stalin had still another means of wreaking vengeance on Trotsky—reprisals against his relatives who remained in the USSR.

As far back as 1926, after Trotsky had declared at a session of the Politburo that Stalin had finally handed in his application to play the role of gravedigger of the party and the revolution, Piatakov, who was then his cothinker, said to him: "He will never forgive you for this, neither you, nor your children, nor your grandchildren."[2] This prognosis was fully realized in the years of the Great Terror. At this time, Trotsky's first wife, A. L. Sokolovskaya, remained in the Soviet Union, as did his two sons-in-law, who were among the most unbending Trotskyists. Both of them were in exile in 1928 and in the middle of the 1930s were transferred to concentration camps; soon they became victims of the first round of executions in the camps. We will tell of Sokolovskaya's fate in Chapter 44.

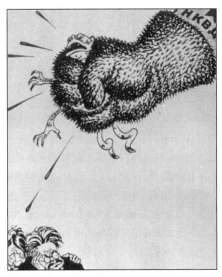

Caricature of Trotsky by the artists   The Yezhov Gauntlet, poster, 1937
Kukryniksy, 1937

These people were not only relatives, but political cothinkers and supporters of Trotsky. Matters were different with Trotsky's son, Sergei Sedov, who had never been interested in politics. "In school he refused to join the Komsomol," wrote N. I. Sedova, "and we allowed him not to. We hoped that when he became older, he would begin to share our interests. But his only passionate interests were mathematics and technology."[3] After refusing to accompany his father into exile and banishment, Sedov devoted himself completely to scientific work.

At the beginning of 1935, Sedov was arrested and brought to trial in the so-called "Kremlin affair." Insofar as it could establish his guilt at all, the Special Board limited itself to making a decision in July of the same year to exile him to Krasnoyarsk for a period of five years.

As an administrative exile, Sedov had the right to independently search for work in his specialty. In Krasnoyarsk he was fortunate in the sense that he was treated in a humane fashion by the director of a machine building plant, A. P. Subbotin, one of Ordzhonikidze's close friends.

At the party meeting where Subbotin was first accused of protecting Sedov, he related the circumstances in which he accepted the latter for work: "A man called Sedov came into my office and proceeded to offer his services as a specialist in gas generators. He stood there before me. I asked him: 'And where did you come from?' 'I,' he says, 'am Trotsky's son.' I must say that I broke out into a bit of a sweat: 'You'll have to wait a while,' I said. And so, Sedov walked around for a while near the factory, and then we gave him a job."

Despite his high position, Subbotin could not independently make such a "responsible" decision. He turned specifically for advice on this question to the first secretary of the Regional Committee, Akulinushkin, who obtained the agreement of the regional directorate of the NKVD in resolving the problem of where Sedov could work.

One of the main reasons which prompted Subbotin to take this risky step was the assignment he had received from the head of the Main Gold-mining Enterprise, Serebrovsky, to arrange the production of gas generator units for motor boats which were needed for the gold extraction industry. Sedov was one of the authors of the monograph, "Light Generators of an Autotransport Type." In September 1935 he was hired at the factory to direct the production of motors. Soon his wife, G. M. Rubenshtein, joined him from Moscow.

Immediately after the trial of the "United Trotsky-Zinoviev Center," Sedov was arrested. When Subbotin appealed to Serebrovsky for help in freeing Sedov as an irreplaceable specialist, he received an unambiguous reply: "If they took him, they did a good thing." At a session of the Regional Committee, Subbotin declared that he had no grounds for accusing Sedov of a careless attitude toward his work, a statement which was followed by Akulinushkin's ominous reply: "An enemy does not do a good job."

From that moment on, two cases were "worked on" in parallel—that of Sedov and Subbotin. At first Subbotin escaped with a party reprimand for "a display of liberalism," and for "dulling his Bolshevik vigilance."[4]

By decision of the Special Board, Sedov was sent along with other Trotskyists to the Vorkuta camps. There is testimony about his fate in the camps from several "Vorkutintsy," whose eyewitness accounts have been preserved in the Nikolaevsky collection. Thus the former prisoner, A. Rakhalov, wrote: "Sedov impressed me as a man who was experiencing a profound inner tragedy. I personally think that he undoubtedly loved his father. It also seems to me that the GPU was often playing games with him, abusing him and them caressing him, and he was fully aware that he would have to long play the role of a martyr for his father.... In any case, his extreme introspectiveness, his fear of saying an unnecessary word, his solitude and pensiveness made him an enigma for me. People told me that he loved his mother very much, and thoughts about her crowded out all others in his mind."[5]

In 1952, Nikolaevsky sent N. I. Sedova a letter in which several political prisoners told about the life of her son in the camps and about the way he was sent from there in a special convoy back to Krasnoyarsk.[6]

In Krasnoyarsk, Sedov was presented with new charges, which were immediately reported in a note in *Pravda* entitled, "Trotsky's Son Sergei Sedov Tried to Poison Workers." It said that Sedov, "a worthy offshoot of his father who had sold out to the fascists," had tried to poison a large group of workers with generator gas.[7]

To lend weight to the "Sedov affair," many factory specialists were added to the case. Sedov was charged with anti-Soviet agitation, wrecking and sabotage activity, and the creation of a terrorist group "together with an agent of German intelligence." After a long investigation, Sedov was sentenced to be shot on 29 October 1937. The sentences in his cases of 1935 and 1937 were overturned only on 28 September 1988—before this the Soviet judiciary had not wanted to address the case of Trotsky's son.

Threads from the "Sedov group" were extended to Subbotin. In April 1937 Akulinushkin wrote to Andreev, the secretary of the Central Committee of the VKP(b): "In 1936 at Stroikrasmash we uncovered a counterrevolutionary organization headed by Sedov—Trotsky's son, Zaks—Zinoviev's nephew, and others. It was established that the head of the construction site and director of the factory, Subbotin, who personally knew the arrested wreckers, placed them in the most important posts and, maintaining very close and intimate ties with them, created with his defense and support the circumstances and conditions for wrecking and sabotage activity."

On 16 June 1937, the arrested Subbotin was accused of heading a right-Trotskyist organization which had engaged in wrecking, espionage and the preparation of terrorist acts. Denying these false charges during the investigation, Subbotin was also not inclined to conceal his oppositional inclinations. At one of the interrogations he declared: "I, of course, could not reconcile myself to inner-party life which denied the rights of a party member to voice his opinions about questions of party policy.... Nor did I share the party line on questions of mass repressions and trials which are sometimes used without any grounds whatsoever against people who do not fully share the policy of the party.... I have never shared the policy of the party with regard to the tempo of industrializing the country, which was then implemented, in my opinion, at the expense of worsening the material conditions of the workers."[8] On 13 July 1938, Subbotin was shot.

In 1937 G. M. Rubenshtein was arrested in Moscow, where she had returned after Sedov's arrest to stay with her parents. A few months before her own arrest, she gave birth to a daughter, Julia. During the search of her apartment, all photographs of Sedov were confiscated, and all books which he had received from his father and which had survived previous searches. In 1952, Nikolaevsky told N. I. Sedova about the account of a former prisoner in Kolyma, who had ended up in West Germany after the war: G. M. Rubenshtein, who had been sentenced by a Special Board to eight years in distant camps, was transferred in November 1938 to Magadan and in 1946, despite finishing her sentence, still remained in a camp.[9] She spent twenty years in all in Kolyma. Sedov's first wife also spent many years in the camps and in exile.

A peculiar "continuation" of the Sedov case is recounted in the confessional work, "My Surroundings. Notes of One Who Happened to Survive," by the famous literary critic, Boris Runin. In the first part, we learn about the many trials which befell the author: spending the first months of the war encircled by the German armies, humiliatingly meticulous interrogations about this encirclement, charges against him in 1949 for being a "rootless cosmopolitan," and so forth. During all this the writer continually stresses that more terrifying than everything he experienced was "a painful secret, a delayed-action secret," the burden of which he carried his whole life and which he decided not to share even with his closest friends.

The author hints that this "secret" was somehow connected with his sister, "who ended up in Siberia because of her husband." However, such facts were so common in those years that they gave no grounds for all-embracing fear. Runin had occasion to become convinced of this when in 1939, in his third year at the literary institute, he was recommended to replenish the authors' collective at *Pravda*, which had been pretty well thinned out during the years of the Great Terror. The first article assigned to him was submitted to the paper but did not appear in its pages. On the next day, Runin was summoned to the editorial offices by its literary specialist, Tregub, who explained that the removal of the article was prompted by the fact that Pospelov, the main editor of *Pravda*, had spotted an unfamiliar name when he perused the pages and had asked that the article be set aside and that he be given information about its author. This news plunged Runin into indescribable horror:

> "So this is it!... What has happened is precisely what I have feared for
> so many years and what sooner or later couldn't help but happen.... And,
> without waiting any further, I said with a faltering tongue: 'Yes, I should
> have told you earlier about a compromising circumstance—my sister has
> been arrested....'
> "But Tregub broke off my words of repentance and impatiently moved
> away from this topic, not even asking what she had been arrested for. By
> the way, at that time, such questions sounded extremely stupid and were
> never asked.
> "'Ah, do you think that's what is involved?!' he suddenly exclaimed,
> obviously annoyed because he was in a hurry to go somewhere. 'Nowadays
> everyone has a sister who has been arrested....'"[10]

It turned out that Pospelov was interested in information about the literary biography of the young author—how old he was, where he had been published, and so forth.

In the second half of the book, the author reveals the content of his "painful secret." The husband of his sister was none other than Sergei Sedov. Immediately after Sedov's second arrest, Runin understood what consequences might
develop for himself and his entire family due to this arrest. Of course, in "the
organs," they knew very well about Sedov's "family ties," but a person could
always be found who on his own initiative might raise this question in order to
open up a new "case." "Through the efforts of the powerful propaganda apparatus," Runin writes, "the name of Trotsky had by that time already begun to
sound Satanic, and any connection to that name not only evoked holy terror
among Soviet philistines, but prompted them—eyes wide with fear—to in-
stantly give a signal to the authorities, without skimping on the most outlandish fabrications."[11]

After the vicious article about Sedov had appeared in *Pravda*, the
Rubenshteins' acquaintances visited their home ever more rarely, and then
they began to walk around it at a distance, as if it were infected by the plague.
"The very sound of this name—Trotsky!—aroused a mystical horror in the
hearts of the contemporaries of the Great Purge," notes Runin. "And the fact
that my sister had some kind of relation to that name automatically turned

not only her, but our entire family, into state criminals, 'collaborators,' 'spies,' 'accomplices,' in short, into 'agents of the greatest villain of modern times, into the most vicious opponent of Soviet power.'"[12]

To admit one's "connection" to Trotsky on the many forms which every working person had to fill out at that time raised the threat of cruel persecution. Therefore, after his sister's arrest, Runin thought it best to leave work and to begin earning money episodically by writing so that he wouldn't come into contact with any personnel departments. Then, Runin recalls, "I deliberately severed all my former relationships, shrinking my circle of friends to an absolute minimum. On the one hand, I did not want to cast a shadow on my comrades—if the whole truth about me became known, then friendship with me might affect them adversely. On the other hand ... I least of all was interested in having people whisper, next to my name, the sacramental name which because of frequent condemnation in the press had become a symbol of world evil. I not only was afraid of harming good people, but I also did not want good people out of the simplicity of their souls to harm me."[13]

Fearing further repressions against members of his family, Runin convinced his parents to separate—"at least then they wouldn't take us away all at once." The writer felt that it was perhaps for this reason that he was left at liberty in 1951, when his parents and fourteen-year-old Julia were exiled to Siberia.

Even after Stalin's death, Runin continued as before to conceal the "peculiarity of his biography," which "still retained its evil power"[14]— for Trotsky was still considered "the most vicious enemy of Leninism." "With this constant secret, fraught with exposure and apparently attached to my biography forever," he writes, "I lived not one year, or two, but almost fifty years."[15]

19. The Anti-Semitic Subtext of the Moscow Trials

AFTER THE NEWS about the second arrest of her son, which left no doubt about his further fate, N. I. Sedova sent a statement to the press, "To the Conscience of the World," in which she despairingly wrote about Sergei's innocence and honesty. "Did anyone speak out in his defense?" she later recalled. "Besides our friends, no one.... Lev Davidovich was crushed by this announcement. 'Perhaps my death would have been able to save Sergei,' he told me, and at times I felt that he was sorry that he was still alive."[1]

Deeply shaken by the fate of his younger son, Trotsky turned attention to one, seemingly insignificant, aspect of his "case," in which he saw an expression of one of the peculiarities of the Great Purge.

"Since the day they were born, my sons have carried the name of their mother (Sedova)," wrote Trotsky. "They never went by any other name—neither at school, nor at the university, nor in their subsequent activity. As for me, for thirty-four years I have borne the name of Trotsky. Throughout the Soviet period, no one ever called me by the name of my father (Bronstein), just as no one called Stalin Dzhugashvili.... After, however, my son Sergei Sedov was brought to court on absolutely incredible charges of preparing the annihilation of workers, the GPU announced to the Soviet and foreign press that the 'real'(!) name of my son was not Sedov, but Bronstein. If these counterfeiters had wanted to emphasize the ties of the accused to me, they would have indicated the name Trotsky, for politically the name Bronstein means nothing to anyone. But they needed something else, namely to stress my Jewish origin and the half-Jewish origin of my son.... If such devices are used at the highest levels, where Stalin's personal responsibility is beyond any doubt, then it is not difficult to imagine what is being done on lower levels, in the factories and especially in the collective farms."[2]

Trotsky also saw an obvious anti-Semitic orientation in the Moscow Trials, at which a disproportionately high number of the defendants were Jewish. At the first show trial, ten (out of sixteen) of the defendants were Jews, at the second, eight (out of seventeen). Trotsky felt that it was particularly monstrous that, of the terrorists supposedly sent by him into the USSR, who were simultaneously working for the Gestapo, all, as if by selection, turned out to be Jews. In all this, Trotsky saw an attempt by Stalin to exploit the anti-Semitic moods that still existed in the country in the struggle against the Opposition.

These statements by Trotsky were met with indignation abroad not only by pro-Stalinists, but also by bourgeois-liberal Jewish circles. Thus the famous American Zionist activist, Stephen Wise, explained his refusal to participate in the commission to investigate the Moscow Trials by the fact that Trotsky was not acting in good faith by raising the Jewish issue in connection with these trials. "If his other charges," declared Wise, "are as unsubstantiated as his complaint on the score of anti-Semitism, then he has no case at all."

Rejecting Trotsky's statements about the continued existence of anti-Semitism in the USSR, B. Z. Goldberg, a journalist who had contributed to the New York newspaper, *Der Tog*, wrote: "In order to beat Stalin, Trotsky considers it right to make Soviet Russia anti-Semitic.... Is this the truth, Mr. Trotsky? Is it honest to write this when it is not true? ... We are accustomed to look to the Soviet Union as our sole consolation as far as anti-Semitism is concerned.... It is therefore unforgivable that Trotsky should raise such groundless accusations against Stalin."[3]

Goldberg's subsequent political fate is noteworthy. At the beginning of 1941, a group of colleagues at *Der Tog*, tried to drive him from the editorial board "for ties with the Comintern and the GPU." During the war years, Goldberg visited the Soviet Union several times, where he was received by Kalinin and Manuilsky. In 1949, the Justice Department in the USA proposed that he register as a foreign agent. In the same year, the MGB "included" Goldberg in the case of the Jewish Anti-Fascist Committee, the leaders of which he had often met during the 1940s. One of the main charges made against the members of this committee was the charge that they passed Goldberg espionage information for the CIA.

For many years, accusations that Stalin was anti-Semitic were refuted not only by foreign Jewish circles, but by members of the Russian emigration. The Israeli historian Nedava reports that even in 1952, that is at the culmination of state anti-Semitism in the USSR, Kerensky told him that in the Soviet Union anti-Semitism had long since been eradicated, and that statements about the existence of anti-Semitism there were invented by supporters of the cold war.[4]

Similar sentiments were shared by many members of the Western intelligentsia, who accepted on faith Stalin's statement made in 1931 in reply to the question from the Jewish Telegraph Agency, located in the US, about the situation of Jews in the USSR. Here Stalin did not hesitate to use the strongest words with regard to anti-Semitism. "National and race chauvinism," he asserted, "is a vestige of misanthropic morals, characteristic of the period of cannibalism. Anti-Semitism, as an extreme form of race chauvinism, is the most dangerous vestige of cannibalism." Stalin declared that "in the USSR, anti-Semitism is legally prosecuted in the most severe manner, as a phenomenon deeply hostile to Soviet society. Active anti-Semites are punished according to the laws of the USSR with capital punishment."[5]

It can hardly be considered accidental that Stalin first published this interview in the Soviet Union on 30 November 1936, i.e., in the interval between the first two Moscow Trials. Whereas the publication of the Jewish Telegraph Agency at the beginning of the 1930s might have remained unnoticed by many Western intellectuals, now the publication of such a responsible declaration in the pages of *Pravda* created a solid reputation for Stalin as "an irreconcilable and sworn enemy of anti-Semitism."[6]

Having accepted this statement by Stalin on faith (much like, it must be said, others of his demagogic statements), many Western intellectuals considered Trotsky's comment about the anti-Semitic aspect of the Moscow Trials to be an invention dictated by his personal hatred for Stalin. Several of them turned to Trotsky with questions, the sense of which can be formulated in the following words: "How is it possible to charge the Soviet Union with anti-Semitism? If the USSR is an anti-Semitic nation, then what else is left?" Such objections and bewilderment, Trotsky stressed, "come from people who have become accustomed to counterposing to fascist anti-Semitism the emancipation of the Jews brought about by the October Revolution. Now it seems to them that the lifebelt is being wrenched from their hands."[7]

Trotsky directed attention to the fact that in the 1930s, "broad circles of the Jewish intelligentsia ... turned in the direction of the Comintern not out of interest in Marxism and Communism, but in search of support against the aggressive anti-Semitism" which had become state policy in Germany.[8] It is natural that in this milieu any comment about Stalin's anti-Semitism would be perceived to be virtually blasphemous.

Trotsky thought it so important to explain the question of anti-Semitism in the USSR that he devoted a special article to it, "Thermidor and Anti-Semitism." Here he first of all recalled how widely anti-Semitism had been spread in tsarist Russia, which was renowned not only for periodic Jewish pogroms, but for the existence of a great number of Black Hundreds' publications, which were printed in enormous press runs for that time. Although the October Revolution liquidated the Jews' lack of rights, this by no means meant that with one blow it had eliminated anti-Semitism. "Legislative acts alone still do not change people," Trotsky wrote. "Their ideas, feelings and views depend on traditions, the material conditions of life, the cultural level, and so forth. The Soviet regime is not yet twenty years old. The elder half of the population was raised under tsarism. The younger half has learned very much from the elder. These general historical conditions alone should force a thinking person to understand that, despite the exemplary legislation of the October Revolution, in the backward masses, nationalistic and chauvinistic prejudices, and anti-Semitism in particular, might still retain great force."[9]

However, Trotsky felt that it was inadequate to explain the vitality of anti-Semitic moods in the Soviet Union as simply the vestiges of the past. He directed attention to new social factors which had arisen during Soviet power and which were creating the soil for the rebirth of anti-Semitism. Soviet Jews belonged primarily to the urban population and composed a very significant portion of it in the Ukraine, in Belorussia and in a greater part of the territory of Russia. The bureaucratic regime which had been established in the USSR "needs a greater number of functionaries than in any other regime in the world. Functionaries are recruited from the more cultured urban population. It is natural that Jews occupy a disproportionately large place in the milieu of the bureaucracy. One may, of course, close one's eyes to this fact and limit oneself to general phrases about equality and brotherhood. But the politics of the ostrich will not move us one step forward."

Under conditions of poverty and a low level of culture for the majority of the population, Trotsky continued, perceptions of social antagonisms are easily sublimated into moods of national ill-will and hostility. "Hatred of the peasants and workers toward the bureaucracy is a basic fact of Soviet life.... Even a priori it is impossible to assume that hatred toward the bureaucracy has not taken anti-Semitic overtones, at least where Jewish functionaries comprise a significant percentage of the population."[10]

Trotsky noted that in awakening anti-Semitic prejudices, a certain part of the guilt lay on the functionaries themselves and the intellectuals from the Jewish milieu. In this regard, he recalled his speech at the republican party congress of the Ukraine in 1923, where he declared that every functionary should be able to speak and write in the language of the surrounding native population. This demand, flowing directly from the principles of Bolshevik national policy, was met with indignation and irony by a definite part of the Jewish intelligentsia which spoke and wrote in Russian and had no desire to study the Ukrainian language.

These sociological factors were joined by the stirring up of anti-Semitic moods by Stalin's policy, which was dictated by the desire of the bureaucracy to escape from social isolation. Along with creating around the bureaucracy a relatively wide layer of new aristocrats with the help of economic and political measures (the Stakhanovites' inordinately high pay, not proportionate to the results of their labor, the introduction of ranks, medals, and so forth) and with pseudo-socialistic demagogy ("socialism has already been built," "Stalin will give, gives and has given the people a happy life"), this policy included an adaptation to the nationalistic feelings of the backward layers of the population. "The Ukrainian functionary, if he is a native Ukrainian, inevitably tries at every critical moment to stress that he is the brother to the muzhik and peasant and not some kind of outsider, and in any case, not a Jew. In devices of this kind, there of course—alas!—is not a trace of 'socialism,' nor even of elementary democratism. But the point is that the privileged bureaucracy, which fears for its privileges and therefore is thoroughly demoralized, is now the most antisocialistic and most antidemocratic layer in Soviet society. In this struggle for self-preservation, it exploits the most hardened prejudices and most backward instincts."[11]

Trotsky gave no small number of examples of how widely anti-Semitic methods were used in the struggle against the legal Opposition of the 1920s. A result of this campaign was the strengthening of corresponding moods in society at large. Confirmation is provided by facts made public at a seminar on anti-Semitism which was led in 1928 by Yuri Larin. Here the worker-propagandists who had gathered from all corners of the nation cited typical questions asked at various meetings. In a number of these questions, which reflected the traditional formulations of anti-Semitism ("Why do Jews always manage to get good positions?", "Why don't Jews want to do heavy labor?", "Won't the Jews betray if there is a war?", and so forth), an important place too was occupied by "new" questions of the type: "Why was the party opposition made up of 76 percent Jews?"[12] It is understandable that this fantastic percentage was suggested by official agitators.

The Moscow Trials provoked a new outburst of anti-Semitism. As an indicator of this fact Trotsky pointed out that in an article on the Trial of the Sixteen, TASS published, in addition to the political pseudonyms of the main defendants, by which they were known to the masses, their "real" names (much as was later done with regard to Sergei Sedov). "The names of Zinoviev and Kamenev are much more famous, it would seem, than the names Radomyslsky and Rosenfeld," Trotsky wrote. "What other motive could Stalin have in introducing the 'real' names of his victims than playing on anti-Semitic moods?"[13]

The most inveterate enemies of Bolshevism detected with great sensitivity the anti-Semitic aspect of the Moscow Trials, as well as the Great Purge in general. In his memoirs, the writer Lev Razgon tells about conversations in Butyrki Prison with a certain Roshakovsky, a prominent Russian aristocrat who had been on friendly terms with Nikolai II. At the beginning of the 1930s, at his own request, Roshakovsky was allowed to return from emigration to the Soviet Union, where he was received with honor, showered with privileges and even met by Stalin and Voroshilov. Arrested in 1937, he nevertheless told his cellmates that he felt happy when he saw the prisons "filled with communists—these Cominternists, Jews, and political intriguers who understood absolutely nothing about what was happening to them." Roshakovsky assured them that the anti-Bolshevik genocide being carried out by Stalin, inseparably intertwined with the persecution of "outsiders," foretold of the "establishment of a great Russian state with its great national tasks." In this state, Roshakovsky declared, we would see the rebirth of "state anti-Semitism. And once again there would be a percentage quota at the universities, once again they would stop accepting Jews into the Department of Foreign Affairs, into the police, into the gendarmerie; they would exclude them from the governmental elite.... In civilized Germany the little-cultured and little-civilized Hitler had come to power by saying: 'Germany—for the Germans!'... Here they will announce the slogan: 'Russia—for the Russians!' Inevitably, unavoidably! And everyone will follow this slogan for whom the Jews are competitors! It will be adopted by bureaucrats, professors, journalists and writers."[14]

At the time, such a prognosis might have appeared to be absolutely outlandish to the overwhelming majority of his contemporaries, but not to Trotsky, who wrote that "in history there has never been an example where the reaction after a revolutionary upsurge was not accompanied by unbridled chauvinistic passions, including anti-Semitism."[15] Confirmation of this emerged in the results of the Great Purge, in which the proportion of Jews (as well as other "outsiders"—Finns, Estonians, Latvians, Poles) by far exceeded their proportion in the nation's population. After 1938, only a few people of Jewish nationality appeared in leading posts in the state and economic apparatus or in the army. The party apparatus, which actually ruled the land, was, practically speaking, completely "cleansed" of Jews. It is not known whether there were secret instructions given on this account, but it remains a fact that among the apparatchiks—"the recruits of 1937," who replaced the previous Bolshevik generation—there were almost no Jews. In Stalin's closest surroundings, there were only two Jews (Kaganovich and Mekhlis), who had committed anti-Semitic operations with no less zeal than other crimes committed by the Stalinist clique.

In her memoirs, S. Allilueva attributes her father's anti-Semitism to his struggle against Trotsky and the Left Opposition in general. In her opinion, in the course of this struggle the anti-Semitism propagated by Stalin was reborn "on a new foundation" and subsequently became an aggressive, official ideology, "spreading far and wide with the speed of the plague."[16]

Nevertheless, even today false conceptions survive which suggest that anti-Semitism on a state level and in everyday life was reborn in the USSR only during the second half of the 1940s. Both the facts cited above and Trotsky's arguments fully refute this version. If Stalin's policy had not facilitated the reanimation of anti-Semitic moods in the pre-war years, a strong outburst of anti-Semitism could hardly have broken out during the war years. Unlike the occupied countries of Western and Central Europe, where Hitler's forces transported Jews into the concentration camps while hiding the plans for their destruction, in the occupied territories of the Soviet Union the extermination of the Jews was carried out openly, with assistance from Hitler's supporters from among the local population. During the same years, on Soviet territory, there could be seen the return of everyday anti-Semitism, and in the circulars of the Central Committee of the VKP(b) there is mention of the "excessive" proportion of Jews in the spheres of science, culture, and so forth.

R. B. Lert, one of the few participants in the dissident movement of the 1960s–1980s who spoke out against the existing regime from communist positions, wrote the following: "Anti-Semitism began to creep into our state and party policy at first unnoticed—before the war; it developed during the war and came into full bloom at the end of the 1940s and the beginning of the 1950s."[17] But even then anti-Semitism was elevated to the position of government policy not openly, as had occurred in Hitler's Germany, but under the guise of false slogans about the struggle against cosmopolitanism, Zionism and so forth. This policy, which during Stalin's lifetime had taken fanatical and terroristic forms (the case of the Jewish Anti-Fascist Committee, the case of the "doctor-killers," etc.), after his death was maintained in the form of cadre limitations, limitations on accepting Jews in the universities, etc. Practical measures of this type were accompanied by ideological outbursts from fervent anti-Semites, in which the name of Trotsky played far from the least role. Thus, in the novella by Shevtsov, "In the Name of the Father and Son," which came out at the beginning of the 1970s, there are attacks against Trotsky as "an agent of world Zionism," written with the drool of a mad dog.

Of course, Shevtsov had to subordinate himself to the laws of Stalinist mimicry by masking his anti-Semitism with ideological labels. For the sake of such mimicry he placed his most intimate thoughts in the mouth of one of the novella's characters—Gertsovich, a Jew who is presented as an Old Bolshevik, imprisoned, no less, during the years of Stalinism. This device was supposed to lend credence to the author's assertions during his anti-Semitic lampoon, delivered by Gertsovich: "Zionism [unlike fascism—V. R.] follows another path, secretly, clandestinely, penetrating all the vital cells of the governments of the entire world, undermining from within all that is strong, healthy, and patriotic, taking people in hand, seizing all the main positions of the administrative, economic and intellectual life of this or that country. Both the fascists and the Zionists ferociously hate Marxism-Leninism and its ideology, particularly the ideas of internationalism, the brotherhood of peoples, with one difference: Zion had gladly sent its agents into the international communist and workers' movement. Sometimes these agents have managed to make it into the leadership of communist parties. And here before Gertsovich there would always arise the image of Judas-Trotsky (Bronstein), whom he considered one of the most typical agents of Zionism, provocateur No. 1." Feeling that he might be going too far here, Shevtsov made the reservation that such thoughts were "the personal point of view of Aaron Markovich, his personal outlook and conviction, which perhaps does not coincide with the theoretical research of philosophers and sociologists."[18]

Later Shevtsov has Gertsovich praise Stalin because he "liberated" the Soviet Union from Trotsky. Declaring that Trotsky "longed to become dictator, counting on dealing with the communists with the arms of inexperienced youths," Gertsovich added: "Trotsky left his cadres in the army. And if Stalin had not spotted him—what would have happened? A nightmare worse than Hitlerism. I know. Let historians say whatever they want to say, but I know: it's a straight path between Zionism and Trotskyism.... What do they agree on? On their desire to rule the world.... Trotsky was a Zionist and his so-called party— is a direct branch of Zionism."[19]

Thus, the arguments of today's "Pamiat," the "Barkashovists" and other anti-Semitic cliques were already being expressed in the pages of the Soviet press twenty-five years ago. Arguments which are close to those in Shevtsov's novella have now even made it into the program of the Communist Party of the Russian Federation, where it states that "bearers of petty-bourgeois ideology [inside the Bolshevik Party—V. R.] viewed the country and national property as 'booty' waiting to be divided up. At first their desires were cloaked by the false, Trotskyist interpretation of the international duty of Soviet Russia."[20]

Ukrainian nationalists also made their contribution to stirring up hatred for Jews and for Trotsky. In 1963, the journal *Dnipro* published A. Dimarov's novel, *Shliakhami zhittia* [The Roads of Life]. One of its central characters was the head of the regional GPU, Solomon Liander, who "took Lev Trotsky as an example for himself; he followed him in all things, even in the smallest details of clothing, even in gestures. And insofar as *Russia could carry on her shoulders only one Trotsky,* Liander decided to be more modest and to be satisfied for the time being with the role of Trotsky on a regional scale [my emphasis— V. R.]." The author adds that Liander inherited "from his father Gersh, and through his father from his grandfather Motele, and through his grandfather from his great-grandfather Chaim—a hatred for 'these damned khokhli [Ukrainians].'"[21] It is noteworthy that the vigilant "communist" censors overlooked all these passages, which advocate national enmity, and arouse Ukrainians against the Jews.

Must one be surprised after all this that during the years of "perestroika" and "democratic reforms," anti-Semitic moods came to the surface, leading to the rebirth of openly Black Hundred organizations with their many publications and even their own armed detachments? Meanwhile, in the anti-Semitic agitation a prominent place was taken by myths about "the vicious Trotskyist plans," which were at one with "the world strategy of Zionism." Not only in the publications of Russian fascists, but in the more "respectable" journals such as *Nash sovremennik* [Our Contemporary], *Moskva* [Moscow], and *Molodaia gvardiia* [Young Guard], a bowing before Stalin as a national leader of the Russian people is combined with frenzied attacks no longer against Trotsky alone, but against all Bolshevism, with claims that the October Revolution was a "Jewish revolution," and so forth. Thus the seeds which were sown by Stalin in the 1930s yielded abundant harvests in the following decades.

20. Why Did They Confess?

A two-way connection existed between the Great Purge, in which hundreds of thousands of people fell victim, and the open trials, at which there were slightly more than one hundred fifty defendants. With their global falsification, the trials were the culmination of the Great Purge. In turn, without these trials, at which political figures widely known throughout the nation and the world confessed to the existence of grandiose conspiracies, the mass terror could not have been carried out.

The defendants at the show trials could not help but assume that their "confessions" would open the door to mass repressions—both against those whom they directly named as their accomplices, and against a multitude of people whom they did not know, who inevitably would be included in the ranks of the executors of their directives on terror, wrecking and espionage. Just before his own arrest, Bukharin openly stated: "My solitary, innocent head will draw in thousands more innocent people. For, after all, they have to create an organization, a Bukharinist organization."[1] Similarly, the other defendants at the show trials—people who were sufficiently sophisticated in politics—could not help but be aware of their political and moral responsibility for "confessions" which had condemned to death not only themselves, but a mass of other, totally innocent people.

The confessions to monstrous crimes were so unbelievable that they fostered many versions about the reasons behind them. One of these was the version according to which "doubles" of the defendants—actors wearing make-up—sat in the courtroom. We can read about this, for example, in the memoirs of A. Larina, N. Joffe, and K. Ikramov. Legends and apocryphal stories of this type made their rounds for decades among circles of the Soviet intelligentsia.

Another version amounts to claiming that the confessions were obtained by using chemical substances which weakened the will of the defendants. This version is most clearly expressed in the story, "The Used Book Dealer," by V. Shalamov, which contains a conversation between the author and a certain captain of the NKVD, Fleming. Arrested like thousands of other Chekists, Fleming told the author of *Kolyma Tales* while he was in the camps:

"Do you know what the greatest secret of our times is?"

"No, which one?"

"The trials of the thirties. How they prepared them. I was in Leningrad at that time. Working under Zakovsky. The preparation of the trials was a matter of chemistry, medicine, and pharmacology. Of suppressing the will by chemical means. There are as many substances like this as you want. And don't tell me you think that if substances for suppressing the will exist, they wouldn't use them. Do you think it's a question of the Geneva Convention or something?"

Shalamov himself was clearly inclined to agree with the sentiments of his fellow prisoner. Commenting on his words, he wrote: "Here and only here lies the secret of the trials of the thirties, of the open trials, open to foreign correspondents and to any Feuchtwanger. There were no doubles at these trials. The secret behind the trials was the secret of pharmacology."

Shalamov juxtaposed this version, as more trustworthy, to the version of the "physicists," i.e., masters of physical torture, which produced the confessions at the open trials. "The physicists," he wrote, "could secure material for the 'special boards,' or for any 'troika,' but for open trials the school of physical actions does not suffice. The school of physical actions (borrowed, it seems, from Stanislavsky) could not stage an open and bloody theatrical spectacle, it could not prepare 'the open trials' which made all mankind shudder. The preparation of such spectacles was, however, well within the means of chemists."[2]

Nevertheless, the version of physical tortures as the main reason behind the confessions still has no small number of supporters. According to this version, the confessions at the open trials were dictated by the defendants' fear of even more terrible tortures in case they refused at the trial to confirm confessions given during the pre-trial investigation. Today, when the materials from many investigatory dossiers have been made public, as well as many memoirs of people who passed through the hell of Stalin's prisons, we are justified in doubting the correctness of this version. We know that many victims of the NKVD endured the most terrible tortures but refused to confess to being guilty of the crimes attributed to them, much less to give the names of their "accomplices." The author of this book managed to meet with several of these people who did not yield to torture because they wanted to preserve their own human dignity and not slander others. One of them was D. B. Dobrushkin, an engineer at the Moscow factory, "Kauchuk" [Rubber]. He passed through a two-year investigation, during which he lost his sight in one eye. Nevertheless, since he never gave any confessions, he ended up in 1939 among those who were set free, having fallen into Beria's "reverse flood."[3]

There were even more who at the trial renounced the testimony which had been forced from them during the pre-trial investigation. This occurred, it is true, only at closed trials, where the rejection of false testimony usually changed nothing in the fate of the defendants. At the public trials, such behavior might have produced an enormous political effect. Both the investigators and their victims could not help but understand that for the "obstinate" defendants at the open trials there would be more of a chance, and simply more physical strength for renouncing their "confessions," than at the closed trials. After all, at the show trials the defendants were supposed to look fairly healthy; therefore for several days before the trial they escaped torture, were well fed, given medicines, and so forth.

The main defendants at the show trials, being sophisticated political figures, could not help but realize what a risk the organization of such trials entailed for Stalin. Without doubt, Stalin himself and his cohorts were also well aware of the risk involved. The renunciation of "confessions" at a court session might break up the entire grandiose provocation and weaken the Great Terror as a whole. For this reason the preparation of the open trials was conducted with a painstaking selection of a few individuals from hundreds of possible defendants.

Two groups being persecuted were not present at the Moscow Trials. The first included unbroken oppositionists who had never capitulated and could not be made to "cooperate" with the investigators no matter what means were employed. Such people, who had not stained themselves by renouncing their views, and who considered Stalin the gravedigger of the revolution, openly told their jailers that they hated Stalin and his regime, or else that they refused to give any testimony in general.

The second group included sincere Stalinists who felt that the extortion of false testimony was the work of "enemies" who had penetrated the NKVD and were consciously exterminating the best people in the land. In Khrushchev's report to the Twentieth Party Congress, documents were cited which showed that even prominent party members fell captive to this version (or else used it in order to renounce their own confessions.). Thus, after an investigation that lasted more than a year, and after enduring the cruelest torture, Rudzutak, a candidate member of the Politburo, completely renounced his confession at trial. He managed to have the following statement included in the trial transcript: "His only request to the court is that information be given to the Central Committee that the organs of the NKVD contain an undiscovered abscess which artificially creates cases, forcing innocent people to confess their guilt.... The methods of the investigation are such that they force victims to invent things and slander innocent people, not to mention themselves."[4]

Another candidate member of the Politburo, Eikhe, conducted himself in a similar fashion. In a letter to Stalin he described the monstrous tortures which were used to extract testimony from him about other party leaders. Eikhe asked that his case be investigated "not for the sake of protecting me, but in order to expose the foul provocation which, like a snake, has entangled many people, particularly because of my faint-heartedness and criminal slander."[5] It is characteristic that in his letter Eikhe explained the false charges made against him not only as "the foul and malicious work of enemies of the party and the people," but as the slander by "Trotskyists" who were trying in such a way to get their revenge because he had sanctioned the arrest of their co-thinkers when he was secretary of the Western Siberian Regional Committee of the party.

Any person who has ever experienced extreme physical pain will agree that at such moments he might be capable of the most irrational steps to escape the pain, including the confession of nonexistent crimes. But this does not mean that he would be prepared to confirm such confessions in the future. Therefore, even though they had obtained the necessary confessions, the investigators might have assumed that at the open trials the accused would tell how their "confessions" had been extorted. Stalin and his satraps (who in such a case would inevitably have paid with their heads) needed to be absolutely certain that the defendants would act obediently at the show trials.

Apparently because the confessions from the accused could not be obtained despite the application of the most inhuman torture, or because the investigators had no confidence that the confessions they had obtained would be "confirmed" by the defendants at trial, many intended open trials were canceled. In Khrushchev's report to the Twentieth Congress, he described the preparations for the trial of a "reserve center," which was supposed to include Eikhe, Rukhimovich, Mezhlauk and others. There was also the trial of the "Leningrad center," which was supposed to have been composed of the former leaders of the Leningrad party organization.[6] We now know about the cancellation of the "Comintern Trial" (which was to include Piatnitsky), the "Komsomol Trial" (with the participation of Kosarev) and others. The intended defendants at these trials were tried before closed doors. The overwhelming majority did not escape death, but at least they avoided the shame of "confessions" at an open trial.

Of course, the very prison conditions and the inquisitional methods of the investigation could not fail to compel the majority of people to give false testimony. A certain parallel to the events of 1937 is provided by the events of the 1980s in Uzbekistan. At a time when the whole country was witnessing a wave of public exposures of the crimes committed a half century before, in this republic similar crimes were committed by two adventurists, Gdlian and Ivanov, and by the investigative groups which they headed. Carefully sensing the new political atmosphere, they adroitly used the growing indignation of the people over the corruption, bribe-taking and embezzling which had drawn into its orbit tens and hundreds of thousands of people. In this regard, a peculiar "championship" belonged to Uzbekistan, where machinations with the records of cotton production allowed even "little people" from the State procurement offices, etc., to squeeze out millions of rubles to be shared with highly-placed bureaucrats who closed their eyes to such crimes. However, Gdlian and Ivanov were not satisfied with finding the actual criminals, they wanted to tarnish all Party and Soviet officials of the republic with accusations that they received or gave bribes; in turn they wanted to show that threads led to Moscow, to "prove" that bribes were given from the Uzbek leaders to members of the Politburo of the Central Committee of the CPSU, and to people who headed judicial bodies of the Soviet Union.

Gdlian and Ivanov built their system of "proof"—fully in the spirit of 1937— only on the confessions of the accused which had been obtained by methods also following Yezhov's traditions, with the exclusion of direct physical torture, which the investigators of the 1980s decided not to employ. Slander and self-slander were forced by threats of execution or of reprisals against the defendants' relatives (many of these relatives were actually arrested, and frequently, whole families), by refusal to provide medical assistance, by sending in cellmates who had beaten people from whom the "necessary" confessions had not been obtained. Widely applying blackmail and intimidation, vulgarity and mockery toward defenseless people, the investigators often forced them (as well as genuine criminals) to write confessions according to dictation or to insert there the "needed" names. Often the transcripts of the interrogations which the accused merely had to sign had been prepared beforehand. In exchange for giving false testimony the arrested were promised freedom and given assurances that they would escape any punishment.

After a careful reinvestigation of the Gdlian cases by a new investigatory group, after expert testimony and the review of the cases in court, fifteen party members arrested by Gdlian-Ivanov were declared innocent. They had all been held in prison from nine months to more than three years.

For their activity in Uzbekistan, Gdlian and Ivanov received promotions and monetary prizes. They spoke out in the press and at "democratic" meetings, and were elected to the Supreme Soviet of the USSR. They organized an even bigger provocation before the Nineteenth All-Union Party Conference (in 1988), when they published a scandalous article in the journal, *Ogonek*, stating that among the delegates to the conference from the Uzbek SSR were "people who had compromised themselves in the field of bribe-taking." Only a year and a half after the article appeared did *Ogonek* list the names of the people, who, it later turned out, had not even been charged, and who had never been questioned.[7]

Returning to the events of the 1930s, let us name one more attempt at an explanation—the version of trial "rehearsals," at which the defendants supposedly denied the charges made against them, but then became convinced of the uselessness of the gesture, since the hall was filled exclusively with NKVD operatives. This version, which served as the basis for the poorly concocted film, "Enemy of the People Bukharin," which appeared during the years of "perestroika," has no foundation in fact. The defendants at the show trials couldn't help but see in the courtroom well-known political figures, journalists, writers, and so forth, as well as famous foreign diplomats and journalists. Thus, they could be certain that if they told the truth, it could not fail to penetrate the walls of the courtroom.

Finally, there is the version presented by A. Koestler, which was carefully developed in his novel, *Darkness at Noon*. According to this version, the defendants were guided by sophisms about the need to "help the party" with their "confessions." Such arguments fill the novel's often-cited "diary" which was kept before the trial by its main character, the Old Bolshevik Rubashov.

If the versions mentioned earlier were politically neutral, then Koestler's version, developed with an artist's sophistication, was sharply tendentious. It proceeds from the existence of a whole "philosophy" which supposedly guided the behavior of the Old Bolsheviks. This "philosophy" was reduced by the author of *Darkness at Noon* to a fetishization of the party and a justification of the most monstrous acts on behalf of this fetish—ranging from unlimited self-degradation to the extermination of millions of innocent people.

The fact that Koestler was close to the communist movement in the 1930s and personally knew several of the defendants at the Moscow Trials facilitated the fact that this version enjoyed people's trust for decades in the West, and then in the USSR, where the book *Darkness at Noon* circulated in the 1960s. As George Orwell noted, in response to the question, "Why did they confess?", Koestler gave the implicit reply: "Because the revolution ruined them." This response was supposed to lead the reader to the conclusion that "the revolution by its very nature includes something negative.... Any efforts to transform society by violent means end in the cellars of the GPU, and Lenin gives birth to Stalin or would himself have begun to resemble Stalin had he lived longer."[8] These ideas were used as weapons by many authors who turned to the theme of the Great Terror—from Koestler and Solzhenitsyn to today's Russian "democrats."

Koestler's book played no small role in the exit of many people in the West from the communist movement and in the strengthening of anti-communist moods among the Soviet intelligentsia.

It is worth noting that all the anti-communist interpreters of the Moscow Trials avoided Trotsky's arguments about the reasons for the defendants' "confessions."

Before beginning an analysis of these arguments, let us note that at all the open trials there were two groups of defendants. One group consisted of accidental people who were chosen from among the thousands of arrested as the most pliable material for confessions. Among the reasons that prompted such defendants to give false confessions, Trotsky named blackmail by the investigators with regard to actual misdeeds they had committed of a criminal or semicriminal nature. "The majority of those shot in the last trial," Trotsky wrote, "were not political figures, but bureaucrats of an average or above average ranking. They had probably committed various mistakes, misdemeanors or perhaps even crimes. The GPU, however, demanded of them confessions to completely different crimes of an historical scale, and then—shot them. Not a single bureaucrat will henceforth feel self-assured or calm. Stalin has dossiers on all somewhat noteworthy political and administrative figures. These dossiers contain records of each and every sin (imprudent dealings with public moneys, amorous adventures, suspicious personal ties, compromised relatives, and so forth). Local satraps keep similar records with regard to their subordinates. At any moment Stalin can bring down and crush any of his colleagues, not excluding members of the Politburo."[9]

Another group of defendants included famous political figures who played leading roles in the oppositions of the 1920s. The number of these people at the first two Moscow Trials was approximately fifteen. Trotsky studied in detail the reasons for the confessions of these defendants in articles dedicated to an analysis of the Moscow Trials.

In one of the first responses to the trials, Trotsky wrote that he did not know and therefore could not say with certainty whether the defendants had been subjected to physical torture or the use of chemical and medical substances which weaken one's willpower. But even without this hypothesis, one could explain why the defendants confessed to nonexistent crimes. For this it was important to first of all turn one's attention to the nature of those whom Stalin ordered to be brought to open trial. Alongside completely unknown people, including known provocateurs who had fallen into the clutches of the NKVD, the defendants' bench included people who had long since broken with the Opposition. "All these were capitulators, people who had recanted several times, who had accused themselves during testimony of the most ignoble actions and filthy intentions; people who had lost any political goal in these confessions, who had lost the meaning of life and any respect for themselves.... For years these internally empty, demoralized, and overstrained ex-revolutionaries were suspended between life and death. Would one additionally need here any specific medications?"[10]

It was enough to know these people and the political atmosphere in the country in order to understand how they were led out of necessity to put the noose around their own necks. The humiliating public recantations which were extorted from them over many years, and which were by no means preceded by physical torture, prepared the "confessions" which were wrested from them at the trials. These recantations bore a "purely ritualistic, standardized character. Their political goal was to teach each and every one to think, or at least to express themselves, in the same way. But precisely for this reason none of the initiated ever took these recantations for good coin. Recantation signifies not a confession, but a contract with the bureaucracy."[11]

Beginning with 1924, every oppositionist, semioppositionist or simply any citizen in disfavor was presented with one demand in order to preserve the right to a piece of bread. He had to "distance himself from Trotskyism and condemn Trotsky; in doing so, the more clamorous and vulgar the denunciation, the better. Everyone grew accustomed to these recantations and denunciations, much like to the automatic rituals of the church."[12] Long before they fell under the millstone of Yezhov's investigations, the main defendants at the Moscow Trials were led to a state of extreme demoralization as a result of their ceaseless confessions to "errors" which lead into the "counterrevolutionary swamp." All these people had renounced themselves several times; they had renounced their own convictions, while heaping praise on Stalin and Stalin's "socialism," the true value of which they knew better than anyone else. "Can an honest person speak of 'confessions,'" Trotsky wrote, "while leaving aside the fact that the GPU had for a number of years prepared and 'educated' the defendants by means of periodic capitulations, acts of self-humiliation, slander, promises, indulgences, persecution and horrifying examples?"[13]

Of course, confessing to political "errors" is still a long way from confessing to terror, espionage, wrecking, a pact with Hitler, and so forth. However, "the GPU had enough time at its disposal to force ever more complete 'confessions' from its victims."[14]

Several of the defendants at the Moscow Trials felt the surveillance of the GPU even while they were members of the Politburo (for example, Bukharin). In the course of unceasing campaigns against "opportunists and double-dealers," they were not only obligated to listen unquestioningly to false charges made against them, but then to publicly confirm these charges. This path logically led them to public confessions at the trials, where they "once again said what could only be said by the most slavish agents of Stalin. Normal people who obey their own will could not conduct themselves during the investigation and trial as Zinoviev, Kamenev, Radek, Piatakov and others conducted themselves. Devotion to their ideas, political dignity, and a simple feeling of self-preservation would force them to fight for themselves, for their individuality, for their interests and for their lives. The only correct and reasonable questions would thus be: who led these people, and how, to a state in which all normal human reflexes are trampled into the ground?"[15]

Hypothetically reconstructing the methods used by the Stalinist inquisitors, Trotsky pointed to their main goal—to link the future defendants collectively by contructing amalgams, that is, by mixing together real and invented facts. "Today A acknowledges a small fact. If B does not confess the same, it means that all of his previous recantations and humiliations were 'insincere' (as an apologist for 'sincerity,' this was Stalin's favorite word). B hurries to confess what A has confessed, and adds a little something extra. Now it is C's turn. In order to avoid contradictions that are too crude, they are given the chance of working out their stories together, if it is advantageous. If D refuses to join in, he risks losing all hopes for salvation. E races ahead in order to show his good will.... The diabolical game continues. The accused are under lock and key. The GPU has time. The GPU also has a Mauser.... If one 'confession' or another turns out in the future to be embarrassing, it is simply discarded as a useless hypothesis." Given such a procedure of interrogations and face-to-face confrontations which break one's will, physical torture might prove to be unnecessary. "The torments of slander, uncertainty and fear destroy the nervous system no less effectively than physical torture."[16]

These psychological means of pressuring the accused were joined by a political means—playing on the military danger which threatened the USSR. In this regard, a certain grain of truth is contained in the "Koestler complex," which was first described by Victor Serge in an article written immediately after the Trial of the Sixteen. Having himself passed through several stages of repression, Serge knew personally several of the defendants of this trial; he also knew the moods and milieu of the capitulators. This is how he described the way the investigators played games with them before the trial:

"You remain, no matter what you have said or done, our irreconcilable opponents. But you are *devoted to the party*, we know this. The party demands from you a new sacrifice which is more complete than all the previous ones: political suicide, the sacrifice of your conscience. You will authenticate this sacrifice by meeting the death penalty halfway. Only in this case will it be possible to believe that you have completely laid down your arms before the Leader. We demand this sacrifice from you because the Republic is in danger. The shadow of war falls upon us, and fascism is rising around us. We must at any price reach Trotsky in his exile, discredit his nascent Fourth International and close ranks in holy unity around the Leader, whom you hate but whom you acknowledge because he is stronger. If you agree, then you may hope for your lives. If you refuse, in one way or another you will disappear."[17]

After Serge, Trotsky described a possible dialogue between investigators and defendants, who long before their arrest had accepted the political formulas used by the Stalinists: "Are you for the homeland (i.e., for Stalin) or against it.... You, of course, have long since recanted, you are no danger to us, you yourselves know that, and we don't wish you any harm. But Trotsky is continuing his ruinous work abroad. He is debunking the USSR (the despotism of the bureaucracy). His influence is growing.... We must once and for all discredit Trotsky. Then the question of you will resolve itself. If you are for the USSR, you will help us. If not, all your recantations were insincere. In view of the imminent war, we will be forced to see you as Trotsky's accomplices and as internal enemies. You must admit that Trotsky prompted you to resort to terror.—But what if no one will believe it?—Leave that side of the matter to us. We have our Duclos and Thorezes, our Pritts and Rosenmarks."[18]

In the course of this outrageous game, some of the defendants, in Trotsky's opinion, not only agreed to collaborate with the investigators, but even helped them to correct the most outlandish aspects of the versions which they would have to present at the trial. Trotsky felt that precisely such a role—as voluntary assistant and "proofreader" for the investigation—was assumed by Radek, who "as a more erudite person apparently demanded to rework the charges." Confirmation of this hypothesis was contained in Radek's testimony that Trotsky proposed to make "concessions" of the Ukraine and the Far East to Germany and Japan, figuring to return these territories after the socialist revolution in the aggressor countries. "The GPU tried to present me as a simple fascist," Trotsky wrote. "In order to lend at least a shade of veracity to the charges, Radek turned me into a potentially revolutionary anti-fascist, but tossed me a 'transitional' plan in the form of a 'temporary' alliance with the fascists and a 'minor' dismemberment of the USSR. Both versions wind throughout the testimony of the defendants: the vulgar provocateur's smear, which originates directly with Stalin, and the complicated military-diplomatic feuilleton à la Radek. These two versions are incompatible. One [Radek's—V. R.] is intended for the educated and 'delicate' 'friends of the USSR' abroad, and the other is for the more mundane workers and peasants in the USSR."[19]

What we have called the "Koestler complex" was seen by Trotsky as only one of the possible motives for the "confessions," capable of influencing only those people who had passed earlier through several stages of self-renunciation. In developing Serge's ideas which assigned great emphasis in the defendants' behavior to their devotion to the party and their respect for its unity, Trotsky wrote: "These people had been spiritually born in the Bolshevik Party, it had shaped them, they fought for it, and it raised them to a gigantic height. But the organization of the masses which had arisen out of an idea, degenerated into an automatic apparatus of the ruling elite. Loyalty to the apparatus became the betrayal of the idea and of the masses. The thinking of the capitulators became hopelessly entangled in this contradiction. They lacked the intellectual freedom and revolutionary courage to break, on behalf of the Bolshevik Party, with those who bore this name. Having capitulated, they betrayed the party on behalf of the unity of the apparatus. The GPU turned the fetish of the party into a garotte, and gradually, without hurrying, tightened it around the necks of the capitulators. During moments of lucidity they could not help but see where this was leading. But the clearer the perspective of moral destruction became, the fewer chances of escaping from the noose remained. If in the first period the fetish of a united party served as the psychological source of the capitulations, then in the last stage the formula of 'unity' served only to cover the convulsive attempts at self-preservation."[20]

The "Koestler complex" can help explain the difference between the behavior of the victims of the Moscow Trials and the behavior of the dissidents from the 1970s and 1980s, who knew quite well that their death in the struggle against the regime was unlikely, and the worst that might happen to them was prison or the camps. But even in that case they expected that foreign governments and world public opinion would fight for their freedom.

However, even a few active dissidents of the 1960s and 1970s (for instance, P. Yakir) spoke at specially organized press conferences and on television with prerehearsed false confessions. Only when hope for freedom and emigration became a reality for the dissidents (as a result of protests by foreign society), did such political renunciation of their past political activity cease.

For the defendants of the 1930s there was no such hope for help from abroad which gave energy to the dissident anti-communists. They could not help but feel the crushing sensation of standing before a mute wall. They had established Soviet power, they had fought for it for long years and now they hoped to preserve at least some of its achievements. This suprapersonal goal stood higher for them than the preservation of their own honor and human dignity.

Finally, the capitulators of the thirties had no "referent group" which for the dissidents of the time of stagnation had been the liberal Soviet intelligentsia, fully aligned on their side. Neither the Stalinists nor the Oppositionists considered the capitulators to be "their own."

Unlike Stalin, who described the Bolsheviks as superhumans ("We communists are people of a special make-up. We are built of special material"; "There are no fortresses in the world which cannot be taken by the workers, the Bolsheviks"[21]), Trotsky often applied Nietzsche's expression to the Bolsheviks: "human, all-too-human." With this expression he had in mind their susceptibility to common human weaknesses and the ability to rationalize, i.e., to justify their abject behavior with supposedly principled motives. If he had noted signs of the "human, all-too-human" among his opponents even when they were in power, then he considered all the more natural such signs when they were in Stalin's prisons. "Perhaps," he wrote, "there are many heroes on the earth who are capable of withstanding all tortures, physical or moral, applied to themselves, their wives and their children. I do not know.... My personal observations tell me that the capacity of human nerves is limited. Through the intervention of the GPU, Stalin can drive his victim into such depths of horror, humiliation, and dishonor that to heap upon oneself the most monstrous crime, with the perspective of unavoidable death or with a slim ray of hope in the future, remains the only escape. If, of course, one doesn't count suicide.... But do not forget that in the prisons of the GPU even suicide often proves to be an unobtainable luxury!"[22]

From letters and personal testimony of his supporters who had passed through Stalin's prisons, Trotsky knew very well that from the end of the 1920s the GPU began to widely use the tortures of sleeplessness, conveyor belt interrogations, and so forth. He could not help but assume that with the transition to the Great Purges such devices had become much crueler. However, he had at his disposal no direct evidence that "measures of physical coercion" had been applied to the victims of the Moscow Trials. Therefore he only indirectly let his readers know that, along with sophisticated psychological pressure, the investigators obtained confessions with the help, too, of inhuman tortures.

Trotsky recalled that the "Inquisition, with much simpler technology, wrenched any confession needed from the accused. Democratic criminal law therefore renounced medieval methods because they led not to the establishment of the truth, but to the simple confirmation of charges dictated by the investigation. The trials of the GPU have all the characteristics of the Inquisition: this is the simple truth behind the confessions."[23] The very fact that the trials used only the confessions of the defendants as court evidence testifies to the return of Stalin's "judiciary" to medieval barbarism. This is sufficient to explain why even Old Bolsheviks and experienced politicians, made, like all people, out of flesh and blood, conducted themselves at the trial like ignorant and illiterate victims of the Inquisition.

At the same time Trotsky stressed that even the official accounts of the trials show what a long and difficult path preceded the shame which the defendants agreed to cast upon themselves at the trial. The transcript of the Trial of the Sixteen, in which the testimony of Smirnov was brazenly abridged and falsely "summarized," nevertheless reveals "a rather clear picture of the tragic struggle of this honest and sincere old revolutionary both with himself and with all the inquisitors."

Less vulnerable, at first glance, were the confessions given by Zinoviev and Kamenev. However, they were completely void of any factual content. "These were agitational speeches and diplomatic notes, but not living human documents. But precisely in this manner they give themselves away. And not only in this manner." The juxtaposition of the confessions from Zinoviev and Kamenev at the Trial of the Sixteen with their confessions in January 1935 and with all their preceding recantations beginning in December 1927 allow one "to establish over the course of nine years a peculiar geometrical progression of capitulations, humiliation and prostration. If one is armed with the mathematical coefficient of this tragic progression, then the confessions at the Trial of the Sixteen arise before us as a mathematically necessary concluding link in a long series."[24]

Of course, in order to convince the defendants to "voluntarily" confess, they were promised their lives in return. But how could the defendants at the second trial believe in this promise when they knew that all their predecessors had been shot after the first trial? Trotsky answered this question in the following way: "The GPU left only a shadow of hope for Radek, Piatakov and the others.—But did you not shoot Zinoviev and Kamenev?—Yes, we shot them because it was necessary, because they were secret enemies; because they refused to confess their ties to the Gestapo, because ... and so forth, and so on. But we have no need to shoot you. You must help us to root out the Opposition once and for all and to compromise Trotsky in the eyes of world public opinion. For this service we will give you your lives. After a certain time we will even return you to work ... etc., etc. Of course, after all that had happened, neither Radek nor Piatakov nor all the others ... could assign great value to such promises. But on the one hand they could expect a certain, inevitable and swift death, while on the other ... on the other was also death, but illuminated with a few sparks of hope. In such instances, people, particularly if they have been trampled, tortured, exhausted, and humiliated, are inclined to seek delay and hope."[25]

The open trials included only those political figures who long before their arrest had publicly emphasized their loyalty to the first commandment of the Stalinist bureaucracy—a furious hatred toward "Trotskyism." Because of their past oppositional activity a "guilt complex" had become reinforced in their consciousness. It was possible to play on this complex in many ways, it could be stirred up in many ways.

The fate of Bukharin and Rykov shows how this was done. Before their arrest, Stalin decided to lead them through a prolonged procedure of new humiliations.

21. Bukharin and Rykov in the Clutches of a "Party Investigation"

In her memoirs, A. M. Larina sketches the following picture of Bukharin's evolution in the months preceding his arrest. After his return from Paris in April 1936, "nothing darkened his moods." Only after he was declared at the Trial of the Sixteen an accomplice of the conspirators did he begin to perceive the terror unfolding in the country as "an unprecedented absurdity."[1]

After the December Plenum, a furious slander campaign was launched against Bukharin and Rykov. The press falsified their entire past political activity, beginning with the first years of their membership in the party, the period of underground and emigration. Despite the fact that *Izvestiia* stood at the forefront of this slander campaign, the newspaper continued until 16 January 1937 to appear under Bukharin's signature as main editor. This gave grounds for Trotsky and Sedov to write that Bukharin was demanding his own head in the pages of *Izvestiia*.

In the period preceding the next plenum of the Central Committee, which was supposed to return to an examination of the Bukharin and Rykov case, interrogations of their former cothinkers continued in the torture chambers of the NKVD. Among those who gave testimony against Bukharin and Rykov were the former secretary of the Moscow Party Committee, Kotov, Rykov's former secretaries, Nesterov and Radin, and the majority of Bukharin's former disciples. Yezhov immediately sent the transcripts of the interrogations to Stalin. From Stalin they then were sent as material for the future plenum to members and candidate members of the Central Committee, including Bukharin and Rykov. In the period between the plenums, about sixty such transcripts were distributed.

Rykov was particularly stunned by the testimony of his former secretary, Ekaterina Artemenko, who was considered virtually a member of his family. She said that he had given her instructions to conduct surveillance of Stalin's automobile in order to organize a terrorist act.[2]

The tactics chosen by Bukharin and Rykov in this period were not identical. In the 1950s, members of the Party Control Commission who were investigating their cases discovered in Stalin's archive no small number of letters from Bukharin with refutations of the slander made against him. At this time, not a single such letter was found from Rykov, who evidently recognized the uselessness of any appeals to Stalin.[3]

According to A. M. Larina, during these months Bukharin's moods changed not only daily but even hourly. At times he made a sober assessment of the character of the events unfolding and their further development. Soon after the December Plenum, he said to his wife about the Central Committee members: "Perhaps the time will come when they will all prove to be unwelcome witnesses to these crimes and will also be destroyed." Reading the testimony sent to him, he said: "This smells of grandiose bloodletting. They will imprison those who were nowhere near Aleksei and me!"; "I am overwhelmed by the horror of foreseeing a terror on an enormous scale." But some time would pass and Bukharin would regain the hope that Stalin would "save" him. At such moments he sent Stalin another letter which began with the words, "Dear Koba!"[4] In a letter from 15 December 1936, Bukharin complained to Stalin: "My morale is in such a state that I am half-alive.... I am dying because of scoundrels, human scum, and despicable villains."[5]

Particularly tortuous for Bukharin and Rykov were the face-to-face confrontations with their former comrades and colleagues. In such a confrontation with Shmidt, Rykov was so shaken that, according to Yezhov, "he clutched his heart, began to run about the room, and pounded his head against the glass."[6]

On 13 January 1937, Bukharin and Rykov were brought face-to-face with Astrov, with Stalin and other members of the Politburo in attendance. Out of all the false witnesses, Astrov won Stalin's particular approval. This apparently can be explained by the fact that Astrov turned out to be the only one of Bukharin's disciples who expressed the readiness to affirm his slanderous testimony to Bukharin's face. As Astrov told the author of this book on 1 May 1993, during the face-to-face confrontation, Stalin turned to Bukharin and said: "What a fine fellow you've ruined for us."

At the confrontation, Astrov said that in the spring of 1932 the "center" of the illegal organization of rightists decided to adopt the tactic of terror. He confirmed Kulikov's testimony that the Riutin Platform had been written by Bukharin, Rykov, Tomsky and Uglanov, and claimed that "Bukharin and Rykov continued to belong to the center of Rightists, remaining at their earlier positions."[7]

In preparing Astrov for the face-to-face encounter, the investigators were particularly stubborn in extracting testimony from him about an illegal conference of "Rightists" which occurred in August–September 1932. Such a conference actually did take place at that time, but Astrov could say very little about it insofar as he participated in only one meeting of former Bukharin supporters in 1932, a meeting which occurred at his apartment. There, in response to a statement by several of his comrades that Stalin should be "removed by force," Astrov declared that he had no intention of participating in any struggle against Stalin. Once they became convinced that this was indeed Astrov's position, the oppositionally inclined "Young Rightists" apparently decided to not include him any more in such discussions which continued at other locations. As Astrov recalled, the investigator in 1933 asked him about the "conference" which occurred in Pokrovsko-Streshnevo and other regions in and around Moscow. Astrov had no information about it.[8] Judging from the material of the investigation of 1933 into the case of the "Bukharin school," and from Bukharin's statements when he was at liberty, Bukharin too knew nothing about this conference; by this time he was refusing to meet with his former pupils.

The subsequent fate of Astrov is noteworthy; he had become a secret agent of the GPU in 1933. He proved to be the sole participant in the "Bukharin school" who not only avoided the death penalty, but who was freed in 1937 on Stalin's personal instructions. His dossier contains Yezhov's resolution: "Set free. Leave in Moscow. Give an apartment and work in history."[9]

In 1949, like many other former oppositionists, Astrov was once again arrested. Having served a seven-year sentence in prison, he was freed in 1956, after which he began vigorously to try to be readmitted into the party. In statements directed along these lines to the Party Control Commission, he said that the "Rightists" had prepared neither a coup, nor terrorist acts, but had simply made separate critical remarks about Stalin's policies.

In the investigation of the case of the "Right-Trotskyist Bloc" at the beginning of the 1960s, Astrov declared that in 1932–1933, the GPU investigators obtained from him "only" the requalification of "oppositional" guilt into "anti-Soviet." The Central Control Commission, which expelled him from the party, also demanded similar testimony from him. "All this combined to morally disarm me," Astrov stated, "and I signed testimony about the counterrevolutionary character of the 'organization of Rightists,' after receiving a three-year prison sentence (in a political prison) from the OGPU Collegium." After his second arrest in 1936, however, the investigation "was intensified by the extreme sharpening of the political situation.... In such conditions, the terrorism of the Rightists became an irrefutable thesis, a position which was personally confirmed to me on behalf of the party by the People's Commissar Yezhov (who was secretary of the Central Committee and, if I am not mistaken, also chairman of the Central Control Commission at that time). This position stripped away any moral stimulus I had to resist the demands of the investigators. Protecting at any cost the members of the Central Committee and the Soviet government from possible attacks on their lives by terrorists who had penetrated the party became for me an imperative necessity, and I gave testimony about the terrorist character of the Rightist organization, without separating myself from them.... Having said 'a', I had to say 'b.' They brought me face-to-face with Bukharin; I confirmed the terrorism of the Rightists, whereas he denied it."[10]

In the 1960s–1980s, Astrov engaged in literary activity. Among his works, the most interesting is the novella, "Krucha" [Steep Slope], which describes "the struggle against Trotskyism" in the 1920s. Depicting this struggle in the spirit of its official interpretation of the 1960s, Astrov presents himself and other participants of the "Bukharin school" under assumed names, but Stalin, Bukharin, Kamenev, Radek and other leading political figures of the time are presented under their own names. It is worth noting that "Krucha" was the only work of the "pre-perestroika" period in which the personality of Bukharin was presented in a rather objective light and even with a certain degree of sympathy.

After Bukharin's rehabilitation in 1988, Astrov published several articles in which he justified his provocateur's behavior during the 1930s by referring to his "loyalty to the party." He explains that he was freed in 1937 because Stalin knew that even before the Fourteenth Congress of the VKP(b) in December 1925 he had broken with Bukharin because of the latter's desire to 'get along with Trotsky in the party.' After that, according to Astrov, he no longer considered himself a disciple of Bukharin, but was incorrectly credited with being in the "Bukharin school" by "Zinovievist oppositionists."[11]

While he was awaiting arrest, Bukharin burned a note he had from Stalin which he had accidentally discovered in 1928 after a session of the Politburo. It read: "We must destroy Bukharin's disciples." According to Larina, in 1937

Bukharin was inclined to think that this note referred not to political, but to physical, destruction.[12]

At one of the confrontations, Stalin raised the question of a "crime" which Bukharin had committed in the distant past. He accused Bukharin of intending to enter into a bloc in 1918 with the Left Social-Revolutionaries and to arrest Lenin. Bukharin replied that the proposal to arrest Lenin for a while and to form a government of Left SR's and "Left Communists"—opponents of the Brest Peace Treaty—was actually made to him by the Left SR leaders; he responded with a decisive refusal and then told Lenin about the episode. Lenin made him swear to tell no one about it. Later Bukharin recalled that the given episode became known only because in 1923, during the party discussion, he broke his oath: "When I was fighting alongside you against Trotsky, I gave this as an example of what a factional struggle might lead to. At the time, it was a bombshell."[13]

The trial of the "Anti-Soviet Trotskyist Center" became a new and bitter experience for Bukharin and Rykov. The defendants claimed that Bukharin, Rykov and Tomsky entered into contact with the Trotskyist "centers" while maintaining their own organization. According to the defendants, all three illegal "centers" had a joint political platform, which had been outlined in the "Riutin Program."

In his concluding word, Radek spoke about "one more fault" which he had: "Although I had already confessed my guilt and unmasked our organization, I stubbornly refused to give testimony about Bukharin. I knew that Bukharin's position was just as hopeless as mine, because our guilt, if not juridically, then in essence, was the same. But he and I are close friends, and intellectual friendship is stronger than any other friendship. I knew that Bukharin was in the same state of shock as I, and I was certain that he would give honest testimony to the Soviet regime. I therefore did not want to deliver him with bound hands to the People's Commissar of Internal Affairs. I also wanted him to be able to lay down his arms, just like our other cadres. This explains why it was only toward the end, when I saw that the trial was fast approaching, that I understood that I could not appear at the trial while concealing the existence of another terrorist organization."[14]

Bukharin approached the trial of the "Trotskyist center" primarily from the standpoint of its consequences for his own fate. As for the lenient sentence given to Sokolnikov and Radek, he explained that "they had earned their lives by slandering him." Nevertheless, even after this trial Bukharin doubted that "Koba would hold a third medieval frame-up trial before the whole world."[15]

After the trial the newspapers began to publish many resolutions from "workers' meetings" which demanded another trial and severe reprisals against Bukharin and Rykov. Soon they received information about the upcoming plenum of the Central Committee, whose agenda included a review of their "case." During these days, as N. A. Rykova recalls, her father often entertained thoughts of suicide. Standing by the window of his apartment in the government house on Granovsky Street, he told her: "If you were to fall out, nothing would be left of you."[16]

Unlike Rykov, who at the end of 1936 had been moved out of the Kremlin, Bukharin and his family continued to live in their Kremlin apartment. A few days before the plenum was to begin, three Chekists appeared at this apartment with an order to evict Bukharin. Immediately after they arrived, the telephone rang: for the first time in several months, Stalin was calling Bukharin to find out about how he was feeling. Bukharin, who was quite distraught, told Stalin that they were getting ready to evict him. In reply, Stalin advised him to tell his visitors to "go to hell." Understanding from Bukharin's responses who was on the other end of the line, the Chekists immediately disappeared. Bukharin unexpectedly received one more ray of hope.

A few days before the plenum, Bukharin learned from his wife about her chance meeting with Ordzhonikidze, who sympathetically told her: "You must be strong!" Interpreting these words as an expression of indirect support, Bukharin wrote a letter to Ordzhonikidze. In it he stated that such a powerful force was at work in the NKVD that he would not be able to understand it until he found himself in the prison torture chambers. "I am beginning to fear," Bukharin added, "that, in the event of my arrest, I, too, might end up in the same position as Piatakov, Radek, Sokolnikov, Muralov and others. Farewell, dear Sergo. You must believe that all my intentions have been honest. I have been honest no matter what may happen to me in the future."[17]

The letter did not reach its addressee, since Larina waited for a few days before sending it. Then came news of Ordzhonikidze's death.

22. The Death of Ordzhonikidze

AT THE BEGINNING of 1937, Ordzhonikidze's position in the party and state hierarchy seemed to be very secure. On 24 October 1936, his fiftieth birthday was celebrated to the accompaniment of many greetings and reports, as well as the renaming of cities, factories, collective farms, etc., in his honor. Ordzhonikidze's name always figured as one of the first among Stalin's "closest comrades-in arms." An even more important sign of Stalin's trust was the mention of Ordzhonikidze's name at the two Moscow Trials among the seven to ten leaders against whom the "Trotskyists" had prepared terrorist attacks.

During all this, Ordzhonikidze was distinguished from the other Kremlin leaders, who had turned into faceless bureaucrats and unquestioning executors of Stalin's will, by such qualities as sincerity, democratism, loyalty to his comrades, and irreconcilability to falsehood and hypocrisy. These vestigial Bolshevik qualities can in large part be explained by Ordzhonikidze's more weighty revolutionary past than among other "comrades-in-arms." Lenin could not have said about any other member of Stalin's Politburo what he said in one of his last works about Ordzhonikidze: " ... I personally belong to his circle of friends and worked with him abroad in emigration."[1]

Clouds began to gather over Ordzhonikidze's head after Piatakov's arrest. Before then, Ordzhonikidze had managed to defend the personnel of his People's Commissariat both in Moscow and in the provinces from unjust accusations and repressions. During the exchange of party documents (spring–summer 1936), out of eight hundred twenty-three people who belonged to the nomenklatura at the People's Commissariat of Heavy Industry, only eleven people were removed from work, out of whom nine were expelled from the party and arrested. Over the last four months of 1936, however, forty-four senior officials were removed from their posts. Thirty-seven of these were expelled from the party and thirty-four arrested. In a file at the department of leading party cadres under the Central Committee where these data were gathered, sixty-six names of nomenklatura staff were also listed who "in the past

I. Stalin and
S. Ordzhonikidze during
their reception of the
Georgian delegation,
March 1936

participated in the opposition and demonstrated vacillation," i.e., who were candidates for future purges. A document prepared by the commissariat's directorate of affairs lists one hundred sixty officials at the central apparatus of the Commissariat of Heavy Industry who in the past had been expelled from the party; ninety-four had been tried for "counterrevolutionary activity."[2]

During the days when his jubilee was being celebrated, Ordzhonikidze was vacationing at Kislovodsk. There he received news about the arrest in Georgia of his older brother Papulii. This was the first instance of the arrest of a close relative of a member of the Politburo (in the future, such arrests would affect virtually all the families of Stalin's "comrades-in-arms"). Ordzhonikidze demanded that Beria keep him informed about Papulii's case, and allow him to meet with his brother. However Beria promised to do this only after the investigation had finished, and then deliberately dragged out the proceedings.

A number of important eyewitness accounts have survived about Ordzhonikidze's moods in the months leading up to his death. In 1966, Mikoyan wrote: "Sergo ... reacted sharply against the repression which had begun in 1936 against party and economic cadres."[3] A more concrete recollection was given by S. Z. Ginzburg, one of Ordzhonikidze's few colleagues who survived: in the mid-1930s, the personnel at the Commissariat of Heavy Industry began to notice that Ordzhonikidze, who was usually cheerful and even-tempered, ever more frequently returned from sessions "up above" in a pensive or despondent mood. "At times, he would exclaim: no, I will not agree with this under any circumstances!" recalled Ginzburg. "I did not know what exactly was being discussed, and of course did not ask any indiscreet questions. But sometimes Sergo asked me about this or that staff member and I was able to guess that apparently 'up there' a discussion was under way about the fate of these people."[4]

At the July Plenum of the Central Committee in 1953, which examined the Beria case, several members of the Politburo told about Beria's intrigues in relation to Ordzhonikidze. "I remember," said Voroshilov, "how at one time, and this is well known to both Comrades Molotov and Kaganovich and in particular the Tbilisi-Georgians, especially those who are here today, what a foul role Beria played in the life of the wonderful communist, Sergo Ordzhonikidze. He did everything possible to slander and discredit this truly crystalline pure person before Stalin. Sergo Ordzhonikidze told not only me, but other comrades too, terrible things about this man."[5] A similar version was outlined by Andreev: "Beria set Comrade Stalin and Ordzhonikidze against each other, and Comrade Sergo's noble heart could not bear this; thus Beria took out of commission one of the best leaders of the party and one of Comrade Stalin's best friends."[6] Mikoyan described how a few days before his death Ordzhonikidze told him in a confidential conversation: "I do not understand why Stalin does not trust me. I am absolutely loyal to him, I don't want to fight with him, I want to support him, but he does not trust me. Here a big role is being played by Beria's intrigues; he gives Stalin incorrect information, and Stalin believes him."[7]

It is not difficult to see that in all these contributions the accent is placed on Ordzhonikidze's boundless devotion to Stalin, and Ordzhonikidze's death is explained—in the spirit of the Stalinist version of 1937—by the fact that his "heart could not bear it" (it is true that this time it was not the news about "Trotskyist" treachery that it could not bear, but Beria's intrigues). The exaggeration of Beria's role in Ordzhonikidze's death was caused primarily by the fact that "Stalin's heirs," who had arrested Beria out of fear for their own security, at first did not know exactly what charges they should lodge against him. In these circumstances, reference to Beria's intrigues against Ordzhonikidze, whose memory was still highly revered among the people, seemed to be the most appropriate solution. While deciding not to speak about the actual reasons for the conflict between Stalin and Ordzhonikidze, the members of the Politburo explained them by referring to Beria's machinations. Such a version corresponded to the line of Stalin's successors at that time: attributing Stalin's crimes to Beria (who, of course, had no few crimes of his own). "In 1953, we created, to put it bluntly, a version about Beria's role, that supposedly Beria was fully responsible for the abuses which were committed under Stalin," Khrushchev would later recall. " ... At that time we still could not free ourselves from the idea that Stalin was a friend to all, the father of the people, a genius, and so forth. It was impossible to immediately imagine that Stalin was a monster and a murderer.... We were captives to this version which we had created in the interests of rehabilitating Stalin: god was not guilty, but his saints, who poorly reported to god, and therefore god sent down hail and thunder and other calamities.... If the people were to learn that the party [by this Khrushchev—fully in the Stalinist tradition—had in mind the party apparatus and in particular the ruling elite—V. R.] is guilty, then that would be the end of the party* ... We were then still prisoners of the dead Stalin and ... gave the party and the people incorrect explanations by blaming everything on Beria. To us, he seemed to be the appropriate figure for this. We did everything to protect Stalin, although we were protecting a criminal and a murderer, for we still had not freed ourselves from our adoration of Stalin."[8†]

Given all this, the version about hostile relations between Ordzhonikidze and Beria rested on real foundations. Although Ordzhonikidze stood immeasurably higher in the party hierarchy than Beria, he was unable in 1932 to prevent the latter's promotion by Stalin to the post of leader of the Trans-Caucasus

---

* This confession, unintentionally wrested from Khrushchev, explains both the half-hearted character of the criticism of Stalin's crimes (stubbornly called "mistakes" in the official propaganda) during the "thaw" years, and the placing of a taboo on further exposés of Stalin during the period of "stagnation," and finally, the utter collapse of the party's authority after the return to these exposés during "perestroika." If the first and second generations of Stalin's heirs had proven capable of consistently developing the line of the Twentieth Party Congress concerning destalinization, the history of our country and of the international communist movement might have developed in a fundamentally different manner.

† Here Khrushchev wrongly credits other Stalinist satraps with "freeing themselves" from adoration of Stalin. However, neither Molotov nor Kaganovich nor Voroshilov ever agreed to recognize Stalin as a murderer.

party organization. The fact that Ordzhonikidze did not want such a promotion for Beria is reported in the memoirs of Ginzburg and A. V. Snegov—one of the leading officials of the Trans-Caucasus Regional Committee in the 1930s. Ginzburg also recalls that Ordzhonikidze's negative attitude toward Beria "in subsequent years deepened, and Sergo did not conceal this."[9]

Similar evidence is contained in a number of investigatory dossiers from the 1930s–1950s. M. Zvontsov, the former second secretary of the Kabardino-Balkarsky district committee who was arrested in 1938, described at his interrogation a discussion between Betal Kalmykov, the leader of the party organization in this republic, and Ordzhonikidze: "Betal asked the question: 'Comrade Sergo, how long will this scoundrel head the Trans-Caucasus Party Organization?' Sergo replied: 'Someone still trusts him. Time will pass and he will expose himself.'"[10]

During the investigation of Beria's case, Bagirov, the first secretary of the Central Committee of the Communist Party of Azerbaidzhan, said that in 1936, Ordzhonikidze questioned him in depth about Beria and spoke of the latter in sharply negative terms. From these conversations it was clear that "Ordzhonikidze already understood the treachery and lack of sincerity shown by Beria ... who had decided to discredit Ordzhonikidze by any means possible."

Beria's hatred for Ordzhonikidze was described by other close cohorts of Beria. "I knew," testified Sharia, "that on the surface Beria thought well of Ordzhonikidze, but in reality he said all kinds of despicable things about him to his circle of confidants." "In my presence, and that of other people," said Goglidze, "Beria uttered some sharply disrespectful comments about Sergo Ordzhonikidze.... I got the impression that Beria was saying this as a result of some personal malice toward Ordzhonikidze and was stirring up others against him."[11]

After Ordzhonikidze's death, Beria made reprisals not only against his older brother, but other relatives as well. In May 1941, Konstantin Ordzhonikidze, Sergo's younger brother, was arrested on Beria's orders. After a three-year investigation, which yielded nothing, he was sentenced by a Special Board to five years of solitary confinement in prison. Later, Beria signed two more directives which prolonged Konstantin Ordzhonikidze's length of imprisonment; the second of these was signed after Stalin's death.

Of course, Beria's intrigues alone cannot explain either Ordzhonikidze's death or his depressed and despondent mood during the last days of his life. In his report to the Twentieth Party Congress, Khrushchev sharply shifted the emphasis in explaining the relations between Stalin, Ordzhonikidze, and Beria. After declaring that "Ordzhonikidze impeded Beria in carrying out his bloody plans ... he was always against Beria, and told Stalin about it," Khrushchev then added unequivocally: "Instead of investigating and taking the necessary measures, Stalin allowed the annihilation of Ordzhonikidze's brother, and led Ordzhonikidze himself to such a state that the latter was forced to shoot himself."[12]

In his memoirs, Khrushchev repeatedly presents a version of Ordzhonikidze's last conversation with Mikoyan which significantly differs from the account given by Mikoyan himself in 1953. In this version, Beria's role is not mentioned when explaining the reasons why Ordzhonikidze felt that the political situation at the time was hopeless. According to Khrushchev, after Stalin's death Mikoyan told him Ordzhonikidze declared that he "could not go on living; he could not fight against Stalin, and he did not have the strength to tolerate what he was doing."[13] At another point in his memoirs, Khrushchev stressed that Ordzhonikidze said to Mikoyan: "Stalin did not trust him; the cadres which he had selected had almost all been destroyed."[14]

Khrushchev's account of Ordzhonikidze's passive suffering is contradicted by evidence of quite another character. In 1937, M. Orakhelashvili, one of the oldest Georgian Bolsheviks and one of Ordzhonikidze's closest friends, testified at his investigation: "I made slanderous remarks about Stalin as the party's dictator, and I considered his politics to be excessively harsh. In this regard, Sergo Ordzhonikidze had a major influence on me; in 1936, when he was talking with me about Stalin's attitude toward the leaders of the Leningrad Opposition at that time (Zinoviev, Kamenev, Yevdokimov, Zalutsky), he said that, with his extreme cruelty, Stalin was leading the party to a split and in the end would drive the nation into a blind alley.... In general I must say that the reception room in Ordzhonikidze's apartment, and on weekends his dacha ... were often the locations of gatherings by participants in our counterrevolutionary organization. While waiting for Sergo Ordzhonikidze, they conducted the most candid, counterrevolutionary conversations, which by no means ended even when Ordzhonikidze himself would appear."[15] If we cleanse the testimony of the expressions "counterrevolutionary" and "slanderous," which were usually written into the transcripts of the interrogations by the investigators, then we

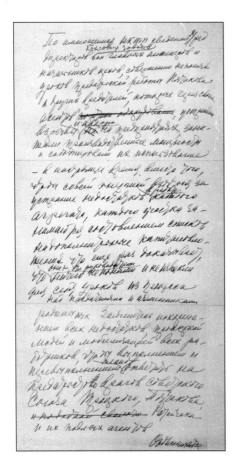

Draft of a telegram by S. Ordzhonikidze to directors of coke factories, 1937

can form an adequate conception of the moods shared by Ordzhonikidze and his closest friends in the mid-1930s.

Stalin himself described of his conflicts with Ordzhonikidze at the February-March Plenum of the Central Committee. According to him, Ordzhonikidze "suffered from the following illness: he would become attached to someone, declare those people personally loyal to him and get along with them, despite the warnings from the party, from the Central Committee [Stalin at that time was used to identifying the party and the CC with himself—V. R.].... How much effort he wasted in order to defend people who are now clearly seen to be scoundrels [Stalin then named Ordzhonikidze's comrades at work in the Trans-Caucasus, whom Ordzhonikidze had defended against slanderous attacks and persecution—V. R.].... How much of his own time he wasted, and how much of ours." Stalin was particularly malicious in speaking about relations between Ordzhonikidze and Lominadze, one of the leaders of the so-called "right-left bloc." Asserting that "Comrade Sergo knew more than any of us" about Lominadze's "mistakes," Stalin announced that in 1926–1928 Ordzhonikidze had received letters "of an anti-Party character" from Lominadze, yet he only told Stalin "eight or nine years after these letters had been written"[16] (all these references to Ordzhonikidze were crossed out by Stalin when the report was readied for printing).

In the last months of his life, Ordzhonikidze repeatedly spoke of the loyalty of the commanders of industry whom he had fostered and of the engineering and technical personnel in general; he said they were loyal to the Soviet regime and defended them from accusations of "sabotage." As he received information about such public statements by Ordzhonikidze, Stalin might have assumed that at the upcoming Plenum of the CC Ordzhonikidze would oppose further reprisals against economic leaders. In order to avoid such an outcome, he had to stir up guilt feelings in Ordzhonikidze because he had harbored "unmasked traitors": Piatakov, Rataichak and others. Stalin was trying to bind Ordzhonikidze, as well as other members of the Politburo, with a bloody guarantee of mutual responsibility, and therefore placed on the agenda of the Central Committee Plenum his report about sabotage in heavy industry. The draft of the resolution on this report, which was presented by Ordzhonikidze, was covered with Stalin's many remarks and comments. He demanded that Ordzhonikidze "speak more sharply" about sabotage and make the center of the report the proposition that economists "must have a very clear conception of the friends and enemies of the Soviet regime."[17]

On his part, Ordzhonikidze prepared an extremely serious countermaneuver. In the draft of the resolution, which he wrote, he included the following point: "To instruct the People's Commissariat of Heavy Industry to report to the Central Committee within ten days about the state of the construction of the Kemerovo chemical combine, the Ural Railcar Enterprise and the Mid-Ural Copper Site, noting the concrete measures taken to liquidate at these building sites the consequences of wrecking and sabotage in order to guarantee the readiness of these enterprises according to the established deadlines."[18] He was referring here to enterprises at which, according to material from the trial of the "Anti-Soviet Trotskyist Center," sabotage had reached a particularly wide scale.

Ordzhonikidze wanted to receive the plenum's sanction for the verification of the situation at these locations, a process already begun at his instigation by people from his commissariat. As he sent a commission to Kemerovo on 5 February, he gave instructions to its chairman, Professor N. Gelperin, to conduct an objective investigation of the facts concerning "sabotage" which had been made public at the trial. In doing so, he used rather cautious formulations. "Keep in mind," Ordzhonikidze said, " that you are traveling to a place which was one of the more active sabotage centers.... Remember that cowardly or insufficiently honest people might be tempted to attribute everything to sabotage, in order, let us say, to submerge their own mistakes in the sabotage trial. It would be fundamentally incorrect to allow this.... You must approach this case as a technical specialist; try to distinguish between conscious sabotage and involuntary mistakes—this is your main assignment."[19]

Gelperin's commission returned to Moscow and prepared a detailed report which did not contain the word "sabotage" even once. Ordzhonikidze managed to receive a similar report from a commission headed by his deputy, Osipov-Shmidt, which investigated the state of the coke industry in the Donbass.

A third commission, which traveled to the construction site of the railway car factory in Nizhny Tagil, was led by the Deputy People's Commissar Pavlunovsky and the head of the Main Construction Industry, Ginzburg. In the middle of February, Ordzhonikidze telephoned Tagil and asked Ginzburg what state the construction was in, and what crimes had been discovered by the commission. Ginzburg answered that the quality of the work at the Ural Railway Car Factory was much higher than at other construction sites in the Urals, "the factory has been solidly built, without any corners being cut, although there were some small overexpenditures in various parts of the financial estimate. At the present time, the construction is at a standstill, and the workers are dismayed."[20] Then Ordzhonikidze asked Ginzburg and Pavlunovsky to return immediately to Moscow and to prepare a note along the way about the status of things at the Ural Railway Car construction site.

When he had returned to Moscow on the morning of 18 February, Ginzburg immediately telephoned Ordzhonikidze and learned from his wife that he had asked several times whether Ginzburg and Pavlunovsky had returned yet. Zinaida Gavrilovna said that Ordzhonikidze was now resting, and asked the leaders of the commission to go to Ordzhonikidze's dacha, where they would soon be joined by her husband.

G. K.
Ordzhonikidze
lying in state,
February 1937

The activity of Ordzhonikidze on the previous day, 17 February, was re-
constructed by a number of investigators on the basis of surviving documents
and eyewitness accounts. From three o'clock in the afternoon, Ordzhonikidze
participated in a session of the Politburo, which discussed drafts of the resolutions for the upcoming Central Committee Plenum. In the evening he went to
the People's Commissariat, where he talked with Gelperin and Osipov-Shmidt.

While Ordzhonikidze was at the Commissariat, a search was conducted of
his apartment. When he found out about this, Ordzhonikidze immediately telephoned Stalin and expressed his indignation. Stalin said in reply: "It's such an
organ, that it might carry out a search at my place. Nothing to get upset about...."
The next morning, Ordzhonikidze had a tête-à-tête discussion with Stalin. After Ordzhonikidze returned home, there was one more telephone conversation
with Stalin—"it was angry and uncontrolled, with mutual insults and recriminations in both Russian and Georgian."[21]

Meanwhile, Ginzburg did not wait for Ordzhonikidze to come to the dacha;
he returned to the commissariat. From there he was soon summoned, along
with other leading members of the People's Commissariat of Heavy Industry,
to Ordzhonikidze's apartment. There he found Stalin and other members of
the Politburo by the bedside of the dead Ordzhonikidze. Stalin distinctly said:
"Sergo worked to the point of exhaustion with a sick heart, and his heart could
not take the strain."

After Stalin's death, Ordzhonikidze's wife told people close to her that when
Stalin was leaving the apartment, he sharply warned her: "Not a single word to
anyone about the details of Sergo's death. Nothing, except the official announce-

Stalin standing beside
Ordzhonikidze's coffin, 1937

Funeral of S.
Ordzhonikidze,
Moscow, 1937

ment, for you know me."[22]

An official statement, signed by the People's Commissar of Health, Kaminsky, and several Kremlin doctors, indicated that Ordzhonikidze "had suddenly died from paralysis of the heart during a daytime nap."[23] All of the people who signed the statement about the cause of death were soon shot.

Any sophisticated person cannot help but notice the close proximity in time of three events: the completion of the trial of the "Trotskyist center," Ordzhonikidze's sudden death, and the February-March Plenum. The plenum's opening, which was originally scheduled for February 20, was postponed for three days because of Ordzhonikidze's funeral. Even during the funeral, a version was circulated linking Ordzhonikidze's death with his shock over the "betrayal" of Piatakov and other "Trotskyists." In his speech at the funeral meeting, Molotov declared: "The enemies of our people, the Trotskyist degenerates, have hastened Ordzhonikidze's death. Comrade Ordzhonikidze never expected that the Piatakovs could stoop so low."[24]

This version, which was widely circulated, made its way even into the article about Ordzhonikidze placed in the "Great Soviet Encyclopedia": "The Trotskyist-Bukharinist degenerates of fascism hated Ordzhonikidze with a bitter hatred. They wanted to kill Ordzhonikidze. The fascist agents failed to do this. But the wrecking activity, the monstrous treachery of the despised right-Trotskyist hirelings of Japanese-German fascism in many ways hastened Ordzhonikidze's death."[25]

In his memoirs, Khrushchev stated that in 1937 he did not know the true cause of Ordzhonikidze's death. According to Khrushchev, he learned about Ordzhonikidze's suicide only after the war, from Malenkov, who in turn had learned about it from a fortuitous conversation with Stalin.[26] Khrushchev's statement is plausible: Stalin could have ordered his closest cohorts—members of the Politburo—to conceal information about Ordzhonikidze's suicide even from "rank-and-file" members of the Central Committee and other high-ranking apparatchiks.

The version of Ordzhonikidze's suicide entered into the conception contained in Khrushchev's report that it was impossible for Stalin's "closest comrades" to oppose his dictates. Ordzhonikidze's suicide was presented by Khrushchev as a peculiar act of personal courage, an expression of the wish not to share in Stalin's crimes.

The version of Ordzhonikidze's suicide was also acknowledged by Molotov, who assessed this event with the insolence and dullness of a fervent Stalinist. Molotov saw the greatest misfortune in the fact that with his death Ordzhonikidze "had put Stalin in a very difficult position." In conversations with Chuyev, Molotov described and characterized Ordzhonikidze's last act in the following way: Ordzhonikidze's brother "spoke out against Soviet power, there was reliable material against him. Stalin ordered his arrest. Sergo got upset. And then he killed himself at home. He found an easy way out [*sic!*—V. R.]. He was thinking about himself. What kind of a leader were you?! ... With his last step he showed that he was nevertheless unstable. It was an act against Stalin, of course. And against the [party] line, yes, against the line. It was a step that was very bad. It couldn't be interpreted otherwise...."

"When Sergo shot himself, Stalin was very angry at him?" (Chuyev asks). "Absolutely," Molotov answers.[27]

There is evidence that Molotov made his own contribution to Ordzhonikidze's persecution. At the June Plenum of the Central Committee in 1957, Rudenko, the General Prosecutor of the USSR, stated that during the investigation of the Beria case, Voroshilov told him: "You should begin to dig around with regard to Sergo Ordzhonikidze; they hounded him, and it is no secret that Viacheslav Mikhailovich [Molotov], when he was chairman of the Sovnarkom, behaved incorrectly toward the deceased."[28]

There are some accounts which call into question the version of Ordzhonikidze's suicide. According to a number of people close to him, during the last days of his life Ordzhonikidze was very energetic and showed no signs whatsoever of depression that would lead to suicide. As Ginzburg stressed, everyone who knew Ordzhonikidze well, "whoever knew his acts, intentions, and plans, particularly towards the end, when he was preparing for the upcoming Plenum of the CC, could not possibly entertain even the thought of his suicide. ... He was assiduously preparing ... to speak out decisively against the mass slaughter of party cadres, of the leaders of industry and construction."[29]

In his memoirs, Ginzburg cites a note addressed to him by his former co-worker at the People's Commissariat of Heavy Industry, V. N. Sidorova. In it she relates facts which were told to her under great secrecy by Zinaida Gavrilovna [Ordzhonikidze's wife]. In the early afternoon on 18 February, a man whom she did not know came to Ordzhonikidze's apartment and said that he must personally deliver to Ordzhonikidze a folder containing Politburo documents. A few minutes after he appeared in Ordzhonikidze's study, a shot

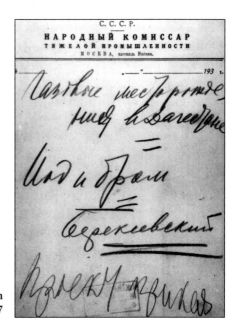

Last entry by G. K. Ordzhonikidze on his notepad at work, 17 February 1937

rang out. Before the man had arrived, Ordzhonikidze had engaged in a sharp telephone conversation with Stalin in the Georgian language.[30]

Several facts recounted by Ginzburg describe Stalin's attitude toward Ordzhonikidze after the latter's death. Thus, all efforts by Ordzhonikidze's comrades to see that the government decree ordering a monument to him be carried out ran up against mute opposition. After the war, Stalin was presented with a list of monuments which had been slated for construction in Moscow. From this list, Stalin crossed out only one name—Ordzhonikidze.[31]

23. Two Letters from Bukharin

THE NEWS OF Ordzhonikidze's death was met with particular anguish in the families of Bukharin and Rykov. When Rykov's wife learned about it, she cried out: "Our last hope!" and fell to the floor, unconscious.[1] Languishing in isolation and inactivity, Bukharin wrote a poem devoted to Ordzhonikidze's memory, and sent a copy to Stalin.[2]

In the days immediately preceding the upcoming plenum, Bukharin prepared two letters. The first was more than one hundred pages long, and was addressed to members and candidate members of the Central Committee, who were about to review his case. In it, Bukharin constructed his defense primarily on assertions of his deep-rooted hatred for Trotsky and Trotskyists, whom he characterized with expressions borrowed from Vyshinsky's lexicon: "Oberbandit Trotsky," "the ober-boss of all the Trotskyist-Zinovievist bands," "ataman of the bandits," "the foul line of Trotskyist traitors," and so forth.[3]

Bukharin referred to *Pravda*'s statement that the Trotskyists, "among other thievish tactical devices, employed the tactic of slandering honest Soviet people." He then added, that for this reason they had decided "after the court testimony during the first trial (and perhaps even earlier) ... to pursue a line of slander regarding collaboration with Bukharin, Rykov and others." Bukharin explained this "line" by the fact that "the Trotskyists were interested directly and immediately in touching up their 'firm,' and they are beginning (or long ago began) to create a myth that others are following after them." He wrote with particular malice about the testimony given by Radek, who, while at liberty, "masked himself before me as he would before an honest party member," but during the investigation and at the trial "inserted pieces of reality into hellish and slanderous fantasies." Bukharin finished this part of his letter with the conclusion that accepting slanders for the truth results from "excessive trust toward people (or to be more precise, toward animals) who by no means are deserving of this trust."[4]

Bukharin used similar arguments in refuting the testimony provided by "rightist false witnesses." He wrote that he fully admitted the possibility of the transformation of many of his former cothinkers into "unbridled counterrevolutionaries" who "had been doing something counterrevolutionary independent of me and without my knowledge." Recalling that he had many times publicly denounced his former disciples who had been imprisoned, Bukharin suggested that perhaps they had decided to get revenge for this by hurling the "most abject slander" at him.

Recognizing that these motives alone were insufficient to explain the falseness of so much testimony, Bukharin cautiously outlined the hypothesis that such testimony might have been extracted by means of provocation on the part of the investigators (of course, he decided not to even hint at the possibility that torture was used during the investigation). For instance, he considered it a provocation to preface the interrogation with assertions of the type: "We already know," "certain people have already testified," "the investigation has facts at its disposal," and so forth. After such phrases, Bukharin noted quite reasonably, people under investigation who knew very well "what they 'had' to say (for the charges had been formulated and were circulating in newspapers throughout the world as almost proven)" would give false testimony out of fear that they would be suspected of "concealment."[5]

Bukharin explained the presence of such a significant amount of slanderous testimony in the following way: "given the overall atmosphere created by the Trotskyist bandits, and the present political situation, and their knowledge of the testimony already given, subsequent false witnesses feel that they have to say approximately the same thing, thus one instance of false testimony bears fruit and multiplies, and assumes the appearance of many, i.e., it turns into many."[6]

Bukharin pointed to the clear absurdities contained in the transcripts of the interrogations which had been sent to him. Thus, his former secretary, Tsetlin, declared that he had belonged to the "organization of rightists" in 1926, and that "the Bukharin school" in 1925 "had in actual fact spoken out against the VKP(b)." Apropos of this statement, Bukharin cited well-known facts: in the years named by Tsetlin there had been not only no organization, but not even a tendency of "rightists," and Stalin, Molotov and other Stalinists were defending the "school" from criticism by the Left Opposition.

Bukharin wrote that he found no less absurd Tsetlin's reply to the question: "Do you know that your organization possesses an archive containing documents of a counterrevolutionary nature?" The archive which Tsetlin named was " ... a filing cabinet in Bukharin's office where he kept various documents he had written: the draft program of the Comintern, folders with material discussed at sessions of the Politburo, and other official documents."[7]

When it came to the more "criminal" testimony (about the formation in 1929 of an underground center of "the organization of rightists," about how this "center" was counting on a peasant uprising, about the preparation of a "palace coup," and so forth), Bukharin was only capable of expressing his unbounded indignation. Insofar as the material composition of these crimes was based only on unsubstantiated testimony from prisoners of the NKVD, it had been impossible to find arguments refuting them.

The only guilt which Bukharin acknowledged was concerning his "politically criminal" conversation with Kamenev in 1928, something for which he had many times repented over the course of almost a decade. Once again agreeing that "the position of the rightists in its development would have led to the victory of the counterrevolution," he declared that by 1930 he had renounced this position and therefore could hardly be counted among the "rightists."[8]

On 20 February, Bukharin sent his letter to the Politburo. He appended a statement that he refused to appear at the plenum and that he was declaring a hunger strike until he was cleared of the charges of treason, sabotage and terrorism. Hoping that the plenum would agree to limit itself to a discussion of this letter in his absence, he explained that he was unable to participate in the work of the plenum because of a severe nervous breakdown: "I cannot walk, I cannot bear the atmosphere that has been created, I am in no condition to speak, nor do I want to sob, fall into hysterics or faint when they revile me on the basis of slanders."[9]

Since he did not exclude the most unfortunate outcome of the party, and then the judicial, investigation, Bukharin prepared another letter simultaneously with the letter to the plenum. It was addressed to "the future generation of party leaders." He asked his wife to memorize this short document, and when he was certain that she had learned every word by heart, he destroyed the letter.

The contents of this letter differed from the contents of the document sent by Bukharin to the plenum. In it he spoke of "the monstrous tangle of crimes which in these terrible days is becoming ever more grandiose, is flaring up like a fire and is smothering the party," and which, in Bukharin's opinion, would be unraveled only after one or more generations.[10]

What was it that Bukharin felt compelled to tell about himself and his times to "a new, young and honest generation of party leaders" (he, of course, did not imagine that the party would not be fated to last until an honest generation of party leaders would appear)? What sum of ideas did he feel compelled to pass on to his descendants and to history in a document which was destined to become his political testament? With what secret thoughts was he prepared to go to his grave?

Alas, even in this secret letter, which, by its design, should have been free from any omissions or reticence, Bukharin said little more than he had outlined in his official appeal to the Central Committee Plenum. The basic content of Bukharin's letter-testament amounted to three fundamental theses: "For seven years" he had harbored "not even a shadow of a disagreement with the party [that is, with the Stalinist clique—V. R.]"; he "had not participated in the secret organizations led by Riutin or Uglanov" and knew nothing about their existence; he "had organized nothing against Stalin."[11]

Thus, the basic thrust of the letter which was forbidden for his contemporaries was Bukharin's desire to convince future "reinvestigators" of his case that from 1930 he had renounced any political struggle against Stalin.

From the content of the letter it is patently evident that Bukharin did not exclude the possibility that, like the victims of the "Trotskyist" trials (whom by that time he had repeatedly denounced in his official letters and statements), he would have to bear false witness against himself and others at an upcoming trial. Foreseeing the possibility of his participation in a grandiose judicial frame-up, he explained that his future "confessions," as well as the entire bacchanalia of lies and terror, would be the result of the activity of "the diabolical machinery of the NKVD," which "employing, *probably*, methods of the Middle Ages, possesses gigantic power" and "the cogs" of which, "to satisfy Stalin's morbidly suspicious nature, *I dare not say more*, and in the pursuit of medals and glory, are doing their foul work [my emphasis—V. R.]."[12] Thus, even in a document written with the intent of being made public after many years, Bukharin held Stalin guilty only for his "morbidly suspicious nature" and feared "to say more," namely, that the "diabolical machinery" was being set in motion by Stalin himself. Nor did he decide to express any certainty that this machinery employed "methods of the Middle Ages," i.e., inquisitional torture. It is understandable that with such ideological baggage Bukharin proved to be defenseless during the completion of the "party investigation" of his case at the Central Committee Plenum.

24. Prelude to the February-March Plenum

THE FEBRUARY-MARCH PLENUM lasted one and a half weeks—much longer than all the other plenums of the Central Committee, regardless of which period in the history of the party was involved. Both with regard to the number of questions discussed, and the number of those speaking, this plenum was second to no other party congress. We could even say that the significance of this plenum for the fate of the party and the nation was greater than the significance of any other plenum of the Central Committee and any other congress of the party. The plenum gave the "theoretical foundations" for the mass terror, sanctified the Great Purge in the name of the party, worked out directives regarding its scale and methods, and finally, prepared the extermination of the greater part of the Central Committee itself.

After becoming familiar with the plenum's material, which became accessible only in recent years, the first question which arises is: why did all the members and candidate members of the Central Committee submissively accept and support the monstrous directives and formulas of the plenum? Why was there not a single voice of protest raised against the crimes which had already been committed and which were being planned? And another question: why in such a case were two-thirds of the participants in the plenum arrested and shot during the next few years?

The answer to the first question is close to the one which was given in response to the question concerning the reasons for the confessions given by the defendants at the open trials. The Central Committee which was elected at the Seventeenth Congress contained people, the overwhelming majority of whom had been "tested" in the previous thirteen years in the struggle against the inner-party opposition. Beginning with the period of the "struggle against Trotskyism" in 1923–1924, politically they had gone downhill, consciously calling black white and repeating all the ideological and historical falsifications of Stalinism. Largely stripped in this struggle of their ideological and moral foundations, for a number of years they had passed over in silence the historical

203

dramas and tragedies unfolding before them; they had ignored the suffering and poverty of the masses, helped Stalin in his reprisals against his former comrades, and sung hymns of praise to Stalinist "socialism." Even before the onset of the great terror they had passed through several circles of political and moral degeneration. They had betrayed the central communist idea—the idea of social equality—by proving to be susceptible to the material privileges and power which Stalin gave them in return for complicity in his crimes and subordination to the perverted norms of party life. They clung to their access to power and privileges at any price, including the price of showering unbridled praise on Stalin, a man whose intellectual narrowness, moral inferiority and capability of committing any crime were well known to them.

The members and candidate members of the Central Committee chosen at the Seventeenth Congress (as well as that part in general of the Old Bolsheviks who obediently followed Stalin), *remained Bolsheviks* to the degree that they retained elements of Bolshevik social consciousness, and selflessly gave themselves to the job entrusted to them, whether it be the development of the economy, defense capability, or the nation's culture. At the same time *they ceased to be Bolsheviks* to the degree that they were transformed from proletarian revolutionaries into bureaucrats, from opponents of social inequality into its defenders, from those expressing the interests of the people into party bigwigs who had torn themselves away from the people.

The main contradiction of the Great Purge was the contradiction between its functional task—the defense of the interests of the ruling stratum, or its monopoly on power—and its main object—the representatives of the same ruling stratum, who, as the totalitarian-bureaucratic regime had solidified, had begun to see the light and were turning into a new potential opposition to Stalinism. The best qualities of the Old Bolsheviks who had remained in power were coming into an ever sharper conflict with the political tasks which Stalin was placing before them. In this I see the explanation for the inevitability of the reprisals against the overwhelming majority of the old party guard, including those who had never joined any anti-Stalinist opposition and who to one degree or another had been subject to the process of degeneration.

Of course, here I am not speaking of the careerists, charlatans, and adventurists who latched onto the ruling party, i.e., not about the foam, which, according to Lenin, not a single great mass political movement in history has managed to escape. I am talking about people who, despite their great political experience and subjective devotion to the ideals of Bolshevism, fell victim to world-historical errors and, in the end, allowed the entire ruling layer to be sent to their execution, although not without a struggle (which will be the focus of the last chapter of this book).

In addressing the more concrete circumstances which determined the passive and silent, or even the active and aggressive support by the plenum's participants for its monstrous resolutions, it is necessary to mention two events which immediately preceded the plenum and which served as a stern warning to members of the CC, a sign that none of them could feel safe from the threat of being counted among "enemies" or "accomplices of enemies."

The first of these events was the Central Committee decree of 2 January 1937, "On the Errors of the Secretary of the Azov-Black Sea Region, Comrade Sheboldaev, and the Unsatisfactory Political Leadership of the Regional Committee of the VKP(b)." In this decree, one of the most influential party secretaries was charged with having displayed "political short-sightedness which is absolutely intolerable for a Bolshevik ... resulting in the fact that the central posts of a number of major cities and regional party organizations in the region until the most recent times were occupied by accursed enemies of the people, spies and Trotskyist wreckers who had conducted their destructive work with impunity." As confirmation, an imposing list was presented of arrested secretaries from the city and regional committees of the party, directors of the largest factories, and staff at the regional committees.

Sheboldaev was dismissed from his post as secretary of the regional committee, "placed at the disposal of the CC," and warned that if he "in his future work does not draw all the lessons from the mistakes he has committed, the CC of the VKP(b) will be forced to resort to more severe measures than a party reprimand in his case."[1] Thus the given resolution juxtaposed a faceless CC and its individual members, which, as we will see later on, permeated all the work of the February-March Plenum.

Another ominous warning immediately directed at a party member of still higher rank was the CC decree of 13 January, "On the Unsatisfactory Party Leadership of the Kiev Area Committee of the KP(b)U, and Shortcomings in the Work of the CC of the KP(b)U." It pointed out that the Kiev area committee "was littered with an exceedingly great number of Trotskyists," and how there were "similar facts of excessive numbers [of Trotskyists]" in other area committees throughout the Ukraine. In confirmation, the decree listed many names of people who were in the closest circles around the second secretary of the CC of the KP(b)U and the first secretary of the Kiev Area Committee, candidate member of the Politburo, Postyshev. Among them were four heads of departments of the Kiev area committee, including one of the people closest to Postyshev—the head of the department of agitation and propaganda, Karpov.

Karpov was an unrestrained Stalinist who had assimilated well those "norms of party life" which had secretly begun to be observed since the beginning of the 1930s. This can be seen in an episode reported by one of the oldest Soviet philosophers, A. Ya. Zis. In 1933, Postyshev, who headed the campaign against "bourgeois nationalism" in the Ukraine, named in one of his speeches the young university instructor Zis as one of the people accused by him of collaborating with "Ukrainian fascism." The immediate cause for being included on this list was that Zis had refused to publicly denounce the renowned Ukrainian philosopher Iurinets, who by that time had been arrested. When Zis appealed for assistance to Karpov, the latter told him: "I know that you are guilty of nothing. But you should understand that not a person will be found in the entire country who would dare to tell a secretary of the CC that he is wrong." Understanding well what consequences Postyshev's passing phrase might bring for Zis, Karpov advised the young man to leave the Ukraine immediately. This saved the life of the young instructor, who became the author of more than twenty scientific monographs and a meritorious scholar of the RSFSR (Russian Republic).[2] As for Postyshev's attitude toward Karpov, see Chapter 33.

The basic blame for having Trotskysts "litter" the Kiev party apparatus was placed on Postyshev, who was duly reprimanded when the CC said, "if similar facts are repeated ... much stronger measures of punishment will be taken against him."[3]

Kaganovich came to Kiev to "explain" to party members the decrees of the CC. Here he met with Nikolaenko, a female graduate student at the Kiev Institute of History, who had been expelled from the party for numerous slanderous statements demanding punishment for "enemies of the people," and then had appealed directly to Stalin. When he returned from Kiev, Kaganovich told Stalin about the favorable impression Nikolaenko had made on him.[4]

Nikolaenko's "vigilance" was so highly valued by Stalin that he devoted a special passage to it in his report at the February-March Plenum. "Nikolaenko is a rank-and-file member of the party," declared Stalin, "she is a typical 'little' person. For a whole year she gave signals about the bad state of affairs in the

Kiev party organization, she exposed ... the domination of Trotskyist wreckers. People brushed her off like an importunate fly. Finally, in order to get rid of her, they went and expelled her from the party. Neither the Kiev organization nor the CC of the KP(b)U helped her to establish the truth. Only the intervention of the party's Central Committee helped unravel this tangled knot. And what became clear after the matter was looked into? It became clear that Nikolaenko was right and the Kiev organization was not right. Nothing more and nothing less.... As you see, simple people sometimes prove to be much closer to the truth than some lofty establishments."[5]

While he was in Kiev, Kaganovich offered Nikolaenko as an example to Postyshev, who had been accused of "political blindness." On 16 January, the Plenum of the Kiev Area Committee, with Kaganovich participating, removed Postyshev from his responsibilities as secretary of the area committee "because of the impossibility of combining the posts of second secretary of the CC of the KP(b)U and first secretary of the Kiev area committee." A month later, the Politburo of the CC of the KP(b)U dismissed from work Postyshev's wife, the Old Bolshevik Postolovskaia. In light of all these facts, it becomes clear why Postyshev in his several speeches and numerous interjections at the February-March Plenum tried to "rehabilitate" himself by demonstrating his profound irreconcilability toward "enemies."

The initial reprisals against Sheboldaev and Postyshev were intended to show all members of the central committee what might happen if they offered the slightest resistance to the repressions which were striking down their closest assistants and colleagues.

Just as earlier, during the sharpest periods of the struggle against the Opposition, Stalin chose the best moment for a "qualitative leap," which in this instance was the February-March Plenum, summoned to serve as a signal for the extermination of essentially the whole party, state, economic and military leadership of the nation. He convened this plenum only after three purges of the party conducted from 1933 to 1936, after two open political trials, and finally after the adoption of the constitution which aroused hope in the consciousness of the majority of Soviet people for the democratization of the country.

It is characteristic that, throughout the years of 1934–1936, Stalin never tired of repeating demagogic formulas which were designed to create the impression that, after a period of material poverty and mass repressions, the So-

viet Union had entered a period of upturn in its well-being and of the flourishing of democracy and of respect for the rights of man. In a speech during a
reception of metallurgists in the Kremlin he declared: "If earlier we one-sidedly
placed the emphasis on technology, on machines, then now the emphasis must
be made on the people who have mastered technology.... We must take care of
every capable and knowledgeable worker, we must take care of and cultivate
him. People must be carefully and attentively nurtured like a gardener culti-
vates his favorite fruit tree. We must raise, help to grow, give perspectives, promote in a timely fashion, and transfer to better work at the right time if a person is not handling his job, without waiting for him to become a complete
failure."[6]

Stalin developed these ideas in a speech at the graduation of students from
the military academies. Here he affirmed that in order to create a modern industry in the shortest possible time, "it was necessary to make sacrifices and
impose the cruelest economizing in everything; we had to economize on food,
on schools, and on manufacture." Now, however, according to Stalin, the period of famine in the realm of technology had been outlived, and the country
had entered "into a new period, I would say, of famine in the realm of people, in
the realm of cadres." Recalling the replacement of the earlier slogan, "technology decides everything," with the slogan, "cadres decide everything," Stalin
declared that "our people" still had not understood "the great meaning of this
new slogan.... Otherwise we would not have had that disgraceful attitude toward people, cadres and workers which we often observe in our practice. The
slogan, 'cadres decide everything,' demands that our leaders show the greatest
concern toward our workers, 'great' and 'small,' regardless of the area in which
they work; they must cultivate them carefully, help them when they need support, encourage them when they show their first successes, move them forward, and so forth.... Meanwhile we have in a whole number of instances facts
of a soulless, bureaucratic and outright scandalous attitude toward workers.
This, by the way, is explained by the fact that people are often tossed about like
stones." In concluding this programmatic statement, Stalin said: "You must
finally understand that of all the valuable capital in the world, the most valuable and the most decisive capital is people, cadres." Depicting himself as a
defender of "cadres" against several of "our leaders," who remained unnamed,
Stalin even declared that it was wrong to attribute all achievements to the
"leaders," while forgetting about the merits of the "cadres."[7]

Stalin began to speak with particular zeal as the ardent advocate of freedom and democracy after the publication of the draft of the new constitution. In a conversation with the American journalist Roy Howard, he stopped to deal with the statement by the latter that the Bolsheviks had "sacrificed personal freedom." Acknowledging that for the sake of building socialism "we had to temporarily restrict our needs," Stalin declared that now socialist society had been built, moreover it had been built "not for the limitation of personal freedom, but in order that the human personality felt itself truly free." He said that the guarantee of this freedom was the new constitution, declaring that it "will be, in my opinion, the most democratic constitution of all those that exist in the world."[8] He repeated this thought in a report to the Eighth Extraordinary Congress of Soviets, polemicizing with those foreign journalists who had stated that the new constitution of the USSR was "an empty promise, calculated in order to make a certain maneuver and deceive people."[9]

This was the ideological background against which the February-March Plenum of the Central Committee unfolded.

25. The February-March Plenum: Bukharin and Rykov Stand Accused

THE FIRST POINT on the plenum's agenda was "the case of Comrades Bukharin and Rykov." The review of this case was intended to serve as a test of the plenum's participants and at the same time was supposed to teach them an inspirational lesson—to show that any member or candidate member of the CC who denied the charges made against him would nevertheless inescapably be sent by his comrades to the scaffold.

A day before the plenum opened, the Politburo passed a resolution: "The Politburo rejects Comrade Bukharin's proposal not to tell the Plenum of the CC that he has declared a 'hunger strike' and is sending his declaration to all members of the CC of the VKP(b), for it feels that the Politburo cannot and should not keep secrets from the CC of the VKP(b)."[1] Under the influence of this decree, Bukharin decided to appear at the plenum without ending his hunger strike. As I. A. Piatnitsky told the members of his family, Bukharin appeared in the hall where the plenum had gathered, and "stood among everyone there, with a full beard and in some kind of old suit.... No one greeted him. Everyone was already looking (at him) as they would a rotting corpse."[2]

Before the plenum opened, Bukharin met Rykov in the vestibule; the latter said to him: "Tomsky proved to be the most farsighted among us."[3] That Rykov had lost any hope for a favorable outcome of their case was caused in large part by the fact that on the eve of the plenum he had been brought to a face-to-face confrontation with his former closest colleagues, Nesterov, Radin, Kotov and Shmidt. In the presence of Stalin and other members of the Politburo, the participants in the confrontation testified that after 1929, the "center of rightists" continued its work and in 1932 developed a program, the authorship of which was attributed to Riutin as a means of camouflage.

The plenum opened with a report by Yezhov, who reported how the People's Commissariat of Internal Affairs had carried out the decision of the previous plenum to continue the investigation of the case of Bukharin and Rykov. Yezhov named many people who had given "exhaustive testimony about the entire anti-Soviet activity of the rightists," and who had confirmed or supplemented the charges made against Bukharin and Rykov with "a great quantity of new facts." As if anticipating the question of the veracity of these testimonies, Yezhov particularly underscored that the members of the Politburo at the confrontations repeatedly asked the people under arrest whether they were slandering Bukharin and Rykov. In response to this, according to Yezhov, all those under arrest "fully confirmed their testimonies and insisted on them."[4]

On the basis of these "irrefutable testimonies" Yezhov declared that in 1930 an illegal center of rightists had been formed which issued directives concerning terror, the organization of a "palace coup" and kulak uprisings. Yezhov named a large number of terrorist groups organized by this "center," a multitude of the names of their participants, and also stated that the mass strikes of workers in Ivanovo and the Ivanovo region which occurred in 1932 had been "artificial" and incited by "rightists."[5]

Following Yezhov, Mikoyan gave a supplementary report in which he said, "The entire Bukharinist group is in prison and almost all have confessed that they were double-dealers and enemies because they studied under Bukharin." Joining together the names of Trotsky, Zinoviev and Bukharin, Mikoyan claimed, "they had created a new type of people, of degenerates, not people, of animals, who speak openly for the party line ... but in actual fact conduct unprincipled and disruptive work against the party."

Calling Bukharin's hunger strike "a political demonstration" and a "brazen ultimatum," Mikoyan spoke with particular malice about how Bukharin in his statement to the plenum had allowed "attacks against the apparatus of the People's Commissariat of Internal Affairs," using "the Trotskyist method of denigrating the apparatus."[6]

After Mikoyan's speech, the floor was given to Bukharin, who as before proceeded from the assumption that it was still possible to prove his innocence to a higher party forum once it had gathered to investigate his case. At the beginning of his speech, Bukharin tried to explain the motives behind his hunger strike and his refusal to appear at the plenum, but even during this attempt he ran into a hail of malicious or mocking interjections which were intended to shift the tonality of his explanations from the tragic to the comic.

Bukharin: Comrades, I beg you not to interrupt because it is very difficult, simply physically difficult for me to speak—for four days I have eaten nothing. I told you, I wrote, why I seized upon it (the hunger strike) in despair, I wrote to a narrow circle because with such charges ... it is impossible for me to live.

    I cannot shoot myself with a revolver because then people will say that I committed suicide in order to injure the party; but if I die much like from an illness, then what would you lose in that case?

Laughter. Voices from the audience: Blackmail!

Voroshilov: What a low-down trick! Keep your trap shut! Scandalous! Think of what you are saying.

Bukharin: But understand, it is difficult for me to go on living.

Stalin: And is it easy for us?

Voroshilov: Just think about it: "I won't shoot myself, I'll just die."

Bukharin: It's easy for you to speak about me. But what would you be losing? After all, if I am a wrecker, a son of a bitch, and so forth, why feel sorry for me: I have no pretensions to anything, I am telling you what I think and what I am going through. If this has anything to do with even the slightest political damage, then unconditionally I will carry out whatever you say. (*Laughter.*) Why are you laughing? Here there is absolutely nothing to laugh at.[7]

Responding to Mikoyan's charges that he was discrediting and "frightening" the Central Committee, Bukharin stressed that in his letter he had called into question not a resolution of the CC, which had still not been made in his case, but the methods used by the investigators during interrogation, which could not help but be influenced by articles in the party press where his guilt was treated as something already proven.

    The only guilt that Bukharin agreed to acknowledge was that in the past he had sometimes stood up for his pupils because he "foolishly confused personal relations with political ones." All the rest of the charges contained in the testimony against him he categorically denied, referring to the many contradictions between the various testimonies and to the fact that "all Trotskyists are innate scoundrels."[8]

    In challenging Bukharin's arguments, the initiative was taken by Stalin, who asked Bukharin question after question about the motives behind the testimony which those under arrest gave against him.

Stalin: Why should Astrov lie? Why should Slepkov lie? For that would not
make things easier for them, would it?

Bukharin: I don't know ...

Stalin: Excuse me, but can't we establish the facts here? At a confrontation
in the offices of the Orgburo, where you were present, we, the members of the Politburo were present, Astrov was there and others under
arrest: Piatakov was there, Radek, Sosnovsky, Kulikov, and so forth.
Then, when I or someone else asked each of those under arrest: "Are
you telling the truth, are you voluntarily giving this testimony or did
they put pressure on you?", Radek even started sobbing at this question—"What do you mean, put pressure? Voluntarily, absolutely voluntarily."

After Stalin was done, Molotov, Voroshilov, and Mikoyan stubbornly repeated the same questions: "Why would these people slander themselves?",
and each time Bukharin was compelled to answer, "I do not know."[9]

In concluding his speech, Bukharin said, "nobody is forcing me to accuse
myself of the monstrous things which people are saying about me, and no one
will get me to do this under any circumstances. No matter what epithets people
have applied to me, I will not make myself out to be a wrecker, make myself out
to be a terrorist, make myself out to be a turncoat, or make myself out to be a
traitor to the socialist motherland."

After these words, Stalin seemed to acknowledge the correctness of
Bukharin's self-defense when he turned to him in a confiding tone: "You should
not, nor do you have the right to, cast aspersions on yourself. That would be
the most criminal thing.... You must put yourself in our position. Trotsky and
his disciples Zinoviev and Kamenev once worked with Lenin, and now these
people have reached an agreement with Hitler. After this can we call anything
monstrous? No we cannot. After all that has happened with these gentlemen,
these former comrades who have reached an agreement with Hitler in order to
sell out the USSR, there are no more surprises in human life. You must prove
everything, and not make a formal reply with question marks and exclama-
tions."[10]

The plenum's first session ended with Bukharin's speech. After this session, Stalin turned to Bukharin in the lobby of the plenum. He raised certain
hopes in Bukharin for a favorable outcome of his case and at the same time

A. I. Rykov

proposed that he publicly apologize for calling the hunger strike. Bukharin agreed to subject himself to this new humiliation. At the start of the morning session which opened on the next day, one more repulsive scene was played out, the scenario of which, we must assume, had been concocted by Stalin and his stooges.

> *Bukharin*: ... I apologize to the Plenum of the Central Committee for my shortsighted and politically harmful act of declaring a hunger strike.
> *Stalin*: That's not enough, that's not enough!
> *Bukharin*: I can give my motivation. I beg the Plenum of the Central Committee to accept my apologies, because it indeed turned out that I placed the plenum of the CC before a kind of ultimatum, and this ultimatum was reinforced by me in the form of this unusual step.
> *Kaganovich*: It was an anti-Soviet step.
> *Bukharin*: By doing this I committed a major political mistake which can only partially be mitigated by the fact that I am in extremely ill health. I ask the Central Committee to excuse me and I give my very profound apologies for this truly and completely inadmissible political step.
> *Stalin*: To excuse and forgive.
> *Bukharin*: Yes, yes, and to forgive.

Stalin: That's right, that's right!

Molotov: Don't you suppose that your so-called hunger strike might be viewed as an anti-Soviet act by some of the comrades?

Kaminsky: Yes, precisely, Bukharin, that's what you have to say.

Bukharin: If some of the comrades might view this in that way (*Commotion in the hall, voices from the audience*: And how could it be otherwise? That's the only way it could be seen). But, comrades, that did not enter into my subjective intentions ...

Kaminsky: But that's what happened.

Shkiriatov: And it could not have been otherwise.

Bukharin: Of course, this makes my guilt even more serious. I beg the CC once again to forgive me.[11]

After this scene, the floor was given to Rykov. Not wanting to fall into Bukharin's position of being charged with "attacks on the NKVD," Rykov began his speech with a high evaluation of the quality of the investigation which had been undertaken. "I must say that the investigation was conducted very quickly, and, in my opinion, very well," he said. "It was conducted in such a way that there are no facts, there is no possibility of saying, that the people who participated in this investigation were somehow interested in making incorrect accusations against either myself or Bukharin.... Given the vigilance of the apparatus [of the NKVD—V. R.], which not long ago was completely restored ... (this apparatus) tried of course, by all means to tell the Central Committee only the truth, only what they have found in good conscience."[12]

In an attempt to convince the plenum's participants of his extreme sincerity, Rykov cited facts which essentially would place several of his "accusers" under the gun. He told about his conversation in 1932 with Radin, who advised him to join the opposition and tried to convince him that the opposition would grow. Summarizing Radin's statements with the sinister formulation, "He proposed that I work against the party and the CC," Rykov declared that he told Radin that he "stood on the edge of a precipice, and I was by no means a fellow-traveler in any way in this endeavor, quite the contrary." Assessing his behavior in connection with their private conversation, Rykov regretted that he "had not gone in good time to the GPU and told what he had recommended for me to do.... If I had taken him at that time where I should have, then my entire situation would have been completely different."[13]

Characterizing the behavior of former supporters of the "right deviation," Rykov said that many of them after 1929 "continued their struggle ... they all moved—some more quickly, others more slowly—onto these anti-Soviet, counterrevolutionary rails." He acknowledged his responsibility for the fact that "a whole number of traitors, criminals and wreckers" were oriented toward him and considered him their inspiration, although he had not given any grounds for this.[14]

Rykov declared that now that he had become familiar with the testimony of those under arrest, he was completely convinced of Tomsky's guilt. "That he (Tomsky) engaged in wrecking ... that he had dealings with the Trotskyist center, this is also beyond any doubt.... That he led, or perhaps became a member of the new center ... —that is absolutely beyond any doubt.... For my own conscience, I cannot allow myself personally to think that Tomsky did not know about the spying activity of the Trotskyists, about the partition of the Soviet Union."[15]

Rykov stated that at the face-to-face confrontation with Shmidt, he asked the latter the question: why did Shmidt not tell him about the sabotage in the Far East, in which he, according to his own words, took an active part. "This ... can only be explained," Rykov added, "by the fact that Tomsky gave him directives not to talk with me about these things."[16]

In order to prove his all-embracing sincerity, Rykov recounted two facts which might be seen as signs of oppositional activity. The first amounted to the following: in 1932, when Rykov was at Tomsky's dacha, a worker came to visit and brought a leaflet from the Riutin group which was being circulated at his factory. "As soon as I heard (it)," Rykov declared, "I cursed this Riutin program, using the foulest words I could find."[17]

Next Rykov repeated the story which had been told at the previous plenum about Zinoviev inviting Tomsky to come to his dacha. According to Rykov, he tried to talk Tomsky out of making this trip, assuring him that "they [the Zinovievists—V. R.] had thought up ... a proposal for an alliance or some kind of bloc for ... a struggle against the Central Committee." After this conversation, as Rykov asserted, he only visited Tomsky once, and on this occasion their wives were present the whole time and "there was not a single minute when Tomsky and I would have been left by ourselves."

Speaking of his relationship to Bukharin, Rykov said that he had experienced a whole series of vacillations in recent times regarding Bukharin's guilt for the crimes which had been attributed to him. "When I had read this mass of material, I even sent the rough outline of a note to Yezhov, stating that where there is so much smoke, there must be fire.... I felt hesitant, particularly when I read Radek's concluding remarks in which he made such charges before the entire nation and the entire world with great expressiveness."

However, continued Rykov, when he called to mind all the facts that he knew about the crucial moments in Bukharin's life, he rejected the thought of the latter's criminal intentions. In this regard, Rykov told how in the beginning of the 1930s, he had once found Bukharin "in a semihysterical state" because Stalin had told him, "You want to kill me." On the same day, Rykov asked Stalin whether he actually felt that Bukharin would be able to kill him. At this point Stalin hastened to turn Rykov's story into a joke: "No, I smiled and said that if you really pick up a knife some time to kill me, then be careful that you don't cut yourself."

After this, Rykov recalled one more episode which testified, as far as he was concerned, in Bukharin's favor. He said that Bukharin told him about the severing of any relations with his pupils and about his approval of "any repressive measures directed at the members of this school." Although Stalin immediately interrupted Rykov with the ominous interjection, "He wasn't telling the truth here either, Bukharin that is," Rykov nevertheless said, "That he (Bukharin) did not sympathize with them in all their criminal dealings and ... had broken with them—of this I am certain to the highest degree."[18]

Like Bukharin, Rykov devoted most of his attention toward proving the falsity of the testimony given against himself. Thus, in Uglanov's testimony there are statements that Rykov attended the funeral of their mutual comrade in the Right Opposition, Ugarov, in 1932. There he received reports and gave directives about "conspiratorial activity." Apropos of this, Rykov stated that at the time of Ugarov's funeral he had been in the Crimea and as proof he showed a postcard from his daughter sent to him on the day of the funeral.

Understanding that nothing he was saying would earn the trust of the plenum, Rykov proposed that the facts he had introduced be investigated "perhaps, through servants," and even by interrogating his wife and daughter. To the laughter of the audience he declared, "My daughter will not deceive you."[19]

Over the next three days discussion proceeded which was devoted to the first point on the agenda. Insofar as the speakers had no new facts at their disposal, they inflated and "interpreted" the facts which were already well known to the plenum's participants. In doing so, the speeches of the participants differed only in shades of meaning and nuances. Thus, Voroshilov found positive words to characterize Bukharin, but only in order to underscore the "indulgence" shown him on Stalin's part. Bukharin, he said, "is a man who combines outstanding and very positive human traits. We cannot deny these traits. He is a very capable man, well-read and perhaps a very useful member of the party; he was a very useful member of the Central Committee at one time, and he was not without use as a member of the Politburo.... Because of these qualities even Lenin at one time forgave many rotten deeds concerning Lenin and our party.... And Comrade Stalin has gotten along with him for fifteen years since Lenin died; he has forgiven him for the most abominable things."

Voroshilov interpreted Tomsky's suicide in the following way: "The third member (of the 'troika') found a solution to his task rather easily.... Tomsky did not facilitate the white-washing of his group, but, in my opinion, he predetermined the charges. He confirmed the charges made against him and his comrades at least by half, if not by 75 percent."[20]

A more savage note was struck by the contribution made by Shkiriatov, who helped Stalin call into question the authenticity of Bukharin's hunger strike. "What could be more hostile, what could be more counterrevolutionary than this action by Bukharin!" Shkiriatov said with unconcealed malice. "In his statement he writes that he began his hunger strike at midnight (*Stalin*: He began his hunger strike at night. *Laughter. A voice from the audience*: After dinner). In doing this Bukharin wants to carry his counterrevolutionary work against the Central Committee to the very end. Read his statement. All these lines are written not with our, a Bolshevik hand, they seethe with hatred for the party."

Shkiriatov interpreted Rykov's explanations in just as tendentious and arbitrary a manner. With regard to the story about meeting with Tomsky in the presence of their wives, he declared: "This immediately suggests that the whole affair is tainted. Why did you take witnesses, to see that you did not trust each other, or were afraid of talking with each other?"

Shkiriatov also saw a criminal subtext in Rykov's "confession" that he and other "rightists" participated in seeing Ugarov off when he was going abroad. "Why did you see him off, what was going on?" asked Shkiriatov. "You did this because he was your cothinker, a participant in your anti-party work, that is why you went to see him off. Later, as is mentioned in the testimonies, under the guise of seeing him off you organized meetings of your center."

At the conclusion of his speech Shkiriatov stated, "These people not only have no place in the CC or the party, their place is in court; the only place for them, as state criminals, is on the defendants' bench. (*Kosior*: Let them prove their case in court.)"[21]

Among fifteen speeches, the only dissonant note was made by Osinsky, who was literally forced onto the tribune by the most zealous Stalinists. And there were serious reasons for this. Osinsky was one of the strongest party theoreticians who retained a certain independence in his judgments. In addition, his career contained a long oppositional past. In 1918 Osinsky was one of the leaders of the "Left Communist" faction, then became a leader of the "Democratic Centralist" group, and together with other members of the group actively participated in the discussions of 1923 on the side of the Opposition. Although abandoning oppositional activity after this discussion, he never added his voice to the hounding of oppositionists. All this explains the scene which unfolded at one of the plenum's sessions. When Molotov announced the next speaker, sudden cries arose from the audience—questions about whether Osinsky had signed up to take part in the discussion.

> *Kosior*: Comrade Molotov, the people are interested, will Osinsky be
> speaking?
> *Molotov*: He hasn't signed up so far.
> *Postyshev*: He's been silent for a long time.
> *Kosior*: He's been silent for many years.[22]

On the next day, Osinsky appeared at the tribune and began by stressing the forced nature of his contribution. "I was summoned, so to speak, to the tribune on the initiative of Comrades Beria, Postyshev and others, and since I was flattered by such attention from the Central Committee, I decided to speak, perhaps, to be of some use." When he was met with caustic remarks, Osinsky managed to put a stop to them and force the audience to hear him out. This happened after the following exchange of heckling and rejoinders:

> *Vareikis*: Lenin called you [Left Communists—V. R.] mad petty bourgeois.
> *Osinsky*: That's true, just as, it seems, that was what he called you (*laughter*), Comrade Vareikis.
> *Vareikis*: But at that time I did not belong to them. In any case, I was for

Brest, everyone knows that, the entire Ukraine knows about it.

Osinsky: But that means that you went mad a bit later, during the Democratic Centralist period (*laughter*).

Of course, Osinsky could not go far beyond the framework of the rules of
the game which had been laid down at the plenum. He declared that he subscribed to the speeches given by members of the Politburo and felt that "all the
necessary logical and juridical grounds existed to put Bukharin and Rykov on
trial." However, his speech was completely free of the abuse which permeated
the contributions of all the other speakers. Osinsky said that before the revolution he "shared a great friendship" with Bukharin and that their political paths
diverged after the dissolution of the Left Communist faction, insofar as
"Bukharin, I must say, followed a more correct path than I. With the ending of
Left Communism, I went farther along the path of democratic centralism,
whereas Bukharin drew closer to the party leadership, to Lenin."[23]

  Then Osinsky spoke in calm tones about his theoretical differences with
Bukharin and about practical differences with him regarding the work of
Izvestiia and the Academy of Sciences, avoiding during his account any political qualifications. The tone of Osinsky's remarks cost him dearly. At the close
of the plenum's work, Mekhlis accused him of "presenting the wretched double-
dealer Bukharin, that complete muddlehead and phrasemonger, as a theore-
tician and great journalist."[24]

  In drawing the balance sheet of the "investigation" into the Bukharin and
Rykov case, we must emphasize that their tragedy consisted in the fact that
since the 1920s they had not managed to recognize those inevitable changes in
political activity which were dictated by the very logic of this activity after the
victory of the revolution. The experience of not only the October, but other
revolutions as well, shows that the activity of the professional revolutionary
and the activity of the professional politician who is in power demand a choice
of differing strategies and tactics in their behavior. Political logic assumes a
swift transition from the stage in which revolutionaries share the psychology
of fraternal cothinkers united by the presence of a common enemy and by relations which flow from their status as the persecuted and oppressed—to a stage
of inevitable differences in view which arise during creative economic work.
Such creative work is always more complex and contradictory than the struggle
to overthrow the regime of exploiters.

At this stage unity of thought inevitably disappears, dispersing into a series of differing "draft" positions, and within the ruling group clashes occur over the adoption of various management decisions. In the absence of the possibility of free political discussions these clashes assume the character of combinations and blocs in the upper echelons, and result in a situation where comradely relations, the attention to and respect for the opinions, convictions, and experiences of comrades in the party grow weaker, and then disappear. The constructive positions of the arguing sides assume an extremely sharp and uncompromising character. The logic of ruthless inner-party struggle comes into play.

Those who did not want, or were unable, to subordinate themselves to this cruel and inhuman logic, which had become established with the active participation of Bukharin and Rykov themselves during the years of the struggle by the ruling faction against the Left Opposition, were doomed. At the February-March Plenum, Bukharin and Rykov on one side and their opponents among the most fanatical Stalinists on the other, spoke in different languages and could not understand one another, even if they had wanted to. Stalin, however, used the given situation in such a way as to deny the plenum participants the possibility of "wanting" to listen to the persecuted and harassed "accused," who just a few years before had been considered the acknowledged leaders of the party.

Meanwhile we should note that far from all of the plenum's participants added their voice to the unbridled badgering of Bukharin and Rykov. This is shown by analyzing the interjections, which allows one to show a sort of "disposition of forces" at the plenum. As a whole, the plenum transcript records about one thousand interjections which were uttered during the discussion of the Bukharin and Rykov case. Not a single one of them was offered as even the most timid defense of the accused, nor did a single one aim to call into question even individual charges made against them. All the interjections were of either a denunciatory or mocking nature.

Approximately a third of the interjections are recorded as "voice (or voices) from the audience"—the stenographers did not manage to establish who had made the interjection. In the remaining instances, the transcript identifies the author of the utterance.

The greatest number of interjections (one hundred, including the extended monologues which interrupted the contributions by Bukharin and Rykov) belonged to Stalin. This number is almost equaled by the number of remarks made by Molotov (eighty-two) and Kaganovich (sixty-seven). The interjections made by the remaining members of the Politburo are listed in descending order: Kosior (twenty-seven), Voroshilov (twenty-four), Mikoyan (twenty-four), Chubar (eleven), and Kalinin (four).

Among the candidate members of the Politburo, the greatest activity was shown by Postyshev (eighty-eight interjections). He is followed by Eikhe (fourteen), Petrovsky (eight), Zhdanov (five) and Rudzutak (one).

The interjections made by people directly connected with the secret police or party investigation appear in the following order: Shkiriatov (forty-six), Yezhov (seventeen), Vyshinsky (who did not belong to a single leading party body but attended the plenum as prosecutor of the USSR) and Yaroslavsky (five each).

Among the "rank-and-file" members and candidate members of the CC, particular activity was shown by Beria (twenty), Mezhlauk (nineteen), Budenny (seventeen) and Stetsky (seventeen). They were followed by Gamarnik (eleven), Polonsky (eight), Yagoda (seven), Shvernik (six), Lozovsky (five), and Khrushchev (four). Five people made three interjections, and fourteen made one or two. Thus, about fifty people made their own contributions to the persecution of the accused—less than half of the overall number of the members and candidate members of the Central Committee attending the plenum.

It must be assumed that Stalin made a careful analysis of the interjections—all the more so since they were each sent for review and editing to the participants in the plenum, and then added to the transcript.

26. Bukharin and Rykov Defend Themselves

After a four-day discussion of their case, Bukharin and Rykov reached a state of extreme exhaustion and despair. N. A. Rykova recalls that during the first days of the plenum her father often repeated: "They want to lock me up." On the days that followed, he almost stopped talking with his relatives, and did not smoke or eat.[1]

In accordance with the scenario of a "party investigation," Bukharin and Rykov had to make closing statements.

Since the lengthy discussion added little to the testimonies sent out before the plenum, Bukharin could not add anything of substance to the arguments he had given before. He unsuccessfully reiterated that he could not "fully or even partially explain a number of questions concerning the behavior of people who are testifying against me."[2]

Vowing that he "absolutely did not want to discredit the new make-up of the Narkomvnudel," Bukharin dared only to recall that according to the theses which Yezhov had presented to the plenum, many double agents had been discovered within the NKVD, and in this regard he suggested: "Perhaps they haven't completely purged the apparatus (of the NKVD)."[3]

The other boundary which Bukharin did not dare to cross was the expression of any doubt over the "Trotskyist trials." When Molotov began to persistently question him whether he found the testimony of the defendants at these trials to be true, Bukharin replied to the accompaniment of laughter from the audience that everything in these testimonies was true except what was said regarding himself.[4]

Throughout his entire speech Bukharin was interrupted by vicious and caustic remarks, the tone of which was set by Molotov and Kaganovich. During one of the more dramatic moments in Bukharin's explanations, Molotov interrupted him with the comment: "The devil only knows what you are doing; we can expect anything from you." When Bukharin began to speak of his former contributions to the party, Molotov tossed out the remark: "Even Trotsky did some good, and now he is a fascist agent, he's sunk that low." At this point Bukharin hastened to say, "That's true, that's true."[5]

Besides the "leaders," Stetsky and Mezhlauk were particularly strenuous in their outbursts; they had been quite frightened when Bukharin mentioned that they had belonged in the past to his "school" (Mezhlauk's name had even figured in a criminal context in one of the testimonies). Bukharin had just managed to deny the charges of "attacking the NKVD" when Stetsky cried out: "You've borrowed all that from Trotsky. During the trial Trotsky wrote the same thing in the American press."[6]

In answering all these malicious attacks, Bukharin continued to make the accusation that a confrontational atmosphere had been created around him consisting exclusively of "Trotskyist double-dealers." "The whole tragedy of my situation," he said, " is that Piatakov and all the others have poisoned the atmosphere so much, the atmosphere has become such that people don't believe human feelings any more—neither emotions, nor the movement of the soul, nor words (*laughter*)."

At the end of Bukharin's speech, people began to shout from the audience: "He should have been put in prison long ago!" Bukharin replied to this with the last words which he would utter in his speech: "Do you think that because of what you are shouting—put him in prison—I will change what I am saying? No I won't."[7]

Rykov began his concluding remarks with words about how he clearly understood that "This meeting will be the last, the last party meeting in my life." He despairingly repeated that the atmosphere at the plenum made him think of slandering himself: "Sometimes I whisper to myself: wouldn't it be better somehow if I go and say what I did not do.... No matter what, the end will be the same. But the thought that perhaps the torment will be less—is very, very seductive. And now, when I stand before this entire series of charges, enormous willpower is required in such conditions, an extraordinarily large amount of willpower to keep from lying."[8]

This tragic confession served as a reason for Stalin to try to push Rykov onto the path of self-slander. He gave him the example of the behavior of the executed defendants from the recent trials. "There are people," declared Stalin, "who give truthful testimony, even though such testimony is terrible, but they do so in order to finally cleanse themselves of the mud which has stuck to them. And then there are people who do not give truthful testimony because they have begun to love the mud which sticks to them, and they don't want to part with it."[9]

In the course of Rykov's speech, he was constantly reminded of the only "crime" to which he confessed—reading the Riutin leaflet along with other "rightists." When Rykov once again mentioned this episode, he was subjected to a flood of reproaches for not having informed about the incident; failure to inform had long ago been elevated by the Stalinists to the rank of a party and state crime.

> *Voroshilov:* If it (the leaflet) was lucky enough to come your way, you should have put it in your pocket and gone straight to the Central Committee ...
>
> *Liubchenko:* At the plenum of the Central Committee why did you not say that you had already read it at Tomsky's?
>
> *Khrushchev:* We have party candidates who, if they come upon an anti-party leaflet, take it to their party cell, but you—are a candidate member of the Central Committee.

Responding to these comments, Rykov declared that he had made "an absolutely obvious mistake." Not satisfied with this response, Molotov reminded Rykov about one more example of his "double-dealing." In 1932, when discussing the Riutin Platform at a plenum of the CC, Rykov announced that if he had known that someone had this platform in his possession, then he would have dragged such a person to the GPU. In reply to this, Rykov said, "Here I am guilty and fully acknowledge my guilt.... I must be punished for what I did, but I should not be punished for what I did not do.... It is one thing if they punish me because I did not drag Tomsky or others where I should have, it is absolutely another thing when they say that I was in solidarity with this program, that this program was my own." Not satisfied with Rykov's qualification of his behavior, Shkiriatov tossed out one more rejoinder: "Since you didn't tell us about it, that means you were a participant."[10]

Trying to show his extreme loyalty to the "general line," Rykov told about his conversation in 1930 with a certain Trofimov, who was indignantly telling him about the process of "dekulakization." "I then answered him," said Rykov, "by saying that in carrying out the type of operation which is now going on in the countryside, there are bound to be certain excesses."[11]

In order to show that his contacts with the "Trotskyists" were precluded, Rykov emphasized his long-standing personal hatred toward them. "I repeat, I was never with any Trotskyist scum, I fought alongside you, with you I never wavered, and never, not for a single minute, was I with them.... I fought with Zinoviev, and did not respect him—ever, anywhere, or in any way.... I always considered Piatakov a hypocrite who could not be trusted ... and the most repulsive person."

In response to Rykov's demarcation from the "Trotskyists," Stalin reminded him of his "bloc with Zinoviev and Kamenev against Lenin the day after taking power." Rykov confirmed this well-known fact concerning the collective resignation of several party activists in 1917 after the majority of the CC refused to form a coalition government with the Mensheviks and SR's: "Yes, that happened." Then Stalin tossed out another charge, this time false, that Rykov had joined Zinoviev and Kamenev in opposing the October uprising. Rykov objected: "That never happened."[12]

At the end of his speech, which proceeded under a hail of ferocious heckling, Rykov despairingly said: "As a man, all is now finished, for me this is beyond dispute, but why do you waste your time mocking me?... This is a savage thing." He ended his speech with the words: "I repeat once again, that to confess to what I did not do, to make of myself ... the scoundrel that I am being portrayed as here—this I will never do.... And I will stick to these words as long as I live."[13]

27. The Plenum Delivers its Verdict

THE DISCUSSION of the Bukharin-Rykov case ended with Yezhov's concluding remarks, in which the main attention was devoted to repudiating the
arguments offered by the accused. In response to assertions that the imaginary members of the "right center" never even met, Yezhov declared: "That's
just the point. Basing yourselves on the experience of the Trotskyists, you were
especially conspiratorial." Even more threatening was Yezhov's answer to
Rykov's comment that in the testimony of those under arrest, nothing was said
about his conspiratorial activity in recent years. "You will be happy to know,
Aleksei Ivanovich," said Yezhov, "that I do not think that we have finished digging. We will get to 1936, too, and also to 1937."[1]

Despite all the curses that had been uttered by Bukharin and Rykov toward the victims of the "Trotskyist" trials, Yezhov asserted as before that during their speeches they "completely avoided the question of evaluating this
entire miserable gang of Trotskyist-Zinovievist riffraff whom we shot long ago."
In this regard, Yezhov declared: Bukharin and Rykov should face "one more
political charge for remaining undisarmed enemies who are giving a signal to
all hostile forces, both here among us in the USSR and abroad (*Voice from the
audience*: Correct).... They are giving a signal to their cothinkers: 'Continue your
work, conspire even more; if you are caught, do not confess.'" To Yezhov's repeated attack, "You are defending this whole miserable gang," Bukharin responded with a cry of protest: "What are you talking about? This is monstrous!...
I am defending nothing of the sort. I am in full agreement with you [i.e., concerning the trials and the execution of the defendants—V. R.]."[2]

Yezhov introduced new "proof" of Bukharin's "criminal" behavior which
showed that during the work of the plenum the NKVD apparatus had fever-
ishly continued the "development" of his case. After mentioning documents
which had been confiscated in Bukharin's office, Yezhov declared: "For some
reason he was terribly fond of collecting, for instance, all the anti-Soviet declarations or letters which came his way. He never gave them to the GPU, but kept

them in a folder."[3]

Yezhov's speech ended with a phrase which left no doubt about the further fate of Bukharin and Rykov: "I think that the plenum will afford an opportunity for Bukharin and Rykov to become convinced in deed of the objectivity of the investigation and to see how an investigation is conducted (*Voice from the audience*: That's right)."[4]

After Yezhov's speech, the plenum chose a commission of thirty-five men to write a resolution.

Members of the commission were unanimous in recommending that Bukharin and Rykov deserved to be expelled from the Central Committee and the party, and arrested. Differences arose only with regard to the procedure of the final reprisals against them. Several members of the commission spoke in favor of the plenum's decree not predetermining the court sentence. The majority proceeded from the previously established practice, according to which the measure of punishment in the most important political cases be determined not by the court, but by the supreme party bodies. Yezhov proposed that the highest measure of punishment be applied to Bukharin and Rykov. A number of the commission's members felt that it was possible not to shoot them, but to "guarantee that they receive a prison sentence of ten years."

After these proposals had been made, Stalin offered his own: "Not to send them to trial, but to send the case of Bukharin and Rykov to the NKVD." On the surface this formulation left alive the hope that the preparatory investigation might not lead to a trial. In reality, it replaced a swift trial with its delay for an indefinite time which was necessary in order to fully break Bukharin and Rykov. And in actual fact another full year of investigation in the torture chambers of the NKVD was required to receive their "confessions" at the trial of the "Right-Trotskyist Bloc."

After further discussion, all the proposals except Stalin's were withdrawn, and the commission unanimously adopted Stalin's resolution.

On the same day, Stalin outlined for the plenum the motives behind the commission's adoption of his proposal. "Of course, the feeling of indignation over the anti-party and anti-Soviet activity of Bukharin and Rykov, as well as their behavior here at the plenum during the discussion about them, was very great in the commission as well as at the plenum," he declared. "But the commission felt that it could not and should not be guided by a feeling of indignation." After stating that a "rather significant number" of the commission's members spoke about the absence of any difference between Bukharin and Rykov, on the one hand, and the Trotskyists and Zinovievists on the other, Stalin said that in the final analysis the commission came to the conclusion that "it was wrong to pile Bukharin and Rykov into one heap with the Trotskyists and Zinovievists, since there is a difference between them, moreover this difference speaks in favor of Bukharin and Rykov." Stalin explained the relative "softness" of his proposal because the difference consisted in the fact that Bukharin and Rykov, unlike the Trotskyists, had not been expelled earlier from the party and the CC.[5]

The resolution indicated that the plenum of the CC had established "as a minimum" that Bukharin and Rykov knew about the terrorist, espionage and sabotage activity of the Trotskyist center and about the organization of terrorist groups by their pupils and supporters, but hid all this from the party, and thereby "encouraged the criminals."

Later the resolution lists the facts of the struggle by Bukharin and Rykov (called as before, "Comrades") "against the party and against Lenin himself both prior to the October Revolution and after the October Revolution." These "facts" included Bukharin's pre-revolutionary polemic with Lenin on theoretical questions, as well as the false accusations against Rykov that he had been "against the October Revolution." These facts, the resolution emphasized, "indisputably suggest that the political fall of Comrades Bukharin and Rykov is neither accidental nor unexpected."[6]

The resolution was adopted unanimously, with two abstentions (Bukharin and Rykov). Immediately after this they were taken into custody.

The fact that not a single one of the plenum's participants besides the accused themselves dared to even abstain during the voting on the resolution does not mean that they all believed in the guilt of Bukharin and Rykov. Thus, soon after the plenum I. A. Piatnitsky told his son that "Bukharin is of course not an enemy. He spoke about Bukharin with great warmth and even greater sorrow."[7]

According to the procedure in the party at that time, the stenographic transcript of the plenum of the CC was sent to all the republic and area organizations. With this in mind, Bukharin carefully corrected the transcript of his speeches, hoping that they would reach at least the party leadership in the provinces. However, in the transcript which was sent out under the seal, "Top Secret," the material of the first point on the agenda, which comprised one-third of the transcript, was omitted. This allowed Stalin's stooges, in discussions of the results of the plenum, to present the contents of the contributions made by Bukharin and Rykov in an unrecognizably distorted form. Thus, in Leningrad, Zhdanov declared: "I do not recall more shameful, more disgusting or more repulsive behavior than the way Bukharin and Rykov conducted themselves.... They declared that we could not stand in judgment over them."[8]

To understand the logic of Bukharin's further behavior in the period separating the February-March Plenum from the trial of the "Right-Trotskyist Bloc," it is important to consider not only what was said at the plenum, but also what was consciously left unstated. We have in mind the story of the so-called "Letter of an Old Bolshevik," which played, apparently, a crucial role in Bukharin's fate.

28. The Fate of the "Letter of an Old Bolshevik"

A T THE END OF 1936 and the beginning of 1937, the pages of the Menshevik journal, *Socialist Herald*, published an article, "How the Moscow Trial was Prepared" (with a subtitle, "From the Letter of an Old Bolshevik"). The goal of this publication was to arouse public opinion in the West to protest against the mass terror, by opening the eyes of Western society to the causes and falsified character of the first trial of Old Bolsheviks.

The actual author of the article, which was presented by the editors as a letter secretly sent from the USSR by an Old Bolshevik, was B. I. Nikolaevsky, who had served in the spring of 1936 as an intermediary in negotiations between the Second International and the Soviet delegation concerning the purchase of the archives of Marx and Engels. During these negotiations Nikolaevsky often met with Bukharin, who was a member of the Soviet delegation. Nikolaevsky described for the first time in 1965 the conversations which had occurred during these meetings. The immediate cause which prompted Nikolaevsky to make public Bukharin's comments was apparently the fact that a number of Western publications printed in May of that year Bukharin's letter, "To the Future Generation of Party Leaders," the text of which had been sent abroad by Larina. It can be assumed that after the appearance of this document, the elderly Nikolaevsky felt that it was necessary to lift the vow of silence which he had voluntarily taken in order not to harm those close to Bukharin who were still among the living, especially A. M. Larina.

In preparing his article for publication in 1936, Nikolaevsky could not help but assume that Stalin had enough agents abroad to accurately learn about both Bukharin's unofficial conversations with him and about the name of the genuine author of the article. Therefore, suspicion of transmitting the information contained in the article might fall on Bukharin. Proceeding from these considerations, Nikolaevsky did not include in the article several episodes told by Bukharin, in order to avoid giving "direct evidence that he was the source of my information."[1] The same goal was apparently pursued by the editors of the

Socialist Herald, who prefaced the publication of the first part of the "Letter" in the issue coming out 22 December 1936, with the following announcement: the letter was received "just before the issue was sent to the printers.... The size of the letter and its late arrival unfortunately deny us any chance of printing its full text in the present issue. We must delay the conclusion of the letter until the first issue of 1937."[2] By writing this preface the editors were giving notice that the facts contained in the letter became known to them not in the spring of 1936, when Bukharin met with Nikolaevsky, but several months later.

In her memoirs, A. M. Larina calls the article, "How the Moscow Trial was Prepared," a deliberate provocation by Nikolaevsky and other Mensheviks in order to "deliver Bukharin's head to Stalin." She ardently rejects the very idea that Bukharin might have conducted any conversations abroad of a political, let alone oppositional, character, with Nikolaevsky or any other Menshevik. According to her, much as during the first years of the revolution, he continued to consider the Mensheviks his worst political enemies. Larina explains the impossibility of such conversations by also referring to the two following circumstances. First of all, in Moscow Bukharin had been given strict directives not to talk alone with any foreigners or emigrants. Secondly, she refers to Nikolaevsky's "unexpected visit" to Bukharin during her presence in Paris. This meeting, in her opinion, was the only time Bukharin talked to Nikolaevsky about the situation in the USSR.

As Larina recalls it, this conversation opened with Nikolaevsky's question: "Well, what is your life like back in the [Soviet] Union?" Bukharin answered: "Our life is wonderful," and then "with sincere enthusiasm" began to develop this train of thought. In doing so, "his statements differed from (his) articles in the press from the recent period only in that he did not mention Stalin repeatedly, which he could not help but do in the Soviet Union." When, however, Nikolaevsky interrupted Bukharin's enthusiastic narrative with a question about his assessment of collectivization, Bukharin said: "At home they write that I spoke out against collectivization, but this is a device used only by cheap propagandists.... Now, in the face of advancing fascism, I can say that 'Stalin has triumphed.'"[3]

This account by Larina completely fits into the conception of her book, according to which, after 1929, "Nikolai Ivanovich felt that he must halt any further struggle. Under Stalin's pressure the party had pursued another path and rejected Bukharin's economic conception. In the circumstances which had developed, Bukharin found nothing more useful than the solidarity of its ranks."[4]

Many documents which have been made public in recent years indicate that Bukharin actually did put an end to any oppositional activity from the beginning of the 1930s. However this does not mean that he remained an unqualified conformist not only in words, but in his heart. And it is hardly possible to agree with Larina's absolute confidence that Bukharin shared with her, still a very young woman at that time, all the political information that he had, and entrusted her with all his political thoughts.

I think that many of the arguments which were introduced in "The Letter of an Old Bolshevik," and which, according to later testimony from Nikolaevsky represented a refashioning of Bukharin's stories, reflect the actual content of Bukharin's political views of that time more adequately than the apologetic statements which Larina describes. We have in mind chiefly the account of how, at the end of 1932 "the situation in the country was much like the situation at the time of the Kronstadt uprising ... in the broadest circles of the party, there was only talk about how Stalin was leading the country with his policies into a blind alley: 'He has put the party at odds with the muzhik'—and that the situation could be saved only by removing Stalin."[5] The "Letter" also repeated almost verbatim Bukharin's thoughts about the tragedy of forced collectivization: "The horrors which accompanied the campaigns in the villages—you have only a faint impression of these horrors, but they, the party elite, were always well informed of what was taking place—were received by many of them very painfully."[6]

As Nikolaevsky recalled in 1965, he also learned from Bukharin's stories about "the details of Riutin's attacks on Stalin." This fact is disputed by Larina with particular vehemence. Noting that the "Letter of an Old Bolshevik" provides more of the contents of the "Riutin Platform" than was contained in the Soviet newspapers, and that the "Letter" described the discussion of the Riutin affair at a session of the Politburo, she reminds us that in 1932 Bukharin was not a member of the Politburo, and "it was not the custom to publicize what occurred at Politburo sessions, let alone at very secret ones."[7] It follows from this logic that Nikolaevsky could have received adequate information about the Riutin group only ... from a member of the Politburo.

In reality, nothing but vulgar abuse and false calumny with regard to the "Riutin affair" was printed in the official or even in the inner-party organs. However, at the beginning of the 1930s, it was still possible to envision a flow of secret information from some members of the Politburo, such as Kirov or Ordzhonikidze, to party activists of Bukharin's stature. There is evidence that the genuine content of the "Riutin Platform" was known to many members of the party. In the 1950s and 1960s, Old Bolsheviks who were campaigning for Riutin's rehabilitation adequately outlined the basic ideas of this forbidden document in conversations with "reinvestigators" from the Party Control Commission.

A. M. Larina correctly notes that the themes raised in the "Letter" were "truly seditious for those times," and that the very fact of transmitting such information to the Mensheviks could have been interpreted by the Stalinist "justice system" only as a criminal act.[8] She uses these correct premises, however, to reinforce the same considerations as before: "The Letter of an Old Bolshevik" "bore a patently provocative character," and its author "consciously undertook to help the executioners." In this regard, she does not exclude the possibility that Stalinist agents specifically provided Nikolaevsky with the information contained in the "Letter" in order to use its publication to compromise Bukharin.[9]

In actual fact the publication of the "Letter" was highly undesirable for Stalin insofar as it not only acquainted world society with facts which Stalin had been concealing for years, but also contained an explanation of his sinister intentions—precisely when he had only begun the extermination of the old party guard. The "Letter" indicated that the decision to hold the Trial of the Sixteen was made as a result of secret police investigations which showed that "the actual mood of the overwhelming majority of the old party activists is sharply hostile to Stalin"; "the party has not reconciled itself to Stalin's one-man dictatorship ... despite all their holiday declarations, in the depths of their souls the Old Bolsheviks think poorly of him, and this negative opinion is not diminishing, but growing.... The enormous majority of those who are now so expressive of their devotion to him, tomorrow, with the first change of the political situation, will betray him." The "Letter" stressed that, after weighing all these facts, Stalin came to the conclusion: "If the Old Bolsheviks, the group which today is the country's ruling layer, are not suited to carry out this function under new conditions, then they must be removed as quickly as possible from their posts and a new ruling layer must be created."[10]

These profound considerations, if combined with the personal experience of members and candidate members of the CC, could have made a very serious impression on them. Therefore, unlike other articles from the emigre press about the situation in the USSR, which were usually distributed to the party elite,* the "rank-and-file" participants in the February-March Plenum were not acquainted with this article from the *Socialist Herald*. In any case, throughout the entire course of the plenum's work, it was mentioned only in the speech of Yaroslavsky, who declared: "If you take the last issue of the *Socialist Herald*, which is entirely devoted to the previous trial, then you will become convinced that Bukharin and Rykov are following the same line of slander which is contained in the *Socialist Herald*, and the *Socialist Herald* has already begun to defend Bukharin and Rykov in advance."[11] Meanwhile, this "defense" of Bukharin and Rykov in the *Socialist Herald* was limited to an article about their "rehabilitation" in September 1936, to which a single sentence was added: "Yezhov now regrets this concession, and quite openly says that he will be able to correct it."[12]

Thus, at the plenum Bukharin was not charged with having held conversations with Nikolaevsky; reference was made only to the coincidence of his views and those found in the *Socialist Herald*.

Meanwhile the question of Bukharin's "secret" negotiations with the Mensheviks had been raised a few months before the plenum—in Radek's testimony at interrogations from 27–29 December, i.e., several days after the appearance in Paris of the issue of *Socialist Herald* containing the first part of the "Letter." Radek declared (supposedly repeating Bukharin's words): "Bukharin asked Dan [the editor of *Socialist Herald*—V. R.], in the event that the members of the "bloc" in the USSR failed, to open a campaign in their defense via the Second International. This then explains the intervention of the Second International in defense of the first center of the bloc of the Trotskyist-Zinovievist organization."[13] The transcript of this interrogation was sent to Bukharin.

Although Radek's testimony dealt not with the article in *Socialist Herald*, but with an official declaration from the leadership of the Second International in connection with the Trial of the Sixteen, the mention of Dan's name alongside Bukharin's was a very ominous sign. Bukharin received an indirect warning that the NKVD possessed some kind of information about his unofficial talks with the Mensheviks. Understanding that the very fact of such confiden-

---

* Throughout the 1920s and 1930s, the *Socialist Herald* continually published articles about events in the internal life of the party which had been carefully hidden by the party elite. The greatest sensation was caused by this journal's publication in 1929 of Kamenev's "Notes" of his negotiations with Bukharin and Sokolnikov. At the time, this publication was distributed to members of the CC in order to prove Bukharin's "double-dealing."

tial discussions could not help but arouse Stalin's extraordinary rage, Bukharin nevertheless remained in the dark about *what precisely* Stalin knew about the contents of these discussions.

In order to more clearly imagine Bukharin's behavior on his trip abroad, let us direct our attention first of all to the fact that Bukharin was traveling abroad for the first time in several years, during which he had been forced to lead an unnatural way of life in the USSR, up to refusing to meet with his closest friends out of fear that he would be suspected of "maintaining a faction." It is understandable that when he found himself abroad, Bukharin felt that he was in an absolutely different atmosphere, and was intoxicated by the apparent freedom from continuous surveillance and the threat of being denounced for the slightest imprudent utterance. In this regard it is appropriate to cite the evidence of another Bolshevik who, according to Nikolaevsky, told him: "There [in the USSR—V. R.], we have forgotten how to be sincere. Only abroad, if we have dealings with a person whom we know we can trust, do we begin to talk sincerely."[14]

With the carelessness that was characteristic of him at times, Bukharin evidently did not consider that the invisible surveillance of the NKVD abroad might be no less thorough and sophisticated than in the USSR. He perhaps remembered this only after Nikolaevsky's untimely visit to his hotel room, when he told his wife in a worried voice that Nikolaevsky apparently learned about the absence of the other members of the commission in the hotel, made a preliminary call to him on the telephone, and appeared especially in order to speak with him alone. It was then that Bukharin expressed his concern about this own lack of caution: "Nevertheless, I blurted out too much to him—about cheap agitation."[15]

According to a number of reliable accounts, in 1935–1936 Bukharin often entertained thoughts about the possibility of a new wave of Stalinist terror in which he would perish. There is nothing surprising in the fact that on the eve of these events Bukharin wanted to tell his secret thoughts, which he had decided to share with almost no one in his own country, to an old socialist whose personal decency was widely known. Moreover, in 1936 Bukharin could not consider Nikolaevsky and other Mensheviks to be the irreconcilable opponents that they were during the first years of the revolution. After all, even the official course of the Comintern at that time included following a policy of the united workers' front, i.e., of an alliance with the parties of the Second International, which included the Russian Mensheviks.

Given all these circumstances, the "Letter of an Old Bolshevik" apparently played no small role in Bukharin's behavior during the investigation and trial. It is characteristic that at the second Moscow Trial Radek did not repeat his version about Bukharin's negotiations with Dan. This version, which was placed in Radek's mouth at the investigation, was set aside until the trial of the "Rightist-Trotskyist Bloc," where it was introduced by Bukharin himself.

We must assume that Stalin saved the "Letter of an Old Bolshevik" in order to put psychological pressure on Bukharin during the prison investigation. From the standpoint of both Bukharin and his executioners, this document was evidence of the main crime which determined the rejection of his attempts to refute all the other charges made against him. This crime was known in the party jargon of the time as "double-dealing."

As we recall, Bukharin left, or to be more precise, was forcibly led away from the plenum of the CC without having confessed to a single of the charges made against him. At the same time, in his speeches at the plenum he never tired of repeating that he considered Stalin's policies to be "brilliant," and Stalin to be the irreproachable leader of the party and the state. Let us now imagine how Bukharin must have felt when after all this he was shown the article from a Menshevik journal which cited his genuine thoughts of an opposite character. According to Stalin's logic, which Bukharin had thoroughly assimilated, this meant that he had continued to remain a "double-dealer" until the last hour that he remained at liberty. The only way to mitigate this "crime," according to the same logic, would have been to agree to "completely lay down one's arms before the party," i.e., to confirm all the other charges made against him.

Bukharin's situation was seriously aggravated by one more circumstance. Even if he had been shown the article in *Socialist Herald* and been acquainted with the agents' reports about his unofficial conversations with Nikolaevsky (strictly banned by Moscow), then even after this he would have remained unsure about what further information about his behavior abroad was at the NKVD's disposal. Moreover, Bukharin was responsible for even more serious "crimes" (about which, it is true, the Stalinist agents might have been unaware).

During his trip abroad, Bukharin held candid conversations not only with Nikolaevsky, but also with F. N. Ezerskaya, formerly the secretary of Rosa Luxemburg. Ezerskaya even proposed that he remain abroad and publish an international organ of "rightists." Bukharin told her that he thought that it was "impermissible to leave the field of battle, all the more so since he felt that the situation [in the Soviet Union—V. R.] was far from hopeless [from the standpoint of the defeat of the anti-Stalinist forces—V. R.]."[16]

Particularly "seditious" was Bukharin's conversation with F. I. Dan. According to the memoirs of L. O. Dan, published after her death, Bukharin appeared at the Dans' apartment unexpectedly and explained his visit by the fact that "it simply would be good for his soul." During this encounter Bukharin gave the impression of a man who felt completely doomed. Telling Dan, "Stalin is not a man, but a devil," who "would devour us [Old Bolsheviks—V. R.]," Bukharin gave a devastating psychological portrait of Stalin: "Here you say that you know little about him, but we know him all too well.... He is even unhappy because he cannot convince everyone, even himself, that he is greater than everyone else, and this is his misfortune, perhaps his only human trait.... But what is no longer human, but something diabolical is that for his 'misfortune' he cannot help but get revenge over people, all people, and particularly those who are higher in some way, or better than him."[17]

It is remarkable that Dan, to the end of his days, never told anyone about his meeting with Bukharin, even his closest friend Nikolaevsky. L. O. Dan explained this by the fact that her husband felt that his tale "might somehow prove dangerous for Bukharin." Nikolaevsky himself called Lidiia Osipovna's comments the "purest invention." Feeling certain that fate had made him "in a certain sense ... Bukharin's executor of sorts,"[18] he could not believe that Bukharin had shared his secret thoughts with anyone else among the emigrants.

It is natural that A. M. Larina, who considers Nikolaevsky's interview "a false document," calls L. O. Dan's memoirs "an even stranger document." Completely rejecting the slightest probability of a sincere conversation between Bukharin and Dan, she raises a question in this regard: why, if this conversation really took place, did Dan, who died in 1947, not tell anyone about it after Bukharin's execution, when "he no longer had to fear any adverse consequences for Bukharin?"[19] It does not occur to Anna Mikhailovna that such extreme caution on Dan's part might have arisen because he knew that the smallest leak of information about the given conversation might bring about her death, and the death of other hostages of the deceased Bukharin who remained in the USSR.

Dan and Nikolaevsky were experienced politicians who carefully followed what was happening in the Soviet Union. They grasped the situation there more accurately than Bukharin, let alone his wife.

Such are some of the circumstances surrounding the "Letter of an Old Bolshevik" and its influence on Bukharin's fate.

29. The February-March Plenum: Questions of Party Democracy

AFTER THE COMPLETION of the Bukharin-Rykov case, discussion at the plenum shifted to a completely different plane. On the surface, the second point on the agenda bore an absolutely "peaceful" and even "democratic" character. It was formulated in the following way: "The preparation of party organizations for elections to the Supreme Soviet of the USSR according to the new electoral system, and the corresponding restructuring of party work." The word "perestroika" [restructuring], which became widely known throughout the world after Gorbachev came to power, was one of the favorite words in the political lexicon of Stalinism.

Zhdanov, who delivered a report on the question, repeated the statements of official propaganda about the beneficial changes connected with adopting "the world's most democratic" constitution and with introducing "the most democratic electoral system." Superficially, these changes looked very impressive. Instead of the previous limitations of voting rights for the so-called "lishentsy [deprived]," (representatives of the former ruling classes), universal and equal elections were introduced, i.e., the right of all citizens of the USSR to participate in them on equal grounds. Whereas earlier the elections had been a multistep process (the delegates to lower Councils [soviets] chose the delegates to higher Councils), now the Councils on all levels were to be elected by the population by means of direct voting. While according to the previous constitution the elections were held in the form of open balloting, the new constitution introduced the secret ballot. Of course, all these changes must have made an enormous impression on the Soviet people, especially the former "deprived," who for the first time felt themselves to be citizens possessing the same political rights as other members of Soviet society.

As one more example of the democratization of the political system, Zhdanov named the introduction by the new constitution of universal polling of the population, or the referendum, regarding the most important questions of state and social life. Such referendums were not held once in the USSR over the more than half a century which passed after the adoption of the constitution of 1936. The first general referendum was the referendum in 1991 on the fate of the USSR, the results of which were trampled a few months later by the deal made at Belovezhskaya Pushcha.

All these "profound transformations," as Zhdanov emphasized, placed two tasks before the party: 1. Preparation for the election battle; 2. Democratization of the activity of all state and public organizations and, most of all, the party itself.

Stalin first spoke about the "election struggle" in a conversation with the American journalist Roy Howard. When the latter expressed doubt whether the new electoral system could guarantee political freedom, Stalin replied: "I foresee a very lively election struggle. We have no small number of establishments which work poorly. It sometimes happens that this or that local organ of power is incapable of satisfying one or another of the multifaceted and ever growing needs of the laborers in the city and countryside. Have you built or not built a good school? Have you improved our housing conditions? Are you a bureaucrat? Have you helped make our labor more effective, and our life more cultured? These will be the criteria with which millions of voters will approach the candidates, tossing out those who are useless, striking them from the ballots, advancing better people and putting forward their candidacy ... universal, equal, direct and secret elections in the USSR will be a whip in the hands of the population against poorly working organs of power."[1]

As was shown by the discussion following Zhdanov's report, some of the plenum's participants perceived the possibility of an "election struggle" in the spirit of the same democratic perspectives outlined by Stalin. Thus, N. K. Krupskaya emphasized that "closed elections [i.e., secret balloting—V. R.] would in fact show how close the party comrades were to the masses and how much they enjoyed authority among the masses."[2]

However, the majority of those who spoke understood very well that Stalin's widely disseminated assurances were aimed at western public opinion, and the "election struggle" would be a struggle against those who dared to take seriously the democratic innovations which had been written into the constitution. Even in Zhdanov's report attention was paid to the possibility that "hostile elements" might become active in the election campaign. The first to be declared to be preparing for the "election struggle" were representatives of the

Church, who after the constitution was adopted had begun to appeal to the local organs of power for the opening of churches, mosques, and so forth.* Hopes for the restoration of religious life often dovetailed with hopes for the liquidation of the collective farms. The secretary of the Azov-Black Sea Area Committee, Yevdokimov, said that while taking the All-Union Census in January 1937 (which soon after the plenum was declared to be an act of "sabotage"), which included a question about attitude toward religion, "enemies" in the village locality said: "The more believers that are registered, the more quickly church affairs will get under way. Everything will return to the way it was, and there will be no more collective farms."[3]

A second hostile group was declared to be the kulaks who had been freed from the camps, then returned to their previous places of residence and were demanding that they be given land and accepted into the collective farms.

The greatest danger was seen to lie among the members of the former socialist parties and among the "camouflaged Trotskyists" who would want to take advantage of the "freedom of the elections." Khrushchev declared that on the eve of the upcoming elections one could see the "active behavior of several hostile groups both in the city and the countryside," and in Riazan an "SR group" had already appeared, the leader of which was recruiting supporters and was telling them "what they had to do in order to work their people into the regional soviet, the village soviet, and the collective farms. From there they do their harm and conduct anti-Soviet, counterrevolutionary work."[4]

Stetsky asserted that it would be difficult for "hostile organizations" to enter their candidates in the elections to the Supreme Soviet, but in the election of lower Soviets, particularly the village soviets, "the electoral struggle will be extremely serious." Stalin immediately supported this idea by declaring that "a number of village soviets might fall into their [enemies'—V. R.] hands." Spurred on by the leader's support, Stetsky stressed that in the elections to the lower Soviets, "the struggle will proceed over the most significant economic needs, questions of everyday life, and great demagogy will be unleashed by hostile elements."[5]

Zhdanov's report indicated that in the course of the election campaign, the dissatisfaction of the masses might erupt over "certain pressure," without which "most difficult campaigns" could not manage. Stating that such pres-

---

* That such episodes actually took place can be seen from the operations summaries of the NKVD (*Neizvestnaia Rossiia. XX vek*, v. II, 1992, pp. 278-279).

sure "enters into the conception of the dictatorship of the working class,"
Zhdanov declared: "We do not renounce this pressure, and in the future it would
be ridiculous to renounce it. There probably will be demagogy concerning the
exaggeration of all kinds of shortcomings of our workers along this line. The
party organizations should be able to take these people (i.e., those who apply
the pressure) under their defense," for agitation "on the part of hostile elements" might be stirred up against them.[6]

In discussing the second aspect of "restructuring"—democratization of
the activity of party and other organizations—a depressing picture was un-
veiled at the plenum regarding the complete suppression of democratic elements on all levels of political and social life. At times it might have seemed
that the party discussion of 1923 had returned, and that the speakers were
repeating the arguments of the earlier opposition.

Zhdanov said that the majority of party committees—starting with the
smallest organizations and ending with the area committees and the CC of the
union republics—had not been reelected after the Seventeenth Congress, i.e.,
for three years—in violation of the party Statutes, which demanded that such
reelections be held once every year to year and a half.[7] Following him, Postyshev
announced that after the Seventeenth Congress, in the Ukraine the regional,
city and area party conferences had not been convened, "and, unfortunately,
there had been no voices which demanded the convening of such conferences....
They were waiting for instructions from above." In reply to Stalin's question:
"And the Statutes?" Postyshev answered sadly, "They forgot the Statutes, Comrade Stalin."[8]

Another blatant violation of party democracy named by the speakers was
the widely spread practice of cooptation onto leading party organs. Examples
were given where 40 to 50 percent of the members of area committees were
coopted, and often such cooptation was done not at plenums, but by referendum. Analogous practices existed in Soviet and trade union bodies: the pre-
sidiums of several city committees consisted completely of coopted members;
in the central committees of many trade unions "the elected members were few
and far between."

Along with being elected, what also disappeared from what the party Statutes stipulated was accountability of elected officials before the organizations
which had selected them. As Postyshev noted, the role of plenums of the party
committees as collectives before which apparatchiks were responsible, had vir-

tually come to an end; the plenary sessions of area committees were reduced to listening to instructive reports from the area committee secretaries, "who not infrequently read lectures to the members of the area committee. There is no situation where the member of the bureau of an area committee has felt responsible to the plenum of the area committee."[9]

As became clear from the report and discussion, virtually all the other elements of party democracy turned out to have been violated. In many regions, the plenums of regional committees had not been convened for seven to ten years. If they had been held, then the elections of apparatchiks at them turned into a system of appointments. Secretaries were chosen ahead of time by higher committees, approved by the Central Committee and then recommended to the plenum, having "two sanctions: the sanction of the area committee and the sanction of the Central Committee." At party conferences the candidacy for the elections to party committees was discussed behind closed doors by a narrow circle of apparatchiks, and then submitted as a list to be voted on, in order to "avoid tiresome criticism on the part of the party masses with regard to one or other of the candidates."[10]

The expulsion of elected members of party committees also proceeded along nondemocratic lines. Insofar as "a whole bunch of people" often were expelled from a regional committee or city committee, "expanded" plenary sessions replete with arbitrarily chosen "party activists" would be called. At one of these "expanded plenums," which removed twelve members of the city committee, only ten members of the city committee were in attendance; thus, "ten people swallowed up twelve people."[11] Evidently, such mass expulsions as those the speakers were discussing occurred under conditions when the people being expelled were under arrest.

In the place of the flouted democratic procedures, what became widely disseminated was the practice of "self-evaluations" by communists before the smallest party organizations. To the accompaniment of general laughter in the hall, Zhdanov gave the example of one such "self-evaluation," after which the party meeting passed the resolution: "Having heard the self-evaluation of communist Sidorov, the meeting resolves: to arrest Sidorov."[12]

The plenum was given many examples of how the apparatchiks were completely estranged from the party masses. Postyshev reported that in Kiev the heads of the CC departments did not feel that they needed to visit the meetings of the smallest party organizations to which they belonged.[13] The secretary of the Dnepropetrovsk area committee, Khataevich, confessed that four to five years ago he felt it was his unconditional obligation once a week to visit party meetings at the factories, collective farms, etc., but for the last year he had not once attended such meetings.[14]

In the primary organizations, the role of party meetings often became a pure formality: "the resolution on this or that question is introduced in good time or is scribbled down by masters of this matter during the very meeting, without any attention to what is being said in the discussion."[15]

From the speeches of the plenum's participants, it followed that democratic principles were being trampled not only in party, but in all state and public organizations. Leading officials who were elected to the Soviets often refused to carry out their most elementary duties as a deputy. An end was put to what had previously been the widespread regular reports to the members of consumer cooperatives, the workers engaged in trade, the communal economy, and so forth.

In the workers' collectives, the role of social organizations amounted to nothing, and the resolution of all problems passed into the hands of a "triangle" consisting of the director of the enterprise, the secretary of the party committee, and the chairman of the trade union committee. This gave rise to an organization, "standing apart from the normal elected organs (party or factory committees), officially and regularly functioning, yet never stipulated by any party or Soviet laws. It meets, passes resolutions and issues directives to be carried out, etc."[16]

The bureaucratization of all social and political life was expressed also in the way the apparatchiks guarded themselves from criticism by their subordinates. As Kosior said, at the congresses of the Soviets, the plenums of executive committees or city soviets, "it was considered to be a great lack of tact if someone accidentally criticized the chairman or anyone else. Even heads of departments considered such criticism to be a deep insult."[17]

"The number one people," who had completely escaped from the control of the masses and become autocratic bosses in their regions, seemed to compete with each other in establishing their own "cults." The authority of a leading official began to be measured by how many collective farms, enterprises and institutions bore his name.[18]

From separate facts and examples the speakers passed on to serious generalizations. In a number of cases, the speaker stressed that instead of democratic centralism, the party was confronted with the growth of bureaucratic centralism. In his concluding remarks, Zhdanov openly stated that among the apparatchiks, the view had taken root that the party was not a self-motivated organization, but "something on the order of a system of lower, middle and higher bodies."[19]

The plenum was supplied with statistics which testified to the unfavorable changes in the social composition of the party, the shrinking portion of workers in it, and the sharp growth of the share of the bureaucracy. For instance, in Voronezh, five thousand five hundred party members worked in state institutions, two thousand in the places of higher education, and around two thousand in the enterprises; worker-communists at the bench numbered only five hundred fifty. In one Voronezh factory, out of three thousand five hundred workers, only three were members of the party.[20]

It would seem that the picture that emerged at the plenum of the degradation of all political institutions should have prompted the speakers to analyze the causes of such a situation and to come to the conclusion that the higher party leadership was responsible. However Stalin, who guided the speakers with his interjections to place the emphasis he needed in their criticism, spurred them to make a new amalgam: to place the blame for the undermining of party democracy on ... "camouflaged Trotskyists."

This idea of Stalin's was grasped best of all by Yevdokimov, who declared, "The counterrevolutionary band of Trotskyists, Zinovievists, rightists, 'Leftists,' and other counterrevolutionary scum has seized the leadership of the overwhelming part of the region's cities. This band set itself the tasks of undermining Soviet and party work, in order to discredit the party and the Soviet regime. It suppressed self-criticism in every way, instilled bureaucratism in the party and soviet organizations, and persecuted people who dared to speak out against them, which was a direct mockery of the inner-party and Soviet democracy." As confirmation of this, Yevdokimov offered the testimony of arrested party functionaries about how, in order to arouse dissatisfaction with the party apparatus, they "suppressed self-criticism, smothered the living word, and left without any consequences the declarations and complaints of the workers. Anyone who tried to criticize these conditions at a meeting was persecuted." In response to Stalin's question about how matters stood with regard to cooptation, Yevdokimov immediately replied, "Cooptation in party organs is widely applied, Comrade Stalin. Of those who have been coopted, a fair number now sit in the organs of the NKVD (*laughter*)."[21]

The resolution on Zhdanov's report (the only plenum resolution which was published in the press), contained no small amount of chatter about democratizing party life, establishing secret balloting in elections to party organs and guaranteeing each party member the unlimited right to reject or criticize the candidates to these organs.

Of course, under conditions of cruel police domination which permeated the entire life of the party and the nation, Stalin would not be worried by "elections without a choice" to organs of state power, or by secret balloting in electing the party organs. This democratic decorum was intended to deceive the masses and foreign public opinion. The only real innovation lay in Stalin's proposal for each leader to prepare his own replacement.

Of course, the plenum's participants did not guess that this unexpected proposal, which was explained by the need to avoid the excessive shuttling of cadres from region to region, had a completely different goal: not to allow complete collapse and chaos in directing the party and the country during the impending total extermination of "number one people" in all chains of the apparatus. Nevertheless, the decree to "prepare replacements" could not help but cause bewilderment and worry among the plenum's participants, the majority of whom were "number one people." These people, who were far from retirement age, could not understand: why did they have to immediately advance candidates to replace all leaders?

However Stalin was not worried by such moods among the high-placed apparatchiks, who were pretty well frightened by recent events and who did not dare to protest against this innovation. Most important for him was to appeal to the future "promotees," for whom his proposal opened the seductive perspective of a rapid ascent up the career ladder. Calling Stalin's proposal "brilliant," Zhdanov emphasized one more of Stalin's theses, declaring, "the shortage of democratism ... was impeding us from seeing new people, and many of our people are stagnating; standing there forgotten, they are becoming a reserve for the dissatisfied within our party." Following these words by Zhdanov, Stalin tossed out a remark which was supposed to underscore the legitimacy of such dissatisfaction: "There are so many talented people, yet they are not promoted in time, and they begin to rot, to stagnate."[22] This idea, which was developed by Stalin in his own report (see Chapter 34), was a direct call to the careerist-minded youth and a promise of swift promotion to high posts.

30. The February-March Plenum on Sabotage

THE NEXT POINT on the agenda was formulated in the following manner: "The lessons of wrecking, sabotage and espionage by the Japanese-German-Trotskyist agents in the People's Commissariats of Heavy Industry and Transport."

Already during the discussion of the problem of party democracy, several speakers, without any connection to the theme of their contributions, introduced "facts" concerning wrecking by "Trotskyists." Thus Yevdokimov said "enemies who had settled down in the Rostov City Committee" deliberately did not supply firefighting equipment when they were building schools. Moreover, as Yevdokimov declared when he referred to the testimony of the "wreckers," they said: "Let the little children study, and after a certain time we will build them such a fire that the entire population of Rostov will curse the Soviet regime until the day they die."[1]

The imagination of the other speakers did not extend to such sinister examples. The secretary of the Sverdlovsk Area Committee, Kabakov, could tell only about how on the day that the congress of Soviets opened in Sverdlovsk, there were bread lines, insofar as "in the organs of the Regional Domestic Trade Council, the entire leadership was focused on planning and the transport system was seized by enemies." Another example cited by Kabakov of "sabotage in trade matters" appeared even more anecdotal: "In one store we encountered the following: Zinoviev's books were being used for wrapping paper, and in another shop, purchases were being wrapped with a report by Tomsky (*laughter*). We checked this out, and it turns out that the trade organizations had bought a respectable number of tons of such literature. Who can say that such literature was being used only for wrapping paper?"[2]

Just as fantastic was the example of "ideological sabotage" given by Bogushevsky. He said that after broadcasting the sentence in the case of the "Anti-Soviet Trotskyist center," the Minsk radio station "played a concert which included the famous B-flat Minor Sonata by Chopin, the third part of which is the "Marche Funèbre," i.e, Chopin's renowned funeral march.... All this was done very subtly: it was not simply a funeral march—that would have been too open and it would have been easier to notice this in the program and prevent it from happening—but the B-flat Minor Sonata; not everyone knows that it contains the march. This, of course, was no accident. It can be explained by the fact that there turned out to be a litter of Trotskyist elements and other absolutely unsuitable people there."[3] According to Bogushevsky, such high musical erudition and sophistication of the "Trotskyist elements" served to express their sorrow on the occasion of the defendants' execution.

Naturally, more impressive "facts" were needed to stun the plenum's members and the nation's entire population with the scale and severe consequences of the "sabotage." They were provided by Molotov's report when he opened the discussion on the agenda's third point. This report was quickly published in *Pravda* and *Bolshevik*, and then issued in a separate edition in a press run of more than a million and a half copies.

To describe the enormous scale which the sabotage had taken, Molotov liberally quoted the testimony of people who had headed the largest enterprises and construction sites. These testimonies contained descriptions of a wide spectrum of sabotage activity: from delaying planning and slowing the tempo of construction, to ruining machinery, organizing accidents and explosions, to poisoning workers with gas, and so forth. All the lack of coordination and the miscalculations connected with forced industrialization, up to the difficult living conditions for the workers (supposedly deliberately created by "wreckers" in order to provoke mass dissatisfaction) and to deception when organizing the Stakhanov movement ("to credit individual workers with work which they had actually not performed" in order to "sow discord between Stakhanovites and non-Stakhanovites"[4]), was explained in the report as the intrigues of "wreckers."

Recalling the "sabotage" trials of non-party specialists at the end of the 1920s and beginning of the 1930s, Molotov unequivocally indicated who it was that now should be dealt the main blow. Noting that the leaders of enterprises "are now almost all communists," he stressed that "the peculiarity of the sabotage being unmasked now is that here ... a party card is used in order to organize sabotage in our state apparatus and in our industry."[5]

After declaring that "recent facts show us the participation not only of

Trotskyists, but of Bukharinists too in the organization of wrecking activity," Molotov quoted the evidence of one of the Bukharinists who was asked: "Did you inform the all-union center of the counterrevolutionary organization of Rightists about your wrecking activity?" He replied: "Yes, I informed Uglanov, a member of the center.... I recall that in one of our meetings at his apartment Uglanov said with satisfaction: 'Good man, Vasya, you have turned out well' (*Postyshev*: Yes, Vasya. *Voice from the audience*: What scum, ah!)."[6]

Molotov spoke with special indignation about the work of the commission created by Ordzhonikidze to verify facts of sabotage at the enterprises of the People's Commissariat of Heavy Industry [NKTP]. In doing so he paid the most attention to the summary note of the Ginzburg-Pavlunovsky commission, which Poskrebyshev demanded be sent to Stalin the day after Ordzhonikidze's funeral. Apropos of this, the following fact is noteworthy: when he learned of Ginzburg's intention to send Stalin the note without amendments regarding "sabotage," M. M. Kaganovich—at that time one of the leading officials in the NKTP—told Ginzburg that in such a case he "had to prepare a small suitcase" (having in mind the possibility of his arrest) and added: "You are not an infant, you know what is going on in our country."[7]

In Molotov's report, the work of the Ginzburg-Pavlunovsky commission was interpreted as "a sign that we are restructuring with difficulty; it is a sign of our inability to develop far-sightedness and vigilance, of our inability to develop insight into all the enemy's moves." Molotov indicated that for many years the head of the Ural Railway Car Construction Site was "the most active wrecker, Maryasan, who then confessed to everything, and for a long period the secretary of the party committee at the same place was a Trotskyist wrecker, Shaliko Okudzhava. This was a closely knit group. It is clear that they performed no small number of wrecking acts against our state. But how can we understand, in the light of all this, that in February of this year, on orders from the NKTP, a commission traveled to the Urals Railway Car Construction Site to check up on wrecking acts and ... stated: 'Wrecking activity at the building site did not develop much...' (*Voice from the audience*: Did not? Nonsense. Did not?) ... And they indicate why they came to that conclusion. But while they were traveling there in February, Maryasan gave new testimony, more concrete testimony, and it does not coincide with such conclusions. How are we to understand this?... Comrades from the Commissariat of Heavy Industry, can't you once again check out both Maryasan and the commission which traveled to the site?* (*Voice from the audience*: Correct!)"[8] This passage from Molotov's report served as an unequivocal warning to party and economic leaders about the inadmissibility of placing under the slightest doubt the veracity of the self-slander generated in the torture chambers of the NKVD.

This idea was even more candidly and cynically expressed in the published version of the text of the report, where it reads: "The political shortsightedness of the commission is absolutely obvious.... It is sufficient to say that this commission did not introduce a single fact of wrecking at the building site. That means that the inveterate wrecker, Maryasan, and the other wrecker, Okudzhava, slandered themselves."[9]

Commenting on the given passage in Molotov's report, Trotsky wrote: "When reading this you do not believe your eyes! These people have lost not only their shame, but their sense of caution.... Further investigation of 'the facts of sabotage' was obviously needed because public opinion did not believe either the charges made by the GPU or the testimony it extorted. However a commission under the leadership of Pavlunovsky, formerly a longstanding member of the GPU, did not uncover a single fact of sabotage."[10]

The story of the Urals Railway Car Construction Site had a noteworthy continuation. After Ordzhonikidze's death Mezhlauk was appointed to the post of People's Commissar for Heavy Industry; he, in turn was soon replaced by Kaganovich. In search of wreckers, Kaganovich traveled to Nizhny Tagil. After inspecting the factory that had been built to make railway cars, he left arm in arm with its new director. That same night, the director of this factory was arrested for the third time, and at the same time almost all of the other leading officials of the factory and the city.[11] Nevertheless, when he returned to Moscow, Kaganovich summoned Ginzburg and, avoiding all discussions about wrecking, reported the outstanding condition in which he found the Ural Railway Car Factory.[12]

After outlining these concrete "facts of sabotage," Molotov began to refute the "arguments and conversations suggesting that sabotage was being strongly

---

* Pavlunovsky was soon arrested and shot. Ginzburg, who survived until recent times, writes in his memoirs that for him it remains a mystery why, after Molotov's words, he not only was not repressed, but even was promoted: he was appointed in 1937 Deputy People's Commissar of Heavy Industry, and in 1939 People's Commissar of Construction for the USSR (*Voprosy istorii KPSS*, 1991, no. 3 , p. 45).

inflated"—sentiments common among leaders of the economy. Stressing that "such arguments are, of course, a vulgar mistake, a mistake of political short-sightedness," Molotov called upon people "to watch for the enemy in good time and to strike him down in good time, tearing away his hands, and when necessary, uprooting him completely, destroying the enemy."[13]

In concluding his report, Molotov expressed confidence that "rooting out the wreckers, saboteurs and spies and other scum in industry and our entire state apparatus" would allow us in the course of "the next several years ... to catch up to and outstrip the leading capitalist countries in technology."[14]

Following Molotov, Kaganovich gave a report which astonished the plenum's participants with its statistics about the scale of the sabotage on railway transport. He said that the Turkestano-Siberian and other railway lines had been "built in a wrecking manner," and that all the journals "dealing with steam engines, railway cars, rails, and so forth" as well as the department of the institutes of higher learning under the jurisdiction of the NKPS were in the hands of wreckers. Almost all the reporters at the dispatchers' conference which had been held in 1934 "turned out to be wreckers and were arrested as Japanese spies and saboteurs." No less horrific was the statistic cited by Kaganovich concerning the scale of the repression in transport. According to him, in merely twenty-six defense lines, four hundred forty-six spies were discovered and "a whole number of other bastards."[15]

It is natural that these statistics would raise the question: how could Kaganovich, who had been working since 1935 as People's Commissar of Transport, overlook such a quantity of wreckers and spies? In this regard, Kaganovich offered a whole series of explanations.

First of all, he repented that he had been "too trustful" and as an example of such trustfulness said he had not paid attention to the fact that one of the officials in his commissariat was a "longtime friend of Serebriakov and each time that he came to Moscow, he always went to visit Serebriakov." After giving a few other similar facts, Kaganovich declared: "My only consolation is that I am not alone, but many of you are in the same situation (*commotion and movement in the hall*), but this consolation is not very pleasant and I think that each of you could provide the same type of examples and monstrosities."[16]

Secondly, Kaganovich said that one of the reasons why the commissariat was so thoroughly "littered" with enemies was that Trotsky had headed transport in 1921.

Thirdly, Kaganovich cited many figures which show that since he had come to this commissariat, he had conducted tireless work in "uprooting" Trotskyists, primarily from among the leading officials in transport. In this regard he announced that on 1 January 1935, out of one hundred seventy-seven heads of departments in the commissariat, thirty-six had participated in the past in oppositional groups; after two years, among two hundred fifty-one department heads (by that time the apparatus of the NKPS had managed to grow significantly), only six former oppositionists remained. Out of ninety-nine leading officials who had been removed from their posts in 1935–1936, thirty-six had been arrested, and twenty-two had been fired before their arrest. In turn, among those arrested, Kaganovich said, in demonstrating his "logic," "three people were listed in questionnaires as former Trotskyists, the rest did not list themselves as former Trotskyists, which means that they were hiding."[17]

Kaganovich announced that in January 1936, he had issued a directive which attributed the main cause for accidents in transport to the wrecking and subversive activity of class enemies. In this directive he advanced the demand "in a month's time to remove all people who *are capable of sabotage* [my emphasis—V. R.].[18] In executing this directive, several thousand people were purged. In the apparatus of the political departments which served railway transport, two hundred twenty-nine Trotskyists were "unmasked," and in the apparatus of the NKPS one hundred nine Trotskyists.[19]

Fourthly, Kaganovich gave examples of his own vigilance with regard to his closest assistants. He reported that "many times, in the presence of a number of people, he looked with suspicion" at his deputy, Livshits, and said to him, "as part of decisively uprooting the last vestiges of Trotskyism ... 'Why do you walk around looking so gloomy? What's wrong with you?... You have remnants of Trotskyism.... There is still some Trotskyism left in you.'"[20]

Kaganovich told about Kniazev, another official who had been shot. Learning by chance that a certain "Kharbinets from the KVZhD [the Chinese-eastern railway]" worked with Kniazev and even lived at his apartment (all former officials of the Chinese-Eastern Railway, which was sold in 1935 by the Soviet government to Manchuria, were placed under suspicion as "Japanese spies"), he, Kaganovich, phoned the NKVD and asked that they organize surveillance of Kniazev.[21]

Kaganovich also described the specific methods he employed to mobilize his own apparatus for the struggle against wrecking. Thus, he "organized something like a war game," by proposing that the commissariat's specialists "imagine themselves to be enemies" and show "how they could create tie-ups at the station, how they could disrupt a schedule."[22] Kaganovich recalled his experience when he worked in the 1920s as the head of the distribution department of the CC, when "we gave each person an hour, maybe an hour and a half; we sat there and heard all about his grandpa and grandma, but in doing so we got to know the person."[23]

Finally, Kaganovich did not let slip the chance to mention the testimony of people under arrest who told how the "iron Narkom" [people's commissar] thwarted their sabotage attempts. Thus, he cited Serebriakov's testimony about how Kaganovich unmasked the "'theory of limitation' which our organization used to camouflage its wrecking activity."[24]

In his report, Kaganovich repeatedly mentioned Stalin's "perspicacity" in uncovering "enemies." He told how "Comrade Stalin observed Shermegorn, who worked on construction, and followed his speeches before the transportation commission. Several times he said, 'This is a bad person, a hostile man.' I do not recall whether he called him an out-and-out wrecker, but in any case he pointed him out directly."[25]

Kaganovich declared: Stalin had "prophetically warned" that the "Trotskyists, Rightists, Right-Leftists and all other opportunist elements which joined them, the majority of them—must inevitably slide into the camp of imperialism. We now see that they have slid into the camp of fascism." One more "foresight," which had been expressed by Stalin in 1933, amounted to the fact that "wrecking in the collective farms and the sabotage of grain collections will in the end play as beneficial a role in the cause of organizing new Bolshevik cadres in the collective farms and Soviet farms as the Shakhty trial in the realm of industry." Having quoted these words, Kaganovich declared that the present reprisals against "wreckers" would play just as "beneficial a role."[26]

Stating that the stoppages, disruptions of schedules, lateness of trains, lowering of norms and, of course, train wrecks, all of this was the work of saboteurs and spies, Kaganovich gave as an example one of the wrecks in which the guilty parties were convicted of negligence. Declaring that this case was now being reviewed at his request in order to reclassify the guilt of those charged as "wrecking," Kaganovich emphasized that "of course, we cannot announce that all [people involved in wrecks—V. R.] have been saboteurs, but in actual fact these were acts of sabotage."[27]

Expressing his satisfaction that "some of these bastards, these wreckers, have been shot," Kaganovich announced that the train wrecks nevertheless had not come to an end. He stated that the recent wreck of a passenger train, which resulted in tens of victims, according to its organizers "was supposed to become widely known and understood to be the response of Trotskyists who remained active in the underground." As proof, he cited the testimony of one of those under arrest: "I was profoundly happy that I avenged the Bolsheviks for the Trial of the Anti-Soviet Trotskyist Center."[28]

Realizing that the wave of repression which was sweeping through transport might cause the mass flight of officials from this branch, Kaganovich proposed that the martial law which was in effect in the defense factories be extended to transport: workers should be stripped of their passports so that they could not transfer to other enterprises.

The discussion of the reports reflected the bewilderment of many participants at the plenum who did not know how concretely they were to "report" about the struggle against wrecking in their departments. In their contributions, the focus was primarily on bureaucratism, economic chaos, deception, petty regulations, voluntarism in planning and other shortcomings in the direction of the economy.

Only the speeches made by Sarkisov and Bagirov contributed to deepening the psychosis over wrecking. Stating that wreckers in the Donbass "had chosen a very clever tactic," Sarkisov cited a letter sent to the NKTP by four directors of coke-chemical factories about blatant deficiencies they had uncovered during construction of these factories. Sarkisov said that this letter had been composed "by Trotskyist bastards ... in order to insure and camouflage themselves."[29]

Bagirov announced that previously, explosions at oil fields had been considered the results of negligence, but "now the people under arrest are testifying that this was not negligence or dereliction of duty, but was done consciously." With great satisfaction Bagirov told how "we arrested, in particular, Ginzburg, a friend of Trotsky's son, Sedov, whom this Ginzburg had recommended for party membership."[30]

Going beyond the bounds of the topic being discussed, Bagirov hurried to announce that in Azerbaidzhan "the Trotskyist-Zinovievist periphery has formed a bloc with counterrevolutionary nationalist elements and through them, with the Musavatists." This bloc, according to him, was engaged in orga-

N. I Yezhov; drawing by A. A. Valter,
Moscow, 1937

Yezhov, Dimitrov and Stalin head for
Red Square, 1 May 1937

nizing rebellious groups in the village areas and had maintained close contact with the nationalists and other "Islamic" republics in order to prepare the separation of these republics from the USSR and the formation of "a powerful Turko-Tatar state under the leadership of Turkey." Along with this, the nationalist elements, according to Bagirov's speech, did not avoid wrecking activity on a smaller scale. For instance, they created "confusion in the realm of orthography and terminology from the Turkish language." Bagirov especially stressed that the majority of the "inveterate counterrevolutionary nationalists" were people who in 1920 had occupied responsible party and Soviet posts.[31]

In order to stimulate a similar course in the remaining contributions, Stalin and Molotov pestered speakers with interjections when they didn't display the necessary zeal in their statements about wrecking in their departments and regions. In this regard their reaction to the remarks by Pakhomov, the People's Commissar of Water Transport, was typical. Although at the beginning of his speech Pakhomov listed many names of the leaders of steamship lines who had been arrested, and declared that more than fifty officials of that level had been arrested, Stalin issued the rejoinder, "Somehow that's not enough." To the accompaniment of "laughter throughout the hall," Pakhomov replied, "Comrade Stalin, I told you that this was only the beginning."[32]

Spurred on by Molotov's interjections such as, "You want to get off with trifles," Pakhomov declared, "We must work in a new way, and for this we must first of all uncover all the wreckers. How can we expose them? If you take a given fact and look at it as you should, if you look at it in a new way to see why something happened, then we will get to the bottom of things and uncover one or two more scum, I assure you. And as soon as we catch two or three scum, these two or three will give two or three more (*laughter*)." However, this statement too did not satisfy the Kremlin leaders. At the end of his speech, Molotov asked Pakhomov a question: "Did the Commissariat find even a single wrecker?" The Narkom replied that he had removed several leaders of steamship lines from work before their arrest. After this statement, the following exchange of remarks occurred between the Narkom and members of the Politburo:

> *Molotov*: You only removed them, but the Commissariat did not explain what was going on.
> *Pakhomov*: I told you, Viacheslav Mikhailovich, what was in the materials. There are no more facts, and I cannot invent things.
> *Kosior*: Which means, there was no sabotage?[33]

A shift in the discussion of the question of sabotage was supposed to be provided by Yezhov's speech, which was accompanied by Stalin's words of encouragement. At the start of his speech, Yezhov expressed his sharp dissatisfaction with the contributions by leaders of departments who "have not fully understood either the meaning or even the raising of the question (*Mezhlauk*: That's right, that's right)." Then Yezhov made it very clear where he and his Commissariat stood in relation to the other People's Commissars and their Commissariats. "The resolution notes the fact that sabotage has not only not been discovered and people have not only failed to take the initiative in this matter," he declared, "but in a number of instances they have impeded matters.... (*Stalin*: Correct. That's putting it mildly.) Yes, Comrade Stalin, that's putting it mildly. And I must say that I ... still do not know of a single instance when, on their own initiative, people have called me and said: 'Comrade Yezhov, this person is somehow suspect, there's something wrong with him, please look into this fellow'... (*Postyshev*: And when you looked into them, they wouldn't give them up). Yes. More often than not, when you raise the question of arrests, people quite the contrary begin to defend these people. (*Postyshev*: Correct.)"[34] Thus, Yezhov was mentioning instances of resistance on the part of high-ranking economic officials to the repressions and, moreover, of their unwillingness to "give up" wreckers from among their own subordinates.

Proceeding from this, Yezhov directed coarse abuse at the People's Commissars. He declared that he had not only not received a single denunciation from them, but in response to his demands to sanction the arrest of people subordinate to them they often said: "And what will I do then, I must fulfill the plan, yet this is my main engineer or the boss of a department, what will I do?" "I usually reply," Yezhov continued, "say thank you, scum, for the fact that we are taking this person away, say thank you because we are taking away a wrecker. You are worth nothing if you defend a person who is carrying out sabotage, when there is enough material on him to arrest him."

Yezhov was indignant that the economic officials saw the struggle against sabotage as "some kind of area for fashionable moods," and were always saying: "They've uncovered sabotage and now they see saboteurs everywhere. They are preventing us from doing our work, they are preventing us from fulfilling the plan." In this regard he declared that "under conditions of our Soviet construction," a wrecker "can harm us only in small ways, when he is already certain that he never will be exposed. (*Stalin*: And he will save up his strength until the moment of war, when he will really do us harm)."

Yezhov shattered any illusions that the discussion should touch only on the two Commissariats mentioned in the agenda. He announced that over the recent months, "One hundred thirty cases had been opened in connection with the People's Commissariat of Transportation, and even more cases remain; in the People's Commissariat of Light Industry, one hundred forty-one people had been given varying sentences, including death by shooting.... In the People's Commissariat of Enlightenment, two hundred twenty-eight had been sentenced (*Voice from the audience*: Oho! That I understand)." On the basis of this, Yezhov drew the conclusion that "not only the People's Commissariat of Heavy Industry is affected [by sabotage—V. R.], not only the NKPS is affected, but all the other Commissariats are affected to no less degree. Therefore to think that these departments, insofar as their reports have not been presented, have simply been skipped over, does not follow from what has been said!" If the People's Commissars are not able to advance the struggle against wrecking, Yezhov continued in a threatening tone, "the CC will find enough strength to teach these people how to learn something, if only they are not hopeless when it comes to learning."[35]

Yezhov's speech completely dispelled the illusions of some Commissars that indulgence might be shown them if the economic plans were successfully fulfilled and overfulfilled by their respective branches of industry (industrial production in the USSR in 1935 and 1936 developed at tempos much higher than the tempos of growth in any of the preceding ten years). Yezhov declared, "All of our plans, essentially speaking, have been lowered. What should we think about overfulfilling a lowered plan? (*Stalin*: Correct.)"

Yezhov began with Gosbank [the State bank] when he opened a concrete discussion about departments. There "we uncovered a rather powerful Trotskyist organization numbering about twenty persons (*Voice from the audience*: Good job! Oho!)." This organization, according to Yezhov, embezzled state funds for financing an underground Trotskyist center and created hard currency bank accounts abroad, for instance, "in case Zinoviev and Kamenev managed to take off across the border." These misappropriations, Yezhov said, were made in the local organizations of Gosbank, and the embezzled resources were squandered not only on "Trotskyist work," but on personal needs: building themselves dachas, homes, and so forth.[36]

Here we encounter one more amalgam which was used by the "organs." Despite the usual conceptions that in the period of Stalinism corruption did not develop widely, many bureaucrats in the 1930s by no means avoided economic crimes. This gave the "organs" the chance to pressure those who were caught squandering funds, embezzling, and so forth, in order to get confessions from them stating that they belonged to Trotskyist wrecking organizations. In exposing this inane mechanism, Trotsky wrote: "The most numerous human material for judicial amalgams is provided by a wide layer of bad administrators, people genuinely or falsely responsible for economic failures, and finally officials who are careless when dealing with public moneys. The boundary between the legal and illegal in the USSR is very cloudy. Along with official salaries, there are innumerable unofficial and semilegal contributions. In normal times, such operations go unpunished. But the GPU has the opportunity at any moment to offer its victim a choice: to perish as a simple embezzler and thief, or to try to save himself as a false oppositionist, recruited by Trotsky to betray the state."[37]

When Yezhov declared that he could "say something about every department," the following exchange of comments took place between him and the
audience:

> *Voice from the audience*: Tell us, it's useful.
> *Molotov*: About the People's Commissariat of Light Industry ...
> *Yezhov*: ... we are only now, essentially speaking, beginning to develop the
>   case concerning the People's Commissariat of Light Industry, although
>   in this department we have condemned a rather significant number—
>   one hundred forty-one persons from among the active wreckers and
>   saboteurs, out of which a rather significant groups has been shot on
>   instructions from the court.... But we have grounds to assume that here
>   we will come across a very large organization of spies and saboteurs
>   which has conducted its work from year to year in this Commissariat.[38]

During the next contributions by the People's Commissars, Molotov and
Kaganovich interrupted them with crude rejoinders which were designed to
emphasize that the speakers were not paying enough attention to the main
task which had now been placed before all the economic specialists, namely,
the independent search for saboteurs in their departments. In this sense, the
dialogue between Molotov and the Commissar of Light Industry, Liubimov, is
instructive:

> *Molotov*: Has your Commissariat exposed any of the wreckers or not? Have
>   there been cases where the Commissariat itself exposed someone or
>   not?
> *Voice from the audience*: He had not prepared for such a case.
> *Molotov*: But nevertheless?
> *Liubimov*: ... I cannot recall a case where our apparatus discovered sabo-
>   tage.
> *Molotov*: That is a major shortcoming.[39]

Much like Kaganovich had extolled Stalin's perspicacity, Liubimov expressed his enthusiasm for Kaganovich's perspicacity: "Lazar Moiseevich has
said very well: if you look into their eyes, you feel that this is a distant person,
there is no fire in his eyes, his soul is not in his work." However, this did not

save the speaker from attacks on the part of the "iron Commissar." When Liubimov said that in his Commissariat there were "idiots who probably were guided by low-ranking wreckers," Kaganovich interrupted here with the remark: "No, these are not low-level wreckers, you are not taking advantage of little people."[40]

The role of a school boy driven into a corner was also played by the People's Commissar of Collective Farms, Kalmanovich. The end of his speech turned into a meticulous and biased interrogation.

> *Kalmanovich*: I think that I am not mistaken if I now talk about those major breakdowns which we have had and to which we must now direct our attention.
>
> *Molotov*: Your are forgetting the main thing ...
>
> *Kaganovich*: ... here we are not discussing the question of your activity, or the shortcomings of your activity, but sabotage, which occurred under your jurisdiction. You are not providing a single fact and you are placing yourself in an awkward position ...
>
> *Kalmanovich*: Did I uncover even a single saboteur? Not a single one [*Restrained laughter*—that is what is recorded in the transcript—V. R.].
>
> *Shkiriatov*: Because you did not know.
>
> *Kalmanovich*: Because I did not suppose that this could possibly be sabotage. I felt that it was poor work. That is where my guilt lies, that is where I made my mistake.[41]

The only Commissar who was not interrupted was Mikoyan. The success of his contribution was determined not only by the fact that the plenum's participants, including the leaders who were directing the course of the plenum, understood very well the difference between "rank-and-file" members of the CC and a member of the Politburo who was close to Stalin. And Mikoyan clearly understood what it was that Stalin wanted to hear from him. Therefore he opened his remarks with ritualistic repentance for missed chances in the search for wreckers in his Commissariat: "The question of sabotage, wrecking and espionage by Japanese-German Trotskyist agents," he said, " ... most of all concerns the food industry. We are now shuddering because, perhaps, tomorrow we might see acts of wrecking and sabotage, because there is no kind of earlier prosperity which guarantees that we will not have unexpected sabotage acts on any given day.... We have few open instances of wrecking, but that by no means can set us at rest. For this only says that the camouflage is more sophisticated and our searches have been insufficiently energetic."

Mikoyan touched on the most ticklish (for authors of the versions about the gigantic scale of the sabotage) question, which could not help but arise in the mind of any intelligent person: why in the "land of victorious socialism" had terror and sabotage assumed a scale which had never before been seen in history? And why did people who belonged to the upper echelons of the ruling circles turn out to be terrorists and saboteurs? "I thought," Mikoyan confessed, " ... that, if Marxists before the revolution had been opposed to terror against the tsar and autocracy, then how could they, people who had passed through the school of Marx, be for terror under the Bolsheviks, under Soviet power? If communists throughout the world who are enemies of capitalism do not blow up factories, how can a person who has passed through the school of Marxism, blow up a factory in his own country? I must say that this never entered into my head. But, evidently, we have to study the question."

Simply raising such dangerous questions at the plenum required no small amount of courage. A person needed the refined flexibility of a true sophist, which Mikoyan possessed, in order to give the answer to this question which Stalin required. As a result of his "study," Mikoyan continued, he had come to an understanding of the following truth: "Evidently the class enemy, the Trotskyists, have fallen to such depths, that it was more than we could imagine, but in actual fact, it was just like Comrade Stalin foretold, as he virtually took us by the hand and said that there is no dirty trick which the Trotskyists and Rightists could not perform."[42]

The discussion of the third point of the agenda ended with the concluding remarks by Molotov, who cited from a "very thick" set of papers from the NKVD containing a list of the number of people arrested over the last five months. This included five hundred eighty-five people from the officials in the People's Commissariat of Heavy Industry and the People's Commissariat of Defense Industry, one hundred thirty-seven from the NKPS (including about ten highway officials), one hundred two from the People's Commissariat of Agriculture, one hundred from the People's Commissariat of Food Production, and so forth.

Molotov expressed his dissatisfaction with the speeches by the majority of People's Commissars, who "cannot boast that they have been participating in the exposure of saboteurs, while the plenum says that no small number of them have impeded the exposure of sabotage."

Appealing to "consider what is useful and correct in every signal" about sabotage, Molotov added that value might be contained in signals "from our enemies, from those who do not deserve our trust, from those who are making these signals with anti-Soviet intentions."[43]

In his remarks, Molotov mentioned that in many branches, the results of the work in the first months of 1937 had proven to be lower than the results achieved in the corresponding period in 1936. However these statistics were introduced by him only in order to preclude the claim that this fall was caused by the numerous arrests of economists and engineers.

The behavior of the plenum's participants in discussing the question of sabotage allows us to sense the inner, psychological distress which is characteristic of people who are in long-term, hopeless and inescapable situations.

Familiarity with the corresponding sections of the transcript of the plenum provides an exceedingly contradictory portrait. People who are directing economic construction and who are responsible for its consequences, both "believe" and do not believe in sabotage. They do not believe because they are well informed of the actual situation and know like nobody else that the majority of the accidents, wrecks and explosions are the result of haste, negligence, and incompetence. They believe, i.e., they force themselves to believe or pretend that they believe, because they know better than others that under conditions of industrial haste, it is impossible to avoid explosions and catastrophes, and consequently, someone must inevitably answer for all this.

It may have appeared at first glance that Stalin was throwing them a life preserver—the possibility of attributing their own failings to the sabotage of their subordinates, leaders of the second echelon. In the beginning of this campaign they felt that they might escape unharmed from the dangerous situation, "having surrendered" only unwelcome subordinates, or even getting out of such a sacrifice, as several had already tried to do. But they underestimated the relentless logic of totalitarian power, which was destroying its own bearers who proved to be incapable of ruthless savagery and blatant falsification.

31. Why Did Stalin Need "Sabotage"?

A T FIRST GLANCE, the charges that the majority of the economic leaders were engaged in wrecking must have been perceived to be absurd, both by the population as a whole, and the apparatchiks. However, this version of Stalin's, which had far-ranging goals, aroused a certain degree of trust, if not among sophisticated politicians, then among the common people. It allowed for an explanation of the fact that the widely trumpeted assurances about the beginning of a "happy life" stood in striking contradiction to what people saw and felt around themselves at every step. Besides a narrow layer of the Soviet aristocracy, few people in the country had begun to live "better and more joyfully," even when compared to the terrible years of the first Five Year Plan. Therefore there was a need to explain the failures of Stalin's policies by referring to the intrigues of saboteurs, in other words to transfer the people's growing dissatisfaction with Stalin and his closest associates onto the leaders of a lower level.

It can be assumed that accusations of sabotage and other forms of hostile activity (in the direct, criminal sense of these words) were Stalin's peculiar reply to the criticism aimed at him in the 1930s by old and new oppositional groups. "The most pernicious enemy of the party and the proletarian dictatorship," the Riutin Platform declared, "the most pernicious counterrevolutionary and provocateur could not carry out any better the work of destroying the party and socialist construction than Stalin is doing.... Stalin objectively is playing the role of a traitor to the socialist revolution.... No matter how monstrous or paradoxical it may seem at first glance, the main enemy of Leninism, the proletarian dictatorship and socialist construction is located at the present moment in our own ranks and even heads the party."[1] How widely such views were spread among communists can be seen from the many letters sent from the USSR and published in the pages of the *Bulletin of the Opposition*. Thus, one of the authors tells about his conversation with a man who had never before decided to criticize the "general line." After his participation in forced collectivization, he said: "If the bourgeoisie were to send us as saboteurs, it would be acting no better than Stalin. It is possible to think that we are confronting a colossal provocation."[2]

The reckless policy of complete collectivization and forced industrialization was not crucially needed for the country to survive, or to guarantee its defense capability in the face of the threat of a fascist invasion. It is well known that as a result of Stalin's extremely crude miscalculations before the war and during its beginning period, Hitler's armies seized territory in the USSR equal to two Frances, in which more than a third of the nation's population lived. In the occupied territory, approximately thirty-two thousand factories, plants and other industrial enterprises, not to mention small enterprises and shops, were fully or partially destroyed and plundered. According to statistics provided in a book by the chairman of Gosplan [State Planning], N. A. Voznesensky, *The Wartime Economy of the USSR During the Great Patriotic War*, the total losses of fundamental and defense funds in the USSR comprised about two-thirds of the national wealth which was located prior to the war on occupied territory.[3] Thus, an enormous part of the national wealth which had been created at the cost of the greatest exertions, sacrifices and deprivation by the Soviet people was squandered during the war years.

In the 1930s, the slightest doubts about the possibility of fulfilling assigned tasks within a schedule dictated from above was called "opportunism" in the party jargon of the time. The furious tempos of construction logically led to many accidents and catastrophes, not to mention the economic disproportions which frequently reduced to nothing the heroic efforts of the enthusiasts of the Five Year Plan. Trotsky repeatedly warned that voluntaristic decisions and their consequences were capable of provoking a grave crisis of confidence in the masses toward the nation's leaders. In order to transfer this crisis of popular confidence one rank lower, Stalin had to invent the sabotage being carried out by People's Commissars, directors and engineers.

In order to more concretely grasp the scale of the poverty of the popular masses, which led to the accumulation of discontent and social protest in the country, it is appropriate to turn to the book by the American journalist John Scott. From January 1933 to the end of 1937 he worked as an electric welder at the building site of one of the most massive industrial giants—the Magnitogorsk Metallurgical Combinat. Arriving in the Soviet Union as an enthusiast of socialist construction, Scott not only carefully observed what was happening around him, but also studied material contained in the combinat's archives (before the period of spy mania in 1937–1938, a foreigner was still able to acquaint himself with documents illustrating the real situation at the construction site). Besides Magnitogorsk, Scott visited a number of other Ural factories, and in the book which he wrote in 1941, presented an objective portrait of what was actually taking place during the industrialization of the USSR.

Scott explained how, from 1928 to 1932, about two hundred fifty thousand people came to the barren place where the Magnitogorsk giant was to be erected. Approximately three-fourths of them came there voluntarily, in search of work, bread cards, and better living conditions. The remaining part consisted of deported peasants and criminals who were placed in corrective labor colonies.

As Scott emphasized, from the very beginning "the tempo of construction was such that millions of men and women starved, froze and were brutalized by inhuman labor and incredible living conditions."[4] Throughout the entire winter of 1932–33, when a particularly difficult situation arose with regard to supplying the site with foodstuffs, even qualified workers received neither meat nor butter, and almost no sugar or milk. In the stores at which they were registered, they were given only bread and a small amount of cereal grain. In the same stores, without using ration cards, they could buy only perfume, tobacco, surrogate coffee, sometimes soap, salt, tea and inexpensive candy. "These latter products, however, were almost never in stock; and when a shipment did come in, the workers sometimes left their jobs, spud wrenches in their hands, to fight their way to half a pound of rocklike candy."[5]

Along with this, in Magnitogorsk there were stores for specialists, engineers and the administrative elite, where goods were sold of a broad assortment. The most abundant was the store for foreign specialists, to which the upper echelons of the engineering and administrative personnel were also assigned. The prices in this store were several times lower than the prices at which workers could obtain similar goods in the commercial stores.

Similarly sharp contrasts existed in living conditions. Almost all the workers lived in settlements without running water or sewage systems, often consisting of temporary barracks, tents and dugouts. In addition, on the outskirts of the city there had been built settlements consisting of one hundred fifty stone houses with metal roofs, running water and central heating. Here the high-ranking officials lived and those foreigners who received their pay in hard currency.

No less onerous than the living conditions were the working conditions, which resulted in an extremely high level of industrial accidents. The situation was made more severe by the fact that the majority of workers were yesterday's peasants with no experience working at industrial sites. Like children, they did not understand what was dangerous. So that they could become skilled workers, as a rule they underwent accelerated professional training "without separation from production," i.e., evening classes after a demanding working day. Under conditions of never-ending stepped-up work, many workers had to work two shifts. All this led to a situation where the hospitals were constantly filled with "men burned with pig iron, who invariably screamed for three days before dying, men rolled like flies in or under cranes or other heavy equipment."[6]

After encountering the unbearable living conditions, many of the recruits were let go and traveled to other places where they heard that life was better. Therefore work which required qualified workers often had to be completed by untrained, unskilled laborers. "The result was that inexperienced riggers fell and untrained bricklayers laid walls which did not stand."[7]

During all this, resources which could have been used to improve the living and working conditions of the workers was senselessly squandered because of the poor organization of labor and production. Not infrequently workers would be sent to pour cement for a foundation before the completion of the digging, or else they were sent to jobs for which they did not have the necessary materials or tools. At the same time, a great amount of material arrived at the construction site which was absolutely not needed, or which would not be needed for several years. "Material and equipment of this kind figured on the books as 'supply plan fulfilled,' whereas their actual value was a minus quality because they had to be stored and cared for."[8]

Since the necessary quantity of peat was not allocated for heating the wooden barracks, during the winter the workers, despite laws establishing cruel punishment for "theft of socialist property," gathered tons of building material which had been designated for production, in order to use them for heating their living quarters.

As a result of all this, "money was spent like water, men froze, hungered, and suffered, but the construction work went on with a disregard for individuals and a mass heroism seldom paralleled in history."[9]

Even after industrialization began to produce a return, the bureaucracy as before paid insignificant attention to questions connected with raising the living standards of the workers. Although the nominal wages grew, their increase was reduced to nothing by incessant inflation. On the basis of his own observations and a study of the statistics for the combine, Scott established that the real wages of the Magnitogorsk workers did not increase from 1929 through 1935. Nor did the economic disproportions decrease which had caused the colossal losses. Thus, because of lack of coordination in getting various components on line, the coke ovens began to work when construction of the chemical factories was not completed. As a result of this, "some twenty-five million gold dollars' worth of valuable chemicals were allowed to escape in smoke every year."[10] Delays in finishing the chemical factories, typical of the chaotic, unsystematic and disorderly construction of productive components during the years of the first Five Year Plans, was declared at the trial of the "Anti-Soviet Trotskyist Center" to be the result of deliberate sabotage by Rataichak and other leading officials in the chemical industry.

Even completed industrial enterprises often could not function without accidents, insofar as insignificant resources, as before, were expended on safety technology. "Equipment was ruined, men were crushed, gassed, and poisoned, money was spent in astronomical quantities."[11] Meanwhile, no one dared to stop production if only for a short time in order to enact the necessary measures to safeguard the work force. The results of such a situation were never-ending catastrophes accompanied by human losses. In describing a powerful explosion at one of the blast furnaces, Scott emphasized that for two whole weeks preceding the catastrophe, everyone whose work was connected with this furnace knew that one of its main components—a tapping hole—was working poorly. The shop foreman told the director of the factory, who in turn passed on the given information to the supervisor of the combinat, Zaveniagin. However, even a telephone call between Zaveniagin and Ordzhonikidze about the problem at the blast furnace did not result in temporarily halting the production process to carry out repairs. "No one wanted to take the responsibility for shutting down the furnace prematurely at a time when the country needed pig iron very badly."[12]

New problems arose during the forced introduction of the Stakhanov movement at the combinat. Shock brigade work performed by the Stakhanovites contributed to an improvement of economic indicators, but the relentless drive by the administration to set records gave birth to a situation where "many things were done which stored up trouble for the future. Equipment was overtaxed, current repairs were neglected ... transport equipment, both rolling stock and rails, was sadly overtaxed."[13] The same situation existed throughout the whole railway transport system of the nation, where daily car loadings rose to 100,000 during the Stakhanovite boom, but in the following years decreased by almost one-fourth. All this led to a new outburst of industrial accidents, the level of which was shown by statistics introduced at the February-March Plenum. Thus, in only one mine in the Kuzbass in 1936, there were one thousand six hundred accidents which resulted in injuries to more than half the miners who worked there.[14]

One of the reasons for the ineffective management, for which the workers paid with their health, and often their lives, was the excessive centralization of the leadership of industry. For instance, the People's Commissariat of Heavy Industry directed thousands of building sites, plants, factories, mines, and work shops scattered throughout the nation's territory. "This commissariat was created by a stroke of the pen and was expected to begin functioning immediately," wrote Scott. "The result was what might have been expected: tremendous enthusiasm, boundless devotion, and hard work; and unbelievable confusion, disorder, and stupidity."[15]

To this was added the obvious lack of preparation on the part of the economic administration when it came to carrying out their management functions. "Whereas most of the workers in the mills were fairly well trained by 1935, had acquired the knacks of electric welding, pipe fitting, or what not, most of the administrators were far from having mastered their jobs. They had not one-quarter the practical experience of men occupying similar positions in industry in America or Western Europe."[16]

The incompetent management of industry prompted many instances of deception, the scale of which can be imagined from the speeches at the February-March Plenum. Thus, Molotov spoke of the "reports of coal extraction in the Donbass, where they dupe us year after year," and of the submission "of reports concerning the starting up of electrostations, workshops, or aggregates, when in actual fact they begin to work six to eight months after the impassioned reports."[17]

All of this—the heightened level of accidents, the violation of norms of manufacturing safety, and other examples of poor economic management— was attributed in 1936–1937 to the sabotage of administrative and engineering or technical personnel. Moreover, it was done in such a form that it was impossible for the managers and specialists to survive no matter what their choice of actions. Thus, Kaganovich demanded strict punishment both for impeding the elevation of overextended technological norms, and for the accidents which resulted from this elevation. Mikoyan declared that reference to technological defects was "code for covering up accidents and damage which had been organized.... We must investigate them in order to follow their tracks and find the saboteurs who are now concealed."[18]

In the beginning, using the activity of saboteurs to explain economic failures aroused even a certain kind of satisfaction among many people, especially sincere Stalinists who believed that finally the reason had been found for the troubling calamities which had occurred in the land of "victorious socialism." Thus, M. A. Svanidze (the wife of A. S. Svanidze, the brother of Stalin's first wife), who had access to the "leader's" closest circles, had a reverential attitude toward him and, of course, did not feel in her everyday life the problems which were shared by millions of common people, nevertheless at the end of 1936 recorded in her diary: "All around me I see sabotage, and I feel like screaming about it.... I see sabotage in the fact that the palace of Soviets is being built on such a space that it will require the destruction of perhaps one hundred well-built and almost new homes.... This during our housing crisis— to destroy beautiful buildings and resettle tens of thousands of people no one knows where ... and the mob which gives the impression of ragamuffins—where is the work of light industry?... Why have prices soared by 100 percent, why can nothing be found in the stores, where is the cotton, flax or wool for which medals were given out when the plan was overfulfilled? What are the officials at Light Industry thinking, if they are not saboteurs? Will they keep being patted on the head for the fact that over the course of nineteen years they haven't been able to properly clothe the people, so that the entire world would stop talking about our poverty which does not really exist—after all we are rich in resources and money and talent? So what then is going on, where is the production, where is the overfulfillment of the plan? And what about the construction of mansions and villas, the outrageous money wasted on maintaining luxurious rest homes and sanatoriums, and the useless squandering of state funds? ... "[19]

At the time of their first arrest, "saboteur"-communists apparently expected that they would suffer a relatively light punishment, much like the nonparty specialists at the beginning of the 1930s, who were given decent living and working conditions after their trial. John Scott tells how in 1932, the GPU sent to Magnitogorsk twenty to thirty engineers who had been convicted in the case of the "Industrial Party." Upon arriving in Magnitogorsk with their families, they were given four-room cottages and automobiles. They worked under contracts according to which they were paid three thousand rubles per month (ten times more than the wage of an average worker). Although they were watched by the OGPU, they were allowed to go hunting on holidays in the forests of the Urals located tens of kilometers from the city. "They were also given highly responsible positions and instructed to work hard in order to prove that they really intended to become good Soviet citizens." One of the former "wreckers" worked as the chief electrician at the combinat, another as the main engineer at a chemical plant. Several of them were decorated with medals for labor achievements. In Scott's opinion, "they would be much more likely to give their wholehearted support to Stalin than to Trotsky, since they are totally out of sympathy with the theory of the World Revolution and the building of a classless society."[20]

It would have been difficult to foresee that the fate of the communist economic specialists would prove to be incomparably more terrible than the fate of nonparty specialists arrested at the beginning of the 1930s. It is true that in the fall of 1936, concern arose among the "red directors" because they were beginning to be turned into scapegoats for the many shortcomings of the bureaucratic planning and management of the economy. At the February-March Plenum, Molotov read a letter which Ordzhonikidze had received from Birman, the director of the Dnepropetrovsk Metallurgical Factory. "The situation being created particularly during the recent period here, in Dnepropetrovsk," wrote Birman, "compels me to turn to you, as an old comrade and a member of the Politburo, for guidance and assistance. It seems to me that the directive of the higher party authorities about completely developing criticism and self-criticism ... has been understood to mean that we must, no matter what, sling mud at each other, and primarily at a certain category of leading officials. This certain category of leading officials consists primarily of economists and the directors of major factories, who, as if with the wave of a secret magic wand, have been made the central target of this part of self-criticism."[21]

To the extent that such "self-criticism" ended all the more frequently with the arrest of directors, engineers and foremen, the enterprises witnessed distrust and hostility on the part of the workers toward officials, and workers' discipline was shattered. As Mikoyan said at the February-March Plenum, "Now, when sabotage is uncovered, the workers look warily at their superiors: 'And is this directive correct or incorrect: Perhaps it is even sabotage?'"[22]

Were there actually any acts of sabotage and wrecking? Scott's book also allows us to answer this question, since he tells of several incidents of genuine sabotage in Magnitogorsk. Thus, one morning ground glass was found in the main bearings of the turbine, something which would quickly destroy the bearings. Not far away there were several buckets with such ground glass, which was used to coat electrodes. As Scott explained this incident, it was obvious that one of the embittered peasants who had been dekulakized and who worked at the combinat, had tossed a handful of this glass into the bearings in order to get revenge against the Soviet regime for his deportation.[23] Scott gives another example of the "blind rage of one of these miserable men," which he managed to see with his own eyes: "I once saw an old peasant throw a crowbar into a large generator and then give himself up to the armed guards laughing gleefully."[24]

One more incident which Scott reports was connected with a foreman he knew well, whose parents came from bourgeois families and perished during the revolution. Changing his name and managing "to lose himself in the crowd," he became a skilled metallurgist and was, by Soviet standards, an extremely successful and well-to-do person. However, he felt that the revolution had destroyed his life and "was rather outspoken in his criticism of the Soviet power. He was a heavy drinker, and under the influence of vodka his tongue would sometimes run away with him. Once he boasted openly in the presence of several foreigners that he would 'wreck the works.' One day not long afterward a heavy Stillson wrench was found in the mashed blades of one of the imported German gas turbines. The frame of the machine was cracked and the whole thing ruined, involving a loss of several tens of thousands of rubles and a good deal of labor. Several days later the foreman was arrested and confessed that he had done the job. He got eight years."[25]

According to Scott, charges of sabotage often were made against common criminals like those who exist in any capitalist city. "A difference was that in Magnitogorsk it was more difficult to embezzle on a large scale than in New York or Chicago; and if caught, one was likely to be accused, not of stealing, but of sabotage and counterrevolution, and had relatively little chance of buying one's self out."[26] To illustrate this, Scott told about the director of the construction office which built houses for the workers. This man built himself a separate home with five rooms, furnished it with good furniture, carpeted it, etc. At the same time, his office fulfilled the construction plan by only 60 percent. In the course of an investigation, it was discovered that he systematically embezzled government resources and funds, introduced a practice of selling building materials to the collective and state farms at speculators' prices, and then pocketed the money he received for this. A public trial was held in the city, and stories about it filled the pages of the local newspapers for days. However, the swindler-director was charged not with theft and corruption, but with conscious sabotage of the construction of housing for the workers. After he confessed his guilt as a saboteur, he was sentenced to be shot.

Scott described the mechanism of fabricating "counterrevolutionary organizations" by giving the example of the director of the coke plant, Shevchenko, who, according to him, "was at least 50 percent bandit—a dishonest and unscrupulous careerist. His personal aims and ideals differed completely from those of the founders of Socialism." Shevchenko's moral credo was expressed in a saying which he often repeated: "All people are whores—except you and me. Work on that basis, and you won't make any mistakes."

In 1935, a powerful explosion occurred at the plant which Shevchenko headed. As a result, four men died and eighteen were injured. At that time, Shevchenko did not suffer any serious punishment. Then in 1937, a trial was held in which he was charged with being a Japanese spy who deliberately organized this catastrophe. About twenty men were tried in the case of the "Shevchenko band." Several of them, according to Scott, were, like Shevchenko, clear crooks, but one was a Ukrainian nationalist. "He felt strongly that the Ukraine had been conquered, raped, and was now being exploited by a group of Bolsheviks, mostly Russians and Jews, who were ruining the country, indeed the whole Soviet Union ... here was a man who was at least a potential menace to the Soviet power, a man who might have been willing to cooperate with the Germans for the 'liberation of the Ukraine' in 1941." As for the other defendants, they were put on trial only because they "were just unfortunate in having worked under a chief who fell foul of the NKVD."[27]

All these episodes suggest that the wreckers' organizations, participation in which led to the arrest of hundreds of people in Magnitogorsk, never in fact existed. Separate acts of sabotage were committed by embittered individuals who hated the Soviet regime, but not by communists, let alone by leading figures in the economy.

Summarizing the testimony about wrecking and sabotage which was given at the second Moscow Trial, Trotsky listed the following methods of sabotage to which the defendants had "confessed": being too slow to develop the plans for constructing new factories, and then continually revising them; dissipating resources throughout various building sites, leading to the freezing of enormous sums of capital; putting unfinished enterprises online; accumulating excessive reserves of ore and raw materials at the enterprises, thereby withdrawing from circulation investment capital; rapacious expenditure of materials, and so forth.

Trotsky recalled that, beginning with 1930, in his articles he had continuously pointed to all these chronic illnesses of the Soviet economy which were created by bureaucratic methods of planning and management. "Perhaps my critical work was simply 'camouflage?'" he wrote in this regard. "By the very meaning of this concept, camouflage would have to be aimed at *covering up* these crimes. Meanwhile, my critical work, on the contrary, *exposed* them. It turns out that while secretly organizing sabotage, I applied all my strength to attracting the government's attention to the acts of "sabotage" and thereby—to those carrying it out. All this would perhaps be very clever, if it were not absolutely absurd."[28]

Trotsky felt that a clear example of the fact that charging "Trotskyists" with sabotage was the "most vulgar part of the judicial frame-up both in its conception and in its execution," was the persecution of hundreds of engineers in railway transport for their adherence to "the theory of limitation." The heart of this theory was that the carrying capacity of railroads has definite technological limitations. After Kaganovich became head of the People's Commissariat of Transportation, "the theory of limitation" was declared to be not only a bourgeois prejudice, but also the invention of saboteurs. "Without any doubt, many old specialists who were trained under conditions of capitalist economy," Trotsky wrote, "clearly underestimated the possibilities contained in planning methods, and therefore were inclined to develop norms that were too low. But from this it does not follow that the tempos of the economy depend only on the inspiration and energy of the bureaucracy. The general material equipment of the nation, the mutual links between various part of industry, transport and agriculture, the degree of skilled labor, the percentage of experienced engineers, and finally the material and cultural level of the population—these are the basic factors which have the last word in determining limits. The desire of the

L. D. Trotsky in his study

bureaucracy to do violence to these factors using naked commands, repression and prizes ('Stakhanovism') inevitably must be paid for in the form of disorder in the factories, the ruination of machinery, a high percentage of subquality products, accidents and catastrophes. There is not the slightest grounds here for putting a Trotskyist 'conspiracy' on trial."[29]

Trotsky pointed out that the Soviet press always wrote about "Trotskyists" as an insignificant group, isolated from the masses and hated by them. However at the trial of Radek-Piatakov, testimony focused on methods of sabotage which would be possible only if the entire administration, from top to bottom, consisted of saboteurs who were carrying out their evil deeds with the active, or at least the passive, support of the workers. Thus Stalin, in trying to terrorize the Soviet people and world public opinion with the monstrosity of the "Trotskyist" crimes, was compelled to expand continuously the number of "exposed" wreckers.

Trotsky saw the particular shamelessness of the Stalinist inquisitors in the fact that at the trial of the "Anti-Soviet Trotskyist Center," after the insistent demands of the prosecutor, the accused testified that they had tried to cause as many human victims as possible. After the trial, even more horrific crimes of the "Trotskyists" were announced. The press declared that in Novosibirsk three "Trotskyists" had been shot for maliciously burning down a school, in which many children died. Recalling that not long before a similar tragedy, which had shaken the whole world, occurred in a school in Texas, Trotsky proposed that people consider for a moment that after such a tragedy "the government of the United States opened a furious nationwide campaign against the Comintern, accusing it of maliciously exterminating children.... Then we would get an approximate idea of Stalin's politics today. Such attacks, conceivable only in the poisoned atmosphere of a totalitarian dictatorship, contain their own rebuttal."[30]

32. The NKVD Stands Accused

FOLLOWING THE DISCUSSION of the question of sabotage, the plenum passed on to a review of hostile activity within the People's Commissariat of Internal Affairs itself. This question was discussed in a closed session, without any of the guests who had been invited to the plenum. Material from this discussion was not included in the secret transcript of the plenum's work.

When Yezhov began his report, he spoke in relatively calm tones. He referred to the shrinking "from day to day of the hostile front" after the liquidation of the kulaks. Along with this the need had fallen away for the mass arrests and exile which had been conducted in the years of collectivization.[1]

As he proceeded, the tone of the report became ever sharper. Yezhov demanded the liquidation of the special prisons for political prisoners (politisolators), in which, according to him, there reigned "a servile and attentive attitude toward the prisoners ... bordering on the curious." Yezhov declared the setting up of recreation courts and permission to have bookshelves in the cells to be such "curiosities." He detected symptoms of impermissibly liberal detention of the condemned in that they were presented the possibility of communicating among themselves, serving their sentences together with their wives, and so forth. With particular malice he quoted from a report about the investigation of the Suzdal isolator, which said, "The cells are large and bright, with flowers by the windows. There are family rooms ... daily walks for the imprisoned husbands and wives for three hours (*Laughter. Beria*: A rest home)." When Yezhov mentioned instructions from the former leadership of the NKVD to give increased rations to political prisoners in the camps, the hall resounded with shouts: "Was that for special services before the Soviet regime?", and "They should have been given half the normal rations."[2]

Yezhov saw one more instance of the liberalism of the former NKVD leadership in the practice of reducing punishment: for instance, out of the eighty-seven sentenced in 1933 in the case of the I. N. Smirnov group, nine were released after a certain time, and sixteen had prison terms replaced with exile.[3]

276

Announcing that from the moment he arrived at the NKVD, he had arrested two hundred thirty-eight officials in the Commissariat who had previously belonged to the Opposition, Yezhov added: "So that this figure does not frighten you, I must say here that we have approached former oppositionists who worked with us with a special, much more severe standard. One fact was enough—if a person concealed from the party and from the organs of the NKVD his former membership in the Trotskyist Opposition, he would be arrested."[4]

Another contingent of arrested Chekists was, according to Yezhov, "agents of the Polish general staff." In this regard he introduced a directive from Stalin, who "after the Kirov events raised the question: Why do you keep a Pole at such a job?"[5] This was one of the first Stalinist directives to drive people out of certain areas of work solely because of their nationality.

Yezhov declared that Molchanov, who had been arrested a few days before the plenum, was the main culprit in "retarding matters" in the NKVD. He accused him of informing Trotskyists about material the NKVD had on them.

During the discussion of Yezhov's report, Yagoda spoke, as did five officials from the NKVD who belonged to higher party bodies. They all acknowledged "a shameful failure in the work of the organs of state security" and promised "to wipe away the shameful stain which lies on the organs of the NKVD,"[6] i.e., their "tardiness" in uncovering "Trotskyist conspiracies." Feeling the threat hanging over them, each of them told in detail about his services in flushing out "counterrevolutionary groups," and tried to shift the blame onto his colleagues, as a result of which nervous squabbling often broke out in the audience.

Understanding that no charge made against the "Trotskyists" would appear excessive, Mironov declared that each of the Trotskyist-Zinovievist organizations "has ties with intelligence agencies of foreign states."[7]

Yagoda apparently still hoped that he would be able to avoid charges of criminal intentions and actions, getting off instead with punishment for "negligence" and "lack of vigilance." Therefore he reacted in horror to Yevdokimov's speech, which called him the main culprit "for the atmosphere created in recent years in the organs of the NKVD." "I think," declared Yevdokimov, "that matters are not limited to Molchanov alone (*Yagoda*: What, have you gone out of your mind?). I am particularly convinced of this. I think that the ex-leader of the NKVD should answer for this matter according to the full extent of the law. We must put Yagoda on trial."[8]

In discussing Yezhov's report, only two contributions struck a slightly discordant note. One of them, no matter how strange this might seem at first glance, belonged to Vyshinsky, who spoke about actual shortcomings in the activity of the NKVD. First of all, he read several transcripts of interrogations which were filled with vulgar abuse from the investigators and which testified to their unconcealed application of pressure on the people under arrest. After citing the words of one peripheral investigator which were directed at a person under arrest: "Do not remain silent and do not play games.... Prove that this is not so," Vyshinsky explained to the plenum's participants that the accused should not have to prove his innocence, but, on the contrary, the investigator has to proved the guilt of the accused. As another example of illegal investigatory procedures, Vyshinsky quoted the "instructions" of the plenipotentiary of the NKVD in the Azov-Black Sea area which directly compelled the investigators to use falsifying methods: "If you are interrogating the accused and he says what is not useful for conviction, finish up with what is useful, and whatever is not, don't write down."[9]

Secondly, Vyshinsky declared that the investigatory material usually suffered from "an accusatory deviation.... It is considered awkward to close a case for lack of proof, as if this would compromise our work.... Thanks to such mores ... the defendants' bench is sometimes occupied by people who consequently prove to be either guilty of something other than what they are charged with, or else completely innocent."[10]

Thirdly, Vyshinsky detected a serious deficiency in the work of the NKVD organs and the Procuracy "in the tendency to build the investigation on the self-confession of the accused," without bothering to reinforce the charges with substantive evidence, facts from expert court witnesses, and so forth: "However, the center of gravity during an investigation should lie precisely in these objective elements of proof."[11]

Such "unexpected" statements coming from the mouth of the prosecutor/ falsifier can be explained, in my opinion, by the following reasons. By demonstrating his strict adherence to juridical norms, Vyshinsky was trying to remove the inner doubts which existed among several of the plenum's participants regarding the legal irreproachability of the recent trials in which he had served as the state prosecutor. In addition, since he understood very well the legal fragility of these trials, he wanted the material prepared by the "organs" to be more convincing at the next public trials. These considerations evidently dictated his warning: "If the accused renounces previously given confessions at the trial itself, then the case might collapse. We then would be completely disarmed, since, without having reinforced a naked confession with anything else, we could not use anything to counter this renunciation of a previously given confession."[12]

If Vyshinsky's speech was dictated by conjunctural considerations, then the other "dissonant" contribution was essentially the only honest speech at the plenum which called into doubt, although in cautious form, the "materials" obtained by the "organs." I have in mind the short speech by M. M. Litvinov, who had not uttered a single word during the entire previous work of the plenum. Seeming not to notice the direction and tone of all the other speeches, Litvinov posed a question about "false" signals made by foreign agents of the NKVD. He described how, with every one of his trips abroad, reports would come from agents about the preparation of "attacks on Litvinov." Ignoring the cries of the most ardent Stalinists, who clearly were dissatisfied with a shift of the discussion onto this plane, Litvinov declared that not a single one of these reports had been confirmed. "When something is being prepared, it never happens that it remains unnoticed, but here not only I did not notice [the preparation of the attacks—V. R.], my bodyguards did not notice, and moreover, the local police, who also provided security, also noticed nothing (*Beria*: What do you expect from the local police?) ... I am saying all this because there are a mass of good-for-nothing agents who, knowing and seeing from the newspapers that 'Litvinov has gone abroad,' report, in order to work things up, that an attack is being prepared against Litvinov. (*Voroshilov*: That is an incorrect philosophy.) An absolutely correct one. This shows that these agents are picked with insufficient discrimination ... and I think that if that's the way matters stand abroad, then perhaps something similar is going on in parts of the agency here in the Soviet Union."[13]

These unequivocal words were not "rebuffed" at the plenum—evidently because the authority of the People's Commissar of Foreign Affairs was too high, and Stalin at this stage did not want to get mixed up in a fight with him. Litvinov's remarks seemed to pass "unnoticed" and disappeared in the mass of "exposures."

In his concluding remarks, Yezhov increased his attacks on Yagoda, most of all for his inability to infiltrate agents into the milieu around Trotsky and Sedov. In reply to Yagoda's rejoinder: "I always, all my life tried to get close to

Trotsky," Yezhov immediately reacted with the following words: "If you tried your whole life and did not get close to him ... this is very bad. We have been trying for a very short while, and we very easily got close to him. This presented no difficulties; you must have the desire, then getting close to him is not so difficult."[14] This statement was no empty boast: Yezhov, we assume, had in mind the recruitment of Zborowski.

The resolution on Yezhov's report repeated the formulation of the September telegram from Stalin and Zhdanov about being late in exposing the Trotskyists. It indicated that the NKVD "already in 1932–1933 had all the necessary threads in its hands to completely expose the monstrous conspiracy of the Trotskyists against the Soviet regime."[15]

The resolution reinforced the liquidation of the last elements of a civilized penal system in the USSR. It said that the previous leadership of the NKVD, having carried out "an incorrect correctional policy, particularly with regard to Trotskyists," had established "an intolerable ... prison regime when it came to the convicts who were the most vicious enemies of the Soviet regime—Trotskyists, Zinovievists, Rightists, SR's and others. As a rule, all these enemies of the people had been sent to so-called political isolators, which ... provided beneficial conditions and were more apt to resemble mandatory rest homes than prisons.... Those under arrest were given the right to enjoy literature, paper and writing utensils in an unlimited quantity, to receive an unlimited number of letters and telegrams, to outfit their cells with personal effects and to receive, along with official nourishment, packages from outside the prison in any quantity and assortment."[16]

The plenum entrusted Yezhov's department with "completing the task of exposing and routing Trotskyists and other agents of fascism, in order to crush the slightest manifestations of their anti-Soviet activity."[17]

33. THE FEBRUARY-MARCH PLENUM ON "PARTY WORK"

A T THE EVENING SESSION on March 3, the plenum turned to the point on the
agenda which read: "On political education of the party cadres and measures to fight against Trotskyists and other double-dealers in party organizations." The special significance of this question was shown by the fact that
Stalin himself delivered the report about it.

Insofar as Stalin's report was published in edited form and became the
basic document for orienting the "cadres" in the laws of the great purge, its
contents will be examined in the next chapter. Here we will dwell only on the
speeches in the discussion which developed the main themes of the report.

All the speakers spoke with enthusiasm of the extraordinary impression
which Stalin's report had made on them. "I, like other comrades, am simply
ecstatic over Stalin's report,"[1] declared Pramnek, the secretary of the Gorky
Area Committee. "Stalin hammers away at one point, which, I swear, otherwise would never make its way into our heads,"[2] confessed Yevdokimov, as if
he were speaking for all the plenum's participants.

Two secretaries who had been having a rough time described the relief
they felt after Stalin's report. "After Comrade Stalin's report," declared
Sheboldaev, "it became easier because the report showed the true dimensions
of what had been weighing me down very strongly, and I think which oppressed
not only me, but also oppressed many others.... Now everything has become
absolutely clear, and besides, he has shown the direction the fight against these
enemies should take. He has shown the way, the means, by which we can be
cured of this illness from which, let us say, I have been suffering, and which has
not been very easy to cure."[3] Seconding Sheboldaev, Postyshev declared: "After
the report by Comrade Stalin ... I somehow felt relieved ... because Comrade
Stalin nevertheless did not give a negative assessment of even those of us among
the secretaries who have made more mistakes than others."[4]

It is worthwhile to focus especially on Postyshev's speech because a fragment of this speech was cited in Khrushchev's report to the Twentieth Party

Congress as the clearest example of the doubts experienced by several participants in the February-March Plenum with regard to the "correctness of the
course that had been set toward mass repressions under the guise of struggling against double-dealers."* Khrushchev cited a fragment about Karpov,
which appeared the following way in Postyshev's speech:† "This is what I think:
we have witnessed such difficult years, there have been such twists and turns,
where people were either broken, or they stayed on their feet, or they went over
to the enemy; there was the period of industrialization, and the period of collectivization, and all the while the party waged a cruel war with enemies during this period. I never assumed that it was possible to live through all these
periods, and then pass over into the camp of our enemies. And now it seems
that he [Karpov—V. R.] fell into the clutches of the enemy from 1934 and became an enemy. Of course, it is possible to believe this or not believe it. I personally think that it is terribly difficult after all these years to go over to the
enemy in 1934. It is very difficult to believe this.... I cannot imagine how it is
possible to pass through these terrible years with the party, and then, in 1934,
to go over to the Trotskyists. It is strange." This fragment from Postyshev's
speech which Khrushchev presented seemed so "bold" and convincing that,
after he had read it at the Twentieth Congress, there was "movement in the
hall," according to the transcript.[5]

However, in Khrushchev's report the given fragment was presented in
deliberately truncated form. In reality, Postyshev's remarks were interrupted
(after the ellipsis) by Molotov's interjection: "It's hard to believe that he only
became an enemy after 1934? Probably he was one even earlier." After this,
Postyshev mentioned his "doubts" once again and then agreed with Molotov's
comment: "Something was always gnawing at him. When this started—in 1926,
in 1924, or in 1930, is hard to say, but evidently something was gnawing at
him."[6]

Despite Postyshev's extreme effort throughout the entire plenum, he turned
out to be one of the "whipping boys," a target of condemnation on the part of
the other speakers. It is true that they did not accuse him of pandering to en-

---

* Khrushchev declared that such doubts were expressed at the plenum "in the speeches of a
number of CC members." Alas, after the most careful study of the plenum materials, we
have not been able to find the expression of such doubts in a single one of the speeches.

† In Khrushchev's report, this fragment was presented in a slightly different variant, not
however, differing essentially from the text in the plenum's published transcript.

emies, but of establishing his own cult, and along with it, toadyism and servil-
ity. Serious proof was offered of these charges. Mekhlis announced that in one
issue alone of a Kiev newspaper, Postyshev's name was mentioned sixty times.[7]
Greater detail on this theme was provided by Kudriavtsev, who had replaced
Postyshev at the post of secretary of the Kiev Area Committee. He said that the
Kiev party organization widely indulged in "ostentation and fanfare, self-glori-
fication and foolish rapture.... Numerous greetings and stormy ovations with
everyone standing greet the leader of the area committee. The atmosphere of
glorification around Comrade Postyshev has reached such proportions that
here and there people speak loudly of Postyshev's closest, most loyal, best and
most devoted comrades-in-arms, and those who have not reached the level of
comrade-in-arms call themselves Postyshevists." Kudriavtsev also told how
Postyshev, who wanted to recommend himself as "friend of the children," sent
extravagant gifts in his own name to children of other republics, and his "syco-
phants presented Comrade Postyshev as a kind and rich uncle who was showering children out of the horn of plenty: there were Postyshev trees, Postyshev
rooms, Postyshev toys, Pioneer palaces, children's playgrounds and parks, etc."

When Kudriavtsev mentioned that "smaller cults" flourished in other cities of the Kiev area ("the secretaries of the Zhitomir organization ... saw nothing wrong in the fact that large and small portraits of them were hung all over
the city"), Molotov directed an ironic remark to the Ukrainian "leaders": "He
(Kudriavtsev) makes a good addition to Kosior and Postyshev."[8]

Developing the theme of "cult worship of local leaders," Mekhlis gave a
number of impressive examples. Thus, the Cheliabinsk newspaper published a
report ending with the words: "Long live the leader of the Cheliabinsk Bolsheviks, Comrade Ryndin!"[9] Criticism of similar episodes let those who had gathered know that from now on, glorification must be limited to Stalin and his
"closest comrades-in-arms."

In trying to determine the differences between party and economic work,
the speakers contradicted themselves and each other. In any case, it was clear
that the party organs should not refuse to intervene directly in economic matters. The counterposing of party and economic work was needed in order to
more clearly define the main task of the party organs: not to limit themselves
to "uprooting" "wreckers," i.e. officials in industry and agriculture, but to focus
their efforts at purging the party apparatus itself. "Party work" was explained
to be the discovery and "uprooting" of "Trotskyists," even if they were to blame

for nothing more than participating in the oppositions of the 1920s. That is precisely how Khrushchev understood the meaning of "party work" when he promised "to embitter and arouse the (Moscow) party organization ... against the Trotskyists and Zinovievists."[10]

A very important aspect of "party work," it followed from the speeches, was to be the encouragement of supplementary reports which had begun to flood into the party organs. Yevdokimov was pleased to announce that a "mass ... of declarations about the ties of various people to unmasked enemies"[11] was now coming into his regional committee. Sheboldaev, who had been transferred a month before to the post of secretary of the Kursk area committee, reported how he tackled this work at the new location: "each day in Kursk we have one hundred to one hundred fifty declarations coming to me, apart from the apparatus; we have to read everything and look into everything, otherwise we will once again miss the boat, the way we did earlier." As proof of the success in "interpreting" the given "signals," Sheboldaev cited facts, according to which they had already arrested seven members of the bureau in the region and four heads of departments of the area committee, as well as twenty-five officials in the agricultural wing alone of the area executive committee.[12]

Andreev spoke about the scale of the impending pogrom of leading cadres, using the example of the Azov-Black Sea region, which had leapt ahead in this regard. He had been sent there two months earlier to "explain" the CC decree to the local regional committee. In reporting the results of this trip, Andreev declared that in the major cities of the region (Rostov, Krasnodar, Novorossiisk, Taganrog, Novocherkassk, Sochi) almost all the first and second secretaries of the city committees, as well as the chairmen and deputy chairmen of the city soviets, "turned out to be Trotskyists." Not satisfied with this, Andreev announced, "There are indications that we shall still have a whole series of proofs showing that Trotskyists were almost everywhere."[13]

For the majority of party secretaries who still did not have the opportunity to boast of such "achievements," all that remained was to lament that they "had overlooked a heap of enemies."[14] Against this background, the only ones who looked "successful" were the most blood-thirsty Stalinists who gave examples of their own "vigilance" and who made suggestions to expand the scale of the terror. Thus, Beria announced that in the past year, about one thousand five hundred former members of "anti-Soviet parties" had returned to Georgia from exile; "with the exception of isolated individuals, the majority of those

returning remain enemies of the Soviet regime, they are enemies who are organizing counterrevolutionary wrecking, espionage, and sabotage." Beria therefore came to the conclusion that "we should not return political exiles to their
previous places of residency."[15]

Mekhlis explained to the plenum how the press must conduct itself in unfolding the campaign of "extirpation." Announcing that in several issues of one
regional newspaper, they had listed fifty-six, and then in another, sixty-eight
"new names of unmasked Trotskyists," he declared that such a "continuous
flow of articles in the newspapers about Trotskyists creates a false impression
about the relative weight of Trotskyists in the country."

In his speech, Mekhlis indicated that while "exposing Trotskyists," one need
not reproduce the statements for which they were being arrested. He spoke
with indignation about how, in uncovering one "Trotskyist," "everything that
he said about Trotsky was printed in the newspaper. They wrote the following,
that Trotsky was a meritorious political figure who did much not only for the
USSR but for the workers and peasants of the entire world. Trotsky even has
more works than Lenin." Mekhlis cited another impermissible incident when
"in a Rostov institute, Shapovalov said that the party needed to have freedom
for groups, and that the whole collective had not exposed Shapovalov."

Finally, Mekhlis declared, "Trotskyists use the type of devices which allow
our editors or newspaper and party simpletons to speak about printing and
typographical errors." As examples, he cited many incidents in the practice of
regional, factory and collective farm newspapers, when the unsuccessful mon-
tage of newspaper materials might produce unwanted associations among
readers; in one newspaper, under the headline, "Vicious enemies of the people,"
someone had placed a portrait of Stalin; in another, under the subtitle, "Shoot
the entire band of hired assassins," Yezhov's photograph stood out vividly.
Mekhlis declared that for such examples of "ideological sabotage," officials in
the press should be ruthlessly punished.[16]

The discussion of the last question on the agenda was completed with
Stalin's closing speech, after which the plenum was declared closed.

34. Stalin Issues Directives

STALIN WORKED for a long time on the text of his speeches at the plenum as he was preparing them for publication. His report was published only on 29 March, and his concluding remarks on 1 April 1937.

The title which preceded this publication, "On the Shortcomings of Party Work and on Measures to Liquidate the Trotskyists and other Double-dealers," differed from the name of Stalin's report in the plenum agenda in that it was more ominous. The word, "liquidate," unequivocally indicated the fate of all those who were considered to be "double-dealers."

Stalin indicated the scale of the proposed "liquidation" just as unequivocally. This scale obviously contradicted the falsified statistics which Stalin had been using for a number of years in order to give the impression of the numerical insignificance of the "Trotskyists." At the Fifteenth Congress of the VKP(b) (December 1927) he cited figures according to which seven hundred twenty-four thousand voted "for the party" in the precongress discussion, and "a few more than four thousand"[1] voted for the Opposition. He made a few correctives to these data at the November 1928 Plenum of the CC. When he declared that less than four thousand people had voted against the CC platform in the previous year's discussion, someone shouted from the audience: "ten thousand." Stalin not only agreed with this figure, but then added: "I think that if ten thousand voted against, then twice ten thousand party members who sympathized with Trotskyism did not vote at all, since they did not come to the conferences. These are the same Trotskyist elements who did not leave the party and who, we must assume, still have not freed themselves from Trotskyist ideology."[2]

At the February-March Plenum, Stalin returned to the figure from 1927 — four thousand people who voted for the "Trotskyists" in the course of the last discussion in the party's history. Adding to this figure two thousand six hundred people who abstained from voting ("assuming that they also sympathized with the Trotskyists"), and 5 percent of those who did not participate in the voting (the number of those not voting comprised 15 percent of the total mem-

286

bers of the party), he arrived at an approximate figure—"twelve thousand party members who sympathized in one way or another with Trotskyism." "Here you have all the forces of Messieurs Trotskyists," Stalin said in commenting on this figure. "Add to this the circumstance that many of this number have become disillusioned with Trotskyism and have left its ranks, then you will get an idea of the insignificance of the Trotskyist forces."[3]

The figure cited by Stalin strikingly contradicted the figures given by other speakers at the plenum. Thus, Kaganovich announced that in the apparatus of the railways alone, in 1934 they unmasked one hundred thirty-six Trotskyists, in 1935 eight hundred seven, and in 1936 three thousand eight hundred, among whom a significant number were arrested.[4]

In reporting the reprisals made against Oppositionists in the army, Gamarnik announced that at the time of verifying party documents (1935–36), two hundred thirty-three Trotskyists and Zinovievists were expelled, during the exchange of party documents (1936) seventy-five, and after the exchange, i.e., from September 1936 to February 1937, two hundred forty-four.[5]

Even more striking were the figures given by secretaries of the republic and area party organizations. Postyshev reported that in only five areas of the Ukraine, during the exchange of party documents three hundred twelve Trotskyists were expelled, and after the exchange one thousand three hundred forty-two. Altogether in the Ukraine from 1933–1937, eleven thousand "enemies of all kinds" were expelled from the party, including slightly more than seven thousand Trotskyists. "Very many of them were imprisoned."[6]

According to Beria, in Georgia alone during 1936, one thousand fifty Trotskyists and Zinovievists were arrested.[7]

Khrushchev reported that in Moscow and the Moscow area, during the verification of party documents one thousand two hundred Trotskyists and Zinovievists were expelled, during the exchange of party documents three hundred four, and after the exchange nine hundred forty-two.[8]

In describing the "purge" activity which had been conducted under his leadership in the Azov-Black Sea area, Andreev said that during the exchange of party documents, "only forty-five Trotskyists" were expelled, but after the exchange they expelled and arrested five hundred Trotskyists.[9]

Naming the approximate number of those purged throughout the whole country in 1933–1934 (609,000), Yakovlev added: "As for the Trotskyists, then it turned out that if they made it through the purge and verification, then after the exchange they were caught. After the exchange, six thousand six hundred people were expelled, just as many as during the verification of party documents, and two times more than during the exchange."[10]

Then Stalin himself, in summarizing the results of the plenum's work, declared that "wrecking, sabotage and espionage by agents of foreign governments, among which an active role has been played by Trotskyists, affected to one degree or another all or almost all our organizations, whether they be economic, administrative or party."[11]

In order to explain the reasons for the appearance of such an abundance of enemies, Stalin referred to his "theory" of the sharpening of the class struggle as the successes of socialism mount. In doing so he sharpened his previous pronouncements on this question. "The further we move ahead, the more successes we have," he declared, "the more embittered will the shattered remnants of the exploiting classes become, the sooner will they pass over to the sharpest forms of struggle, the more they will play dirty tricks on the Soviet state, and the more they will latch onto the most desperate means of struggle, as the last means of those who are doomed."*[12]

Warning against conceptions that the Trotskyists no longer were dangerous insofar as the overwhelming majority of them were in prisons and camps, Stalin sharply condemned the idea that "the Trotskyists ... had apparently reached the end of their last cadres." In this regard, he unexpectedly transferred his "denunciations" beyond the borders of the USSR by calling a whole number of foreign groups and organizations "Trotskyist reserves." Not skimping in his expressions of malice, he included in these groups "the Trotskyist counterrevolutionary Fourth International, two-thirds of which is composed of spies and saboteurs," "the group of the scoundrel Scheflo in Norway, who gave refuge to the ober-spy Trotsky," "another group led by just as bad a scoundrel ... Souvarine in France," "various gentlemen in Germany, every kind of Ruth Fischer, Maslow and Urbahns, who have sold their souls and bodies to the fascists," and a "famous horde of writers in America led by the famous

---

* As monstrous as it is, the program of the KPRF (the most massive of the Russian parties calling themselves communist) states: "To a significant degree, one example of foresight has proven to be justified: to the extent that socialism is created, the resistance of forces hostile to it not only does not diminish, but often assumes the cruelest and most monstrous forms" (*Pravda*, 31 January 1995). Obviously the program's authors feel that the periods of stagnation and "perestroika," which preceded capitalist restoration in the USSR, were periods of the successful "creation of socialism."

artist Eastman, all of these bandits of the pen who make their living by slandering the working class of the USSR.*"[13]

The report directly stated that "the Trotskyists" must be seen not as ideological or political opponents, but as criminals of the lowest order. Several times Stalin reproached "our party comrades" for the fact that they had not noticed that "Trotskyism had ceased to be a political tendency in the working class as it had been seven to eight years ago. Trotskyism had turned into a frenzied and unprincipled band of wreckers, saboteurs, spies and assassins, acting on the orders of the intelligence organizations of foreign states." Therefore, "in the struggle against contemporary Trotskyism, what we now need is not the old methods, not the methods of discussion, but new methods, the methods of uprooting and routing."[14] Such a directive freed Soviet and foreign Communists from the ideological struggle against "Trotskyists," which demanded at least some kind of, even falsified, exposition of their political views.

Later Stalin explained what must be understood by "a political tendency in the working class": "This is a group or party which has a certain political physiognomy, platform or program, which does not hide and cannot hide its views from the working class, but, on the contrary, propagandizes its views openly and honestly."[15]

Avoiding the question of how the Trotskyists could propagandize their views in the USSR, Stalin referred only to the "lessons" of the previous trials. "During the trial of 1936, if you remember, Kamenev and Zinoviev vigorously denied that they had any kind of political platform," he declared. "They had a full opportunity to outline their political platform at the trial. However, they did not do this ... because they were afraid of revealing their genuine political face.... At the trial in 1937, Piatakov, Radek and Sokolnikov followed another path.... They acknowledged that they shared a political platform, they acknowledged and outlined it in their testimonies. But they outlined it not in order to appeal to the working class, to appeal to the working class for support for the Trotskyist platform, but in order to curse it as a platform which was against

---

* O. Scheflo was one of the leaders of the Norwegian Labor Party; B. Souvarine was one of the leaders of the French Communist Party in the 1920s who was expelled from it for supporting the Left Opposition in the USSR; Ruth Fischer and A. Maslow were leaders of the German Communist Party until the mid-1920s, when they were expelled for being close to the Left Opposition; M. Eastman was a left-wing American journalist who was a sympathizer of the Left Opposition until the end of the 1930s.

the people and against the proletariat." In this, one of the most cynical passages of his report, Stalin portrayed the trials as the type of arena in which the
defendants possessed "the full possibility" of "appealing to the people" for support of their views. According to Stalin's report, they did not do this only because the platform "of contemporary Trotskyism" amounted to the most repulsive things: wrecking, terror, espionage, the restoration of capitalism, the
territorial dismemberment of the Soviet Union, and so forth. As Stalin declared,
this platform was concealed by the defendants on Trotsky's orders even from
the "Trotskyist masses," and from the "leading Trotskyist elite, composed of a
small group of about thirty to forty people."[16]

   However, even after all these passages, Stalin tossed a life preserver to the
former Trotskyists who still remained at liberty. The first step in this direction
had been made at the plenum by Molotov, who warned against wild reprisals
against all former Trotskyists (let us recall that some of them, for instance
Rozengolts, were in the plenum's audience). "Now, comrades, we often hear
the following question," said Molotov. "What should we do if a person is a former
Trotskyist, does it mean that we can have nothing to do with him?... Moreover,
not long ago, in connection with exposing Trotskyist sabotage activity, somewhere people began to go too far, going after both those who were guilty and
innocent, without correctly understanding the interests of the party and the
state."[17] In the published text of Molotov's report, this situation is explained in
a more "expanded" and "liberal" manner: "We cannot consider a mistake every appointment of a former Trotskyist to a responsible post. We cannot refuse
to employ a former Trotskyist in responsible work only because he once, at one
time, spoke out against the party line."[18]

   Similar reservations were contained in Stalin's report, when he left former
oppositionists a certain sliver of hope for salvation. "Do we have to beat and
uproot not only genuine Trotskyists," Stalin asked, "but also those who once
vacillated in the direction of Trotskyism, and then, long ago, abandoned
Trotskyism, not only those who are really Trotskyist agents of sabotage, but
also those who once had the occasion to walk down the street which one or
another Trotskyist once walked down? In any case, such voices were raised
here at the plenum." Just as during the sharpest moments of the legal struggle
against the Oppositions of the 1920s, Stalin superficially was distancing himself from the extremist moods of CC members and was speaking in favor of
"flexible" decisions. He declared, "you cannot measure all people by the same

yardstick.... Among our leading comrades there are a certain number of former Trotskyists who long ago abandoned Trotskyism and are now waging a battle against Trotskyism no worse, and even better than a few of our respected comrades who did not have the occasion to waver in the direction of Trotskyism." This carefully conceived passage pursued two goals: 1. To tell people "who had wavered" in the past that a condition of their survival was special activity in supporting and carrying out reprisals against their former cothinkers; 2. To warn those who "did not have the occasion to waver in the direction of Trotskyism," that this would not serve as an indulgence if they did not take an active part in the impending purge.

Leaving it to the local leaders to decide independently the issue of how to decipher the metaphor he had given them ("who once had occasion to walk along the same street that one or another Trotskyist walked along"), Stalin "defended" one more category of "our comrades"—those who "ideologically always stood against Trotskyism, but, despite this, maintained personal ties with individual Trotskyists, ties which they quickly severed as soon as the practical physiognomy of Trotskyism became clear to them. It is of course not good that they ended their personal ties of friendship with individual Trotskyists not immediately, but after some delay. But it would be foolish to lump all these comrades together into one group with the Trotskyists."[19] This passage indirectly indicated that "personal ties of friendship with individual Trotskyists" might become a reason for repression, if the ties were not severed "in time."

The fact that all links in the party and governmental system were thoroughly "littered" with Trotskyists was explained by Stalin in the following way: party cadres, distracted by "the colossal successes on the front of economic construction," lost their vigilance and became infected with "the idiotic disease of carelessness."

There actually were certain grounds for claiming economic successes. In 1935–36, Soviet industry reached tempos of growth in the productivity of labor which were unknown in the previous decade. But the economic successes even in those years were not as great as Stalin portrayed them. The chronic diseases of the Soviet economy had not been eliminated: the disproportions between the various branches of the national economy, the low quality of production, the high percentage of waste, and so forth. Now all these shortcomings were being ascribed to the machinations of wreckers, and the economic leaders were receiving a stern warning for the puzzled questions which had arisen among them in connection with the demand to uncover saboteurs in all enterprises, including even those which had achieved higher economic indicators. "Success after success, achievement after achievement, overfulfillment of the plan after overfulfillment," Stalin asserted, "gives birth to moods of carelessness and self-satisfaction, creates an atmosphere of ostentatious triumphs and mutual congratulations ... a thick atmosphere of conceit and self-satisfaction, an atmosphere of parade spectacles and noisy self-praise." Condemning these phenomena which he had been fostering in the party and in the nation for years, and which could not help but arouse either indignation or bewilderment in any thoughtful person, Stalin presented them as the cause for "political blindness," expressed in such statements as: "Strange people sit there in Moscow, in the party's CC they think up all kinds of questions, they go on about some kind of sabotage, they never sleep, and they never let others sleep ... "[20]

To put an end, once and for all, to such moods, Stalin invented and then refuted six "rotten theories" which stood in the way of "finally routing the Trotskyist band." With these "theories" he had in mind common sense arguments, in particular doubts about how the leaders of enterprises which always fulfilled or overfulfilled economic plans could be saboteurs. In this regard, Stalin demanded that "we smash and drive back ... the rotten theory which says that the systematic fulfillment of economic plans reduces sabotage and the results of sabotage to nothing." He explained that this "theory" did not take into account that "saboteurs usually schedule their wrecking activity not for peaceful times, but for the period on the eve of war or during the war itself."[21]

In his report Stalin directly pointed to those whom he saw to be the main social support in carrying out the Great Terror. As opposed to the "cadres," who, according to his theory of 1935, "decide everything," he now was advancing the category of "little people," who were capable of proposing the best economic solutions and of effectively exposing "enemies." Thus, he told how the CC three times rejected the draft of measures proposed by the People's Commissariat of Heavy Industry to overcome "delays" which had been discovered in the Donbass. "Finally we decided to summon from the Donbass several workers and rank-and-file economic and trade union officials. We talked with these people for three days. And all of us who are members of the CC had to admit that these rank-and-file workers, these 'little people,' were able to suggest the correct solution."[22]

As another example of the perspicacity of "little people," Stalin praised the denunciations made by Nikolaenko. This passage was an open call for careerists among the "little people" to make denunciations of the leaders at any level without fear of reprisals.

Stalin was just as specific in indicating who should be selected as the object of total extermination. Comparing today's saboteurs to the "saboteurs of the Shakhty period," he declared that the strength of the latter had consisted of their technical knowledge, which "our people" did not have at that time. Now, however, according to Stalin, "tens of thousands of genuine, technologically prepared Bolshevik cadres have grown up among us." In comparison to them, Piatakov and other "Trotskyists" were "apprentices." The strength of these "modern-day saboteurs," Stalin stated, was that they possessed party cards which gave them "access to all our institutions and organizations," thereby making them "an out-and-out godsend for the intelligence services of foreign states."[23]

Stalin's report outlined a well thought-through plan for "a cadre revolution," which would go far beyond the bounds of "uprooting" the participants in the earlier oppositions and which assumed practically a full replenishment of all the apparatuses of power. In this regard, Stalin listed the approximate numbers of the "leading staff of our party," dividing it into hierarchical steps. Using military terminology from pre-revolutionary times (which by itself could not help but grate on the ear of anyone who retained a Bolshevik mentality), he declared: "In the composition of our party, if you have in mind its leading layers, there are approximately three to four thousand high-ranking leaders. This, I would say, is the general staff of our party."

"Then there are thirty to forty thousand midlevel leaders. This is our party's officer corps."

"Further, there are about one hundred thousand to one hundred fifty thousand in the lower party command staff. These, so to speak, are our noncommissioned officers."[24]

Stalin then virtually proceeded to make public a plan for fully replacing the representatives of all these layers with a new, young generation of promotees who were yearning for power and privileges. He openly declared that "we have tens of thousands of capable and talented people. We must only get to know them and promote them in time so that they not remain in their old places and begin to rot. Seek and ye shall find."[25] This was a direct challenge issued not to the party leaders, but to those who should replace them: in order to find an outlet for their ambitious strivings, only one thing was required, which was by no means the most difficult condition—they had to show their zeal in "exposing enemies of the people."

Serious social meaning was contained in the juxtaposition by Stalin of the youth and the old cadres. It appeared to Stalin that he could simultaneously and effectively resolve two issues—to frighten and then remove the layer of leaders which was dangerous for him and to open a vertical channel of mobility for the youth who would be ardently devoted to him because they did not know the truth about his past and the past of the party in which, at the dawn of soviet power, completely different morals and relations had dominated.

Stalin's insidious plan was aimed at using monstrous and inhuman methods to resolve one of the main contradictions of post-revolutionary society: the contradiction between the Old Bolsheviks who occupied leading posts in the party and state apparatus, and the young generation which wanted to grow and attain social advancement. Trotsky had first pointed to this contradiction in the article, "The New Course" (1923), where he warned against the consolidation of "apparatus-bureaucratic methods of politics, which turn the young generation into passive material for education and aggravate the inevitable alienation between the apparatus and the masses, between the 'old-timers' and the young." In order to ward off this danger, Trotsky proposed "to refresh and renew the party apparatus ... in order to replace those who have become bureaucratized with fresh elements who are closely linked with the life of the collective or who are capable of establishing such links."[26]

Insofar as the ideologues of the ruling faction immediately and falsely interpreted these proposals as Trotsky's attempts to flatter the youth, defame the "old guard," and so forth, Trotsky felt that it was necessary to devote a special article to this question, "The Problem of Party Generations." In it he indicated that the main danger of the old course consisted in "the tendency to ever increasingly counterpose several thousand comrades who comprise the leading cadres to the remaining masses as an object to be acted on."[27] Trotsky suggested that ways of overcoming this danger would be to strengthen the independence of the party, democratize its internal life, periodically rotate and renew the leading cadres, and inculcate in the party youth the ability to form their own opinion and to fight for it.

The rejection of this alternative in the course of a bitter inner-party struggle led to what Trotsky had predicted: the degeneration of the party "simultaneously at both poles." Nevertheless, the "upper pole," i.e., the representatives of the old party guard, continued to present a serious danger to the Stalinist regime. The consciousness of the majority of these people maintained a Bolshevik mentality and a nostalgia for the traditions of party life which were being trampled on. In these conditions, what was preferable for Stalin was a shift in the center of the regime's social support to the youth, who had grown up in Stalinist conditions and who perceived discussions as something impermissible; in addition, they thought that a regime of personal power was an inviolable law of party and political life.

One more important political factor was at play here. In principle, securing the social advancement of the youth is one of the main, and vitally important, tasks of post-revolutionary society. Their living standards are usually low, their work difficult, and the only thing which allows people not to lose hope in social equality is the extent to which the slogan of the social revolution is brought to life: "We have been naught, we shall be all."

The deliberate social policy in the realm of education which was begun immediately after the October Revolution allowed thousands of people coming from a working class or peasant background to receive an education which was sufficient for a professional start in management. However the layer which had come to power after the revolution was not inclined to "make room" for the youth.

Undertaking to resolve the problem of generations not with democratic methods, as the Left Opposition was proposing, but with totalitarian ones, Stalin ran into one of the most fundamental defects of totalitarianism. He not only fell into the trap himself, but left several generations of Soviet people in it.

Totalitarian management guarantees a swift growth of the economy on the basis of mobilizing the population with the aid of a "monolithic" ideology. This sterile ideology, which amounts to an assortment of dogmas not open to discussion or criticism, can function only under conditions of the absolute political loyalty of its leaders at all levels. Their strict political selection is therefore inevitable, and professional criteria (competence, specialized knowledge, etc.) recede into the background. That is what happened during the Stalinist years, when a well-mobilized populace ended up under the management of leaders like Voroshilov and Kaganovich.

Apparently, Stalin at first believed that it was not only necessary but possible to combine the political and professional demands of leaders, that these demands would get along with each other. However, under conditions of cardinal changes in the very ideology of the ruling party and in the character of the political regime, a distortion in the direction of political reliability (in the sense of unreservedly accepting Stalin's model of society as "socialist") proved to be inevitable and overwhelming.

Taking political criteria into account when promoting leaders is vitally important for the creation of a system based on a nationalized economy and its planned management. However, for such a system to successfully function, what is needed is the democratization of all social and political life, protecting against the omnipotence of the bureaucracy with its desire to crush all dissident thought. What inevitably changes in a bureaucratic system is the ideology, which turns into an amazing mixture of myths and phantoms, masked by abstractions from the socialist lexicon.

In the first years after Stalin's death, it had already become obvious that to overcome the sharply felt breach between word and deed, there would have to be a practical and intellectual renunciation of the malignancies of the past and an uncompromising adherence to the truth in an analysis of the present. However the achievement of these goals in the post-Stalinist period proved to be impossible, insofar as it contradicted the interests of the "recruits of 1937," who retained the key posts in the party and state apparatus. This layer blocked the channels of vertical mobility for the following generations with much greater force than had been done by the generation of fifty- and forty-year-olds in the 1930s. However, insofar as there was some vertical mobility, if only due to natural causes, the party gerontocracy of the 1970s and 1980s did prepare its own replacements, consisting of cynics and careerists to whom ideology was essentially a matter of indifference. And the very leaders of the epoch of stagnation, who had remained in power for a half-century, proved to be indifferent to the ideological side of life and politics since they had adopted a course of narrow pragmatism. Bound up with all this, the weakening of the role of the political factor in cadre policy led to the promotion of a new generation of partocrats, technocrats and pseudo-scholars who served them. They relatively quickly shattered the existing system, first by knocking out its ideological struts and then destroying it politically.

The source of these destructive processes must be sought in the "cadre revolution" of 1937, the plan for which Stalin announced at the February-March Plenum. Calling for the infusion of "fresh forces, who await their promotion" into the "command cadres," and the preparation "of not one, but several shifts which can replace the leaders of the Central Committee of our party," he demanded that all party leaders, from the secretaries of the smallest cells to the secretaries of republic organizations, "select in the course of a certain period, two people, two party members who are capable of serving as their acting deputies."[28]

All these ominous directives, which essentially obligated the party leaders to prepare the conditions for their total extermination, were camouflaged by widely trumpeted assurances about the widening of inner-party democracy. Stalin promised an end to reducing the elections to party bodies to an empty formality; he promised to stop the transformation of party forums into clamorous demonstrations, and to put a halt to "the soulless, bureaucratic attitude ... toward the fate of individual party members." Apropos of this, he condemned "certain of our party leaders," who remained unnamed, but who "drive out (party members) ... wildly and indiscriminately, who expel thousands and tens of thousands from the party.... They consider the expulsion of thousands and tens of thousands to be a trifling matter, comforting themselves with the fact that the party has two million members, and tens of thousands of expulsions cannot change anything in the party's position." Having presented the monstrous practice of expelling "tens of thousands" from the party as simply the defect of "certain leaders," which could easily be corrected by the all-powerful CC, Stalin promised to punish those who "artificially produce a number of dissatisfied and embittered people," and to guarantee "an attentive attitude toward people, toward party members, toward the fate of party members."[29] This closing fragment of his speech was designed to give some hope to the communists who had been expelled from the party in 1937, not by the tens of thousands, but by the hundreds of thousands, after which, in the majority of cases, they had been deprived of their work and their freedom.

35. The Election Campaign in the Party

THE ELECTION CAMPAIGN to party organs, which was launched immediately after the plenum, was designed to serve as a test of how well prepared the party organizations were to uncover "enemies of the people" in their own ranks. On 6 March *Pravda* published an information bulletin about the plenum. Then it began to publish instructive articles which contained two types of orientation material: the first was demagogically "democratic," and the second was a call to "vigilance." A demand was placed before all party organizations to put an end to their "conceit, complacency and obliviousness to the interests of party members."[1] Blame for these unhealthy party mores, however, was not placed on the party regime which had taken root, but on "the wolves in sheep's clothing, who by deception have broken into our party home."[2] "Inordinate praise of leaders who have a weakness for flattery" was called "a weapon of struggle against the party, and a barrier to vigilance" which was used by the "Trotskyist cuckoos."[3] The demand was made to promote to party organs people "who have truly been tested in the struggle against all enemies of the working class, people who are endlessly devoted to the party of Lenin-Stalin and its Central Committee."[4]

In a speech to the June (1957) Plenum of the CC, Khrushchev spoke very vividly about the mechanics of conducting "democratic elections" which were fostered by these conditions. Khrushchev recalled that at the party conferences of 1937, even the elections of a presidium often dragged on for a week—because the delegates were so eager to use the right they had been granted to "unrestrictedly reject" candidates. "After all you know," Khrushchev said, "how people told about their biographies, and how they were asked about their grandfathers and grandmothers. Some of the comrades who are here can remember these things."[5]

Many years later, in his memoirs Khrushchev recounted in greater detail the atmosphere in which these conferences were held. "It was a terrible period," he recalled, "terrible because we felt that we were surrounded by enemies, and that these enemies ... had occupied an important position in the economy and in the army, had seized a majority of commanding posts.... The party was demoralized ... the leaders did not feel that they were leaders."[6]

In this atmosphere, the "initiative" of those delegates who had more of a penchant for "vigilance" was combined with behind-the-scenes machinations which were prompted by the "organs." Khrushchev said that the candidates which were nominated to the Moscow Area and Moscow City Committees of the party had passed a preliminary review and been confirmed by the NKVD. "To tell the truth, at that time we considered that this would help the party organs in studying the cadres and exposing enemies who had penetrated even into the leadership. That's how we had been taught."[7]

During the work of the Moscow Party Conference, Yezhov telephoned Khrushchev and said that in the elections they had to reject one of the candidates who had already been applauded as he was placed on the list for secret balloting. The reason given for this demand was that this person was "linked up with enemies" and soon would be arrested. Thirty years later, Khrushchev recalled what efforts it had cost him to carry out the behind-the-scenes work in carrying out Yezhov's instructions. In doing so "such psychological damage was done, and it had such a foul affect on the conference delegates.... They rejected him. He was bewildered: what was going on? The next night he was arrested, and the question was cleared up for everyone."[8]

To an even greater extent Khrushchev was surprised to receive instructions to arrange the electoral defeat of Yaroslavsky, who for many years had played the role of Stalin's main assistant in the fight against "Trotskyists." Meanwhile, Yezhov was explaining his demand by the fact that Yaroslavsky "had been insufficiently active in waging the struggle against the Opposition, and he sympathized with Trotsky."[9] Khrushchev, who was well versed in apparatus mechanics, understood that the application of such a directive to Yaroslavsky could only have come directly from Stalin. "It was very hard for me personally," Khrushchev recalls, "however I had to carry out my assignment and began to tell the secretaries of the party cells to carry out the corresponding agitation among the delegations, but they must do so in such a way that it not reach Yaroslavsky himself, who had already been placed on the list of nominees." When she learned about these instructions, the Old Bolshevik Zemliachka thought that it was the personal initiative of Khrushchev, and sent an indignant letter on this question to the CC. "I could not explain to her immediately,"

Khrushchev, Molotov and Stalin at a special session devoted to the opening of the Moscow-Volga Canal, 1937

Khrushchev writes, "that I was carrying out the will of the CC [the concepts of "Stalin" and the "CC" by that time had firmly and unreservedly become identified in the minds of the apparatchiks—V. R.]. She understood this later. Of course, her letter produced no results."[10]

Several episodes recounted by Khrushchev show how the selection of candidates took place at the Moscow conferences. The first episode was connected with the head of one of the departments of the Moscow Committee, Brandt, who before the conference told Khrushchev that he always was having to explain whether he was the son of a colonel in the tsarist army named Brandt who headed the anti-Soviet uprising in Kaluga in 1918. Although Brandt would always say that his father had truly been a colonel, but another, who had never disgraced himself before the Soviet regime, he was sure that this time they would begin to slander him with particular cruelty, and therefore he was entertaining thoughts of suicide. Imagining all too well the atmosphere which would dominate at the conference, Khrushchev understood that it "might prove to be fatal for Brandt," and decided to tell Stalin himself about this case, in order to save his comrade and colleague. After he had received assurances from Khrushchev that Brandt was "a person who had been tested," Stalin ordered that "he not be subjected to insults." As a result, Brandt was elected a member of the Moscow Committee.[11] In light of this episode, one can easily imagine how, for many people who did not have the opportunity to obtain Stalin's personal protection, such "misunderstandings" ended tragically at the time.

The second episode involved Malenkov, who occupied one of the most responsible positions in the CC—he headed the department of leading party organs. Despite his position, Malenkov felt to the fullest degree the "democratic" zeal of the conference participants. At the June Plenum of 1957, when there was a settling of longstanding accounts between members "of the collective leadership," Khrushchev reminded Malenkov how he had come to his rescue "so that they didn't tear you to pieces. They were asking you who you really were, and where you had come from."[12]

Khrushchev described this episode in greater detail in his memoirs. He had left the conference for talks with Stalin, and when he returned, Khrushchev found a discussion going on about Malenkov's candidacy. "Malenkov was giving explanations. They told me that he had already been standing there for an hour or more, and every one of his answers led to another question about his party career and about his activity during the Civil War ... the situation was developing in which Malenkov might be rejected."[13] Khrushchev's account is confirmed by the transcript of the conference, from which it is clear that Malenkov was having the most trouble with the question of whether he was in Orenburg when this city was seized by the Whites in 1918 (let us recall that at that time Malenkov was seventeen years old). When Malenkov answered this question affirmatively, cries rang out in the hall: "That means he was with the Whites." Khrushchev saved the situation. He assumed his place as chairman and explained to the delegates: "Comrades, I think that such questions might lead the conference astray. The Whites may indeed have been on the territory of Orenburg at that time, but Comrade Malenkov was not on their side."[14] Only after this "explanation" was Malenkov left on the ballot.

The third episode involved the fate of Khrushchev himself. Knowing that during the discussion of candidacies, the slightest affiliation of each candidate in the past to "Trotskyism" would be presented, inevitably in an especially biased manner, Khrushchev was terrified that some of the delegates might remember a dangerous page in his biography: during the discussion of 1923 he had spoken in support of Trotsky on the question of inner-party democracy. Understanding that if this fact became known in the heated atmosphere of the conference, he "would find it very difficult to give an explanation," Khrushchev decided to confess directly to Stalin. Imagining what consequences this confession might entail, he sought advice from Kaganovich, who at that time was very favorably disposed toward him. Kaganovich, who "had been entrusted with observing the Moscow Conference," began to strongly dissuade Khrushchev from his intentions to tell Stalin about his "Trotskyist vacillations." Despite his warnings, Khrushchev nevertheless decided to tell Stalin "about the mistake committed in 1923," so that he would not appear at the conference to be a man "who had concealed compromising information."

After he had told Stalin about his "mistake," Khrushchev added that he "had been taken in at that time by Kharechko, who was a rather well known Trotskyist." Stalin reacted to his words: "Kharechko? Oh, I knew him. He was an interesting man." (Kharechko at that time was in a Kolyma concentration camp). Khrushchev asked Stalin whether he should speak at the conference about his "mistake" from the distant past. Stalin answered: "As far as I'm concerned, you don't have to mention it. You have told us, and that is enough." Molotov, who was present during this conversation, objected: "No, it would be better if he spoke." Stalin agreed: "Yes, you had better speak about it, because if you don't, then someone might latch onto it, and then they will shower you with questions, and us with denunciations."

Thirty years after the event, Khrushchev recalled that this discussion produced a certainty in him that "those who had been arrested were truly enemies of the people, even though they had acted so craftily that we were unable to notice because of our inexperience, political blindness and trustfulness. Stalin ... seemed to rise up even higher on the pedestal: he saw everything, knew everything, judged people's mistakes fairly, defended and supported honest people, and punished those who were undeserving of trust."[15]

Kaganovich treated this episode somewhat differently in his discussions with Chuyev. Kaganovich reported that Khrushchev came running to him with tears in his eyes: "What am I to do? Should I speak at the conference or not?" Kaganovich promised to seek advice on this question from Stalin. When he learned that Khrushchev "had been a Trotskyist," Stalin asked, "And what about now?" Kaganovich replied, "He is very active, and fights sincerely." Then Stalin said: "Let him speak, let him tell about it. Then you should speak and say the CC knows about this and trusts him...." As Kaganovich recalls, "That's what was done."[16]

The episode of Khrushchev's "Trotskyist past" had a noteworthy continuation. At the session of the Presidium of the CC in June 1957, when Molotov and Kaganovich proposed to remove Khrushchev from his post as First Secretary of the CC, one of their main arguments was reference to Khrushchev's "Trotskyism." Kaganovich was particularly impassioned in exposing

Khrushchev as a "Trotskyist." When several participants at the session began to protest against this "inadmissible method," Molotov declared, "But it all happened."[17]

Even two decades after 1937 and a third of a century since his "mistake," Khrushchev himself invested this charge with such significance that he devoted a major portion of his speech to it at the June Plenum of 1957. Declaring that "we correctly infused our party with hatred toward Trotskyists, Zinovievists, and Rightists," he—in a thoroughly Stalinist spirit—gave casuistic explanations of his position in 1923. After describing how, at the time of "the discussion, foisted [on the party] by the Trotskyists," he had spoken out against the violations of inner-party democracy which had been allowed in his party organization, Khrushchev added: "And so it turned out that my comments at that time, that is, during the first days of the discussion, were objectively in support of the Trotskyists, although in essence I never had acted together with the Trotskyists. I quickly understood that I had made a mistake, that my remarks might be interpreted as contributions from incorrect positions."[18]

Mikoyan felt that it was necessary to defend Khrushchev at the plenum from the charge of "Trotskyism." He recalled how in 1923, "Trotsky advanced the slogan of inner-party democracy and appealed to the youth.... During this discussion, at one of the first meetings, Comrade Khrushchev spoke in favor of this position of Trotsky's, but then, when he figured out what was what, actively campaigned against Trotsky in the same organization and therefore enjoyed the support of the party organization."[19]

The facts we have cited show how deeply the specter of "Trotskyism" was embedded in the consciousness of Stalin's successors even after his death. As before they used it in the struggle for power and in settling personal accounts.

The episode of Khrushchev's "Trotskyist past" shows indirectly that many communists who had just as distant a relationship to "Trotskyism" as Khrushchev, but who did not have the chance to enjoy Stalin's direct protection, were in the course of the election campaign of 1937 branded as "Trotskyists" and then added to the ranks of those arrested. In any case the election campaign achieved the goal which Stalin had set: it created among all party members, including the most highly placed apparatchiks, a feeling of helplessness and fear with regard to the possible charges that could be made as a provocation.

The drafting of final resolutions proved to be no less difficult for the conference organizers than the holding of elections. They had to find, at their own risk, a balance between the "liberal" line of the February-March Plenum concerning inner-party democracy, and the "severe" line of the same plenum concerning "the uprooting of enemies of the people." It turned out to be easiest of all for Khrushchev to find his way out of the difficulty, because in the given instance he used his privilege of personal access to Stalin to show him the draft resolution of the Moscow Conference. Many years later Khrushchev recalled how relieved he felt when Stalin crossed out particularly vulgar language in the resolution which was directed against "double-dealers." "If I myself had proposed such a resolution," noted Khrushchev, "then things would not have turned out well for me: it did not follow the tone of our party press, and seemed to soften or blunt the sharpness of the struggle."

When Postyshev read the Moscow resolution, he was extremely surprised by its "liberalism." Khrushchev was forced to explain that Stalin "had, with his own hand, crossed out sentences which sharpened the struggle against enemies." Hearing this, Postyshev said with evident satisfaction, "Then we will also act in the same way. And we will use your resolution as an example."[20]

It would seem that the results of the February-March Plenum and the election campaign which followed had reinforced Stalin's absolute power. Neither among the CC members, nor among the delegates of local conferences, was a single voice of protest heard against the ominous formulas and directives being foisted upon the party. However, Stalin's position at the time was far from being as firm as it might appear at first glance. The purge which was unfolding in the party and across the nation evoked active protest both in the USSR and beyond its borders. In order to reveal the actual scale of the resistance to Stalin's terror, let us turn first of all to the reaction which this terror encountered abroad.

36. The Dewey Commission

MEETING WITH DISBELIEF on the part of Western public opinion toward the charges made at the Moscow trials, the Stalinists decided to mobilize public organizations in the West which were under their control. This included, for instance, the French League of the Rights of Man, which created a commission presenting a report by the lawyer Rosenmark, underscoring the juridical irreproachability of the Trial of the Sixteen. A statement of an opposite nature, which was presented by Magdeleine Paz, one of the League's members, was rejected by the League and remained unpublished.

The character of Rosenmark's report is suggested by its final conclusion: in any other country, Trotsky would be sentenced to death in absentia for his "crimes"; the Moscow court, however, had demanded "only" to arrest Trotsky and place him on trial if he appeared on the territory of the USSR. Commenting on this statement, Trotsky made the following entry in his diary: "This bourgeois sharpster thus feels that my 'terrorist' activity in league with the Gestapo has been proven. Must we be surprised by this? If one begins to dig around in French newspapers of 1917 and subsequent years, then it is not hard to become convinced that all the Rosenmarks of the time considered Lenin and Trotsky agents of the German general staff.* The French democratic patriots therefore continue a tradition: only in 1917 they were against us in a union with tsarist diplomats, with Miliukov and Kerensky, whereas now they serve as official 'friends' of Stalin, Yagoda and Vyshinsky."[1]

Meanwhile in Europe and America a movement was gathering force which called into question the charges of the Moscow Trials. Soon after the Trial of the Sixteen, several hundred French writers, scholars, deputies in parliament and trade union leaders appealed to Western public opinion to conduct an international investigation of these charges. At the beginning of 1937, a com-

---

* This wild accusation, never substantiated by any trustworthy documents, was once again made by Russian "democrats" of the 1990s. It served as the most substantive argument in the frenzied campaign to discredit Bolshevism.

mittee was formed in Paris to investigate the Moscow Trials, and in the USA, a committee for the defense of Leon Trotsky. On the basis of these committees, a commission was formed, with the participation of seventeen scholars and social activists from various countries, which worked in parallel in Paris and New York. It included, among others, Wendelin Thomas, a former Reichstag deputy from the German Communist Party and a leader of an uprising among German sailors in 1918; Otto Rühle, a German Social-Democrat and previously an associate of Karl Liebknecht; and the famous American sociologist, Edward A. Ross. The legal adviser to the commission was the American lawyer John Finerty, who had served as defense counsel at the trials of Tom Mooney and Sacco and Vanzetti. Heading the commission was the major American philosopher, seventy-eight-year-old John Dewey.

Among members of the commission, Marxists were in a minority. Its core consisted of people with liberal-democratic views. The only member of the commission who was politically and personally close to Trotsky was A. Rosmer, member of the Executive Committee of the Comintern in 1920–1921, and main editor of the newspaper *L'Humanité* in 1923–24. The remaining members had never met Trotsky and did not sympathize with "Trotskyism."

The commission invited representatives of the Soviet embassies and sections of the Comintern in the USA, France and Mexico, as well as famous "friends of the USSR," including D. Pritt and L. Toledano, to take part in its work. However all these organizations and individuals declined the invitation. Members of the Second International refused to join the commission of inquiry out of their fear for the fate of the Popular Front in the European countries.

Also refusing to take part in the inquiry were major writers in the West, including those who did not believe in the Moscow frame-ups and who preserved their respect for Trotsky. Objecting to the very idea of a counter-trial, Bernard Shaw declared: "The strength of Trotsky's case was the incredibility of the accusations against him.... But Trotsky spoils it all by making exactly the same sort of attacks on Stalin.... Now I have spent nearly three hours in Stalin's presence and observed him with keen curiosity, and I find it just as hard to believe that he is a vulgar gangster as that Trotsky is an assassin." The arguments of André Malraux were steeped in even greater sophistry: "Trotsky is a great moral force in the world, but Stalin has lent dignity to mankind; and just as the Inquisition did not detract from the fundamental dignity of Christianity, so the Moscow Trials do not detract from the fundamental dignity [of com-

Bulletin of the Opposition, no. 56–57, July-August 1937. Lead article by Trotsky: "The Decapitation of the Red Army"

munism]."[2]

Surprisingly enough, among Western cultural figures such arguments were not so rare at that time. On 5 December 1936, Stefan Zweig emphasized in a letter to R. Rolland that genuine friends of the USSR "should do everything so that such things as the Zinoviev trial are never again repeated." However, immediately after this, Zweig noted that, in his opinion, Trotsky "did not possess enough sense of dignity to remain silent, and his writings have brought much—too much!—benefit to reaction."[3]

Playing on moods of this type, Soviet diplomats abroad made enormous efforts to discredit the activity of the Dewey Commission in the eyes of world public opinion. Particular zeal in the defense of the Moscow trials was shown by the Soviet ambassador to the United States, Troyanovsky, and the consul Umansky (both men proved to be among the few diplomats who survived the years of the Great Terror).

Trotsky, Sedov and their comrades accomplished titanic work in gathering documents and testimony which demolished the accusations of the Moscow Trials. Testimony concerning the methods which the GPU employed in forcing confessions from their victims was given to the commission by Soviet and foreign prisoners who had managed to escape from the USSR. A German communist-emigrant, who left the Soviet Union in 1935, said that after his

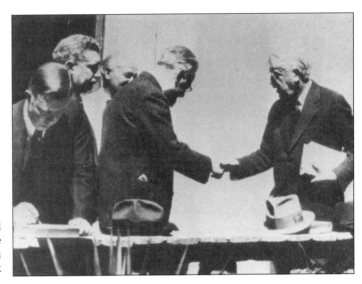

Trotsky and
Dewey as the
commission
begins its work

arrest he was not allowed to sleep for several months. They threatened him
with execution, forcing him to confess to espionage on behalf of Germany.[4]
Tarov, a Russian worker-oppositionist who escaped abroad after six years in
Stalinist prisons and exile, told about the savagery during collectivization, and
about provocations and mockery of Oppositionists, which drove some of them
to insanity or to suicide. He said that many oppositionists who did not yield to
"treatment" were tortured in prisons and concentration camps, and that the
"overwhelming majority of capitulators had left the opposition exclusively because they could not withstand the inhuman repression of the GPU." As an
example of the provocations performed by the Stalinist inquisitors, Tarov mentioned the attempt to saddle him during his exile with a new case that charged
him with plans to build a radio station in order to establish contact with
Trotsky.[5]

At the first stage of its work, the Dewey Commission set out to establish
whether enough facts and arguments were at Trotsky's disposal to predicate
the need for a counterinvestigation. With this goal in mind, hearings were held
in Trotsky's house, which was located in the suburb of Coyoacan. Journalists
from many countries around the world attended the hearings.

In opening the hearings, John Dewey declared: "If Leon Trotsky is guilty of
the acts with which he is charged, no condemnation can be too severe.... That
he has been condemned without the opportunity to be heard is a matter of

utmost concern to the Commission and to the conscience of the whole world."[6]

On 9 May 1937, at an enormous meeting in New York, Dewey outlined the basic conclusions of the preliminary inquiry. His speech ended with the words: "Trotsky has fully demonstrated the need for further inquiry. We recommend therefore to continue the work of this commission to the end."[7]

The report of the Coyoacan hearings (the first volume of the Commission's work) was published in London and New York. Consisting of six hundred pages, it included the transcripts of thirteen sessions. After reading the report, the former American communist Bertram Wolfe wrote an article in which he said: "The writer owns that his previous position was to give credence rather to Stalin than to Trotsky, but a rereading of the Moscow confessions together with the present work ... carried literally overwhelming conviction that Trotsky could not have done the things charged against him in the Zinoviev-Kamenev and Radek-Piatakov trials."[8]

The refutation of the charges made against Trotsky did not leave a stone standing of the charges made against the defendants of the Moscow Trials, since, according to the official version, all their crimes were carried out on Trotsky's orders.

Members of the commission did not limit themselves to the immediate task, a careful verification of the foundations of the charges made at the Moscow Trials. They questioned Trotsky in detail about his political biography, his relationship to Lenin, and the movement for the Fourth International. They also raised the question of whether there was a connection between Stalin's crimes and the actions of the Bolsheviks during the revolution and civil war. In other words, the hearings in Coyoacan thoroughly examined the problems which, over the following decades, would become the subject of sharp historical and political discussions about the relationship between Bolshevism and Stalinism.

37. TROTSKY IN THE CURVED MIRROR OF ANTI-COMMUNISM

TROTSKY'S ANSWERS to the questions submitted by participants in the Coyoacan hearings are of enormous interest when it comes to assessing the traditional conceptions that bourgeois historians have of the October Revolution and Bolshevism.

Bourgeois historiography, despite its superficial objectivity and respectability, is politicized and tendentious to no lesser degree than the Stalinist school of falsification. This becomes abundantly clear upon reading the most substantive work devoted to the history of the great purge, Robert Conquest's book *The Great Terror*. Without touching on the numerous other mistakes and juggling of facts which we have found in this work, let us stop to examine the contents of the three pages (and no more) which the author felt were sufficient to illustrate Trotsky's views and activities. On these pages, Conquest managed to present no less than ten theses which remain unsupported by citations or by any other evidence, and which do not withstand criticism if they are juxtaposed with actual historical facts. Let us name several of these theses, after arranging them, so to speak, according to the chronological framework of the falsifications.

1. Trotsky "firmly crushed the democratic opposition within the party."

2. Trotsky was a "leading figure among the 'Leftist' Old Bolsheviks, that is, those doctrinaires who could not agree with Lenin's concessions to the peasantry. These people, and Trotsky in particular, preferred a more rigorous regime even before Stalin began to carry out such a line."

3. Trotsky "never expressed a word of sympathy for the deaths of millions during collectivization."

4. "Even in exile during the 1930s, Trotsky was not by any means a forthright revolutionary out to destroy a tyranny."

5. Trotsky did not oppose Stalin ideologically, nor did he expose him as the gravedigger of the revolution, but "simply quarreled with Stalin about which

'phase' of evolution toward Socialism had been attained" in the Soviet Union.

6. Trotsky "stood, in fact, not for the destruction of the Stalinist system, but for its takeover and patching up by an alternative group of leaders."

7. Trotsky's political judgment was "unbelievably inept."

8. Trotsky's influence in the USSR during the thirties "was practically nil."

9. All these points are logically crowned with "an alternative prognosis" or "a prognosis aided by hindsight": if Trotsky had come to power, then he would have ruled only "less ruthlessly or, to be more precise, less crudely, than Stalin."[1]

All these points were copied down with the accuracy of diligent students by Russian dissidents of the 1970s and by "democrats" of the 1980s and 1990s; they were then expressed in a pseudo-scholarly way in Volkogonov's book, *Trotsky. A Political Portrait.*

In turn, Conquest did not think up the arguments cited above, which bear the stamp of lightweight journalistic escapades. Rather he copied them from the works of anticommunist ideologues of the 1930s. In doing so, the English historian did not bother to investigate the arguments which Trotsky introduced in his polemics with the Conquests and Volkogonovs of his time.

The reader who has read my book in a thoughtful and unbiased way will easily discover the true value of Conquest's judgments. A more detailed refutation of them is contained in my three previous monographs on the history of the inner-party struggle of the 1920s and 1930s. Nevertheless, in order that the reader may clearly see how the ideas of the many "Trotsky specialists" of the past and present stand in relationship to historical truth, it is fitting to outline the basic arguments advanced by Trotsky in 1937, when he was compelled to expose not only Stalinist slanders, but also the slanders coming from the camp of bourgeois reaction and from the renegades of communism.

38. Trotsky on Bolshevism and Stalinism

URING THE COYOACAN HEARINGS, Trotsky answered questions which reflected the interest of the Commission's members in whether or not there
was any similarity between Stalinist totalitarianism and the Bolshevik regime.
These were the same questions which in our times have been raised anew by
Russian "democrats" of the Volkogonov type, who categorically state: Lenin
and Trotsky were the main architects of the totalitarian-bureaucratic system,
which "would always find its Stalin."[1]

Even before the hearings, Wendelin Thomas, one of the members of the
Dewey Commission, sent Trotsky a letter in which he raised a number of historical, sociological, philosophical and ethical questions which tried to establish: Were not the Stalinist judicial frame-ups and mass terror the inevitable
consequence of the Bolsheviks' "amoralism?" In reply to Thomas, Trotsky
stressed that arguments about "amoralism" as some kind of "original sin" of
Bolshevism were just as false as the Stalinists' declaration that "Trotskyism" is
"original sin" which fatally leads to sabotage, deals with German fascism, and
so forth. The basic difference between Bolshevism and Stalinism, as Trotsky
pointed out, was the following: "In the period when the revolution was fighting
for the liberation of the oppressed masses, it ... had no need for forgeries. The
system of falsifications flows from the fact that the Stalinist bureaucracy is
fighting for the privileges of a minority and is compelled to conceal and camouflage its actual goals."[2]

Thoughts about the fundamental difference between "the regime of Le-
nin-Trotsky" and the "regime of Stalin" (members of the Dewey Commission
formulated the problem in such terms) were developed by Trotsky at the
Coyoacan hearings.* Here Trotsky stressed that, according to his conceptions,

---

* In outlining Trotsky's statements, we are using not only his own publications, but also the
notes of Albert Glotzer, who participated in the sessions of the Dewey Commission as a
court reporter. In 1989, Glotzer published a book, *Trotsky: Memoir & Critique*, part of which
is devoted to an account of the Coyoacan hearings.

The Coyoacan
hearings:
(left to right)
Jean van
Heijenoort,
Albert
Goldman,
Trotsky,
Sedova,
Jan Frankel

the main criterion in assessing a political regime is the degree to which it satisfies the material and moral needs and interests of the popular masses, to which constitutional amendments must be subordinated. Proceeding from this criterion, it is easy to see that the Stalinist bureaucracy did not simply change the democratic organization of the party and the Soviets which existed in the first years of the revolution, but turned it into its opposite, an antipopular organization defending the privileges of a new ruling caste.

With regard to arguments that Stalin's crimes were the inevitable consequence of the establishment of the dictatorship of the proletariat, Trotsky declared the dictatorship of the proletariat is "not an absolute principle which logically produces benign or malignant consequences, but an historical phenomenon which, depending on concrete conditions, both domestic and foreign, can develop in the direction of workers' democracy and the full abolition of power, as well as degenerate into a Bonapartist apparatus of oppression."[3]

As for the statements of the bourgeois press along the lines that the Bolsheviks in the epoch of the ascendancy of the Russian Revolution had used the same methods which Stalin was now using, Trotsky emphasized that the poisoned weapon of slander was organically foreign to the revolutionary policies of the rebellious masses who were following the Bolsheviks. This weapon, which was always part of the arsenal of reaction, was being used by Stalinism which had usurped power from the Soviet proletariat. "No matter what the sanctimonious adherents of pure idealism say," Trotsky wrote, "morality is a function of social interests, and consequently, a function of politics. Bolshevism might have been cruel and ferocious towards its enemies, but it always called things by their own names. Everyone knew what the Bolsheviks wanted. We had nothing to hide from the masses. It is precisely on this central point that the morality of today's ruling caste in the USSR radically differs from the morality of Bolshevism.... The Stalinist oligarchy has made defamation and slander against those who think differently the most important weapon of self-preservation. With the help of systematic slander which embraces everything, be it political ideas, work obligations, family relations or personal ties, people are driven to suicide, insanity, prostration and betrayal."[4]

In reply to the question of whether the existence of the bureaucracy is inevitable in a socialist state, Trotsky said that the socialist state is a transitional form necessary for the construction of socialist society. "The relationship between bureaucratism and democracy cannot be changed in twenty-four hours. These relations depend on the level of material prosperity and the cultural level of the population. The more the abilities of the population are developed, the easier it will be for everyone to carry out the simple intermediary functions of regulation in the realm of distribution. The bureaucrat in a cultivated, civilized country has not the possibility of becoming a demi-god."[5]

When the lawyer Goldman asked if the growth of the bureaucracy had started during Lenin's time, Trotsky answered that at that time the Bolsheviks had done everything possible in order to avoid the bureaucratic degeneration of the Soviet regime. Even in conditions of civil war, when the militarization of the party and the Soviets was almost inevitable, he added, "I myself tried in the army—even in the army on the field—to give a full possibility to the Communists to discuss all military measures. I discussed these measures even with the soldiers and, as I explained in my autobiography, even with the deserters."[6]

Apropos of this, it is appropriate to make one historical digression concerning the "episode with deserters." This episode (without, of course, mentioning Trotsky's name) was described in one of Vasily Aksenov's early short stories. Here the author tells (apparently using the eyewitness account of his father, an Old Bolshevik, whose fate is the focus of the story) about the arrival "of a high-ranking Moscow commissar" at a gathering place of deserters who made up an "unbridled horde of morally empty and wildly yelling people."

He drove up in a large black car, whose bronze ornaments shone in the sun. He was all in leather, wore glasses, and, what surprised us most, absolutely unarmed. Nor were those traveling with him armed.

He got up onto a dangerously wobbly tribune, placed his hands on the railing and turned his narrow, pale face toward the soldiers who had deserted.

Things began to happen! The whole field began to roar, and shook from wild anger.

"Down with him!"—the deserters yelled.

"Snakes are coming here to give us orders!"

"He should feed the lice in the trenches!"

"Get going while the getting's good!"

"Oh, if I had my gun I'd knock off those damned glasses!"

"Brothers, why are we looking at his filthy specs?!"

"Let's go, boys!"

... suddenly the voice of the commissar rolled like thunder across the field...

"Before us stand not White-Guard scum, but revolutionary fighters! Remove the escort!"

In the silence which followed, a deserter's cap suddenly flew up over the field and someone's voice shouted out a solitary "Ura."

"Comrade revolutionary fighters!" the commissar intoned. "The scales of history are tilting in our favor. Denikin's bands have been smashed near Orel!"

"Ura" rolled across the whole field, and in five minutes each phrase coming from the commissar evoked triumphant shouts and cries.

"Death to the bourgeois!"

"Give us world revolution!"

"Everyone to the front!"

"Ura!"

And we, the escorts, whom everyone had forgotten, shouted something, rooted to the spot from youthful enthusiasm, looking at the small figure of the commissar with his fist shaking above his head against the enormous sky of a crimson sunset."[7]

After juxtaposing this scene to the attitude shown toward deserters, "en-

Trotsky gives
his concluding
speech at the
hearings in
Coyoacan

circled troops" and military prisoners during the war of 1941–1945, the reader
will easily sense the abyss between the epochs of Bolshevism and Stalinism.

In his concluding speech at the Coyoacan hearings, Trotsky once again
touched on the theme of civil war and his conduct in it. "For three years I directly led the Civil War. In this harsh work I was obliged to resort to drastic
measures. For these I bear full responsibility before the world working class
and before history. The justification of rigorous measures lay in their historical
necessity and progressive character, in their correspondence with the fundamental interest of the working class. To all repressive measures directed by the
conditions of civil war, I gave their real designation, and I have given a public
accounting for them before the working masses. I had nothing to hide from the
people, as today I have nothing to hide from the Commission."[8]

Repression during the period of the Civil War and repressions of the Stalinist
regime, Trotsky showed, fulfilled absolutely different social functions and served
the attainment of political goals which were different in principle. In the first
case, the issue was the defense of the fundamental interests of the people in
the fight against hostile forces. In the second—the defense of the selfish interests of the bureaucracy in its fight against the people. This determined the
opposed direction and methods of Bolshevik and Stalinist repression. The first
was directed at armed conspirators, the second at unarmed people who were
dissatisfied with the ruling regime, or who were being subjected to completely

arbitrary violence. Insofar as the bureaucracy "does not dare to look the people in the eye,"[9] and does not dare to openly declare its interests, it follows a course of falsifying the conceptions and actions of its opponents, accusing them of nonexistent crimes. In order to give weight to these charges, it reinforces them with new repressions, embracing an ever-wider circle of people. This logic of the political struggle pushed Stalin onto the path of ever newer frame-ups and amalgams.

After the Civil War, Trotsky stressed, the Bolsheviks hoped that the possibilities of establishing democracy would become much wider. But two different but closely interlinked factors impeded the development of Soviet democracy. The first factor was the backwardness and poverty of the country. On this basis the bureaucracy grew up, which in turn became a second, independent factor impeding the democratization of Soviet society. Then the struggle in society once again became, to a certain degree, a class struggle.[10]

Trotsky devoted significant attention in his Coyoacan speech to the statements by the bourgeois press, according to which his criticism of Stalinism was motivated by his personal hatred for Stalin and by the wounded pride of one who has suffered defeat. He said that such arguments were borrowed from official Soviet propaganda, where they fulfill an important political function by serving as the flip-side of the glorification of the "leader." "Stalin creates a 'happy life,' while his defeated opponents are capable only of envying him and of 'hating' him. Such is the profound 'psychoanalysis' of lackeys!"[11]

In subsequent years, Trotsky repeatedly returned to the question of the relationship between Bolshevism, Stalinism and "Trotskyism." He entered into polemics not only with bourgeois ideologists, but also with several of his former supporters who had turned to anticommunism. Shock over the monstrous scale of the Stalinist terror caused in the consciousness of a definite section of the supporters of the Fourth International something of a psychological aberration, much like that which arose among many who were seeking explanations of the causes behind Stalin's climb to power. Trotsky stressed that in the works not only of the Stalinists, but also Stalin's opponents, one could see "a stubborn attempt to shift Stalin's activity back in time," resulting in an involuntary exaggeration of his political role in events happening before 1923. In this attempt Trotsky saw "an interesting optical-psychological phenomenon, when a man begins to cast a shadow back onto his own past."[12]

A similar attempt to "cast the shadow" of Stalin's crimes onto the past of the Bolshevik Party was observed after 1937 among several "disillusioned" revolutionaries who renounced their own past and passed over to the positions of bourgeois democracy. Such people tried to find the sources of Stalin's crimes in the methods of the Bolsheviks, which in turn had been drawn from the catechism of Bakunin and the practical activities of Nechaev.

In refuting this version, which for many years had been in the arsenal of anticommunism, Trotsky pointed out that Nechaev's methods even in the nineteenth century had been decisively rejected by genuine revolutionaries, and that the very word "Nechaevism" entered into the revolutionary lexicon as a strong condemnation of "terrorist materialism." Among Bolsheviks, the question of the acceptability of Nechaev's practices was simply never raised. Only after the victory of the bureaucracy over the Left Opposition did some young Soviet historians try to discover an ideological kinship between Bolshevism and Bakunin's "revolutionary catechism." In such attempts Trotsky saw nothing more than a false historical analogy. He stressed that as the bureaucracy became more estranged from the masses, "in the struggle for its self-preservation it saw itself to be ever more in need of resorting to the methods ... which Bakunin recommended in the interests of sacred anarchy, but which he himself renounced in horror when he saw their application by Nechaev."

If Nechaev's methods in many ways coincided with the methods of the Stalinist bureaucracy, the goals of the latter were immeasurably more reactionary than the goals set before themselves by Bakunin and Nechaev, who preserved to the end of their days a subjective devotion to the revolutionary cause. "With methods which the mass movement cannot accept, Nechaev tried to fight for the liberation of the masses, whereas the bureaucracy fights for their enslavement. According to Bakunin's catechism, every revolutionary is doomed; according to the catechism of the Soviet bureaucracy, everyone is doomed who fights against its domination."[13]

Trotsky also called an historical slander any attempt to deduce Stalinist methods from the pre-revolutionary activity of the Bolsheviks as professional revolutionaries, which supposedly engendered a moral nihilism. In speaking of the morality of the professional revolutionary, he noted that the latter "in any case must have been much more deeply imbued with the idea of socialism, in order to meet the deprivations and sacrifices, than a parliamentary socialist for whom the idea opened up a seductive career. Of course, even the professional revolutionary might have been guided by, or to be more precise could not have helped but be guided by, personal motives, i.e., concern about his comrades' good opinion, ambition, thoughts about future victories. But that type of historical ambition, which almost completely dissolves the personality in itself, in any case is higher than parliamentary careerism or stale, trade union egoism."[14]

In reviewing the evolution of Bolshevism, Trotsky polemicized with arguments that the Bolshevik Party, which had acted with unanimity under Lenin's leadership, supposedly depended completely on him. Consequently, after his death, it was inevitably doomed to bankruptcy. Noting that such arguments were devoid of historical concreteness, Trotsky wrote: "That brilliant people are not born in droves is beyond dispute, just as the fact that they exert extraordinary influence on their party and on their contemporaries in general. Such was Lenin's fate." His brilliance was expressed in the way he opened new historical roads, and discovered new political formulas and perspectives around which the party could coalesce. This, however, does not mean that the party was intellectually passive. Its inner life was constructed in such a way that "each Bolshevik, from Lenin's closest collaborators to the provincial worker, should have, on the experience of innumerable discussions, political events and actions, become convinced of the superiority of Lenin's ideas and methods."[15]Addressing charges made against the Bolsheviks of revolutionary maximalism, cruelty and violation of the principles of formal democracy, Trotsky noted that there were plentiful grounds to direct these charges at one of their first authors—Plekhanov. In this regard, he recalled that at the Second Congress of the RSDLP, Plekhanov admitted the possibility after the revolution of limiting voting rights for representatives of the former ruling classes, the application of the death penalty to the tsar and his satraps, and the dispersal of a representative assembly chosen through universal suffrage.

Finally, Trotsky dealt with the fate of his prognosis which had been used by many anticommunists to prove that Stalinism grew out of Lenin's organizational methods. This prognosis, which was issued in 1904 in a polemic with Lenin's plan of party building, was summarized in the following words: "The party apparatus replaces the party, the Central Committee replaces the apparatus and, finally, a dictator replaces the Central Committee." Noting that these words did give a rather full portrayal of the process of degeneration of the Bolshevik Party which had begun in the middle of the 1920s, Trotsky said that nevertheless his prognosis "is by no means distinguished by the historical pro-

Bulletin of the Opposition, no. 58–59, September-October 1937, containing articles about the murder of Ignace Reiss

fundity which several authors have wrongly attributed to it."

Trotsky noted that when he was writing his youthful brochure, he felt that Lenin's centralism was excessive. He therefore resorted to the logical *reductio ad absurdum*. However, not only centralism can be taken to impermissible extremes, but also the second organizational principle on which the Bolshevik Party was built, democratism. "It is not difficult to 'foretell' in a purely logical manner that unrestrained democracy leads to anarchy or atomization, or that unrestrained centralism leads to personal dictatorship." However, in the political practice of Bolshevism, democratism and centralism acted not as abstract principles, but as concrete elements of party organization, and the relationship between them did not always remain unchanged. After the confusion and isolation of local party organizations in 1898–1903, "the drive to centralization could not help but assume exaggerated and even caricatured forms. Lenin said that when a stick is bent in one direction, you have to bend it back in the other." In subsequent years, Lenin's organizational policies did not represent a straight line. More than once he had to speak out against excessive centralism and appeal to the lower ranks of the party against its leaders. Due to the flexibility of its organizational policies the Bolshevik Party in the heroic period of the Russian Revolution achieved the combination in its inner life "of the broadest democracy, which gives expression to the feelings and thoughts of the broadest masses, and centralism, which guarantees a firm leadership."

The destruction of the equilibrium between democracy and centralism during the period of Stalinism was not the logical result of Lenin's organizational principles, but the political result of the social degeneration of the party, of its transformation into an organization which served the interests of the bureaucracy. "Revolutionary centralism became bureaucratic centralism; the apparatus, which cannot and dares not appeal to the masses in order to resolve internal conflicts, is compelled to seek a higher instance above itself. Thus bureaucratic centralism inevitably leads to personal dictatorship."[16]

Trotsky pointed out that the merging of the bureaucracy's social qualities and interests with Stalin's personal qualities and motives guaranteed both the possibility and the success of the great purge. "Stalin united the cause of his personal revenge with the cause of exterminating the opponents and enemies of the new ruling caste.... Since the entire Soviet oligarchy is an organized and centralized mediocrity, Stalin's personal instincts coincided in the best possible manner with the basic features of the bureaucracy: its fear of the masses, from whom it emerged and whom it betrayed, and its hatred for any form of superiority."[17]

Out of the social position of the ruling layer which had raised Stalin to power grew the necessity for the ideological and judicial forgeries which in the end came crashing down on the representatives of this layer. "The Soviet bureaucracy is a caste of upstarts which fears for its power, for its income, fears the masses and is prepared to punish them with fire and sword not only for every assault on its rights, but for the slightest doubt about its infallibility." However, the ruling caste could not bring bloody repressions down upon the heads of those who were dissatisfied and who were criticizing them by charging them with hating the despotism and privileges of the bureaucracy. Therefore it was compelled to resort to never-ending falsifications.

Thus Trotsky explained the transformation of repressions and the accompanying forgeries into a system by the logic of the class struggle which was prompted by the promotion of a new ruling layer whose interests contradicted the traditions and former composition of the Bolshevik Party. The revolutionary struggle for social equality against the old privileged classes was replaced by the establishment of a new system of social inequality and reactionary terror needed for the defense of this system. It was, in essence, a counterrevolutionary revolt, the success of which in no small measure was due to the fact that it was camouflaged with the defensive flag of Bolshevism, of defending the gains of the October Revolution. "Stalin came from a school of revolutionary fighters who never had stopped before the most decisive measures of action, or before the sacrifice of their own lives.... But the ruthless decisiveness and firmness of the old revolutionaries Stalin redirected toward serving a new caste of privileged people. Under the guise of continuing the old struggle, Stalin put under the mauser of the Cheka and exterminated the entire old generation of Bolsheviks and all the most independent and self-sacrificing representatives of the new generation."[18]

Such an outcome of the struggle, even in the first half of 1937, was not fatally preordained. Very much in the final victory of Stalinism depended at the time on international circumstances which were favorable to it. In order to create such conditions, Stalin applied his main political resources—slander and terror—to the struggle against supporters of the Fourth International in foreign countries.

39. The Hunting Down of Trotskyists Abroad

"No other faction in the history of the workers' movement," wrote Trotsky in 1937, "was subjected to such malignant and vicious persecution as the so-called 'Trotskyists.'"[1] These words characterized the situation of Trotsky's supporters not only in the USSR, but also in the capitalist countries.

At a time when "Trotskyists" in the Soviet Union were being shot on charges of collaborating with the German secret police, Hitler's regime was persecuting defenders of the Fourth International in Germany. At the end of 1936 in Danzig, an illegal Trotskyist group called "Spartakus" was uncovered. Out of sixteen members, ten were tried on charges of conducting antifascist propaganda and speaking out against Germany's participation in the war in Spain.

The verdict indicated that the Danzig Trotskyists "dragged through the mud everything that is German, and on the contrary, extolled Soviet Russia." In turn, the German Stalinists declared not long before the trial that "the Trotskyist branch in Danzig has long since been an espionage and provocateurs' center of the Danzig Gestapo."

In response to the Danzig trial, Trotsky noted that the defendants at it, unlike the defendants at the Moscow Trials, did not renounce Trotskyism, but openly spoke of their solidarity with the movement of the Fourth International. Another difference between the Danzig and Moscow Trials Trotsky saw in the fact that in Danzig the court limited itself to relatively short sentences of imprisonment and did not accuse the defendants of imaginary crimes. Trotsky explained this by saying that "the totalitarian regime in Danzig is still young, and public opinion of the ruling party itself is not prepared for such undertakings.... The GPU is giving the Gestapo lessons."[2]

A few months later, a local group of Trotskyists was put on trial in Hamburg. The accused were sentenced to five to ten years of imprisonment. At the time of the investigation they were subjected to torture, and one of them committed suicide in order to put an end to the torment.

In bourgeois-democratic countries, Stalin's agents tirelessly provoked regimes into persecuting Trotskyists. In this regard, a provocative role was played also by the Soviet press, which declared foreign Trotskyists to be agents of the fascist secret police, conducting subversive work against local governments. In just February and March of 1937, the pages of *Pravda* published such articles as "Trotskyists under the Aegis of Polish Intelligence," "Subversive Activity of Trotskyists in Belgium," "The Unmasking of Trotskyists in the USA," "The Intrigues of Franco's Trotskyist Agents," "The Wretched Comedy of Franco's Trotskyist Accomplices," and so forth.[3] The article, "Espionage International (Trotskyists at the Service of Fascist Intelligence)," "unmasked" Ciliga, "the Italian spy and agent of the Yugoslav secret police," "the degenerates Ruth Fischer and Maslow," "the old spy A. Nin," "the arch-adventurist, the scoundrel Souvarine, who in his filthy pamphlets, on the orders of his boss, the bandit Trotsky, praises the murderers of Comrade Kirov [i.e., the victims of the Trial of the Sixteen—V. R.]" and many other activists of the Trotskyist and other anti-Stalinist communist groups in various countries. "All this Trotskyist scum, led by the ober-spy Trotsky and his offshoot Sedov," the article said," "is united in an international espionage organization directed by the German Gestapo, and the Japanese, Italian and other intelligence services." With unconcealed indignation the article's author wrote about L. Cardenas, charging him with the following: "Thanks to the pressure and direct threats of reactionary and Fascist circles in America ... he has allowed Trotsky to live in Mexico." "Hounded by the curses and hatred of the working class," the author wrote in concluding his article, "the foul serpent Trotsky feels most secure under the protection of the police and secret service. That's the way it was in Norway, and that is what has happened in Mexico."[4]

Following in the footsteps of the Soviet press, the foreign organs of the Stalinists disseminated unfounded claims about the subversive activity of Trotskyist groups. Jacques Duclos, one of the leaders of the French Communist Party, declared that terrorist acts in Paris were the work of Trotskyist hands; the police had not managed to find the culprits. The New York newspaper, the *Daily Worker*, published an article accusing the Chinese Trotskyists of ties with the Japanese General Staff.

This propaganda campaign of the Stalinists went hand in hand with attempts to provoke "Trotskyist" trials abroad. In the spring of 1937, Slutsky, the head of the foreign section of the NKVD, told Krivitsky that the former leader of the Soviet agents in the United States, Markin, who had been murdered three years earlier in mysterious circumstances, had filled the entire Soviet intelligence service in America with Trotskyists. This "comment about 'Trotskyists' in the American service of the OGPU," Krivitsky would later report, "evidently meant that something had been prepared precisely in the USA. The word 'Trotskyists' was used by Soviet high-ranking people for signifying any opponents of Stalin."[5] According to information which Krivitsky had, the NKVD tried to provoke a "Trotskyist-fascist" trial in the United States, planning to entangle in it American Trotskyists and other opponents of Stalin from among former members of the Communist Party of the USA.

The Stalinist agents worked particularly actively in those countries which maintained friendly relations with the Soviet Union. "Using international difficulties, hirelings of the Comintern who are prepared to do anything, and, not the least in importance, the resources of an expanded gold industry," Trotsky wrote. "Stalin hopes to achieve the application of the same methods [which are used in the USSR—V. R.] in other countries as well." These efforts are facilitated by the fact that "reaction everywhere is not against getting rid of revolutionaries, especially if the work of frame-ups and murders on the sly is undertaken by a foreign 'revolutionary' government, with the assistance of domestic 'friends,' paid out of the same foreign budget."[6]

In the spring of 1937, Stalin tried to organize a "Trotskyist trial" in Czechoslovakia, where the government was feeling ever-increasing pressure from Germany and therefore was trying to draw closer to the Soviet Union. Anton Grylewicz, one of the oldest activists in the German workers' movement, who had been expelled from the KPD in 1927 for participating in a group of Left Oppositionists, was chosen to be the main victim of the projected trial. From 1930, Grylewicz directed a publishing house which printed Trotsky's books; he was official publisher of the *Bulletin of the Opposition* and editor of the journal *Permanent Revolution*, organ of German supporters of the Fourth International. In March 1933, storm troopers raided his apartment, after which he emigrated to Czechoslovakia, where he continued to publish Trotsky's works.

In his "Notes," I. Reiss tells how Stalinist agents gave the Czech police material depicting Grylewicz as an agent of the Gestapo, and how Stalin often telephoned Yezhov to find out how the "Grylewicz affair" was progressing. Reiss noted that Stalin was "prepared to do everything to have a Trotskyist trial in Europe."[7]

This testimony supplements Krivitsky's account of Slutsky's telephone conversation with Yezhov. After this conversation, which Krivitsky happened to overhear by chance, Slutsky told him:

"Stalin and Yezhov think that I can arrest people in Prague just like in Moscow."

"What do you have in mind?" asked Krivitsky.

"They want a trial of Trotskyist spies in Europe," answered Slutsky. "It would have an enormous effect, if it can be arranged. The Prague police must arrest Grylewicz. Generally speaking, they are prepared to collaborate [with the NKVD—V. R.], but we cannot deal as simply with the Czechs as we do with our own people. Here in Moscow we just have to open the gates of the Lubianka a bit wider and drive through as many people as we need. But in Prague there are still legionnaires [former members of the Czechoslovak legion which rose up in 1918 in an anti-communist rebellion.—V. R.] ... and they are sabotaging our activity."[8]

In June 1937, Grylewicz was arrested by the Prague police, who presented him with a suitcase he had left with one of his comrades. In it were pamphlets, leaflets and business letters, none of which could be used as substantive evidence of espionage activity. Therefore they had thrown into the suitcase fake passports, a roll of film with photographs of espionage documents and a German seal which granted the right to cross the border with Germany. Grylewicz was able to prove that none of these things belonged to him. Then the police began to question Grylewicz regarding his opinion of the Moscow Trials. In doing so, according to Grylewicz, they "very sharply, and even maliciously defended the Stalinist frame-up trials."[9] After several months imprisonment in an investigatory prison, Grylewicz was handed a decree forbidding him from residing in Czechoslovakia. On these grounds they moved him to a transfer prison, and then forced him to cross the Austrian border.

Not limiting themselves to such provocations, the Stalinist agents organized terrorist acts against foreign Trotskyists. A special group under the foreign section of the NKVD was formed for this purpose; it included political emigrants who were assigned there by the leadership of the Comintern.

The most sensational political assassination was the savage murder of Ignace Reiss, one of the leading members of Soviet counterintelligence in Europe.

40. The Breakthrough and Death of Ignace Reiss

THE BIOGRAPHY of Reiss, who became the first "non-returnee" among the Old Bolsheviks, was the typical biography of a proletarian revolutionary. Having joined the revolutionary movement before the October Revolution, Reiss carried out illegal work for many years in the countries of Central and Eastern Europe, where he was repeatedly arrested and imprisoned.

In the middle of the 1930s, Reiss and Krivitsky, who headed the foreign intelligence service in Western Europe, gathered information about Germany's military preparations. As the Swiss historian Peter Hube notes, they "did not consider themselves agents in today's understanding of the term, they called themselves soldiers of the world revolution. For them, the October Revolution was the first shot in the war declared against social inequality and national oppression."[1]

When he had come to the conclusion that the Stalinist regime was degenerating into fascism, Reiss made contact with Sneevliet (deputy of the Dutch parliament who shared Trotsky's views) and told him that the decision had been made in Moscow to use any means possible to eliminate Trotsky's most active foreign supporters.

Having finally decided to break with Stalin, Reiss wrote a letter to the CC of the VKP(b) in which he declared: "It is true that the record-setting pilots will find it easier to attract the attention of American ladies and the youth of both continents who have been poisoned with sports, than it will be for us to win over public opinion and shake the conscience of the world! But ... nothing will be forgotten and nothing will be forgiven.... The 'brilliant leader, father of the people, and sun of socialism' will have to answer for all these matters." Reiss declared that he felt within himself "enough strength to 'start all over again.' And that is precisely the point: to 'start all over again' in order to save socialism." The letter ended with an appeal: "Back to Lenin, to his teachings and to his cause.... Forward to new battles for socialism and for the proletarian revolution! For the organization of the Fourth International!"[2]

S. M. Spiegelglass

Along with his letter, Reiss sent to Moscow the Order of the Red Banner which he had been awarded in 1928. In explaining this act, he wrote that he refused to wear a medal which now was being awarded to the executioners of revolutionaries. As confirmation, Reiss wrote that not long before in *Izvestiia* he had read a list containing the names of people being decorated who were carrying out death sentences.

Reiss entrusted the letter to be passed on to Moscow to L. Grozovskaya, who worked in the Soviet trade representation in Paris. Grozovskaya gave the letter to the deputy head of the foreign department of the NKVD, Shpigelglaz [Spiegelglass], who had come abroad to carry out a purge of the Soviet intelligence services, including the kidnaping and murder of intelligence officers who refused to return to the USSR.

After showing the letter to Krivitsky, Shpigelglaz demanded that he participate in the swift liquidation of Reiss. Immediately after this conversation, Krivitsky warned Reiss about the danger which threatened him. The next morning, Reiss fled Paris.

After Reiss's disappearance, Stalinist agents began hunting for him. The role of a "decoy duck" was entrusted to the Soviet intelligence agent Schildbach, who had been connected with Reiss during many years of joint work. Reiss trusted her insofar as she had told him about her own misgivings and her intention to follow his example. Coming to visit Reiss in Switzerland, Schildbach proposed that they spend an evening at a restaurant not far from the city of Lausanne. As they were leaving the restaurant, an automobile drove up. Several men jumped out and seized Reiss. The next morning, his bullet-riddled body was found by the Swiss police.

In 1956, at hearings before the American Subcommittee on Internal Security, Lola Dallin revealed several details about Reiss's murder. She said that, because of security considerations, Sedov not only did not tell his closest collaborators Reiss's name, but for some time would not even meet with him. Their first meeting was scheduled in the French city of Rheims, where Reiss was supposed to go immediately after his meeting with Schildbach. Later the Swiss and French police established that a reserve group of killers waited for Reiss in Rheims in case the terrorist act in Switzerland failed.[3]

Altogether, no less than twenty people took part in organizing the murder of Reiss. This included a group of Russian emigrants led by S. Ya. Efron, a former White-Guard officer and the husband of Marina Tsvetaeva. Efron belonged to the emigré tendency of "Eurasians," who at the beginning of the 1930s declared their pro-Soviet orientation. In these circles much was said about Stalin's realization of the "fatally important Russian idea," and of how the Trotskyists were in its way.

One of the paradoxes of the 1930s was that at the time when the number of people in the Soviet Union who dreamed of fleeing abroad in order to escape the nightmare of Stalin's purges was growing, in the ranks of the emigration there was a growth in the number of "returnees," who enthusiastically embraced the changes occurring in the USSR and who tried to return to the Motherland. One of these was Efron, who applied in 1931 to the Soviet embassy for a Soviet passport and expressed his readiness "to mitigate his guilt" before the Soviet regime by means of carrying out assignments from the GPU. As Tsvetaeva wrote to her close friend, "S. Ya. has completely gone over to the Soviet Union, he sees nothing else, and in it he sees only what he wants to see."[4]

In 1934, Efron became general secretary of "The Union of Return to the Motherland," an emigré organization supported by the GPU. As the *Bulletin of the Opposition* explained, the "Union of Returnees" was actually the central

Г. П. У. УБИВАЕТ И ЗАГРАНИЦЕЙ

ИГНАТИЙ РАЙСС

4 сентября вблизи Лозанны было обнаружено изрешетенное пулями тело. На убитом был найден паспорт на имя чехословацкого гражданина Германа Эбергарда. В действительности это был — Игнатий Райсс, работник нелегального советского аппарата заграницей, за несколько недель до убийства порвавший со Сталиным и ставший под знамя Четвертого Интернационала.

Игнатий Райсс родился 1 января 1899 года в мелкобуржуазной еврейской семье в Польше. Еще на гимназической скамье он примкнул к революционному движению, которое захватило его целиком, когда он учился на юридическом факультете Венского университета. Будучи членом австрийской КП,

И. Райсс в 1920 г. посылается на нелегальную работу в Польшу. Вскоре последовал арест, пытки и приговор к пяти годам тюрьмы. Но через полгода тов. Райссу удалось (под залог) снова получить свободу. Совсем молодым, в героическую эпоху русской революции, Райсс вступает в непосредственную связь с Москвой, по заданиям которой он с того времени работает: в 1923-1926 г.г. — нелегально в Германии (в Рурской области); вернувшись в Вену, и проведя там некоторое время в тюрьме, он в 1927 году едет в Москву и становится членом ВКП. Ближайшие годы проходят на нелегальной работе в разных странах Центральной и Восточной Европы; в 1929-1932 г.г. — в центральном аппарате в Москве, затем снова заграницей.

Тов. Райсс верил или старался верить, что служит делу рабочего класса, а не сталинской клике. Но сомнения мучили его все больше. В 1936-1937 г.г. ускорившееся разложение сталинщины, и в частности, московские процессы, глубоко потрясшие Райсса, толкнули его к выводу, что нужно резко и навсегда порвать со сталинской кликой. Большое моральное и личное мужество требовалось, чтоб вычеркнуть из жизни многие годы самоотверженной работы, чтоб пойти на разрыв со Сталиным — Ежовым. Игнатий Райсс, лучше, чем кто бы то ни было, знал, что ему грозит. Но решение его было непреложно.

Связавшись весной этого года со сторонниками Четвертого Интернационала, И. Райсс прежде всего предупредил их о том, что в Москве принято решение любыми средствами «ликвидировать» заграничных троцкистов и антисталинских коммунистов *).

В июле 1937 г. тов. И. Райсс посылает — под псевдонимом Людвиг — письмо в ЦК ВКП (см. стр. 23) о разрыве со Сталиным и покидает тот весьма ответственный пост, который он занимал. В ответ на

*) В порядке этой директивы — в Испании агенты ГПУ убили Андреа Нина; в Чехословакии Сталин — Ежов инсценировали дело старого оппозиционера и бывшего издателя «Бюллетеня» А. Грилевича, по обвинению в шпионаже в пользу Гитлера. Все это только «скромное» начало гораздо более широкого плана.

Игнатий Райсс

Obituary of Ignace Reiss in the *Bulletin of the Opposition*

recruitment office of the GPU in Paris.[5]

Members of the "Union of Return" received money from the NKVD agents and were proud to do so as proof that Soviet Russia had forgiven her repentant sons. The agent's work performed by Efron was so "handsomely" paid for that for the first time in many years he was able to take care of his family's material needs. Tsvetaeva knew that the several hundred francs which Efron, who was without work, brought home each month was payment for collaborating with the GPU-NKVD. In October 1937, in a conversation with the correspondent from the emigré newspaper *Poslednie novosti* (Latest News), she said: "His Soviet sympathies are known to me, of course, just as well as to everyone who has ever met with my husband."[6]

Efron and his friends in the "Union" participated in the foulest foreign operations of the NKVD. In November 1936, they were the ones who broke into the Nikolaevsky institute in order to steal Trotsky's archives there. From 1935 on, Efron's group was assigned to conduct systematic surveillance of Sedov. As the emigrant V. B. Sosinsky was to recall, Efron "definitely wanted to meet Trotsky's son.... He kept telling me: 'I simply want to have a look at him.' He came. I showed him Sedov. And then Sergei Yakovlevich [Efron] walked right up to him, under the pretext of an interview which he supposedly wanted to take for some newspaper. Sedov drove him off. In actual fact, Sedov had come in order to get a look at his face, and he recognized him."[7]

In a letter to Trotsky on 1 November 1937, Sedov reported some of the results of the investigation into Reiss's murder. It had been established that the group which prepared the murder had first been engaged in following Sedov. At the address next to the one in which Sedov lived, the emigrant Smirensky moved in (later arrested in the Reiss case); he, together with Renata Steiner (an emigrant recruited by Efron) and other accomplices followed Sedov's movements. When Sedov went on vacation, Steiner stayed in the same *pension*; meanwhile Efron and Smirensky were based in the same village where they received daily reports from her. In January 1937 the Efron group was preparing to kill Sedov in the city of Mulhouse, where Sedov was supposed to go to meet with a Swiss lawyer who had participated in the inquiry into the Moscow Trials. This attack was broken off because of Sedov's sudden illness, which prevented his trip to Mulhouse. For five days, the terrorists waited for him there. The hunt for Sedov was temporarily discontinued because Spiegelglass ordered Efron's group to join the hunt for Reiss. In Moscow, finding Reiss was felt to be a more pressing matter. Sedov said that Efron was the main organizer of Reiss's murder, and that none of the immediate killers had been caught.[8]

In the book *Agents of Moscow*, A. Brossa correctly calls Reiss and Efron "the two polar opposites of Stalinism." "Primordial communism, from which originates ... the world outlook held by Reiss, with his rejection of the growing strength of Stalinism, Efron perceives to be a hostile culture which disgusts him.... On one side was the heritage which was passed on to Stalinism, which they were destroying while pretending that they were carefully preserving it, and that they were proud of it; on the other—a new radicalism, lacking roots and the slightest semblance of legitimacy, a pseudo-romanticism of brute force and cruelty."[9]

The final transcript of the French police devoted to the case of the Reiss murder states: "If Efron in actual fact did not participate in the organization of Reiss' liquidation, then it is only because the significance of the case worried him and it seemed preferable to entrust this function to one of his comrades."[10]

The automobile driven by Reiss's killers had been rented by Renata Steiner. Soon after the murder the Swiss police discovered the abandoned car with traces of blood, and arrested Steiner. Her testimony led the investigation to other participants from Efron's group.

The French police questioned Tsvetaeva, showing her copies of telegrams sent by Efron to participants in the murder. Tsvetaeva declared that she was certain that Efron had no part in this crime and refused to identify his hand-writing on the telegrams.

Because of his threatened arrest, Efron was sent to the USSR, where Ariadna, his daughter who shared his views, had arrived a few months earlier. The Efrons and several other of their closest "returnees" were settled into Tomsky's dacha.

In June 1939, Tsvetaeva and her fourteen-year-old son returned to the USSR. Two months later, arrests of the "returnees" began. On 22 August, Ariadna was arrested, and on 10 October, Sergei Efron and several of his comrades.

According to published material from Efron's investigatory dossier, it is clear that during the investigation he gave the names of about thirty people whom he recruited for "secret work" under the direction of the NKVD. This list contains several people whom the French and Swiss police interrogated in the case of Reiss' murder.[11]

The trial of Efron and several other "returnees," who were charged with "working for French intelligence" and desiring "to damage friendly relations between the USSR and Germany," took place in July 1941. All the defendants were sentenced to be shot. Ariadna Efron, who was tried in a separate case, spent long years in prisons and exile. In a statement sent after her rehabilitation to the military prosecutor, she wrote: "My father, in the past a White emigré, and then paying for his mistakes and his guilt before the Motherland, did everything to make up for them. For many years he conducted intelligence work abroad, and organized in France a powerful group of intelligence agents." In another appeal for Efron's rehabilitation, she spoke of "the assignment given by Spiegelglass to the group headed by my father."[12]

The rehabilitation file devoted to Efron's case, which was compiled by the investigatory department of the KGB, indicates: "For a number of years Efron

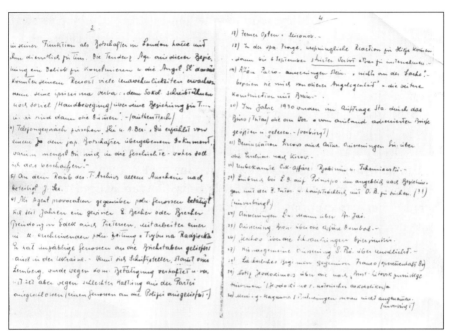

Reiss's "Notes"

was used as a group leader and active informant-recruiter; with his participation a number of White emigrants were recruited by the organs of the NKVD....
In the Soviet Union Efron lived under the name of Andreev at the expense of the organs of the NKVD."[13]

While investigating the murder of Reiss, the Swiss police established that four members of the Soviet trade representation in Paris had participated in the murder. Three of them were able to leave France in a timely fashion. The French police managed to arrest only Grozovskaya, whose extradition was demanded by the Swiss authorities. However, soon she was freed on bail, paying a large sum, and, despite her promise not to leave, disappeared from France.

The fates of the other participants in the murder unfolded in different ways. Schildbach fled to the USSR and in December 1938 was sentenced to five years exile in Kazakhstan. Abbiat, the murderer of Reiss, disappeared without a trace; his mother, who lived in Paris, received a check from Moscow for ten thousand Francs.[14]

After Reiss's murder, Yezhov's agents began to search for his archives, which were located with his widow. A Soviet intelligence agent who visited Krivitsky reported in despair that they were forcing him to stop at nothing to steal Reiss's notes and letters. Krivitsky gave him advice on how to sabotage the assignment.[15] Part of Reiss's notes, which exposed the machinations of the Moscow Trials, were published in the December issue of the *Bulletin of the Opposition* in 1937.

In the article, "The GPU Murders Abroad As Well," Leon Sedov wrote: "'The father of the people' with his Yezhovs knows all too well how many potential Reisses there are in the entire apparatus [of the USSR and Comintern—V. R.]. The Lausanne murder should serve as a warning to all of them—and not only them.... The workers' press and workers' organizations are obliged to apply all the more energy to exposing Stalin's crimes. Only wide publicity given to the crimes can put a muzzle on the mad usurpers."[16]

41. "Stay Out of Range of the Artillery Fire!"

The revolutionary movement in Spain unfolded after 1931, when the monarchy was overthrown. On 27 April 1931, Trotsky sent a letter to the Politburo in which he warned that if the unity of revolutionary forces were not achieved in Spain, then they would inevitably suffer a defeat which "almost automatically would lead to the establishment in Spain of *genuine fascism* a la Mussolini." Stalin distributed this letter to members of the Politburo with an accompanying malicious inscription: "I think that Mister Trotsky, this ringleader and Menshevik charlatan, should be whacked in the head by the ECCI [Executive Committee of the Communist International]. Let him know his place."[1]

For the next five years, Stalin paid no attention to the events in Spain. The situation changed after the Popular Front won in the elections of February 1936, and then five months later the fascist rebellion of General Franco occurred. From the very beginning, Franco was given aid by Germany and Italy, who sent their expeditionary forces to Spain. On July 30—one hundred days before the first Soviet planes joined the Republican army—German and Italian squadrons had already bombed Madrid and other Spanish cities. The unlimited domination of the Spanish skies by hostile planes, which were mercilessly annihilating the civilian population, seriously weakened the Republican forces.

In these conditions, the French Prime Minister, Leon Blum, declared the principle of nonintervention in the Spanish events. The "democratic" governments of Europe refused to give aid to the legitimate government in Spain in its struggle against rebels who were being supported by the open intervention of Fascist powers. This policy took refuge behind an international pact concluded in September 1936 banning the export or transit of arms and war materiel to Spain. A "Committee of Non-Intervention" was formed to control this pact. Twenty-six countries participated, including the Soviet Union.

Despite their participation in the committee, Germany and Italy by no means decreased their aid to the Spanish rebels. In the fall of 1936, one hun-

335

dred fifty thousand Italians and fifty thousand Germans were fighting on Franco's side. German and Italian ships were blockading the shores of Spain.

On September 4 in Madrid, a government was formed which was headed by the Left Socialist Largo Caballero. All parties of the Popular Front entered into this government, including the Communist Party. The regime began to maintain an orientation toward the Soviet Union, from which it expected active aid in the struggle against the insurgents and interventionists.

"The Soviet intervention [in the Spanish war—V. R.]," wrote Krivitsky, "might have been decisive at certain moments had Stalin taken the risks on the Loyalist side that Mussolini took on the Franco side. But Stalin risked nothing ... he took no chances of involving the Soviet Union in a great war." To this was added Stalin's distrust of the Popular Front, which he felt was useful only for one thing: "to elect, with the aid of 'fellow travelers' and dupes, governments friendly to the Soviet Union." Under these conditions, Stalin was prepared to abandon international revolutionary tasks and impede the growth of revolutionary actions by the popular masses into socialist revolutions. He proceeded from the fact that foreign communists who were obedient to his commands "would drop their opposition to the ruling powers and, in the name of 'democracy,' join forces with other political parties."[2]

As he took his first look at the events in Spain, Stalin employed delaying tactics in sending aid to the Republicans. As was already indicated in the "Notes" of Ignace Reiss, "As for the Spanish question—the first reaction [of Stalin—V. R.] was to help, then there was a strict ban on any undertakings until September 6 [1936]."[3]

The only thing which Stalin allowed during the first period was for the Comintern and Soviet society to join the movement which had arisen throughout the world in support of republican Spain. In connection with the Spanish events, the concept of international duty entered into Soviet propaganda and was enthusiastically embraced by the Soviet people. "The Spanish Republic of 1936–1939 and its International Brigades," recalls Lev Kopelev, "became unusually close to us precisely because they united people of various nations and various parties. It seemed that in Madrid and Catalonia, the proletarians of all lands had actually united in a general struggle against fascism and in a general desire for justice and liberty. Spain awakened our old ideals and our dreams about international brotherhood. They awakened precisely at a time when shameless lies and unrestrained terror raged around us."[4] Kopelev tells how he and his comrades jealously studied the Spanish language and wrote several times in vain to Stalin, Voroshilov and Mikhail Koltsov, begging to be sent to the front in Spain.

In his novel *For Whom the Bell Tolls*, Ernest Hemingway wrote about the same feelings which had seized thousands of people in the capitalist countries. His book is the most honest and moving work of art in the twentieth century devoted to the theme of revolution and civil war. The hero of the novel, the American journalist Robert Jordan, several times repeats the idea that the Spanish war "might prove to be the turning point in the fate of mankind."[5]

Many people of both communist and noncommunist convictions assumed that Stalin's actions were dictated by his orientation toward world revolution. Walter Krivitsky, who was well versed in Stalin's political maneuvers, decisively refuted this notion, stressing that "the problem of world revolution had long since ceased to be real to Stalin. It was solely a question of Soviet Russia's foreign policy." Knowing about this, none of the Soviet leading officials who were connected with international affairs ever took seriously the campaign raised by the Comintern in defense of the Spanish republic. "This organization [the Comintern], then already nicknamed the 'gyp joint' [that is what Stalin called it in his closest circle—V. R.], had been relegated to a quiet suburb of Moscow and from being the intended torch of international revolution, had become a mere adjunct of Stalin's foreign policy—sometimes useful in indirect ways, other times a considerable nuisance.... To a few veteran leaders of the Comintern, still inwardly devoted to the ideal of world revolution, the fighting in Spain brought new hope. These old revolutionists really thought the Spanish Civil War might once more kindle the world. But all their enthusiasm produced no munitions, no tanks, no planes, none of the war supplies for which Madrid was pleading, and with which the fascist powers were supplying Franco. The real function of the Comintern at this time was to make enough commotion to drown the louder noise made by the silence of Stalin."[6]

Meanwhile, the Spanish government, which did not have its own war industry, was in ever greater need of modern armaments for conducting the war. However the governments of the bourgeois-democratic states forbade any shipments of arms to the Spanish republic; the ban first applied to state and then privately owned weapons produced by capitalist firms. The Soviet Union became the only hope for the republicans.

In the fall of 1936, the position of the Spanish Republic became ominous.

Stalin and
Molotov
among
delegates from
republican
Spain,
Moscow, 1937

Franco's troops, joined by colonial Moroccans as well as German and Italian regular forces, were driving towards Madrid. Out of seven major highways that connected the capital with the country, six were seized by the fascists. Only then did Stalin make the decision to reply to the desperate appeals by the republican government. However, he did this in such a way as to derive enormous material benefit from his "aid." He entered into negotiations with the Spanish leaders over payment for the arms with the republic's gold reserves, which were about six hundred tons. In order to mask this operation, Stalin ordered the People's Commissar of Foreign Trade to publish a decree banning the "export, re-export and transit to Spain of any kinds of arms, munitions and military vessels." This decree, understood throughout the world to be the consequence of the policy of nonintervention, camouflaged the creation by Stalin's agents abroad of a network of "private firms" to conduct export-import operations. These firms obtained diplomatic papers from East European, Latin American and Asian governments verifying that the purchase of weapons was being made for their countries. Using these papers, huge purchases of arms were made from French, Czechoslovakian, Polish and Dutch military industrialists. The market's "freedom of trade" was at the time so great, that even the German "cannon kings," who felt themselves to be relatively independent of Hitler's totalitarian regime, sold shipments of the latest weapons to its opponents.[7]

Soviet counterintelligence worked so effectively that the ships carrying weapons managed to sail from Odessa, under changed names and the flags of foreign states, traveling through the Mediterranean straits where German and Italian agents were maintaining strict surveillance of the movement of seagoing vessels. Then these ships unloaded in ports located on territory controlled by the Republican forces, changed their names into Russian ones and, under Soviet flag, returned to Odessa.

Even before major shipments of arms from the Soviet Union, an enormous shipment of Spanish gold arrived in Odessa. Supervision of this operation in Spain was assigned to A. Orlov, who for conspiratorial reasons went under the name of "Mister Blackstone from the National Bank of the USA."

In 1957, at hearings before the Senate Subcommittee of the USA on Questions of National Security, Orlov significantly added to the details of the "gold operation." He said that this operation was unique, and had been assigned to him personally by Stalin.

On 20 October, Orlov received a coded telegram informing him of Stalin's demand to immediately transfer the gold to the USSR. Officially it was felt that the gold was destined to be kept in the Soviet Union in order to save it from possible seizure by Franco's forces who were marching on Madrid.

The loading of gold onto Soviet ships was conducted under the greatest secrecy. In the Odessa port, officers of the NKVD spent several days carrying by hand heavy boxes with gold through the cordoned off area separating the pier from the railway station, and then loaded them into freight cars which were sent to Moscow. The leaders of this special detachment were decorated with the Order of the Red Banner, which usually was awarded for combat exploits.

When the foreign press published articles about the Soviet Union receiving Spanish gold, Moscow officially denied the "fabrications" about the conclusion of this deal.

At a banquet dedicated to the transfer of the gold to the Soviet Union, Stalin said in the presence of members of the Politburo: "The Spaniards will never see their gold any more than they will see their own ears."[8] Thus, under the flag of "international aid," the Spanish republic was stripped of its main national wealth. This action was not the product of any official agreement, but the result of a secret deal between Stalinist emissaries and a small group of people in the Spanish leadership.

When he had become convinced of the success of the gold operation, which showed the dependence of the Spanish government on Moscow, Stalin out-lined a plan at a session of the Politburo for cautious intervention in Spain—under the cover of official declarations of neutrality. In developing this plan, Stalin proceeded primarily from geopolitical considerations. He assumed that Spain was fated to join either the Italo-German or the Anglo-French bloc. Un-derstanding that with the sharpening of inter-imperialist contradictions, a friendly Spain was vitally needed by both Paris and London, Stalin came to the conclusions that even without the Soviet Union's open participation in the war he would be able to install a regime in Spain which would be under his control. In doing so he would be able to reach an agreement with France and England for an alliance with the USSR. Then he proposed either to enter into such an alliance, or turn it into a bargaining chip, in order to achieve his coveted goal—an alliance with Hitler's Germany (exploratory negotiations between Soviet diplomats and German political figures about such an agreement had been held throughout 1936).

A second motive which prompted Stalin to act on the side of the Spanish republicans was the desire to enlist the support of foreign antifascists in the prelude to the Great Purge. As Krivitsky emphasized, the Western world was unaware "how tenuous at that time was Stalin's hold on power, and how essen-tial it was to his survival as dictator that he should be defended in these bloody acts by foreign Communists and eminent holders of idealistic views [among the latter Krivitsky had in mind Western humanists of such magnitude as Romain Rolland, Bernard Shaw, H. G. Wells and others—V. R.]. Their support was vitally important to him. And his failure to defend the Spanish republic, combined with the shock of the Great Purge and the treason trials, might have cost him their support."[9]

Finally, Stalin's decision to shift to "cautious intervention" in Spain was dictated in no small part by the fact that among the Republicans during the initial stages the Communists comprised a small minority. In June 1936, the Communist Party of Spain had eighty-four thousand members. In the ranks of the leftist forces in Spain, socialists, syndicalists and anarchists dominated, and the Trotskyists had a party headquarters. On the territory which remained in the hands of the republicans, there were three governments—a pro-Soviet central government in Madrid, an independent government in the Basque re-gion, and a Catalonian government in Barcelona, where the anti-Stalinist forces were particularly strong, especially the POUM (Workers' Party of Marxist Unification). The Catalonian front was one of the most important sectors in the defense of the republic; the divisions there were made up of anarchists and POUMists.

Insisting on the consolidation of all anti-Stalinist revolutionary forces in Spain, on 10 August 1936 Victor Serge proposed in a letter to Trotsky to appeal to the anarchists and syndicalists with the following message: "We, revolutionary Marxists, feeling that it is necessary to reinforce the homefront of the revolution with a firm hand, simultaneously declare that the proletarian dictatorship must be and will be true freedom for the toilers. We will fight with you for the reinforcement of freedom of opinion within the revolutionary movement and we give a solemn vow to do everything to deny the bureaucracy any possibility whatsoever of turning the revolution into a prison for workers in the Stalinist manner."[10]

Similar moods were shared by many of the volunteers who kept coming to help the republicans not only from all of Europe, but from the United States, Canada, Latin America, Australia, South Africa, the Philippines, and even from fascist countries—Germany and Italy. Among them were no small number of Trotskyists and other socialist-minded people who were opposed to Stalin and Stalinism. Thus, the possibility existed that powerful antifascist and at the same time anti-Stalinist forces might arise in Spain who would be able to take an active part in the defense of the Spanish Revolution.

In describing the atmosphere which reigned in the general staffs of the International Brigades during the first months of the civil war, Hemingway wrote: "At either of those places you felt that you were taking part in a crusade. That was the only word for it although it was a word that had been so worn and abused that it no longer gave its true meaning. You felt, in spite of all bureaucracy and inefficiency and party strife, something that was like the feeling you expected to have and did not have when you made your first communion. It was a feeling of consecration to a duty toward all of the oppressed of the world which would be as difficult and embarrassing to speak about as religious experience and yet it was as authentic as the feeling you had when you heard Bach, or stood in Chartres Cathedral or the Cathedral at León and saw the light coming through the great windows; or when you saw Mantegna and Greco and Brueghel in the Prado. It gave you a part in something that you could believe in wholly and completely and in which you felt an absolute brotherhood with the others who were engaged in it."[11]

This feeling of revolutionary solidarity which seized thousands of people was capable of creating in Spain a mighty army of the future international socialist revolution, independent of Stalin. It was precisely for this reason that Stalin decided to begin with Spain when transferring NKVD methods onto the international arena. Arriving in Europe on an inspection tour, Slutsky gave Krivitsky Stalin's instructions: "We cannot allow Spain to become a free camping ground for all the anti-Soviet elements that have been flocking there from all over the world. After all, it is our Spain now, part of the Soviet front ... and as for the anarchists and Trotskyists, even though they are antifascist soldiers, they are our enemies. They are counterrevolutionists, and we have to root them out."[12]

Guided by the above considerations, Stalin issued a statement which testified to the beginning of the USSR's intervention in the Spanish events. In his message to the leader of the Spanish Communists, José Diaz, he said: "The toilers of the Soviet Union are simply carrying our their duty by giving all possible aid to the revolutionary masses of Spain.... The liberation of Spain from the knout of fascist reactionaries is not the private affair of Spaniards, but the general cause of all leading and progressive humanity."[13] In this missive, which was widely distributed throughout the world, the formula of "progressive" humanity for the first time replaced the class and revolutionary-internationalist formulas of Bolshevism.

A week later, the Soviet government officially announced that "it cannot consider itself bound by the pact of nonintervention to any greater degree than any of the other participants in this accord."[14] On 29 October, Caballero addressed the army and population of Madrid, announcing the beginning of arms shipments from the USSR. "Now," the document said, "... we have tanks and powerful aviation.... Now that we have tanks and airplanes, let us advance. Victory will be ours!"[15]

This declaration resounded at a critical moment in the civil war, when four columns of rebel troops and interventionists had reached the outskirts of Madrid. General Mola, the leader of the offensive, declared that he had a "fifth column" of spies and diversionary agents in Madrid and in general among the rear of the Republican forces. From that moment, this concept entered into the world lexicon. It immediately began to be used by Stalinist propaganda for justifying the terror in the USSR and in Spain.

Soviet troops began to arrive in Spain under the guise of volunteers. How-

Orlov's
diplomatic
passport

ever Stalin, worried as before about the USSR being openly drawn into the Spanish war, gave categorical orders that Soviet people "must not cross the line which can be reached by artillery fire."[16] This directive remained unshakeable throughout the entire Spanish war. Only Soviet pilots and tank troops, who fought under other, non-Russian names, participated directly in battle. The main part of the Soviet military personnel performed the functions of instructors or technical specialists. All the officers and soldiers of the Red Army were quartered in such a fashion that they had no contact with the Spanish civilian population. They had no access to local political circles and no ties with the public at large. The vigilant control over them by agents of the NKVD was formally explained by the need to keep their presence in Spain a secret. In actual fact, this control was exerted "in order to avoid infecting the ranks of the Red Army in any way with heretical political ideas."[17]

As Hemingway wrote, the Spanish war did not produce "military geniuses.... Not a single one. There was not even a semblance of one."[18] This also was a consequence of Stalin's policies, since he did not wish to send to Spain a single one of the leading Soviet military commanders. At a session of the Military Council which preceded the trial of the Soviet generals (see Chapter 49), Stalin declared: "Tukhachevsky and Uborevich have asked to be sent to Spain. We say: No, we do not need any big names. To Spain we will send people who are little known ... we will send people without big names, our lower and midlevel officer staff."[19]

The Soviet armed forces were subordinated to two men personally chosen by Stalin. One of them was the Old Bolshevik Ya. K. Berzin, who had earlier headed Soviet military intelligence. Stalin's second emissary was Stashevsky, a Soviet Communist of Polish origin who officially occupied the post of trade representative in Barcelona.

Berzin, who did not have great talent as a military leader, nevertheless played a major role in organizing the defense of Madrid at the end of 1936. He made a significant contribution to the formation of a modern regular army out of undisciplined and uncoordinated Spanish armed detachments.

At the head of one of the International Brigades was General Stern, who before this, according to Stalin, "was secretary to Comrade Voroshilov, and nothing more."[20]

Besides the military personnel, a large group of NKVD officials headed by Alexander Orlov was sent to Spain. The experienced intelligence officer Lev Feldbin operated under this name. Orlov's official post was military adviser to the Spanish government.

For almost two years Orlov carried out Stalin's secret assignments in Spain. When he received information from the Soviet Union about reprisals against old Chekists, he had no doubt that his turn would soon be next. "At the fronts in Spain," he later recalled, "especially when I traveled to a front line zone during preparations for an offensive of republican forces, I often came under hostile bombardment. During these moments I often caught myself thinking that, if they killed me while I was carrying out my duties, the threat which was hanging over my family and our close friends who had remained in Moscow would immediately dissipate. Such a fate seemed to me to be more attractive than an open break with Moscow. But this was a sign of faintheartedness. I continued my work among the Spaniards, who praised me for my courage, and I dreamt that perhaps Stalin would fall at the hand of one of his cohorts or that the horror of the nightmarish Moscow 'purges' would pass somehow by itself."[21]

On 9 July 1938 Orlov received a telegram from Yezhov with instructions to immediately leave for Antwerp and meet on board a Soviet steamship there "with a comrade whom you know personally … to find out about an important upcoming assignment."[22] Being well enough versed in Stalin's plans and activities, Orlov understood that they were preparing a trap for him: as soon as he stepped foot on board the Soviet steamer, he would quickly be arrested and forcibly returned to the USSR for "liquidation." Immediately after receiving

André Marty
and
Luigi Longo
among
International
Brigade troops

the telegram, Orlov flew with his wife and daughter to Canada, and from there to the United States, where he lived under another name for fifteen years. He decided to publish his book, *The Secret History of Stalin's Crimes*, only at the beginning of 1953. It did not, however, include accounts of the crimes committed in Spain with his active participation.

After the appearance of Orlov's book, the American authorities became interested in him. At hearings before the Senate Subcommittee on Internal Security, Orlov described his activity in Spain and insisted that he had been an adviser to the government on questions of intelligence, counterintelligence and the waging of partisan war behind enemy lines. When, however, the senators asked him about his participation in reprisals against Trotskyists and POUMists, Orlov unreservedly called such evidence slander.

In actual fact Orlov, who headed the Soviet Military Intelligence Headquarters, set up highly effective work in training agents and informers and in coordinating their activity on the territory seized by the insurgents. However, no less important was another side of his work, consisting of the execution of Stalin-Yezhov directives outlining reprisals against independent-minded revolutionaries. He coordinated this work with the leadership of the Spanish and other Communist parties. Their activity was controlled by Palmiro Togliatti, who occupied the post of Comintern representative in Spain.

One of the main assignments Stalin gave his emissaries from the NKVD and the Comintern was to maintain unflagging control over the international voluntary forces. Thirty-five thousand foreign volunteers were fighting from fifty-three countries, the majority of whom joined the International Brigades. At the beginning of the Civil War, according to Krivitsky, "From the Soviet Union [were] dispatched as soldiers to Spain scores of foreign Communists who, outlawed in their own countries, had been living as refugees in Russia. Stalin was glad to get rid of them."[23]

In other countries members of the International Brigades were recruited primarily by local Communist parties. After arriving in Spain, their passports were taken away, and a significant number of them were sent to Moscow to be transferred to agents of the NKVD who were being sent to the corresponding countries. The ranks of the volunteers were filled with provocateurs who kept watch over their reading and conversations and who eliminated people whose political views differed from Stalinism.

One of the leaders of reprisals against genuine and imaginary Trotskyists was the secretary of the ECCI, André Marty. In the novel *For Whom the Bell Tolls*, Hemingway gives a vivid description of Marty's activity in exterminating the internationalists. A corporal of the Republican army tells Spanish partisans who were being held by Marty: "He has a mania for killing people.... That old one kills more than the bubonic plague.... But he doesn't kill fascists like we do.... He kills rare things. Trotskyists. Divigationers. Any type of rare beasts.... When we were at Escorial we shot I don't know how many for him. We always furnish the firing party. The men of the Brigades would not shoot their own men. Especially the French. To avoid difficulties it is always us who do it. We shot French. We have shot Belgians. We have shot others of diverse nationality. Of all types.... Always for political things."[24]

The famous Soviet journalist, Mikhail Koltsov, spread disinformation to "justify" the Stalinist terror. According to Hemingway, Koltsov, "in direct communication with Stalin, was at this moment one of the three most important men in Spain."[25] After carrying out the most important and confidential Stalinist assignments, Koltsov had a long conversation with Stalin and his closest lackeys during one of his trips to Moscow. Koltsov told them in detail about the situation in Spain and received further instructions.

Officially Koltsov was in Spain as a correspondent for *Pravda*, which regularly published his articles about the civil war, including deceitful articles about

"Trotskyist conspiracies." By the end of 1936 he had written about the "counterrevolutionary and traitorous role of the Catalonian Trotskyists," who demanded the "launching of absolutely inappropriate economic experiments." He claimed that "Catalonia will create a new government."[26] A month later Koltsov wrote that Trotsky had been giving directives to the POUM, as a result of which the POUM "had restructured in the usual Trotskyist fashion," was focusing on "provocations, raids and murders" and "is shifting ever more to terrorism." In the spirit of the official cliches of Soviet propaganda, Koltsov asserted: "Wherever Trotsky extends his foul hand, he sows lies, treachery and murders ... everything that is dark, malignant, criminal, all scum and human riffraff beckon to his call for foul acts of banditry."[27]

An objective description of the POUM's activity was provided by George Orwell, who characterized the POUM as "one of those dissident Communist parties which have appeared in many countries in the last few years as a result of the opposition to 'Stalinism'.... Numerically it was a small party, with not much influence outside Catalonia, and chiefly important because it contained an unusually high proportion of politically conscious members."[28] The POUM's militia, in which Orwell fought, was distinguished by its spirit of social equality. "General and private, peasant and miltiaman still met as equals; everyone drew the same pay, wore the same clothes, ate the same food and called everyone else 'thou' and 'comrade'; there was no boss class, no menial class, no beggars, no prostitutes, no lawyers, no priests, no bootlicking, no cap touching. I was breathing the air of equality, and I was simple enough to imagine that it existed all over Spain. I did not realize that more or less by chance I was isolated among the most revolutionary section of the Spanish working class."[29]

It was precisely the genuinely socialist spirit that reigned in the ranks of the POUM which prompted the Stalinists to disseminate the most malicious fabrications about this party. "The Communists contended that the POUM propaganda divided and weakened the governmental forces and thus endangered the war.... Tentatively at first, then more loudly, they began to assert that the POUM was splitting the government forces not by bad judgment but by deliberate design. The POUM was declared to be no more than a gang of disguised fascists, in the pay of Franco and Hitler, who were pressing a pseudorevolutionary policy as a way of aiding the fascist cause.... This implied that scores of thousands of working class people, including eight or ten thousand soldiers who were freezing in the front line trenches and hundreds of foreign-

ers who had come to Spain to fight against fascism, often sacrificing their live-
lihood and their nationality by doing so, were simply traitors in the pay of the
enemy. And this story was spread all over Spain by means of posters, etc., and
repeated over and over in the Communist and pro-Communist press of the
whole world."[30]

To the extent that the Soviet Union intervened in Spain, there were essentially two civil wars being fought. One was the official war of the Republicans
versus the Franco forces, and the second was a secret war against all who shared
an anti-Stalinist orientation and who were not inclined to subordinate themselves unconditionally to the orders of the Soviet and Comintern emissaries.

This second, filthy war, which carried away a multitude of honest and courageous antifascists and divided the forces which were fighting on the side of
the Republic, was one of the main reasons for the military defeats of the Republicans. Another reason was the internal policy of the Spanish government,
which drove away from revolutionary struggle thousands of potential fighters
in Spain and throughout the world.

42. Trotsky on the Spanish Revolution

In describing the atmosphere of the first months of the civil war, Erenburg stressed that not only the workers, but also "the petty bourgeoisie, the peasantry and intellectuals hated the Spanish military which had flouted the national pride.... The word 'freedom,' which had long since been devalued in many countries of Europe, was still inspiring everyone here."[1]

The Spanish republic enjoyed active support throughout the world. On the side of the Republicans were not only such remarkable Spanish writers as Garcia Lorca (savagely murdered by the fascists) and Raphael Alberti, but writers who came to the country such as Pablo Neruda, André Malraux, Nikolas Guillén, John Dos Passos, Antoine Saint-Exupéry, and prominent political figures (Pietro Nenni, Luigi Longo and many others).

The logic of the class struggle inexorably demanded the transformation of the Spanish Revolution into the socialist revolution. It was around this very question that the political struggle unfolded in the ranks of the Republicans.

Resistance to the insurgents during the first days was accompanied by active revolutionary actions by the Spanish working masses. Peasants seized the landlords' estates. Workers nationalized factories and transport. As soon as the rebellion began, the workers demanded that they be given arms from government arsenals, something to which the authorities, although with great hesitation, were compelled to agree. Organs of workers' power were created: revolutionary committees, workers' patrols which replaced the old bourgeois police, and detachments of a workers' militia organized by the trade unions. The revolutionary character of the events in Spain caused great disquiet among "liberals" in the capitalist countries. In exposing the class nature of this distress, George Orwell, who took an active part in the Spanish war, wrote: "Foreign capital was heavily invested in Spain. The Barcelona Traction Company, for instance, represented ten millions of British capital; and meanwhile the trade unions had seized all the transport in Catalonia. If the revolution went forward there would be no compensation, or very little."[2]

349

The Spanish Communist Party, as paradoxical as this might seem at first glance, held a position similar to the liberals and did everything possible to prevent the further development of the revolution. Its leaders stated that they must strive not for the social revolution and the seizure of power by the workers, but for the defense of bourgeois democracy. Given conditions in which "the country was in a transitional state that was capable either of developing in the direction of Socialism or of reverting to an ordinary capitalist republic,"[3] they stubbornly defended a nonrevolutionary course. Such a line was dictated by Moscow, under whose orders the Communist press propagated the following slogans: "At present nothing matters except winning the war; without victory in the war all else is meaningless. Therefore this is not the moment to talk of pressing forward with the revolution.... At this stage we are not fighting for the dictatorship of the proletariat, we are fighting for parliamentary democracy. Whoever tries to turn the civil war into a socialist revolution is playing into the hands of the fascists and is in effect, if not in intention, a traitor."[4]

Such a line flowed directly from Stalin's international strategy. "The only unexpected feature in the Spanish situation—and outside Spain it has caused an immense amount of misunderstanding," wrote Orwell, "is that among the parties on the government side the Communists stood not upon the extreme left, but upon the extreme right. In reality this should cause no surprise, because the tactics of the Communist Party elsewhere, especially in France, have made it clear that Official Communism must be regarded, at any rate for the time being, as an anti-revolutionary force. The whole of Comintern policy is now subordinated ... to the defense of USSR, which depends upon a system of military alliances.... The clue to the behavior of the Communist Party in any country is the military relation of that country, actual or potential, towards the USSR.... In Spain the Communist 'line' was undoubtedly influenced by the fact that France, Russia's ally, would strongly object to a revolutionary neighbor."[5]

Such political strategy and tactics alienated many potential fighters from the Spanish Civil War. "Once the war had been narrowed down to a 'war for democracy' it became impossible to make any large-scale appeal for working class aid abroad. If we face facts we must admit that the working class of the world has regarded the Spanish war with detachment. Tens of thousands of individuals came to fight, but the tens of millions behind them remained apathetic. During the first year of the war the entire British public is thought to have subscribed to various 'aid Spain' funds about a quarter of a million pounds—probably less than half of what they spend in a single week on going to the pictures. The way in which the working class in the democratic countries could really have helped her Spanish comrades was by industrial action—strikes and boycotts. No such thing ever even began to happen. The Labour and Communist leaders everywhere declared that it was unthinkable; and no doubt they were right, so long as they were also shouting at the tops of their voices that 'red' Spain was not 'red.' Since 1914–1918 'war for democracy' has had a sinister sound. For years past the Communists themselves had been teaching militant workers in all countries that 'democracy' was a polite name of capitalism. To say first 'Democracy is a swindle,' and then 'Fight for democracy!' is not good tactics. If, with the huge prestige of Soviet Russia behind them, they had appealed to the workers of the world in the name not of 'democratic Spain,' but of 'revolutionary Spain,' it is hard to believe that they would not have got a response."[6]

The grotesqueness of the situation which had developed in the Spanish war, Orwell wrote, was seen in the fact that the Communists "showed themselves willing to go a great deal further than the Liberals in hunting down the revolutionary leaders."[7]

Precisely for these reasons, the majority of antifascists in Spain and in other countries did not have an adequate conception of what was actually happening in the course of the Civil War. The Communist Party of Spain in 1937 increased its ranks to two hundred fifty thousand. This was more than the membership of the other left parties. "There was an enormous growth in the membership of the party, and the influx was largely from the middle class—shopkeepers, officials, army officers, well-to-do peasants, etc. ... the Communists had gained power and a vast increase of membership partly by appealing to the middle classes against the revolutionaries, but partly also because they were the only people who looked capable of winning the war. The Russian arms and the magnificent defense of Madrid by troops mainly under Communist control had made the Communists the heroes of Spain. As someone put it, every Russian airplane that flew over our heads was Communist propaganda."[8]

Meanwhile the possibility remained of consolidating Communist and other left forces that did not belong to the Comintern. It was precisely this possibility which frightened Stalin and explains in many ways the monstrous terror which was unleashed in Spain in 1937.

Among the independent revolutionary parties which functioned as an ac-

Возможна ли победа в Испании ?

Установим еще раз основные факты. Армия Франко создана под прямым покровительством Асаньи, т.-е. Народного фронта, включая социалистических и сталинских, а затем и анархистских вождей.

Затяжной характер войны есть прямой результат консервативно-буржуазной программы Народного фронта, т.-е. сталинской бюрократии.

Чем дольше политика Народного фронта сохраняет свою власть над страной и революцией, тем больше опасность изнурения и разочарования масс и военной победы фашизма.

Ответственность за это положение ложится целиком на сталинцев, социалистов и анархистов, точнее — на их вождей, которые, по примеру Керенского, Церетели, Шейдемана, Эберта, Отто Бауэра и др. подчинили народную революцию интересам буржуазии.

Значит-ли это, что, при сохранении нынешней политики, военная победа Кабальеро над Франко немыслима? Учесть заранее материальные и моральные ресурсы и возможности борющихся лагерей невозможно. Только самый ход борьбы может дать проверку действительного соотношения сил. Но нас интересует не военная победа сама по себе, а победа революции, т.-е. победа одного класса над другим. Всеми силами надо помогать республиканским войскам; но победа армии Кабальеро над армией Франко еще вовсе не означает победы революции.

— «Какую революцию имеете вы в виду, — возразят нам филистеры из Народного фронта: демократическую или социалистическую? Победа армии Кабальеро над армией Франко будет означать победу демократии над фашизмом, т.-е. победу прогресса над реакцией».

Нельзя слушать без горькой усмешки эти доводы. До 1934 года мы не уставали разъяснять сталинцам, что и в эпоху империализма демократия сохраняет преимущество над фашизмом; что во всех тех случаях, где они враждебно сталкиваются друг с другом, революционный пролетариат обязан поддержать демократию против фашизма.

Однако, мы всегда прибавляли: защищать буржуазную демократию мы можем и должны не методами буржуазной демократии, а методами классовой борьбы, которые и подготовляют замену буржуазной демократии диктатурой пролетариата. Это значит, в частности, что в процессе защиты буржуазной демократии, в том числе и с оружием в руках,

Bulletin of the Opposition: "Is Victory Possible in Spain?"

tive, independent force in the Spanish war, the leading place belonged to the POUM, which was headed by the prominent figure in the workers' movement, Andrés Nin. Despite the claims of the Stalinists, who called the POUM a "Trotskyist party,"[*] the POUM belonged to the movement for the Fourth International only until 1933, and then broke away from it. Having expelled the Trotskyists from its ranks, it continued to maintain a critical position with regard to Stalinism.

Andrés Nin, who assumed the post of Minister of Justice in the autonomous government of Catalonia, spent nine years when he was younger in Moscow, where he worked as general secretary of the International of Red Trade Unions. After his break with the Comintern, from 1931 to 1933 Nin conducted a friendly correspondence with Trotsky which was then discontinued because of political disagreements between them.

Noting that the POUM, after breaking with the Fourth International, was

---

[*] In the spirit of the Stalinist tradition which called all different-minded revolutionaries "Trotskyists," Soviet historiography for many years numbered POUM and Nin among the "Trotskyists." This tradition was followed by Erenburg, too, who carefully carried out all assignments for the Stalinists in Spain and knew very well the real disposition of political forces there, yet thirty years later in his memoirs called the POUM, as before, a Trotskyist party.

supporting reactionary persecution of "Trotskyists," and that its leaders "vow and apologize at every step: 'We are not for the Fourth International, we are not Trotskyists,'" Trotsky wrote: "Outside of the line of the Fourth International there is only the line of Stalin-Caballero. The leadership of POUM traces between these two lines helpless zigzags.... For precisely this reason, every new stage in the revolution takes them unawares."[9]

In the article, "Is Victory Possible in Spain?", written in April 1937, Trotsky noted that the Stalinists and bourgeois liberals declare: "The victory of Caballero's army over Franco's army will mean the victory of democracy over fascism, i.e., the victory of progress over reaction." Such statements concealed the class nature of the events in Spain and most of all the fact that "power is already in the hands of the military agents and the bureaucracy in alliance with the Stalinists and anarcho-reformists."[10] In Trotsky's opinion, victory in the war with Franco could be guaranteed only by the growing over of the Spanish Revolution from the bourgeois-democratic into the socialist revolution. Given the sharp leftward movement of the masses both in Spain and in the entire world, such a strategy would have been capable of attracting to the side of the republic significantly broader masses not only in Spain, but outside its borders.

Trotsky demonstrated that "the prolonged character of the war is the direct result of the conservative-bourgeois program of the Popular Front, i.e., the Stalinist bureaucracy. The longer the policy of the Popular Front maintains its power over the country and the revolution, the greater will be the danger of the exhaustion and disillusionment of the masses, and of the military victory of fascism."[11]

The POUM, which was capable of becoming a serious counterweight to Stalinism on the international arena, occupied a vacillating, halfhearted position on decisive questions of the Spanish Revolution. It is true that Nin warned that "the revolution is retreating," and called for the "deepening of the revolution." However he never decided to openly counterpose the POUM to the Spanish government. In characterizing the position of the POUM's leaders, Trotsky wrote that they "plaintively *try to persuade* the government to take the path of the socialist revolution."[12]

Placing his hopes on the revolutionary rebuilding of the POUM, Trotsky appealed to this party with the following demands: "You must break from the petty-bourgeois parties.... You must descend into the masses, into the deepest

Books by
Trotsky
published
in 1937

and most oppressed lower ranks.... You must inseparably tie your fate to theirs. You must teach them to create their own fighting organizations—soviets—in opposition to the bourgeois state."[13]

Interesting testimony about the relationship between Trotsky and the POUM has been published recently by a former POUM activist, Bartolome Costa-Amik. He recalls that in November 1936, he traveled for the first time from Catalonia to Mexico—as the head of a sports delegation which was touring the countries of Europe and America on a propaganda mission to appeal for support for the struggling republic. During this trip he met with Cardenas and transmitted to him a request from the POUM leadership to grant Trotsky political asylum. In 1937 Costa-Amik met three times with Trotsky and participated in detailed discussions with him. "The events in Spain interested Trotsky very much," he recalls. "In addition, our Catalonian party was the first Marxist party in the world to speak out against the unfortunately well-known 'Moscow Trials,' which had been arranged by Stalin in order to deal with his political opponents. No, we were not Trotskyists, and we even categorically differed with Trotsky on many questions. But we could not accept Stalinism, which was trying to crush beneath it the entire world revolutionary movement."

Trotsky remained in the memory of the Spanish revolutionary as "very sure of himself, of his correctness. Our party was not very large, but nevertheless Trotsky felt that we must without fail take power in Spain. I argued that this was absurd and that you could not draw a parallel between Spain and the Russia in which the Bolsheviks carried out a revolution. He answered in his characteristic passion, in a very emotional manner ... meanwhile, despite how impassioned he was during our arguments, Trotsky impressed me as a sincere and charming man. Without doubt this was an outstanding personality, and, I must confess, I became somewhat intimidated before him. Yet we parted very warmly."[14]

In response to arguments that the POUM was incapable of taking power into its own hands because the party was too small, Trotsky wrote: "How many members does the POUM now have? Some say twenty-five thousand, others say forty thousand [in February 1917 the Bolshevik Party had twenty-four thousand members—V. R.]. This question does not have, however, decisive significance. Neither twenty-five thousand nor forty thousand can by itself guarantee victory.... Forty thousand members with a hesitant and vacillating leadership are capable of only lulling the proletariat, thereby preparing a catastrophe. Ten thousand, with a firm and insightful leadership, can find the road to the masses, break them away from the influence of the Stalinists and Social Democrats, charlatans and windbags, and guarantee not only the episodic and fragile victory of the Republican forces over the fascists, but the complete victory of the toilers over the exploiters. The Spanish proletariat has shown three times that it is capable of achieving such a victory. The whole question lies in the leadership!"[15]

The need to rebuild the POUM in a revolutionary manner was dictated by the fact that the central government, which included right-wing socialists, liberals and Communists, was increasingly taking away the revolutionary conquests of the masses. By the beginning of 1937, the local committees had been dissolved, and the workers' patrols and detachments of the workers' militia had been disbanded, replaced by a "unified army" with a privileged officer caste. "It would, however, have been quite possible to reorganize the militias and make them more efficient while keeping them under direct control of the trade unions," wrote George Orwell in this regard. "The main purpose of the change was to make sure that the Anarchists did not possess an army of their own. Moreover, the democratic spirit of the militias made them breeding grounds for revolutionary ideas. The Communists were well aware of this, and inveighed ceaselessly and bitterly against the POUM and Anarchist principle of equal pay for all ranks. A general 'bourgeoisification,' a deliberate destruction of the egalitarian spirit of the first few months of the revolution, was taking place. All happened so swiftly that people making successive visits to Spain at intervals of a few months have declared that they seemed scarcely to be visiting the same country; what had seemed on the surface and for a brief instant to be a workers' state was changing before one's eyes into an ordinary bourgeois republic with the normal division into rich and poor."[16] Orwell considered expressions of this transformation to be the official declaration by the "socialist" Minister, Negrin that "We respect private property," and the return to territory occupied by the Republicans of deputies to the Cortes (the Spanish parliament before 1936) who had fled from Spain at the beginning of the war because they feared persecution for their pro-fascist views.

These changes were accompanied by the stripping away of real power from the trade unions and "the general movement ... away from working class control and towards centralized control, leading on to state capitalism or, possibly, towards the reintroduction of private capitalism."[17] As more power was taken away from the working class and ever more revolutionaries ended up in prison, it became increasingly clear that "in reality it was the Communists above all others who prevented revolution in Spain." In stating this fact, Orwell added: "Please notice that I am saying nothing against the rank-and-file Communist, least of all against the thousands of Communists who died heroically round Madrid. But these were not the men who were directing party policy. As for the people higher up, it is inconceivable that they were not acting with their eyes open."[18]

In analyzing the tragic changes in the character of the Spanish Revolution, Trotsky wrote that the Stalinists' use of violence against the left wing of the working class was due to a desire to prevent the revolutionary rebuilding of the leadership of workers' organizations. This violence, which was supposedly being carried out "in the name of discipline" and "army unity," was "nothing but the school of Bonapartism." Trotsky warned the POUM's leaders that "the most ominous challenges lie ahead."[19]

These challenges, for which the POUM and other revolutionary forces in Spain were not prepared, occurred in May 1937, when the Stalinists provoked the so-called "Barcelona uprising," allowing them to finally transform Spain into an arena of bloody terror against revolutionaries—the opponents of Stalinism.

43. The Barcelona Uprising

THE HEROIC DEFENSE of Madrid and the victory of the Republicans at Guadalajara greatly elevated the prestige of the USSR and the Spanish Communist Party. Using this, Stalin opened a new phase in the intervention in the Spanish war and in spreading his power to the entire territory occupied by the republicans.

The main obstacle to turning Spain into an obedient vassal of the Kremlin was Catalonia. A vivid description of the atmosphere in this heroic province is contained in Upton Sinclair's novella, "No Pasaran!" ["They Shall Not Pass"], in which he tells about the arrival in Barcelona of American volunteers.

The thing that struck the Americans most was the perfect order in this great city. War had not touched it—only revolution, and that had been over in forty hours. It was an industrial city; the unions called themselves Anarcho-Syndicalists, believing in the free association of workers in control of individual factories.[*] It was these educated workers and their wives who had charged machine-guns with carving-knives and pieces of board with nails sticking out. Now they had a city to direct; they had lost their chains, and gained a world.... These workers who laughed and sang and pounded on the table—these were the people who had made history three months ago, when by radio and telephone and steam-whistles the word had been spread that the troops were marching from their barracks. The workers had poured out into the streets—having been well taught about Fascism, and what was being plotted against the workers' state. It was they who had charged the barricades, and captured arsenals and barracks; there had been furious fighting up and down that broad boulevard, Las Ramblas, with sixteen hundred killed....

---

[*] In the Russian translation of 1937, this sentence reads: "Barcelona was an industrial center and there were many workers there." The Soviet censors banned any positive reference to the role played by the Anarcho-Syndicalists in the war. *Trans.*

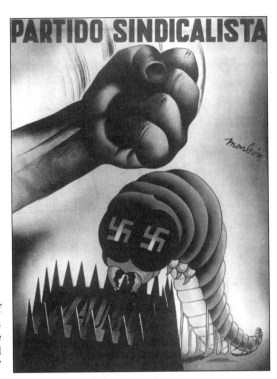

Poster of the Party of Syndicalists, issued in connection with the mobilization to defend Madrid; Valencia, 1937

This workers' city lay in a workers' province, Catalonia, which for generations had been struggling for independence from the reactionary monarchy of Spain. Now they had their own government; but they were forced to realize that they could not survive if the Fascists took the rest of the country. So they had the problem of cooperating with Madrid; also the problem of working out compromises among the various parties and factions of the workers.[1]

The influence of the official Communist Party in Catalonia was not great. Here the leading role was played by the Anarchists and POUMists.

One of the main goals which Stalin had set in Spain was to weaken and then overthrow the Catalonian government, which resembled to a large degree the government of a sovereign state. In pursuit of this goal, Stalin prohibited the unloading of a Soviet ship carrying aircraft in Barcelona. He ordered the ship to be redirected to the port of Alicante, which was being blockaded by Franco's ships. This action delayed the availability of these planes for the republican forces, who were suffering from an acute shortage of aircraft. "This fantastic development," wrote Krivitsky, "was part of Stalin's fierce but silent battle to gain complete control of the Loyalist government, a battle which went on behind the open theater of war. If Stalin was to make Spain a pawn in his power game, he must subdue all opposition in the Spanish republic. The spearhead of that opposition was in Catalonia. Stalin was determined to support with arms and manpower only those groups in Spain which were ready to accept without reservation his leadership. He was resolved not to let the Catalonians lay hands on our planes, with which they might win a military victory that would increase their prestige and thus their political weight in the republican ranks."[2]

As the Soviet intervention in Spain increased, Stalin made ever more belligerent demands upon the central Spanish government to deal with the Catalonian opposition. On his orders, Slutsky told a minister of the Republican government, the Communist Hernandes, that it was necessary to crush the POUM, since this party had criticized the Moscow Trials. Hernandes describes this in a book which came out in 1953 in Mexico.[3]

However Caballero did not agree to launch terror in Catalonia, although the Soviet consul Rosenberg repeatedly told him that Stalin personally was insisting on the liquidation of the POUM. Caballero continued to support the Catalonian government which was desperately resisting the Stalinist purges.

By December 1936, the terror was raging not only in Barcelona, but in Madrid and Valencia. In February 1937, *Pravda* announced that on the orders of the Committee for the Defense of Madrid, the arrest had been made of a Madrid POUMist group at the radio station. The closing down of the radio station was officially explained by the fact that it "systematically disseminated attacks against the legitimate government of the republic, against the Popular Front." At the same time, the publication of the POUM newspaper, *Red Comrade-in-arms*, was halted for "not observing the rules of censorship and for its campaign against organizations which were in the Popular Front." The same issue of *Pravda* republished the article from the organ of the Spanish Communist Party, *Frente Rojo*, which demanded the dissolution of the POUM. "We are talking about bandits left by fascism in our midst," the article said. "We demand that a people's tribune put on trial the fascist cadres of this organization."[4]

A month and a half later, TASS published "details of the Fascist-Trotskyist conspiracy in Valencia." These articles indicated with unconcealed satisfaction that "the Trotskyist accomplices of Franco ... heroes of the fascist underground sit under lock and key. Many of them have confessed their guilt."[5]

The number of the arrested republicans and International Brigade members reached into the hundreds by this time. Agents of the NKVD kidnapped and murdered people. As the *Bulletin of the Opposition* wrote, "In Barcelona, Valencia and Madrid, the GPU has its own prisons where there is no access not only for relatives of those who have disappeared, but also for the state police and even the central government."[6] The methods of torture, forced confessions and mass shootings which had been developed in Moscow were widely used in these prisons. "Treason" was felt to be any unfavorable remarks about the Stalinist regime, criticism of the methods of conducting the war, and association with bearers of "heretical" views. Thus Spain became the launching pad for transferring into other countries the experience of the struggle against "enemies of the people," which was repeated in all "People's Democratic" countries after the Second World War.

The members of the central government reacted with ever growing indignation to the activity of the NKVD's extensive network, which was absolutely independent of the Spanish authorities, and to the ruthless purges of all dissident voices, whom the Spanish Communist Party indiscriminately branded as "Trotskyists." Caballero vigorously protested against the terror which was reaching the members of his party and its political allies.

Soviet military figures warned Stalin that the Spanish leaders were upset with the NKVD's shameless repressive activity and with the spying by Soviet agents in governmental circles. In a report sent to Voroshilov and Yezhov to be passed on to Stalin, Berzin said that these agents were compromising the Soviet Union by their unceremonious interference in Spain's domestic affairs. He proposed that Orlov immediately be recalled from Spain. Slutsky showed Krivitsky this document, expressed his complete agreement with Berzin, and added that Orlov's people were conducting themselves in Spain in the same way that colonizers usually handled natives.[7]

Like Berzin, Stashevsky cautiously tried to suggest to Stalin that the NKVD should have mercy on the existing left political parties in Spain. He also communicated these thoughts to Tukhachevsky, who was in favor of calling to order those who were acting in Spain as if they were in a subjugated country.[8]

However Stalin ignored all these considerations, and tried as before to gain full control over Spain. To achieve this goal, he had to subordinate Catalonia to his authority and remove Largo Caballero.

The Stalinist agents centered their choice on Negrin, the minister of finance, who was selected to replace Caballero as prime minister. Negrin saw the salvation of his country in support from the Soviet Union and the establishment of an iron fisted regime in Spain. He "welcomed the purging of the 'uncontrollables' and 'troublemakers' in his country by any hand, even the foreign hand of Stalin.... He was ready to go along with Stalin in everything, sacrificing all other considerations to secure this aid."[9]

In order to finish off the POUMists and execute the plan of replacing the government's cabinet, Stalin's agents provoked an uprising in Barcelona.

Krivitsky said that before the May events in Catalonia he happened to see two documents which testified to the provocative preparation of a "conspiracy" in Barcelona. One of them was a report by José Diaz, the leader of the Spanish communists, to Dimitrov, in which he described the activity of the Communist Party in undermining the ranks of the anarchists and socialists from within. The other was a report from an NKVD agent who was the leader of a Paris group of Russian émigré-anarchists sent to Barcelona. Gaining the trust of the anarcho-syndicalist leaders, he incited them to engage in risk-laden activities which would require the intervention of the army to suppress disturbances and unrest behind the front lines.[10]

The stirring up of various political groups in Catalonia against each other ended in the fratricidal conflict which erupted in May 1937. Five days of bloodletting resulted in five hundred deaths and more than a thousand wounded.

In the words of George Orwell, who gave the most truthful description of the Barcelona uprising, by May "things had reached a point at which some kind of violent outbreak could be regarded as inevitable.... There was a certain amount of resentment among the working classes because of the growing contrast of wealth and poverty and a general vague feeling that the revolution had been sabotaged."[11]

The immediate cause of the conflict was the governmental decree that the workers surrender their private weapons. At the same time a decision was made to arm to the teeth the "nonpolitical" police, which refused to accept any members of the trade unions. On May 3, on orders from the government, groups of Civil Guards seized the telegraph and other important public buildings. In response, the workers stopped work. On the next morning, barricades sprang

J. Hernandes, J. Duclos and M. Koltsov at a plenum of the Central Committee of the Spanish Communist Party

up in the city. Battles broke out with renewed force when the Civil Guard tried to disarm the workers. However, the workers had neither a unified leadership nor a clear plan of action. The leaders of the POUM tried to limit their activity to passive defense. Therefore the six thousand assault guards which arrived from Valencia on May 7 were able to take control of Barcelona into their own hands. The government issued an order to begin disarming all irregular troop detachments.

The official version of the Barcelona tragedy was that traitors—Trotskyists and anarchists—had risen up in order to "stick a knife in the back of the Republican government." A leading role in the dissemination of this disinformation belonged to Mikhail Koltsov. In his book *Spanish Diary*, which summarizes the contents of his voluminous correspondence from Spain, he states that a fascist espionage organization had been uncovered in Madrid, and that its tracks led to Barcelona. Along with leaders of the reactionary aristocracy and "Francoist Phalange," leaders of the POUM participated in this organization. The spies had their own radio station which secretly broadcast to the insurgents information about the disposition and regroupment of Republican troops.

With Olympian detachment and even a certain amount of irony with regard to the Republican police, Koltsov told how they "vacillated and swung back and forth for a long time, bartered at length with the Justice Minister, Irujo, and finally grew impatient; they began to liquidate the major nests of the POUM and arrest the Trotskyist leaders." This "restructuring" was aided, according to Koltsov, by the fact that the socialist, republican and non-party members of the Madrid police, who previously had felt that the struggle against the Trotskyists was a private affair of the communists, "suddenly came upon such acts by the POUMists that they became completely upset." The police rapidly arrested two hundred spies who were found to be holding documents which forced them to confess to preparing an armed uprising. The main document among them was a map of Madrid containing a message written in invisible ink on the reverse side. After the message was developed, it became clear that it was a letter to Franco, although the major portion of it was encoded. While trying to decipher it, "the police wandered around in the dark" until the general staff gave them some of Franco's code books which had been captured. One of the codes was the exact one used in the letter. With the help of this code book, as Koltsov tells it, the following text was deciphered: "Your order to infiltrate our people into the ranks of the extremists and the POUM is being carried out successfully. In carrying out your order, I was in Barcelona, where I met with N.—the leading member of POUM. I relayed to him all your instructions.... He promised me that he would send new people to Madrid in order to facilitate the work of the POUM. Due to these measures, the POUM will become both in Madrid and Barcelona the real support of our movement."[12]

Not until 1992, as a result of an investigation conducted by members of a Catalonian television station, was the plan for fabricating the false document found in the archives of the KGB. It was this forgery that Koltsov presented as a document sent by a Fascist agent. The coded text with the letter "N" (Nin) was prepared in response to an order from Orlov by two members of the Republican secret police, A. Castalia and J. Jimenez. The participants in the investigation found not only the forgery itself, which was preserved in Spain's national historical archive, but also Jimenez, who survived until recent times. On the television screen he confirmed his participation in the forgery's preparation.[13]

After suppressing the unrest in Barcelona, Orlov ordered the general director of security, the Communist Ortega, to sign, without consulting the Minister of Internal Affairs, a large number of orders for the arrest of leaders and

Убийство
Андрея Нина
агентами Г. П. У.

Когда Андрей Нин, руководитель ПОУМ'а был
арестован в Барселоне, не могло быть ни малей-
шего сомнения в том, что агенты ГПУ не выпустят
его живым. Намерения Сталина раскрылись с исклю-
чительной ясностью, когда ГПУ, которое держит з
своих когтях испанскую полицию, опубликовало за-
явление, в котором Нин и все руководство ПОУМ'а
обвиняются в том, что они являются «агентами»
Франко.

Вздорность этого обвинения ясна всякому, ко-
му известны хотя бы самые простые факты испан-
ской революции. Члены ПОУМ'а героически боро-
лись против фашистов на всех фронтах Испании.
Нин — старый и неподкупный революционер. Он за-
щищал интересы испанского и каталонского наро-
дов против агентов советской бюрократии. Именно
поэтому ГПУ избавилось от него при помощи хоро-
шо подготовленного «рейда» на барселонскую тюрь-
му. О том, какую роль сыграли в этом деле офици-
альные испанские власти можно делать только пред-
положения.

Article in the
Bulletin of the Opposition **about**
the murder of Andres Nin

activists in the POUM. On 15 June the activity of the POUM was outlawed. In
Orwell's words, "[they] arrested everyone connected with the POUM whom
they could lay hands on, including even wounded men, hospital nurses, wives
of POUM members and in some cases, even children."[14]

On 10 June Andrés Nin was arrested; at the beginning of the year he had
been driven out of the Catalonian government. He was imprisoned in the small
town of Alcala de Enares, where he fell into the hands of Stalinist agents headed
by Orlov and Vittorio Vidali, a member of the Comintern who later participated in the organization of Trotsky's murder. As Julian Gorkin, a surviving
leader of the POUM, was to say in 1962, Nin was subjected to inhuman torture,
but he refused to give the testimony demanded of him.

Nin enjoyed such authority throughout the world that after his arrest a
campaign for his liberation was launched in many countries. In France a committee in defense of the POUM was formed. A group of famous French writers
(A. Gide, F. Mauriac, Roger Martin Du Gare and others) demanded the organi-

zation of a fair trial for the POUM and for Nin.

Then Orlov's team incited the kidnaping of Nin from the secret prison. According to an official statement, the kidnaping was performed by Gestapo agents. In reality, Orlov and four accomplices—one Soviet and three Spaniards— carried out Nin's murder. The killers buried Nin's body by the marker for the "seventeenth kilometer" on the road near the town of Alcala de Enares. On 24 July Orlov sent the "Center" a report under the code name "Nikolai," which outlined the kidnaping and murder of Nin.[15]

In 1992, the government of the province of Madrid published a decree ordering the search for Nin's grave and the establishment of a monument on the approximate location of his burial.

In August 1937, an international commission headed by James Maxton, a member of the British parliament, came to Spain to verify the charges against the POUM and the facts connected with Nin's disappearance. Insofar as its efforts proved to be unsuccessful, in December another commission arrived which was also headed by a member of the British Parliament, John McGovern. Despite permission signed by the minister of justice and the director of Spanish prisons, the members of this commission were not allowed to visit the "secret prison" set up in Barcelona by the Communist Party. The Minister of the Interior directly stated to members of the commission, "We have received aid from Russia and have had to permit certain actions which we did not like."[16]

While remaining silent about foreign protests, *Pravda* spent several months after the Barcelona events publishing articles about "cleansing the rear lines of Trotskyist-fascist provocateurs and spies."[17] One of these articles stated that the Valencia police published a list of those arrested in June, which contained the names of "six hundred forty-five fascists, Trotskyists, and people without documents."[18] Even more arrests were made in Catalonia.

Trotsky reacted to the attacks on the POUM with the article, "Beginning of the End," in which he stressed: "The methods of amalgams and forgeries worked out in Moscow are being transported in ready-made form to the soil of Barcelona and Madrid. The leaders of the POUM, who can only be accused of opportunism and indecisiveness with regard to the Stalinist reaction, are suddenly declared 'Trotskyists' and, of course, allies of fascism. The GPU agents in Spain 'found' chemical letters which they wrote themselves and in which the link between Barcelona revolutionaries and Franco is established according to all the rules of Moscow forgery. There is no shortage of scoundrels who are willing to carry out these bloody assignments."[19]

Not knowing the leading role that Orlov was playing in provoking the Barcelona uprising and in the subsequent persecution of the POUMists, Trotsky named another active participant in these bloody events, a person who acted under his own widely known name. This was the former oppositionist V. A. Antonov-Ovseenko, who wrote a shameful article during the Trial of the Sixteen in which he told about a letter he had sent to Kaganovich. In it he said that when it came to Zinoviev and Kamenev, he "would carry out any instruction from the party. It was clear, yes, even if that meant shooting them as clear counterrevolutionaries."[20]

A few weeks after this article appeared, Antonov-Ovseenko was summoned to see Stalin, who told him that he had been appointed general consul in Barcelona. At this post, as Stalin made it very clear, Antonov-Ovseenko could compensate for his "Trotskyist past," i.e., for his participation in the Left Opposition in the 1920s.

"The former revolutionist, Antonov-Ovseenko, who repented in 1927 for his oppositional sins and became mortally afraid in 1936 of ending up on the defendants' bench," wrote Trotsky, "declared in *Pravda* that he was fully prepared to strangle Trotskyists 'with his own hands.' They immediately sent this person to Barcelona under the guise of a consul and told him precisely who it was that he should strangle.... Such responsible assignments are made under the direct supervision of the 'general secretary.'"[21]

The ideological "justification" for the bloody reprisals in Catalonia was provided by Mikhail Koltsov. Vivid testimony about this can be found in Hemingway's novel *For Whom the Bell Tolls*, where Koltsov is introduced under the name of Karkov. The writer portrays Karkov with undisguised sympathy, is delighted with his mind and even looks at him (through the eyes of his hero) as if he were gazing upwards from below. However, as one reads the novel, one senses that with Hemingway, who did not fully understand the political mosaic of the time, several of Koltsov's statements which he confided to the author evoked a feeling of alarm that was not fully conscious. Characteristic in this sense is the description of the conversation between Karkov and Robert Jordan (whose image to a certain extent is the author's alter ego). When Jordan hears from Karkov words about the admissibility of individual terror, a sharp dialogue unfolds between them, in which Karkov alternates between the banal clichés of Stalinist propaganda and his own cynical statements and lies.

"I thought that you did not believe in political assassination....

"We do not believe in acts of terrorism by individuals," Karkov had smiled. "Not of course by criminal terrorist and counterrevolutionary organizations. We detest with horror the duplicity and villainy of the murderous hyenas of Bukharinite wreckers and such dregs of humanity as Zinoviev, Kamenev, Rykov and their henchmen. We hate and loathe these veritable fiends," he smiled again. "But I still believe that political assassination can be said to be practiced very extensively."

"You mean — "

"I mean nothing. But certainly we execute and destroy such veritable fiends and dregs of humanity and the treacherous dogs of generals and the revolting spectacle of admirals unfaithful to their trust. These are destroyed. They are not assassinated. You see the difference?"[22]

From this excerpt it is quite obvious that with a cynical smile Karkov was counterposing political murders without investigation or trial, which were widely practiced in Spain, to the imaginary terrorist actions of "double dealers." And as he went along he was trying to convince his listener of the difference between "assassination" and "liquidation" carried out according to the sentences passed during the Moscow trials.

Karkov's answers to Jordan's questions about the "POUM putsch" sounded even more ambiguous:

"The POUM was never serious. It was a heresy of crackpots and wild men and it was really just an infantilism. There were some honest misguided people. There was one fairly good brain and there was a little fascist money. Not much. The poor POUM. They were very silly people."

"But were many killed in the putsch?"

"Not so many as were shot afterwards or will be shot.... Poor POUM. They never did kill anybody. Not at the front nor anywhere else. A few in Barcelona, yes."

"Were you there?"

"Yes. I have sent a cable describing the wickedness of that infamous organization of Trotskyite murderers and their fascist machinations all beneath contempt but, between us, it is not very serious, the POUM. Nin was their only man. We had him but he escaped from our hands."

"Where is he now?"

"In Paris. We say he is in Paris. He was a very pleasant fellow but with bad political aberrations."

"But they were in communication with the fascists, weren't they?"

"Who is not?"[23]

It is likely here that Hemingway is presenting almost verbatim the content of his conversations with Koltsov about the Barcelona uprising and its consequences. With a sophist's refinement, Koltsov let his listener know the difference between the way he described the events in Barcelona in his dispatches, and the way he actually assessed them. The official version which was concocted by Koltsov for the press depicted the POUM as "a foul organization of hired assassins"; proceeding from this version, more POUMists were shot than died during the time of the putsch. Yet Koltsov told Hemingway that the putsch was "just an infantilism," the POUM had not killed anyone, and Nin was "a very pleasant fellow." From his story about Nin's fate one thing obviously follows: one of Koltsov's functions in Spain was to misinform foreign journalists and public officials about the most vicious crimes committed by the Stalinists.

Koltsov also performed this function in the summer of 1937 at the international writers' congress held in Spain, where he said: "Our country is fully insured against the adventures of big and little Francos. It is insured by its vigilance and decisiveness, it is insured by the fact that with the first step of the Trotskyist Francos, Soviet security organs will block their path, and the military courts will punish them with the support of the entire population."[24]

After reprisals against the POUM, there was a marked increase in the number of kidnappings and summary executions of "uncontrolled elements." One of the victims of the Stalinists was Trotsky's former secretary, Erwin Wolf, who had come to Spain in May 1937. Two months later he was arrested, but soon released from prison. Three days after being set free Wolf disappeared without a trace.

Caballero and the majority of other members of the Spanish government refused to believe the charges made against the POUMists. The Minister of Justice Irujo declared that he had become familiar with the case of the POUM and that he was certain that not a single bit of evidence presented there concerning treason and sabotage would withstand criticism, and the documents which allegedly had been signed by Nin were forgeries. Irujo stated that the police had exceeded their authority and had fallen under the control of foreign communists.[25]

Immediately after the crushing of the Barcelona uprising, the second point of the Stalinist plan began to be implemented: the replacement of the governmental cabinet. The Spanish Communists, who were not content with the dispersal of the POUM, the banning of its press, and the arrests of its leaders on slanderous charges, demanded from Largo Caballero the liquidation of all anti-Stalinist groups and the establishment of full control over all newspapers, radio stations and assembly halls. After Caballero refused to meet these demands, the communist ministers announced their exit from the government. The decision to do this was made at a session of the Politburo of the Spanish Communist Party which was attended by representatives of the Comintern, Togliatti and Gerö (the future head of the Hungarian government who was swept from his post by the popular uprising in 1956).

As a result of this démarche, Caballero was forced to retire on May 15. Two days later a second government of the Popular Front, now headed by Negrin, was formed. It finished the attacks on the POUMists, formed a new Catalonian government and disarmed all the "uncontrolled elements."

The terror which was unleashed by the Stalinist forces on the territory held by the Republicans sharply weakened the Republican forces. Describing the events in Spain after the assault on the POUM, Krivitsky noted: "the fascist powers became more and more aggressive in the West. Italy and Germany intervened openly on Franco's side.... If Stalin were to capitalize on his achievements in Spain, he would have to give her now the full measure of help needed to defeat Franco and his allies. But now more than ever, he was loath to risk a major war.... He intervened there in the hope that he might, with the stepping stone of a Spanish dependency, build a road from Moscow to London and Paris, and so ultimately to Germany. His maneuver was unsuccessful. He lacked real audacity. He played his game boldly against the independence of the Spanish people, but feebly against Franco. He succeeded in murderous intrigue, but failed in waging war."[26]

After the destruction of the POUMists and other anti-Stalinist forces, the civil war in Spain continued for almost two more years, but the initiative passed into the hands of the republic's enemies. The atmosphere in the camp of the Soviet advisers changed dramatically. In describing the setting at the hotel "Gaylord's," which had become a virtual apartment-headquarters, Hemingway wrote, "It was the opposite of the puritanical, religious communism" which had been characteristic of the headquarters of the International Brigades during the first months of the civil war.[27] To Robert Jordan, who was visiting Gaylord's for the first time, "it seemed too luxurious and the food was too good for a besieged city and the talk too cynical for a war.... And the talk that he had thought of as cynicism when he had first heard it had turned out to be much too true.... It was there [at Gaylord's] you learned how it was all really done instead of how it was supposed to be done."[28]

Hemingway described the gathering of "grand society" at Gaylord's when the Soviet military men and journalists openly exchanged information about the confusion and chaos which reigned among the republican troops. Here Karkov, who during the first months of the civil war "was not cynical ... when he talked,"[29] spoke in another vein altogether when he commented on reports about current events at the front. The following episode is characteristic. "A man of middle height [I. Erenburg—V. R.] with a gray, heavy, sagging face, puffed eye pouches and a pendulous underlip called to him in a dyspeptic voice." After repeating to Karkov some obvious nonsense that Dolores Ibarruri had just reported, he commented on her account with the bombastic words: "It was one of the greatest moments of the war to me when I heard the reports in that great voice where pity, compassion and truth are blended." Karkov reacted to this retort with cynical indifference: "Write it.... Don't tell it to me. Don't waste whole paragraphs on me. Go and write it now."[30]

There is great significance in the way Hemingway portrayed the contrasting moods which seized his hero during the first months of the civil war and during the period when Soviet domination in Spain had sunk its roots deeply. Before carrying out a dangerous assignment, Robert Jordan recalls: "you fought that summer and that fall for all the poor in the world, against all tyranny, for all the things that you believed and for the new world you had been educated into.... It was in those days, he thought, that you had a deep and sound and selfless pride—that would have made you a bloody bore at Gaylord's, he thought suddenly.... You were too naive. You were in a sort of state of grace.... There was not any Gaylord's then."[31]

The transformation of the civil war in Spain—from an arena of struggle "against all tyranny" into a means for implementing Stalin's geopolitical maneuvers and into an arena for exterminating communist dissidents—determined the defeat of the Spanish Revolution. The damage done by Stalinist provocations and reprisals was not limited to Spain alone. These actions had a fatal impact on the fate of the entire worldwide communist movement. The most terrible consequence was that the Stalinist terror, which was conducted in Spain even more openly and ruthlessly than in the USSR, began to be associated in the minds of the majority of people with the concept of "communism."

In summarizing the events which occurred in Spain after the Barcelona uprising, George Orwell wrote: "Anyone who has given the subject a glance knows that the Communist tactic of dealing with political opponents by means of trumped-up accusations is nothing new. Today the key word is 'Trotsky-fascist'; yesterday it was 'social-fascist.' It is only six or seven months since the Russian State trials 'proved' that the leaders of the Second International ... and prominent members of the British Labour Party, were hatching a huge plot for the military invasion of the USSR [this refers to the trial of the "Right-Trotskyist Bloc"—V. R.].... I doubt whether this kind of thing pays, even from a sectarian point of view. And meanwhile there is no possible doubt about the hatred and dissension that the 'Trotsky-fascist' accusation is causing. Rank-and-file Communists everywhere are led away on a senseless witch-hunt after 'Trotskyists,' and parties of the type of the POUM are driven back into the terribly sterile position of being mere anti-Communist parties. There is already the beginning of a dangerous split in the world working class movement. A few more libels against lifelong socialists, a few more frame-ups like the charges against the POUM, and the split may become irreconcilable. The only hope is to keep political controversy on a plane where exhaustive discussion is possible.... To make the wrong decision may be to land ourselves in for centuries of semi-slavery. But so long as no argument is produced except a scream of 'Trotsky-fascist!' the discussion cannot even begin. It would be impossible for me, for instance, to debate the rights and wrongs of the Barcelona fighting with a Communist Party member, because no Communist—that is to say, no 'good' Communist—could admit that I have given a truthful account of the facts."[32]

The spectacle of Stalinist crimes demoralized and drove away from the communist movement many people who participated in the Spanish war. In this regard, the fate of Arthur Koestler is instructive. Before the war in Spain he had been an exemplary Stalinist, and he traveled widely in the USSR as a correspondent for Western left newspapers, depicting Soviet reality in an apologetic light. In Spain he was captured by Franco's troops, and he miraculously managed to avoid being shot. In the summer of 1937, his book *Unprecedented Vic-*

tims was published in Moscow. At the end of 1939 he was put into an internment camp by the French police. After being released, Koestler went to England, where he was arrested as a "suspicious alien." Like many other Western Stalinists, he made a sharp turn in the direction of anticommunism.

A significant part of the Soviet participants in the Spanish war were ruthlessly exterminated. In 1937, Berzin and Stashevsky were arrested and shot. At the end of 1938, Mikhail Koltsov was arrested, and after a prolonged investigation, he was shot in 1940. The fate of José Diaz ended tragically; in 1942 he committed suicide by throwing himself out of the window of his Moscow apartment.

After returning from Spain, Stern and the main Soviet aviation advisor, Smushkevich, were promoted in rank and awarded the highest governmental honors (Smushkevich was one of the first military figures to be twice honored as Hero of the Soviet Union). At the Eighteenth Congress, Stern was elected a member of the Central Committee, and Smushkevich a candidate member. Along with other heroes of the Spanish war (for instance, the legendary pilot Rychagov), they were arrested immediately before the outbreak of World War II and in October 1941 were shot without a trial.

In exterminating the participants in the civil war in Spain, Stalin was guided by two considerations. First of all, he was trying to prevent information leaks about the provocations and crimes of his agents in Spain. Secondly, he was afraid that the revolutionaries who had taken part in the Spanish war might become infected with the "Trotskyist" heresy—for they had enjoyed access not only to "Trotskyist' literature, but even direct contact with Trotskyists and other anti-Stalinists.

A new stage in the persecution of participants in the Spanish war began at the end of the 1940s. One of the goals of the trials of communists in the countries of "People's Democracy" was the desire to prove the existence of a "Trotskyist underground" which had been born during this war. At the Hungarian trial of 1949, the main defendant was the former member of the International Brigades, Laszlo Rajk, who was forced to "confess" that the majority of Interbrigadistas were influenced by "Trotskyism."

At the Czechoslovakian trial of Slansky-Klimentis (1952), the former International Brigade member Arthur London was declared a Trotskyist. He was sentenced to a long prison term and freed after Stalin's death. In his book *Confession* London tells how first a trial was planned around "the Trotskyist conspiracy" of former fighters in the international brigades. Testimony was obtained from London against such famous Interbrigadistas as the Politburo member of the Italian Communist Party, Luigi Longo, and the Politburo member of the French Communist Party, Raymond Guyot. One of the investigators considered it a personal achievement to include in the transcript of the interrogation the formulation: "the Trotskyist group of International Brigade volunteers."

Recalling how long pogromist attitudes were maintained in his country toward members of the International Brigades, London reported how even after Stalin's death the Czechoslovak state security organs sent a circular to all departments in which participants in the International Brigades were equated with officials from the police and army in the protectorate of Czechia and Moravia, which had been set up by Hitler's supporters, and with former officers of the Slovakian Fascist Guard.

Meanwhile, even after the experience of his own investigation, trial and imprisonment, London remained to a large degree in the power of Stalinist amalgams; he apparently had participated in fabricating such amalgams in the 1930s. Recalling the interrogations of the 1940s, he wrote: "The testimony of suspicious elements, whom we rapidly exposed in Spain or in the camps of France, is now being used in order to slander us. They won't even stop at calling them good communists, or at making them victims of our 'Trotskyist band'.... What a pleasure it was for them [the "dubious elements" who had not been "fully beaten"—V. R.]. To get their revenge on us and to use the situation in order to assert their political innocence."[33] Thus the charge of "Trotskyism" returned like a boomerang to London from those whom a few years earlier he had persecuted as "Trotskyists."

The nightmare of the Stalinist terror, both in Spain as well as in the USSR, served not only to destroy genuine Trotskyists or persons close to them in political convictions, but also to tarnish those deceived or careerist-minded communists with participation in political murders.

The scale of the "anti-Trotskyist" terror shows how many communist opponents of Stalin remained abroad in 1937. But no fewer remained in the Soviet Union, and, perhaps there were more genuine Trotskyists who continued their heroic battle even in Stalin's prisons and concentration camps.

44. Trotskyists in the Camps

In describing the atmosphere in Moscow in 1937, the legendary antifascist counterintelligence agent Leopold Trepper wrote the following:

> The glow of October was being extinguished in the shadows of underground chambers. The revolution had degenerated into a system of terror and horror; the ideals of socialism were ridiculed in the name of a fossilized dogma which the executioners still had the effrontery to call Marxism.... All those who did not rise up against the Stalinist machine are responsible, collectively responsible. I am no exception to this verdict.
>
> But who did protest at that time? Who rose up to voice his outrage?
>
> The Trotskyists can lay claim to this honor. Following the example of their leader, who was rewarded for his obstinacy with the end of an ice ax, they fought Stalinism to the death, and they were the only ones who did. By the time of the great purges, they could only shout their rebellion in the freezing wastelands where they had been dragged in order to be exterminated. In the camps, their conduct was admirable. But their voices were lost in the tundra.
>
> Today, the Trotskyists have a right to accuse those who once howled along with the wolves. Let them not forget, however, that they had the enormous advantage over us of having a coherent political system capable of replacing Stalinism. They had something to cling to in the midst of their profound distress at seeing the revolution betrayed. They did not "confess," for they knew that their confession would serve neither the party nor socialism.[1]

After the first Moscow Trials, Trotsky wrote that all the Old Bolsheviks who had stood trial had capitulated in 1927–1929 and since then had repeatedly made public renunciations of the Opposition. "The GPU has been able to knead these people like dough. In the Soviet Union there are, however, genuine

374

Trotskyists: thousands of them are in prison or in exile. These people were not appropriate for the GPU amalgams. Therefore they were set aside. Now, however, after the trials and executions, they will all fall under the barrel of the ultimatum: either repent and 'confess,' or die. It is possible that some of them will falter under this hellish pressure and will be used for a new court spectacle."[2]

Today we know that many of the "undisarmed" Trotskyists were brought to Moscow in 1936 from their prisons and places of exile for reinvestigation, whereupon they endured monstrous tortures (this has been expressively told in A. Rybakov's novel, *1935 and Other Years*). However not a single one of them agreed to give the testimony that was demanded, and not one of them was tried during the open show trials.

Even at the first stage of the Great Purge it became clear that, despite all the preceding slander campaigns and furious repression, a new, young generation of Trotskyists had grown up in the Soviet Union; their courage amazed even their executioners. In his memoirs Krivitsky introduces a story which had been told to him by Slutsky. "We belong to the generation which must perish. Stalin has said that the entire pre-revolutionary and war generation must be destroyed as a millstone around the neck of the revolution. But now they're shooting the young ones—seventeen and eighteen years of age—girls and boys who were born in the Soviet state and never knew anything else.... And lots of them go to their deaths crying, 'Long live Trotsky!'"[3]

In his book *Smolensk Under Soviet Rule*, which is based on material from the Smolensk archive of the NKVD (the only archive of this kind which was seized and carried away by Hitler's forces, thereby ending up in the West after the war), the American historian Merle Fainsod introduces a number of examples of reprisals against genuine Trotskyists in the Smolensk area (then the Western area), where "Trotskyism" was less influential than in other regions.

In 1936 all Trotskyists who were in exile or in political prisons were transferred to concentration camps. The Old Bolshevik Z. N. Nemtsova recalls that on the steamship carrying prisoners to Vorkuta, she met an enormous group of Trotskyists. Here a fight broke out between Trotskyists and Stalinists who shared the same fate. In the course of the fighting, according to Nemtsova, "we called them fascists, and they called us the same."[4] In these mutual recriminations, the two sides were guided by fundamentally different considerations: the arrested Stalinists continued to believe that the Trotskyists were fascist agents; the Trotskyists, however, were calling the Stalinist regime a fascist regime.

Nemtsova considers herself fortunate that in 1936 she was convicted according to the article KRD (counterrevolutionary activity), and not KRTD (counterrevolutionary Trotskyist activity). For those whose sentence contained the letters "KRTD," life in the camps was much worse than for the others: they were subjected to a particularly difficult regimen. Many other memoirists who passed through Stalin's camps write about this too. Thus, Evgenia Ginzburg called those who were convicted under article KRTD "camp pariahs. They were given the most difficult outdoor work, they were not allowed to work at their 'specialties,' and sometimes on holidays they were locked in isolation cells."[5]

Even Solzhenitsyn, in listing the various lettered subdivisions of the articles which were used by the Special Board for convictions, reluctantly notes when he comes to the article "KRTD": "This letter 'T' would later make the life of a prisoner in the camp much more difficult."[6]

The works of Varlam Shalamov describe in greater detail than anywhere else the fate of those who bore the burden of this article. Shalamov himself was first arrested on 19 February 1929 in a trap that was set for workers in one of the underground Trotskyist print shops. In his "Brief Biography," he writes that members of the Left Opposition were those who "were the very first to try, by sacrificing their lives, to prevent that bloody deluge which went down in history as the Stalin cult. The Oppositionists were the only people in Russia who attempted to organize active resistance to this rhinoceros."[7]

In the novella, "The Glove, or KR-2," Shalamov proudly writes that he "was a representative of those people who opposed Stalin." In doing so, among the Oppositionists, "no one ever felt that Stalin and the Soviet regime were one and the same thing."[8]

After actively participating in the underground activity of the Opposition in 1927–1929, Shalamov refused to give testimony at his interrogations and was sentenced by a Special Board to three years in the concentration camps. He called this sentence "the first camp sentence given to Oppositionists."[9]

Shalamov was sent to the Vishersky division of the Solovki camps, where he worked as the head of the economics department of the Bereznikovsky chemical combine which had been built primarily by prison labor. At that time, the use of "politicals" in the camps not for physical labor but according to their specialty was a common occurrence. At a meeting of workers at the Vishersky chemical plants, the prisoners were told that "the government is restructuring the work of the camps. From now on, the main goal will be education through corrective labor. Any prisoner may demonstrate through his labor his right to be set free. Administrative posts, up to the very highest, can be assigned to prisoners."[10]

Of course the conditions in the camps differed from those in exile. Exiled oppositionists conducted a lively correspondence, including the sending of news about recent opposition activity, and articles or declarations by opposition leaders and theoreticians. Such material also circulated between exiles and their comrades who were at liberty. Shalamov recalls that he himself conducted such correspondence for more than a year. Therefore his comrades did not immediately understand that "a camp was not exile, where such letters might pass without great difficulty. They received my address and selected people who were supposed to send me everything, to write, maintain contact, and send the addresses of exiles for correspondence, but all this fell into the hands of the camp supervisors. To condemn me for such things would have been going too far—1937 was still eight years away—but neither Stukov nor Ushakov (heads of the camp) wanted to keep such a dangerous person around."[11]

Although, according to Shalamov, "in 1930 the Trotskyists were no longer anything new in the camps. And in 1931, even less so," their situation there was by no means as severe as it would be in five to seven years. In 1930, Shalamov met the Oppositionist Bliumenfeld in the camp; he had been convicted of participating in the activity of an underground Trotskyist center and was working as the head of the economic planning department of the Vishersky camps. "With regard to my case, Bliumenfeld gave the solemn assurance in the name of the underground of that time that, if 'we had known that even one Oppositionist had received the camps rather than exile or political prison, then we would have obtained your release. At that time our brothers were not being sent to the camps. You were the first.'

"'What kind of leaders are you,' I said, 'if you do not know where your people are?'

"Bliumenfeld was probably in contact through his own channels with people in Moscow, and it was not difficult to find out who I was."[12]

In the fall of 1930, Shalamov and Bliumenfeld submitted a statement to the government, not asking for amnesty, but protesting against the severe conditions for women in the camps.

In 1931 the camp supervisors received a directive from the deputy chairman of the OGPU which ordered the immediate release of all prisoners occupying administrative posts in the camp who had no additional penalties—and it ordered that all their rights be restored, including the right to live anywhere in the country. This was one of the camp "unloadings" which occurred at the beginning of the 1930s. As a result of this "unloading," Shalamov was freed before his sentence was up. In 1932 he returned to Moscow and worked there until 1937 as a writer and journalist, publishing many sketches and stories in the central newspapers and journals.

During these years Shalamov no longer participated in opposition activity. Having never been a member of the party, he had several chances to escape future arrests. However, at the insistence of his relatives, in 1936 he called attention to his oppositional past by writing an official declaration renouncing "Trotskyism." Recalling this event, Shalamov wrote that his family "at a difficult moment betrayed me lock, stock and barrel, although they knew all too well that by condemning me, by pushing me into a deep pit, they too would perish."[13]

On 12 January 1937, Shalamov was once again arrested in Moscow and sentenced according to article "KRTD" to five years in the Kolyma camps. A half year later, his wife was exiled to Central Asia.

At the beginning of his second sentence, Shalamov was still able to enjoy "Berzin's rules" in Kolyma. "When we came to the gold mine," he recalled, "people were still living the 'happy' life as before. Those who had just arrived were given a new winter outfit.... The sick bay stood empty. Newcomers were not even interested in that establishment.... The work was hard, but you could earn a lot—up to ten thousand rubles in the summer months. A bit less in the winter. In severe cold—more than fifty below zero—people didn't work. In the summer people would work ten hours with a shift change every ten days (in winter—four to six hours)." A medical review divided all the prisoners into four categories—healthy, not completely healthy, capable of light physical labor and invalid. The norms for the prisoners were established with their state of health being taken into account.[14]

In *Kolyma Tales*, Shalamov writes of the time when the head of the Dalstroi was the Old Bolshevik E. P. Berzin. At that time the accounting was practiced in such a way that "people with ten-year sentences could return after two or three years. The food was excellent, the clothing too.... The pay for the prison-

ers was colossal, allowing them to help their families and return to the main-
land after finishing their sentence as well-to-do people....

"The prisoners' cemeteries at that time were so few in number that one
might think that Kolyma residents were immortal.

"These few years ... were 'the Golden Age of Kolyma.'"[15]

After Berzin's arrest in the middle of 1937, everything in Kolyma changed
dramatically for the worse, especially for "lettered convicts, who possessed the
most dangerous letter 'T.'" Their personal dossiers contained "special directives": "during time of imprisonment, deny all telegraph and postal contact,
use only for heavy physical labor, and report on their behavior once every quarter." These "special directives," Shalamov stressed, "were an order to kill, to
not let them out alive. All those who fell under the 'special directives' knew
that this piece of cigarette paper obligated all future bosses—from the convoy
guard to the head of the camp administration—to persecute, inform on, and
take measures; if any small-scale boss was not active in destroying those who
possessed 'special directives,' then his comrades, his fellow workers would inform on this boss."

There is hardly any other book which is more insightful than *Kolyma Tales*
in depicting the fate of the "letter convict," who was "hunted by the entire
convoy of all the country's camps in the past, present and future—not a single
boss in the world would want to show any weakness in destroying such an
'enemy of the people.'"

One of the most memorable heroes of *Kolyma Tales* is the oppositionist
Krist, whose fate bears an undeniable resemblance to the fate of Shalamov
himself. Receiving his first sentence as a nineteen-year-old, Krist "was put on
active status in all the card files of the Soviet Union, and when the signal came
for persecution, he left for Kolyma with the fatal brand of 'KRTD.'" It was practically impossible to protect oneself against the fate which this article carried.
"The letter 'T' in the article applied to Krist was a mark, a brand, and a sign
according to which people persecuted Krist for many years, not releasing him
from the icy gold mines in Kolyma's sixty-below cold. It meant killing him with
heavy labor, with impossible camp labor ... killing him with beatings by the
camp bosses, clubbings with prison guards' rifle butts, jabs by the barbers, and
the elbows of his comrades." An innumerable number of times Krist was forced
to conclude that "no other article of the criminal code was as dangerous for the
state as his article with the letter 'T.' Neither betrayal of the Motherland, nor

terror, nor the entire terrifying bouquet of points under Article 58. Krist's four-letter article was the mark of an animal which must be killed, which had been ordered to be killed."

Krist paid close attention to the fate of those few people who lived to see their release date, "despite having in their past the brand with the letter 'T' in their Moscow sentence, in their camp passport or prison record, and in their personal dossier." He knew that even after the sentence had run out and they had been set free, "their entire future would be poisoned by this important information about their criminal status, their article, and the letters 'KRTD.' These letters would block the path in any future that Krist had. They would block the road for the rest of his life in any part of the country, and at any job. This letter not only took away one's passport, but made it impossible to find work for all time, and did not allow one to leave Kolyma."[16]

The fate of those who bore this "letter" in the camps served as a serious touchstone for Solzhenitsyn, who underscored his own desire to avoid this theme in *The Gulag Archipelago*. "I am writing for the Russia that is mute," he declared, "and therefore will say little about the Trotskyists: they are all people of letters, and those who managed to survive most likely have already prepared detailed memoirs and will describe their dramatic epic more fully and more precisely than I would be able to do." The cynicism of this statement can be judged for what it is worth if we note what Solzhenitsyn knew perfectly well: from among the thousands of "undisarmed" "cadre" Trotskyists, only a few individuals had managed to survive. For this reason, among the hundreds of memoirs written by prisoners of Stalin's camps, those which belong to "Trotskyists" can literally be counted on one's fingers.

However Solzhenitsyn, who was pretending to create a virtual encyclopedia of Stalinist terror and who was well aware of the availability of certain information about the fate of Trotskyists abroad, nevertheless felt that it was necessary to write "something" about the Trotskyists "for the sake of the general picture." Never does this writer contradict himself more than on those few pages which he devotes to telling about the Trotskyists. Noting that "in any case, they were courageous people," he immediately supplements this indisputable statement with the traditional anticommunist "prognosis aided by hindsight": "I fear, by the way, that if they had come to power, they would have brought us a form of madness that would have been no better than Stalin's."

Another comment by Solzhenitsyn is just as devoid of any proof. Following his account of the organizational activity and of the mutual assistance which Trotskyists displayed during the struggle against their jailers, Solzhenitsyn writes: "I get the impression (but do not insist upon it) that they were overly fussy [?—V. R.] in their political 'struggle' in camp conditions, which produced a shade of the tragicomic." Having supplied this passage with reservations ("impression," "I do not insist upon it"), the writer proceeds to comment in a mocking tone about stories that have come to him about the behavior of Trotskyists in the camps (Solzhenitsyn was not able to meet with Trotskyists themselves, insofar as almost none of them remained in the camps by the mid-1940s—the overwhelming majority had been shot because of camp trials or had been worn out by the regimen established for them). Solzhenitsyn attaches particularly sarcastic comments to his account of acts of resistance by the Trotskyists: the singing of revolutionary songs as they parted, the reciting of anti-Stalinist political slogans, the hanging of mourning flags on the tents and barracks on the twentieth anniversary of the October Revolution, and so forth. Since personally he had not encountered a single similar act of protest (after the destruction of the Trotskyists such collective actions in the camps no longer were carried out), Solzhenitsyn writes that, in his opinion, these actions contained a "mixture of something bordering on hysterical enthusiasm with a sterility that was becoming ridiculous." It is natural that, for a writer who described sympathetically in his "artistic investigation" the hopes of the prisoners for foreign intervention, and who considered such moods the expression of genuine opposition to the regime, the devotion of the arrested Trotskyists to Bolshevik symbols cannot help but seem "ridiculous" and "hysterical." However Solzhenitsyn was nevertheless forced to end his ironic tale about the Trotskyists with the significant words: "No, they were true politicals. There were many of them, and they sacrificed themselves."[17]

Solzhenitsyn treats this theme much more objectively in his novel *The First Circle,* which was written in the years before the writer had made the final passage to positions of zoological anticommunism. Here, in the portrayal of the character and fate of the Trotskyist Abramson, artistic truth clearly gets the upper hand over the political prejudices and predilections of the author. Let us recall that the majority of the inhabitants of the "sharashka" described in the novel were arrested in the "postwar levy," including those who had served in Hitler's forces. Among these people, who were thoroughly anticommunist in spirit, the only exceptions were the Stalinist Rubin and the Trotskyist Abramson.

The latter had not been "shot at the proper time, worn out at the proper time, or trampled at the proper time," but miraculously had managed to survive: he alone survived among hundreds of his comrades and co-thinkers who perished. Whereas Rubin was constantly ridiculed for his views by the other prisoners, Abramson was never subjected to such derision. Moreover, Nerzhin, the main hero of the novel, in whom the reader can easily discern Solzhenitsyn himself, unintentionally feels Abramson's moral superiority, although the latter was not inclined to share his political views with him.

What is particularly attractive in the novel is the profound artistic insight into the ideological and spiritual world of Abramson, who was serving his third decade of imprisonment. Abramson felt that the wave of arrests to which Rubin and Nerzhin belonged "was gray, these were helpless victims of the war, but not people who had voluntarily chosen political struggle as a way of life.... It seemed to Abramson that these people could not be compared with those giants who, like himself, at the end of the twenties freely chose Yenisei exile rather than renounce their own words that had been spoken at party meetings and remain in comfort—such a choice had been given to each of them. These people could not bear the distortion and defamation of the revolution, and were prepared to sacrifice themselves for its sake." It would be difficult to speak more honestly and accurately about the fate of "cadre" Trotskyists and about the way they differed from representatives of all the subsequent dissident currents in the USSR.

Despite everything he had endured, Abramson "preserved within himself, somewhere behind seven seals, not only a vivid but the most morbid interest in the fate of the world, and in the fate of that doctrine to which he had sacrificed his life." Since he did not find in his intellectual world anything in common with the views of the other inhabitants of the "sharashka," he felt that it was senseless to enter into political debates with them. He listened silently to their mocking arguments about Bolshevism and the October Revolution (such arguments, of course, could not help but make their way through the countless stool pigeons to the jailers, but they were punished with nowhere near the ruthlessness and frenzy as the slightest recurrence of "Trotskyist" ideas). Abramson refrained from participating in conversations on political themes because for him it was "just as impossible to reveal his deeply-held and often violated thoughts to the 'young' prisoners as to show them his naked wife."[18]

Let us pass from artistic examples to memoir accounts of the fate of

Trotskyists during the Great Terror. Here, interesting reminiscences are provided by the Old Bolshevik D. Baitalsky, who was in the Left Opposition. He tells about the progress of a group of prisoners, the majority of whom were Trotskyists, as they traveled from Karaganda to Vladivostok in 1936. They had their own council of seniors which in Kolyma merged with the senior councils of other Trotskyist prison convoys. Among the participants in this convoy were no small number of Bolsheviks with pre-revolutionary party service who had been prominent party leaders in the past. But most of them were "hot-headed youths, inexperienced in political struggles, who considered themselves to be the true fighters for Leninism." In the camp, all these "rock-hard Trotskyists ... instead of taking the line of passive submission in order to physically preserve their lives ... pursued a course of resistance to Stalinism, of fighting against the powerful apparatus of the NKVD."

It was precisely into this milieu that the "organs" sent a particularly large number of provocateurs and informers. Baitalsky recalls how he met at a Kolyma gold mine with a certain Kniazhitsky, whom he had once given a recommendation to join the party. Kniazhitsky reported that during the years of the legal inner-party struggle he "had always voted for the line of the Central Committee, but distributed Trotskyist literature in the underground." Having tracked him down, GPU agents used his presence on an official business trip abroad to threaten that "they would make a spy out of him." In exchange for avoiding this disgrace, Kniazhitsky was given the chance to sign an agreement to follow the participants of the Trotskyist underground. Thus he became a secret agent and provocateur. At the beginning of the 1930s they arrested him and sent him into exile so that there he would "throw light on the life of the Trotskyist colony." In May of 1936, this entire colony was sent to Kolyma camps, including Kniazhitsky and many other provocateurs. In recounting this shameful chapter of his life, Kniazhitsky said: "I hate the NKVD agents, and if Stalin fell into my clutches, I would strangle him with my own hands. But I am obligated to 'work,' to carry out my assignments and put people behind bars: I gave them my signature."[19]

In recent years, several excerpts have been published from the denunciations of informers which reveal the political moods among the Trotskyists at their places of imprisonment. Thus, at the beginning of 1936, an undercover agent among the prisoners informed the prison chief at one of the camps: "A group of Trotskyists located in barracks no. 8 is conducting systematic agitation against the party, and in particular against Comrade Stalin.... Martynov said: 'Our boys are working everywhere, they have only formally routed us Trotskyists, but in actual fact we are working; all that is needed is patience, and Trotskyists have plenty of that'.... Stebiakov said: 'The leadership of Stalin is a leadership of violence, and such a system of corrections will lead to nothing positive, but, on the contrary, people are made even angrier—not against the regime, but against its leaders.' Martynov replied to this: 'We need not only to talk, but to act. We need new forms and methods of work'.... In a discussion Martynov declared: 'The fact is that neither Trotsky, nor I, nor a number of others will bow down to Stalin.'"

The Trotskyists expressed views of this type not only in private conversations between themselves. A report of surveillance against a Trotskyist convoy of prisoners being sent from Kazakhstan to the transfer camp of Vladivostok says that in Krasnoyarsk the prisoners yelled through the windows of the train cars, "Down with the counterrevolutionary Central Committee of the VKP(b), headed by Stalin!", and, "Comrade workers! Before you stand political prisoners of the Stalinist regime, Bolshevik-Leninist-Trotskyists who are being taken to Kolyma for physical extermination. The best part of the proletariat is languishing in Stalinist prisons. A gang of functionaries and bureaucrats, headed by Stalin, is sitting in the government."[20]

In Vladivostok, as their ship pulled into port, the Trotskyists unfurled a banner with the slogan: "Down with Stalin!" and began to shout: "They write that there are no political prisoners, but they are sending political prisoners in bunches into the camps. Workers! Look—before you are Communists-Bolsheviks-Leninists, surrounded by a convoy of fascism."[21]

On the steamship traveling to Kolyma, in working out the demands to be sent to the Central Executive Committee and the Comintern, the Trotskyist Poliakov said: "Gather your strength for the difficult struggle that lies ahead. Some of us will retreat before the difficulties, they will be bought by easing their living conditions, but we must prepare for great tribulations, and perhaps even death."[22]

In her memoirs, N. Gagen-Torn tells about those in the camps who preserved "some kind of hope which gave them the strength to live, without being broken." Most of all she includes among them the "'unrepentant Leninists,' as they called themselves," whom she met in the camps. The views of these people, who did not hide their membership in the Opposition, amounted to the following:

"1. (The demand) to publish Lenin's dying letter which Stalin had concealed, thereby violating party democracy.

"2. Stalin had turned the dictatorship of the proletariat into the dictatorship over the proletariat, and then launched an impermissible terror.

"3. Collectivization, which had been introduced in a violent way, with the full enslavement of the peasantry, was not bringing socialism any closer, but leading to the hypertrophy of the state.

"4. The tactics of the party headed by Stalin were discrediting the idea of communism.

"Only the sacrificial blood of communists who were fighting against the Stalinist line could save this idea. They accepted the challenge. From exile on the way to Kolyma, about one hundred of them were herded through Vladivostok. They walked along and sang: 'You fell victim in the fatal struggle, dying with unbounded love for the people.' The guards beat them with rifle butts, but the singing continued. They were driven into the hold of the ship, but even from there the singing could be heard. In Kolyma they declared a hunger strike, demanding a political regimen: correspondence, permission to read, separation from common criminals. On the fifteenth day, forced feeding began. They refused to give in. On the ninetieth day the administration promised to meet their demands. They called off the hunger strike. They were transferred to various camp locations; the camp bosses promised that they would find the conditions they had demanded. Then gradually they were once more taken to Magadan and put in a terrible prison—'Vaska's house.' A new case was opened against them. They knew that they would be shot, but remained unbowed. These were courageous people. It is most likely that they all perished, but they preserved their faith in the necessity of fighting for communism as they understood it."[23]

As long as Berzin was the head of Dalstroi, and the head of the secret-political department [SPO]of the Magadan UNKVD was Mosevich (the former head of the SPO of the Leningrad UNKVD who was sentenced in the trial of the Leningrad Chekists), the Trotskyists managed to achieve the fulfillment of the demands they had made during the collective hunger strikes: the chance to work according to their specialty, permission for families to live together, etc. After the mass hunger strike of Trotskyists who were scattered among different gold mines, but who maintained contact with each other, agreement was reached with the Dalstroi administration about easing the camp conditions.

B. M. Eltsin
with his
daughter and
granddaughter
in exile

Small cells were built in the barracks, separated from each other by low walls made of planks; they were then assigned to the families of Trotskyists who had won the hunger strike. The strike, which had lasted for several months, was accompanied by the slogans: "Socialism cannot be built on the bones of the working class"; "Stalin is pumping our blood, the blood of Bolsheviks, into the gold fields."[24]

One of the leaders of the underground committee which led the hunger strike was the long-time Oppositionist, the sixty-two-year-old Boris M. Eltsin, who never signed any statements of capitulation.

Among the Kolyma Trotskyists was A. L. Sokolovskaya, Trotsky's first wife, who had passed through tsarist prisons and exile. By this time she had lost her two daughters: the younger died from tuberculosis in 1928, and the older, who had gone abroad, committed suicide in 1933. "Despite all her simplicity and humanity," recalls N. A. Joffe about Sokolovskaya, "she struck me as a figure out of some ancient Greek tragedy."[25]

In her memoirs, Gagen-Torn describes Sokolovskaya's subsequent fate. In an Irkutsk transfer prison, she met "a woman with an intelligent and sorrowful Jewish face," who was being sent from Kolyma to Moscow. The first conversation they had unfolded in the following manner:

"KRD?"

"KRTD. They don't take KRD's such a long distance for a new investigation," she grinned.

"Have you been in long?"

"They took me in 1930, first into exile, then to a political prison..."

"Who were you with in prison?" she asked.

"A wide, wide range of people. Among those who might interest you, I met Katia Gusakova."

She shuddered. I looked at her closely.

"Had she been in prison long?"

"She spent a year in solitary. They brought her to us in our cell looking like she had just been taken down off the cross. She was all eyes and long braids. Her body was transparent. She said that she had been on a prolonged hunger strike."

The woman sat in silent expectation. She nervously straightened her greying hair.

"It was from her that I first heard about Trotskyism," I said, looking straight at her. "She told me about the political prison and exile, but most of all, she asked about life outside, about the dekulakization of 1930–1934. Many things became clearer to me. Our conversations helped us both. I gave her facts, and she told me about the conceptions of Aslan David-ogly [the conspiratorial name which prisoners used when referring to Trotsky*—V. R.]."

The woman gave a start and brightened with some kind of inner light.

"You know that name? That means that Katia trusted you," she said with a sigh. "I will have to trust you too. You are going to Kolyma, and I am coming from there. Many of our people are there. They do not hide the fact that they are Trotskyists, and therefore I will ask you to tell them that they are taking me for a reinvestigation. This is very important for them." Only after this did Sokolovskaya say that she was Trotsky's first wife.

"I have ... a grandson from my older daughter," Sokolovskaya continued. "I was so worried about the boy! He is now fourteen years old. They say that he has been taken away too."

"Where? To prison? What a horrible childhood."

"In tsarist times they did not take away the children.... But this one—he wants to annihilate everyone. To the seventh generation. Liova resembles his

---

* In a number of Eastern languages "Aslan" means "lion."

grandfather and, like him, seems to be talented. What will happen to him?"

N. Gagen-Torn writes that Sokolovskaya told her "about things which I had never suspected, she spoke about Aslan David-ogly and—as if a cloth had wiped the exhaustion and old age from her face—she became young again. When she received my promise to tell about her fate to her friends, Sokolovskaya said:

"'From a Magadan camp they took me to "Vaska's house," and no one knows anything about me after that. And I do not know who else was taken. Who remains? It is important to know this, because they want to open a new case. I know that in the Magadan camp Lolo Bibneishvili remained behind, this is the wife of Lado. The same Lado who in tsarist times was renowned throughout Georgia. He was a most active Bolshevik.... So, tell Lolo that I have heard nothing at all about any of our other comrades. I don't feel bad, and I am in good spirits. After all, I am old, and they worry about me. I send greetings to my comrades, I believe in their courage and good spirits.... Tell them that there, abroad, Aslan David-ogly will be able to do many things.'

"She looked at me with radiant eyes, proud of her memories of him, of her love for him. And I, who had yet to understand the tribulations of old age, sat in silent wonder at this woman, and the glow of her reminiscences."[26]

In the camps the Trotskyists were divided into "those who had left" and "those who remained." The first included those who at the end of the 1920s and beginning of the 1930s had openly renounced their views and for the most part were returned to the party; the second included those who refused to declare that they were renouncing the Opposition, and therefore who remained in exile and in political prisons right up until 1936–1937, when they were transferred to the camps of harsh regime. Naturally, "those who remained" were faced with much more severe conditions in the camps. Hardly a single one of them survived the prison camp executions at the end of the 1930s. "If I had been a Trotskyist," writes V. Shalamov, "I would have been shot long ago, annihilated, but even temporary contact branded me for eternity. That is the degree to which Stalin feared (the Trotskyists)."[27]

It is a paradox that the Trotskyist-capitulators were sentenced in 1936 to still relatively short sentences. Much more severe sentences were given to people who fell under the article "KRTD" in 1937—the majority of whom had nothing to do with the Opposition in the past. A few "who had left" managed to be freed after serving their terms. Among them was A. S. Bertsinskaya, who with her husband, T. Sh. Askendarian, took an active part in establishing Soviet power in Azerbaidzhan. Belonging to the Opposition in the 1920s, in 1928 they were sent into exile in Minusinsk. After giving statements of capitulation, they were set free, but in August 1936 they were arrested once more and sentenced by a Special Board to five years in the camps. In Magadan they were placed in barracks along with Trotskyists "who remained." There representatives of both categories of prisoners waged a battle for the observance of the labor code concerning an eight-hour, and not the ten-hour, working day which had been established for prisoners. They fought for the observance of days off, which were completely canceled during the summer, and for other demands. On Sundays they were locked up for refusing to go to work.[28]

The spring of 1937 in Kolyma witnessed the beginning of camp trials involving those Trotskyists who had participated in hunger strikes and other forms of collective protest. The trial material in the "case of the political center of Trotskyists in Kolyma," aside from clearly fantastic charges ("preparing an armed uprising with the support of Japan and the USA," and so forth), contains characteristic excerpts from statements made by the defendants: "Chichinadze considers our entire land of the Soviets to be a concentration camp".... Shuklin said: "Now Stalin has no authority among the world proletariat because he is bloodthirsty and, in addition, is the most wretched figure.... Stalin wants to destroy all his opponents, intelligent people, the true leaders of the nation, people who according to their intellectual level are much higher than he is." Meshcherin said: "Who among the Old Bolsheviks is being arrested and shot at this time? It is clear that they want to destroy all the old leaders. After all, no one knew Stalin as a leader."[29]

Five of the defendants at this trial were sentenced to be shot, and the rest to ten years of imprisonment. But even after this the struggle of the Trotskyists against their executioners continued. In her memoirs Bertsinskaya tells about the fate of the Old Bolshevik Zakharian, who belonged to those who "were ferociously irreconcilable and steadfastly unbending." After she was transferred from the gold mine to Magadan, they took away her young son who had been with her. When in 1942 Bertsinskaya was told about the end of her sentence, she saw things in the camp warehouse which belonged to Zakharian and others "who remained," and who by this time had been shot.[30]

V. Shalamov writes about a "famous brigade" which was located at the Kolyma gold mine, "Partisan." This brigade, which included "Trotskyists who refused to work at all," conducted a number of hunger strikes in 1936. As a result, they received permission from Moscow not to work, while receiving the "productive" rather than the punitive ration. "Food was divided into four 'categories'—the camp used philosophical terminology in the most inappropriate places: 'Stakhanovite,' for fulfilling the norm by 130 percent and more—1,000 grams of bread; 'shock brigade,' for 100–130 percent—800 grams of bread; 'productive,' 90–100 percent—600 grams, and punitive—300 grams of bread. Those who refused to work when I was there were transferred to the punitive ration, bread and water. But that is not how it always was. A struggle unfolded in 1935 and 1936—and through a series of hunger strikes the Trotskyists at the 'Partisan' gold mine won the legitimate 600 grams. They were denied their 'stalls' and camp shop purchases, but they were not forced to work." On their own initiative they prepared wood for the whole camp. One night in 1937 they were all taken away to an investigatory prison. After this, no one ever saw a single one of them again.[31]

Recently published material from their investigation dossier tells about the further fate of the members of this brigade. Not a single one of them admitted any guilt, and four refused to reply to questions asked by the investigators. All fourteen defendants in this case were sentenced to be shot in September 1937. The group included a professor who directed a trust, a writer, and some workers, engineers, economists and teachers.[32]

N. I. Gagen-Torn tells how by 1939 in Kolyma she witnessed the disappearance of all her "friend-opponents, who adhered to the sacred belief that 'the idea of communism which was flouted and discredited by Stalin would have to be reborn with our blood.' And they willingly gave this blood. I had an immeasurable respect for the Russian intelligentsia's tradition of sacrifice which was embodied in them."[33]

There were even more Trotskyists in the Vorkuta camps than in Kolyma. Here, too, they were the only group of prisoners who offered organized resistance.

The Nikolaevsky collection contains no few memoirs of former camp prisoners on the events which later became known as the Vorkuta tragedy. Its beginning is vividly described in the memoirs of A. Rakhalov. He says that until 1936 the majority of Trotskyists who had not capitulated were still in exile, where they carried with them their small libraries and theoretical works that contradicted the "general line." Their children lived with them and went to schools where "often they heard the conversations conducted by their teachers about the happy childhood of Soviet children under the Stalinist sun, and about the difficult but successful war being waged by their leader against the enemies of the people (this of course meant their parents). Their 'leprous' parents quickly tired of the poison which was being given to their children in massive doses at school, and withdrew them in order to turn them into 'simply literate people' at home."

In 1936, the Trotskyists in exile together with their families were loaded into railway cars and sent to Arkhangelsk. From there they were sent to the arctic Vorkuta, where the prisoners learned that in their sentences the word, "exile" had mechanically been replaced with the word "camp." As a result, they were turned from "administrative exiles" into prisoners. Moreover, an additional five years was added to their previous sentences without any explanation.

"This was the beginning of the tragedy.

"The food supplies which they had were quickly exhausted, and the prisoner's ration was far from adequate for them to feel satisfied even for fifteen minutes. The children did not ask for an extra crust of bread. They understood that their fate was bound up completely with the fate of their parents."

Among this group of prisoners was Sergei Sedov; Poznansky, Trotsky's former secretary; V. Kosior, the former head of the oil industry (his brother was S. Kosior, a member of the Politburo); and "a whole pleiade of former prominent party leaders, beginning with the secretaries of area committees ... and ending with the secretaries of regional committees, Gosplan officials and members of other organizations."

As the author of the memoirs notes, "the mood of those who had arrived [in Vorkuta] was far from despondent, but, on the contrary, keen-spirited, energetic and ... angry." The arrival of Oppositionists in Vorkuta coincided with the discussion of the draft of "the Stalin constitution." The Trotskyists subjected it to a withering criticism, and one of them, after listening to a radio broadcast, "calmly summed things up: everything is clear, comrades—this is not a Stalinist constitution but Stalinist prostitution."

"The Trotskyists undoubtedly had great experience in revolutionary battles and, thanks to this, were able to close their ranks, working cordially and courageously, and they were able to take certain measures of caution in their work and struggle." When the author of the memoirs advised V. Kosior "to reconcile himself to his fate and to save his strength for serving out his prison sentence," insofar as "no actions of protest would help," Kosior replied: "In a certain sense you are right. But do not forget that we are not a band of criminals and we are not accidental political criminals, we are opponents of Stalin's policies and we desire only the best for our country.... If our situation is indeed wretched, then we at least want to know what Moscow thinks about it. Today we are justified in assuming that the local Chekists are displaying their own initiative when they violate our most elementary rights, even as prisoners, and we want to know Moscow's opinion about this—then much will become clear for us."

In October 1936, the culminating point in the Vorkuta tragedy began to unfold—all the Trotskyists who were in the surrounding camps declared a hunger strike.

The hunger strikers demanded an open trial (the majority of them had received camp sentences in absentia, determined by a Special Board), the release of their wives and children, with the right to freely choose their place of residency, the transfer of the elderly and of invalids from polar regions to regions with a less severe climate, the separation of political prisoners from criminals, and the establishment of the same food for all prisoners regardless of fulfilling quotas.

All the memoirs mention one and the same length of the hunger strike—an unprecedented one hundred thirty-two days. More than a thousand prisoners participated in it, and several people died. Soon the participants in the hunger strike were taken from all the camp sites to a settlement that was several dozen kilometers from the mine. But even from there, the rest of the prisoners began to receive information that the hunger strike was continuing and that the Trotskyists had no intention of giving in. "Not even the free employees at the camps dared to express their hatred for the 'insulting behavior of the damned counterrevolutionaries,' since evidently the tragedy of the starving people found some kind of response in their hearts.... The Chekists took all measures to prevent this hunger strike from becoming the object of world public opinion and the press."[34] In the spring of 1937, on orders from Moscow, the hunger strikers were told that their demands would be met. They were all sent to the "Brick Factory," a former site for special punishment, where in the fall of 1937, mass shootings of the prisoners began.

45. "The Bureaucracy Is Terrorized"

T HE OPPONENTS of Stalinism were not limited to the camp population. Their numbers grew steadily outside the camps as well.

In stimulating the relentless publication of articles about ever newer "exposed Trotskyists," Stalin was not embarrassed by the fact that the abundance of such articles created the impression that a huge number of people supported the thoroughly reviled Trotsky. His main goal was to arouse horror at the scale of the conspiratorial activity headed by Trotsky and at the monstrosity of the crimes committed by the participants in this all-embracing conspiracy.

However, when they observed that ever newer faces were falling out of the ruling wagon, simple people could not help but ask themselves: Who is ruling us? Why have people who fought for Soviet power and were its favorites until yesterday suddenly turned into serious criminals?

Despite the inescapable victimization which would follow the slightest expression of doubt over the correctness of the repression, indignant voices of protest still resounded even at party meetings. In her memoirs, O. Adamova-Sliozberg tells about her encounter in a prison cell with a textile worker from Ivanovo, the Old Bolshevik and participant in the civil war O. I. Nikitina, who had worked for thirty-five years in the mills. Nikitina received ten years because, with the directness that was one of her traits, she declared at a meeting: "'You say that they are all traitors. What, does that mean that Lenin was blind, that he did not see the people who lived all around him?' And here she was, sitting for days on end, whispering to herself, trying to convince herself that she had done the right thing."[1]

Even when it came to Trotsky, who for many years had been portrayed by the official propaganda as the leader of the "vanguard of the counterrevolutionary bourgeoisie," words of sympathy and respect were spoken in public more often than might be expected. Thus Kozlov, a student at the industrial workers' training program in Rostov-on-the-Don, said at a combined party and Komsomol meeting: "Trotsky made colossal contributions to our country ... he was one of the most popular leaders of the revolution." In spite of demands by the "organs," assistant prosecutor Startsev refused to sanction Kozlov's arrest for his statement, declaring, "After all, Trotsky did occupy the positions which Kozlov said at the meeting."[2]

Similar, even though scattered, voices of protest prompted Stalin to gradually widen the circle of those being persecuted. In planning the show trials, he apparently did not foresee the consequences that they would entail. His primary political goal was to exterminate his most hated opponents and strike a fatal blow against the Fourth International. However he did not calculate the force of the blow. In explaining the inner logic of the subsequent repression, Trotsky wrote: "Stalin's unbroken successes [in the fight against the inner-party oppositions—V. R.], beginning in 1923, gradually led him to conclude that he could deceive or do violence to the historical process. The Moscow Trials are the highpoint of this policy of deception and violence. In addition ... each new deception requires a double deception in order to be successful; each act of violence widens the radius of necessary violence.... The world is struck not so much by the strength of his will and inflexibility, as by his meager intellectual resources and political capabilities. One can neither deceive nor do violence against the historical process. The trials apparently staggered the entire bureaucracy, with the exception of an insignificant group of initiates. No one understood why these trials were needed, no one believed that the threat from the Opposition was so great."[3]

Confirmation of these words can be found in the informers' reports which are preserved in the party archives. In Kolomna, Sominsky, a member of the party since 1918, made statements at a party study circle "in which he defended enemies of the people, expressed sympathy for them, praised their activity and compared unfavorably the present leadership of Stalin to that of Lenin." In the same Kolomna, a worker at the steel mill declared, "Trotskyists and Bukharinists are not the bad people they are being made out to be." The chauffeur Pavlov in Zaporozhets called the Trotskyists "meritorious revolutionaries." In discussions with his comrades, a worker at the Zaporozhets alcoholic beverage plant who was a candidate member of the party, said, "I feel very sorry for such people as Kamenev and Zinoviev, innocent people who are suffering." During interrogations at the NKVD he confirmed these words and added, "No one has forbidden me from feeling sorry for anybody: you feel sorry for them, and we will feel sorry for someone else."[4]

Chetkin, a member of the VKP(b) since 1919, was expelled from the party because he "conducted clearly Trotskyist conversations about the case of the defendants Zinoviev and Kamenev, denigrating the concluding indictment speech made by the prosecutor of the USSR." The same fate befell Tydman, a Moscow engineer and member of the party from 1917, who at a meeting devoted to the Zinoviev and Kamenev trial "delivered a clearly counterrevolutionary speech, praising these bandits and emphasizing their positive role in the revolution."[5]

Analogous moods found expression not only in the cities, but also in rural areas. The reports of NKVD officials in the Voronezh area tell that in one of the collective farms the following statements were made: "Zinoviev and Kamenev were prominent people and enjoyed the respect of the people, they would have been elected to the government if there was secret balloting, but to prevent this from happening, the authorities shot them." "It's a pity that they shot the Zinovievists. In new elections we would have voted for them."[6] In one of the agricultural regions of the Kursk area the tractor operator Korobov was expelled from the party because at a meeting devoted to the results of the Trial of the Sixteen, he declared: "Trotsky had accomplishments which should go into the encyclopedia, whereas these events should be seen as a falling out between members of the Central Committee."[7]

These facts, selectively taken from just a few regions (and they could be multiplied easily using only published materials) show convincingly the absence of any universal "blindness" or "silence." The dissident statements, as we would call them today, came not only from the milieu of rank-and-file communists, but people who enjoyed widespread fame in the party and the country dared to make them as well. In his book *The Campfire's Glow*, Yuri Trifonov introduces the story told by the Old Bolshevik Nakoriakov about a speech given by A. A. Solts, who for more than ten years had worked as a member of the Presidium of the Central Control Commission, and in 1937 occupied the post of assistant to the prosecutor of the USSR in the trial sector. At a meeting of regional party activists in Moscow, Solts sharply criticized Vyshinsky's activity and demanded that a commission be created to investigate it. "Part of the audience froze in horror, but the majority began to shout: 'Down with him! Get him off the tribune!! A wolf in sheep's clothing!' Solts continued speaking. Some volunteers, seized with rage, ran up to the old man and dragged him from the podium."[8] Solts's subsequent fate differed somewhat from the fate of his colleagues and comrades. He was hidden away in an insane asylum and, after being released, remained in a state of deep depression until his death in 1945.

The show trials aroused the greatest anxiety among the bureaucrats who stood closest of all to their victims. Previously, bureaucrats who were loyal to the "general line" could be sure not only of their personal security, but of preserving their posts and privileges. Now, however, Stalin was "probing the living tissues of the ruling elite with his knife. The bureaucracy became frightened and terrorized. For the first time it was seeing Stalin not as the first among equals, but as an Asiatic despot, a Genghis Khan, as Bukharin had once called him. Under the influence of the tremor which he himself had initiated, Stalin became convinced that he was by no means an unquestionable authority for the entire layer of the party and Soviet bureaucracy (which remembers his past and for this reason alone is incapable of yielding to the hypnosis). Around his own circle, Stalin has been forced to take his knife and draw another concentric circle with a large radius. Fear and horror grew along with the number of lives which have been touched and the interests which have been threatened. In the old elite, no one believed the charges, and under the influence of the terrible shock, they all began talking about this with each other."[9]

Of course, such conversations were held in private, as a rule, or in an intimate circle of friends who were bound together by bonds of mutual trust. But there were exceptions. N. Zaporozhets recalls an episode which occurred in the summer of 1937 at a rest home for party activists. During lunch, P. I. Smorodin, the second secretary of the Leningrad area committee, who had been a legendary leader of the Komsomol, turned to those sitting at the table: "Don't you think it is time that we began thinking about what is happening in our country? We have to act before they take us all one at a time, like chickens from their roost!" At first everyone was stunned, and then they hurriedly began to leave. The only one left with Smorodin was his old friend, P. F. Dorofeev (the stepfather of Natalia Zaporozhets).[10]

Even Stalin's closest stooges had to encounter expressions of concern, however timid or indirect, about the trials. Khrushchev recalls how he witnessed a remarkable conversation between Demian Bedny, Kaganovich, and Ordzhonikidze. The poet was admitting that he simply couldn't write any verses about the Trial of the Sixteen: "I cannot, I simply cannot. I have tried as hard as I can, but I am unable to do it. It's like an attack of sexual impotence when I begin to think about them." Although Demian Bedny soon "mastered" himself and wrote no small amount of repulsive doggerel filled with condemnation of the trials' victims, many of whom he had been close to personally in the past, this conversation is symptomatic. No less symptomatic is Khrushchev's reaction at the time to the poet's words: "I was struck by such candor. This means that he retained some degree of sympathy for those who were on the defendants' bench."[11]

In order to reduce such inclinations to a minimum, and even more so their public expression, Stalin subjected each bureaucrat to a daily "loyalty test." Krivitsky, who left the Soviet Union in the summer of 1937, told Leon Sedov: "As for the struggle against Trotskyism, I will tell you only one thing. One gets the impression that Stalin thinks about nothing else, that for him no other questions even exist.... When some other question or problem does arise, people approach it primarily from the standpoint of the struggle against Trotskyism. Whether a person is doing his work poorly or well—is not important. What is important is whether or not he is fighting against Trotskyism. If you give a report on a serious question, you notice that almost no one is listening to you. Toward the end, they ask: And as for the Trotskyists, how are you managing there?"[12] The only satisfactory answer to this "cardinal" question could be a series of denunciations of one's co-workers, subordinates or superiors.

In characterizing what was new in Soviet life after the first show trials, Trotsky wrote: "Before 1936, Stalin simply violated the conscience of people by forcing them to say what they were not thinking. Beginning with 1936, he openly began to play games with the heads of his colleagues. A new period opened up! With the assistance of the bureaucracy, Stalin crushed the people; now he is terrorizing the bureaucracy itself.... Stalin's closest colleagues are exchanging glances, silently asking each other: Whose turn will it be tomorrow?"[13]

After the first two Moscow Trials, a final separation could be noted between Stalin and that section of the party which retained its loyalty to the traditions of Bolshevism and the October Revolution. The danger for Stalin began to come not only from the irreconcilable Oppositionists, and not only from the participants of the former oppositions who had capitulated, but from all the Old Bolsheviks, with the exception of a few people who belonged to his inner circle. "The old guard," wrote Trotsky in June 1937, "has long since been liquidated *politically*. Its *physical* extermination is now being carried out in true Stalinist fashion, combining sadistic bestiality with bureaucratic pedantry." The relative ease with which this destruction was being accomplished was due to the fact that "the bureaucracy has lost control over its own reflex mechanisms and means of self-defense. The new forms of persecution, which transgress all bounds of the comprehensible, are forced upon it by the progression of the old forms of persecution."[14]

If the bureaucracy, which had long ago entrusted all the decisive levers of power to Stalin, had lost control over its self-defense reflexes, (which, it would seem, should have stimulated resistance to the course aimed at its total annihilation), then Stalin still preserved an amazing degree of self-control during the bacchanalia of the Great Terror. He unleashed the Great Terror without grasping the scale on which it would unfold in the future. But the unrest which arose in the circles of the bureaucracy forced him to discard from the ruling elite not only the participants in the former oppositions and the basic core of Old Bolsheviks in general, i.e., the generation of fifty-year-olds, but also the younger generation which for the most part had not participated in the oppositions of the 1920s. After the reprisals against the old party guard, wrote Trotsky, "the mauser of the GPU is aimed at the next generation, which began its ascension with the civil war.... Thousands and thousands of functionaries and commanders who came from Bolshevism or who joined Bolshevism have supported Stalin until recent times not out of fear, but according to their conscience. But the latest events have awakened in them a fear for the fate of the regime and for their own personal fate. Those who helped Stalin rise to the top are proving to be ever more ill-suited for the job of supporting him at such dizzying heights. Stalin is forced to reforge the weapons of his rule ever more frequently."[15]

The generation of forty-year-olds—people who were at the zenith of their physical and intellectual powers—was capable of actively opposing Stalinism to a greater degree than the former members of the oppositions who were demoralized after retreating for many years from their own convictions. As Trotsky emphasized, "the verification of the forty-year-olds, i.e., the generation which helped Stalin to deal with the old guard, is assuming a systematic character. We are no longer talking about accidental figures, but about stars of the second magnitude." The verification of this "intermediate formation" showed Stalin that "the upper echelon of the privileged elite is headed by people who are still not entirely free of the traditions of Bolshevism." Stalin therefore cannot help but fear that "from the milieu of the bureaucracy itself and particularly the army, opposition will arise to his dictatorial plans. This means that ...

Stalin will try to destroy the best elements of the state apparatus."[16]

Among the generation of forty-year-olds, the greatest threat to Stalin came from the leaders of the Red Army, which, according to Leopold Trepper, was "the last bastion to be removed; it alone still eluded his control."[17] Because of their functional nature, the general staff and officer corps were highly organized and possessed the material resources for active resistance to Stalin. Hopes for such resistance were deeply rooted in the consciousness of many Old Bolsheviks. As M. V. Raskolnikova-Kanivets recalled: "Raskolnikov was amazed that the Red Army, with its marshals and generals, had not reacted to this bloody 'purge.' At that time Fedya still hoped that within the USSR resistance would finally be found."[18]

All Soviet and foreign historians who have written about 1937 agree that such resistance did not exist in the USSR, and that the total destruction of the Soviet general staff was prompted by Stalin's notorious and unfounded suspiciousness. The "conspiracy of the generals" is one of the most dramatic and enigmatic pages in the history of the Great Terror. In examining it I will therefore resort to historical hypotheses more often than I did in the previous sections of the book. I hope that further archival research will allow us to more fully explain one of the most essential questions which arises in the course of analyzing the events of 1937: Was there in this year an anti-Stalinist military-political conspiracy?

46. Reasons for Reprisals against the Generals

EVEN IF WE SET ASIDE the version of the existence of a military conspiracy which will be examined below, it is not difficult to see that Stalin had very serious grounds for conducting a purge of the army's commanding staff.

First of all, the Red Army was a powerful material force, and its commanders felt more self-confident and independent of Stalin's dictates than people in the civilian sectors. Officials in the military circles, as Krivitsky stressed, "lived outside that special party world in which people were forever 'deviating' from the correct Stalinist course, 'recanting,' 'deviating,' again and again 'recanting,' each time with increasing penalties and with a progressive breakdown of the will. The job of the generals, the building of a powerful army and system of national defense, had preserved their morale. Stalin knew that Tukhachevsky, Gamarnik, Yakir, Uborevich and the other ranking generals could never be broken into the state of unquestioning obedience which he now required of all those about him. They were men of great personal courage."[1]

Second, the commanding staff of the army contained thousands of people who had served in 1918–1924 under Trotsky's leadership. Among the army communists were a great number of people who had sided in 1923–1927 with the Left Opposition. At the February-March Plenum Voroshilov said: "By 1923–1924, the Trotskyists had on their side, as you recall, and you should recall, almost all Moscow and the military academy as a whole, with the exception of a few individuals.... And the school of the Central Executive Committee here, and the various schools for the infantry, artillery and other parts of the Moscow garrison—all of them were for Trotsky (*Gamarnik*: And the headquarters of the Moscow Military District, where Muralov was located, was for Trotsky)."[2]

In February 1937, Shchadenko, the head of the Frunze Military Academy, reported to Gamarnik that in the discussion of 1923 the majority of the communists at the academy "adopted Trotskyist positions." At that time forty-eight people voted for the resolution of the Central Committee, and two hundred four for the resolution of the Opposition.[3]

Of course, the repression of the preceding years had not passed by the army. At the beginning of the 1930s, several thousand former tsarist officers were discharged. Some of them were arrested and condemned on false charges of conspiratorial activity.

At the February-March Plenum, Voroshilov declared: "Without great fanfare, which was unnecessary, we threw out a large number of unsuitable elements, including Trotskyist-Zinovievist rabble, and every type of suspicious scum. In the time since 1924 ... we purged from the army a great number of people from the command and supervisory staff. Do not be frightened by the figure which I will give, because this includes not only enemies, but also people who were simply useless, and some good people whom we had to retire [apparently due to age or for health reasons—V. R.], but then again there were very many enemies too. In the course of these twelve to thirteen years we purged approximately forty-seven thousand people." In 1934–1936 alone, said Voroshilov, "we threw out of the army for various reasons, but mainly because they were worthless and politically unreliable, around twenty-two thousand people, out of whom five thousand were tossed out as oppositionists and as low quality elements of various kinds in a political sense."[4]

Although the percentage of expelled army communists in 1933–1935 was lower than in civilian departments, in absolute numbers those expelled amounted to three thousand three hundred twenty-eight people, of whom five hundred fifty-five were purged "for Trotskyism and forming counterrevolutionary groups." Among these five hundred fifty-five, four hundred were immediately discharged from the army.

Nevertheless, the high command remained basically the same which it had been since the end of the Civil War. Of course, such prominent Trotskyists as Mrachkovsky and Muralov were driven out of the army. However, many oppositionists who had submitted statements of capitulation remained in high positions right up until the middle of 1936. At the time of the February-March Plenum, according to Voroshilov, the army still contained seven hundred former Trotskyists, Zinovievists and Right Oppositionists—people with party cards or who had been expelled from the party, but whom "commissions at various times felt could be left in the army."[5]

Third, the commanders and political personnel to a certain degree reflected the dissatisfaction of the peasantry, from whom the rank-and-file soldiers in the army were largely drawn. As Krivitsky emphasized, at every period critical for Stalin, i.e., "during forcible collectivization, hunger, and rebellion, the generals had supported him reluctantly, had put difficulties in his path, had forced deals upon him."[6] At certain moments even Voroshilov had taken such a position; once, along with Tukhachevsky and Gamarnik, he declared at a session of the Politburo that it would be necessary to ease the repression in the villages in order to preserve the army's reliability.

Trotsky assumed that a link existed between the leaders of the Right Opposition and the highest military commanders, even if it only took the form of political sympathy. He felt that the differences between the military leaders and Stalin over questions of domestic policy had sharpened after 1932, when the consequences of forced collectivization assumed a particularly ominous character.[7]

Fourth, differences arose in the 1930s and deepened over the years between Stalin and the generals grouped around Tukhachevsky over Soviet military doctrine. Stalin and Voroshilov made superficial and boastful statements about conducting a future war exclusively on enemy soil and with little bloodshed. Tukhachevsky counterposed a conception of a wide-scale military conflict into which the Soviet Union would inevitably be drawn. Making a realistic assessment of the scale of Germany's rearmament, he declared at one of the higher government forums that he was fully convinced of the possibility that war might unfold on the territory of the USSR.

Unlike Stalin, who tried after Hitler came to power to establish an alliance with the "superpower" which he considered Germany to be, Tukhachevsky maintained a firm antifascist orientation. On 31 March 1935, *Pravda* published Tukhachevsky's article, "The Military Plans of Today's Germany." The manuscript of the article had been edited by Stalin, who softened a number of formulations in it about the anti-Soviet character of Hitler's military preparations. Nevertheless, Tukhachevsky's article provoked sharp dissatisfaction in German governmental and military circles. On 4 April the German ambassador, Schulenberg, told Litvinov about their negative reaction to this article. On the same day Hartman, the German military attache in Moscow, told Gekker, the head of the Foreign Relations Department of the General Staff of the RKKA [Red Army], that "he had been instructed to report the negative effect which Tukhachevsky's article had made on the commanding staff of the Reichswehr."[8]

Several of Tukhachevsky's biographers have turned to Lidiia Nord's book, *Marshal M. N. Tukhachevsky*, which was first published in 1950 in the Russian émigré press. It has not yet been established who lurks behind this pseudonym. The author of the book, who calls herself the widow of one of Tukhachevsky's associates, displays undoubted familiarity with many details of the latter's life. Although the book contains quite a few obvious fabrications, some of its passages are unquestionably interesting. This relates most of all to the account of Tukhachevsky's attitude toward Stalin's "Germanophilia." According to Nord, in the circle of his close friends, Tukhachevsky said: "Now I see that Stalin is a secret, but fanatical, admirer of Hitler. I am not joking.... Hitler would only have to make a step in Stalin's direction, and our leader would throw himself with open arms at the fascist. Yesterday when we were speaking privately, Stalin justified Hitler's repressions against the Jews by saying that Hitler was clearing the path of everything that prevented him from obtaining his goal, and that from the standpoint of his ideas, Hitler was right. Hitler's successes impress Iosif Vissarionovich too much, and if you look closely, you will see that he copies the Führer in many ways.... And what is even sadder, there are people who, instead of putting him in his place, look at him with rapture and hang on his every word as if they expected to hear brilliant thoughts."[9]

The differences between Stalin and the group around Tukhachevsky also involved questions of the modernization and mechanization of the armed forces, the role of the cavalry and motorized units in a future war. In 1930, a sharp conflict arose between Tukhachevsky, on the one hand, and Stalin-Voroshilov, on the other, when Tukhachevsky proposed to significantly increase the size of the army and to outfit it with tanks, artillery and airplanes. Tukhachevsky apparently sent a note with these proposals first to Ordzhonikidze, who then passed it on to Stalin with the comment: "Soso. Read this document. Sergo."[10] At the same time, this note was sent to Stalin by Voroshilov, who added to it his own condemnation of Tukhachevsky's "radicalism." In a letter of reply to Voroshilov, Stalin severely sharpened this evaluation. "I think," he wrote, "that the 'plan' of comrade Tukhachevsky is the result of a fashionable enthusiasm for 'left' phraseology, the result of an enthusiasm for bureaucratic and paper maximalism.... To 'realize' such a plan would certainly mean to destroy both the country's economy and its army. It would be worse than any counterrevolution."[11]

After Voroshilov read this letter aloud at a session of the Military Council, Tukhachevsky sent a letter to Stalin in which he said that such an assessment of his proposals would absolutely exclude in the future his "possibility of broadly discussing a number of questions concerning the development of our defense capability." Only after a prolonged silence did Stalin in May 1932 send a letter to Tukhachevsky acknowledging the correctness of the general's position and the error of his own reaction to it. "Now," wrote Stalin, " ... when several vague questions have become clearer to me, I must admit that my evaluation was too sharp, and the conclusions of my letter were not entirely correct.... It seems to me that my letter to Comrade Voroshilov would not have been so sharp in tone, and it would have been free of several incorrect conclusions with regard to you, if I had placed the debate at that time on a new foundation. But I did not do this since, apparently, the problem was not yet clear enough for me. Don't be angry with me because I have decided to correct the shortcomings of my letter after a certain period of delay."[12] It may well be that this is the only instance when Stalin not only admitted the erroneous nature of his position, but virtually asked forgiveness from the person he had defamed and insulted.

Nevertheless, during the 1937 trial of Tukhachevsky and the other defendants, the conceptions of accelerating the formation of tank units at the cost of reducing the cavalry and the budget for it were considered to be a wrecking operation.

Fifth, Tukhachevsky and the generals close to him most fully expressed the dissatisfaction of the general staff with the limitations and incompetence of Voroshilov and the persons close to him, primarily members of the former First Cavalry. They were dissatisfied with the arbitrary and group spirit displayed by Voroshilov's supporters, which had such a destructive influence on the quality of the Soviet armed forces. The degree of this dissatisfaction can be seen in the diary entry written on 15 March 1937 by Kutiakov, a Civil War hero who, after Chapaev's death, had led his division: "As long as 'the iron-man' stands at the helm, there will be disorder and toadyism; everything stupid will be honored, and everything intelligent will be denigrated."[13]

Tukhachevsky and the generals close to him expressed similar views, although in not such sharp form, even in Stalin's presence. On 1 June 1937, in a report to the session of the Military Council, Voroshilov said: "The fact that these people—Tukhachevsky, Yakir, Uborevich and a number of others—were close to each other, this we knew, this was no secret.... Last year, in May, at my apartment, Tukhachevsky accused me and Budenny, in the presence of Comrades Stalin, Molotov and many others, of gathering around ourselves a small group of people with whom I conducted and directed all policy, and so forth.

Tukhachevsky
speaking at
the Seventh
Congress
of Soviets

Comrade Stalin said at that time that there had to be an end to personal squabbles, and that we must convene a session of the Politburo at which we would investigate this matter in detail. And at such a session we looked into all these questions, and once again arrived at the same result.

Stalin: He withdrew his accusations.

Voroshilov: Yes, he withdrew them, although the Yakir and Uborevich group behaved themselves rather aggressively at the session when it came to me. Uborevich kept quiet, but Gamarnik and Yakir behaved very badly toward me."[14]

Only members of the military at that time could allow themselves such sharply critical statements about one of Stalin's closest associates, who was, moreover, their immediate boss.

Another indication of the sharp conflict between Voroshilov and the Tukhachevsky group is a letter from Uborevich to Ordzhonikidze, the sole member of Stalin's Politburo to whom the military leaders could appeal. In this letter, written 17 August 1936, Uborevich states: "Voroshilov does not consider me capable of carrying out major military or state work.... I must say that he has an even lower estimation of Tukhachevsky. In my opinion, Tukhachevsky has lost much of his former capacity for work because of these blows and assessments.... If Comrade Voroshilov considers me a commander who is little suited for major work, then I must speak very sharply both to his face and in

his absence about his views concerning the most important contemporary problems of war."[15]

At the trial of 1937, the defendants confessed that they held discussions
among themselves about the need to remove Voroshilov from leadership of
the army.

Sixth, Stalin could not help but feel alarmed at the genuine prestige and
respect which the leading officers had won among the people. As Krivitsky
stressed, even during the last years of collectivization, when Stalin's authority
was lower than ever before, "these generals, especially Tukhachevsky, had enjoyed enormous popularity not only with the officers corps and the rank and
file of the army, but with the people."[16] Such extraordinary recognition remained
with them even in the years to follow. In describing Tukhachevsky's speech at
the Seventh Congress of Soviets in 1935, A. Barmine, a "non-returnee" who was
close to Soviet military circles, noted: "When Tukhachevsky appeared on the
platform, the whole room rose to its feet and greeted him with a storm of applause. The ovation was marked out from all others by its force and sincerity."
In commenting on this account, Trotsky wrote: "Stalin undoubtedly distinguished well the tone of this ovation, he noted it and remembered Tukhachevsky
a few years later."[17]

At the trial of the "Right-Trotskyist Bloc," Bukharin declared that in the
milieu of "conspirators" he called Tukhachevsky "a potential 'little Napoleon,'"
because he feared his Bonapartist inclinations. In discussing this topic, A. M.
Larina notes that she learned from Bukharin that Stalin had called
Tukhachevsky a "little Napoleon" in a conversation with Bukharin. The latter
had then persuaded Stalin that Tukhachevsky had no desire whatsoever to
take power.[18]

Seventh, the officers of the Red Army knew better than anyone else the
true value of Stalin's "exploits" during the Civil War, which were becoming the
subject of ever louder claims in the official press. This propaganda campaign
was initiated essentially by Stalin himself. At a session of the Politburo and the
Presidium of the Central Control Commission in September 1927, in response
to Trotsky's criticism of his many mistakes during the Civil War years, Stalin
declared: "There are a number of documents, and this the entire party knows,
showing that the Central Committee sent Stalin from front to front for three
years, going to the south, the east, the north and west, whenever things became difficult at the front."[19] This boastful self-characterization was para-

First Marshals
of the Soviet
Union, 1935;
seated:
Tukhachevsky,
Voroshilov,
Yegorov;
standing;
Budenny,
Bliukher

phrased and amplified by Voroshilov in his obsequious article, "Stalin and the
Red Army," where he states that Stalin "was, perhaps, the sole person whom
the Central Committee sent from one military front to another, choosing places
that were the most dangerous and the most troublesome for the revolution."[20]

Certain memories could not be blotted out of the consciousness of the
Soviet military leaders. Despite the officially cultivated version about the "heroic" role of Stalin and Voroshilov in battles around Tsaritsyn, the generals
knew that the Central Committee had removed them from the Military Council of the Southern Front, and then recalled them from Tsaritsyn because of
their arbitrariness, insistence on partisan warfare, and refusal to reckon with
the decisions of the Central Committee and to subordinate themselves to the
Revolutionary Military Council of the Republic.

Right until the middle of the 1930s a subject of unceasing discussion in
military circles was the question of the reasons behind the defeat of the Red
Army in the Polish campaign of 1920. The participants in the campaign knew
well that Stalin, who occupied the post at that time of member of the Military
Council of the Southwestern Front, refused to carry out the decision of the
Central Committee and the directive coming from the Commander-in-Chief
to send the First Cavalry and the Twelfth Army to assist the Western Front,
headed by Tukhachevsky, who was launching an offensive against Warsaw.

This was one of the main reasons for the disruption of the offensive and the failure of the entire Polish campaign. Starting in 1923, a whole series of works on military history were published which were devoted to this chapter of the Civil War. In several of them, for instance in *Lvov-Warsaw*, the book by Yegorov, the former commander of the Southwestern Front, blame for the defeat of the Red Army was placed on Tukhachevsky. Similar arguments were presented during the discussion of the Soviet-Polish War which occurred in 1930. During this discussion one of the speakers declared: "In general, Tukhachevsky should have been hanged for 1920."[21]

In other works, including the third volume of the *History of the Civil War*, the analysis of the reasons for the defeat of the Red Army mentioned errors by the commanders of the Southwestern front (Yegorov and Stalin). The last of the works to objectively examine the history of the Polish campaign was the book by Kutiakov, *Kiev Cannae*, which was written in 1935. In diary entries for the end of 1936 and the beginning of 1937, Kutiakov wrote about the inevitable reprisals which would befall him for this book: "My *Cannae of 1920* is a noose around my neck; it will destroy me at the first opportune moment. That means I must be prepared for this." "*Cannae* was written with my blood, and then with my entire heart; despite this, both in the past and now, it has brought me and will bring me nothing but terrible misfortune."[22]

At a session of the Military Council on 2 June 1937, Stalin burst into a stream of coarse abuse directed at Kutiakov, calling his book "a rotten thing," the goal of which was to "expose the Red Cavalry." In passing, Stalin berated Sediakin, a commander of the second rank, for having written a preface to this book which "aroused doubt and even suspicion."[23]

As we can see, Stalin had plenty of reasons for harboring distrust and hostility toward the Soviet general staff.

We must also add that provocative versions about the intentions of the Soviet military leaders to overthrow Stalin were constantly being fabricated in foreign and émigré circles. In the creation of these scenarios, which were designed to continuously arouse Stalin's suspicions, no small contribution was made by *Red Marshals*, the book published in 1932 by the White émigré writer, Roman Goul (the sketch devoted to Tukhachevsky in this book had first been published a bit earlier). With his lively pen, Goul claimed that the "big shots" in the Red Army were "freeing themselves from the control of the party apparatus. I think that it is correct to say that the replacements for the terrorist-communist dictatorship will emerge from a group of military leaders in the Red Army, which will rest mainly upon the peasantry."[24]

In Goul's book, which is an amazing mixture of genuine facts and the author's overactive imagination, candidates for the "liquidation of the communist dictatorship" were declared to be Tukhachevsky and Bliukher. In addition, Goul called Tukhachevsky a protégé of Trotsky, and claimed that the general was completely obliged to the latter for his promotion in the services. Even more fantastic was Bliukher's biography as it was presented by Goul. The author called the official Soviet facts about Bliukher "falsified," and juxtaposed to them his own version of Bliukher's secret life. He called the general a "soldier living under a pseudonym," "a name he had borrowed for himself from the man who conquered Napoleon at Waterloo." The book offers conflicting accounts from the foreign and emigre press, including such pearls as: "Bliukher speaks with a strong German accent," "Bliukher is a German officer who became a prisoner of war; he is the former right-hand man of Colonel Bauer," "Bliukher is a well-groomed man with polished nails," and so forth.[25]

After praising Bliukher's military successes in the civil war in China, where Bliukher worked in the mid-1920s as a military advisor to the Kuomintang, Goul then goes on to provide a provocative story about Bliukher's ties to the leaders of the so-called "Right-Left Bloc" who had been driven from their posts in 1930. Demonstrating a knowledge of certain actual circumstances surrounding the activity of this oppositional group, Goul turns it into a "conspiracy" which proceeded under the "darkest conspiratorial cover" and had as its goal the organization of a "palace coup." He announces that the "conspirators" had even drawn up a list of the new government, in which Bliukher would become Commissar of War. After Stalin uncovered this "conspiracy," as Goul assures us, Bliukher remained at his post only as a result of Voroshilov's protection. "Such people, like Marshal Bliukher, who came out of nowhere but has firmly gone down in Russian history," the author writes in concluding his narrative, "make people take note of them if they do not die."[26]

To the "unreliable" Tukhachevsky and Bliukher, the wily White-émigré scribbler counterposed Voroshilov, by clearly exaggerating his military exploits to please Stalin. Knowing Stalin's special attitude toward the First Cavalry, Goul stated that "the First Cavalry under Budenny played the decisive role in the victory of the Reds over the Whites in the Civil War." Voroshilov was the political commissar in the First Cavalry. According to Goul, this army had nothing

in common with the communist spirit: "with a truly nationalistic, patently anticommunist Cossack and peasant force of the steppes, Voroshilov routed the
armies of the White generals which were considered to be nationalistic."

Calling Voroshilov "truly the *first* marshal of the republic," Goul hinted
that he was the only Soviet military leader who presented no threat to Stalin.
"Voroshilov might 'grapple' with Stalin in Politburo debates, pound his fist on
the table and raise a ruckus. But Stalin, who is a master of Machiavellian combinations, is able to pacify Voroshilov, despite all the noise and his pounding
on the table."[27]

Similar writings by the opponents of the Soviet regime had an unmistakable influence on Stalin. Voroshilov and his cohorts in the First Cavalry were
the only commanders from the Civil War who survived the Great Terror. They
were the ones who were placed by Stalin at the head of the Red Army in the
early period of the Second World War, and it is their "art of warfare" which the
Soviet armed forces can thank in no small measure for their initial defeats.

47. Prelude to the Purge of the Army

U NDERSTANDING THAT, when it came to the army, a lack of caution might result in a serious counterblow, Stalin prepared the purge of the army gradually, slowly and patiently.

At the February-March Plenum, Voroshilov announced that until then six people with the "rank of general" had been arrested: Primakov, Putna, Turovsky, Shmidt, Sablin and Ziuk, as well as two officers: Colonel Karpel and Major Kuzmichev.[1] This was an insignificant figure in comparison with the number of those arrested by the time of the plenum in any other area.

The people named by Voroshilov had belonged to the Left Opposition in 1926–1927, but had then left it. Their names had been mentioned at the first two show trials as participants in a "military-Trotskyist organization" within the Red Army.

At the Trial of the Sixteen, it was said that in his letter to Dreitser, Trotsky gave instructions to organize illegal cells in the army. However the defendants named only Primakov and Putna as military figures in contact with the "United Trotskyist-Zinovievist Center." Besides these names, the trial mentioned only Shmidt and Kuzmichev as people who had prepared terrorist acts against Voroshilov.

Before their arrest, Shmidt and Kuzmichev served in the Kiev Military District under Yakir's leadership. Yakir managed to arrange a meeting with Shmidt at the NKVD. During this meeting Shmidt confirmed his confession, but in parting, secretly slipped Yakir a note addressed to Voroshilov, in which he denied the charges made against him. However, on the next day, Voroshilov called the reassured Yakir and said that during a new interrogation Shmidt had returned to his previous testimony.[2]

Whereas the interrogators managed to obtain confessions (for the time being only about terror) from Putna, Shmidt and Kuzmichev by August-September 1936, Primakov held out considerably longer—for nine months—despite the fact that they systematically tormented him with sleep deprivation

Moscow delegation at the Eighth Extraordinary Congress of Soviets. In the first row: Andreev, Yezhov, Khrushchev, Zhdanov, Kaganovich, Voroshilov, Stalin, Molotov, Kalinin, Tukhachevsky

and his interrogations not infrequently ended in heart attacks. At the end of August, the investigator told Primakov that he had been expelled from the party in absentia by the Party Control Commission [PCC] for participating in a "military counterrevolutionary Trotskyist organization." In a statement sent 31 August from prison to the PCC, Primakov wrote: "In 1928 I acknowledged my Trotskyist mistakes and broke with the Trotskyists. Moreover, in order to prevent my Trotskyist past from dragging me backwards, I broke not only in principle, but stopped meeting with any Trotskyists, even with those who were closest to me (Piatakov and Radek)." On 5 October, the PCC refused to review Primakov's case.[3] On 16 October Primakov sent a letter to Stalin in which he confessed only to being guilty "of not fully severing my personal ties with Trotskyists who were my former comrades in the Civil War, and in meeting with them (with Kuzmichev, Dreitser, Shmidt and Ziuk) up until 1932, I spoke in a hostile manner about Comrades Budenny and Voroshilov."[4]

Right up until May of 1937, other future defendants in the "Tukhachevsky affair" felt themselves, as before, to be people enjoying full trust. On 10 August 1936, i.e., immediately before the Trial of the Sixteen, the Politburo approved Voroshilov's proposal to remove from a number of generals, including Kork, the severe party reprimands which they had received in 1934–1935. A month and a half before that, also at the request of Voroshilov, the party reprimands which had been made in 1932 were removed from another group of generals, including Kork and Uborevich. In September-October 1936, the Politburo passed a resolution to send Eideman on an official trip abroad. At the VIIIth Extraordinary Congress of Soviets (November-December 1936), a group photograph was taken showing Tukhachevsky sitting in the front row alongside Stalin and other members of the Politburo.

On 17 March 1937, a sugar factory in the Kiev area which had previously borne Piatakov's name was now given Yakir's name. On 27 April Gamarnik was confirmed as a candidate member of the newly formed Defense Committee of the USSR, which included Stalin and other members of the Politburo.[5]

It may well be that the only incident which could have caused alarm among the military leaders was the unexpected mention of Tukhachevsky's name during cross-examination of Radek at the trial of the "Anti-Soviet Trotskyist Center." In telling of his "conspiratorial" discussion with Putna, Radek announced that this conversation had occurred when Putna came to him on an official assignment from Tukhachevsky. After this statement, Vyshinsky began to question Radek about Tukhachevsky. In response to the prosecutor's questions, Radek declared that he "never had and could not have had any unofficial dealings with Tukhachevsky connected with counterrevolutionary activities, because I knew Tukhachevsky's attitude to the party and the government to be that of an absolutely devoted man."

Krivitsky recalls that when he read this part of the court transcript, he immediately said to his wife, "Tukhachevsky is doomed." In response to what would seem to be a reasonable objection from his wife ("But Radek again and again absolved Tukhachevsky of any connection with the conspiracy"), Krivitsky noted: "Do you think that Tukhachevsky needs any absolution from Radek? Do you think for a moment that Radek would dare of his own accord to drag Tukhachevsky's name into that trial? No, it was Vyshinsky who put Tukhachevsky's name in Radek's mouth, and it was Stalin who put Vyshinsky up to it."

Krivitsky added to his account: "Tukhachevsky's name was mentioned eleven times by Radek and Vyshinsky in that brief passage, and to those versed in the OGPU technique, this could have but one meaning. To me, Stalin and Yezhov had forged a ring round Tukhachevsky and perhaps other ranking generals of the high command."[6] It goes without saying that Tukhachevsky himself and the generals close to him could interpret this episode from the trial in only that way. It is significant that the trial transcript published in Russian did not include this episode. It appeared only in the trial transcript published in English which was intended for foreign public opinion.

Nevertheless, over the next several months the mass arrests continued to bypass the army. There were only individual preventive measures with an outcome that was still unclear. Thus in January 1937, Gamarnik, the head of the Political Directorate of the Red Army, sent a directive to all localities demanding that all party archives at military institutions be checked in order to uncover army communists who had at any time voted for the "Trotskyist Opposition." By 9 February, the assistant head of the Frunze Military Academy reported to Gamarnik that he had reviewed the academy's archives and opened personal card files for each former oppositionist who had been "uncovered."[7]

At approximately the same time, Malenkov sent Stalin a note which included a detailed list of personnel at the People's Commissariat of Defense [NKO] and the military academies who had belonged to the Left Opposition in the 1920s. Opposite each name in the lists was specific information about the "sins" of the given communist: "voted for the Trotskyist resolution, signed Trotskyist documents in 1924 in the newspaper *Pravda*"; "spoke in defense of Trotskyist theses on the peasant question"; "voted in 1921 for the Trotskyist line on the trade unions, shared Trotsky's platform prior to the Tenth Congress."[8]

In January 1937, Gamarnik signed a document, "On the Application of the Conventional Code 'O. U.' (Special Registry) to People from the High Command, Dismissed For Political and Moral Reasons." If that secret code appeared on an order to dismiss a commander from the army, such a commander could not enlist in the armed forces even during the opening phase of a war. Later on, this order would serve to indicate that if people discharged with such a code were found at their place of residency, they were to be arrested immediately by the organs of the NKVD.[9]

Right up until the February-March Plenum, similar preventive measures still gave no grounds to assume that the terror would descend upon the army with as much force as on the civilian branches of the economy. Evidently even Voroshilov believed at the plenum that the army purges carried out in previous years were sufficient, and that further mass repressions would avoid the army. In the conspectus of his speech at the plenum he wrote that, of the three corps commanders who had been arrested, two of them (Primakov and Shmidt) "have not yet confessed their guilt. The most to which they would admit is that they did not like Voroshilov and Budenny, and they confess that right up until 1933 they allowed themselves to sharply criticize Budenny and me." It is true that, in trying to speak in unison with the other orators, Voroshilov wrote at the end of his notes: "It is not excluded, on the contrary, it is even probable, that even in the ranks of the army there are quite a few undiscovered, unrecognized Japanese-German, Trotskyist-Zinovievist spies, saboteurs and terrorists."[10]

In his speech at the plenum, Voroshilov said: "at the present moment, in the Workers' and Peasants' Red Army, fortunately or unfortunately, and I think that it is to our great good fortune, we have not yet found very many enemies of the people.... When I say 'fortunately,' I hope that in the Red Army there are few enemies in general. That is as it should be, for the party sends its best cadres into the army; the country selects is healthiest and most steadfast people."[11] As we can see, Voroshilov's position at the plenum was in many ways similar to Ordzhonikidze's position during the initial period of the extermination of cadres in the People's Commissariat of Heavy Industry.

However, very quickly Voroshilov's "optimistic" prognosis was reduced to virtually nothing by Molotov, who said in the concluding remarks to his own speech: "I have not touched on the War Department, but now I will turn to the War Department. In actual fact, the War Department is a very large matter, the job of checking up on it will not proceed now, but a bit later, and it will be a very thorough review." In speaking about the "military economy," Molotov declared: "If we have wreckers in all branches of the economy, can we imagine that only there we have no wreckers? It would be absurd, it would be wishful thinking, incorrect wishful thinking.... I can say that at first we had intended to hear a special report here about the War Department, then we decided not to, having in mind the importance of this matter. And for the time being only minor symptoms have been discovered there of work done by wreckers, of work done by Trotskyist spies and saboteurs. But I think that even here, if we approach things more carefully, there must be more."[12]

Given all these statements, apparently neither Voroshilov nor even Molotov suspected that in order to destroy the supreme commanders of the army, Stalin would embark on a special provocation which was of unprecedented insidiousness—a provocation which would be implemented with the assistance of Hitler and the upper echelons of the German intelligence services.

48. The Stalin-Hitler Provocation

DOZENS OF MEMOIRS and research articles have been devoted to the history of the "foreign" pages of the "Tukhachevsky affair." Taken together, they provide a rather complete picture of what happened during the fabrication of "evidence" pointing to conspiratorial ties between leaders of the Red Army and the German General Staff.

The connecting link between Stalin and Hitler was the White-Guard General Skoblin, one of the leading members of the Russian General Military Union (ROVS), an organization formed in 1924 out of the officers and generals of the former White armies. On 10 September 1930, Skoblin appealed to the Central Executive Committee of the USSR for a personal amnesty and the granting of Soviet citizenship. He volunteered to provide information "about all the actions directed at undermining the power of the Soviet Union which become known to me."[1] From that moment on, Skoblin became an agent of the OGPU, and was assigned the nickname "farmer." On assignment from Soviet intelligence, he moved in White-Guard circles, while at the same time establishing contact with the German secret services. In 1935, Skoblin was promoted in his official work: he was appointed deputy chairman of the ROVS and leader of its secret section, the main task of which was to fight against penetration of the ROVS by agents of the NKVD.

The enactment of the provocation was facilitated by the fact that Tukhachevsky and other Soviet military leaders had played a leading role in implementing the agreements reached by the Soviet and German governments after they signed a Soviet-German peace treaty in the Italian town of Rapallo in 1922. An important aspect of these agreements was the establishment of cooperation between the high command of the Red Army and the leadership of the Reichswehr, the German armed forces, which were limited according to the Versailles Treaty to having no more than 100,000 troops. The German pilots, as well as artillery and tank specialists, were then able to enroll in military schools created in the Soviet Union to study the mastery of modern armaments which

Germany was forbidden to own by the Versailles Treaty. Thus, Germany was given the chance to prepare new officer cadres, also banned by the Versailles Treaty, which the Soviet government refused to recognize from the moment it was signed. In turn, the Soviet officers and generals studied problems of strategy and tactics in the Academy of the German General Staff. Later on, the cooperation was also extended into the area of armaments. In exchange for permission to build German military plants on the territory of the USSR, the Reichswehr presented the Soviet side with military patents, and the Soviet Union ordered strategic materials and complex equipment from German industry.

Tukhachevsky directed the work which concerned military orders and cooperation with the Reichswehr. His assistant in these dealings was Putna, who worked in 1929–1931 as military attache in Germany.

The Soviet-German military ties were more beneficial to the Soviet Union than to Germany. Strict control was exercised over the Reichswehr by the victorious powers in the First World War, which limited Germany's ability to become stronger even with the assistance of the USSR. The Soviet Union, however, which was not bound by such limitations, was given the chance through its alliance with the Reichswehr to soften the consequences of the military blockade which had been imposed by England and France.

Among the German generals and military industrialists were people very upset by the "pro-Soviet orientation" of the Reichswehr. They tried to forge ties with political and military-industrial circles in the capitalist countries in order to fight against the "Bolshevik threat." Pursuing the "Rapallo line," therefore, corresponded to the political interests of the Soviet Union.

The situation changed after the Nazis seized power. Despite Stalin's desire to continue the Soviet-German military cooperation even under these conditions, Hitler refused to do so. By unilaterally abrogating the restrictive military clauses of the Versailles Treaty in 1935, and by introducing universal military conscription, Hitler began a rapid buildup of the Wehrmacht (as the German armed forces now began to be known).

The secret archives of the German general staff contained documents reflecting the business relations between military circles in the USSR and Germany until 1933, including letters from Tukhachevsky and official documents which he had signed. The presence of these documents then became the basis for the provocative action launched on Hitler's orders in response to a maneuver instigated by Stalin.

The mechanism through which this provocation was carried out is described in the posthumously published memoirs of Walter Schellenberg, the director of Nazi Germany's foreign intelligence.

In December 1936, Heydrich, the chief of the German political police, received information from Skoblin that Tukhachevsky and other high-ranking commanders in the Red Army were preparing a conspiracy against Stalin and maintaining ties with several generals in the Wehrmacht who also wanted to free themselves from the tutelage of the "party bureaucracy" in their own country. Although Skoblin did not present documentary evidence confirming this information, Heydrich detected in it the possibility of sapping the strength of the Red Army. Janke, who was adviser to Hitler and Hess on intelligence matters, expressed his doubts to Heydrich about the accuracy of Skoblin's information. Basing himself on information received from Japanese intelligence, and also on information at his disposal about Skoblin's wife, Plevitskaya (a famous singer of Russian folk songs), as a longtime agent of the GPU, Janke declared that Skoblin's message had been inspired by Stalin. He felt that Stalin was using this disinformation to destroy a generals' "Fronde" headed by Tukhachevsky, and at the same time to strike a blow at the commanders of the Wehrmacht. In Janke's opinion, Stalin, who was guided by considerations of inner-party policy, wanted the motive for the removal of Tukhachevsky and his cohorts to come from the USSR's most dangerous foe, which at that time was considered to be Hitler's Germany.

Heydrich not only rejected Janke's warning, but declared that he was a weapon in the hands of German military circles and subjected him to house arrest for three months—long enough to carry out the "operation." Skoblin's version was sent by Heydrich directly to Hitler, who ordered documents confirming it to be prepared for Stalin. According to Schellenberg, Hitler proceeded in his calculations from the fact that "the weakening of the Red Army as a result of the 'decimation' of the Soviet high command would, at a certain time, secure his rear lines in a war against the West."[2]

Feeling that success in the given operation "would be the greatest catastrophe for Russia since the revolution," Heydrich told his closest aides: "Even if Stalin only wants to confuse us with this information from Skoblin, I will supply our uncle in the Kremlin with enough evidence to turn his lie into pristine truth."[3]

It was decided to prepare documents about secret contacts between the

Soviet generals and Wehrmacht commanders with the aid of a rather crafty maneuver. On Hitler's orders, a nighttime burglary was performed at the building which housed the secret archives of the German armed forces. During the raid, the burglars stole originals of Tukhachevsky's handwritten letters, records of conversations between representatives of the Soviet and German commanders, and so forth. In order to cover the tracks of the nighttime break-in, a fire was set which destroyed the section of the archives containing materials about the Soviet-German military collaboration.

Using the stolen documents, a forged letter from Tukhachevsky was fabricated, carefully reproducing not only his handwriting, but his style of correspondence. On this letter, which spoke of plans by Tukhachevsky and his cothinkers to take power into their own hands, the forgers placed genuine stamps from the office of the Abwehr (the counterintelligence service of the German general staff): "Top Secret" and "Confidential." When he familiarized himself with this forgery, Hitler scrawled a resolution on it demanding surveillance of the German generals who allegedly were linked with Tukhachevsky.

The dossier personally examined by Hitler also contained forged receipts signed by Soviet generals about large sums they had received for the secret information they provided, reports of "secretly monitored" conversations between German officers about the "conspiracy," and materials from "investigations" by the German secret services of ties between military figures in the USSR and Germany.

The next task was to deliver all this material to Stalin. To do this, the disinformation efforts were shifted to Czechoslovakia, whose government at that time was oriented toward the USSR in order to counterbalance Germany's expansionist plans. This stage of the operation is described in the memoirs of Beneš, the Czechoslovakian president, which were published after the war. He recalls that in February 1937, Mastny, the Czechoslovakian envoy in Germany, told him that the German ruling circles expected the rapid replacement of the government in Moscow by a powerful conspiratorial group of generals. On 8 May Beneš sent a secret communique to Stalin in which he reported the conspiracy in the Red Army and the ties between the conspirators and a group of German generals—opponents of the Nazi regime who were also preparing to seize power in their own country.

Even before these events, the German special services had surreptitiously given Soviet agents disinformation material about the military leaders. Thus, in January 1937, Klimov, the correspondent for *Pravda* in Berlin, said that persistent rumors were circulating in German officers' circles about ties between the fascists and the heads of the general staff of the Red Army, and that "in this regard the name of Tukhachevsky was mentioned."[4]

On 9 April 1937, S. Uritsky, the head of the counterintelligence department of the RKKA, reported to Stalin that in Berlin rumors were being inflated about the existence of opposition to the Soviet leadership among the general staff of the Red Army. At approximately the same time, a note from Yezhov came to Stalin referring to information from the ROVS that a group of the highest military commanders headed by Tukhachevsky was preparing a governmental coup.

In the first months of 1937, rumors about a conspiracy between Soviet and German generals were widely circulating also among governmental and diplomatic circles in England and France. In March 1937, Potemkin, the USSR ambassador to France, sent a telegram to Litvinov about his confidential conversation with the French War Minister, Daladier, who had said that he possessed information about negotiations between Soviet and German generals.

In creating a version about the pro-German orientation of Tukhachevsky and the generals around him, White-Guard circles in Czechoslovakia played no small role. They gave the Czechoslovak leaders information indicating that, as a result of the military conspiracy in the USSR, friendly relations would be established between the Soviet Union and Germany, and the Soviet-Czech mutual aid pact would be abrogated.

During the war, the Gestapo agent Giering boasted to the Soviet intelligence agent Leopold Trepper about the mechanism for carrying out the Stalin-Hitler provocation. Basing himself on this information, Trepper wrote that in the course of this provocation "Stalin and Hitler had divided up the work. The first had had the idea for the plot, and the second had carried it out."[5]

Among Soviet sources, the most valuable information on the fabrication of the "Tukhachevsky affair" is contained in Krivitsky's memoirs. According to him, Stalin's plan, which pursued the goal of disgracing Tukhachevsky and the generals close to him, began to be implemented at least half a year before the "discovery of the military conspiracy." In December 1936, a special courier who had come to The Hague, where Krivitsky was then located, gave him an order to place at the disposal of the foreign service of the NKVD two agents from the Soviet military intelligence who would be capable of playing the role of German officers. Soon afterwards there was a meeting in Paris between Krivitsky and

Slutsky, in the course of which the latter explained that the given order came directly from Yezhov. Slutsky then added, "We've got to have [these people] at once. This job is so important that nothing else matters!"[6]

In March 1937, Krivitsky traveled to Moscow, where he met with Furmanov, the head of the counterintelligence department which was engaged in infiltrating anti-Soviet émigré organizations. From what Furmanov said, Krivitsky understood that his agents had been put in contact with a White-Guard group in France.

In September 1937, Krivitsky discovered the key to unraveling the "conspiracy such as history has never known"when he read in the Paris newspapers about the mysterious disappearance of General Miller, the head of the ROVS. On the day of his disappearance, as he left his study, Miller handed his aide a sealed envelope which he asked him to open only if he never returned. When the envelope was opened, the following note was found inside: "I have an appointment at 12:30 today with General Skoblin ... he is to take me to a rendezvous with two German officers.... Both of these men speak Russian well. The meeting has been arranged at the initiative of Skoblin. It is possible that this is a trap, and that is why I am leaving you this note."[7]

When he read this article, Krivitsky understood that the two "German officers" who had acted in unison with Skoblin were the agents he had put at the disposal of the NKVD.

When Miller's colleagues demanded explanations from Skoblin, he started by trying to prove his alibi for Miller's kidnapping. When, however, he was shown Miller's note, he slipped out of the room and drove away in an automobile that was waiting for him. After his disappearance, documents were found in his apartment which left no doubt about his work for the NKVD.

Skoblin's wife, Plevitskaya, was arrested by the French authorities on charges of espionage, and in December 1938, was sentenced to a prison term of no less than twenty years. The severity of her crimes can be seen by the fact that such a severe sentence is very rarely applied by the French justice system to women.*

---

* At the end of the 1980s, a Soviet journalist asked the KGB to provide material for an article about the "remarkable Soviet intelligence agent, Plevitskaya." In this regard, the deputy head of the intelligence department indicated in a letter to the deputy chairman of the KGB that "to write about Nadezhda Plevitskaya is inexpedient because of operative considerations" (*Novoe vremia*, no. 21 (1991), pp. 49–50).

Krivitsky saw a close link between the information about Skoblin and the report given to him by Spiegelglass, according to which the facts about the "military conspiracy" fell into the hands of Stalin and Yezhov through the so-called "Guchkov circle," headed by the former Minister of War under the Provisional Government. As a central figure in the monarchist wing of the Russian emigration, Guchkov was in contact with the German special services and repeatedly sent his agents into the USSR. Agents of the NKVD were infiltrated into the Guchkov circle, among whom the leading role was played by Guchkov's daughter. She had married the English communist R. Trail, who died in Spain in 1937. Vera Trail traveled to Moscow more than once, where she met with Yezhov. Later she said: "At one time, Yezhov worshiped me (of course, in an absolutely innocent sense)."[8]

Skoblin, who worked as secretary of the Guchkov circle, told the latter about the "conspiracy" of the Soviet generals. Miller, who was well informed on this matter, was a person who might leak information about the connection between Stalin, Hitler and the White-Guard organizations. Therefore Miller was "put out of the way."[9]

The Paris group of the Left Opposition was well informed about the link between Skoblin and the NKVD, and about the reasons for Miller's kidnapping. In December 1937, the *Bulletin of the Opposition* announced, "Miller was kidnapped in order to put the White-Guard organization—through Skoblin and Co.—at the service of the GPU."[10]

The final stage in the provocation was described in an article by Alexander Orlov which was published in 1956. According to Orlov, an NKVD agent named Izrailovich worked in the Soviet embassy in Berlin. One of his duties was to maintain contact with two informers who occupied important posts in the German general staff. Because a meeting with these people in Nazi Germany, i.e., in the zone of control belonging to the ubiquitous Gestapo, was too risky, Izrailovich arranged regular meetings with them in Czechoslovakia. After one of these meetings, he was arrested by the Czechoslovakian police, who discovered that he was carrying film which he had just received from the German officers. When he was charged with espionage on behalf of the Nazis, Izrailovich, whom Orlov "knew to be a pathological coward," fell to pieces and declared that, on the contrary, the German officers were his agents and the film he had received from them contained photocopies of secret documents belonging to the German general staff. When he learned about this incident, Beneš, "who was trying with all his might to maintain cordial relations with communist Russia because of the growing threat to Czechoslovakia from Germany ... personally handed the police report and Izrailovich's testimony to the Czech ambassador in Moscow with instructions to give the information about this matter, if possible, personally to Stalin." After the generals of the Red Army had been liquidated, Stalin told the Czechs that Izrailovich had actually maintained contact with German intelligence as an intermediary for Tukhachevsky. "Although the Czechs knew what had really happened, they needed Stalin's assistance against Hitler even more than a year earlier. They obediently spread Stalin's false version about Izrailovich as if it were true."[11]

After Soviet intelligence learned about the intention of the highest-ranking figures in the Reich to give Stalin a dossier about the "conspiracy," Stalin's personal representative came to Berlin supplied with official papers bearing Yezhov's signature.

As Schellenberg recalls, "to everyone's surprise, Stalin offered to pay money for the material about the 'conspiracy.' Neither Hitler, nor Himmler, nor Heydrich had counted on being rewarded. Heydrich demanded three million gold rubles—in order, as he said, to save 'face' before the Russians." When the documents were received, the Stalinist emissary paid the given sum in installments. According to Schellenberg, this "Judas money" was given to German agents in the USSR, who were arrested when they attempted to use them. "Stalin had made the payment in large bills, and all the numbers were registered with the GPU."[12]

Even after the Tukhachevsky trial, German official circles continued to spread disinformation which was designed to reinforce Stalin's suspicions of the reliability of the Red Army generals. According to information which Krivitsky received from one of his agents, at an official reception in Berlin, someone asked Hitler's personal secretary on political questions, Wiedemann, whether there was any truth in the charges made at the trial against Tukhachevsky? Wiedemann boastfully replied: "We hadn't nine spies in the Red Army, but many more. The OGPU is still far from on the trail of all our men in Russia."

Krivitsky, as an experienced intelligence officer, "knew only too well the character of such talk. So would any Military Intelligence officer of any nation. It was designed for wide circulation, with a view to undermining the morale of the enemy."[13]

Only in October 1938, when the purge of the Red Army was basically over, did the official organ of the Wehrmacht, *Deutsche Wehr*, say that Tukhachevsky and his colleagues had been slandered by a "traitor, the famous General Skoblin, who betrayed to the Bolsheviks Generals Kutepov and Miller."[14]

The provocation against Tukhachevsky and other supreme military commanders served the interests of both Stalin and Hitler. Stalin was given the chance to destroy the last organized force in the country which was capable of moving against him. Hitler seized the opportunity to decapitate the Red Army, using Stalin's hands in destroying the flower of the Soviet high command.

As Schellenberg correctly noted, "the Tukhachevsky affair was the first illegal prologue to the future alliance between Stalin and Hitler."[15]

49. Preparing the Trial of the Generals

AFTER THE FEBRUARY-MARCH PLENUM, the scale of the repressions directed against the commanding cadres increased sharply. Whereas five hundred seventy-seven people had been dismissed from the Red Army for political reasons between 1 January and 30 March 1937, from 1 April to 11 June (the day that newspapers carried the article about the impending trial of eight military leaders)—four thousand three hundred seventy people were removed. Each day in April and May, Leplevsky, the head of the Special Section of the NKVD (which was investigating state crimes in the army), sent for Voroshilov's and Gamarnik's sanction lists of the commanders and political workers to be arrested. Voroshilov and Gamarnik reviewed hundreds of such lists.[1]

According to Krivitsky, by the end of April it was no secret in elite Moscow circles that the fate of Tukhachevsky and a number of other figures from the General Staff had already been decided. "It was felt to be dangerous to enter into a conversation with them. They remained isolated, surrounded by a zone of silence."[2]

It was during these days that Stalin organized the next provocation. On 21 April Yezhov presented Stalin with a memorandum proposing to cancel Tukhachevsky's scheduled visit to the coronation of the English king, since information had been received from "a foreign source deserving full confidence" that the German special services were preparing a terrorist act against Tukhachevsky during his trip to England. Stalin added a resolution to the note: "However sad it might be, I must agree with Comrade Yezhov's proposal." He then ordered that the document be distributed to members of the Politburo, and that it be shown to Tukhachevsky himself. On 22 April the Politburo voted to send Orlov, the Deputy People's Commissar of Defense, to London in place of Tukhachevsky. Apparently, such an action, which seemed on the surface to be a sign of concern over Tukhachevsky's security, was aimed at denying the general, who expected his arrest, the chance to become a "non-returnee."

During these same days, testimony was being obtained in the torture chambers of the NKVD from the former head of the Special Section of the NKVD, Gai, and the former Deputy People's Commissar of Internal Affairs, Prokofiev, about conspiratorial ties linking Tukhachevsky and other generals to Yagoda. Volovich, the former deputy head of this department of the NKVD, gave testimony about the preparation of a military coup by Tukhachevsky. At the next session, Yezhov demanded that the investigators handling Gai and Prokofiev treat these cases as a "social command" coming from Stalin.[3]

On 1 May 1937, Stalin induced a state of shock among the military commanders who were present at a festive dinner held in Voroshilov's apartment. According to the eyewitness account given by Uritsky, who was head of the Intelligence Directorate of the RKKA at that time, at this dinner "the leader said that enemies would be exposed and that the party would grind them into dust. He then proposed a toast to those who remained loyal and would be worthy of taking their places at the table of honor during the anniversary of the October Revolution."[4] Upon hearing this ominous warning, the military leaders could only guess who among them had been earmarked by Stalin to be the next victims.

In order to deprive the generals of any opportunity to take responsive measures, Stalin decided to tear them away from their usual surroundings. The "reshuffling" of the commanding cadres began in the middle of April, when Feldman was transferred from his post as head of the directorate of the command headquarters of the NKO to the post of deputy commander of the troops of the Moscow Military District, and two deputies to Uborevich were transferred to jobs beyond the borders of the Belorussian Military District.

On 10 May the Politburo passed a decree about a number of new reassignments among the upper military leadership. In particular, Yakir was transferred from his post as commander of the Kiev Military District to the post of commander of the Leningrad Military District. Tukhachevsky received a sharp demotion in his service status. He was dismissed as deputy People's Commissar of Defense and appointed troop commander of the Volga Military district, a position of secondary significance. Three days after this decision was made, Tukhachevsky was received by Stalin, who told him that the reason for his transfer to Kuibyshev was the arrest of his acquaintance, Kuzmina, and his former messenger on charges of espionage.[5] Tukhachevsky's last article appeared in the newspaper *Krasnaia zvezda* [Red Star], on 6 May 1937.

At the beginning of May, Stalin passed a resolution in the Politburo about

V. M. Primakov

the liquidation of the unified military and political command in the Red Army. The resolution also established Military Councils (consisting of the commander and two members of the Council) in districts, fleets and armies, and instituted military commissars in all military units, starting with the regiment and any unit which was larger. This measure removed the right of commanders of all ranks to make decisions and issue orders without the sanction of the Military Councils and political commissars.

Prior to this, the Military Councils and the commissars had existed only in the Civil War years, when they were created to guarantee control by communists over the activity of the command staff, which to a large degree was composed of former officers in the tsarist army. In 1937, however, 90 percent of the officers were party members. Commenting on the rebirth of dual power in the army, Trotsky wrote: "The military councils of 1937 are designed to help the oligarchy, which has raised itself above the revolutionary class, to protect the power it has usurped from the attack of its own marshals and generals."[6]

On 6 May Medvedev, the former head of the Directorate of Anti-Aircraft Defenses, was arrested. He had been expelled from the party in 1934 and worked prior to his arrest as deputy head of the construction of a hospital. His arrest, as Radzivilovsky,* the investigator in the Medvedev case would say in 1939, was ordered by Yezhov "with the intention of beginning with him in assembling a case concerning a military conspiracy in the RKKA."[7]

According to Radzivilovsky's testimony, the Deputy People's Commissar of Internal Affairs, Frinovsky, demanded that he "provide a picture of a major and deeply rooted conspiracy in the Red Army.... In doing so, the enormous role and contribution made by Yezhov and Frinovsky in uncovering this conspiracy was to be made clear to the Central Committee."[8]

At the beginning of May, Primakov began to confess. This began after he was summoned to a session of the Politburo, where, according to his account, he "continued to resist and play down his guilt in every way possible." Stalin then declared, "Primakov is a coward; to refuse to speak out in such a case is cowardice." After this rebuke, Primakov wrote a statement to Yezhov in which he declared his readiness to give testimony about his "Trotskyist work." At first he limited himself to confessing his criminal "ties" with Shmidt and Putna, who had been already arrested, and with Mrachkovsky and Dreitser, who had already been shot. On 14 May Primakov named Yakir as a "co-participant" whom "the Trotskyist organization" allegedly had designated to assume the post of People's Commissar of Defense. After another week, Primakov testified that Tukhachevsky headed the conspiracy, and that he was connected with Trotsky. During the same interrogation, Primakov gave the names of forty more prominent military personnel who had taken part in the "military-Trotskyist conspiracy."[9]

As can be seen from the material in Primakov's investigation dossier, in May-June 1937 he gave not only fantastic information about a "fascist conspiracy." During the investigation he also spoke about the genuine moods of many commanders which were bound up, first of all, with dissatisfaction over forced collectivization and its consequences (destruction of livestock, disruption of the countryside, absence of the "master's hand" in the peasant economy) and, secondly, with Voroshilov's activity in the army. Thus, according to Primakov, corps commander N. V. Kuibyshev said: "Voroshilov needs either

---

* In 1938, a large group of investigators who participated in preparing the trial in the case of the "military conspiracy" was arrested. During the investigation they gave detailed testimony about how the case was fabricated and about the sadistic methods used against the defendants.

lackeys like Khmelnitsky, or fools like Kulik, or else old men who are willing do anything they are told, like Shaposhnikov."[10]

It was during this period that Putna gave testimony that he had delivered a letter in 1935 to Tukhachevsky from Trotsky, after which Tukhachevsky supposedly told Putna that "Trotsky could count on him." Putna named a large number of participants in the "military Trotskyist organization" who were immediately arrested. Among them were the future defendants at the trial of the generals, Eideman, Feldman and Kork. The latter two apparently showed the greatest readiness to collaborate with the investigation and the trial. This hypothesis is supported by the fact that their speeches at the trial filled up twelve and twenty pages of the court transcript respectively, whereas the interrogations of the other defendants proceeded in question-and-answer form.[11]

On 14 May the Politburo passed a decree removing Kork from his post (without explaining why), and on 15 May, it rescinded the resolution passed a month earlier appointing Feldman deputy commander of the troops of the Moscow Military District. On 20 May Yakir's appointment to a new post was canceled, Uborevich was transferred to the post of troop commander of the Central Asian Military District, and Gamarnik was appointed member of the military council of the same district. On 22 May Eideman was dismissed as chairman of Osoaviakhim [Society for the Promotion of Defense, Aviation and Chemistry]. On the same day eight people (including Kork and Feldman) were removed from the Military Council of the People's Commissar of Defense in connection with their discharge from the RKKA or else with dismissal from the positions they held. The decision to expel five more people from the Military Council, including Tukhachevsky and Eideman, was made on 26 May—after they had already been arrested. On 3 June, the same decision was made with regard to five more people who had been arrested, including Yakir and Uborevich.[12]

After they had received the transcript of the interrogations of Kork and Feldman about the preparation of a military coup, Stalin, Molotov, Kaganovich, and Voroshilov (Stalin allowed only these three members of the Politburo to read the materials of the investigation) gave their sanction for Tukhachevsky's arrest, which was carried out on 22 May.

In his memoirs, Lieutenant-General P. A. Ermolin tells of Tukhachevsky's last days at liberty. He met Tukhachevsky at a party conference in the Volga Military District. "I felt that Mikhail Nikolaevich was not quite himself," recalled Ermolin. "Sitting not far from him at the presidium table, I furtively

kept glancing at him. His temples had turned gray, and his eyes were somewhat swollen. At times he would lower his eyelids, as if the light had become
brighter. With his head bowed, his fingers nervously played with pencils which
lay on the tablecloth. I had managed to observe Tukhachevsky in many set-
tings ... but I had never seen him looking like this."[13]

On the morning of the next day, Tukhachevsky appeared once again at the
conference's presidium. By the evening session, where he was supposed to speak,
he was already absent.

On 24 May the Politburo passed a resolution on "the conspiracy in the
RKKA." It mentioned the message from Beneš to Stalin and indicated that the
conspirators were planning "in coordination with the German general staff and
the Gestapo to overthrow Stalin and the Soviet government through a military
coup, as well as all organs of the party and Soviet power, and to establish ... a
military dictatorship."[14]

The Politburo decided to ask the members and candidate members of the
Central Committee to vote on a resolution calling for the expulsion of
Tukhachevsky and Rudzutak from the party and for the submission of their
case to the NKVD. The explanation for this resolution was that the Central
Committee "had received information pointing to the participation of CC member Rudzutak and CC candidate member Tukhachevsky in an anti-Soviet
Trotskyist-Rightist conspiratorial bloc and in espionage against the USSR on
behalf of fascist Germany."[15] The corresponding resolution was formulated by
means of a referendum of members and candidate-members of the CC on 25–
26 May. Budenny displayed special zeal during the voting; on his ballot he wrote:
"Unreservedly 'for.' We must execute these bastards."[16]

On 28 May Yakir was arrested, and on 29 May Uborevich. The Central Committee resolution on their expulsion from the party was also passed after their
arrest—on 30 May-1 June. In this resolution Yakir and Uborevich were accused
of "participating in a military-fascist Trotskyist-Rightist conspiracy" and of
espionage activity on behalf of not only Germany, but also Japan and Poland.[17]

In the course of investigations which were conducted in the mid-1950s
and the beginning of the 1960s, people who had participated in preparing the
trial of the generals said that the military leaders were subjected to "inhuman
and cruel interrogation methods." Investigators who were arrested in 1938 said
the same thing. Thus, for instance, Ushakov declared after the same methods
which he had applied to the generals had been applied to him: "In Lefortovo

(and not only there) I had occasion to beat enemies of the party and of the Soviet regime, but I never had any conception of the torment and feelings experienced by the defendants."[18] The same Ushakov said, "B. M. Feldman confessed to me that he participated in an anti-Soviet military conspiracy.... On 25 May they had me question Tukhachevsky, who confessed on the twenty-sixth, and on the thirtieth I received Yakir. Working on these three alone, without assistants (or 'mates'), and having instructions that the case must be finished for hearings in a few days, I almost never lay down to sleep, but dragged a few more facts out of them, a few more conspirators. Even the day the trial began, early in the morning I obtained additional testimony from Tukhachevsky about Apanasenko and a few others." Among the "others," for instance, was Timoshenko.[19]

In 1961, Surovnitskikh, a former investigator, testified that in the course of the interrogations in the case of the military conspiracy, the investigators suggested names of their "co-participants" to the arrested people in order to reinforce the "'solidity and seriousness' of the conspiracy as Yezhov demanded."[20]

The use of inhuman torture against the victims is mentioned not only in the testimony of the investigators, but can be seen from the spots of blood discovered on Tukhachevsky's interrogation transcript.

During the last ten days of May, Stalin received Yezhov almost every day and read transcripts of the interrogations. On 30 May, at his instigation, the Politburo passed a resolution to remove Gamarnik from his job in the People's Commissariat of Defense as a person in "close group connection with Yakir, who has been expelled from the party for participating in a military-fascist conspiracy."[21] On the next day Voroshilov sent two officials from the Commissariat of Defense to visit the apartment of Gamarnik, who was ill, in order to deliver the order of his dismissal from the RKKA. Immediately after they left, Gamarnik shot himself. The reasons for this act were explained in the following way in an official statement: "The former member of the CC VKP(b), Ya. B. Gamarnik, who became entangled with anti-Soviet elements and apparently feared exposure, committed suicide on 31 May."[22]

On 1 June, in the stunned atmosphere which had been created by all these announcements, an expanded session of the Military Council was opened. The participants included its members, the members of the Politburo and one hundred sixteen military officials invited from the central apparatus of the NKO and from various localities. By this time, one-fourth of the members of the

Military Council (twenty people) had been arrested.

On the same day the Politburo passed a decree demanding that twenty-six people be stripped of their decorations because of "treason and counterrevolutionary activity." On this list, among others, were the names of five military leaders (Gorbachev, Peterson, Garkavy, Kork and Eideman), eleven former leading officials in the NKVD (Yagoda, Molchanov, Volovich, Gai, Prokofiev, Pogrebinsky, Boky, Bulanov, Firin, Pauker, Chertok) and five "civilians" (Rykov, Yenukidze, Kabakov, Ukhanov, Gvakhariia).[23] Most of these people had been arrested several days before this resolution was passed.

Before the session of the Military Council opened, its participants were shown the testimony of Tukhachevsky and other "conspirators." These testimonies were widely used in Voroshilov's report, "On the Counterrevolutionary Conspiracy in the RKKA, Discovered by the Organs of the NKVD." Voroshilov confessed his own "enormous guilt" which consisted of the fact that he "not only did not notice the rotten traitors, but even when some of them (Gorbachev, Feldman and others) had already begun to be exposed, he did not want to believe that these people, who it seemed had been working irreproachably, were capable of such monstrous crimes." At the same time, Voroshilov warned the assembled commanders that he had never once received from them "a warning signal" about the existence of "counterrevolutionary conspirators" in the Red Army. Challenging them "to verify and purge the army down to its smallest nooks and crannies," Voroshilov warned that a result of this purge "we might inflict huge casualties from the standpoint of numbers."[24]

On the next day Stalin delivered a major speech at the Military Council. It is difficult to name another speech given by Stalin which is as confused as this one. Stalin often repeated himself, jumped from one subject to another, digressed from the subject, and so forth. At the same time, the transcript of the speech demonstrates his great self-control, the ability to construct his speech in calm and measured tones, filled with considerable irony toward the "conspirators." What is most disturbing is that, as at the February-March Plenum, "laughter rippled through the audience" more than once in the course of Stalin's remarks.

Stalin declared that the organs of the NKVD had uncovered "a military-political conspiracy against the Soviet regime, instigated and financed by the German fascists." The political leaders of the conspiracy he named were Trotsky, Bukharin, Rykov, Rudzutak, Karakhan and Yenukidze, and the heads of the conspiracy "in the military" were Yagoda, Tukhachevsky, Yakir, Uborevich, Kork, Eideman and Gamarnik. Stalin called ten of these thirteen people German spies, and the other three (Rykov, Bukharin and Gamarnik)—"organizers and facilitators of espionage on behalf of the German Reichswehr."[25]

Stalin repeated several times that the conspiracy was not prompted by domestic political reasons, insofar as the successes on all fronts of domestic policy were "extraordinary," "the economy has been flourishing and will continue to do so," etc. According to Stalin, the conspiracy was rooted "not so much in native soil, as in foreign conditions; it was connected to policy not so much of the inner life of our country as to the policy of the German Reichswehr."[26] Throughout his speech Stalin repeatedly mentioned that the conspirators intended "to arrest the government in the Kremlin," but each time accompanied this declaration with the provision that this action was being prepared on orders coming from the "German Reichswehr."

After raising the question as to why people occupying such high posts would voluntarily turn themselves into "slaves" and "chattels" of the Reichswehr, Stalin explained that several people were dissatisfied with the fact that they were not being "promoted." He also pointed to the activity in Germany of "the experienced intelligence agent and beautiful woman," Josephine Gensi, who "used her feminine charms" to recruit Karakhan, Yenukidze, Tukhachevsky and Rudzutak.[27]

Announcing that "we have arrested around 300–400 men in the military," Stalin called for further "signals," in which, "if there is even 5 percent of the truth, then that is already something."[28] In saying this, he was trying to convince those gathered that their "signals," even based on dubious suspicions and containing 95 percent slanders, would be encouraged. In conclusion, Stalin emphasized that "among our people ... there are still comrades who have been accidentally affected.... It would be good to introduce the practice, if such people come forward and themselves tell us about everything—of forgiving them."[29] As at the February-March Plenum, Stalin declared his readiness to give indulgences to former Trotskyists who "have left Trotskyism, left it for good and who are putting up a very good fight against it." Having said that he could "count twenty or thirty" such people, Stalin named as an example the Politburo member Andreev, who "had been a very active Trotskyist in 1921," but now "was fighting very well."[30]

Of course, Stalin's speech was far from convincing, particularly in explaining the reasons for the transformation of major governmental figures and military leaders into "puppets and dolls in the hands of the Reichswehr." However the session's participants understood all too well that in the atmosphere of totalitarian hysteria which dominated at the Military Council, it would not be appropriate to ask Stalin any questions.

In the discussion following Voroshilov's report, forty-two people spoke, of whom thirty-two were arrested in 1937–1938, and two more (Kulik and Meretskov) were arrested in later years. Of those who spoke, eight people who were particularly venomous in branding the "traitors" were chosen by Stalin to form a new legal body which Stalin had invented—the Special Judicial Office of the Supreme Court of the USSR. From these people, who condemned their former comrades, four (Alksnis, Belov, Dybenko and Goriachev) were shot over the next two years, one (Bliukher) died while being interrogated and one (Kashirin) committed suicide while awaiting arrest. Only Budenny and Shaposhnikov died in their beds.

After the designation of the members of the military court, Primakov, who had by now been completely broken, gave damaging testimony about three of his future judges: Kashirin, Dybenko and Shaposhnikov. Knowing full well the value of this testimony, Stalin not only waited for a year before dealing with Dybenko and Kashirin, but he also preserved Shaposhnikov's life, putting him to use in a special way. Shaposhnikov, a former colonel in the tsarist army who joined the party only in 1930, was elected a member of the CC at the Eighteenth Congress of the VKP(b), and spent almost the entire war as head of the General Staff.

On 5 June Stalin, Molotov, Kaganovich and Yezhov selected eight defendants for the upcoming trial out of a large group of arrested military leaders. Then the individual dossiers containing material from the investigation of these people were joined together into one group case.

The composition of the defendants was such that the trial made its own contribution to creating the atmosphere of distrust toward "aliens" which Stalin had been propagating in those years. Uborevich and Putna were Lithuanians, Yakir, Gamarnik (named in the court indictment as a participant in the conspiracy) and Feldman were Jews, Kork an Estonian and Eideman a Latvian.

Relatively few facts have been published about the course of the hasty trial against the main defendants. We know, for instance, that on 7 June Yakir sent Yezhov a letter in which he told of the falsification of a number of cases in the

Ukraine, where material "was prepared according to the following principle: if the last five reports and testimonies are not enough, we will send five more; and if they turn out to be insufficient, we will add some more. This would be said when it was unclear: would there be any more, and where would we get them?"[31]

Tukhachevsky's behavior at the investigation appears more enigmatic. He was arrested on 22 May, brought to Moscow on 24 May and interrogated for the first time on 25 May. On the day following the first interrogation, he wrote a statement to Yezhov, in which he acknowledged the existence of a "military-Trotskyist conspiracy" and promised "to present the investigation independently with everything concerning the conspiracy, hiding none of its participants, nor a single fact or document." "The beginning of the conspiracy," Tukhachevsky writes, "goes back to 1932. Those participating in it were Feldman, Alafuzo, Primakov, Putna and others, and I will testify about it in detail later."[32]

A few days after this statement, Tukhachevsky sent Stalin a letter which was called, "Plan of Defeat." An analysis of the contents of this document fully excludes the possibility that it was dictated to Tukhachevsky by the investigators. The document displays the author's profound knowledge of the international political situation of the time, high professionalism and erudition in military questions. It is written in the language of military-scholarly literature, which was obviously inaccessible to the incompetent investigators of the NKVD. The letter, which is written in a calm and businesslike tone, includes many references to German military theoreticians and to the experience of previous wars. The basic ideas of the letter are illustrated with maps that are appended to it.

From the contents of the letter it is clear that at the time it was written, Tukhachevsky was familiar with the testimonies of other military leaders about "wrecking activity" in the army. However, the separate fragments found in it about "wrecking" (without which the investigators obviously would not agree to send the letter as it was intended) are presented in such a way that they virtually repudiate the testimony given by the other defendants.

At the beginning of the letter Tukhachevsky indicates that "the center of the anti-Soviet military-Trotskyist conspiracy carefully studied material and sources which can answer the question: what are Hitler's operational plans through which he intends to guarantee the domination of German fascism in

Europe?"[33] The remaining contents of the letter include a painstaking analysis of the possible variants of Germany's military actions against the USSR and the strategic operations which might arise during the first stages of war.

Tukhachevsky found it "absolutely fantastic" that Hitler would assume the task of completely routing the USSR with a drive on Moscow. He stated that Hitler would be able to pursue only limited goals in a war with the Soviet Union, hoping in the best case only to wrest away separate territories from the USSR. Such considerations corresponded to the real relationship of Soviet and German armed forces at that time, which were much more advantageous for the USSR than in 1941, when Germany's military and economic resources had grown significantly, and the Red Army had been drained to the utmost by the earlier purges.

Proceeding from the political situation of the time, Tukhachevsky assumed that Germany could enter into a military and political alliance with Poland and that she would try to seize Czechoslovakia prior to invading the USSR. Considering that such a seizure might be possible in the nearest future and in the shortest possible time, Tukhachevsky stressed: "A situation is not excluded in Europe in which not a single one of the parties will be able to support Czechoslovakia in time against Germany.... France might prove to be in such a state at the beginning of the war that she will not be able to fulfill the duties stipulated in her peace treaties and will not move against Germany."[34]

Analyzing in detail the possible theaters of Germany's military actions against the USSR from the economic point of view, Tukhachevsky came to the conclusion that the most probable direction of Hitler's military strike would be the Ukraine. It would not be superfluous to note that Stalin mechanically applied this evaluation, which corresponded to the disposition of forces in 1937, to the military and strategic situation which developed in 1941. As a result of this miscalculation, when the war broke out, the Western front lagged behind the South-Western and Southern Fronts both in manpower and in war materiel. Only on 27 June 1941 was Marshal Shaposhnikov able to convince Stalin, after he had analyzed German documents seized by Soviet troops which showed that two out of four tank groups in the Wehrmacht were advancing in the western sector, that the conception of the main blow from Hitler's forces coming on the southwestern sector was a major strategic blunder.[35]

In examining the different ways the Red Army might repulse a joint invasion by Germany and Poland, Tukhachevsky disclosed the strong and weak sides of each variant. In doing so, he indicated that the Soviet Union enjoyed superiority over possible aggressors in aviation and cavalry (the latter advantage was, in his opinion, illusory, since cavalry would sustain very heavy casualties from the enemy's air force). Along with this, Tukhachevsky noted the weakness of the artillery, tank, and machine gun reserves of the Main Command of the Red Army and the absence in the Red Army of motorized divisions and a major system of roads. The main danger as he saw it was that the operational plan of the General Staff was constructed as if they expected only a war with Poland. After citing the number of possible divisions which would be put into operation by Germany and Poland taken together, he criticized the operational plan for intending to mobilize a significantly smaller number of divisions, and indicated how many divisions would be needed to actively repulse the aggressors. Describing conditions under which the Red Army "might suffer a serious defeat in its first operations," Tukhachevsky once again turned to the shortcomings of the authors who had written an operational plan in which the actions of the Belorussian Front would not be secured with the necessary forces and supplies. As a result of this, in his words, "defeat is not excluded even without any wrecking activity whatsoever." In order to underscore the weak sides of the operational plan adopted by the Politburo, Tukhachevsky declared that the "wrecking activities" worked out "by the center" amounted to the decision to "leave in place the current plan which consciously had not been secured with the necessary forces."[36]

The same device was used by Tukhachevsky when he mentioned the way the "conspirators" had reckoned with the defeatist directives from Trotsky and "the instructions from General Rundstedt." In actual fact he testified that in his activity he tried to reduce to nothing the consequences of these imaginary "directives" and "instructions." In this regard he referred to the fact that during the strategic war games in April 1936 he had proposed that Yakir "facilitate the work of the Germans by handing over the Leplevsky fortified region in an act of sabotage and wrecking" (such an action, according to the testimonies of the other defendants, entered into the plans of the "conspirators"), and he proposed that Uborevich (acting on behalf of the "Germans") "have diversionary groups of sappers in the area of his railroads." Following this scenario, Tukhachevsky went on to explain what must be done to reduce to a minimum the consequences of the possible blowing up of railroad bridges by the enemy.[37]

To put more pressure on the defendants, Stalin ordered that face-to-face encounters be arranged in the presence of members of the Politburo (or rather, in the presence of the usual Molotov, Voroshilov and Kaganovich). The confrontations were apparently designed to convince the future defendants that it would be useless to deny the charges in court. As Dagin, the former head of security at the NKVD, was to say at an interrogation in 1938, "all investigators were warned ahead of time about face-to-face confrontations, and they never stopped 'pumping' their victims right up until the moment of the encounter. The one who worried more than anyone else was Yezhov. He was always summoning the investigators to find out if the arrested people would pass muster during the confrontation. He was not interested in the heart of the case itself, but only whether or not the investigation would disgrace itself in the presence of Politburo members, or whether the prisoners would renounce their own testimony.... On the eve of the face-to-face confrontations, new transcripts would hastily be prepared which would record the testimony that the prisoners were supposed to give during the confrontation itself."[38] It is curious that Dagin's testimony exposing Yezhov's role in falsifying the investigations was given several months before the latter was arrested.

By the way, Yezhov didn't need to worry that the statements made by the prisoners to Stalin's envoys about the fabrication of false charges or about inhuman methods of investigation would improve their fate. In confidential conversations with Chuyev, Molotov never once mentioned his presence at the face-to-face confrontations with the military figures, but he did describe in detail how such encounters proceeded with his deputies at the Council of People's Commissars, people whom he knew much more intimately than the generals. Molotov was particularly vivid in describing the confrontation with Rudzutak, attended by several members of the Politburo. According to Molotov, Rudzutak told them that he did not admit to the crimes ascribed to him. The following dialogue between Chuyev and Molotov dealt with this issue:

"Could it really be that you were unable to stand up for him if you knew him so well?"

"I couldn't do so simply because of personal impressions! We had material at our disposal."

"If you were certain ..."

"I was not 100 percent certain. How could I be one hundred percent certain when people were saying that ... after all, I wasn't all that close to him. He was my deputy. We met at work. He was a good and intelligent man. But at the same time, I saw that he was very busy with his own personal affairs, he was mixed up with somebody, who knows, with some women [according to the "logic" of Stalin-Molotov, this was already an appropriate reason to distrust him politically—V.R.] ..."

"What charges were made against him?"

"I do not remember now. He said: 'No, this is all wrong. I strongly deny it. And they tortured me. They forced me. I will sign nothing.'"

"And this was reported to Stalin?"

"Yes. He cannot be excused. 'Act the way you see fit,' Stalin said. And Stalin thought highly of Rudzutak."

"And he shot him?"

"Yes, he shot him."

"And maybe he was innocent?"

"But I cannot fully vouch for him, I cannot say that he behaved honestly. He was friends with Antipov, Chubar [other deputies under Molotov who were arrested after Rudzutak – V. R.]."

Molotov concluded the discussion of Rudzutak's fate with a particularly cynical passage: "I consider him a guilty person who displayed enormous obstinacy and resistance. That fact alone—that he didn't want to talk to Chekists. Who else would he want to speak to if he had fallen into such a situation?"[39]

If fifty years later Molotov assessed the behavior of his deputy at the Sovnarkom in this way, it is easy to imagine what an impassable barrier must have arisen between him and the generals during the face-to-face confrontations. And it would have been even more senseless for the generals to have appealed to Voroshilov, since hostile relations had developed with him long ago.

Before the trial, it was proposed that the defendants appeal in a written statement to Stalin. In a statement written on 9 June, Yakir wrote: "All my conscious life has proceeded in honest and self-sacrificing work in plain sight of the party and its leaders—*then came the descent into a nightmare, into the incorrigible horror of treachery.... The investigation is over. I have been charged with state treason, I have confessed my guilt, and I have fully repented. I unreservedly believe in the correctness and wisdom of the decision made by the court and the government.... Now each word I speak is the truth—I will die with words* of love for you, the party and the country, and with unbounded faith in the victory of communism" [my italics—V. R.].[40]

This letter was read aloud by Zhukov at the June Plenum of the Central Committee in 1957, and then by Shelepin at the Twenty-Second Congress of the CPSU.[41] However, both times it was presented in a deliberately truncated and therefore falsified form. The words shown above in italics were omitted. This omission consciously gave the impression that after he had been falsely charged, tortured and humiliated, and sensing his unavoidable execution, the completely innocent Yakir was trying to accomplish one thing, to convince Stalin of his personal loyalty.

The only people Stalin allowed to read such documents were the same "troika" from the Politburo, who therefore were being subjected to one more loyalty test. Stalin wrote on Yakir's letter, "Scoundrel and prostitute," and sent it to Voroshilov. Voroshilov then made the obsequious addition: "An absolutely precise definition," under which Molotov also signed his name. Kaganovich felt compelled to add the unprintable words: "For a bastard, scum and whore, there is one punishment—the death penalty."[42]

In the days immediately preceding the trial, Stalin repeatedly received Vyshinsky and Yezhov in the presence of Molotov, Kaganovich, and Voroshilov. The end result of these meetings was the final preparation of the act of indictment, which was signed by Vyshinsky.

On the day of the trial, Stalin sent a telegram to the Central Committees of the Communist Parties in the republics, and to the regional and area committees, ordering them to organize meetings of workers at which they must "pass a resolution about the need to apply the supreme measure of punishment."[43]

50. The Trial of the Generals

ON THE DAY OF THE TRIAL, the newspapers published an article from the Procuracy of the USSR about the conclusion of an investigation into eight generals who had been charged with "violation of military duty (the oath), betrayal of the motherland, betrayal of the peoples of the USSR, and betrayal of the Workers' and Peasants' Red Army [RKKA]." The article said that the investigation had established the participation of the accused, as well as Gamarnik, "in anti-state links with leading military circles from one of the foreign states conducting unfriendly policies toward the USSR." Of course it was easy to guess that the "one foreign state" that the paper had in mind was Germany. Later it stated that the defendants were in the service of the military intelligence of this state, and that they systematically had gathered for its military circles espionage information about the state of the Red Army, carried out wrecking activity to undermine its strength, prepared its defeat in the war and, finally, "intended to expedite the restoration of a regime of land-owners and capitalists in the USSR."[1]

This article was squeezed out of the act of indictment, which said that the "center" of the military-Trotskyist organization to which the defendants belonged was formed in 1932–1933 on direct orders from Trotsky and the German General Staff, and acted in close concert with the "centers" of the Trotskyists and Rightists.

Unlike the transcripts of the open show trials, the transcripts of this trial were edited and corrected by the NKVD officials who had shortly before been conducting the investigation. In the course of an investigation at the beginning of the 1960s, many instances of distortions of the testimony were found in the transcripts. Thus, in 1962, when one of the stenographers at the trial compared her original stenographic notes to the corrected transcript, she pointed to arbitrary additions made to Feldman's testimony and to Tukhachevsky's concluding remarks. These additions spoke, in particular, about connections with the Japanese General Staff and about espionage on behalf of various foreign governments.[2]

Even the text of the transcript which had been edited in such a way testifies that the majority of the defendants denied their participation in espionage. Thus, in response to Dybenko's question, "When did you personally begin concretely to conduct espionage work for the German general staff?" Yakir replied: "Personally, I never directly began this work." When Dybenko asked a similar question, "Did you directly conduct espionage work with the German General Staff?" Uborevich replied, "I never did."[3]

When Ulrich asked when he had begun his espionage activity, Tukhachevsky replied, "I do not know if this could be considered espionage activity." Concretizing these words, Tukhachevsky said in his closing remarks: "I had a passionate love for the Red Army, a passionate love for my homeland which I have defended since the civil war.... As for the meetings and conversations with representatives of the German General Staff, and their military attaches in the USSR, then they were official in nature; they occurred at maneuvers, or at receptions. The Germans were shown our military technology, they had the opportunity to observe the changes taking place in the organization of our troops, or in their equipment. But all this happened before Hitler came to power, when our relations with Germany sharply changed."[4]

Important evidence about the behavior of the defendants during the trial is contained in notes presented after the trial by members of the Special Judicial Office. From a note by Budenny addressed to Stalin, it seems that Primakov, who confirmed many other charges, "very stubbornly denied the fact that he led a terrorist group against Comrade Voroshilov consisting of Shmidt, Kuzmichev and others." Budenny wrote that Tukhachevsky, "from the very beginning of the trial, during the reading of the indictment and during the testimony of all the other defendants, shook his head, emphasizing therefore that, from his standpoint, not only the trial, but the investigation and all that was recorded in the indictment—all this was not always true, or did not correspond to reality." Later Budenny wrote that Tukhachevsky started by trying to deny the testimony given at the pre-trial investigation, and even "tried to popularize his own official ideas before those sitting in the audience at the trial." From Budenny's further account of Tukhachevsky's testimony it follows that Tukhachevsky said that he had reported to the government about the small size of the Red Army in comparison with the German and Polish armies, but that "no one listened to" his ideas about the possible defeat of the Soviet Union as a result of this imbalance of armed forces. After these words, as Budenny reported, Ulrich cut off Tukhachevsky and asked him about his work "as an agent of the German intelligence services since 1925." In reply "Tukhachevsky declared that he, of course, might be taken for a spy, but that in actual fact he never gave any information to German intelligence."[5]

Belov's notes to Voroshilov, which were presented a month after the trial, produce a painful impression. In describing his observations of the defendants' bearing at the trial, Belov makes shameful comments which are meant to convince Voroshilov of his hatred for his former comrades. "Bourgeois morality says at every step: 'A man's eyes are the mirror of his soul,'" writes Belov. "During this trial, in the course of a single day I was able to convince myself more than I had been able to do throughout the rest of my life, that this statement is false. The eyes of this entire gang revealed nothing which would allow one to detect the limitless perfidy of the defendants sitting on the bench. As a whole, each one of them looked ... unnatural. The imprint of death was already present on their faces. In general, the color of their faces was what is called sallow.... Take Eideman. This type looked more pitiful than the others. He had completely fallen apart, had a hard time standing up, and didn't speak, but babbled in a muffled, unsteady, spasmodic voice." Like Budenny, Belov noted that at the trial Tukhachevsky "tried to demonstrate both his vast operational and technical erudition ... and tried to make the trial see his role as a positive one, and to minimize his role as a traitor."[6]

In private conversations at the beginning of 1938, when the danger of arrest was hanging above his own head, Belov spoke about his impressions of the trial in quite another way. In Erenburg's memoirs, he describes a "terrible day" at Meyerhold's apartment, when "Vsevolod Emilievich was visited by one of his friends, corps commander I. P. Belov. He was very agitated and, paying no attention to that fact that Liuba and I were in the room besides Meyerhold, began to tell how they tried Tukhachevsky and the other military men... 'This is how they sat—right opposite us. Uborevich looked me straight in the eyes....' I remember one more thing that Belov said: 'And tomorrow they will put me in their place.'"[7]

Unlike the open show trials, which lasted for a week or more, the closed military trial was over in one day. In the course of this day, Ulrich managed to visit Stalin, who, in the presence of Molotov, Kaganovich, and Yezhov, gave orders to sentence all the defendants to be shot. The sentence was read by

Ulrich at 11:35 P.M., and that night it was carried out in the presence of Ulrich and Vyshinsky.

On 12 June, both the sentence and a report that it had been carried out were published in the press. A day later, Voroshilov's order of the day to the army was published, which contained the following words: "World fascism will once again learn that its faithful agents, the Gamarniks and Tukhachevskys, Yakirs and Uboreviches, and other traitorous carrion who serve as capitalism's lackeys, have been wiped from the face of the earth. Their memory will be cursed and then forgotten."[8]

A few days after receiving information on the trial, Trotsky wrote an article, "The Decapitation of the Red Army." In it he stressed that the defendants were the flower of the Soviet high command. Yakir and Uborevich had been entrusted with the defense of the western border, and they had prepared for years for their future role as the country's defenders against German invasion. Even more significant military figures were Tukhachevsky and Gamarnik, who greatly surpassed Voroshilov in military talent and knowledge. During the Civil War years, Voroshilov had displayed a complete lack of the qualities needed for military leadership. "Neither Stalin nor the other members of the Politburo had any ... illusions about Voroshilov as a military leader. They tried therefore to prop him up with qualified personnel."[9] The real leader of the army was not Voroshilov, but Tukhachevsky, who fulfilled the function as its "mechanizer" and in any future war should have played the role of supreme commander.

Trotsky noted that the majority of the defendants had never belonged to the Left Opposition. Prior to 1928, only Primakov and Putna had been in its ranks. In 1924, Gamarnik, who worked at that time in the Ukraine, was also considered a "Trotskyist." The "troika" that ruled the party at that time (Zinoviev, Stalin and Kamenev), who had tried to tear the most capable "Trotskyists" away from their usual surroundings and buy them off with the perspective of a high-ranking career, transferred Gamarnik to the Far East. After a radical break from "Trotskyism," Gamarnik quickly climbed up the administrative ladder. After he became a member of the Central Committee and the senior representative of the party in the army, Gamarnik "played a leading role in all the army purges, doing along the way whatever was demanded of him."[10]

In the article Trotsky paid attention to the fact that, before the trial, Soviet newspapers called only Primakov, Putna and Gamarnik "Trotskyists," "but no one ever called the others this terrible name. What restrained them from turning Tukhachevsky, Yakir, Uborevich, Eideman and others into Trotskyists was not only the absence of any overt links, but also the absence of any desire to overly inflate the strength of Trotskyism in the army." Only in Voroshilov's order of the day, published the day after the execution of the generals, were all the generals declared to be Trotskyists. "Falsification, as we see, also has its own logic," Trotsky wrote in commenting on these facts. "If the generals, along with the Trotskyists, have served Germany in order to 'restore capitalism,' then Germany could not help but join them together in its own interest. In addition, 'Trotskyism' has long been a collective concept which embraces all who must be exterminated."[11]

The absurd and shameful accusation that the generals were serving Hitler's Germany, Trotsky stressed, was needed by Stalin in order to "justify with strong pretexts the murder of the most talented and independent people before the Russian workers and peasants. He is counting on the hypnotic action of the totalitarian press and the no less totalitarian radio." As for Stalin's innovation—the inclusion of major military leaders into the makeup of the court—this was a "diabolical test of loyalty. The military leaders who remain alive are henceforth beholden to Stalin by the shame with which he deliberately covered them."[12]

Trotsky stated that accusing the Soviet generals of collaboration with Germany pursued important foreign policy goals. It was designed to destroy the opinion in the West that "an alliance with Germany, regardless of its state form, was an axiom of the Soviet Union's foreign policy."[13] Using savage means, Stalin decided to demonstrate to the bourgeois-democratic states that he had broken with the pro-German orientation which he had been trying to preserve even after Hitler had come to power. In order to show loyalty to his new allies, especially France and Czechoslovakia, Stalin "needed scapegoats for the policy which he had renounced yesterday."[14]

All the defendants in the Tukhachevsky trial were rehabilitated in 1957, and Gamarnik in 1955. However the question of the reasons for their victimization apparently continued to bother Khrushchev. This, in my opinion, explains the fact that in 1961 a new commission was created by a resolution of the Presidium of the Central Committee of the CPSU. Its task was to review the charges made against Tukhachevsky and other military figures, and to clarify the reasons and conditions for opening their "case." The results of this work, which continued for more than three years, were outlined in a detailed report sent on 26 June 1964 to Khrushchev by the commission's chairman, Shvernik.

First of all, the commission rejected the charges of espionage ties between the generals and the German special services. One thing used in this process was the testimony of a former major general in the German army, Schpalke, who was engaged in intelligence gathering in the Soviet Union from 1925 to 1937. Arrested in 1947, Schpalke testified during the investigation that from 1926 on, he had been assigned to the commanders of the Red Army who traveled to Germany to study in the military academy; however he never received any espionage material from them. Schpalke was closely linked to the German military attache in Moscow, Koestring, who, according to the material of the investigation, received military secrets from the defendants. According to Schpalke, after the trial of the generals Koestring became indignant and stated that he had never had any espionage connections with the defendants.[15]

On the basis of expert testimony given by personnel from the General Staff of the Soviet Army, and other investigative actions which the investigators and the court should have performed in 1937 but did not, the commission reconfirmed the total groundlessness of the charges of wrecking made against the defendants.

The commission's report does not contain any answer to many legitimate questions which arise in an analysis of the generals' case. I have in mind first of all of the reasons for the confessions made by the defendants, and for the servile letters they wrote to Stalin before the trial. In the majority of historical works devoted to the Tukhachevsky case, these confessions are explained exclusively by the use of physical torture. However, such an explanation is inadequate for a number of reasons.

First of all, the defendants at the trial of the generals were strong and healthy people, most of whom had only recently crossed the threshold of their fortieth birthday. Unlike the main defendants at the open trials, they had not spent long years before their arrest engaged in endless acts of self-deprecation and humiliation. For this reason, one might expect significantly greater resistance from them than, for instance, from Zinoviev or Bukharin.

Second, the stunning speed with which the confessions were obtained draws our attention. The majority of the defendants at the open trials did not give such confessions for several months. The trial of the generals, however, was prepared in record-setting time. From the arrest of the main defendants to the trial itself, slightly more than two weeks passed. Such a time period was clearly insufficient to break these courageous men who had many times looked death in the eye.

Third, unlike the defendants at the open trials, where the judges were faceless bureaucrats, the defendants at the trial of the generals were appearing before their former comrades-in-arms. This fact should have filled them with hope that the truth, if spoken in their presence, would inevitably make it beyond the courtroom's walls.

Fourth, we know of many cases when the most savage torture proved to be incapable of extracting false confessions from those being investigated. No confessions were given during investigation or trial, for instance, by General Gorbatov, or by Gnedin, who headed the press department of the People's Commissariat of Foreign Affairs, or even by a woman, the secretary of the Central Committee of the VLKSM [Komsomol], Pikina, despite the fact that they all were subjected to cruel tortures. Why, then, should the defendants at the trial of the generals have proven to be weaker than these people?

51. Looking Ahead Fifteen Years

THERE IS ONE MORE VERSION of why the defendants "confessed." It is most clearly expressed in the testimony given by the investigator Zalpeter, in which he gave the following explanation of the causes behind the repression and the self-defamation which came from "responsible party members": "The mass repressions of leading officials in the People's Commissariats (including the People's Commissars) can be explained by the fact that Stalin ruled the country with dictatorial methods. He decided everything himself, did not tolerate objections, did not consider the opinion of others and subjected to mass operations those who contradicted (or criticized) him. These people were by no means counterrevolutionaries. In this sense, a correct characterization of Stalin is given in the Trotskyist document, the so-called 'Testament,'* which says that he was intolerant of those who thought differently."

Later, asking the question why the prisoners gave "false testimony," Zalpeter explained that "in essence, their fate had been decided before their arrest in the Central Committee." Understanding this and feeling that their situation was hopeless ("once they had died politically, what meaning did physical life have for such people"), these people, who lived in a state of absolute isolation and were subjected to physical interrogation methods, "would give any testimony against themselves, and when the investigators declared that the other people in their case had confessed—would include the latter in their testimony."[1]

This statement by a courageous and principled Chekist, which essentially reproduces the "Koestler complex," deserves careful consideration. However it ignores the indisputable fact that many victims of Stalin's terror signed the confessions beaten out of them at the pre-trial investigation, and then renounced them during the trial because they didn't want to cover themselves

---

* It is curious that Zalpeter, who was expressing his obviously negative opinion of Stalin, nevertheless called Lenin's "Testament" a "Trotskyist document." Of course, it cannot be excluded that these words were inserted into his testimony by the investigators.

with any more shame before their deaths. For instance, Medvedev, whom we have mentioned earlier, was tortured by the same investigators who tortured the generals appearing before a military trial. Then, on 17 June 1937, at a closed session of the court, Medvedev declared that all his testimony from the pre-trial investigation was false. Similar conduct by the defendants during their trial, where the judges were military leaders who knew them well, could have produced a much greater effect than the renunciation of a confession before three members of a Military Collegium who put their stamp on dozens of death sentences each day.

In order to clarify whether physical torture was always able to guarantee that the defendants would slander themselves and others at frame-up trials, let us turn to the transcript of the trial of the Jewish Anti-Fascist Committee [EAK], a case which was fabricated by the MGB [Ministry of State Security] in 1949–1952. Without addressing other aspects of this trial, let us deal only with those sides which are connected with explaining the reasons for defendants' "confessions" during pre-trial investigations and the renunciation of these confessions in the courtroom.

Unlike the extremely hasty preparation of the trial of the generals, the investigation in the case of the EAK lasted for about four years. During this entire time, the defendants were in the hands of extremely active falsifiers who used the multifaceted "experience" of the NKVD-MGB in dealing with people under investigation. In all senses it was easier to obtain "confessions" from the defendants in this case than from the victims of the trial of the generals. First of all, the majority of them were much older than the generals were in the 1930s; therefore there was a high probability that these people would not stand up to torture. Secondly, the people who were brought to trial from the EAK were in the clutches of the investigators for more than three years—much longer than the generals. Consequently, even in this regard, the situation of the generals was more auspicious than it was for the "EAKists." Thirdly, the defendants from the EAK were writers, scholars, and actors; it would appear to have been much easier to force them to give false confessions than the military leaders.

However, at the trial of the EAK, all the defendants completely denied their guilt and declared that the confessions they had given during the pre-trial investigation were forced from them and obtained as a result of the investigators' savage methods.

During the first court sessions the defendants still had not decided to speak about these methods. The poet Kvitko said only that "he had found it very difficult to fight with the investigator" and that "circumstances"[2] prompted him to give false testimony. The poet Gofshtein said: "During the investigation I was in such a state that I simply was not aware of what I was signing, or what I was doing.... I was trapped in such a chain of events, and in such conditions, that I agreed with everything that the investigator told me.... I was in a state of insanity."[3]

A scholar from the Institute of History, Iuzefovich, cautiously tried to tell the court how the defendants had been reduced to such a state: "Both the prison administration and the medical unit know what state I was in, how I was suffering, when they gave me transcripts to sign even though I was in complete disagreement with them. I do not want to elaborate, but if need be, I will testify about this in detail, only not here before everyone, but directly before the Military Collegium. But I do want to say one thing—I think that it fits into the transcript—I was prepared to confess even that I was the Pope's nephew and that I was acting in his name and on his direct orders."[4]

The journalist Talmy and the Deputy Minster of State Inspection Bregman explained that they confessed during the pre-trial investigation because they had been overwhelmed by long interrogations and sleepless nights. Bregman declared that at the time of the investigation he was "morally crushed and physically unwell.... In 1952 I became physically healthier, sorted many things out in my mind, analyzed them and finally declared that I was guilty of nothing."[5]

The actor Zuskin said: "I had no use for the type of life which I led in prison. Life in prison oppressed me, and I told the investigator, 'Write what you want, I will sign any sentence, but I want to live until the trial where I can tell the whole truth.'"[6]

The first to describe the investigators' methods, which forced the defendants to slander themselves and others, was the Deputy Minister of Foreign Affairs and Central Committee member Lozovsky. He said that the head of the investigation, Colonel Komarov, told him: "I should acknowledge all the charges, otherwise he would hand me over to his investigators ... then comes a 'mathematical formula which wouldn't fit into the transcript' [apparently Lozovsky had in mind the abusive language which the investigators were accustomed to using with the prisoners—V. R.], then he said that they would let me rot in prison and beat me with rubber truncheons so that I would no longer be able to sit down. Then I told them that it would be better to die than endure such torture. They told me in response that they would not allow me to die quickly, that I would die a slow death.... Then I decided that it would be better if I slandered myself and signed everything that they had written into the transcript, and then I would tell at the trial ... how Komarov conducts investigations."[7] Lozovsky said that in pursuing such a tactic, he slandered not only himself, but Zhemchuzhina (Molotov's wife), and also L. S. Shtern, and he asked the latter's forgiveness at the trial.

Even more terrible things were reported by the main physician at the Botkin Hospital, Shimeliovich, who said: "They threatened Lozovsky that they could beat him and do other things, and he slandered himself, and perhaps some others, so that later during the trial he could deny everything. I did not take this road. I argued for three years and four months, and if the opportunity presents itself, I will argue in the future, both with the investigator and, if necessary, with the prosecutor."

During the first round of questioning at the trial, Shimeliovich said that an hour and a half after he had been arrested and "made to look in the corresponding fashion," they took him to Abakumov, the Minister of State Security, who said right away, "Look, what a mug," after which he spoke the word, "Beat." When he later came up against Shimeliovich's stubborn refusal to confess, Abakumov once again repeated the order: "Beat him until he dies."

"If they only threatened Lozovsky," Shimeliovich continued, "then I must, unfortunately ... declare that for a month (January-February 1949) I received approximately, give or take a few in either direction, eighty to one hundred blows per day, and altogether, I think that I received about two thousand blows. I was repeatedly subjected to physical punishment, but you will hardly find an investigator who will say that even under all these circumstances I changed my testimony. No, whatever I knew I said, and never, neither standing, nor sitting, nor lying down, did I ever utter what is written down in those transcripts." The only time he signed a transcript was on a day of particularly savage beatings, when he was reduced to such a state that the investigators stopped several times to ask, "Can you hear?" He would answer, "I can hear, I can hear." This transcript, as Shimeliovich recalled, was put together by one of the main executioners and organizers of the EAK case, Riumin. Only after Riumin read excerpts from this transcript at the next interrogation did Shimeliovich learn that it contained his signature. Then he wrote a statement to Riumin in which he said: "The transcript which was put together by the investigation in March 1949 was signed by me when I was in a difficult psychological state—I was barely conscious. I was in such a state because of methodical beatings over the course of a month, day and night. I will not mention the insults and mockery. I ask that my present statement from 15 May 1949 be added to my dossier." After he had reported this at the trial, Shimeliovich added: "I felt that this course [of torture—V. R.] was apparently not finished, for the investigator Shishkov said to me: 'You see, everything that I promised you I will do. If you are in no condition to walk to the interrogations, then we will bring you on a stretcher and then we will beat you and beat you.'" Riumin personally did not touch him, but was present "at the beatings, where besides him there were seven people who directly participated in beating me."[8]

Shimeliovich signed the second transcript, which was also compiled by Riumin, after he had endured a new "course of beatings," and was in a "semiconscious and depressed state." He never said what was written down in this transcript, and "when he was in a clear frame of mind, renounced it even at the investigation."[9]

Iuzefovich testified at a closed session of the court (that is, in the absence of the other defendants), that Abakumov had told him: "If I didn't confess, then he would transfer me to the Lefortovo Prison, where they would beat me. And even before this they had already been 'working me over' for several days. I refused Abakumov, then they took me to Lefortovo Prison where they began to beat me with a rubber truncheon and stomp on me with their feet when I fell down. I decided to sign any confession if only to live until the day of the trial."[10]

As far as we can judge from the court material, such cruel tortures were not applied to the women; the investigators limited themselves to threatening that they would be used. As the translator, Vatenberg-Ostrovskaya, said, "they interrogated me with a rubber truncheon on the table.... They kept threatening that they would beat me terribly, that they would turn me into a cripple, and so forth.... This frightened me terribly, and I was in some kind of frenzy. Every day and night I heard from the investigator that they would beat me and beat me horribly."[11]

The academician L. S. Shtern reported that she had been taken three times from the inner prison to Lefortovo because she had not wanted to sign "the novel written by the investigators." The chairman then asked, "Well, there it's a prison and here it's a prison, what difference does it make?" Shtern answered:

"There—is the gateway to hell, perhaps sometime you [the judges—V. R.] might be able to go there and see what is going on.... The floor there is cement, the cells are poorly heated, there are small windows which do not always open, and the food is such that I could do nothing with it.... My cellmate told me that I would nevertheless sign everything during the investigation. And there truly were moments when it seemed to me that I was going mad, and at those times I could have told lies about myself and others.... After all, there were days when they questioned me twice. After you spend all night at an interrogation, you come to your cell in the morning, but they not only do not let you sleep, you cannot even sit down."[12]

At a closed session of the court, the poet Fefer said that on the night of his arrest Abakumov declared: "'If I would not give a confession, then they would beat me.' I therefore became frightened, which was why I gave false testimony at the pre-trial investigation, and then partially confirmed the lies during the trial.... I was so frightened, that during the face-to-face confrontation with Zhemchuzhina at the Central Committee, I said that I had seen her at the synagogue, although this had never really happened."[13]

Besides physical torture, the investigators used "psychological methods of coercion" in order to demoralize the prisoners. This included anti-Semitic outbursts which were supposed to make the prisoners become depressed. Thus, Lozovsky recounted how, over the course of eight nighttime interrogations, Komarov repeated many times, "'Jews were a rotten people, that Jews were crooks, good-for-nothings and scum, that the whole opposition was made up of Jews, and that all Jews sputter at the Soviet regime, that Jews want to exterminate all Russians.' And naturally, if he had wanted to, he could have written whatever he desired. That is how the forty-two-volume tree developed which lies before you, in which there is not a single word of truth about me."[14]

Along with beatings and threats, the investigators resorted to false promises to allow the prisoner to go free if he gave the required testimony. Thus the poet Markish was told by the investigator, "they condemn only the leading figures, but they would let me go. Riumin told me as early as 1950 that I could even begin thinking about a new book."[15]

The defendants told the court about other illegal methods used by the investigators. They said that the investigators not only wrote up the transcripts before the interrogations, but also resorted to direct distortion of testimony. "The investigator does not write down everything that the prisoner says, and, besides, he interprets this testimony in a completely different spirit than it was given," said the editor of a publishing house, Vatenberg. "They understand it in the following way: 'Nothing which serves the defense of the prisoner is to be entered into the transcript'... I could give tens, if not hundreds of (such) examples.... I declare that the dossier does not contain correctly formulated transcripts."[16]

Kvitko said with a certain measure of irony: "It seems to me that we have exchanged roles with the investigators, for they are obliged to charge us with facts, and I, a poet, am obliged to create imaginative works. But the opposite has happened."[17]

Lozovsky directed the judges' attention to the fact that the majority of the confessions of the most diverse people were fabricated according to the same standard. "You have studied these forty-two volumes better than I," he said to the judges, "and I think that you, as experienced people, noted that all the defendants testified in the same way and all the formulations are identical. However the people whose testimonies are gathered together in this case are people of varying cultural levels and status. It turns out that someone reached an understanding with regard to the formulations. Who, the arrested? I think not. That means that the investigators reached an understanding, otherwise it would be impossible to obtain identical formulations from different people."[18]

As one more method of falsification, Lozovsky named the replacement of "material evidence ... with the immaterial fabrications of the investigator."[19] He emphasized that the accusations made against him of passing espionage material to the Americans were not substantiated by any materials of the investigation. In this regard, Lozovsky declared: "Not as a member of the Central Committee, but simply as a rank-and-file Soviet man, do I have the right to know for what reason I am supposed to be executed?... How in general could you conceal such things? After all, this means that several heads will fall. It means not only my own head, but the heads of my family and a number of others which are here today. What is this, does the Soviet method of investigation mean to charge a man with espionage and then to hide from him and the court the very material for which he must be executed?"[20]

Several defendants rejected not only the slanders made against themselves, but also against people sitting next to them on the defendants' bench. "I consider Lozovsky an honest man," said Iuzefovich. "I do not believe, and even in the other world I will not believe, that he is a criminal. He might have made mistakes ... but for him to commit a crime is the same thing as to say that if I were to commit a crime, I must choose to commit suicide and become the murderer of my young daughter."[21]

To refute the charges, the defendants chose the tactics of offense rather than defense. In this regard, Lozovsky's declaration is characteristic when he addresses one of the main charges—that EAK activists wanted to create a Jewish republic in the Crimea to turn it into a beachhead for the USA. "From Fefer's testimony which he gave earlier," said Lozovsky, "it follows that they promised (the Americans) to fight for the Crimea. Who? These two musketeers, Fefer and Mikhoels—would fight for the Crimea, against the Soviet regime. This once again is slanderous fictionalizing. And who made it up? Fefer himself, and this served as the foundation of the entire trial, this was the starting point of all the charges, including that of treason. But today something else emerges from Fefer's testimony. But I, for instance, cannot be held responsible for everything that Fefer has woven together, and now is changing."[22]

In proving the absurdity of the premise in the indictment about the "direct pact [of EAK figures—V. R.] with representative of reactionary American circles," Lozovsky said: "I ask, where have the reactionary circles of America come from, where have they jumped out from? This is from newspapers of 1952, not 1943. When Mikhoels and Fefer were in the USA, there was at that time the government of Roosevelt, with whom we were in alliance.... What right did the investigator have to apply the alignment of forces in 1952 to the alignment of forces in 1943?"

In examining the history of how the version of the Crimea arose, Lozovsky said that this version first appeared in Fefer's testimony about the beautiful Crimean landscapes which attracted Jews to the Crimea. "As more and more prisoners were questioned, this formulation began to grow, and each investigator added a bit, and in the end the Crimea became overgrown with such a pelt that it turned into a monster. That's how the beachhead arose. Why, where from, and on what grounds? Someone supposedly said that the American government intervened in this matter. That means Roosevelt. I must say that in the fall of 1943 Roosevelt met with Stalin in Teheran. May I be so bold as to assure you, that I know more than all the investigators put together what they were discussing in Teheran, and I must say that nothing was said there about the Crimea.... Why then did they have to sharpen this formulation until it smells of blood?... Because the investigators reached an agreement among themselves, some added a bit, others added some more, and it turned out that Lozovsky wanted to sell the Crimea to reactionary American circles.... The myth-making about the Crimea is something absolutely legendary, and here is would be appropriate to use Pomialovsky's expression, that it was 'fiction in the neural substance'... The investigation will not be able to dress Lozovsky in the collar of an agent of reactionary circles from the USA."[23]

Summing up his testimony, Lozovsky declared: "The indictment against me is fundamentally false. It does not stand up to criticism from a political or from a legal point of view. Moreover, it contradicts the truth, logic and common sense."[24]

Throughout the trial, Shimeliovich acted with extreme courage. In his closing remarks he said, "These people from the MGB did not succeed in breaking me. I want to emphasize one more time that in the course of the trial, the indictment has been demolished." Shimeliovich appealed to the court to bring to trial those guilty of falsifying the whole case against the EAK and of using criminal methods during the investigation. "I ask the court to go to the appropriate authorities with a request to ban corporal punishment in the prisons," he said. " ... On the basis of what I have said during the trial, I would ask that several MGB agents be held strictly responsible ... including Abakumov."[25]

In additional testimony Kvitko said, "The facts on which the crimes ascribed to me are based—do not exist, and the charges are based on false testimony from several dishonest and self-seeking people."[26]

When speaking about her ideological inclinations, Shtern said, "From my point of view, that with which I am charged—cosmopolitanism—is internationalism."[27] Then she added, "I waited for this trial with great impatience and feared that I would not live to see it. I did not want to die with the charges which lay upon me."[28]

In her closing remarks, Shtern declared, "With my arrest the Soviet Union has suffered a much greater blow than from all the activity of the EAK, since it is now possible to discredit my work and to destroy all that has been achieved.... For me, my work is important, and for good work I would have to witness the restoration of trust in me, as well as my full rehabilitation."[29]

The defendants' renunciation of the slanderous charges did not save them from destruction (Stalin ordered to leave among the living only L. S. Shtern), but it did save them from having to cover their own names with dishonor.

In this regard, let us ask the question: why did Tukhachevsky, Yakir and other generals not conduct themselves during the trial as the defendants at the trial of the EAK conducted themselves in 1952? In turn, this question is inexorably bound up with another: Was the trial of the generals the purest falsification (like the trial of the EAK) or was it an amalgam, that is, the combination of false charges of espionage, etc., with charges having a factual basis? In other words, was there a military-political conspiracy against Stalin?

52. Was There a Military Conspiracy?

In works written during the last years of his life, Trotsky returned several times to the question of whether a conspiracy of the generals actually had existed. In the article, "Decapitation of the Red Army," he analyzed the social and political reasons which might have given rise to the plans, intentions and agreements of the military leaders against Stalin. The army was basically a peasant army in its composition. Besides the army's dissatisfaction with collectivization and its consequences, Trotsky saw other reasons, such as the contradictions between the military and civilian bureaucracies which arise in a totalitarian regime. "When the bureaucracy frees itself from popular control," he wrote, "the military caste inevitably tries to free itself from the supervision of the civilian bureaucracy.... It is true that there has not yet been a conspiracy. But it is on the agenda. The dispute has had a preventive character. Stalin has used a 'fortuitous' opportunity to give the officers a bloody lesson."[1]

Trotsky developed this idea in his book *Stalin*, where he stressed that the military apparatus "finds it hard to put up with the limitations placed upon it by politicians and civilians." Foreseeing the possibility that conflicts might arise with the army apparatus, headed by independent and experienced military leaders, Stalin used the GPU to prepare a noose for the flower of the high command.[2]

Trotsky saw another reason for the discontent of the generals: in the face of a growing threat of war, the most responsible commanders could not help but feel alarm over the fact that such a limited and militarily untalented person as Voroshilov headed the army. "One can be sure that in these circles people advanced the candidacy of Tukhachevsky to take his place.... The generals may have held discussions about how they should free the army in general from the supervision of the Politburo. From here it is still a long way before reaching a direct conspiracy. But under conditions of a totalitarian regime, this is already the first step towards one."[3]

In his book *Stalin*, Trotsky compared the official reports of the trial of the generals with the reports of the trial in the case of the "Right-Trotskyist Bloc," which took place in March 1938. There was an obvious contradiction between these accounts. The sentence in the military trial accused the generals of obtaining espionage information for the government of a hostile state and of preparing the defeat of the Red Army in the event of war. At the trial of the "Right-Trotskyist Bloc," the question of the Tukhachevsky conspiracy was once again raised with new aims now being attributed to it. The generals who had been shot nine months before "were subjected along the way to a new trial, and, forgetting to dismiss the overly fantastic charges of espionage, [Stalin's cohorts] charged them with preparing a military conspiracy."

In response to the question, "Was there in fact a military conspiracy?" Trotsky replied in the following way: "It all depends on what people call a conspiracy. Every sign of discontent, every time dissatisfied people draw closer together, every criticism or argument about what must be done in order to halt the devastating policies of the government—is, from Stalin's standpoint, a conspiracy. And under a totalitarian regime, without any doubt every opposition is the embryo of a conspiracy." Trotsky considered the attempt of the generals to protect the army "from the demoralizing intrigues of the GPU" to be such an "embryo." "They protected the interests of defense."[4]

It would be appropriate to move from Trotsky's hypotheses to statements by leaders of foreign states, who devoted no small amount of thought to the question of how much truth there was in the official reports about a military conspiracy in the USSR. An analysis of this question, as well as the question of the causes and background of the Great Terror in general, occupied a prominent place in Churchill's work, *The Second World War*. In the corresponding section of his book, Churchill not only made a number of factual errors and slips, but, like many other bourgeois politicians, also showed an inability to understand the domestic events happening in the USSR.* On the one hand, he felt that it was "highly improbable that the communists from the old guard had united with the military and vice versa." On the other hand—in complete contradiction with the given argument—on the same page he acknowledged

---

* The weakness of Churchill's conceptions of the structure of the regime in the USSR can be seen, for instance, in his comments on the disagreements which supposedly existed between Stalin and the other members of the Politburo during the war. On the whole, even in this book, written at the height of the "cold war," Churchill did not conceal his enthusiasm for Stalin, whom he called a great Russian statesman and military leader.

that it was completely possible that there was "a so-called conspiracy of the military and the old guard of the communists who tried to overthrow Stalin and establish a new regime on the basis of a pro-German orientation." Apparently not having information that Stalin himself was inclined to adopt a pro-German orientation long before the "Molotov-Ribbentrop Pact," Churchill attributed it to the Old Bolsheviks and the Soviet military leaders, who held consistently anti-fascist positions.

Churchill saw another motive for a possible confrontation between representatives of these two groups and Stalin. He thought that "they undoubtedly were filled with envy toward Stalin, who was pushing them aside." Proceeding from this conception, Churchill felt that Stalin was justified in trying to "deal with them all at once in accord with the customs of a totalitarian state."

Filled with unconcealed respect for Stalin, Churchill called the attitude of Chamberlain and the general staffs of England and France exaggerated when they thought that the purge of 1937 was "an internal defeat of the Russian army" and that "obvious hatred and feelings of revenge were tearing apart the Soviet Union." In contrast to these arguments, Churchill declared that "a system of rule based on terror could quite well be reinforced by a ruthless and successful consolidation of its power." Proceeding from these premises, he virtually approved of the "ruthless, but perhaps, useful purge of the military and political apparatus in Soviet Russia and the series of trials ... at which Vyshinsky performed so brilliantly [sic!—V. R.] in the role of state prosecutor."[5]

More substantial comments were made by Hitler with regard to the "grandiose purge of the general staff carried out by Stalin." Hitler, better than anyone else, knew the true value of the documents handed over by his special services to Stalin which served as the basis for putting the generals on trial. Nevertheless, in one of his table conversations with those close to him, Hitler made the significant remark: "Even now it is still not clear if the differences between Stalin, on the one hand, and Tukhachevsky and his colleagues on the other, really went so far that Stalin was forced to seriously fear for his life, the threat to which came from this circle of people."[6] It is possible that Hitler's reasoning here was not a purely speculative hypothesis, but rested upon some facts that were at his disposal.

Let us now turn to accounts which come, so to speak, from the opposite flank, from people who were the closest to Stalin and who joined him in preparing the trial of the generals. In this area, we are largely indebted to Feliks

Chuyev, an inveterate Stalinist who nourished a burning desire to rehabilitate and glorify Stalin, and for this reason enjoyed the trust of Molotov and Kaganovich, who answered his most "ticklish" questions. In conversations with Chuyev, both of these Stalinist stooges categorically denied the fact that they agreed to the rehabilitation of the military leaders. However, the decision in favor of the legal rehabilitation of the latter was made by the Military Collegium of the Supreme Court of the USSR on 31 January 1957 (and for Gamarnik, in 1955), and the decision on their party rehabilitation was made at a session of the Presidium of the Central Committee of the CPSU on 25 April 1957, that is, when Molotov and Kaganovich were members of this Presidium. At the June plenum of the CC in 1957, where they were directly charged with reprisals against Tukhachevsky and his comrades, they did not say a single word about their opposition to the rehabilitation of the military leaders.

Many years later, in defending the version that the generals were guilty of the crimes with which they were incriminated at the trial of 1937, Kaganovich offered very unconvincing arguments: "Nevertheless, there was some kind of grouping in the high command, there couldn't help but be. It was there. All this upper layer had studied in Germany, and was connected with the Germans. We received information, Stalin had facts, that we had a group that was connected with the fascists.... Tukhachevsky was, by all accounts, a man of Bonapartist inclination. A capable man. He could have had such pretensions."[7]

Kaganovich replied no more intelligibly to the concrete questions Chuyev asked:

"Was he (Tukhachevsky) a conspirator?"

"I fully allow that he was."

"People are now writing that their confessions were beaten out of them by Chekists."

"The confessions are not the point, it was the material which we had before the trial," said Kaganovich.

"But they were given to Stalin by the Germans via Beneš."

"People say that it was English intelligence. But I allow that he was a conspirator. At that time, anything was possible."[8]

Molotov outlined his version of the conspiracy more coherently and with greater assurance. When Chuyev read him an excerpt from Churchill's book— about the information received from Beneš as the starting point for the organization of the trial—Molotov said: "I am not sure that this question is being correctly presented.... Stalin could not have believed a letter from a bourgeois leader when he far from always trusted his own people. The point is that we knew about the conspiracy even without Beneš, we even knew the date of the coup."[9]

Molotov readily talked about the "Tukhachevsky conspiracy" with other writers, too, who adhered to Stalinist views. In a book with the significant title *Confession of a Stalinist,* Ivan Stadniuk said that in a conversation about this conspiracy "Molotov spoke in detail about who was supposed to kill him and Stalin, Voroshilov and Kaganovich, and when it was supposed to happen."[10]

One more writer with whom Molotov shared his reminiscences and views was V. Karpov, the first secretary of the Union of Soviet Writers and a member of the Central Committee of the CPSU. In his book about Zhukov, Karpov tells how he once raised the question of the victimization of the generals in a conversation with Molotov:

> "These were major military leaders who did so many good things during the Civil War. You knew them all well, didn't you have some doubts about their hostile activity?"
>
> Molotov answered firmly and even, I would say, cruelly:
>
> "With regard to these military figures, I never had any doubts, I knew them as Trotsky's protégés—they were his cadres. He put them in place with far-ranging goals, back when he was aiming at becoming the head of the state. It was very good that we managed to neutralize these conspirators before the war.... I always knew Tukhachevsky to be a sinister figure."[11]

Molotov's reminiscences are interesting primarily as a reflection of the somber psychology of this man who until the last days of his life tried to justify his own crimes. This, however, does not exclude the fact that some fragments of his testimony might, as I will soon show, be taken into account when discussing the question of whether a "military conspiracy" existed.

Unfortunately, the Russian and foreign researchers who have returned time and time again to unraveling the Tukhachevsky affair, have practically not a single disinterested account from anyone who participated in this tragedy. In such instances, the historian is compelled to acknowledge the existence of what is called a "white spot." And it is white precisely because it lacks color, i.e., evaluation, in the historical sense. Everyday thinking finds it hard to reconcile itself with such indifference, it tries to lend color to history in order to continually find guilty ones and their victims. The historian is duty-bound to leave unpainted spots in the picture he presents until he finds objective and irreproachable evidence and testimony.

This does not mean that unexposed crimes and incompletely explained tragedies teach us nothing in politics. The history of the "generals' plot" offers a lesson which is no less important than the history of the still unexplained Kennedy assassination.

When a group of influential people (or even one man, such as John Kennedy) is the strongest weapon in a clash of powerful political forces, it often proves to be very difficult to know the truth, or to find reliable accounts of what happened. The more significant the scale of the political intrigue, the more important it becomes for its organizers to remove all traces. Therefore usually all immediate witnesses are eliminated. But an even more reliable way to conceal the truth, is to bury it, i.e., genuine events and their motives, under several layers of carefully prepared lies. When a researcher finds himself in such a room of mirrors, he might easily lose the orientation of his historical quest. All the divergent versions seem to be true since they are entangled not only with clear fabrications, but also with half-truths. And at the same time not one of these various accounts, which offer, at first glance, an exhaustive range of alternatives, leads to the truth.

Finding out that each successive discovery has turned out to be a new variant of lie and disorientation, the researcher might be prompted to recognize whatever version that suits him as the historical truth. However, there is always a chance that he will not end up buried under the rubble of the many versions being foisted upon him. For this he must answer the age-old question: *cui prodest*? Who would benefit from the "unmasking" of the "generals' conspiracy?"

It would benefit Stalin, for it would allow him to eliminate potentially dangerous political opponents. It would benefit Hitler, insofar as it would permit him to weaken the Red Army. It would benefit the leaders of the major capitalist powers, insofar as the weakening of the Red Army would improve the probability of the successful outcome of their scenario: "Let the Soviets and fascists slaughter each other." If the geopolitical forces of such a scale and with such a purpose were interested in some kind of conspiracy, then it would "take place," even though in fact it might be more symbolic than practical, or it might actually be carried out by people quite apart from those who were "unmasked," or the intentions of the people "unmasked" might have been infinitely remote from the motives which are attributed to them.

Even if one of the interested parties did not manage to, could not, or did not participate in the "unmasking" of the conspiracy, the sum of their intersecting interests creates the historical field on which it must have arisen.

The lessons of each major political conspiracy are extremely valuable, for they firmly remind us that large-scale politics not only reshuffles or shatters human destinies, it hourly creates a new historical reality—a rationally constructed, controllable world which often exerts decisive influence on the fates of millions of people.

It is unlikely that we will someday find the eyewitness accounts of people who directly participated in the "military conspiracy." All the people who could have known about it were destroyed during the years of the Great Terror (nine days after the trial of the generals, the number of people arrested who were charged with being accomplices in this conspiracy had already reached almost one thousand).

All the more important are the accounts received, so to speak, secondhand. Although they are not considered evidence in the courtroom, for the historian they might provide important assistance, especially when they come from a man who deserves to be trusted. In this regard, let us briefly dwell on the fate of a man who provided important evidence of the existence of an anti-Stalinist conspiracy in 1937.

53. The Ballad of General Orlov

> The style of the ballad is by no means young
> But if the words are painful
> And the words say that they are painful,
> Then the style of the ballad grows young.
> *Vladimir Mayakovsky*

THIS CHAPTER IS PERHAPS the most difficult chapter in the book. It talks about the fate of a man who played no small role in the history of the twentieth century, a man with one of the most contradictory biographies in modern history. He was a man whose exploits in various years evoke revulsion and indignation, or understanding and respect. The reader has often met with this man's name—Alexander Orlov—in the pages of our book. From the previous chapters one draws the irrefutable conclusion that, in 1936–1938, Orlov played the role of the "Spanish Yezhov" (while immeasurably surpassing the latter in intellect, erudition and the mastery of an intelligence agent). Unlike the "bloody dwarf," who was blindly devoted to the "leader," when Orlov was carrying out Stalin's most sinister orders he was filled with an ever-growing hatred for him.

The story of Orlov's fate is made easier by the fact that we now know much more about it than about the fate of any other of the Soviet figures on this level. Orlov's biography is treated in detail in the major monograph *Deadly Illusions*, written by the Russian journalist Oleg Tsarev and the English historian John Costello. This thorough and conscientious investigation is based on an analysis of Orlov's accessible and voluminous dossiers which are contained in Soviet and American archives. The authors deserve to be commended for the fact that their book, which came out in New York in 1993, i.e., at the height of the anticommunist hysteria which had been unleashed in the republics of the former Soviet Union, is almost devoid of any tendentious or anticommunist passages.

Orlov with his daughter, 1938

After he fled to the USA, Orlov was fully justified in fearing that the same fate would befall him as had earlier befallen Reiss. Therefore, with the help of his relatives and childhood friends who were in the USA, he obtained permission to live in this country under an assumed name. Nevertheless, he reasonably assumed that Stalin's agents would search for him throughout the world in order to "liquidate" him.

In his book *The Secret History of Stalin's Crimes,* Orlov wrote that, in trying to prevent himself and his family from being killed by Stalin's gangsters, he sent Stalin a letter in which he warned that if his family were harmed, he would publish information about Stalin's crimes which was known only to him outside the Soviet Union (a list of these crimes was included with the letter). If the killers reached Orlov himself, these exposures would be published by his lawyer.

It is most likely that this version is a deliberate obfuscation by Orlov. Careful searches in the Soviet archives have not revealed any traces of such a letter.

As the authors of the book *Deadly Illusions* correctly note, Orlov must have known that his warning would hardly frighten Stalin. "The cynical dictator would surely have scoffed them off as the undocumented allegations of an embittered Trotskyist traitor."[1]

In actuality, Orlov resorted to a much more effective means to restrain Stalin-Yezhov from chasing after him. In the NKVD archive, an eleven-page letter was found which he sent to Yezhov soon after he fled to the United States. In this letter Orlov promised his complete silence if they left him in peace, and at the same time unequivocally, although vaguely, warned that if they dealt with him or his relatives, a statement would be made public about the spy network which he had created in England in the 1930s, which included agents of such caliber as Philby, Maclean, Burgess and others.[2]

The term "repentance," which has been thoroughly vulgarized by today's "democrats," could properly be applied to Orlov during this period of forced emigration. Or to be more precise, we must speak of true repentance of his own crimes, which Orlov decided in some measure to mitigate through political actions which were dangerous for him. At the end of 1938, he sent a letter to Trotsky in which he said that an agent-provocateur of the NKVD named "Mark" had been infiltrated into the milieu of the Paris Trotskyists and the editors of the *Bulletin of the Opposition*. Not knowing Zborowski's last name, Orlov gave information he knew about the spy which left no doubt about whom he meant: his appearance, family situation, official place of work, etc.

Legitimately fearing that the letter might be seized by NKVD agents, Orlov did not mention his own name in it. The letter was written in the name of Stein, a naturalized American Jew (Orlov warned Trotsky that this name was not genuine). In order to win Trotsky's trust with regard to his message, "Stein" wrote that he had received the information about "Mark" from his relative, the NKVD official Liushkov, who had fled in 1938 to Japan.[3]

Not long ago, it became known that a second letter was sent from "Stein" to Trotsky. It was written in connection with an article appearing in the Western press that Trotsky was expecting the arrival in Mexico of his grandson. Not knowing that this referred to the boy who was living in France, Orlov revealed a plan worked out long ago by the NKVD: to send Trotsky, in the guise of his grandson living in the Soviet Union, a completely different child accompanied by a person who would be assigned to kill Trotsky. He begged Trotsky to be extremely careful, reporting how insistent Stalin was in demanding that his satraps carry out the murder as soon as possible.

Unfortunately, the communication between Orlov and Trotsky remained onesided. Responding to "Stein's" request to establish systematic contact, Trotsky placed an ad in an American newspaper, inviting the author of the warning letters to appear in the editorial offices of the Trotskyist newspaper in New York and to meet there with one of its staff. Orlov visited this office, but the appearance of the man Trotsky had designated caused him, who knew about the intensive penetration of Stalinist agents into Trotskyist organizations, to lose confidence: he suspected that the man was an agent of the NKVD. After this, Orlov decided to phone Trotsky (at that time to call from the USA to Mexico was not as simple as it is today). He managed to place a call, but fearing that his telephone conversation would be monitored, decided not to tell the secretary who came to the phone his name or the goal of his call. Trotsky refused to come to the phone, thinking that some unknown but persistent journalist was imposing himself in order to get an interview.

Orlov's warning with regard to Zborowski did not achieve its goal. Soon after receiving the letter, Trotsky showed it to Lola Estrine, who had arrived in Mexico. She managed to convince him that this letter was sent by Stalinist agents who were trying to pry away from him one of his devoted followers.

The very fact that Orlov sent the letters to Trotsky is very significant. It shows that even such a man as Orlov, who had carried out Stalin's orders to exterminate Trotskyists in Spain, was trying in every way possible to warn Trotsky about the dangers which threatened him.

For a long time after his arrival in the USA, Orlov did not make himself known. Only after *Life* magazine published his articles in 1953, which later went into his book *The Secret History of Stalin's Crimes*, did the American authorities learn that a former NKVD general had been living on the territory of their country for fifteen years. The FBI immediately became involved with Orlov. For more than ten years Orlov was repeatedly questioned by members of this organization, and he also spoke before special hearings organized by the Senate Subcommittee on Internal Security. As a result of these interrogations, the American Pinkertons were sure that Orlov had told them everything he knew about the activity of Soviet intelligence. However the former Soviet agent clearly "outplayed" his American colleagues. Having created an impression of complete sincerity, he did not provide a single name of the agents he had recruited who were successfully continuing their work for the USSR. The only NKVD agent whom Orlov was happy to expose was Zborowski, who had moved in 1942 to the USA. The final result of this exposé was the opening of a legal investigation into Zborowski, who was finally sentenced to five years in prison.

The Secret History of Stalin's Crimes is the most complete and reliable account of the mechanism of Kirov's murder and the organization of the Moscow Trials, especially the first, which occurred when Orlov was in the USSR. According to Orlov, he received information about the other trials from NKVD officials who traveled to Spain in 1937–1938. The majority of facts contained in Orlov's book have been confirmed by official investigations conducted in the USSR in the 1950s and 1960s.

The least interesting chapter in the book was the chapter devoted to the "Tukhachevsky affair," which Orlov treated hastily and in many ways inaccurately. Only at the end of this chapter does he let slip an enigmatic phrase: "When all the facts connected with the Tukhachevsky case become clear, the world will understand that Stalin knew what he was doing."[4]

Orlov made public a new version of the "Tukhachevsky affair" only after the Twentieth Congress of the CPSU. On 23 April 1956, his article appeared in *Life* under the title, "The Sensational Secret Behind Damnation of Stalin." Both the facts contained in the article and the fate of the article itself deserve the most careful analysis.

54. The Secret of the Tukhachevsky Affair

IMMEDIATELY AFTER THE TRIAL of the generals, their close friends and relatives were arrested, and the majority of them were shot. The sole defendant's
wife remaining at liberty turned out to be L. Yu. Brik, who had been married to
Primakov before his arrest. She apparently was saved by the circumstance that
in 1935 she had attracted Stalin's attention when she wrote him a letter about
what she considered to be the negligent attitude of leading literary circles toward the works of Mayakovsky, her earlier husband. On this letter, Stalin outlined a resolution addressed to Yezhov, which contained the famous words
about Mayakovsky as "the best, most talented poet of our Soviet epoch."

In his book *Unfinished Novels*, the writer Iulian Semenov tells about his
conversation with L. Brik, who recalled, "I spent all of 1936 in Leningrad.... And
during that whole time I noticed—and the longer it went on, the more I noticed—that in the evenings military figures would come to visit Primakov. They
locked themselves in his study and sat there until late at night. Perhaps they
truly wanted to topple the tyrant?"[1]

In connection with this statement, Iu. Semenov made public for the first
time in the Soviet press the following version. The Chekists, who had received
the order from Stalin to find documents in the tsarist archives which would
compromise the pre-revolutionary past of the victims of the show trials, unexpectedly found documentary evidence of Stalin's activity as an agent-provocateur of the tsarist secret police. After they related this news to their cothinkers
in the military, the latter "began to prepare a coup in order to save the country
from the tyrant: the grounds for overthrowing Stalin were absolute.[2]

Evidently the writer borrowed this version from Orlov's article in *Life*, which
he could have been able to read only abroad, since the issue with this article
was removed from the special depositories of all the Moscow libraries sub-
scribing to this journal.[3] (This very fact suggests the serious alarm in the Soviet leadership over Orlov's exposés).

Orlov opened his article by telling about his meeting in the fall of 1937 in

470

EX-NKVD GENERAL IS FINALLY FREE TO DISCLOSE DEEDS SO SHOCKING REDS MUST DISOWN OLD IDOL

In the 1930s Alexander Orlov was one of the Soviet Union's highest ranking NKVD officers and with the late Andrei Vishinsky was a prosecutor at the Soviet Supreme Court. Just prior to his defection to the West in 1938, Orlov served as the Soviet's chief intelligence officer with the Loyalist forces during the Spanish civil war.

In 1953, in a series of articles in LIFE, later published in book form as The Secret History of Stalin's Crimes, Orlov for the first time revealed the background of the notorious purges and judicial frame ups

whereby the dictator consolidated on the country his personal rule by terror. The authenticity of Orlov's account has now been confirmed in many instances by no less an authority than Nikita Khrushchev, speaking for the present leadership of the Soviet Union. But at that time Orlov did not dare—and he explains why on page 13 —to disclose Stalin's guiltiest secret of all.

In this article Orlov discloses that secret and offers it as a cogent reason for the sensational turnabout of Russia's bosses in denouncing and downgrading Stalin.

by ALEXANDER ORLOV

IN the autumn of 1937, visiting Paris from my post in Spain, I ran into Paul Alliluyev, brother-in-law of Stalin and a friend of mine, at the Soviet pavilion of the International Exhibition. Sensing that he was deeply depressed and eager to tell someone his troubles, I arranged to meet Alliluyev very same evening.

We walked along the Seine for a long time and ended up in an obscure little cafe. Our conversation ranged far and wide over the horrendous landscape of the blood purges then under way in the Soviet Union. At one point, quite naturally, I asked him what was behind the most spectacular single episode in the cruel events: the execution of Marshal Mikhail Tukhachevsky and other Red army marshals and generals.

Paul's eyes narrowed and he spoke slowly, evidently anxious that I take his words to heart. "Alexander," he said, "don't ever inquire about the Tukhachevsky affair. Knowing about it is like inhaling poison gas."

I wondered then—and again two years later, in New York, when I read the announcement of Paul's sudden but never explained death—how much of the poison gas

to history as Stalin. It was a secret that obsessed Stalin's mind and spelled death for those whom he suspected of knowing it.

In my book, The Secret History of Stalin's Crimes, published in 1953, I declared that "when all the facts of the Tukhachevsky affair are disclosed, the world will realize that Stalin knew what he was doing. . . . I am making this assertion because I know from an absolutely unimpeachable and authoritative source that the case of Marshal Tukhachevsky was tied up with one of Stalin's most horrible secrets which, when disclosed, will throw light on many things that seemed so incomprehensible in Stalin's behavior."

Today the same disclosure will also throw a revealing light on the panicky behavior of Khrushchev and Co, as they hasten to disown Stalin's crimes and to demolish the myth of his greatness.

At the 20th Congress of the Soviet Communist party this February, Nikita Khrushchev astonished Russia and the world by declaring:

Stalin had fabricated charges of trea-

Orlov's article in *Life* magazine

Paris with Stalin's brother-in-law, Pavel Alliluev, who had come there on official business. According to Orlov, Alliluev looked very depressed. The conversation they had "revolved around a terrible picture of the bloody purges which were then taking place in the Soviet Union." When Orlov asked a question about the background to the Tukhachevsky case, Alliluev answered, "Alexander, don't ever inquire about the Tukhachevsky affair. Knowing about it is like inhaling poison gas."[4] A year later, P. S. Alliluev died a sudden and mysterious death.

Following this, Orlov said that Alliluev did not suspect that he, Orlov, was the only man outside the borders of the USSR who was familiar with the events which prompted Stalin to purge the Red Army. Orlov then added that now he was describing these events for the first time, including the "most sensational and certainly the best kept secret in the monstrous career of Josef Dzhugashvili.... It was a secret that obsessed Stalin's mind and spelled death for those whom he suspected of knowing it.... I am making this assertion because I know from an absolutely unimpeachable and authoritative source that the case of Marshal Tukhachevsky was tied up with one of *Stalin's most horrible secrets*, which,

Illustration to
Orlov's article in *Life*

when disclosed, will throw light on many things that seemed so incomprehensible."[5]

"The authoritative source," to use Orlov's words, was his cousin, Z. B. Katsnelson, who in 1937 occupied the post of Deputy People's Commissar of Internal Affairs of the Ukraine.* Katsnelson was not only Orlov's close relative, but his longtime friend who trusted him deeply. This is how Orlov explained the secret confessions which Katsnelson made during their meeting in February 1937 in a Paris clinic where Orlov was being treated for injuries received in Spain from an automobile accident (The official goal of Katsnelson's trip to Paris was, as Orlov indicated, a meeting with two NKVD agents who were there).

In Orlov's account, Katsnelson's story about the conspiracy against Stalin began with a description of the pre-history of this conspiracy and of the motives which prompted the generals to follow such a risky course.

During the preparations of the first show trial, Stalin said to Yagoda: "It

---

* In order to elevate one's trust in this "source" Orlov clearly exaggerated the political role of Katsnelson by saying that he was a member of the CC VKP(b) (which Katsnelson never was) and met daily with Stalin.

would be useful if the NKVD could show that some of the intended victims of the purge had been agents of the Okhrana, the tsarist secret police"[6] (a revolutionary's service in the tsarist secret police was considered the most disgraceful crime in the USSR).

Yagoda ordered an officer of the NKVD, Shtein, to search in the police archives for documents compromising the Old Bolsheviks who were to be brought to trial. Shtein was unable to find such documents, but then he unexpectedly discovered documents of the deputy director of the department of the tsarist police, Vissarionov, among which were handwritten reports from Stalin, irrefutable proof of his work for the Okhrana over many years.

Understanding the fate which awaited him if he handed these documents over to Yagoda, Shtein hid them from his boss. He left for Kiev in order to show these documents to a friend, the People's Commissar of Internal Affairs, Balitsky. Balitsky and Katsnelson made a careful examination of the documents which left not the slightest doubt about their authenticity. They then spoke about the documents to people who enjoyed their complete trust: Yakir and Kosior. Yakir in turn passed the news to Tukhachevsky, "whose personal dislike of Stalin was well known."[7] Among the people who were let in on the secret, Katsnelson also named Gamarnik and Kork.

"The sudden realization that the tyrant and murderer responsible for the piled-up horror was not even a genuine revolutionary but an impostor, a creature of the hated Okhrana, galvanized the conspirators into plans for action. Together they decided to stake their lives to save their country by ridding it of the enthroned agent provocateur."[8]

The people who were planning the conspiracy could not have helped but understand that only the violent removal of Stalin could halt the nightmare of the bloody purges which threatened to swallow an ever greater number of party and military leaders. Only in this way could Tukhachevsky, Yakir and their comrades remove the sword which implacably hung over their heads.

As Katsnelson told Orlov, the generals were still at the stage of "gathering forces" and had not worked out a final and firm plan for the coup. Tukhachevsky was inclined to adopt the following course of action. He intended to convince Stalin and Voroshilov to gather the senior officers to discuss the existing problems of the country's defenses. At this meeting the conspirators were to arrest Stalin, while two specially chosen regiments of the Red Army cut off access to the Kremlin in order to block the possible advance of NKVD troops which were loyal exclusively to Stalin and Yezhov.*

Two points of view were held among the conspirators concerning what should be done with Stalin after his arrest. Tukhachevsky and other generals thought that Stalin should be shot immediately, after which a plenum of the CC should be convened and the documents exposing him would be revealed. Kosior, Balitsky and other people, who did not belong to the military circles, felt that it was necessary to deliver Stalin to the CC plenum and charge him there with being an agent and provocateur prior to the revolution.

When he had finished telling Orlov about everything, Katsnelson expressed fears that the conspiracy would fail. In reply Orlov said that he felt such failure to be unlikely, since "Tukhachevsky is the respected boss of the army. The Moscow garrison is in his hands. He and his generals have passes to the Kremlin. Tukhachevsky reports to Stalin regularly and is not suspected." Orlov added that the usual risk associated with any conspiracy in this case was excluded since "nobody in his right mind would go to Stalin and tell him about the police file, since immediate liquidation would be the reward for such a disclosure."[9]

A few days after this conversation with Katsnelson, Orlov returned to Spain, where he anxiously waited for news about the success of the conspiracy. Instead, he learned that the generals had been tried and, a month later, that Katsnelson had been shot.

Orlov explained the frenzied outburst of terror which unfolded after this trial, and the unbelievable scale of the ferocious purge of the high command of the army, as Stalin's desire to destroy "others who might conceivably have learned something about the file [of Vissarionov—V. R.] or who were friends of those who had been executed. Every military man who owed his post, directly or indirectly, to one of the executed top generals became a candidate for death. Hundreds, and soon thousands, of officers were hauled from their commands and homes to the extermination cellars."[10]

Even in *The Secret History of Stalin's Crimes,* Orlov had carefully served notice that an attempt at a military-political coup had actually taken place. It is true that in this regard he referred only to the statement by Spiegelglass, who told him in the fall of 1937 about the panic which had seized the Stalinist

---

* Events developed according to the same approximate schema during the arrest of Beria in 1953.

leadership several months before: "All passes to the Kremlin were suddenly declared invalid. Our detachments [i.e., the NKVD troops—V. R.] were placed on alert! As Frinovsky said, 'The whole government was hanging by a thread.'"[11] In approximately the same words, Orlov related Spiegelglass's story in his article of 1956. In the light of these statements, we can place a certain amount of confidence in Molotov's words which we cited earlier: "We even knew the date of the conspiracy."

Orlov repeated the version about the conspiracy in 1965 before the Senate Subcommittee on Internal Security. Here he added that he learned from Katsnelson about photocopies of the police file which had been hidden by the conspirators in reliable places. Orlov declared that for many years he had been thinking about ways in which he might look for the hidden documents. He had even considered using plastic surgery to change his appearance, and then traveling to the USSR (for instance, as an American tourist) in order to look for these documents.[12]

In connection with all this material, the question arises: Why did Orlov not report the conspiracy against Stalin in his book *The Secret History of Stalin's Crimes*, which he prepared over many years? Why did he wait until three years after it was published? Orlov said that immediately after Stalin's death he had decided not to publicize this version because it seemed to him that Stalin's successors were maintaining his cult and therefore they would persecute a person who revealed this most terrible of Stalin's secrets with as much fury as Stalin himself would have done. Proceeding from these considerations, Orlov continued, he limited himself in 1953 to placing in the safe of an American bank a packet with the information he published three years later. He left instructions to open this safe and the packet after his death. "Happily," Orlov added, "the current turn of events in the Soviet Union [i.e. Khrushchev's speech at the Twentieth Congress of the CPSU—V. R.] has made it possible for me to publish the facts myself."[13]

Orlov claimed that only the fact that "Stalin's inheritors" learned of his shameful secret can explain their decision to expose Stalin's crimes. "It is obvious," he wrote, "that Khrushchev and the others must have realized that by indicting Stalin they would gravely endanger themselves.... Their sudden attack on Stalin was bound to rouse in the minds of the Russian people angry recollections of how Khrushchev, Bulganin, Kaganovich, Mikoyan and Malenkov had glorified Stalin and his policies before huge audiences of Communist Party activists, how they had justified Stalin's bloody Moscow Trials and how they had hailed the shooting of the Red Army generals as a 'just punishment to traitors.' The bosses of the Kremlin no doubt knew that in the minds of the Russian people pertinent questions were bound to arise as to their complicity in Stalin's crimes and their fitness for continuing as leaders of the Soviet Union and of world Communism."[14]

These ideas of Orlov's were not far from the truth. We know from Khrushchev's memoirs how stubbornly the other members of the Politburo opposed his wish to give his report about Stalin; they openly declared that if he did they would appear tarnished in the eyes of Soviet and world public opinion. It is worth noting that even Churchill, who met with Khrushchev in England soon after the Twentieth Party Congress, recommended that he halt the campaign of destalinization.* Churchill said: "You must give the people time to digest what you have told them, otherwise it will turn against you." When he told delegates of the Italian Communist Party about Churchill's words, Khrushchev added: "I think that this was sincere advice. The old fox Churchill fears that if, as a result of our unwise actions, we are removed from the leadership of the country, then a government will come to power which will return to Stalinist methods of sharp irreconcilability. I told Churchill: 'We will keep this in mind.'"[15]

In evaluating the situation which arose after the Twentieth Congress, Orlov said that only "Stalin's main crime" [i.e., his activity as a provocateur—V. R.], which became known to Khrushchev, prompted the latter to begin the campaign of destalinization. In developing this thought, Orlov wrote that only the disclosure of the secret about Stalin's activity as an agent of the Okhrana would allow Khrushchev and other members of the "collective leadership," who did not have similar crimes in their record, to effectively distance themselves from Stalin.

Stating that in the near future one might expect the disclosure of "Stalin's guiltiest secret" in the Soviet Union, Orlov stated that one of the goals of his article was to accelerate this action.

It seems to me that here Orlov was unsuccessfully trying to outwit the Kremlin leaders, much as he had clearly toyed with the American intelligence

---

* Here I am using this concept in a narrow sense—as the disclosure of the truth about Stalin's crimes.

agents and Senators. Orlov's genuine motives were much more complex that those he indicated. The publication of *The Secret History of Stalin's Crimes* occurred soon after Stalin's death, when in Western public opinion (and it was primarily to this that Orlov was appealing) Stalin's name was surrounded with the aura of the victor in the Second World War, of a man to whom the Soviet Union owed its return to the status of a superpower. In this regard, the Great Purge was considered justified and necessary not only by the Communists of all countries, but also by such people as Churchill, who wrote that it saved the USSR from "a fifth column" during the war. In these conditions, to report an anti-Stalin conspiracy might only reinforce this version and raise Stalin's prestige, i.e., produce an effect which directly contradicted the one which Orlov was trying to achieve. As for Stalin's past as a provocateur, for Western public opinion of the 1950s this fact did not have the significance that it had for Bolsheviks of the 1930s.

After the Twentieth Congress of the CPSU, a fundamentally different situation developed. The exposure of Stalin's crimes, which resounded at the supreme party forum in the USSR, shook the entire world. Before tens and hundreds of millions of people in the Soviet Union and beyond its borders Stalin appeared as he truly was—as a villain and murderer. Khrushchev's report deprived Stalin of the aureole of a great military leader and statesman, and confirmed the most onerous charges which until then had been considered the inventions of "Trotskyists." In these conditions, the conspiracy against Stalin might have appeared fully justified to world public opinion.

It is no accident that in his carefully planned article Orlov named G. K. Zhukov as the initiator of the exposure of Stalin's crimes. Orlov understood all too well that his sensational article, published in one of the major American magazines, could not help but make its way to the highest Soviet leaders, including Zhukov, who at that time occupied the posts of candidate-member of the Politburo and Minister of Defense. Zhukov was one of the few members of the "collective leadership" who not only was not stained with participation in Stalin's crimes, but, on the contrary, had been in Stalin's disfavor for a number of years. Khrushchev spoke in his report to the Twentieth Congress about Stalin's wish to "denigrate the role and military capabilities of Marshal Zhukov."[16]

Knowing all this, Orlov did not skimp in his praise of Zhukov when he declared that he personally had been given the chance to become convinced of his honesty and courage. For the sake of this he even invented the information about how he met with Zhukov in Spain, where he had arrived as a military observer during the Civil War (in actuality, Zhukov never had been in Spain). We can assume that Orlov hoped that, as a result of further tumult in the Soviet leadership, Zhukov would end up as the country's head and would effectively continue the process of destalinization.

Therefore Orlov appealed to Zhukov's military conscience, which, according to him, would have to be suffering from the "stain of 1937, which blemished the honor of the Red Army." He expressed certainty that "the defeats attributed to the generals in World War II and the victories unfairly ascribed to Stalin must have rankled."[17]

In all this, Orlov displayed his profound political insight. Zhukov actually did play a crucial role in removing Beria and, a few years later, the so-called "anti-party group." At the June Plenum of the CC in 1957, Zhukov spoke immediately after the colorless introductory speech by Suslov. He was able to master and define the further course of the plenum's work by parrying the critical (and in many ways correct) comments by Molotov, Kaganovich and Voroshilov, who claimed that Khrushchev had transferred the discussion onto a different plane when he charged these Stalinists with having victimized the military leaders. Here it is worth recalling that Khrushchev "showed his gratitude" to Zhukov for this support in a purely Stalinist manner. Fearing the further growth of Zhukov's political influence and authority, a few months after the June Plenum he arranged to remove the marshal from all his posts, lodging both justified and unjustified charges against him.

Orlov made one more political maneuver when he included in the list of Stalin's crimes exposed at the Twentieth Congress "Khrushchev's declaration" that "Stalin had fabricated charges of treason against Marshal Mikhail Tukhachevsky and seven other leaders of the Red Army in 1937, had them executed without trial and followed up those assassinations with the murder of five thousand innocent officers."[18]

In this fabricated "declaration," Orlov attributed to Khrushchev his own mistaken assumption that there had been no trial of the military leaders. The main "imprecision" that was consciously introduced by Orlov is the fact that in Khrushchev's report there was no mention at all of the Tukhachevsky affair. It is true that Khrushchev devoted special attention to the losses suffered by the Red Army from the purges. He said that "from 1937–1941, as a result of Stalin's suspicious nature, several layers of command cadres were repressed on slanderous charges ... beginning literally with the company and battalion and ending with the highest army centers."[19] However Khrushchev named in this connection only a few of the victimized commanders, who "had sat in prison" and then been set free to take an active part in the Second World War.

We may assume that after he had carefully studied Khrushchev's report, Orlov became convinced that it had ignored the exposures contained in *The Secret History of Stalin's Crimes* (with the exception of the cautious statement that "the circumstances connected with the murder of Comrade Kirov still contain much that is unclear and enigmatic," and the supposition that the leaders of the Leningrad UNKVD had been shot in 1937 in order to "cover the tracks of the organizers of Kirov's assassination"[20]). Although these statements essentially repudiated the charges made against the victims of the three open trials, clearing them of the sole crime that was actually committed, the trials themselves were not called into question in Khrushchev's report.

In these conditions, Orlov apparently made the decision to prompt the Soviet leaders to review as soon as possible at least the Tukhachevsky trial, in which the majority of the defendants had not belonged to any oppositions. Such a review was indeed carried out a few months after Orlov's article appeared.

The rehabilitation of Tukhachevsky and his comrades at the beginning of 1957 occurred for two basic reasons.

First of all, the open trials were attended by leaders of the Western Communist Parties, who then relied on their "personal impressions" to vouch for the correctness of the charges made against Zinoviev, Bukharin and other Old Bolsheviks. According to Khrushchev it was these figures who persuaded him not to review the open trials by directly stating that this would cause harm to their prestige and would lead to the loss of many members from their parties. The trial of the generals, however, was closed, and in connection with the review of this trial, there would be no need to fear a negative reaction on the part of the leaders of the "fraternal parties."

Secondly, the rehabilitation of Tukhachevsky and his comrades was dictated in large part by considerations of the upper-echelon struggle for power which had unfolded after Stalin's death. Documents found by Zhukov and Serov (who was then Minister of State Security) in the secret archives proved irrefutably that Molotov, Kaganovich, and Voroshilov had taken an active part in organizing the trial of the generals. The accusation that they had participated in

destroying the best Soviet military leaders facilitated the political discrediting
of these people.

In reviewing Tukhachevsky's case the version claiming the absence of any
guilt whatsoever on the part of the defendants, including the attempt to overthrow Stalin, was left untouched. The version of the anti-Stalin conspiracy which
Orlov had outlined was not made public in the USSR, not only during
Khrushchev's reign, but during the course of the "full disclosure" campaigns of
1987–1993, directed first against Stalinism and then against Bolshevism. The
article from *Life* was first published in the USSR (which had already become
the "former USSR") by E. Plimak and V. Antonov at the beginning of 1994.

Even more surprising is the fact that almost none of the foreign works
about the "Great Terror" contain any reference to this article. Plimak and
Antonov explain this silence in the following way: "Whereas the book, *The Secret History of Stalin's Crimes,* quickly became a bestseller, the letter to *Life*
from 23 April 1956 simply became lost in the flood of information which
emerged after the Twentieth Congress about Stalin's crimes."[21]

In my mind, the matter is hardly that simple. The silence surrounding the
account presented by Orlov can be explained by the fact that it sharply contradicted the conception of the absolute arbitrariness of all the repressions carried out by Stalin. This conception became firmly established in western
Sovietology and then was repeated in the 1980s-1990s with the assiduousness
of first disciples by our "perestroishchiks" and "democrats." The account of an
anti-Stalinist conspiracy threatened to demolish this conception, which denied the existence of any resistance to Stalin and Stalinism in the Bolshevik
milieu.

This version, however, is much more persuasive in explaining the behavior
of the military leaders at the investigation and in the courtroom than the traditional reasons given for their "confessions," which rely exclusively on the use
of physical torture (the conception of literary works addressing this theme—
the novels *Fear* by Anatoly Rybakov and *The Conspiracy against the Marshals*
by Eremei Parnov—rest on this type of explanation).

Two or three weeks of torture, no matter how brutal, could hardly break
these courageous people to such a degree that they would lose their human
dignity and their ability to resist the provocative slanders being heaped upon
them.

Orlov's version allows us to construct a logical chain of events, both for

Stalin and for his victims. The military leaders (evidently in an alliance with several Old Bolsheviks) began to prepare the anti-Stalin conspiracy at the end of 1936. Separate rumors, not fully verified and not completely reliable, apparently reached Stalin, who immediately began to prepare a preventive retaliatory strike. With these goals in mind, the operation to obtain forged "documents" about the defeatism, spying and wrecking activity of the generals was conceived and carried out. These "documents" were supposed to exude an air of "unimpeachability" because the information about them had come from the head of a state that was friendly to the Soviet Union (Beneš), and the documents themselves had been obtained through a circuitous route by Soviet intelligence agents from the intelligence services of a hostile state (the Gestapo).

A new amalgam was concocted during the investigation and trial in the Tukhachevsky affair. Tukhachevsky and his comrades were condemned not for a conspiracy against Stalin, but for serving the fascist powers. The charge of preparing an anti-Stalinist coup was made against them with hindsight, several months after their execution, and it came from the mouths of Bukharin, Rykov and other defendants at the trial of the "Right-Trotskyist Bloc." Of course, this charge, too, was amalgamated with false charges of wanting to restore capitalism, of preparing the defeat of the USSR in a future war and of coming to an agreement with the ruling circles of fascist states.

The generals hardly wanted to establish a military dictatorship in the USSR. They wanted to restore the Bolshevik regime and therefore chose the motif of overthrowing Stalin, which could win over to their side the majority of the CC. Of course, even if Stalin had been an actual agent of the Okhrana (this fact, which is disputed by many serious historians, has still not been fully clarified), this crime did not compare with the crimes he committed while he was in power. But the crimes of Stalin the dictator either were backed by the official sanction of higher party organs (for instance, the deportation of the "kulaks" or the punishments for oppositional activity), or were committed in an atmosphere of the strictest secrecy, unbeknownst even to the party leaders (the assassination of Kirov, the fabrication of falsified cases and trials). The activity then of Stalin as an agent-provocateur against his own party, from the standpoint of the party mentality of that time, would have served as the most convincing evidence of the illegitimacy of his rule.

We can assume that in the course of the extremely hasty investigation, which was accompanied by torture and humiliation, the investigators managed to convince some of the defendants of the false character of the documents exposing Stalin as a provocateur, thereby sowing in their minds a "guilt complex" toward Stalin. This would explain both the false confessions as a means of atoning for this "guilt" and the abject character of Yakir's farewell letter to Stalin, and a whole number of other mysteries in the behavior of the generals during the investigation and trial.

In conclusion, let us touch on the difference between the goals which stand before us and which stood before the authors of the rehabilitation files for the trials of 1936–1938. The goal of these files was to conceal the obvious lack of coordination, the contradictions and outright forgeries in the materials of the investigation and trial, and on this basis to overturn *all* the charges made against the victims of the trials.

Our goal has been to unravel the Stalinist amalgams, i.e., to separate the fantastic and absurd charges from the evidence of the defendants' genuine anti-Stalinist activity. In following this path, we can also explain the events occurring at the June Plenum of the Central Committee in 1937, which removed the last obstacles in the way of the Great Purge.

55. The June Plenum of the Central Committee

B y the end of March 1937, a relatively small part of the Central Committee chosen at the Seventeenth Congress had been driven out. In 1935, one had been expelled (Yenukidze), and in 1936, two more (Sokolnikov and Piatakov). It would take almost half a year (from August 1936 until the end of February 1937), in order to expel two former leaders of the "Rightists" from the CC. Judging from the speeches at the February-March Plenum, the speakers felt that Bukharin and Rykov would be the last victims from the Central Committee at that time. Even Yaroslavsky, who knew better than others of Stalin's hatred for former oppositionists, said in his speech, "It must be hoped that we are discussing for the last time in the Central Committee of our party the question of betrayal by members and candidate members of the CC."[1]

Even after the February-March Plenum the tempo of expulsions did not increase immediately. The next in line turned out to be Yagoda, whose persecution had passed through several stages. Several months after his transfer from the post of People's Commissar of Internal Affairs to the post of People's Commissar of Communications, he was sent into the reserves of the NKVD while retaining his title as general commissar of security (in January 1937 this title, equal to a marshal's rank in the army, was also given to Yezhov). At the February-March Plenum, Yagoda was accused of negligence at work rather than of open state crimes.

On 31 March 1937, the Politburo sent all members of the Central Committee the following statement: "Due to the discovery of common crimes and crimes against the state committed by the People's Commissar of Communications, Yagoda, while he was People's Commissar of Internal Affairs, and also after his transfer to the People's Commissariat of Communications, the Politburo of the CC of the VKP(b) considers that it is necessary to expel him from the party and order his immediate arrest. The Politburo of the CC of the VKP informs members of the CC of the VKP, that in view of the danger of leaving Yagoda at liberty for even a single day, it is compelled to give orders for Yagoda's immediate arrest. The Politburo of the CC VKP asked members of the CC VKP to sanction Yagoda's expulsions from the party and his arrest. On behalf of the Politburo of the CC VKP, Stalin."[2]

Yagoda's arrest was the first instance in which a member of the Central Committee was arrested *prior* to passing the resolution mandated by the party statutes to remove him from the Central Committee (not to mention that, despite the party statutes, the adoption of such resolutions began to be carried out through referendum, without discussing the question of expulsion at a plenum of the CC in the presence of those being expelled). On 3 April the Politburo passed a resolution, according to which Yagoda was "relieved of his duties as People's Commissar of Communications ... due to the discovery of instances of criminal malfeasance in office."[3] Thus, outside of a narrow circle of initiates, no one, including members of the CC, was clear whether the former head of the omnipotent secret police had been arrested for purely criminal activity or for "participation in a conspiracy." Only one thing was obvious—the arrest of Yagoda, who had a firm reputation of being an executioner and adventurist, was greeted by the majority of CC members with genuine approval.

In 1937, the process of expelling people from the Central Committee assumed the following character. Members and candidate-members of the CC were sent blanks containing the text of the Politburo resolutions. The blanks were to be filled out at one's discretion. On the blanks concerning Yagoda, we meet a wide range of remarks—from the laconic "I am for" (Krzhizhanovsky) to emotional comments such as "For!!! And I offer particular congratulations that the bastard has been unmasked" (Zhukov); "I consider the actions of the Politburo to be absolutely correct, I endorse them fully and I vote to expel the traitor Yagoda from the party and the CC (Ivanov)."[4]

The next round of repressions, in which members and candidate-members of the CC unanimously approved the expulsion and arrest of their comrades in the Central Committee, began at the end of May 1937—in connection with "the discovery of the military-political conspiracy." Even before the arrest of Tukhachevsky, Rudzutak, Yakir and Uborevich, several of the "civilian" members and candidate members were expelled from the CC. On 17–19 May, two resolutions were passed which approved the corresponding proposals submitted by the Politburo. The first of them indicated: "On the basis of material at our disposal in which member of the CC VKP(b) Kabakov is charged with belonging to the counterrevolutionary center of Rightists, be it resolved to expel Kabakov from the CC VKP(b) and from the party, and to send his case to the NKVD." The second resolution was connected with the mass repressions which had been unleashed in Georgia. Candidate member of the CC Eliava and member of the Central Inspection Commission Orakhelashvili were expelled from these bodies on charges that they "knew about the counterrevolutionary activity of the Georgian Trotskyist Center, but concealed this information from the CC."[5]

On 20–22 May, one more Politburo resolution was approved by referendum: "In view of the fact that, according to the testimonies of a number of arrested participants in the anti-Soviet organization of Rightists (Yagoda, A. P. Smirnov, Prokofiev, Karakhan, Giber and others), member of the CC VKP(b) Ukhanov has been exposed as an active member of a counterrevolutionary conspiracy against the Soviet regime, be it resolved that Ukhanov be expelled from the CC VKP(b) and from the party, and that his case be sent to the organs of the NKVD."[6]

Thus, before the June Plenum of the Central Committee, thirteen of its members had been expelled and two (Tomsky and Gamarnik) committed suicide before they could be arrested.[*]

The voting blanks attached to the transcript of the June Plenum show that the remarks made on them, as a rule, repeated in shorter or expanded form the formulations contained in the Politburo resolutions. Some of the remarks show the mortal fear for their own fate which gripped the people voting, and their desire to demonstrate the special zeal with which they supported the proposals to expel and arrest their comrades. Thus, on 26 May, candidate member of the CC Veinberg sent to the CC VKP(b) (or to be more precise, to Stalin's office) a letter with the following content: "Today, when I voted for the expulsion from the party of Rudzutak and Tukhachevsky, I recalled that, in voting for the expulsions from the CC and the party of Kabakov, Ukhanov, Eliava, and Orakhelashvili, I accidentally forgot to add the words: 'and send their cases to the NKVD.' I now state that I am voting not only for the expulsion from the party of all these counterrevolutionaries who have betrayed the party, the Soviet regime and the Motherland, but also for sending their cases to the NKVD and dealing with these most vicious enemies of the people with all the severity of the laws of the USSR."[7]

Immediately on the eve of the plenum, the Politburo passed two more reso-

---

[*] Besides this, two members of the Central Committee which had been elected at the Seventeenth Congress (Kirov and Ordzhonikidze) died a violent death and three (Kuibyshev, Menzhinsky and Tovstukha) died before 1937.

Leon Trotsky, 1937

lutions on cadre questions. One of them (from 14 June) dismissed Rozengolts from his post as People's Commissar of Foreign Trade. Nevertheless, Rozengolts, who had belonged to the Left Opposition in the 1920s, was not expelled from the Central Committee at the June Plenum.

The second resolution (from 16 June) freed CC member Rumiantsev from his duties as first secretary of the Western regional Committee of the CPSU "in view of the discovery of former ties ... with enemy of the people Uborevich" (the Western, now Smolensk, region was part of the Belorussian military district headed by Uborevich).

By the time of the June Plenum, the resolution of such questions had completely become the province of the "little Politburo" or, to use the official language, of the standing commission under the Politburo composed of Stalin, Molotov, Voroshilov, Kaganovich, and Yezhov (the latter was not at that time even a candidate member of the Politburo). This commission, which was formed on 14 April 1937, was created "in order to prepare for the Politburo—and in cases of special urgency, to resolve—questions of a secret nature, including questions of foreign policy."[8]

Before examining the work of the June Plenum, let us turn our attention to one fact that apparently in many ways determined the special ferocity of its decisions. In June 1937, Trotsky sent a telegram to the Central Executive Committee of the USSR, which formally was the highest organ of the state at that time. "Stalin's policies," wrote Trotsky, "are leading to a crushing defeat, both internally and externally. The only salvation is a turn in the direction of Soviet democracy, beginning with a public review of the last trials. In this endeavor I offer my full support."[9]

At first glance, this telegram, and the very fact that it was sent, speak of Trotsky's naiveté, since it suggests he thought that the rebirth of Soviet democracy was possible at this time, and even that he could participate in it. It might seem just as strange that Trotsky was appealing to the Central Executive Committee, which by that time had lost even the insignificant amount of real power it previously had wielded. However Trotsky was not a person who was given to taking senseless or impulsive steps. Despite the fact that the motives of his appeal remain unclear even today, it is natural to assume that Trotsky possessed information which showed that the true devotion to Stalin by the majority of party and Soviet leaders was in inverse proportion to their official proclamations of this devotion, and that Stalin's position was extremely fragile and unstable. This might have been the source of Trotsky's hopes that, under conditions of the Great Terror, which was tearing one prominent member after another from the party ranks, a consolidation of leading figures in the country would be possible which would be aimed at overthrowing Stalin and his clique.

Trotsky's telegram ended up not at the CEC, but the NKVD, where it was translated from English (only in this way was the Mexican telegraph able to accept it for transmission) and sent to Stalin as a "special communiqué." After he had read the telegram, Stalin wrote the following resolution on it, which testified clearly to his loss of self-control: "Mug of a spy! Brazen spy for Hitler!"*

---

* This document, as well as many other documents of the Politburo, and even the personal correspondence of its members, show that Stalin and his "closest comrades-in-arms" expressed themselves in a conventional code which was designed to give the impression that they believed in the amalgams they were creating. Otherwise Stalin, who hardly believed in the existence of contacts between Trotsky and Hitler, would not have written such words on a document intended only for his most immediate circle.

His signature beneath these words was joined by the signatures of Molotov, Voroshilov, Mikoyan and Zhdanov, who expressed their agreement with Stalin's assessment."[10]

In order to better understand the events which unfolded at the June Plenum, we must keep in mind that the members of the CC at that time understood all too well that the real power in the country was held not by the CC but by the Politburo. They had been able to learn from experience that for many years the job of the CC had been reduced to voting mechanically for resolutions that had already been passed by the Politburo. They knew that the slightest statement in opposition would attract immediate sanctions—removal from the CC and dismissal from high posts. That is what had happened at the beginning of the 1930s to the members of the newly formed opposition groups: Syrtsov, Lominadze, A. P. Smirnov and others. In this regard, one might recall that during interrogations at the CCC and OGPU the participants of the group around A.P. Smirnov and Eismont named members of the CC who were not in agreement with Stalin, but who obediently voted for Stalin's resolutions. Almost none of the people they named were re-elected to the CC at the Seventeenth Congress. The vulnerability of rank-and-file members of the CC was also expressed in the fact that surveillance was established over each one of them, especially over former oppositionists.

However in 1937, even people who had reconciled themselves to these Stalinist "norms of party life" began to feel that something was now happening which earlier had seemed to be beyond belief. Each one of them could not fail to be aware of the grave danger that hung over all the Old Bolsheviks. Whereas at the preceding plenums of the CC the participants had made a deal with their own consciences by not daring to express even a shadow of a doubt with regard to the growing reprisals, by now many of them had begun to search for ways of consolidating against Stalin. Even when it came to devoted Stalinists who previously had concealed their concern even from themselves, their eyes began to open to the terrorist regime which they had helped in no small measure to create. This explains, in our view, the opposition to the terror which arose at the June plenum.

Until recently this plenum, which took place from 23–29 June, has been a blank spot in the history of the party. Official accounts of the plenum say that it approved a new electoral law—a proposal about elections to the Supreme Soviet of the USSR—and reviewed three narrowly economic questions: improving the seed stock, introducing correct crop rotation and measures to improve the work of the Machinery and Tractor Stations.[11]

As can be seen from the plenum's transcript, these questions were actually reviewed at its sessions on 27–29 June. However this official and amazingly peaceful agenda camouflaged the main content of the work of the plenum. The first point was the discussion of Yezhov's report about how the NKVD has discovered a grandiose conspiracy which involved the participation of prominent figures in the party and the country.

At the end of May, the members and candidate-members of the CC were sent a Politburo resolution from 20 May, according to which the plenum of the Central Committee was to convene on 20 June. Then it was agreed that the plenum's agenda would consist of four points, and the plenum's draft resolutions were approved. However at a session of the Politburo on 15 June, the opening of the plenum was postponed to 23 June. On 19 June the Politburo approved a "final agenda" for the plenum, according to which the first point was set to be "Comrade Yezhov's report."[12]

As the plenum approached, Stalin and other secretaries of the CC received many requests to be allowed to attend. Such a request came, for instance, from Dimitrov, who asked that he and two other leaders of the Comintern be admitted to the plenum. Voroshilov asked to allow "leading officials from the Red Army and the fleet," and Kaganovich his closest assistants in the NKPS. Especially vivid was the letter to Kaganovich from a member of the Inspection Commission, Chutskaev, which was sent when the plenum had already begun its work. After stating that he had not received an invitation to the plenum, Chutskaev wrote: "In light of the facts which are now pouring down upon us, and in light of the consequences which have affected many members of the central party organs which were elected at the last congress of the party, I cannot help but understand the refusal to allow me to participate in the plenum of the CC VKP(b) to be anything but an expression of political lack of confidence. I want to know why I am being denigrated, and in what way.... I have committed no sins, either in thought or in deed, against either the CC or against Comrade Stalin."

All these letters contain notes by Kaganovich, Andreev, Zhdanov or even Poskrebyshev: "Against" (allowing them to attend the plenum) or (allow them in) "after the first point."[13]

The discussion of Yezhov's "report" occupied the first four days of the plenum's work. Yezhov stated that the latest testimony obtained by his department led to the conclusion that the scale of the conspiracy was so great that the country was on the brink of a civil war. Only the organs of state security under the direct leadership of Stalin could prevent this civil war. On this basis Yezhov, with Stalin's support, demanded that his commissariat be granted extraordinary powers.

On the first day of the Plenum, twenty-six members of the CC were expelled. These expulsions were formulated in a resolution which consisted of two points. The first expressed "political lack of confidence" in three members (Alekseev, Liubimov, Sulimov) and four candidate members of the CC (Kuritsyn, Musabekov, Osinsky and Sedelnikov). These people, whose names were mentioned in the resolution with the prefix of "Comrade," were expelled from the CC without any indication that their cases should be sent to the NKVD.

The second point was the approval of a Politburo decree about expelling, "for betrayal of the party and the motherland and for active counter-revolutionary activity," nine members of the CC (Antipov, Balitsky, Zhukov, Knorin, Lavrentiev, Lobov, Razumov, Rumiantsev, Sheboldaev) and ten candidate members of the CC (Blagonravov, Veger, Goloded, Kalmanovich, Komarov, Kubiak, Mikhailov, Polonsky, Popov, Unshlikht). It was resolved to send the cases of these people (of course, no longer called "comrades") to the NKVD.[14]

The overwhelming majority of these twenty-six men had not given speeches at the previous plenum, nor had they tossed out any rejoinders; several of them had spoken only on the insistence of Yezhov and other Stalinists.

In this way, forty-six members and candidate members of the CC which had been elected at the Seventeenth Congress did not take part in the work of the June Plenum. Nevertheless, among the remaining participants at the plenum there were people who decided to speak out against the Stalinist terror.

There is almost no information available about the speeches of these people, or about what happened in general during the discussion of the first point on the agenda. Material from the plenum which is kept in the former central party archive contains a note that is unprecedented in the history of the plenums of the CC: "The sessions of the plenum for 22–26 June were not stenographically recorded."[15] We can get an idea of what happened during these tragic days only from a few incomplete excerpts contained in corresponding archival dossiers, or from a few memoirs.

The events which unfolded at the plenum sharply deviated from the scenario worked out by Stalin. The June Plenum became the first and last attempt by a part of the Central Committee to stop the Great Terror by relying on the party statutes. Several of the plenum's participants protested against the granting of extraordinary powers to the NKVD and proposed the creation of a party commission to investigate its activity.

These contributions were preceded by secret meetings which were provisionally called "cups of tea" by their participants. In 1963, the Old Bolshevik Temkin said that when he was in the same prison cell with I. A. Piatnitsky, he learned from him that at the "cups of tea," people discussed the question of removing Stalin from the leadership of the party at the plenum.[16] One of the participants told Stalin about the content of these discussions, giving him the chance to prepare a retaliatory blow which consisted most of all, it appears, in the preventive expulsions from the party of a large group of members and candidate-members of the CC.

Khrushchev, who repeatedly returned in his memoirs to the events of 1937–1938, said almost nothing about the work of this or other subsequent plenums of the CC at which two-thirds of the Central Committee was expelled. The only event which he often described (without mentioning that it occurred at the June Plenum) was the speech by G. N. Kaminsky.

The recollections by members of the Presidium of the CC about one fragment of this speech played an important role in the arrest of Beria in 1953. When members of the post-Stalin "collective leadership" decided to get rid of Beria, according to Khrushchev, they had no direct evidence of his crimes, "everything was based on intuition."[17] Then Khrushchev recalled Kaminsky's speech at the June Plenum, where "each speaker was supposed to criticize someone." This phrase which Khrushchev uttered in passing says much about the atmosphere which had developed at the plenum. Apparently, Stalin demanded that its participants tell everything that they knew which compromised other party members, even if these facts were connected with the distant past. Following this directive, Kaminsky declared: "Here everyone who speaks is telling all that they know about others. I also would like to speak so that this was known to the party." Then he spoke of the persistent rumors which circulated among the Baku communists that during the occupation of Baku by English troops and the activity there of the Musavatist government, Beria worked for the Musavatist intelligence service, which in turn was connected with English intelligence.[18]

Kaminsky
and I. P. Pavlov
at a conference
of medical
scientists

As Khrushchev recalls, at the June Plenum no one else touched upon this sensitive topic, which was bound up with the dark pages in the biography of the sinister Stalinist monster. Beria himself did not give any explanations of this matter. However at the next session of the plenum, Kaminsky did not appear in the audience. "This was then quite common," commented Khrushchev about this event. "Many members of the CC who attended one session did not come to the second; they ended up as 'enemies of the people' and were arrested."[19]

Sixteen years later, at a session of the Presidium of the CC which had gathered for the arrest of Beria, Khrushchev began his speech by recalling Kaminsky's speech. The charge which had been made in this speech served as the basis for calling Beria an "English spy" and as grounds for his arrest. This charge was presented in official articles in such a manner that Beria appeared to be an "English spy" not only in the Civil War years, but also in the later years of his activity.

In his memoirs, Khrushchev mentioned only this aspect of Kaminsky's speech. However Kaminsky accused Beria at the June plenum not only of having dubious ties twenty years earlier, but of crimes committed during the time he was leader of the Transcaucasian party organization. Kaminsky expressed doubt about the official versions of the suicide of the first secretary of Armenia, Khandzhian, and the untimely death of the chairman of the Abkhasian Central Executive Committee, Lakoba. It became clear during the investigation of the Beria case that Khandzhian had been shot personally by Beria, and Lakoba had been poisoned by him.

Kaminsky clearly understood what might await him after such a speech. As he left for the Kremlin on 25 June, the day on which his speech was scheduled, he warned his wife that he might not return from the plenum. The night before he cleaned all papers out of his safe and desk drawers in his office. When his deputy, Karmanova, who was watching these actions, asked if he was getting ready to be transferred to other work, Kaminsky replied, "No, I am doing this to be ready for anything."[20]

The rehabilitation materials for the Kaminsky case indicate that he was arrested on 25 June. The next day, the plenum passed a decree: "To expel Kaminsky, as a person not worthy of trust, from his candidacy for membership in the CC VKP(b) and from the party."[21]

The second, sharper speech at the plenum was given by Piatnitsky, a member of the party since 1898, who declared that falsified cases were being fabricated in the NKVD and illegal methods of investigation were being used; therefore a thorough verification of the activity of this commissariat was needed.[22]

It was not as simple to deal with Piatnitsky as with other members of the CC who had been expelled by lists, or with the forty-two-year-old Kaminsky. Piatnitsky was not a bureaucrat of the second rank, but one of the oldest Bolsheviks who had played a major role in the Comintern from its foundation until 1935, and who had headed the political-administrative department of the CC VKP(b) since then.

In one of his few confidential conversations about the events of 1937, Kaganovich stated that after Piatnitsky's speech, in the recess between sessions of the plenum, members of the Politburo "surrounded Piatnitsky and tried to convince him to retract his words; he replied that he had expressed his opinion and that he would not withdraw it."[23]

The next day, Yezhov announced that Piatnitsky had been a provocateur in the tsarist secret police. However, unlike other members of the CC, Piatnitsky was not immediately arrested. In a brief statement before the closing of the plenum Stalin said that with regard to Piatnitsky, a "verification" was proceeding which would be finished in a few days.[24]

As Piatnitsky's wife, Iu. N. Sokolova, relates in her diary which has survived, over the next week Piatnitsky called Yezhov each day, demanding face-to-face confrontations with people who had given testimony against him.

Yezhov postponed a meeting with Piatnitsky several times; only on 3 July was he invited to appear at the NKVD. Piatnitsky returned from there at dawn. "This was a completely exhausted and unhappy man. He said only one thing: 'It was awful, Iulia.'"[25]

Piatnitsky told members of his family that a face-to-face confrontation had been arranged with former Comintern personnel who slandered him. "He said that he was guilty of nothing before the party, that he did not acknowledge his guilt, and that he would fight for the truth. But that a very long period might pass until he was declared innocent."[26]

On 7 July Piatnitsky was arrested. He was expelled from the party at the next plenum of the CC in October, i.e., four months after his arrest.

As in the "case of the generals," a provocation put together by the Gestapo played a certain role in the fabrication of Piatnitsky's case—but this time it was on their own initiative. Leopold Trepper describes the mechanism of this complex fabrication in his memoirs. The Gestapo agent Giering told him that in 1937 the Gestapo decided to use the spy mania which existed at the time in the USSR in order to create a version about a "German agent" who was in the leadership of the Comintern. Piatnitsky was chosen for this role because he had headed the delegation of the VKP(b) in the Comintern for many years and through him it would be easy to strike a blow against the best cadres of the Comintern.

With these goals in mind, the Gestapo recruited two arrested German communists who were then set free. They then handed over a fabricated dossier on Piatnitsky to Moscow. This helped destroy the old revolutionary, and along with him hundreds of Comintern personnel. As Trepper emphasized, "this was one of the best services which Stalin performed for Hitler."[27]

The fact that, besides Hitler's forces, White-Guardists who were collaborating with them participated in this provocation can be seen from the letter from one of the leaders of a White-Guard organization in Prague, Colonel Gegelshvili, to the White-Guard General von Lampe. In this letter, written in 1943, he says: "You and I torpedoed this dreadnaught 'World Revolution' in 1937, when the head of its technical bureau, Piatnitsky, was arrested."[28]

In a report assembled in the summer of 1937, the Russian General Military Union emphasized: "The Yezhov provocation against Piatnitsky pursues one goal—to compromise a prominent Bolshevik who has known too many of the secrets of the Kremlin-Comintern ... his removal was an unavoidable condition of establishing more intimate contact between Stalin and Hitler. For a long time, Piatnitsky held in his hands all the ties and all the agents of international Bolshevism. His fall and arrest signify the sunset of the Comintern's activity. Now Stalin will proceed with his imperial policy after having made Hitler his ally."[29]

These comments are very insightful. The Comintern cadres were raised in an uncompromisingly antifascist spirit. Without a bloody purge of these cadres, it would have been impossible to force the foreign communist parties to support the deal between Stalin and Hitler, as was done in 1939.

The Piatnitsky case was supposed to evolve into a "Comintern trial." This was prevented by Piatnitsky's amazing fortitude; as was revealed during the investigation into his case, he was subjected to two hundred twenty hours of interrogation accompanied by torture.

Piatnitsky, who never belonged to any opposition, chose as a weapon of defense at the investigation to express his irreconcilability toward "Trotskyism." On 23 January 1938 he handed his investigator Laftang a letter, addressed to the Politburo, in which he said: "I have been in prison for six and one-half months already. I have lived with the hope that the investigation will establish my absolute innocence. Now, apparently, everything is lost. I am seized by the horror.... I cannot, I do not want to, and I should not sit in a Soviet prison and be tried for Right-Trotskyist counterrevolution, to which I never belonged; I fought against it."[30] This letter never arrived where it was intended; it was discovered only twenty years later during Laftang's arrest. All this time he had kept the letter to himself.

The memoirs of M. Mendeleev show the significance which Stalin attached to the Piatnitsky case. In May 1938, his cellmate, Melnikov, the former leader of the communications department of the Comintern, reported that he had been taken on Yezhov's orders to the Kremlin for a night confrontation attended by Stalin, Molotov, Voroshilov, Kaganovich, and Krupskaya. In Mendeleev's version events unfolded the following way:

"I heard Stalin's voice: 'Comrade Krupskaya says that she does not believe and does not allow that Piatnitsky was a spy. Comrade Yezhov will report to you and convince you with the facts.' Yezhov ... began to ask me certain questions. I answered according to instructions. And suddenly I heard N. K. Krupskaya's sharp and indignant voice:

"'He's lying! He is a fascist, he is a scoundrel!' And she began to shout:

'Viacheslav Mikhailovich! Kliment Efremovich! Lazar Moiseevich! You know Piatnitsky well. He is after all the most honest man. Lenin loved him and respected him very much.'

"Krupskaya rushed about, she looked for sympathetic eyes. The answer was an oppressive silence ... the silence was broken by Stalin's voice:

"'Comrade Krupskaya does not trust Melnikov's testimony. Well, we will continue to verify things.'"[31]

Piatnitsky's case was reviewed on 19 June 1938 in Lefortovo Prison, along with the cases of Rudzutak and seven other members and candidate-members of the CC. Among other charges, Piatnitsky was accused of infiltrating Trotskyist agents into the Comintern and of introducing "Trotskyist formulations" into the translations of Marxist literature into foreign languages. At a regular formal session of the Military Collegium of the Supreme Court, Piatnitsky, who did not admit his guilt, was sentenced to the supreme measure of punishment.

Who among the participants at the June Plenum supported Kaminsky and Piatnitsky? The record of Stalin's speech at the end of the plenum helps us to answer this question. We shall cite the record fully.

> *Stalin.* I must announce, comrades, that in view of irrefutable information which we have received concerning CC members Kodatsky and Chudov and candidate member Pavlunovsky, showing that they participated in the criminal activities of the conspirators, we had to arrest them. We have Komarov's testimony about this, it will be distributed to you. We must remove these former members of the CC and one candidate member of the CC from the CC.
>
> *Voices from the audience.* Correct.
>
> *Andreev* (chairing the session): There is a proposal to accept this proposal by Comrade Stalin. Who is in favor of approving this proposal? Who is against? No one. It is accepted ... the plenum's agenda is exhausted. I declare this session of the plenum of the CC closed.

This whole text is crossed out with a thick line, and on the page is written by hand: "This announcement was made by Comrade Stalin at the end of the 29 June 1937 Plenum of the CC VKP(b). Crossed out by Comrade Stalin, since it should not go into the transcript."[32]

In the transcript which was sent to the localities all that remained was the plenum's decree formulated after it had closed. It speaks about the expulsion of the three people Stalin had named, to whom was added the name of candidate member of the CC Struppe, for "belonging to a counterrevolutionary grouping."[33]

Thus, as the curtain was falling, Stalin announced to the remaining participants of the already completely submissive plenum, as if it were simple conference routine, that several members and candidate members of the CC had been arrested, after which he demanded that they vote for their expulsions from the CC.

How this resolution from the June Plenum was "explained" in the localities can be seen in the speech of the Old Bolshevik D. A. Lazurkina at the Twenty-Second Congress of the CPSU. She recalled how Zhdanov "gathered us together, the leading members of the [Leningrad] regional committee, and announced that two enemies had been discovered in our ranks—the former second secretary of the regional committee, Chudov, and the chairman of the Executive Committee of the Leningrad Soviet, Kodatsky.... We could not say anything. It seemed that our tongues had frozen. But when this meeting was finished, and Zhdanov was leaving the hall, I said to him: 'Comrade Zhdanov, I do not know Chudov, he has not been long in our Leningrad organization. But I can vouch for Kodatsky. He is an honest member of the party. He has fought against all the oppositions. It's unbelievable! It must be looked into.' Zhdanov looked at me with cruel eyes and said: 'Lazurkina, put an end to this discussion, otherwise things will go badly for you.'"[34]

Altogether, thirty-one people were expelled at the June Plenum—many more than during all the preceding years, starting with 1927, when this measure was first used (against Trotsky and Zinoviev).

After the plenum, which gave extraordinary powers to the NKVD, Stalin-Yezhov were in a position where their hands were fully untied for further crimes. One part of the extraordinary powers was the Politburo decree officially allowing the use of torture against arrested victims.

The existence of this shameful document is known from the coded telegram sent by Stalin on 10 January 1939 to the secretaries of the central committees of the national communist parties, regional and area committees, and also the leaders of commissariats and directorates of internal affairs. This telegram was a reply to questions from local party apparatchiks who had arrived at their posts only recently and in a number of instances, due to their naiveté, had protested against the use of the "method of physical coercion" by members of the NKVD. Stalin explained that the application of this "method" "in the practice of the NKVD has been allowed since 1937 with the approval of the Plenum of the CC VKP(b)."[35]

The document itself which contains their "approval" has never been found, although the corresponding telegram, according to Molotov, was sent to all members of the CC and all regional committees. We can assume that Stalin made sure to remove all traces of this action. Evidently, a directive was sent to all localities with the order to return it to the CC to be destroyed. That such a practice was widespread during those years can be seen by the fact that the original of Stalin's telegram from 10 January 1939 has also never been found in the archives of the CC, and a copy of it was found in only one area committee of the party (in Dagestan).[36]

The fact that the directive about the use of torture was formulated by a special decree of the Politburo can be seen by the admissions at the June Plenum of the CC in 1957 by Molotov and Kaganovich, who had been backed into a corner. Khrushchev asked Molotov the questions: "What was the basis for passing the resolution about torturing arrested people and extorting testimony from them?... Who signed this document about interrogations and beatings?" The following exchange then took place:

Molotov. The use of physical measures was a general resolution of the Politburo. Everyone signed it.

Voice. There was no such resolution.

Molotov. There was such a resolution.

Voice. Show us.

Molotov. It was secret. I do not have a copy.

Khrushchev. Tell us how it was signed. Repeat what you said.

Kaganovich. All the members of the Politburo signed for.... With regard to spies, to apply extreme measures of physical coercion ...

Khrushchev. I want to add one point of information. Kaganovich and Molotov obviously will not refuse to repeat that we had the following discussion. On the eve of the Twentieth Congress or after the congress, if I remember, Kaganovich said that there was a document where all [members of the Politburo—V. R.] signed to allow arrested people to be beaten. Kaganovich proposed to find this document and destroy it.

We gave the assignment to Malin [at that time head of the general department of the CC in charge of party archives—V. R.] to find this document, but they did not find it, it had already been destroyed....
You then even said how this resolution was written and who signed it.
Kaganovich. Yes, I told how. Everyone was sitting right there, at the session, the document was written out by hand and signed by everyone [all members of the Politburo—V. R.] ...
Khrushchev. Who wrote this document?
Kaganovich. Stalin wrote it by hand.[37]

Official permission to use torture opened the road to an even greater outburst of terror, which led to the virtual liquidation of the former Bolshevik Party and a significant part of the cadres of the international communist movement. I propose to describe the main events of the Great Purge which followed the June Plenum in my next book, *The Party of the Executed.*

Notes

Introduction

1. *Inostrannaia literatura* [Foreign Literature], no. 4 (1988), p. 170.
2. *Literaturnaia gazeta* [Literary Gazette], 27 July 1988.
3. *Reabilitatsiia: Politicheskie protsessy 30–50–x godov.* (Moscow: 1991), p. 63.
4. Ibid., pp. 65–66.
5. *KPSS v rezoliutsiiakh i resheniiakh s"ezdov, konferentsii i plenumov TsK,* ninth edition, vol. 9, p. 120.
6. *Voprosy istorii* [Problems of History], no. 6–7 (1992), p. 83.
7. Ibid., p. 87.
8. *Voprosy istorii*, no. 2–3 (1992), p. 76.
9. *Voprosy istorii*, no. 12 (1991), pp. 62–63.
10. *Voprosy istorii*, no. 2–3 (1992), pp. 76, 80.
11. Ibid., p. 79.
12. See, for example: *Velikaia Otechestvennaia voina Sovetskogo Soiuza. 1941–1945. Kratkaia istoriia* (Moscow: 1965), p. 39.
13. Valentinov, N. V., *Nasledniki Lenina* (Moscow: 1991), pp. 215–216.
14. Ibid., p. 215.
15. Ibid., p. 214.
16. Ibid., p. 216.
17. Ibid., pp. 218–219, 223.
18. Chuev, F., *Sto sorok besed s Molotovym* [One Hundred Forty Conversations with Molotov] (Moscow: 1990), p. 135.
19. Allilueva, S. I., *Tol'ko odin god* (Moscow: 1990), p. 135.
20. Valentinov, *Nasledniki Lenina*, p. 219.
21. *Novyi mir* [New World], no. 4 (1988), p. 101.
22. Lenin, V. I., *Polnoe Sobranie Sochinenii* [PSS], vol. 43, p. 383/*Collected Works* [CW], vol. 32, pp. 323–324.
23. *Biulleten' oppozitsii* [Bulletin of the Opposition], no. 58–59 (1937), p. 3.
24. *Biulleten' oppozitsii*, no. 68–69 (1938), p. 3.
25. Voslenskii, M., *Nomenklatura. Gospodstvuiushchii klass Sovetskogo Soiuza* (Moscow: 1991), pp. 103, 105.
26. Cited in: Trotskii, L. D., *Portrety revoliutsionerov* [Portraits of Revolutionaries] (Moscow: 1991), pp. 157–158.
27. *Literaturnaia gazeta*, 27 July 1988.
28. *Molodaia gvardiia*[Young Guard], no. 8 (1970), p. 319.
29. Ibid., p. 317.
30. Tvardovskii, A., *Poemy* (Moscow: 1988), p. 325.
31. Okudzhava, B., *Stikhotvoreniia* (Moscow: 1984), pp. 11–12.
32. Trotskii, L. D., *Stalin*, vol. 2 (Moscow: 1990), pp. 215–216.

1. Preparations for the First Show Trial

1. *Reabilitatsiia. Politicheskie protsessy 30–50–x godov,* (Moscow: 1991), p. 175.
2. *Voprosy istorii*, no. 12 (1994), pp. 16–17.
3. *Reabilitatsiia*, p. 176.
4. *Voprosy istorii*, no. 2 (1995), p. 17.
5. Trotsky Archives, Houghton Library, Harvard University, nos. 9437–9942, 3664–3674, 12881–12886.
6. Trotskii, L. D., *Prestupleniia Stalina* [Stalin's Crimes] (Moscow: 1994), p. 145.
7. Trotsky Archives, nos. 15204, 15205, 15199.
8. *Rasstrel'nye spiski*, Issue. 1 (Moscow: 1993), pp. 27, 32.
9. *Voprosy istorii*, no. 2 (1995), p. 17.
10. *Reabilitatsiia*, p. 180.
11. *Voprosy istorii*, no. 10 (1994), p. 26; no. 2 (1995), p. 18.
12. *Voprosy istorii*, no. 12 (1994), p. 17.
13. Ibid., p. 18.
14. *Reabilitatsiia*, p. 179.
15. *Voprosy istorii*, no. 12 (1994), p. 18; *Reabilitatsiia*, p. 179.
16. *Voprosy istorii*, no. 2 (1995), p. 18.
17. *Reabilitatsiia*, pp. 184–185.
18. *Izvestiia*, 21 March 1990.
19. Orlov, A., *Tainaia istoriia stalinskikh*

prestuplenii (Moscow: 1991), pp. 121, 129.
20. Ibid., pp. 124, 137.
21. Larina, A. M., *Nezabyvaemoe* [This I Cannot Forget] (Moscow: 1989), p. 66.
22. Orlov, *Tainaia istoriia stalinskikh prestuplenii*, pp. 126–127.
23. Ibid., pp. 135–136.
24. Chuev, F., *Tak govoril Kaganovich. Ispoved' stalinskogo apostola* [Thus Spake Kaganovich. Confession of a Stalinist Apostle] (Moscow: 1992), p. 140.
25. Vyshinskii, A. Ia., *Sudebnye rechi* [Trial Speeches] (Moscow: 1955), pp. 419.
26. Krivitskii, V., *Ia byl agentom Stalina* (Moscow: 1991), p. 216.
27. *Biulleten' oppozitsii*, no. 60–61 (1937), p. 13.
28. Krivitskii, *Ia byl agentom Stalina*, pp. 217–219.
29. *Reabilitatsiia*, p. 185.
30. *Oktiabr'*, no. 8 (1992), p. 167.
31. Orlov, *Tainaia istoriia stalinskikh prestuplenii*, p. 103; *Rasstrel'nye spiski* (Moscow: 1993), p. 26.
32. *Reabilitatsiia*, p. 187.
33. Orlov, *Tainaia istoriia stalinskikh prestuplenii*, p. 81; *Pravda*, 20 August 1936.
34. *Reabilitatsiia*, pp. 186, 201, 202, 205.
35. Ibid., p. 186.
36. Ibid., p. 210.

2. The Trial of the Sixteen
1. *Pravda*, 15 August 1936.
2. *Biulleten' oppozitsii*, no. 52–53 (1936), p. 14.
3. Vyshinskii, *Sudebnye rechi*, pp. 416–417.
4. Ibid., p. 393.
5. *Biulleten' oppozitsii*, no. 27 (1932), p. 6.
6. *Pravda*, 22 August 1936.
7. Orlov, *Tainaia istoriia stalinskikh prestuplenii*, p. 70.
8. *Reabilitatsiia*, p. 183.
9. Ibid., p. 181.
10. Trotskii, *Prestupleniia Stalina*, p. 81.
11. *Pravda*, 23 August 1936.
12. Vyshinskii, *Sudebnye rechi*, p. 422.
13. Ibid., p. 395.
14. *Pravda*, 22 August 1936.
15. Ibid.
16. *Pravda*, 24 August 1936.
17. *Reabilitatsiia*, pp. 205–206.
18. *Pravda*, 22 August 1936.
19. *Pravda*, 24 August 1936.

20. Trotskii, L. D., *Dnevniki i pis'ma* [Diaries and Letters] (Moscow: 1994), pp. 51–52.
21. Ibid., p. 91.
22. Volkogonov, D. A., *Trotskii*, book 2. (Moscow: 1992), p. 126.
23. *Pravda*, 21 August 1936.

3. "Thirst for Power" or "Restoration of Capitalism"?
1. *Reabilitatsiia*, pp. 207–209.
2. *Pravda*, 20 August 1936.
3. Vyshinskii, *Sudebnye rechi*, p. 390.
4. Trotskii, *Prestupleniia Stalina*, pp. 63–64.
5. Vaznetsov, A., "Revstavratory kapitalizma i ikh zashchitniki," *Pravda*, 12 September 1936.
6. Trotskii, *Prestupleniia Stalina*, p. 209.
7. *Izvestiia*, 21 August 1936.
8. Stalin, I. V., *O nedostatkakh partiinoi raboty i merakh likvidatsii trotskistskikh i inykh dvur-ushnikov* [On Shortcomings of Party Work and of Measures to Liquidate Trotskyists and other Double-dealers] (Moscow: 1937), pp. 15–16.

4. "The Molotov Affair"
1. *Pravda*, 20 August 1936.
2. Vyshinskii, *Sudebnye rechi*, p. 387.
3. *Biulleten' oppozitsii*, no. 52–53 (1936), p. 47.
4. *Biulleten' oppozitsii*, no. 58–59 (1937), pp. 18–19.
5. Ibid., p. 19.
6. *Biulleten' oppozitsii*, no. 50 (1936), p. 15.
7. Orlov, *Tainaia istoriia stalinskikh prestuplenii*, pp. 155–156.
8. *Reabilitatsiia*, pp. 223–224.
9. *Pravda*, 23 November 1936.
10. *Reabilitatsiia*, pp. 231–232.
11. *Protsess antisovetskogo trotskistskogo tsentra* [Trial of the Anti-Soviet Trotskyist Center] (Moscow: 1937), p. 96.
12. *Reabilitatsiia*, p. 224.
13. *XXII s"ezd Kommunisticheskoi partii Sovetskogo Soiuza*, Stenograficheskii otchet, vol. 2. [22nd Congress of the CPSU] (Moscow: 1962), p. 216.
14. Chuev, *Sto sorok besed s Molotovym*, p. 302.
15. *Biulleten' oppozitsii*, no. 58–59 (1937), pp. 20–21.

5. Results of a "Rotten Compromise"
1. *Pravda*, 5 February 1936.

2. Cited in: Trotskii, *Prestupleniia Stalina*, p. 72.
3. Vyshinskii, *Sudebnye rechi*, p. 423.
4. Trotskii, *Prestupleniia Stalina*, p. 72.
5. *Izvestiia*, 2 September 1992.
6. Orlov, *Tainaia istoriia stalinskikh prestuplenii*, p. 335.
7. Trotskii, *Stalin*, vol. 2, pp. 270–272.

6. Political Repercussions of the Trial of the Sixteen

1. *Minuvshee. Istoricheskii al'manakh* [The Past. Historical Almanac], no. 7 (Moscow: 1992), p. 100.
2. *Pravda*, 23 August 1936.
3. *Pravda*, 24 August 1936.
4. *Pravda*, 4 September 1936.
5. *Pravda*, 24 August 1936.
6. Feikhtvanger, L., *Moskva 1937: Otchet o poezdke dlia moikh druzei* [Moscow 1937: Account of the Trip for My Friends] (Moscow: 1937), p. 91.
7. Cited in: Motyleva T., "Druz'ia Oktiabria i nashi problemy," [Friends of October and our Problems] *Inostrannaia literatura*, no. 4 (1988), p. 167.
8. Ibid., pp. 164–165.
9. Ibid., p. 165.
10. Cited in: *Biulleten' oppozitsii*, no 52–53 (1936), p. 52.
11. *Pravda*, 21 August 1936.
12. *Sotsialisticheskii vestnik* [Socialist Herald], no. 17 (1936), p. 10.

7. Trotsky Interned

1. *Pravda*, 12 September 1936.
2. *Bol'shevik*, no. 18 (1936), p. 30.
3. Cited in: Trotskii, *Prestupleniia Stalina*, p. 48.
4. Sedova, N. I. & Victor Serge, *The Life and Death of Leon Trotsky*, p. 209.
5. *Poslednie novosti* [Latest News], 10 November 1936.
6. Cited from: Trotskii, *Dnevniki i pis'ma*, p. 252.
7. "Scope of Soviet Activity in the United States, Hearing before the Subcommittee to Investigate the Administration of the Internal Security Act," 6 March 1956, Washington, p. 137.
8. *Pravda*, 24 August 1936.
9. Trotskii, *Prestupleniia Stalina*, p. 119.
10. "Scope of Soviet Activity in the US," (hearing),

29 February 1956, Washington, p. 89.
11. *Biulleten' oppozitsii*, no. 52–53 (1936), p. 2.

8. Leon Sedov's *Red Book*

1. *Biulleten' oppozitsii*, 52–53 (1936), pp. 2–3.
2. Ibid., p. 4.
3. Ibid., pp. 4–5.
4. Ibid., p. 5.
5. Ibid., p. 20.
6. Ibid., p. 17.
7. *Pravda*, 21 August 1936.
8. *Biulleten' oppozitsii*, no. 52–53 (1936), p. 17.
9. Ibid., p. 18.
10. Ibid., p. 18
11. Ibid., p. 21.
12. Ibid., pp. 20–21.
13. Ibid., p. 19.
14. Ibid., p. 43.
15. Ibid., pp. 43–44.
16. Ibid., p. 46.
17. Ibid., p. 4.
18. Ibid., p. 27.
19. Ibid., p. 47.
20. Ibid., pp. 47–48.

9. Ten Percent of the Truth, or What Really Happened

1. *Reabilitatsiia*, p. 181.
2. *Biulleten' oppozitsii*, no. 52–53 (1936), p. 24.
3. Ibid., p. 25.
4. Ibid., p. 37–38.
5. Getty, J. Arch, *Origin of the Great Purge: The Soviet Communist Past Reconsidered: 1933–1938* (Cambridge University Press: 1985); Broué, P., "Trotsky. A bloc des opposition de 1932," *Cahiers Leon Trotsky*, no. 5 (Paris: 1980).
6. Broué, P., "Party Opposition to Stalin (1930–32) and the First Moscow Trial," in: *Essays on Revolutionary Culture and Stalinism* (Slavica Publishers, 1985), p. 166.
7. Trotsky Archives, document no. 4782.
8. Broué, "Party Opposition to Stalin," p. 101.
9. Ibid., p. 105.
10. *Voprosy istorii*, no. 10 (1994), pp. 22–23.
11. Trotsky Archives, document no. 13224.
12. Trotsky Archives, document no. 4858.
13. Ibid.
14. Broué, "Party Opposition to Stalin," pp. 107–108.
15. Ibid., p. 110.

10. Candidate Defendants at Future Trials

1. Piatakov, Yu., "Besposhchadno unichtozhat' prezrennykh ubiits i predatelei," [Mercilessly Annihilate the Despicable Murderers and Traitors] *Pravda*, 21 August 1936.
2. Radek, K., "Trotskistsko—zinov'evskaia fashistskaia banda i ee getman—Trotsky," [The Trotsky-Zinoviev Fascist Band and its Hetman—Trotsky] *Izvestiia*, 21 August 1936.
3. *Pravda*, 22 August 1936.
4. *Reabilitatsiia*, p. 219.
5. *Voprosy istorii*, no. 1 (1995), p. 10.
6. *Pravda*, 22 August 1936.
7. *Reabilitatsiia*, p. 245.
8. *Pravda*, 23 August 1936.
9. Trotskii, L. D., *Portrety revoliutsionerov* (Benson [USA], 1988), pp. 230–231.
10. Recounted to the author by N. A. Rykova.
11. Larina, *Nezabyvaemoe*, p. 292.
12. *Istochnik* [The Source], no. 2 (1993), p. 6.
13. Ibid., p. 12.
14. Shelestov, A., *Vremia Alekseia Rykova*, [The Times of Aleksei Rykov] (Moscow: 1988), p. 285.
15. Larina, *Nezabyvaemoe*, p. 300.
16. *Znamia* [Banner], no. 12 (1988), p. 136.
17. *Istochnik*, no. 2 (1993), p. 11.
18. Ibid., pp. 7–8.
19. Ibid., p. 7.
20. Ibid., p. 15.
21. *Voprosy istorii*, no. 1 (1995), p. 21.
22. *Istochnik*, no. 2 (1993), p. 16.
23. Ibid., p. 17.
24. Larina, *Nezabyvaemoe*, pp. 295–296.
25. Ibid., p. 305–306.
26. Ibid., p. 305.
27. *Voprosy istorii*, no. 1 (1995), p. 21.
28. *Istochnik*, no. 2 (1993), p. 17.
29. Larina, *Nezabyvaemoe*, pp. 308–309.
30. *Pravda*, 10 September 1936.
31. *Biulleten' oppozitsii*, no. 52–53 (1936), pp. 46–47.
32. Larina, *Nezabyvaemoe*, pp. 310–312.
33. *Voprosy istorii KPSS*, [Problems of the History of the CPSU] no. 11 (1988), p. 49.

11. From Charges of Terror to New Amalgams

1. Orlov, *Tainaia istoriia stalinskikh prestuplenii*,

p. 173.
2. Vyshinskii, A. Ya., *Sudebnye rechi*, p. 423.
3. *Istoriia i istoriki* [History and Historians] (Moscow: 1965), p. 257.
4. Trotsky, *Prestupleniia Stalina*, pp. 81–82.
5. *Biulleten' oppozitsii*, no. 54–55 (1937), p. 9.
6. Trotsky, *Prestupleniia Stalina*, p. 82.
7. *Biulleten' oppozitsii*, no. 52–53 (1936), p. 48.
8. Ibid.
9. Ibid., no. 54–55, p. 17.

12. The Beginning of the Yezhov Period

1. *Pravda*, 1 September 1936.
2. Recounted to the author by B. N. Lesniak.
3. *Voprosy istorii*, no. 8 (1993), p. 19.
4. "Vysoko derzhat' znamia stalinskoi bditel'nosti," [Raise High the Banner of Stalinist Vigilance] *Pravda*, 5 September 1936.
5. *Izvestiia*, 29 August 1936.
6. *Pravda*, 3 September 1936.
7. "Pokaznaia bditel'nost'," [Ostentatious Vigilance] *Pravda*, 7 September 1936.
8. *Voprosy istorii*, no. 8 (1993), p. 19.
9. Khlevniuk, O. V., *Stalin i Ordzhonikidze: Konflikty v Politburo v 30-e gody* (Moscow: 1993), pp. 64–65.
10. *Reabilitatsiia*, p. 32.
11. *Stalinskoe Politburo v 30-e gody* (Moscow: 1995), p. 150.
12. Ibid., p. 148.
13. *Reabilitatsiia*, p. 246.
14. *Sovetskoe gosudarstvo i pravo*, [translation] no. 3 (1965), p. 24.
15. *Reabilitatsiia*, pp. 246, 248.
16. *Pravda*, 28 October 1936.
17. *Reabilitatsiia*, p. 182.
18. Riutin, M. N., *Na koleni ne vstanu*, pp. 349–350.
19. *Reabilitatsiia*, p. 182.
20. Riutin, *Na koleni ne vstanu*, pp. 349–350.
21. Ibid., p. 311.
22. *Voprosy istorii*, no. 8–9 (1992), pp. 22–23.

13. The Kemerovo Trial

1. *Pravda*, 21, 22, 23 November 1936.
2. *Biulleten' oppozitsii*, no. 54–55 (1937), p. 45.

14. The December Plenum of the Central Committee

1. Larina, *Nezabyvaemoe*, pp. 269–270.

2. Shelestov, *Vremia Alekseia Rykova*, p. 286.
3. Larina, *Nezabyvaemoe*, p. 314.
4. *Voprosy istorii*, no. 1 (1995), p. 21.
5. *Voprosy istorii*, no. 1 (1995), pp. 5-7; RTsKhIDNI, f. 17, op. 2, d. 575, l. 11-51.
6. RTsKhIDNI, f. 17, op. 2, d. 575, l. 44, 54-55.
7. *Voprosy istorii*, no. 1 (1995), p. 6.
8. RTsKhIDNI, f. 17, op. 2, d. 575, l. 59, 68.
9. RTsKhIDNI, f. 17, op. 2, d. 575, l. 68-93.
10. *Voprosy istorii*, 1995, no. 1, pp. 9-11.
11. RTsKhIDNI, f. 17, op. 2, d. 575, l. 94-106.
12. *Voprosy istorii*, no. 1 (1995), p. 8.
13. RTsKhIDNI, f. 17, op. 2, d. 575, l. 107-110.
14. Ibid., l. 122.
15. Ibid., l. 138-143.
16. *Voprosy istorii*, no. 1 (1995), pp. 8-9.
17. RTsKhIDNI, f. 17, op. 2, d. 575, l. 167, 172-174.
18. *Voprosy istorii*, no. 1 (1995), pp. 11-17.
19. Ibid., pp. 12-17.
20. *Voprosy istorii*, no. 6-7 (1992), p. 25.
21. Ibid., p. 26.
22. Ibid., p. 23.
23. Chuev, *Tak govoril Kaganovich*, p. 137.
24. Ibid., p. 152.
25. *Voprosy istorii*, no. 1 (1995), pp. 18-19.
26. Ibid., p. 19.
27. Ibid., p. 4.

15. The Trial of the "Anti-Soviet Trotskyist Center"
1. Larina, *Nezabyvaemoe*, p. 308.
2. *Reabilitatsiia*, p. 222.
3. Orlov, *Tainaia istoriia stalinskikh prestuplenii*, p. 193.
4. Ibid.
5. *Izvestiia*, 21 August 1936.
6. *Ogonek* [The Flame], no. 52 (1988), p. 29.
7. *Voprosy istorii*, 1995, no. 1, p. 10.
8. Orlov, *Tainaia istoriia stalinskikh prestuplenii*, p. 198.
9. *Reabilitatsiia*, p. 225.
10. Sedova & Serge, *The Life and Death of Leon Trotsky*, p. 216.
11. *Biulleten' oppozitsii*, no. 54-55 (1937), pp. 16-17.
12. Trotskii, *Prestupleniia Stalina*, pp. 167-168.
13. Ibid., pp. 171-172.
14. Sedova & Serge, *The Life and Death of Leon Trotsky*, p. 217.
15. *Protsess antisovetskogo trotskistskogo tsentra*,

pp. 40-43, 60, 61, 158.
16. Vyshinskii, *Sudebnye rechi*, pp. 444-445.
17. *Protsess antisovetskogo trotskistskogo tsentra*, p. 231.
18. *Pravda*, 24 January 1937.
19. Vyshinskii, *Sudebnye rechi*, p. 447.
20. *Protsess antisovetskogo trotskistskogo tsentra*, p. 225.
21. Ibid., pp. 96-97.
22. Trotskii, *Prestupleniia Stalina*, p. 23.
23. Volkogonov, *Trotskii*, book 2, p. 194.
24. Trotskii, *Prestupleniia Stalina*, pp. 188-189.
25. *Protsess antisovetskogo trotskistskogo tsentra*, p. 224.
26. Ibid., p. 68.
27. Ibid., p. 136.
28. Vyshinskii, *Sudebnye rechi*, p. 483.
29. Ibid., pp. 431, 435, 437.
30. Ibid., p. 478.
31. Ibid., p. 480.
32. Ibid., p. 482.
33. *Biulleten' oppozitsii*, 1933, no. 36-37, p. 9.
34. Vyshinskii, *Sudebnye rechi*, pp. 475-476.
35. Trotskii, *Prestupleniia Stalina*, pp. 196-197.
36. *Protsess antisovetskogo trotskistskogo tsentra*, pp. 214-215.
37. Ibid., p. 222.
38. Ibid., p. 115.
39. Ibid., p. 230.
40. Ibid., pp. 256-258.
41. *Izvestiia*, 2 September 1992.
42. Trotsky Archives, document no. 13225.
43. "Prigvozdit' trotskizm k pozornomu stolbu," [Nail Trotskyism to the Pillar of Shame] *Pravda*, 8 February 1937.
44. *Pravda*, 30 January 1937.
45. Feikhtvanger, *Moskva 1937*, p. 102.
46. Ibid., p. 91.
47. Ibid., pp. 104-105.
48. Ibid., p. 103.
49. Ibid., p. 86.

16. Trotsky Returns to Battle
1. Trotskii, *Prestupleniia Stalina*, p. 29.
2. Ibid., p. 53.
3. Deutscher, I., *Trotskii v izgnanii* [Trotsky in Exile], p. 385.
4. *Biulleten' oppozitsii*, no. 54-55 (1937), pp. 21-22.
5. Trotskii, *Dnevniki i pis'ma,*, p. 163.

6. Ibid.
7. Ibid., p. 154.
8. Ibid., p.156.
9. Trotskii, *Prestupleniia Stalina*, p. 7.
10. *Izvestiia*, 21 August 1990.
11. Trotsky Archives, document no. 5809.
12. *Biulleten' oppozitsii*, no. 54–55 (1937), p. 2.
13. Ibid., p. 3.
14. Ibid., p. 20.
15. Ibid., p. 14.
16. Ibid., p. 4.
17. Ibid., p. 33.
18. Ibid., p. 7.
19. Hoover Institute Archives, Nikolaevsky Collection, box 295, folder 16, p. 163.

17. Trotsky on the Goals of the Moscow Trials

1. *Znamia*, no. 5 (1988), p. 69.
2. See, for instance, Volkogonov, *Trotskii*, book 2, p. 97.
3. Trotskii, *Prestupleniia Stalina*, p. 38.
4. *Biulleten' oppozitsii*, no. 54–55 (1937), p. 11.
5. Ibid., p. 32.
6. Trotskii, *Prestupleniia Stalina*, p. 237.
7. Ibid., p. 203.
8. Ibid., p. 39.
9. *Biulleten' oppozitsii*, no. 54–55 (1937), pp. 13–14.
10. Trotskii, *Prestupleniia Stalina*, p. 204.
11. Ibid., p. 39.
12. *Biulleten' oppozitsii*, no. 54–55 (1937), pp. 13–14.
13. Trotskii, *Prestupleniia Stalina*, p. 40.
14. Ibid., pp. 206–207.
15. *Biulleten' oppozitsii*, no. 54–55 (1937), p. 8.
16. Trotskii, *Prestupleniia Stalina*, p. 237.
17. Ibid., pp. 237–238.
18. Ibid., p. 236.
19. *Biulleten' oppozitsii*, no. 54–55(1937), p.17.
20. Trotskii, *Prestupleniia Stalina*, pp. 204–205.

18. A Tyrant's Revenge

1. *Izvestiia*, 5 February 1937.
2. Trotskii, *Dnevniki i pis'ma*, p. 115.
3. Sedova & Serge, *The Life and Death of Leon Trotsky*, p. 219.
4. *Voprosy istorii*, no. 10 (1993), pp. 157–158.
5. Hoover Archives, Nikolaevsky Collection, box 279, folder 10, p. 40.

6. Ibid., box 628, folder 13.
7. *Pravda*, 27 January 1937.
8. *Voprosy istorii*, no. 10 (1993), pp. 159–160.
9. Hoover Archives, Nikolaevsky Collection, box 628, folder 13.
10. Runin, B. M., *Moe okruzhenie. Zapiski sluchaino utselevshego* [My Milieu. Notes of One Who Accidentally Survived] (Moscow: 1995), p. 73.
11. Ibid., p. 136.
12. Ibid., p. 139.
13. Ibid., p. 141.
14. Ibid., p. 189.
15. Ibid., p. 143.

19. The Anti-Semitic Subtext of the Moscow Trials

1. Sedova & Serge, *The Life and Death of Leon Trotsky*, p. 219.
2. Trotskii, *Prestupleniia Stalina*, pp. 219–221.
3. Cited from the book: Nedava, J., *Vechnyi komissar* [Eternal Commissar] (Jerusalem: 1989), pp. 151–152. [See: Nedava, J., *Trotsky and the Jews* (Philadelphia: 1972), pp. 186–187].
4. Ibid., p. 138 [p. 172].
5. Stalin, I. V., *Sochineniia*, vol. 13, p. 28.
6. Ibid.
7. Trotskii, *Prestupleniia Stalina*, p. 216.
8. Ibid., p. 85.
9. Ibid., pp. 216–217.
10. Ibid., p. 217.
11. Ibid., pp. 217–218.
12. Larin, Yu., *Evrei i antisemitizm v SSSR* [The Jews and Anti-Semitism in the USSR] (Moscow-Leningrad: 1929), pp. 241–242.
13. Trotskii, *Prestupleniia Stalina*, p. 221.
14. Razgon, L., *Nepridumannoe* [True Stories] (Moscow: 1991), p. 77, 80–81.
15. Trotskii, *Prestupleniia Stalina*, p. 221.
16. Allilueva, *Tol'ko odin god*, p. 159.
17. Lert, R. B., *Na tom stoiu* [Here I Stand] (Moscow: 1991), p. 249.
18. Shevtsov, I., *Vo imia ottsa i syna* [In the Name of the Father and the Son] (Moscow: 1970), pp. 378–379.
19. Ibid., pp. 382–383.
20. *Pravda*, 31 January 1995.
21. *Dnipro* [Dnepr], no. 10 (1963), p. 33.

20. Why Did They Confess?

1. Larina, *Nezabyvaemoe*, p. 363.
2. Shalamov, V. *Kolymskie rasskazy* [Kolyma Tales], book 1, (Moscow: 1992), p. 325, 327.
3. Information recounted to the author by D. B. Dobrushkin.
4. *Reabilitatsiia*, p. 37.
5. Ibid., pp. 35–36.
6. Ibid., pp. 36, 38.
7. Iliukhin, V., "Zapretnaia glava," [Forbidden Chapter] *Pravda*, 16 November 1994.
8. Oruell, D., *Esse, stat'i, retsenzii* [Essays, Articles and Reviews], vol. 2, Perm' (1992), p. 181.
9. *Biulleten' oppozitsii*, no. 54–55 (1937), pp. 32–33.
10. Ibid., p. 15.
11. Ibid., p. 14.
12. Ibid., p. 15.
13. Ibid., p. 17.
14. Ibid., p. 16.
15. Ibid., p. 4.
16. Ibid., pp. 16–17.
17. Cited from: Trotskii, *Dnevniki i pis'ma*, pp. 151–152.
18. *Biulleten' oppozitsii*, no. 54–55 (1937), p. 17.
19. Ibid., pp. 31–32.
20. Trotskii, *Dnevniki i pis'ma*, p. 152.
21. Stalin, *Sochineniia*, vol. 6, p. 46; vol. 11, p. 58.
22. *Biulleten' oppozitsii*, no. 54–55 (1937), p. 7.
23. Ibid., pp. 6–7.
24. Trotskii, *Dnevniki i pis'ma*, p. 157.
25. *Biulleten' oppozitsii*," no. 54–55 (1937), pp. 17–18.

21. Bukharin and Rykov in the Clutches of a "Party Investigation"

1. Larina, *Nezabyvaemoe*, p. 289.
2. Shelestov, *Vremia Alekseia Rykova*, pp. 286–287.
3. Communicated to the author by N. A. Rykova.
4. Larina, *Nezabyvaemoe*, pp. 317, 319, 324.
5. *Voprosy istorii*, no. 1 (1995), p. 21.
6. *Voprosy istorii*, no. 2 (1993), p. 31.
7. *Reabilitatsiia*, p. 251.
8. Communicated to the author by V. N. Astrov.
9. *Reabilitatsiia*, p. 258.
10. Ibid., pp. 258–259.
11. *Literaturnaia gazeta*, 29 March 1988.
12. Larina, *Nezabyvaemoe*, pp. 340–341.
13. *Reabilitatsiia*, p. 251.

14. *Protsess antisovetskogo trotskistskogo tsentra*, p. 231.
15. Larina, *Nezabyvaemoe*, p. 331.
16. Communicated to the author by N. A. Rykova.
17. Larina, *Nezabyvaemoe*, p. 333.

22. The Death of Ordzhonikidze

1. Lenin, *PSS*, vol. 45, p. 361.
2. Khlevniuk, *Stalin i Ordzhonikidze* (Moscow: 1993), pp. 88–89.
3. *Pravda*, 27 October 1966.
4. *Voprosy istorii KPSS*, no. 3 (1991), p. 90.
5. *Izvestiia TsK KPSS*, [Information of the CC CPSU] no. 2 (1991), p. 175.
6. Ibid., p. 183.
7. Ibid., p. 150.
8. *Voprosy istorii*, no. 6–7 (1992), pp. 86–87.
9. *Voprosy istorii KPSS*, no. 3 (1991), p. 90.
10. Vaksberg, A., *Neraskrytye tainy* (Moscow: 1993), p. 123.
11. *Beriia: konets kar'ery* (Moscow: 1991), p. 360.
12. *Reabilitatsiia*, p. 56.
13. *Voprosy istorii*, no. 6–7 (1992), p. 83.
14. *Voprosy istorii*, no. 4 (1990), p. 81.
15. *Beriia: konets kar'ery*, p. 378.
16. *Voprosy istorii*, no. 11–12 (1995), pp. 14, 16.
17. Khlevniuk, *Stalin i Ordzhonikidze*, p. 97.
18. Ibid., p. 96.
19. Gel'perin, N., "Direktivy narkoma," [A People's Commissar's Directives] "Za industrializatsiiu," [For Industrialization] 21 February 1937.
20. *Voprosy istorii KPSS*, no. 3 (1991), p. 92.
21. Dubinskii-Mukhadze, I., *Ordzhonikidze* (Moscow: 1963), p. 6.
22. *Voprosy istorii KPSS*, no. 3 (1991), pp. 92–93.
23. *Pravda*, 19 February 1937.
24. *Pravda*, 22 February 1937.
25. *Bol'shaia Sovetskaia Entsiklopediia*, vol. 43 (Moscow: 1939), cols. 299–300.
26. *Voprosy istorii*, no. 6–7 (1992), pp. 82–83.
27. Chuev, *Sto sorok besed s Molotovym*, pp. 191–192.
28. *Istoricheskii arkhiv*, [Historical Archive] no. 1 (1994), p. 60.
29. *Voprosy istorii KPSS*, no. 3 (1991), p. 96.
30. Ibid., p. 97.
31. Ibid., p. 98.

23. Two Letters from Bukharin

1. Shelestov, *Vremia Aleskeia Rykova*, p. 288.

2. Larina, *Nezabyvaemoe*, p. 346.
3. *Voprosy istorii*, no. 2–3 (1992), pp. 5–6, 12, 19.
4. Ibid., pp. 7, 10, 17.
5. Ibid., pp. 30–32.
6. Ibid., p. 6.
7. Ibid., pp. 24–25.
8. Ibid., pp. 18, 19, 26, 29.
9. Ibid., p. 6.
10. Larina, *Nezabyvaemoe*, p. 363.
11. Ibid., pp. 363–364.
12. Ibid., pp. 362–363.

24. Prelude to the February-March Plenum
1. RtsKhIDNI, f. 17, op. 3, d. 983, l. 14–15.
2. Communicated to the author by A. Ya. Zis.
3. RtsKhIDNI, f. 17, op. 3, d. 983, l. 110–111.
4. *Istoricheskii arkhiv*, no. 5 (1993), pp. 42–43.
5. Stalin, *O nedostatkakh partiinoi raboty*, pp. 54–55.
6. *Pravda*, 29 December 1936.
7. *Pravda*, 6 May 1935.
8. *Pravda*, 1 March 1935.
9. *Pravda*, 26 November 1936.

25. The February-March Plenum: Bukharin and Rykov Stand Accused
1. *Voprosy istorii*, no. 2–3 (1992), p. 43.
2. *Dodnes' tiagoteet*, vyp. 1, p. 283.
3. Larina, *Nezabyvaemoe*, p. 350.
4. *Voprosy istorii*, no. 4–5 (1992), pp. 4, 12.
5. Ibid., pp. 11, 13, 15.
6. Ibid., pp. 16–18, 21.
7. Ibid., p. 24.
8. Ibid., pp. 25–26, 33.
9. Ibid., pp. 32, 33.
10. Ibid., p. 36.
11. *Voprosy istorii*, no. 6–7 (1992), p. 3.
12. Ibid., p. 4.
13. Ibid., pp. 6–7.
14. Ibid., pp. 15–16.
15. Ibid., pp. 11–12.
16. Ibid., pp. 5–6.
17. Ibid., p. 14.
18. Ibid., pp. 11–13.
19. Ibid., p. 7.
20. Ibid., pp. 23–24.
21. Ibid., pp. 20–23.
22. *Voprosy istorii*, no. 10 (1992), p. 16.

23. *Voprosy istorii*, no. 11–12 (1992), pp. 3–4.
24. *Voprosy istorii*, no. 7 (1995), p. 15.

26. Bukharin and Rykov Defend Themselves
1. Communicated to the author by N. A. Rykova.
2. *Voprosy istorii*, no. 2 (1993), p. 17.
3. Ibid., p. 8.
4. Ibid., p. 6.
5. Ibid., pp. 12–13.
6. Ibid., p. 5.
7. Ibid., p. 17.
8. Ibid., p. 18.
9. Ibid., p. 20.
10. Ibid., pp. 21–22.
11. Ibid., p. 20.
12. Ibid., p. 23.
13. Ibid., p. 26.

27. The Plenum Delivers its Verdict
1. *Voprosy istorii*, no. 2 (1993), p. 29.
2. Ibid., pp. 26–27.
3. Ibid., p. 33.
4. Ibid.
5. *Voprosy istorii*, no. 1 (1994), pp. 12–13.
6. *Reabilitatsiia*, pp. 255–256.
7. *Dodnes' tiagoteet*, vyp. 1, p. 283.
8. *Oktiabr'*, no. 12 (1988), p. 115.

28. The Fate of the "Letter of an Old Bolshevik"
1. Fel'shtinsky, Iu., *Razgovory s Bukharinym* (Moscow: 1993), p. 25.
2. *Sotsialisticheskii vestnik*, no. 23–24 (1936), pp. 20–21.
3. Larina, *Nezabyvaemoe*, pp. 256–257.
4. Ibid.
5. *Sotsialisticheskii vestnik*, no. 23–24 (1936), p. 20.
6. Ibid., p. 22.
7. Larina, *Nezabyvaemoe*, pp. 262, 263.
8. Ibid., p. 262.
9. Ibid., pp. 271–273.
10. *Sotsialisticheskii vestnik*, no. 1–2 (1937), p. 23.
11. *Voprosy istorii*, no. 11–12 (1992), p. 11.
12. *Sotsialisticheskii vestnik*, no. 22–23 (1936), p. 24.
13. *Voprosy istorii*, no. 2–3 (1992), p. 8.
14. *Sotsialisticheskii vestnik*, 1965, book 4, pp. 83–84.

15. Larina, *Nezabyvaemoe*, p. 258.
16. Fel'shtinsky, *Razgovory s Bukharinym*, p. 19.
17. *Novyj zhurnal*, New York, no. 75 (March 1964), pp. 180–181.
18. Fel'shtinsky, *Razgovory s Bukharinym*, pp. 24, 27.
19. Larina, *Nezabyvaemoe*, pp. 286–288.

29. The February-March Plenum: Questions of Party Democracy
1. *Pravda*, 5 March 1936.
2. *Voprosy istorii*, no. 7 (1993), p. 14.
3. Ibid., p. 10.
4. *Voprosy istorii*, no. 6 (1993), p. 18.
5. *Voprosy istorii*, no. 7 (1993), pp. 5–6.
6. *Voprosy istorii*, no. 5 (1993), p. 6.
7. Ibid., p. 7.
8. *Voprosy istorii*, no. 7 (1993), p. 13.
9. Ibid.
10. *Voprosy istorii*, no. 5 (1993), pp. 9, 10.
11. Ibid., p. 8.
12. Ibid, p. 11.
13. *Voprosy istorii*, no. 7 (1993), p. 14.
14. *Voprosy istorii*, no. 6 (1993), p. 13.
15. *Voprosy istorii*, no. 5 (1993), p. 11.
16. Ibid., p. 12.
17. *Voprosy istorii*, no. 6 (1993), p. 9.
18. Ibid., p. 26.
19. *Voprosy istorii*, no. 7 (1993), p. 17.
20. Ibid., p. 4.
21. Ibid., pp. 8–9.
22. *Voprosy istorii*, no. 7 (1993), p. 19.

30. The February-March Plenum on Sabotage
1. *Voprosy istorii*, no. 7 (1993), p. 9.
2. *Voprosy istorii*, no. 6 (1993), p. 28.
3. *Voprosy istorii*, no. 5 (1993), p. 22.
4. *Voprosy istorii*, no. 8 (1993), p. 6.
5. Ibid., p. 11.
6. Ibid., pp. 12–13.
7. *Voprosy istorii KPSS*, no. 3 (1991), pp. 93–94.
8. *Voprosy istorii*, no. 8 (1993), pp. 17–18.
9. Molotov, V. M., *Uroki vreditel'stva, diversii i shpionazha iapono-nemetsko-trotskistskikh agentov* (Moscow: 1937), p. 31.
10. Trotskii, *Prestupleniia Stalina*, p. 214.
11. *Voprosy istorii KPSS*, no. 5 (1989), pp. 99–100.
12. *Voprosy istorii KPSS*, no. 3 (1991), p. 95.
13. *Voprosy istorii*, no. 8 (1993), p. 11.

14. Ibid., pp. 24–25.
15. *Voprosy istorii*, no. 9 (1993), pp. 6, 14.
16. Ibid., pp. 24–26.
17. Ibid, p. 23.
18. *Istoricheskii arkhiv*, no. 5 (1993), p. 42.
19. *Voprosy istorii*, no. 9 (1993), p. 27.
20. Ibid., p. 26.
21. Ibid., pp. 23–23.
22. Ibid., p. 10.
23. Ibid., p. 27.
24. Ibid., p. 7.
25. Ibid., p. 12.
26. Ibid., pp. 30, 31.
27. Ibid., pp. 15, 17.
28. Ibid., p. 16.
29. *Voprosy istorii*, no. 1 (1994), p. 17.
30. Ibid., pp. 22, 24.
31. Ibid., p. 25–27.
32. *Voprosy istorii*, no. 2 (1994), pp. 15–16.
33. Ibid., pp. 17–18.
34. Ibid., pp. 19, 21.
35. Ibid., pp. 21–22.
36. Ibid., pp. 21–23.
37. Trotskii, *Prestupleniia Stalina*, p. 70.
38. *Voprosy istorii*, no. 2 (1994), p. 28.
39. *Voprosy istorii*, no. 6 (1994), p. 11.
40. Ibid., pp. 7, 10.
41. Ibid., pp. 22–23.
42. Ibid., pp. 14, 16–17.
43. *Voprosy istorii*, no. 8 (1994), pp. 18, 20.

31. Why Did Stalin Need "Sabotage"?
1. *Reabilitatsiia*, pp. 432, 437.
2. *Biulleten' oppozitsii*, no. 17–18 (1930), p. 38.
3. Voznesensky, N. A., *Voennaia ekonomika SSSR v period Otechestvennoi voiny* [The Military Economy of the USSR during the Patriotic War] (Moscow: 1947), pp. 159, 162.
4. Skott, Dzhon, *Za Uralom. Amerikanskii rabochii v russkom gorode stali* (Sverdlovsk: 1991), p. 83. [For an English edition, see Scott, John, *Behind the Urals* (Bloomington: Indiana University Press, 1989), p. 64.] [Hereafter, the first page number will be from the Russian edition, the second from the English edition].
5. Ibid., pp. 97–98/pp. 78–79.
6. Ibid., p. 68/p. 44.
7. Ibid., p. 92/p. 73.
8. Ibid., p. 96/p. 77.
9. Ibid., p. 111/p. 92.

10. Ibid., p. 164/p. 155.
11. ibid., p. 147/p. 137.
12. Ibid., p. 150/p. 140.
13. Ibid., pp. 172–173/p. 163.
14. *Voprosy istorii*, no. 6 (1994), p. 5.
15. Scott, *Behind the Urals*, p. 182/ p. 174.
16. Ibid., p. 183/ p. 175.
17. *Voprosy istorii*, no. 8 (1994), p. 19.
18. *Voprosy istorii*, no. 6 (1994), pp. 17–18.
19. *Iosif Stalin v ob"iatiiakh sem'i* (Moscow: 1993), pp. 183–188.
20. Scott, *Behind the Urals*, pp. 282–284/pp. 286–288.
21. Molotov, *Uroki vreditel'stva, diversii i shpionazha iapono-nemetsko-trotskistskikh agentov,* [Lessons of Wrecking, Diversion and Espionage by Japanese-German-Trotskyist Agents] pp. 41–42.
22. *Voprosy istorii*, no. 6 (1994), p. 20.
23. Scott, *Behind the Urals*, pp. 194–195/pp. 186–187.
24. Ibid., p. 279/p. 283.
25. Ibid., p. 193/p. 186.
26. Ibid., p. 193/pp. 185–186.
27. Ibid., pp. 183, 187–188, 192–193/pp. 176, 179, 180.
28. Trotskii, *Prestupleniia Stalina*, p. 137.
29. Ibid., p. 134.
30. Ibid., p. 138.

32. The NKVD Stands Accused

1. *Voprosy istorii*, no. 10 (1994), p. 15.
2. Ibid., pp. 18–20.
3. Ibid., p. 16.
4. Ibid., p. 20.
5. Ibid., pp. 21–22.
6. *Voprosy istorii*, no. 12 (1994), pp. 3, 22.
7. *Voprosy istorii*, no. 2 (1995), p. 10.
8. Ibid., p. 7.
9. Ibid., pp. 12–13.
10. Ibid., p. 12.
11. Ibid., p. 11.
12. Ibid.
13. Ibid., p. 8.
14. Ibid., p. 18.
15. Ibid., p. 24.
16. Ibid., p. 23.
17. Ibid., p. 25.

33. The February-March Plenum on "Party Work"

1. *Voprosy istorii*, no. 4 (1995), p. 7.
2. Ibid., p. 13.
3. Ibid., p. 14.
4. *Voprosy istorii*, no. 5–6 (1995), p. 3.
5. *Reabilitatsiia*, p. 34; *Voprosy istorii*, no. 5–6 (1995), p. 4.
6. *Voprosy istorii*, no. 5–6 (1995), p. 4.
7. *Voprosy istorii*, no. 7 (1995), p. 12.
8. Ibid., p. 19.
9. Ibid., p. 12.
10. *Voprosy istorii*, no. 8 (1995), p. 22.
11. *Voprosy istorii*, no. 4 (1995), p. 9.
12. Ibid., pp. 16–17.
13. *Voprosy istorii*, no. 8 (1995), pp. 3–4.
14. *Voprosy istorii*, no. 7 (1995), p. 22.
15. *Voprosy istorii*, no. 5–6 (1995), pp. 10–11.
16. *Voprosy istorii*, no. 7 (1995), pp. 11–13.

34. Stalin Issues Directives

1. Stalin, *Sochineniia*, vol. 10, p. 336.
2. Stalin, *Sochineniia*, vol. 11, pp. 277–278.
3. Stalin, *O nedostatkakh partiinoi raboty*, pp. 57–58.
4. *Voprosy istorii*, no. 9 (1993), p. 27.
5. *Voprosy istorii*, no. 7 (1995), p. 4.
6. *Voprosy istorii*, no. 5–6 (1995), pp. 6–7.
7. Ibid., p. 10.
8. *Voprosy istorii*, no. 8 (1995), p. 22.
9. Ibid., p. 7.
10. *Voprosy istorii*, no. 5–6 (1995), p. 19.
11. Stalin, *O nedostatkakh partiinoi raboty*, p. 5.
12. Ibid., p. 29.
13. Ibid., pp. 32–33.
14. Ibid., pp. 14, 17, 26–27.
15. Ibid., p. 14.
16. Ibid., pp. 15–17.
17. *Voprosy istorii*, no. 8 (1993), p. 18.
18. Molotov, *Uroki vreditel'stva, diversii i shpionazha iapono-nemetsko-trotskistskikh agentov*, p. 33.
19. Stalin, *O nedostatkakh partiinoi raboty*, pp. 43–44.
20. Ibid., pp. 23–24.
21. Ibid., pp. 30–31.
22. Ibid., pp. 53–54.
23. Ibid., pp. 10–20,
24. Ibid., p. 35.
25. Ibid., p. 36.

26. Trotskii, L. D., *K istorii russkoi revoliutsii*, [Towards a History of the Russian Revolution] (Moscow: 1990), pp. 201–202.
27. Ibid., p. 167.
28. Stalin, *O nedostatkakh partiinoi raboty*, pp. 36–37.
29. Ibid., pp. 56–58, 60.

35. The Election Campaign in the Party
1. *Pravda*, 14 March 1937.
2. *Pravda*, 29 March 1937.
3. *Pravda*, 10 March 1937.
4. *Pravda*, 7 March 1937.
5. *Istoricheskii arkhiv*, no. 2 (1994), p. 45.
6. *Voprosy istorii*, no. 4 (1990), pp. 73, 75.
7. *Voprosy istorii*, no. 2–3 (1992), p. 84.
8. Ibid.
9. *Voprosy istorii*, no. 4 (1990), p. 74.
10. *Voprosy istorii*, no. 2–3 (1992), pp. 84–85.
11. *Voprosy istorii*, no. 4 (1990), pp. 76–77.
12. *Istoricheskii arkhiv*, no. 2 (1994), p. 45.
13. *Voprosy istorii*, no. 4 (1990), p. 78.
14. *Trudnye Voprosy istorii* [Difficult Problems of History] (Moscow: 1991), pp. 208–209.
15. *Voprosy istorii*, no. 4 (1990), pp. 77–79; *Istoricheskii arkhiv*, no. 2 (1994), p. 45.
16. Chuev, *Tak govoril Kaganovich*, p. 99.
17. *Istoricheskii arkhiv*, no. 3 (1993), p. 62.
18. *Istoricheskii arkhiv*, no. 2 (1994), pp. 43–45.
19. *Istoricheskii arkhiv*, no. 4 (1994), p. 41.
20. *Voprosy istorii*, no. 4 (1990), p. 79.

36. The Dewey Commission
1. Trotskii, *Dnevniki i pis'ma*, pp. 155–156.
2. Cited from: Deutscher, *Trotsky v izgnanii*, p. 409.
3. Cited from: *Inostrannaia literatura*, no. 4 (1988), p. 165.
4. *Biulleten' oppozitsii*, no. 56–57 (1937), pp. 26–27.
5. Trotsky Archives, document no. 17301.
6. *Biulleten' oppozitsii*, no. 56–57 (1937), p. 17.
7. Ibid., p. 19.
8. Cited from: *Biulleten' oppozitsii*, no. 62–63 (1938), p. 3. [See: *Writings of Leon Trotsky:1937–38* (New York: 1976), p. 56.

37. Trotsky in the Curved Mirror of Anticommunism
1. Konkvest, R. *Bol'shoi terror* (Firenze: 1974),

pp. 816–818. [For an English version, see: Conquest, Robert, *The Great Terror. A Reassessment* (Oxford University Press, 1990), pp. 412–414].

38. Trotsky on Bolshevism and Stalinism
1. Volkogonov, *Trotskii*, book 1, p. 134.
2. *Biulleten' oppozitsii*, no. 56–57 (1937), p. 14.
3. *Biulleten' oppozitsii*, no. 56–57 (1937), p. 19.
4. Trotskii, *Dnevniki i pis'ma*, p. 154.
5. Glotzer, A., *Trotsky: Memoir & Critique* (New York: 1989), p. 263.
6. Ibid., pp. 260–261.
7. Aksenov, V., *Na polputi k lune* [Halfway to the Moon] (Moscow: 1966), pp. 13–15.
8. Trotskii, *Prestupleniia Stalina*, p. 76. [In English: *The Case of Leon Trotsky* (New York, 1969), p. 473].
9. Ibid., p. 92.
10. Glotzer, A., *Trotsky*, p. 261.
11. Trotskii, *Prestupleniia Stalina*, p. 76.
12. Trotskii, *Stalin*, vol. 2, pp. 152–153.
13. Ibid., pp. 136–137.
14. Ibid., p. 138.
15. Ibid., pp. 138–139.
16. Ibid., pp. 139–141.
17. Ibid., pp. 251–252.
18. Ibid., p. 252.

39. The Hunting Down of Trotskyists Abroad
1. *Biulleten' oppozitsii*, no. 56–57 (1937), p. 16.
2. Ibid., p. 12.
3. *Pravda*, 2 February; 21, 22, 29 and 31 March 1937.
4. *Pravda*, 21 July 1937.
5. Krivitskii, *Ia byl agentom Stalina*, p. 198.
6. *Biulleten' oppozitsii*, no. 58–59 (1937), p. 2.
7. *Biulleten' oppozitsii*, no. 60–61 (1937), p. 12.
8. Krivitskii, *Ia byl agentom Stalina*, pp. 195–196.
9. *Biulleten' oppozitsii*, no. 60–61 (1937), p. 15.

40. The Breakthrough and Death of Ignace Reiss
1. Khube, P., "Smert' v Lozanne," *Novoe vremia*, [New Times] no. 21 (1991), p. 36.
2. *Biulleten' oppozitsii*, no. 58–59 (1937), p. 23.
3. "Scope of Soviet Activity in the US," (hearing),

2 March 1956, pp. 140–141.
4. Kagan, Iu. M., *Marina Tsvetaeva v Moskve. Put' k gibeli* [Marina Tsvetaeva in Moscow. Path to Destruction] (Moscow: 1992), p. 194.
5. *Biulleten' oppozitsii*, no. 60–61 (1937), pp. 18–19.
6. *Poslednie novosti*, 24 October 1937.
7. Losskaia, V., *Marina Tsvetaeva v zhizni* [Marina Tsvetaeva in Life] (Neizdannye vospominaniia sovremennikov) [Unpublished Memoirs of Contemporaries] (Moscow: 1992), p. 190.
8. Trotsky Archives, document no. 4921.
9. *Inostrannaia literatura*, no. 12 (1989), pp. 240–241.
10. Losskaia, *Marina Tsvetaeva v zhizni*, p. 313.
11. *Stolitsa*, [Capital] no. 39 (1992), pp. 59–60.
12. *Stolitsa*, no. 38 (1992), p. 56; *Novoe vremia*, no. 4 (1993), p. 49.
13. *Stolitsa*, no. 39 (1992), p. 59.
14. *Novoe vremia*, no. 21 (1991), pp. 36, 38.
15. Krivitskii, *Ia byl agentom Stalina*, p. 266.
16. *Biulleten' oppozitsii*, no. 58–59 (1937), p. 22.

41. "Stay Out of Range of the Artillery Fire!"
1. Cited in: Volkogonov, *Trotskii*, book 2, pp. 295–297.
2. Krivitskii, *Ia byl agentom Stalina*, pp. 129–30.
3. *Biulleten' oppozitsii*, no. 60–61 (1937), p. 13.
4. Kopelev, L., *I sotvoril sebe kumira*, [And He Made Himself an Idol] (Ann Arbor), p. 148.
5. Kheminguei, E., *Sobranie sochinenii v 6 tomakh*, vol. 4, (Moscow: 1993), p. 40.
6. Krivitskii, *Ia byl agentom Stalina*, pp. 129–131.
7. Ibid., p. 137.
8. "Testimony of Alexander Orlov," (hearing) 14–15 February 1956, Washington, pp. 3429–3431.
9. Krivitskii, *Ia byl agentom Stalina*, pp. 132–133.
10. Trotsky Archives, document no. 5020.
11. Kheminguei, *Sobranie sochinenii v 6 tomakh*, vol. 4, pp. 188–189. [For an English version: Hemingway, *For Whom the Bell Tolls* (New York: 1940), p. 235.] [Hereafter, the first page number will be from the Russian edition, the second from the English edition.]
12. Krivitskii, *Ia byl agentom Stalina*, p. 150.
13. *Pravda*, 16 October 1936.

14. *Pravda*, 24 October 1936.
15. *Pravda*, 30 October 1936.
16. Krivitskii, *Ia byl agentom Stalina*, pp. 129–145.
17. Ibid., p. 145.
18. Kheminguei, *Sobranie sochinenii v shesti tomakh*, vol. 4, p. 187.
19. *Istochnik*, no. 3 (1994), p. 83.
20. Ibid.
21. Orlov, *Taianai istoriia stalinskikh prestuplenii*, p. 11.
22. Ibid., p. 13.
23. Krivitskii, *Ia byl agentom Stalina*, p. 131.
24. Kheminguei, *Sobranie sochinenii v shesti tomakh*, vol. 4, p. 326/pp. 418–419.
25. Ibid., p. 331/p. 424.
26. Kol'tsov, M., "Podlye manevry ispanskikh trotskistov," [Foul Manuevers by Spanish Trotskyists] *Pravda*, 14 December 1936; "Gnusnye manevry trotskistov v Katalonii," [Rotten Maneuvers by Trotskyists in Catalonia] *Pravda*, 17 December 1936.
27. Kol'tsov, M., "Agentura trotskistov v Ispanii," [Trotskyist Agents in Spain] *Pravda*, 22 January 1937.
28. Oruell, D., *Pamiati Katalonii* (Paris: 1976), pp. 76–77 [English edition: Orwell, *Homage to Catalonia*, (New York: 1952), p. 60]. [Hereafter, the first page number will be from the Russian edition, the second from the English edition].
29. Ibid., p. 85/pp. 66–67.
30. Ibid., p. 82/p. 64.

42. Trotsky on the Spanish Revolution
1. Erenburg, I., *Sobranie sochinenii*, vol. 9, p. 101.
2. Orwell, *Homage to Catalonia*, p. 65–66/p. 51.
3. Ibid., p. 67/p. 52.
4. Ibid., p. 76/p. 59.
5. Ibid., pp. 72–73/pp. 56–57.
6. Ibid., p. 88/pp. 68–69.
7. Ibid., pp. 73–74/p. 57.
8. Ibid., pp. 69, 80/pp. 54, 63.
9. *Biulleten' oppozitsii*, no. 56–57 (1937), pp. 14–15.
10. Ibid., pp. 10, 14.
11. Ibid., p. 10.
12. Ibid., p. 12.
13. Ibid., p. 15.
14. *Trud*, [Labor] 22 February 1994.

15. *Biulleten' oppozitsii*, no. 56–57 (1937), p. 16.
16. Orwell, *Homage to Catalonia*, pp.71–72/pp. 55–56.
17. Ibid., p. 185/p. 152.
18. Ibid., pp. 86–87/pp. 57, 67–68.
19. *Biulleten' oppozitsii*, no. 56–57 (1937), pp. 12, 15.

43. The Barcelona Uprising

1. Sinkler, E., *No pasaran!, Roman gazeta*, no. 8 (1937), pp. 57–58. [For the English edition: Sinclair, *No pasaran! [They Shall not Pass]*, (Pasadena: 1937), pp. 78–80.]
2. Krivitskii, *Ia byl agentom Stalina*, pp. 141–142/pp. 91–92.
3. Hernandes, Jesus, *Yo fui un ministro de Stalin* (Mexico: 1953).
4. *Pravda*, 8 February 1937.
5. *Pravda*, 28, 29 March 1937.
6. *Biulleten' oppozitsii*, no. 60–61 (1937), p. 18.
7. Krivitskii, *Ia byl agentom Stalina*, p. 153/ p. 106.
8. Ibid., pp. 153–154.
9. Ibid., p. 149/p. 101.
10. Ibid., pp. 154–155/p. 108.
11. Orwell, *Homage to Catalonia*, pp.182–183/ p. 150.
12. Kol'tsov, M., *Ispaniia v ogne*, [Spain in Flames] vol. 2 (Moscow: 1987), p. 155; see also: Kol'tsov, M., "Fashistsko-shpionskaia rabota ispanskikh trotskistov," [Fascist-Espionage Work of the Spanish Trotskyists] *Pravda*, 19 June 1937.
13. *Izvestiia*, 26 November 1992.
14. Orwell, *Homage to Catalonia*, p. 210/p. 173.
15. Costello, J. & Tsarev, O., *Deadly Illusions* (New York: 1993), pp. 291–292.
16. Orwell, *Homage to Catalonia*, pp.211–213 p. 175].
17. Tamarin, E., "Trotskistskie naemniki Franko i interventov" [Trotskyist Hirelings of Franco and the Interventionists], *Pravda*, 7 June 1937; "Fashistsko-shpionskaia rabota ispanskikh trotskistov" [Fascist-espionage Work of the Spanish Trotskyists], *Pravda*, 19 June 1937; "Aresty trotskistskikh banditov v Ispanii" [Arrests of Trotskyist Bandits in Spain], *Pravda*, 17 July 1937; Kol'tsov, M., "Trotskistskie shpiony v Ispanii" [Trotskyist Spies in Spain], *Pravda*, 25 August 1937.
18. "Aresty Fashistsko-trotskistskikh agentov v

Valensii" [Arrests of Fascist-Trotskyist Agents in Valencia], *Pravda*, 8 July 1937.
19. *Biulleten' oppozitsii*, no. 58–59 (1937), p. 2.
20. *Izvestiia*, 24 August 1936.
21. *Biulleten' oppozitsii*, no. 58–59 (1937), p. 2.
22. Kheminguei, *Sobranie sochinenii v shesti tomakh*, vol. 4, p. 196/pp. 244–245.
23. Ibid., p. 198/p. 247.
24. *Pravda*, 8 July 1937.
25. Orwell, *Homage to Catalonia*, p.211–212/ p. 174.
26. Krivitskii, *Ia byl agentom Stalina*, p. 158 p. 115.
27. Kheminguei, *Sobranie sochinenii v shesti tomakh*, vol. 4, p. 188/p. 234.
28. Ibid., pp. 184–185/pp. 228, 230.
29. Ibid., p. 190/p. 237.
30. Ibid., p. 282/pp. 357–358.
31. Ibid., pp. 189–190/pp. 236–237.
32. Orwell, *Homage to Catalonia*, pp. 216–217/ pp. 178–179.
33. *Inostrannaia literatura*, no. 4 (1988), p. 176.

44. Trotskyists in the Camps

1. Trepper, Leopol'd, *Bol'shaia igra*, pp. 59–60. [For an English version, see: Trepper, *The Great Game* (New York: McGraw-Hill, 1975), pp. 56–57.]
2. Trotskii, *Dnevniki i pis'ma*, p. 160.
3. Krivitskii, *Ia byl agentom Stalina*, p. 186 [p. 151].
4. *Ogonek*, no. 27 (1988), p. 5.
5. *Daugava*, no. 12 (1988), pp. 8–11.
6. Solzhenitsyn, A. I., *Sobranie sochinenii* [Collected Works], vol. 5, (Moscow: 1991), p. 204.
7. Shalamov, V. *Voskreshenie listvennitsy* (Paris: 1985), p. 13.
8. Shalamov, V., *Perchatka ili KR-2*, (Moscow: 1990), p. 37.
9. Ibid., p. 9; *Voskreshenie listvennitsy*, p. 14.
10. Ibid., p. 17.
11. Ibid., p. 48.
12. Ibid., pp. 104–105, 109.
13. *Shalamovskii sbornik*, first issue, Vologda: 1994, p. 62.
14. Ibid., pp. 45–46.
15. Shalamov, V., *Kolymskie rasskazy*, book 1, (Moscow: 1992), p. 532.
16. Ibid., pp. 265–269.

17. *Daugava*, no. 10 (1989), pp. 89–90.
18. *Novyi mir*, no. 3 (1990), pp. 105–107.
19. *Minuvshee. Istoricheskii al'manakh*, vol. 2 (Moscow: 1990), pp. 347–353.
20. *Khotelos' by vsekh poimenno nazvat'* [I Would Like to Name Them All By Name] (Moscow: 1993), pp. 109–113.
21. Ibid., p. 115.
22. Ibid., p. 118.
23. Gagen-Torn, N. I., *Memoria*, (Moscow: 1994), pp. 206–207.
24. *Khotelos' by vsekh poimenno nazvat'* (Moscow: 1993,) p. 122.
25. Joffe, N. A., *Vremia nazad*, [Back in Time] (Moscow: 1992), p. 111.
26. Gagen-Torn, *Memoria*, pp. 73–76.
27. *Shalamovskii sbornik*, first issue, p. 57.
28. *Kraevedcheskie zapiski*, [Notes of Local History] Vyp. 18, Magadan: 1992, pp. 32–35.
29. *Khotelos' by vsekh poimenno nazvat'*, pp. 126–127.
30. *Kraevedcheskie zapiski*, Vyp. 18, pp. 34–35.
31. Shalamov, V., *Perchatka ili KR-2* (Moscow: 1990), pp. 207–208.
32. *Khotelos' by vsekh poimenno nazvat'*, pp. 145–147.
33. Gagen-Torn, *Memoria*, pp. 91–92.
34. Hoover Archives, Nikolaevsky Collection, Box 279, Folder 10, pp. 34–49.

45. "The Bureaucracy Is Terrorized"

1. *Dodnes' tiagoteet*, [Unto This Day a Burden] pp. 46–47.
2. Khlevniuk, O. V., *1937-i, Stalin, NKVD i sovetskoe obshchestvo* [1937, Stalin, the NKVD and Soviet Society] (Moscow: 1992), p. 64.
3. Trotskii, *Stalin*, vol. 2, p. 267.
4. *Kommunist*, no. 1 (1990), p. 81.
5. Khlevniuk, *1937-i*, pp. 144–145.
6. *Neizvestnaia Rossiia. XX vek* [Unknown Russia. 20th Century], vol. 2 (Moscow: 1992), pp. 278–280.
7. Khlevniuk, *1937-i*, p. 146.
8. Trifonov, Iu. V., *Sobranie sochinenii*, vol. 4 (Moscow: 1987), p. 24.
9. Trotskii, *Stalin*, vol. 2, pp. 267–268.
10. *Dodnes' tiagoteet*, p. 537.
11. *Voprosy istorii*, no. 5 (1990), p. 53.
12. *Biulleten' oppozitsii*, no. 60–61 (1937), p. 9.

13. *Biulleten' oppozitsii*, no. 54–55 (1937), p. 33.
14. *Biulleten' oppozitsii*, no. 56–57 (1937), p. 1.
15. Ibid., pp. 2, 6.
16. Ibid., pp. 2, 7.
17. Trepper, *The Great Game*, p. 67.
18. Raskol'nikov, F. F., *O vremeni i o sebe* [About My Times and Myself], p. 531.

46. Reasons for Reprisals against the Generals

1. Krivitskii, *Ia byl agentom Stalina*, pp. 235–236/p. 224.
2. *Voprosy istorii*, no. 8 (1994), p. 5.
3. *Voprosy istorii KPSS*, no. 6 (1991), p. 20.
4. *Voprosy istorii*, no. 8 (1994), p. 12.
5. Ibid., p. 13.
6. Krivitsky, *Ia byl agentom Stalina*, p. 236/p. 224.
7. Trotskii, *Stalin*, vol. 2, pp. 277–278.
8. Voennye arkhivy Rossii [Russia's Military Archives], issue 1 (1993), p. 71.
9. Nord, L., *Marshal M. N. Tukhachevskii*, (Paris: 1976), pp. 116–117.
10. RTsKhIDNI, f. 85, op. 27, d. 65, l. 1.
11. *Voennye arkhivy Rossii*, Vyp. 1 (1993), pp. 78–79.
12. Ibid., pp. 79–80.
13. Ibid., p. 84.
14. Ibid., p. 47.
15. *Fakel 1990. Istoriko-revoliutsionnyi al'manakh*, (Moscow: 1990), pp. 237–238.
16. Krivitskii, *Ia byl agentom Stalina*, p. 236 [p. 224].
17. Trotskii, *Stalin*, vol. 2, p. 275. [For the Barmine quote, see: Barmine, Alexander, *One Who Survived* (New York: 1945), p. 221.]
18. Larina, *Nezabyvaemoe*, p. 185.
19. *Voennye arkhivy Rossii*, Vyp. 1 (1993), p. 76.
20. *Stalin. Sbornik statei k piatidesiatiletiiu so dnia rozhdeniia* [Stalin. Anthology of Articles Celebrating His Fiftieth Birthday] (Moscow-Leningrad: 1930), p. 9.
21. *Voprosy istorii*, no. 9 (1989), p. 60.
22. *Voennye arkhivy Rossii*, Vyp. 1 (1993), p. 84.
23. *Istochnik*, no. 3 (1994), p. 82.
24. Gul', R., *Krasnye marshaly* [Red Marshals] (Moscow: 1990), p. 128.
25. Ibid., pp. 172–173.
26. Ibid., pp. 203–206.
27. Ibid., pp. 169–171.

47. Prelude to the Purge of the Army

1. *Voprosy istorii*, no. 8 (1994), p. 6.
2. *Komandarm Iakir* [Army Commander Yakir] (Moscow: 1963), pp. 224–225.
3. Parnov, E., *Zagovor protiv marshalov* [Conspiracy Against the Marshals], 1991, pp. 320–322.
4. *Reabilitatsiia*, p. 283.
5. *Stalinskoe Politburo v 30-e gody* [Stalin's Politburo in the 1930s], p. 33.
6. Krivitskii, *Ia byl agentom Stalina*, pp. 229–230/pp. 216–217.
7. *Voprosy istorii KPSS*, no. 6 (1991), pp. 18–19.
8. RTsKhIDNI, f. 17, op. 71, d. 50, l. 1–30.
9. Karpov, V., *Marshal Zhukov. Ego soratniki i protivniki v gody voiny i mira* [Marshal Zhukov. His Comrades and Opponents During War and Peace] (Moscow: 1994), p. 72.
10. *Voprosy istorii KPSS*, no. 6 (1991), p. 28.
11. *Voennye arkhivy Rossi*, Vyp. 1 (1993), p. 8; *Voprosy istorii*, no. 8 (1994), p. 5.
12. *Voprosy istorii*, no. 8 (1994), pp. 24–25.

48. The Stalin-Hitler Provocation

1. Karpov, *Marshal Zhukov*, p. 59.
2. Shellenberg, V., *Memuary* (Moscow: 1991), pp. 43–44.
3. Shchetinov, Iu. A., Starkov, B. A., *Krasnyi marshal* (Moscow: 1990), p. 283.
4. *Reabilitatsiia*, p. 303.
5. Trepper, *The Great Game*, pp. 68–69 [p. 67].
6. Krivitskii, *Ia byl agentom Stalina*, pp. 228 [p. 215].
7. Ibid., p. 247/p.238; *Poslednie novosti*, 24 September 1937.
8. Brossa, A., "Gruppovoi portret s damoi", [Group Portrait with a Lady] *Inostrannaia literatura*, no. 12 (1989), p. 243.
9. Krivitskii, *Ia byl agentom Stalina*, pp. 249 p. 240.
10. *Biulleten' oppozitsii*, no. 60–61 (1937), p. 19.
11. *Life*, vol. 40 (1956), no. 17, p. 39.
12. Shellenberg, *Memuary*, p. 45.
13. Krivitskii, *Ia byl agentom Stalina*, p. 244 [p. 234].
14. Cited from: *Novaia Rossiia* [New Russia], Paris, (1938), no. 57, p. 13.
15. Shellenberg, *Memuary*, p. 45.

49. Preparing the Trial of the Generals

1. *Voprosy istorii*, no. 6 (1991), pp. 28–29.
2. Krivitskii, *Ia byl agentom Stalina*, p. 238.
3. *Voennye arkhivy Rossii*, Vyp. 1 (1993), pp. 32–35.
4. Ibid., p. 35.
5. Ibid., pp. 40–41.
6. *Biulleten' oppozitsii*, no. 56–57 (1937), p. 3.
7. *Voennye arkhivy Rossii*, Vyp. 1 (1993), pp. 35–36.
8. *Reabilitatsiia*, p. 286.
9. *Voennye arkhivy Rossii*, Vyp. 1 (1993), pp. 36–37.
10. Sledstvennoe delo V. M. Primakova.
11. *Voennye arkhivy Rossii*, Vyp. 1 (1993), pp. 37–38, 53–54.
12. RTsKhIDNI, f. 17, op. 3, d. 987, l. 57.
13. *Marshal Tukhachevskii* (Moscow: 1965), p. 128.
14. Shchetinov & Starkov, *Krasnyi marshal*, p. 290.
15. *Voennye arkhivy Rossii*, Vyp. 1 (1993), pp. 41–42.
16. RTsKhIDNI, f. 17, op. 2, d. 615, l. 8.
17. *Voennye arkhivy Rossii*, Vyp. 1 (1993), p. 45.
18. *Reabilitatsiia*, p. 309.
19. *Voennye arkhivy Rossii*, Vyp. 1 (1993), p. 44.
20. Ibid., p. 35.
21. Ibid., p. 46.
22. *Pravda*, 1 June 1937.
23. RTsKhIDNI, F. 17, op. 2, d., 615, l. 8.
24. *Reabilitatsiia*, p. 309.
25. *Istochnik*, no. 3 (1994), pp. 73, 76.
26. Ibid., pp. 76–77.
27. Ibid., p. 75.
28. Ibid., pp. 78, 80.
29. Ibid., p. 85.
30. Ibid., p. 74.
31. *Voprosy istorii*, no. 12 (199), p. 69.
32. *Voenno-istoricheskii zhurnal* [Journal of Military History], no. 8 (1991), p. 44.
33. Ibid., p. 45.
34. Ibid., pp. 47, 51.
35. Bargramian, I. Kh., *Velikogo naroda synov'ia* [Sons of a Great People] (Moscow: 1984), pp. 177–178.
36. *Voenno-istoricheskii zhurnal*, no. 8 (1991), pp. 48, 52; no. 9 (1991), pp. 56, 59, 62..
37. *Voenno-istoricheskii zhurnal*, 1991, no. 9 (1991), p. 58.
38. *Reabilitatsiia*, p. 291.
39. Chuev, *Sto sorok besed s Molotovym*, pp. 412–

413.
40. *Voennye arkhivy Rossii*, Vyp. 1 (1993), p. 50.
41. *Istoricheskii arkhiv*, no. 3 (1993), p. 18; *XXII s"ezd Kommunisticheskoi partii Sovetskogo Soiuza* , vol. 2, p. 403.
42. *Voennye arkhivy Rossii*, Vyp. 1 (1993), p. 50.
43. Ibid., p. 55.

50. The Trial of the Generals
1. *Pravda*, 11 July 1937.
2. *Voennye arkhivy Rossii*, Vyp. 1 (1993), p. 54.
3. Ibid., p. 65.
4. Shchetinov & Starkov, *Krasnyi marshal*, p. 295.
5. *Voennye arkhivy Rossii*, Vyp. 1 (1993), pp. 55–56.
6. Ibid., p. 56.
7. Erenburg, *Sobranie sochinenii*, vol. 9, p. 190.
8. *Pravda*, 13 June 1937.
9. *Biulleten' oppozitsii*, no. 56–57 (1937), pp. 3, 5.
10. Ibid., p. 4.
11. Ibid., p. 6.
12. Ibid., p. 5.
13. Trotskii, *Prestupleniia Stalina*, p. 6.
14. *Biulleten' oppozitsii*, no. 56–57 (1937), p. 6.
15. *Voennye arkhivy Rossii*, Vyp. 1 (1993), pp. 68–69.

51. Looking Ahead Fifteen Years
1. *Voennye arkhivy Rossii*, Vyp. 1 (1993), pp. 34–35.
2. *Nepravednyi sud: Poslednii stalinskii rasstrel.* (Stenogramma sudebnogo zasedaniia nad chlenami Evreiskogo antifashistskogo komiteta) [Unjust Trial: Stalin's Last Executions (Transcript of the Trial of the Members of the Jewish Anti-Fascist Committee)] (Moscow: 1994), p. 92.
3. Ibid., pp. 113, 120.
4. Ibid., p. 125.
5. Ibid., p. 229.
6. Ibid., p. 303.
7. Ibid., p. 194.
8. Ibid., pp. 198–199.
9. Ibid., pp. 205, 211.
10. Ibid., p. 235.
11. Ibid., p. 361.
12. Ibid., pp. 321, 332.
13. Ibid., p. 234.
14. Ibid., p. 345.

15. Ibid., p. 367.
16. Ibid., pp. 271–272.
17. Ibid., p. 369.
18. Ibid., pp. 166–167.
19. Ibid., p. 343.
20. Ibid., p. 172.
21. Ibid., p. 135.
22. Ibid., p. 179.
23. Ibid., pp. 341, 342, 344.
24. Ibid., pp. 340–341.
25. Ibid., pp. 371–372.
26. Ibid., p. 348.
27. Ibid., p. 373.
28. Ibid., p. 332.
29. Ibid., pp. 373–374.

52. Was There a Military Conspiracy?
1. *Biulleten' oppozitsii*, no. 56–57 (1937), pp. 6–7.
2. Trotskii, *Stalin*, vol. 2, p. 276.
3. *Biulleten' oppozitsii*, no. 56–57 (1937), p. 5.
4. Trotskii, *Stalin*, vol. 2, p. 277.
5. Cherchill', U., *Vtoraia mirovaia voina* [The Second World War], vol. 1 (Moscow: 1991), pp. 132–133.
6. Piker, G., *Zastol'nye razgovory Gitlera* [Hitler's Table Conversations] (Moscow: 1993), pp. 446–447.
7. Chuev, *Tak govoril Kaganovich*, p. 45.
8. Ibid., pp. 100–101.
9. Chuev, *Sto sorok besed s Molotovym*, pp. 441–442.
10. Stadniuk, I. *Ispoved' stalinista* [Confesssion of a Stalinist] (Moscow: 1993), p. 343.
11. Karpov, *Marshal Zhukov*, p. 69.

53. The Ballad of General Orlov
1. Costello & Tsarev, *Deadly Illusions*, p. 308.
2. Ibid., pp. 308–310.
3. Trotsky Archives, document no. 6137.
4. Orlov, *Tainaia istoriia stalinskikh prestuplenii*, p. 232.

54. The Secret of the Tukhachevsky Affair
1. Semenov, Iu., *Nenapisannye romany* [Unwritten Novels] (Moscow: 1990), p. 183.
2. Ibid., p. 182.
3. *Oktiabr'*, no. 3 (1994), p. 167.
4. *Life*, vol. 40 (1956), no. 17, p. 34.

5. Ibid.
6. Ibid., pp. 35–36.
7. Ibid., pp. 36–37.
8. Ibid., p. 37.
9. Ibid., pp. 37–38.
10. Ibid., p. 38.
11. Orlov, *Tainaia istoriia stalinskikh prestuplenii*, p. 233.
12. Costello & Tsarev, *Deadly Illusions*, p. 411.
13. *Life*, vol. 40 (1956), no. 17, p. 43.
14. Ibid., pp. 43–44.
15. *Istochnik*, no. 2 (1994), pp. 82–83.
16. *Reabilitatsiia*, p. 48.
17. *Life*, vol. 40 (1956), no. 17, p. 44.
18. Ibid., p. 34.
19. *Reabilitatsiia*, p. 45.
20. Ibid., p. 32.
21. *Oktiabr'*, no. 3 (1994), p. 175.

55. The June Plenum of the Central Committee

1. *Voprosy istorii*, no. 11–12 (1992), p. 10.
2. RTsKhIDNI, f. 17, op. 2, d. 614, l. 95.
3. Ibid., f., 17, op. 3, d. 985, point 126.
4. Ibid., f. 17, op. 2, d. 614, l. 103, 105.
5. Ibid., l. 135.
6. Ibid., l. 308.
7. Ibid., l. 377.
8. *Stalinskoe Politburo v 30-e gody*, p. 55.
9. *Novoe vremia*, no. 50 (1994), p. 37.
10. Ibid.

11. *KPSS v rezoliutsiiakh*, vol. 6, p. 392.
12. RTsKhIDNI, f. 17, op. 2, d. 780, l. 2, 5, 9, 12.
13. RTsKhIDNI, f. 17, op. 2, d. 779, l. 18, 22.
14. RTsKhIDNI, f. 17, op. 2, d. 614, l. 1–2.
15. Ibid., l. 1.
16. *Stranitsy istorii KPSS. Fakty. Problemy. Uroki* (Moscow: 1988), pp. 600–601.
17. *Voprosy istorii*, no. 2–3 (1992), p. 98.
18. *Beriia. konets kar'ery*, pp. 242–243.
19. *Voprosy istorii*, no. 2–3 (1992), p. 98.
20. *Oni ne molchali*, pp. 200–202.
21. RTsKhIDNI, f. 17, op. 2, d. 614, l. 2.
22. *Oni ne molchali*, pp. 220.
23. *Dodnes' tiagoteet*, p. 265.
24. RTsKhIDNI, f. 17, op. 2, d. 622, l. 220.
25. *Dodnes' tiagoteet*, pp. 265–266.
26. Ibid., p. 279.
27. Trepper, *The Great Game*, pp. 54–55.
28. *Oni ne molchali*, pp. 225.
29. Ibid., p. 224.
30. Ibid., p. 222.
31. *Stranitsy istorii KPSS. Fakty. Problemy. Uroki*, p. 603.
32. RTsKhIDNI, f. 17, op. 2, d. 622, l. 220.
33. Ibid., f. 17, op. 2, d. 614, l. 93.
34. *XXII s"ezd Kommunisticheskoi partii Sovetskogo Soiuza*, vol. 3, pp. 120–121.
35. *Reabilitatsiia*, p. 40.
36. *Istoricheskii arkhiv*, no. 3 (1993), p. 89.
37. Ibid., pp. 86, 88–89.

Name Index

A

Abakumov, V. S., 451-453, 456
Abbiat, 333
Adamova-Sliozberg, O. L., 393
Adler, F., 48
Agranov, Ya. S., 1, 4
Aksenov, Vasily P., 314
Akulinushkin, P. D., 149-150
Alafuzo, 435
Alekseev, P. A., 490
Alksnis, Ya. I., 434
Alliluev, Pavel E., 471
Alliluyeva, S. I., xvi, 160
Andersen-Nexø, M., 128
Andreev, A. A., 32, 73, 110, 150, 187, *412*
    at February-March Plenum, 284, 287, 433
    as former Trotskyist, 433
    at June 1937 Plenum, 489, 496
Andreev, as Efron alias, 333
Antipov, N. K., 439, 490
Antonov, V., 480
Antonov-Ovseenko, V. A., 366
Apanasenko, I. R., 431
Arkus, 21
Arnold, V. V., 32-33, 97, 116, 126
Artemenko, Ekaterina, 179
Askendarian, T. Sh., 389
Aslan David-ogly, 387-388
Astrov, V. N., 180-181, 213
Avtorkhanov, A., 12

B

Bagirov, M. D., 189, 254-255

Baitalsky, M., 383
Bakaev, I. P., 23, 25
Bakunin, M. A., 318
Balitsky, V. A., 473, 490
Barmine, A., 406
Bauer, O., 40
Becher, Johannes, xi, xx
Bedny, Demian, 396-397
Beliavsky, 88
Beloborodov, A. G., 91
Belov, I. P., 434, 453
Beneš, E., 419, 422-423, 430, 461, 481
Berdyaev, N. A., xxvii
Beria, L. P., 101, 166, 492-493
    as alleged Musavatist agent, 491
    as alleged target of terrorism, 117
    case against in 1953, 187-189, 197,
        474n, 478, 491-492
    at February-March Plenum, 219, 222,
        276, 279, 284-285, 287
    and Ordzhonikidze, 186-190
Berman-Yurin, K. B., 20
Bertsinskaya, A. S., 388-389
Berzin, E. P., 378-379, 385
Berzin, Ya. K., 344, 360, 372
Bibneishvili, Lado, 388
Bibneishvili, Lolo, 388
Birman, 270
Bismarck, Otto von, 58
Blagonravov, G. I., 490
Bliukher, V. K., *407*, 409, 434
Bliumenfeld, 377
Bliumkin, Ya. G., 115
Blum, Leon, 132, 335
Bogdan, 19, 57

519

Testament of, 16, 68, 385, 448, 448n
and Trotsky, 285, 309, 312
Leplevsky, G. M., 425
Lert, R. B., 160
Lesniak, B. N., 87
Lie, Trygve, 47-49, 130-131
Liebknecht, Karl, 130, 306
Litvinov, M. M., 279, 402, 420
Liubchenko, P. P., 225
Liubimov, I. E., 259, 490
Liushkov, G. S., 17, 467
Livshits, Ya. A., 116, 116, 252
Lobov, S. S., 490
Lombardo Toledano, Vicente, 135, 306
Lominadze, V. V., 64, 75-76, 192, 488
suicide of, 76n, 103
London, Arthur, 372-373
Longo, Luigi, *345*, 349, 373
Lorca, Garcia, 349
Lozovsky, S. A., 222, 450-451, 453-456
Lugovoi, A. V., 92
Lukacz, G., 344
Lurie, M. I., 12, 19-21, 56
Lurie, N. L., 12, 19-21, 56
Luxemburg, Rosa, 130, 237

M

Maclean, D., 467
Malenkov, G. M., xxiv, 196, 301, 414, 475
Malin, 499
Malraux, André, 306, 349
Mann, Thomas, 41-42
Mantegna, 341
Manuilsky, D. Z., 155
Markin, 325
Markish, P. D., 453
Marty, André, *345*, 346
Martynov, 384
Maryasan, L. E., 249-250
Maslow, A., 288, 289n, 324
Mauriac, F., 364

Maxton, James, 365
Mayakovsky, Vladimir V., 465, 470
McGovern, John, 365
Medvedev, M. E. , 427-428, 449
Medvedev, S. P. , 63
Medvedev (of Leningrad NKVD), 7
Medvedev, R., xx
Mekhlis, L. Z., 160, 220, 283, 285
Melnikov, B. N., 495-496
Mendeleev, M., 495
Menzhinsky, V. R., 485n
Meretskov, K. M., 434
Meshcherin, 389
Meyerhold, Vsevold Emilievich, 443
Mezhlauk, V. I., xv, 167, 222, 224, 250, 256
Mikhailov, V. M., 490
Mikhoels, S. M., 455
Mikoyan, A. I., 31-32, 110, 475, 488
on Beria and Ordzhonikidze, 186-187, 190
at February-March Plenum, 211-213, 222, 260-261, 269-270
and Khrushchev, 303
Miliukov, P. N., 45, 305
Miller, E. K., 421-422, 424
Mironov, L. G., 6-7, 9, 277
Mola, 342
Molchanov, G. A., 1, 4, 8, 17, 277, 432
Molotov, V. M., xvi, 10, *34*, 40, *300, 338, 412*, 451, 486-488, 495
as alleged target of terrorist attack, 33-35, 110, 117, 120, 462
and Bukharin, 73, 75, 110, 110n
as Chairman of Council of People's Commissars, 30, 91
conversations with F. Chuyev, xvi, 34, 197, 438, 461
at December Plenum, 100
at February-March Plenum, 95, 213-215, 219, 222, 223, 225, 248-251, 250n, 255-256, 259, 261-262, 268, 270, 282-283, 290, 415

Subject Index

A

Abwehr, 419
Academy of Sciences, 126, 220
Aftenposten, 121
Agents of Moscow, 331
All-Union Census, 241
All-Union Congress of Soviets, 99
"All-Union Trotskyist Center," 4, 97
Amalgam, method of, xxx, 59, 74, 143, 173,
    457, 482
    of corruption and sabotage, 258
    at Moscow Trials, 65-66
    in Spain, 365, 373
    Trotsky on, 51, 258, 317
American Committee for the Defense of
    Trotsky, 135
Anarchists:
    Russian, 361
    in Spain, 340-342, 355-358, 357n, 361-
        362;
Anti-Semitism, in Germany, 156, 161
    of Moscow Trials, 154-156
    in NKVD, 453
    social roots of, 157-158, 160
    in Soviet Union, 155-163
    Trotsky on, 154-160;
"Anti-Soviet Trotskyist Center," case of. *See*
    Moscow Trial, second
Anti-Stalinist bloc, 61-66, 90
Anti-Stalinist forces, in Spain, 341-342, 369
Anti-Stalinist military conspiracy, 399-400,
    478-481
Anticommunism
    and analysis of Great Terror, xx, xxv,

xxix, 138, 170, 319
    embraced by former party bosses, xix
    and people of the '60s, xxiii, 143, 170,
        175
    and Solzhenitsyn, 380-381
April Conference of 1917, 95
Arbeiderbladet, 46
Archives
    of Marx and Engels, 231
    of Trotsky, 2, 49-50, 62, 64, 331
Asylum, right of, 48, 130, 354
Azerbaidzhan, 189, 254, 389

B

Barcelona uprising, 356, 357-373
Barkashovists, 162
Black Hundreds, 157, 162
Bolshevik, 248
Bolshevik-Leninists, 143, 384
Bolsheviks, xii, xviii, 141, 190, 261
    anticommunist view of, xxx, 44, 138,
        209, 310, 312
    in conflict with Stalinism, 204, 309-322,
        480-481
    falsification of by Stalinism, 9, 13, 142-
        143
    and internationalism, 342
    as label in post-Soviet Russia, xix, xxvi
    national policy of, 158
    opponents of, xxi, 57, 159, 163, 272, 480
    and repressive actions during revolu-
        tion, 309, 313-314, 316, 355
    as target of Stalin's crimes, xxii, 9, 53-
        54, 145, 160, 175, 383, 499

and EAK trial, 448-453
by Gestapo, 323
by NKVD, 56-57, 176, 179, 184, 308
of Nin, 364
permitted by 1937 Politburo decree, 497-
 499
of Piatnitsky, 495
and purge of Red Army, 428n, 430-431,
 446-447, 480-482
and second Moscow Trial, 124-125
Totalitarian hysteria, 434
"Totalitarian idiotism," 19, 21, 102
Totalitarian regime, xvii, xxviii, 138, 145,
 204, 445, 460
 contradictions of, 80, 458
 in contrast with Bolshevism, 312
 methods of, 262, 275, 295
Trial of the Sixteen, xxix, 14-25, 29, 36, 83,
 159, 366
 and Bukharin, 107, 179, 192
 defendants at, 14, 68, 71, 78, 173-174, 324
 and "Molotov Affair," 30-31, 91
 political motives for, 53, 84-85, 234
 political repercussions of, 40-45, 128, 309
 and purge of Red Army, 411
 and Rakovsky, 54
 reasons for confessions at, 36-38, 55-56;
  Sedov on, 51, 54-62, 64, 86
 Stalin on, 289
 transcript of, 116, 177
 Trotsky on, 46, 50-51, 159
 true facts in, 17, 60-65.
 See also Kamenev, Zinoviev, Old
  Bolsheviks.
Trotsky, A Political Portrait, 311
Trotsky: Memoir & Critique, 312n
"Trotsky's curse," 130
Trotskyism, 143, 306, 317
 Bukharin attack on, 107-108
 Stalinist attacks on, 114, 132, 142, 182,
  203, 290, 372-373
Trotskyist-Zinovievist bloc

according to Broué, 66
alleged, 70-71, 91, 245, 254, 277
in army, 401, 414-415
and Bukharin, 100-101, 199, 227, 235
as pretext for Trial of the Sixteen, 27-28,
 40, 118
Stalin on, 2, 13, 90
"Trotsky-Zinoviev Center," 13, 22-23, 32, 35,
 72, 85, 87
Trotskyists, 284, 287, 329, 381, 393
 actual activities and support for, 56, 61,
  63-64, 140, 147, 374
 American, 325
 capitulators from, 61, 290-291, 388, 433
 charged as agents of fascism, 97, 104-
  105, 127, 196, 280, 323-324
 charged with espionage, 100, 216, 247,
  260, 288
 charged with sabotage, 85, 91-92, 96-97,
  100,104, 167, 205-207, 247-249, 253-
  254, 258, 273-275, 288
 charged with terror, 185
 Chinese, 324
 excessive hysteria against, 87-90
 frame-ups of, xii, xxv, 1, 4-5, 26-29, 83-
  84, 95, 140, 477
 in France, 43
 liquidation of, 3, 139-140, 146, 252, 283-
  286, 289, 375, 445
 persecuted in capitalist countries, 323-
  326
 in prison camps, 104-105, 280, 373-392
 in Red Army, 400-401, 428, 445
 and second Moscow Trial, 118-119, 122,
  125
 in Spain, 340-342, 345-347, 360, 362-
  363, 365-368, 372-373
 Stalinist caricature of, 99-100, 102, 141,
  211, 241, 245
 Trepper on, 374-375
Tsarism, xviii, 117, 157, 305, 319, 388
 former officers of, 401, 427, 434